ENCYCLOPEDIA OF JEWISH-AMERICAN LITERATURE

Gloria L. Cronin
Alan L. Berger

Facts On File
An imprint of Infobase Publishing

Encyclopedia of Jewish-American Literature

Facts On File, Inc.
An imprint of Infobase Publishing
132 West 31st Street
New York NY 10001

Library of Congress Cataloging-in-Publication Data

Cronin, Gloria L., 1947–
    Encyclopedia of Jewish-American literature / Gloria L. Cronin, Alan L. Berger.
        p. cm.
    Includes bibliographical references and index.
    ISBN-13: 978-0-8160-6085-6 (hc : alk. paper)
    1. American literature—Jewish authors—Encyclopedias. I. Berger, Alan L., 1939–   II. Title.
    PS153.J4C76 2008
    810.9'8924003—dc22   2008007872

Facts On File books are available at special discounts when purchased in bulk quantities for businesses, associations, institutions, or sales promotions. Please call our Special Sales Department in New York at (212) 967-8800 or (800) 322-8755.

You can find Facts On File on the World Wide Web at http://www.factsonfile.com

Text design by Rachel L. Berlin
Cover design by Takeshi Takahashi

Printed in the United States of America

VB KT 10 9 8 7 6 5 4 3 2 1

This book is printed on acid-free paper and contains 30 percent postconsumer recycled content.

TABLE OF CONTENTS

⟪❦⟫

Introduction   vii

Acknowledgments   xi

A Survey of
Jewish-American Literature   xiii

A-to-Z Entries   1

Primary Source Bibliography   332

Bibliography of
Secondary Sources   345

List of Contributors   362

Index   364

INTRODUCTION

About This Volume

The entries in this volume introduce more than 100 Jewish-American writers and their literary works. The majority of these writers are American-born, with some notable exceptions: Saul Bellow was born in Canada, Isaac Singer in Poland, and Elie Wiesel in Romania. Bellow and Singer spent most of their lives in America; Wiesel continues to live in America. Bellow and Singer were both Nobel laureates in literature, while Wiesel is a Nobel Peace Prize winner. Their disparate voices have helped weave the complex fabric of Jewish-American literature, while at the same time expressing the relationship between Jewish particularity and the tradition's universal message of freedom as articulated in the master narrative of the Exodus. This narrative is also emphasized by other writers, such as Emma Lazarus, a Jewish-American poet, whose poem "The New Colossus" appears on the base of the Statue of Liberty, which after 1886 welcomed new immigrants to American shores. Most of the Jewish-American authors in this book, like most of the Jews in America, trace their roots to the Ashkenazim from eastern and central Europe, although some few claim descent from the Sephardim of Spain and North Africa.

Defining a Jewish-American Writer

Given the long history and many wanderings of the Jewish people, we might well wonder what the term *Jewish-American* means. The long-standing debate concerning just who qualifies as a Jewish writer has often been symbolically embodied in the argument over whether to refer to oneself as an American-Jewish author or a Jewish-American author. The three major Jewish writers from mid-to-late-20th century, Saul Bellow, Bernard Malamud, and Philip Roth, all at one time strenuously rejected the label "Jewish writer." Malamud even universalized the definition of Jewishness, which he might have characterized as the ability to grow morally as a result of suffering. Roth has aggressively contended that he has no desire to do public relations for the Jewish community. Of the three, only Bellow finally acceded to being labeled a Jewish-American writer, and then only near the very end of his life. All three asserted strongly that they wrote about issues central to the human condition. However, the current stress on ethnicity and multiculturalism within the American academy and Jewish America's rediscovery of its Judaic religious dimension have caused the debate to flare up again. Wendy Shalit, in her recent critique of American literary portrayals of

Orthodox Judaism, divides writers according to their status as "outsiders" and "insiders." She then dismisses what she calls "Outsider insiders." These are Jews she calls the formerly Orthodox, or those pretending to be religious. She sanctions only works written by insiders who paint favorable portraits of Orthodox Judaism. (See "The Observant Reader," in the *New York Times Book Review,* January 30, 2005. For an intelligent discussion of this article, see Sara R. Horowitz's "Mediating Judaism: Mind, Body, Spirit and Contemporary North American Jewish Fiction" in the *AJS Review* 30, No. 2, pp. 231–253.) This formula is too rigid to encompass all of Jewish expression and omits the variety within Orthodoxy itself. Shalit's prescription is not likely to have much long-term impact on Jewish-American writers, always notorious for being iconoclasts.

For the purposes of this volume, a Jewish-American writer is of Jewish origin, resident in America, aligned or not aligned with Jewish religious life in North America, and generally acculturated as a Jewish person. Practically speaking, however, the writers included in this volume are all self-identified as Jewish Americans and incontestably considered Jewish-American writers by the American publishing industry, scholars, and the reading public. Not surprisingly, these writers reflect a wide variety of attitudes toward Jewish religion, ritual, and culture. What they hold in common is their shared sense of their Jewish and American heritages.

The Scope of This Book

We have designed this volume for high school and college readers, academics and their students, and the general public; to that end, we have reexamined the scope of Jewish-American literature. The important *Jewish American Literature: A Norton Anthology* (2000) gives considerable weight to the very early beginnings of Jewish-American literature and the pre-1970s moment but in some ways fails to reflect the veritable explosion of Jewish literature of the last 40 or so years. This encyclopedia, although informed by history, takes its shape from the thinking of the post-1960s American cultural studies movement, committed to redraw-

ing the expanding American literary map subsequent to the civil rights movement, the women's movement, and the multicultural movement. We have concentrated primarily on writers of fiction, poetry, and drama, those genres most likely to be of interest to teachers and students in high school and college-level literature classes. By necessity, we have left out the equally rich body of American Jewish literary and social documents: letters, personal journals, Yiddish theater, song, radio, television, and film script, despite their powerful shaping influence on the American imagination. Thus we have gone beyond the Norton anthology's emphasis on the very earliest beginnings of this tradition, by giving deliberate weight to the tradition that emerges during the decades leading up to and following World War II, the rapidly escalating Jewish-American literary tradition of the second half of the 20th century, and the remarkable literary energy evident in this, the first decade of the 21st century. We have also given much attention to the post-1980s resurgence of Jewish-American women writers, the second and now third generation of post-Holocaust writers, postmodern writers, the so-called Jewish-American Literary Revival, and the New York Resurgence. By carefully considering the literary outpouring of the last 30 years, we hope to provide a snapshot of the richest decades of Jewish-American literature and a clear sense of the literary accomplishments of the children and grandchildren of the decades dominated by Bellow, Roth, and Malamud.

Useful Resources

We recommend several other useful resources for users of this encyclopedia. The 1654–1880 period is most thoroughly covered in *Jewish American Literature: A Norton Anthology* (2000), which also covers the 1950–70 period reasonably well. Its headnotes are truly indispensable. The three-volume critical history by Louis Harap—*Creative Awakenings: Jewish Presence in Twentieth-Century American Literature 1900–1940s, In the Mainstream: Jewish Presence in Twentieth Century American Literature 1950s–1980s,* and *Dramatic Encounters: The Jewish Presence in Twentieth-*

Century American Drama, Poetry, Humor and the Black-Jewish Relationship—contains very detailed coverage on the early history of this tradition. Andrew Furman's *Contemporary Jewish American Writers and the Multicultural Dilemma: Return of the Exiled* (2000) provides useful multicultural critical/historical treatment of the post-1980s writers and their works. Ezra Cappell's important *American Talmud* (2007) connects the contemporary tradition of Jewish-American literature with the ancient theological and ethical tradition of Talmudic Midrashric commentary. Alan L. Berger's *Crisis and Covenant: The Holocaust in American Jewish Literature* captures the tension between historical theology and the hovering presence of the Holocaust while exploring the usefulness and transformation of the traditional theologi-

cal understandings in the post-Holocaust world; Berger's *Children of Job: American Second Generation Witnesses* analyzes the international transmission of trauma and the role of covenantal Judaism in the works of daughters and sons of Holocaust survivors; Alan and Naomi Berger's *Second Generation Voices: Reflections by Children of Holocaust Survivors and Perpetrators* extends the study of trauma by featuring essays of children of Jews and Germans. Gloria L. Cronin and Blaine H. Hall's *Jewish American Fiction Writers: An Annotated Bibliography* is an extensive collection of materials that cover the critical conversation on 62 Jewish American authors.

Note: Many of the entries in this book on Saul Bellow and his works are adapted and expanded from Gloria L. Cronin's previously published work.

Acknowledgments

This volume is lovingly dedicated to Professor Dan Walden and his wife, Bea, in acknowledgment of Dan's foundational work in Jewish-American literary scholarship and of their gracious friendship to us all.

Our gratitude goes to the many contributors to this encyclopedia, coming as they do from a variety of backgrounds and religious traditions, for their shared passions for Jewish-American literature. Their keen insights into the works and authors about which they write provide the substance of this volume.

Special thanks are also due to Robert Means, humanities librarian of the Harold B. Lee Library at Brigham Young University; Andy Schultz and Jack Mallard in Gloria Cronin's office, for their invaluable editing, technical assistance, and project management; Bonnie Lander in Alan Berger's office, for her superb administrative assistance; and our Facts On File acquisitions editor, Jeff Soloway, for his astute guidance.

Gloria L. Cronin
Alan L. Berger

A SURVEY OF JEWISH-AMERICAN LITERATURE

Jews in American History

Jews originated from the desert cultures of the Middle East more than 4,000 years ago. Their history and their literary culture find form in the Hebrew Bible (or TaNaK), the Mishnah, the Talmud, and the Midrashim. These are the beginning and foundation of what would eventually become Jewish literature. Its American incarnation, however, came after millennia of political autonomy, self-division, eventual dispossession, exile, and dispersion under the various empires of the Egyptians, Assyrians, Persians, Greeks, and Romans. As recently as 900 C.E. the Jews began their European sojourn, some settling in Spain, or elsewhere in Iberia, and others in Italy, France, and Germany. Iberian, or Spanish, Jews came to be called Sephardim, and developed over time a Judeo-Spanish language known as Ladino, as well as their own unique rituals. The Jews who settled in central Europe became known as Ashkenazim. These people developed the Yiddish language and their own distinctive ritual life. With the Christian persecutions of Jews in western Europe during the Crusades and during the plague of the 14th century, Jews moved from central and southern Europe into eastern Europe to live in small villages, or shtetls. Mostly isolated from a large part of Europe, they maintained their Yiddish language and their intense devotion to their religious culture and Hebrew sacred texts. By the 19th century, they constituted the single-largest group of Jews living anywhere and had created such famous centers of learning as Vilna, Slobodka, Galicia, and others. By this time, a Yiddish literary culture, oral and written, was highly developed. Yiddish is a development of Middle High German, with approximately 15 percent of its lexicon deriving from Hebrew and Aramaic, with additional traces of Old French, Italian and, eventually, Slavic. It is that rich linguistic archive containing more than 1,000 years of European Jewish culture that waves of Jewish immigrants brought to America, the Golden Land, beginning in the 1880s. After relative isolation in Europe, these essentially medieval, orthodox, and mostly Hasidic Jews arrived in America in an increasing flood. Many of them had been dislocated by pogroms (government-sanctioned violence) unleashed against them in the political aftermath of the assassination of the Russian czar Alexander II. Today, the descendants of both Sephardic Jews and the more numerous Ashkenazim continue to thrive in the United States, though assimilation has taken its toll.

1492–1880: Jews and American Settlement

Jewish history in the New World began with the arrival of the Spanish explorer Christopher Columbus in 1492. This was well before John Smith established Jamestown in 1607 Virginia and well before the Pilgrims arrived at Plymouth Rock in 1620. The first European Jew to set foot in the New World (actually Cuba) was Christopher Columbus's interpreter Luis de Torres. Though Torres spoke Spanish and Hebrew, and knew Aramaic, Arabic, and Latin, he disappointed Columbus because he was unable to communicate with the "Natives." The falling out with the Natives that followed caused Torres and several other Spanish Marranos ("swine," or crypto-Jews forced to convert to Christianity, who, nevertheless, secretly held to their Jewish faith) to remain behind with him. Hence, in 1492 Torres and his coreligionists became the first Jews to settle in the New World. News quickly spread that Jews were settled and trading lucratively in the New World. As the Spanish Inquisition took an increasingly violent toll of Jews, (they were compelled to convert to Christianity or be killed), many Spanish and Portuguese Jews soon migrated to the Americas. In the American Southwest, Spanish Marranos participated in the 16th-century conquest of these desert territories. Jews were also settling in Virginia as early as 1621, just one year after the Pilgrim fathers landed in Massachusetts. In 1654, 23 Dutch Jews fleeing Recife, Brazil, from which they had been expelled when Portugal recaptured the colony from the Dutch, arrived in the Dutch colonial port of New Amsterdam on the French ship *Sainte-Catherine*. This ship was known later to Jewish historians as the "Jewish *Mayflower*."

Jews also sought to settle in New Amsterdam, later called New York, then only a wretched, muddy fort settlement that had been founded in 1625 by the Dutch West India Company. This small settlement of 1,500 people, mainly involved in the beaver pelt trade, was rimmed by rough wooden palisades designed to repel Algonquin Indians. Its north side eventually became the famous Wall Street, home of the New York Stock Exchange. Peter Stuyvesant, then director general of Colonial New Amsterdam, sought to bar the Jews from New Amsterdam, relying on the traditional Christian anti-Semitic belief that Jews were enemies of Christ. The directors of the Dutch West India Company located in Amsterdam overruled Stuyvesant on both financial and moral grounds. The directors wrote Stuyvesant: "[M]any of the Jewish nation are principal shareholders" in the West India Company. Addition-

ally, they noted the "considerable loss" suffered by the Jews in Brazil. The directors therefore decreed that Jews could "travel, trade, live, and remain" in New Netherland as long as "the poor among them shall not become a burden to the company or to the community, but be supported by their own nation" (Jonathan D. Sarna, *American Judaism: A History*, New Haven, Conn.: Yale University Press, 2004, p. 2). By 1680 the first Jewish burial ground in the United States was established in what is now Chatham Square, lower Manhattan. The year 1682 saw several Jewish trading posts scattered along the Delaware River into southeastern Pennsylvania.

With the arrival of William Penn that same year, and the founding of Philadelphia as a tolerant Quaker city committed to religious freedom, Philadelphia became the first real center of Jewish settlement in America in the 18th century. From this amazingly tolerant city the beautiful Jewish society figure Rebecca Gratz (b. 1781) emerged as a brilliant letter writer. A noted philanthropist, she planned the first Hebrew Sunday school in America. There were also Jews in the Port of Charleston early in the 1680s, and by 1702 Carolina Jews were able to vote in elections. Unfortunately, those Jews who settled in Louisiana in 1724 have left almost no record of their lives. In 1706 the New York Jewish community established Kehilot Kodesh Shearith Israel, Holy Congregation, Remnant of Israel, the oldest Jewish congregation in America. Once the British took over the colonies, the rules of worship were relaxed and other Jewish congregations began to form. The Massachusetts Bay colony of Rhode Island, founded in 1635 by Roger Williams, and the Providence Plantations on Narragansett Bay, became early colonial American refuges for Jewish pioneers.

By 1759 the Newport congregation of Jeshuat Israel had begun to build the Touro Synagogue, now a national historic site. Jewish merchants began arriving in Boston during the early 1700s. By 1776 several Jews enlisted as soldiers during the Revolutionary War. In Charleston, South Carolina, Jews quickly numbered among the Southern gentry, and many even owned slaves. In the Southeast, Mississippi, and Alabama, Jews settled before 1783 and increased in number after the Louisiana Purchase in 1803. Especially large numbers of Jews are recorded as moving into the early New Orleans parishes. In the early 19th century, records show Jews listed in active service in the War of 1812, the Second War of Independence. According to historian Seymour Kurtz, despite the prevailing atmosphere of anti-Semitism during these years Jews, who numbered about 6,000 just before the American Revolution, were engaged in every walk of life in the original 13 colonies.

As the nation headed into the Revolutionary War, many Jews were active in pioneering activities from the Atlantic to the steadily expanding western frontier, and on into the American Southwest. In the ensuing years they participated in every phase and in every geographic region of pioneering settlement in America: the American South, the Gulf States, the Texas borderlands, the American Southwest, the Mexican Territory, and eventually the West. According to historian Juanita Brooks, in 1826 Emmanuel Lazarus is listed as part of a 16-man trapping and exploring party looking for trade routes to California and the Northwest. Arriving in 1844, Moses Shalienberger spent the next four years camping around the Great Salt Lake while assessing its mineral resources. In 1849 Brigham Young formed the provisional State of Desert to shelter Mormons driven out of Missouri; several Jews are numbered among these early settlers. These pioneers and explorers entered the American West by various routes. Some traveled overland from Independence, Missouri. Some sailed the all-water route down the Atlantic and around Cape Horn to the Pacific Ocean, there joining wagon trains formed in San Francisco and bound for California, Oregon, Arizona, Nevada, Utah, and Idaho. Still others crossed the Isthmus of Panama, traveling through the jungle by mule, and eventually ending up in Los Angeles and San Francisco. Jewish merchants were present among the earliest Mormon settlements in Utah and Idaho, where they found religious tolerance and even official welcome while Salt Lake City was still Mexican territory. (See Juanita Brooks, *History of the Jews in Utah and Idaho,* Salt Lake City: Western Epics, 1973.)

These early Jews, shaped in the colonial milieu of North American settlement, number significantly among America's religious pilgrims, explorers, pioneers, trappers, traders, religious leaders, settlers, soldiers, merchants, actors, peddlers, lawmakers, bankers, financiers, philanthropists, abolitionists, Revolutionary War soldiers, Civil War heroes, theologians, and patriots. Collectively, their presence served to force America to the test of religious freedom guaranteed by the Constitution. Since the Hebrew Bible and language exerted significant influence in early American life, Jews, the original Chosen People of the biblical tradition, no doubt felt included in the founding Puritan mythic narrative of the New Eden and the new "Chosen People." Jews and Puritans, like their literal and spiritual desert ancestors, were still bound in a covenantal relationship with God. It could not have been lost on these early American Jews that Puritan preachers quoted extensively from the Holy Scripture, and compared the situation of the Puritans in America to that of the Israelites who entered the biblical Promised Land. They must have been aware as well that the laity also read and knew Hebrew Scriptures, and that the Puritans used biblical names such as Daniel, Ezra, Rachel, and Esther for their children. Many place names in the New World also reflected this biblical heritage: Zion National Park, Bethlehem (house of bread), Salem (peace), Goshen, Canaan, and others. (See Abraham I. Katsh, "Hebraic Influences on Puritan America." In *Encyclopaedia Judaica Yearbook, 1975/6.* Jerusalem: Keter, 1977.) Benjamin Franklin was later to propose that the Great Seal of the United States of America should portray the Israelites crossing the Red Sea. Historian William Lecky, among others, suggests that this biblical narrative and these generations of Jews were the Hebraic mortar which cemented the foundations of American democracy.

1881–1920: The Eastern European Immigrants

Jewish Americans who attained distinction from colonial times to 1880 were for the most part native-born Ashkenazim. Religiously, they were more Protestant than Jewish in observance, and were quite outside Yiddish culture. By contrast, those who arrived after 1881 were predominantly orthodox Yiddish-speaking Jews from eastern Europe fleeing pogroms and other systematic government-sanctioned violence against Jews. Anti-Semitic upheavals in Russia and Poland following the 1881 assassination of Czar Alexander II spurred the massive eastern and southern European immigration of Jews into North America, and lasted until the discriminatory Johnson Act of 1924 effectively stopped this flood of eastern European Jews. Even though the doors of Ellis Island had suddenly slammed shut, however, this influx of Jews had already introduced Yiddish literary culture and speech into mainstream American culture, along with their various European languages and centuries of Jewish and Hebrew religious learning. Within a generation these Jews would powerfully affect newspaper, entertainment, radio, movie, television, and literary culture in America. Religiously speaking, the arrival of eastern European Jews meant that Reform, or Liberal, Judaism would cease being the dominant form of Jewish expression in America, and that both the Orthodox tradition and a vibrant secularism would now vie for the allegiance of America's Jews.

The literature of these more recent Jewish immigrants and their children would be powerfully marked by their experience with the infamous Ellis Island National Immigration Center. Passing the Statue of Liberty, a gift of the French government which had been dedicated in 1886, they then experienced a bewildering variety of miserable physical and mental assaults. For several days these frightened immigrants were fed nonkosher as well as totally unfamiliar foods. Given bananas, a fruit unknown to them, they did not know to peel off the skins before eating them. They were shouted at in English, had their names badly transliterated or totally altered by indifferent immigration officials, their politics questioned, and their bodies poked. The most excruciating physical torment was having their eyelids raised by fishhook-like instruments as medical personnel searched for evidence of the highly contagious "red eye." Their IQs and mental health were then checked through a series of bizarre and primitive psychological tests. Those who failed these extensive tests were promptly separated from their families and sent back on the return voyage. This cruel circumstance sometimes separated family members forever, and too often resulted in shipboard suicides. Emma Lazarus's words written on the base of the Statue of Liberty might have been a beacon of hope to the entering immigrants, but they were a cruel irony to those sent home:

> Keep, ancient lands, your storied pomp! Cries she.
> With silent lips. Give me your tired, your poor,
> Your huddled masses, yearning to breathe free,
> The wretched refuse of your teeming shore,
> Send these, the homeless, tempest-tossed to me.
> I lift my lamp beside the golden door.

It was Emma Lazarus's father, Moses, who had founded Manhattan's famous Knickerbocker Literary Club.

In the 1920s anti-Semitic xenophobia had reached fever pitch. As the gates of Ellis Island closed in 1924, Jewish immigrants realized that they were at this time the dominant "ethnic" or immigrant cultural group of their day and marked off as inferior stock by the majority Christian culture. All of this was exacerbated by the Great Migration, that huge demographic shift that brought unprecedented numbers of southern blacks flocking to New York and other American cities. At this same moment the Jewish-American population, which had been 226,042 in 1887, had added to it 3,384,695 eastern European immigrants by 1920 (*Encyclopaedia Judaica*, 2nd ed.). America's newly arrived Jews were now subject to the bitter realities of American racism and anti-Semitism. The appalling ghetto conditions in the major cities, coupled with terrible labor relations and constant neighborhood physical violence, all play out in the writings of these first generations of Jews who loudly voiced the demand that America live up to its constitutional promise of religious tolerance.

Before the arrival of the eastern European Jews these American-born Jewish populations had produced few writers. In Joseph Lebowich's 1906 bibliography of American Jewish writers, "The Jew in

American Fiction" (*The American Hebrew* 78 [May 4, 1906]), he cites only 18 American Jewish authors for the years 1900–1906. Ten years later Rebecca Schneider's more comprehensive *Bibliography of Jewish Life in the Fiction of America and England* lists 41 Jewish-American writers who published fiction between 1900 and 1916. Most of these earlier authors were of German-Jewish origin, and had begun writing in the 1890s. With the exception of Abraham Cahan, few of the late 19th-century eastern-European immigrants wrote in English. This process usually took two generations. Issues of assimilation and labor unrest dominate this early work. Due to the traditional domestic scripting of orthodox Jewish women, there were few Jewish-American women writers in these first generations. In fact no Jewish woman produced significant fiction or poetry in America until the appearance of Rebecca Gratz and Emma Wolf. Anzia Yezierska did not begin publishing fiction until 1905, Fannie Hurst's works had just begun to emerge in 1910, and Mary Antin's *The Promised Land* did not appear until 1912. Even the prolific Edna Ferber did not produce her major novel, *So Big,* until 1924.

The first Jewish-American writer of real stature was Abraham Cahan, whose classic *The Rise of David Levinsky* (1917) underscored the impossible tensions generated by a population caught between Jewish tradition and American modernity. The religious reaction the young David Levinsky receives from his rabbi on announcing he was going to America says it all. The holy man responded: "To America! Lord of the World! But one becomes a Gentile there." In Cahan's distinctly Jewish version of America's favorite Horatio Alger rags-to-riches narrative, David arrives in the New World with four cents in his pocket. Unlike most Jewish immigrants, by novel's end he is a millionaire and a giant presence in the garment industry. Yet he muses, "I cannot escape from myself. My past and my present do not comport well." Cahan's book became a paradigm for future assimilationist novels whose protagonist's Old World religious identity remains forever in conflict with a secular America. Despite the overwhelming success of *The Rise of David Levinsky,* at the dawn of the 20th

century, Jewish-American writers were a distinctly marginal presence in American letters.

The Proletarian Writers, 1920–1930

By the 1920s over two-thirds of the newly arrived 3,384,695 Jews, plus the original 226,042 non-Yiddish-speaking resident Jews, had settled in cities where not only housing and employment opportunities were lacking (*Encyclopaedia Judaica,* 2nd ed.). The mostly Irish-Catholic and northern and eastern European Protestant immigrants were often extremely hostile to them. Ivy League universities rapidly imposed strict quotas (*numerus clausis*) on the number of Jewish students they would admit. Hotels and other establishments often refused service to both African Americans and Jews. Rapid industrialization created serious labor unrest, and this fueled Jewish radicalism, which took the form of an unyielding embrace of social justice. This Jewish-American tendency to political leftism fueled a socialist politics strongly committed to forming trade unions. Understandably, the clash of competing ethnic groups formed a principal theme for Jewish-American writers for the next two generations.

One of the most poignant records of these new generations of Jewish Americans is to be found in the many political propaganda magazines, the most popular of which was Abraham Cahan's Yiddish-language *Forvorts,* or *Jewish Daily Forward.* Cahan developed this comprehensive newspaper to include fiction, poetry, political, religious, and cultural commentary, scholarship, daily news, and theater reviews. Its famous Bintel Brief (a bundle of letters) section, was the forerunner to the modern-day Letters to the Editor, and Dear Abby columns. Here the displaced immigrant generations wrote heartbreaking accounts of abandonment, divorce, poverty, family dislocation, and terrible homesickness. They lamented the younger generation's rapid assimilation into American culture, their abandonment of the elderly, their general disregard of the Jewish orthodoxy of the medieval European shtetl, and the culture of their parents. It is a heartbreaking tale of marital and family breakdown, economic impoverishment,

ghetto life, organized crime, and health crises. A rich source of information for social historians and literary scholars alike, *Foorworts* also records the progress between 1909 and 1914 of the Jewish labor union movement, which it actively nurtured through its editorials and stories on the appalling and exploitive sweatshop and factory conditions in which Jewish and other immigrant men, women, and children worked. The socialist or proletarian literature that emerged out of this period records the heroism of Jews and others who protested outrageous economic exploitation and their effective disenfranchisement from the American dream. By the 1920s the first English-speaking generation of American Jews was poised to write their accounts of these deprivations, violence, anti-Semitism, and ghetto conditions in America's industrial cities.

Simultaneously, such large numbers of linguistically talented Jews concentrated in America's major industrial cities created an exponential increase in the number of Jewish-American writers who would appear in the post–World War I decades. This emerging literary culture received major impetus from two sources: (1) the Anglo-American and European modernist moment including avant-gardists such as Waldo Frank, Lewis Mumford (half Jewish), Paul Rosenfeld, and Gertrude Stein; and (2) the appearance of several sympathetic and influential WASP writers and literary critics. Though few Jewish-American women writers emerged during these decades, Anzia Yezierska and Mary Antin bridge the period. By 1922 the *American Jewish Yearbook, 1922,* edited by Harry Schneiderman, listed 275 Jewish-American writers of various genres.

Acceptance into the WASP literary establishment for American Jews was slow in coming. In American literature there had been two major literary "renaissances," that of the 1840s and 1850s, which saw the appearance of Emerson, Thoreau, Hawthorne, Melville, and Whitman, and that of the 1920s, which saw the appearance of T. S. Eliot, Eugene O'Neill, F. Scott Fitzgerald, Ernest Hemingway, William Faulkner, Willa Cather, Sherwood Anderson, Thomas Wolfe, and many others. All of these writers were of Anglo and northern European ancestry. In retrospect, this was to be the last

exclusively Anglo-Saxon and northern European moment in American letters. Jews and African Americans alike faced northern European racial superiority fueled by Social Darwinism, primitivism, the eugenics movement, and colonial Western racial ideologies when they challenged the closed club of the American mainstream literary culture.

The American literary establishment until well past the middle of the 20th century took as its fundamental assumption a universalist notion of literary aesthetics and of who was capable of producing "Literature." In recent decades cultural critics have unveiled the nationalist, racial, and religious foundations of this "universalism," which now sometimes appears to have been an anti-Semitic, racist notion which excluded many writers. For decades Jews and other so-called minority American writers were largely unread since they were not writing in the Anglocentric or northern European "voice," reflecting the traditional experiences and aesthetic formulas. By this cultural measure, peoples of Native American, African, Jewish, Asian, and Latina/o descent were deemed constitutionally and culturally incapable of entering the American literary arena. Truth, beauty, and verbal excellence belonged only to European and British cultures. Not surprisingly, the unwelcome presence of Yiddish-speaking Jews in America was recorded negatively in nearly all the early works of these reflexively patrician novels by Anglo-Saxon American writers of the late 19th and early 20th centuries.

For their part, a majority of these early 20th-century immigrant generations lived in accordance with norms of Jewish orthodoxy forged since the Middle Ages in Europe's Jewish ghettoes. Surprising numbers, however, were infused with Zionist ideals and poised to enter both modernity and the American experience minus what some viewed as the shackles of Jewish orthodoxy. For the American ghetto-born children of both groups, assimilation proved highly seductive. Many were embarrassed by the Yiddish of their "foreign" parents, and the intergenerational conflict that ensued marks all subsequent Jewish-American and other immigrant literatures. With the entry of these first American-born generations into the American public school

system, city libraries, art galleries, and universities, family dislocation was intensified. Now trilingual (European language, Yiddish, and English), the language-rich children of the Jewish immigrants sought entry into the American mainstream. However, their Jewish-Yiddish identity remained mapped on their tongues and apparent in such cultural markers as their choice of food, humor, European culture, socialist politics, religious views, commitment to social justice, and intellectual style. Themes of resistance, protest, Jewish socialism, Jewish family disruptions, Jewish labor unrest, Jewish religious orthodoxy, and Jewish assimilation mark all of their writings. Notable among the writers to emerge in the post–World War I and immediate post-Depression years were Nathanael West, Henry Roth, Meyer Levin, Mike Gold, Clifford Odets, Muriel Rukeyser, Hortense Calisher, Arthur Miller, Delmore Schwartz, and Isaac Rosenfeld. All had grown up in the shadow of a fundamentally WASP and Roman Catholic America that had violently rejected them. For their part, Jewish-American writers activated by Yiddish socialism vigorously sought to redress social injustice and the evils of capitalism, which they associated with anti-Semitic gentiles. Interestingly, many Jewish-American writers are listed among the 93 prominent writers, artists, and intellectuals who protested the miscarriage of justice displayed in the infamous seven-week Sacco and Vanzetti trial of 1921.

Proletarian Literature of the 1930s

By the 1930s, Jews were very visible among the ranks of those writers who participated in the short-lived tradition known as American proletarian literature. Their work was promoted by such avant-garde journals as the *New Masses, The Comrade, The Liberator,* and the *Partisan Review,* this latter being initially the principal organ for the John Reed Clubs, which encouraged and published "revolutionary literature." Jewish-American writers and editors were also prominent among mainstream WASP and black antibourgeois writers protesting American injustice and the ill effects of American capitalism. The six-member editorial board of *The New Masses* included three Jewish

editors, one of whom was the notable proletarian novelist Mike Gold. All 12 of the original editors who made up the 1934 *Partisan Review* editorial board were Jewish, including the influential poet, fiction writer, and literary critic Philip Rahv (born Ivan Greenbaum). Eleven Jews were listed among the 17 executive committee members of the First American Writers Congress of 1935. The Jewish-American writer Waldo Frank became its chairman. Granville Hicks's *Proletarian Literature in the United States* (1935) features 63 American writers, half of whom are American Jews. Mike Gold's *Jews without Money* (1930), no longer much read, was reprinted many times within the first year of publication. By 1935 it had been translated into 15 languages. This decade also saw the emergence of Meyer Levin's numerous and popular works, including his later *The Settlers* (1972) and *The Harvest* (1978), Daniel Fuchs's influential *Williamsburg Trilogy* (1934–37), and Henry Roth's acknowledged classic, *Call It Sleep* (1934).

Though relatively short-lived, this class-conscious, assimilationist, revolutionary, and literarily crude work left two principal legacies: the entry of American Jews into American literary life, and the crucial moral energy that would energize American Jewish intellectuals and writers about to be confronted with global fascism, capitalist excesses, Stalinist atrocities, Hitlerism, and the Holocaust. Jewish-American socialist writers reminded America once more that it was failing in its democratic promise, and thus contributed further to the "Hebraic mortar" that was still shoring up the American democracy. The trickle of American Jewish writers who emerged in the decades of the 1920s and 1930s became a torrent by the 1950s.

Into the Mainstream, 1940–1950

By the 1940s, the prevailing Eurocentric universalist aesthetics, literary formalism, and political indifference of the American literary establishment could no longer keep a socially conscious Jewish-American literature from entering the mainstream. The Jewish-American writers who came of age after decades of American anti-Semitism, World War II, and the Shoah wrote with extraordinary passion about the issues of Judaism in the American context. The new Israelite exiles in the American Babylonia asked the ancient question: "How shall we sing the Lord's song in a foreign land?" Marjorie Morningstar, the protagonist of Herman Wouk's novel of the same name, struggles with the temptation to marry someone Jewishly unacceptable—and remains loyal to her Jewish values. Meanwhile, Henry Roth's youthful immigrant protagonist, David Searle, learns the difficult lessons of a Jewish youth in a radically secular America.

The official moment of American Jewish entry into the literary mainstream was signaled by the 1944 symposium "Under Forty," published in the *Contemporary Jewish Record* of the American Jewish Committee. Eleven of the respondents were American Jews and included such prominent figures as Muriel Rukeyser, Alfred Kazin, Delmore Schwartz, Lionel Trilling, Howard Fast, and Isaac Rosenfeld. Following this publication, the organizers wisely realized that a significant new American Jewish literary presence had arrived in the mainstream of American letters. They retired the *Contemporary Jewish Record* and replaced it the following year with *Commentary.* This publication, along with the politically toned-down *Partisan Review,* would feature the early work of such distinguished American Jewish writers as the future Nobel laureate Saul Bellow, Delmore Schwartz, Alfred Kazin, and Isaac Rosenfeld.

When in 1948 the *Partisan Review* published its symposium on "The State of American Writing," it included three American Jewish writers with the six non-Jewish authors. Despite the collapse of Jewish socialism and the American political Left, young Jewish writers like Leon Uris and Norman Mailer produced socially conscious novels that examined the existential absurdity of war, anti-Semitism in the American military, and the impact of the establishment of the state of Israel in 1948, and provided critiques of mainstream American bourgeoise culture. (Jewish-American literature, with the exception of Edward Lewis Wallant's novel *The Pawnbroker,* would not confront the Holocaust directly until the 1970s.) Saul Bellow's first two novellas, *Dangling Man* (1947) and *The Victim*

(1949), were written out of postwar exhaustion and the metaphysically gloomy formulas of early modernist despair, engaged European models and philosophical ideas, and reflected the ennui of the moment. With the publication of *The Wasteland* (1946), Jo Sinclair arrived as the first prominent Jewish lesbian literary voice. Alan Ginsberg's *Howl* (1955) is arguably the great work of the American Beat poets. Isaac Rosenfeld and Paul Goodman were other up-and-coming writers.

Coming of Age in the Literary Mainstream, 1950–1970

In the 1950s, called by some the Jewish decade of American literature, several American Jewish writers entered the literary mainstream. The early works of Isaac Rosenfeld, Delmore Schwartz, Norman Mailer, Saul Bellow, Bernard Malamud, J. D. Salinger, Herman Wouk, Leon Uris, Grace Paley, Edward Lewis Wallant, Isaac Bashevis Singer, and Philip Roth all appeared in this decade. So too did the essays and reviews of the influential literary critics Lionel and Diana Trilling, Alfred Kazin, and Leslie Fiedler. J. D. Salinger's *The Catcher in the Rye* (1951), a novel that immediately assumed the status of a cult classic, prophetically pointed to the coming revolution among the young. Arthur Miller's *Death of a Salesman* (1951) and *The Crucible* (1953) transformed the American stage and reflected the paranoia of the cold war era. Themes of anti-Semitism in the workplace, Jewish social life, intellectual life in America's universities, religious crisis, assimilation, the Jewish humanistic legacy, the disappearance of *Yiddishkeit,* political disillusionment, retreat into the private realm, consumerism, McCarthyism, black/Jewish race relations, and a host of related topics preoccupy these writers. Significantly, they wrote remarkably little about the Shoah, though its monumental effects can be seen behind much of their work. These second-generation children of immigrants were writers whose roots lay in the moment of the Great Depression, the spiritual devastation of World War II, the Shoah, and the establishment of the fledgling state of Israel in 1948. Many of these writers had succeeded far beyond the Jewish family and neighborhood. They spoke unaccented English and had largely abandoned traditional religious ritual. Many writers now, realizing an era was passing, reproduced American Jewish urban life with a nostalgic sociological fidelity; some embraced Zionism, and nearly all imaginatively revisited Jewish-American life of earlier decades. Jewish-American authenticity becomes an increasingly urgent concern for all of them.

As the decade of the 1950s ended, there was no question about the growing importance of American Jewish writing in the mainstream tradition. The Jewish-American Beat generation poet, Alan Ginsberg, author of *Howl* (1956) and *Kaddish and Other Poems* (1961), dominated the Beat movement's brief literary moment. However, when the *Times Literary Supplement* (November 6, 1959) published an article entitled "A Vocal Group: The Jewish Part in American Letters," the other side of the story was revealed—the catastrophic loss of faith and the humanist intellectual crisis within Jewish-American religious and secular life. The moment registered literarily in bewildering ways: the Jewish-American recourse either to Greenwich Village bohemianism or the bourgeois escape to the suburbs, the Beat poets registering their various howls, not to mention the future Nobel laureate in literature Saul Bellow, who was busily reading European philosophy and the modernists to assess the effects on Western culture of French existentialism. If *Dangling Man* (1947) and *The Victim* (1947) register his examination and rejection of European nihilism, *The Adventures of Augie March* (1953) signals his renewed optimism for postwar America. However, the themes of Jewish-American alienation in the aftermath of modernity, World War II, and the Holocaust continue to appear in the work of such writers as Herman Wouk, Chaim Potok, Bernard Malamud, and Philip Roth, all literary artists and innovators who came of age during World War II. Together they would dramatically alter the formal, linguistic, and aesthetic limits of mainstream American literature. But it was Saul Bellow who patented the distinctively nuanced voice of urban America and forever changed Anglo-Saxon–based American everyday speech within the country's literary record.

Perhaps it was the gigantic shadow of the murdered 6 million that drew Jewish-American writers to pay more attention to the rapidly disappearing religious life, dietary regulations (laws of kashruth), extended family life, Jewish neighborhoods, food ways, family kitchens, and traditional humor. Much of the literature of this period contains lovingly crafted and memorable depictions of immigrant grandparents, birth families, religious education, and synagogue membership. Most notable of these many casualties of assimilation was the disappearance of the Jewish-American Yiddish linguistic legacy and the diminishment of the previously vibrant American Yiddish theater tradition. The emergence of Yiddish studies as a university discipline in this generation is illustrative of cultural loss. It explains the writerly fascination with the disappearing legacy of eastern European immigrant culture, secularization, intermarriage, and the loss of American Jewish family life. But none of these issues has had the lasting effects on the tradition that the Holocaust has. It has steadily become the dominant single subject in Jewish-American literature.

The Emergence of Jewish Women Writers

The escalating crises of the cold war, the bankruptcy of the Marxist religious vision, the aftermath of the atomic bomb, the American youth revolution, the drug culture, neomysticism, liberal hedonist simplicity, and the birth of New Age religion transformed Jewish-American literature by the 1970s. During the 1960s and 1970s significant numbers of Jewish-American women writers had been energized by the social freedoms accorded women during World War II, and the first wave of the feminist movement emerged. Questioning the patriarchal constructions of traditional Judaism, along with the entire social structure of the male-dominant American establishment, they too lent their genius to American literary life. This distinguished cadre included such writers as Susan Sontag, Cynthia Ozick, Norma Rosen, Grace Paley, Erica Jong, Hortense Calisher, Esther Broner, Tova Reich, Anne Roiphe, and Tillie Olsen, to name just a few. Tillie

Olsen writes of Jewish socialist themes on behalf of the laboring class and single mothers, as does Grace Paley. In her *The Little Disturbances of Man* (1959) she emphasizes feminist outrage, cold war political protests, peace marches, and related themes in Jewish women's lives. Esther Broner's *A Weave of Women* (1975) focuses on the fraught intergenerational relationships between Jewish mothers and daughters, while Susan Fromberg Schaeffer's *Anya* (1974) treats similar themes of intergenerational mother-daughter relationships as affected by modernity, and the events of the Holocaust. Anne Roiphe in her provocative novel *Lovingkindness* (1974) frames the collision between an emergent Jewish feminist movement and traditional orthodoxy. Erica Jong and Susan Sontag, preeminent feminists and philosophical theorists, expanded the feminist debate and entered the wider fields of philosophical, cultural, and social criticism. The influence of Jewish women's issues has steadily escalated throughout the subsequent decades. Only the Shoah would eclipse these thematic issues.

The Shoah, Existential Crisis, 1960–1970

Deepening awareness of the impact of the Shoah on the meaning of Jewish identity and on the subsequent theological crisis concerning the role of God in history continued to change everything. Of works by Holocaust survivor writers who found refuge in America, Elie Wiesel's searing memoir *Night* (1958) has become the classic Holocaust memoir. Appearing in English translation in 1960, it catalyzed the American-born writers. The dislocation of the Holocaust survivor is also famously registered in American-born Edward Lewis Wallant's *The Pawnbroker* (1961), and again in Saul Bellow's *Mr. Sammler's Planet* (1970).

Clearly during the decades of the 1960s and 1970s American Jewish writers were also still puzzling over Jewish identity in America, and still attempting to recapture the increasingly distant immigrant world. In historical fictions such as those of Saul Bellow, Philip Roth, Bernard Malamud, and E. L. Doctorow, Jewish life before and after the Holocaust is brought into radical juxtaposition. Moreover, from the 1970s on, American

Jewish literature came to dominate the American literary mainstream with psychologically insightful, artistically gifted, metaphysically engaged masters of their craft, such as Bellow, Erica Jong, Jerzy Kosinski, Malamud, Ozick, Paley, and Hugh Nissenson. Nissenson's work especially is marked by an awareness of the Holocaust and the evident triumph of evil in a godless universe. Critic Andrew Furman calls these decades the "bear market years" of the Jewish-American literary tradition, and adds as a corollary that Bellow, Roth, Malamud, and Ozick seemed "to have largely devoured their literary children." He also points out that by the 1980s "their literary grandchildren were about to set the stage for the current resurgence of Jewish American literature" (*Contemporary Jewish American Writers and the Multicultural Dilemma: Return of the Exiled,* Syracuse, N.Y.: Syracuse University Press, 2000, p. 177).

The Jewish-American Literary Resurgence, 1980 to the Present

The literary grandchildren of the 1970s giants include writers like Nessa Rappoport, Rebecca Goldstein, Robert Cohen, Allegra Goodman, Melvin Bukeit, Thane Rosenbaum, Jonathan Rosen, Steve Stern, Helen Epstein, Art Spiegelman, Julie Salamon, Jonathan Safran Foer, Nathan Englander, and Michael Chabon, to name just a few. By the 1980s we see the appearance of a Jewish-American literature that privileges the Jewish tradition, if not necessarily Orthodox Judaism, over and against the norms of American mainstream culture. Arthur A. Cohen's *In the Days of Simon Stern* (1973) and Cynthia Ozick's *The Pagan Rabbi* (1971), *Bloodshed* (1976), and *Levitation* (1982) all employ Jewish myth and mysticism as a standard by which to critique the state of Judaism in America, and to frame the seismic upheaval of the Holocaust. In 1993 a special issue of *Contemporary Literature,* "Contemporary American Jewish Literature," first signaled this resurgence. In 1996 *Response: A Contemporary Jewish Review* published a special issue entitled "Perspectives on Jewish American Literature."

In 1997 *Prairie Schooner,* an old and respected literary quarterly, published a special issue labeled

"Jewish-American Writers," providing also a reading list of some 30 emerging Jewish-American writers. One year earlier, the ALA Jewish American and Holocaust Literature Symposium, held in Del Ray Beach, Florida, began to devote its annual meetings to "The Jewish Literary Revival." It has continued to the present to focus scholarly attention on this current Jewish-American literary resurgence. In 1998 *Shofar* produced a special issue focusing on Jewish-American literature about Israel, and Israeli literature about America. Inclusion, not marginalization in the contemporary multicultural moment, will help this resurgence flourish, even though these writers, Philip Roth notwithstanding, will never have the kind of international or even national readership enjoyed by a writer like Ernest Hemingway. The year 2000 saw the landmark appearance of *Jewish American Literature: A Norton Anthology*.

Beyond the catastrophic reverberations of the Holocaust, the 1980s also witnessed the paradigm shifting effects of the postmodern moment as reflected in a remarkably rich outburst of Jewish-American literature by a new generation of women writers, such as playwright Wendy Wasserstein, and novelists Alix Kates Shulman, Anne Michaels, and Rebecca Goldstein. Postmodern male writers like Michael Chabon and Steve Stern continue to explore the ramifications of the Holocaust and Jewish identity by utilizing the myths, symbols, and language of Jewish religion and mysticism. These decades also witnessed the emergence of a second-generation literary response to the Holocaust. Unlike Bellow's *Mr. Sammler's Planet* (1970), which focused on the life of a survivor who observes the moral decay of Judaism and the American city, the daughters and sons of Holocaust survivors do not attempt to imagine the horrors of the Holocaust. Rather, most of them write of the continuing generational and religious aftermath of the catastrophe. Thane Rosenbaum in *Second Hand Smoke* (1999) calls them the most articulate of the second generation, the "survivors of the survivors." Many of these writers seek a twofold goal: to remind the world of the Jewish catastrophe and to help prevent future genocides.

This is the subject matter of Helen Epstein's *Children of the Holocaust* (1979) and *Where She came From* (1997), Julie Solomon's *White Lies* (1987), and Rosenbaum's post-Holocaust trilogy *Elijah Visible* (1996), *Second Hand Smoke* (1999), and *The Golems of Gotham* (2002).

The New Millennium, the Jewish Literary Revival, and the New York Resurgence

The richness of the current moment in Jewish-American literature defies Irving Howe's now famous public statement made over 30 years ago that Jewish-American writing would soon cease to be a distinct and vibrant literature. Referencing Philip Roth's *Portnoy's Complaint*, Howe writes that it "reflected the point of which the underground springs of both Yiddish culture and the immigrant experience had finally dried up" (Irving Howe, *World of Our Fathers*, Simon & Schuster, 1976, p. 597). Mark Schechner made a similar prediction during his address at the 1997 ALA Jewish American and Holocaust Literature Symposium at Del Ray Beach, Florida. From the 1980s, the various and abundant postmodern tradition in American Jewish literature puts to rest any notion that the Jewish-American literary tradition has peaked and waned. In this volume we have given much space to showcasing these most recent writers in the belief that they will be of major interest to high school and college readers in the coming decades. No true picture of Jewish-American literature could slight them. These current writers, by sheer virtue of their numbers, their established literary expertise, and their relative youth, constitute a virtual literary renaissance within the tradition. Women writers like Dara Horn, Joan Legant, Allegra Goodman, and Jacquie Osherow have moved their readers to new levels of understanding about what Judaism means to more than half of the members of the tradition whose orthodox voices were for too long silenced. Like their forbears, the works of these Jewish women writers demonstrate a wide variety of affiliations across a spectrum ranging from Orthodox Judaism, to *Yiddishkeit,* to Jewish ethnic descent, and American secularism.

The role of religion in current Jewish-American fiction is both vigorous and controversial. Writers like Nessa Rappoport, in *Preparing for Sabbath* (1989), Allegra Goodman in *Total Immersion* (1989), and all of Cynthia Ozick's works reflect the virtues of Jewish-American particularism and are expressed in traditional observance. Elie Wiesel continues to lend his eloquent voice and haunted memory to portraying what was lost to Judaism—and the world—in the Nazi extermination of the Jewish people. Steve Stern writes of an imaginary ghetto— "the Pinch"—in humorous detail, while portraying the life and times of its Jewish inhabitants. The contemporary discussion of how Orthodox Judaism is portrayed in Jewish fiction has sometimes assumed a strident note. The contention that only the religiously observant themselves are entitled to write novels about Orthodox Jews provides much impassioned discussion. Writers who were formerly religious, or who pretend to be, they argue, cannot write accurately about orthodoxy. While such a position may be maintained, this attempt to "fence the pasture" will not prove any more successful than other attempts to contain and suppress the Jewish-American creative spirit. The untenable assumption of this position, that the Judaic tradition is unchanging, is an especially problematic notion in the postmodern and multicultural era.

The work of the current generation of young Jewish-American writers frequently reflects not only the impact of the Holocaust, but the continuing hold of Jewish mythic and mystical material. Michael Chabon's Pulitzer Prize–winning novel *The Amazing Adventures of Kavalier and Clay* (2000) utilizes the mythical figure of the golem (a creature made of earth and animated by the utterance of a magical formula) in order to cope with difficulties confronting the Jewish community. Thane Rosenbaum's *The Golems of Gotham* (2002) utilizes the golem figure as a dybbuk, or soul of a deceased person, in bringing back to life six iconic Holocaust writers who committed suicide after the *Shoah*. Nathan Englander in *For the Relief of Unbearable Urges* (1999) writes of Hasidic Judaism and its response to the Holocaust. The unabashed

recovery of Jewish rites and rituals marks this generations' embrace of the tradition, albeit in frequently unorthodox ways.

A marked New York resurgence within the Jewish-American literary revival has also greatly enlivened this current moment in Jewish-American letters. As Melvin Bukiet writes in the introduction to his anthology *Scribblers on the Roof: Contemporary American Jewish Fiction* (2006), many of these writers are associated with the New York City's Congregation Ansche Chesed located within that culturally rich three-square-mile area between Central Park West and Riverside Drive from Lincoln Center at 64th Street to Columbia University at 116th Street. It is here that noted Jewish-American writers such as Diana and Lionel Trilling, Philip Roth, I. B. Singer, and a host of characters from numerous Jewish-American novels have lived. For the last several years, on Monday nights through June, July, and August, he reports, a very successful series of readings sponsored by the congregation's adult-education program have been held on the roof top of the shul overlooking Riverside Drive. This prestigious series of readings has included such notable writers as Melvin Bukiet, Pearl Abraham, Myra Goldberg, Jonathan Rosen, Steve Stern, and the many others featured in *Scribblers on the Roof,* edited by Bukiet and David Roskies. As both writers point out in their introduction, a number of Jewish-American writers still reside in this historic epicenter of New York Jewish-American literary culture.

The prophesied falling after the high point of the Bellow, Malamud, and Roth years has become instead a resurgence. As this volume goes to press, it is Philip Roth who dominates the current moment in Jewish-American literature. A descendant of the Yiddish-speaking generation, and just a little younger than the recently deceased (2005) Saul Bellow, he began his long and illustrious writing career in the late 1950s. Rumored to be a Nobel laureate nominee, and one of only three American writers to have his entire work published by the Library of America, he belongs to an acknowledged handful of writers who dominate the early 21st-century American literary mainstream.

A-TO-Z
ENTRIES

⌒⌒⌒

The Adventures of Augie March
Saul Bellow (1953)

The Adventures of Augie March, unlike SAUL BEL-LOW's first two dark, formal European experi-ments, is a hilarious picaresque tale chronicling Depression and post–World War II era Chicago. Influenced by H. G. Wells's London, James Joyce's Dublin, and Theodore Dreiser's Chicago, it is a realist chronicle of American melting-pot democ-racy. Its lasting legacy, however, is its distinctly 20th-century American urban voice compounded of immigrant street language, Yiddish, biblical influences, and the mandarin voices of the great English, American, and European writers.

Bellow's talent for portraiture is also evident in the rich Hogarthian snapshots of the Russian-Jew-ish March family. There is the ambitious Ameri-canized older brother, Simon, the dreamy younger brother, Augie, their ineffectual, gentle mother, the fierce Russian Grandma Lausch, and her annoying poodle, Winnie. Later there are scenes of Mexico, World War II, lovers, and wives. However, Chicago itself is the central presence. Bellow once com-mented in an interview with Joyce Illig:

> All of civilized mankind is entering this pecu-liar condition in which we [Chicagoans] were pioneers. That's why Chicago is significant. . . . We experienced the contemporary condition before others were aware of it. . . . Chicago is, I believe, the symbol of it. In Chicago, things were done for the first time, which the rest of the world later learned and imitated. Capital-ist production was pioneered in the stockyards, in refrigerator cars, in the creation of the Pull-man, in the creation of farm machinery, and with it also certain urban political phenomena which are associated with the new condition of modern democracy. All that happened here. It happened early.

Bellow began writing this book in postwar Paris after recovering from a deep depression induced by seeing the condition of that city. Slowly he recov-ered his American-born optimism. Apocalyptics similar to those of James Joyce and D. H. Lawrence would not do. The human self had survived two world wars, the atom bomb, and even the Holo-caust. While Bellow and Ralph Ellison roomed to-gether in Paris, Bellow's *Augie March* and Ellison's *Invisible Man* took shape. Both reveal the identity issues, voices, and vernacular cultural capital of two distinct but marginalized groups of Americans.

Bellow's exuberant mixture contains Cervan-tesque chivalric allusions, Dickensian caricature, Yiddish wit, Bellow's family history, classical lore, and Whitmanesque catalogs of the street, the bar, the poolroom, the gangsters, the sharpsters, and the Northside Chicago immigrants. Ultimately this is a tale of two brothers, a dreamer and a ma-terialist, who together reflect the contemporary American condition. While Simon sinks into un-happiness and consumerism, Augie learns that fate is determined not by biology or environment, but by character. Like his predecessor, Huckleberry Finn, he will always be "lighting out" for that new unspoiled territory.

Bibliography

Alter, Robert. "Heirs of the Tradition." *Rogue's Progress: Studies in the Picaresque Novel.* Cambridge: Harvard University Press, 1964.

Amis, Martin. "A Chicago of a Novel." *Atlantic,* October 1995, 114–120, 122–127.

Illig, Joyce. "An Interview with Saul Bellow." *Publishers Weekly,* 22 October 1973: 74–77.

—Gloria L. Cronin

Against Interpretation Susan Sontag (1966)

Against Interpretation (1966), SUSAN SONTAG's first collection of essays, has attained the status of an intellectual classic. In it she drew on her Jewish heritage and social sensibility, as well as her acute awareness of the Holocaust, as she addressed post–World War II American culture. It was a groundbreaking book that blurred the hitherto rigid cultural boundaries between high and popular culture and sought to reconnect American intellectual life with international culture. The essays in this collection are alternately explosive, acerbic, subversive, trenchant, campy, teasing, provocative, and overtly political.

Breaking out of the confines of established intellectual rhetoric and reconceiving her intellectual audience as nonacademicians was subversive enough. But she also engages popular culture, politics, and intellectual life within the same horizon. Her subject matter encompasses such diverse topics as camp culture, the Vietnam War, psychoanalysis, Sartre, Camus, Ionesco, Weil, Godard, Beckett, Lévi-Strauss, Leiris, Lukacs, Bresson, the imagining of disaster, science fiction, movies, contemporary piety, religious thought, the artist as sufferer, cultural philistinism, communism, and fascism. Many essays indict the white race, address sexism, suggest a radical displacement of heterosexuality, and call American culture a parochial sort of happenstance derived from polyglot foreigners who act as if they are engaged in a "drive through." In these

matters she belonged to a group of women intellectuals including the equally renowned Mary McCarthy, Hannah Arendt, and Elizabeth Hardwick who lent their brilliance to the New York cultural scene. Alongside her provocative cultural politics, however, Sontag places her rather conservative literary agenda. As an aesthete she wants to cultivate the readers' intuitive responses to literature.

In the lead essay, "Against Interpretation," she encourages readers to experience the transparency and luminousness of the object of literature itself, and to pursue language as a profound private happiness. Accordingly, she attacks professional commentators and current practices of interpretation, even suggesting that criticism is the revenge critics enact on writers and their works. She argues for the primacy of style and aesthetics over content, and demands a proper balance of moral and aesthetic content. In place of a hermeneutics, she wants an erotics of art privileging an unmediated emotional and sensory response to the work.

Critics of Sontag's aesthetics point out that this stylish and persuasive essay is not nearly as systematic, thought through, or innovative as its author would like to think. Victorian critic Matthew Arnold had repeatedly expressed the notion of "transparency" and direct reading experience, while early modern critics like T. S. Eliot, in the wake of Matthew Arnold's and Walter Pater's aesthetics, felt that such a response was severely limited by the experience and background of the individual reader. Most generally agree that Sontag's separation of form and content is a false one, as is the notion of the unlocated universal reader. In the wake of postmodernism and multiculturalism, her espousal of the notion of a universal aesthetics now seems naive. Clearly the academy ignored Sontag's plea—for the past 40 years it has trained its critical readers to identify the dominant ideology in a work before aesthetics. Erotic reader responses based in sensation and emotion are no longer thought to preclude political and cultural reading strategies.

When the essays in *Against Interpretation* appeared in 1966, they stunned and outraged the stuffy mid-1960s cultural establishment, including the then aging Jewish radicals of the old *Partisan Review* crowd. This generation felt betrayed by one so young, so female, so activist, so ready to embrace celebrity, and yet so impeccably trained in literature and philosophy. Traditionalists abhorred the idea of a literary intellectual creating such a potpourri of high culture, popular culture, radical politics, aesthetics, and academy-based intellectual life with such wicked pleasure and scholarly panache. By insisting that such reviewers, critics, and social commentators leave works of art and readers alone, Sontag also earned the increasing displeasure of deconstructionists. Those on the old left, those on the right, and those in the middle as well all found themselves under indictment for their collective political indifference and ethical superficiality. Susan Sontag's successful attainment of high media visibility as a public intellectual and political activist didn't please the establishment either. Though she was intensely private about her personal life, Sontag was extrovertedly telegenic, deliberately posed, and self-consciously poised in her public life. In retrospect, these essays announced the official credo that would undergird her lifelong intellectual, political, and public work.

Viewed from nearly half a century later, some of these essays seem somewhat dated, yet, a few seem almost prophetic. In one Sontag states her early dissatisfaction with heterosexuality long before the gay rights movement had gathered its current momentum. Her comments on a mostly European cinema and photography is filtered through a markedly gay sensibility. In another she accurately predicts the fall of official communism some 20 years before it actually happened. In yet another she accurately predicts the primacy of photography and the image in 20th-century culture. *Against Interpretation,* constantly in print since 1966, has been translated into 32 languages. It was highly influential in energizing the social protest movement of the mid-sixties and in reorienting a rather parochial post-fifties American culture. It has influenced generations of writers all over the world and initiated Susan Sontag's rise to intellectual celebrity. Sontag, who died in December 2004, was tall, elegant, good-looking, and charismatic;

for most of her life she sported a trademark white swoosh in the front of her hair and refused to talk about her private life as a bisexual. She gave her own personal style and politics to *Against Interpretation,* while it in turn contributed to her status as an iconic figure of the age.

Bibliography
Fox, Margalit. "Susan Sontag, Social Critic with Verve, Dies at 71," *New York Times,* 29 December 2004, pp. A1, 18.
Hitchens, Christopher. "Susan Sontag: Remembering an Intellectual Heroine," Slate. Available online. URL: http://www.slate.com/id/2111506/. Accessed Dec. 29, 2004.
Rollyson, Carl E. *Susan Sontag: The Making of an Icon.* New York: Norton, 2000.
—Gloria L. Cronin

Aleichem, Sholem (1859–1916)

The writer who adopted the pen name Sholem Aleichem (the English spelling of his first name varies widely) was born Solomon (or Shalom) Rabinowitch in the town of Pereyeslav, Ukraine, in 1859. He left his home in 1906 and settled for a time in New York City. His pen name means "Peace be unto you" in Yiddish and Hebrew, and is quite similar in Arabic. He became a world famous writer and humorist, owing to the vivid depiction and popularization of the everyday life of Jews in eastern Europe, mostly in the Pale of Settlement, a region on the western border of imperial Russia where Jews were allowed to settle permanently under czarist rule. Three czars reigned during Sholem Aleichem's lifetime: Alexander II (1855–81), Alexander III (1881–94), and Nicholas II (1894–1917). Jews within the Pale endured more than czarist hatred and degrading segregation. There was latent and sometimes overt anti-Semitism, the continuing possibility of persecution, and even the occasional pogrom, such as the one that took place in 1905 in Chişinău. Not to be overlooked is the fact that this kind of déclassé existence induced in Jews a deep-rooted sense of inferiority and sustained that effect over generations. Yet there was the human response of wry acceptance of the "eternal outsider" condition, and ironic humor if not outright cheerfulness to lessen the misery. And there was one more element that Sholem Aleichem captured so effectively in his depiction of the passing parade of Jews under the yoke. That was the propensity to kvetch (in the vernacular), to complain, especially to complain to God about what was going on, and not necessarily about such serious issues as the deadly dangers that Pale of Settlement Jews were exposed to.

Literary treatments of Sholem Aleichem's life tend sooner or later to bring up the matter of his reputed meeting with Mark Twain (1835–1910), by way of showing the former writer's universality and especially his secure place among the most important (non-Jewish) writers. According to this anecdote or story, Mark Twain claimed that he had wanted to meet him, because of having heard that he, Twain, was the American Sholem Aleichem. According to one account of this so-called meeting, Sholem Aleichem reversed the hearsay line by saying he, Sholem, had heard that he himself was the Jewish Mark Twain. There is a good reason to refer to this oft-mentioned meeting. A close reading of material on Sholem Aleichem's life reveals amazing parallels between the two writers.

Sholem Aleichem won great fame, and profited hugely for a time, from his voluminous literary output. Through mishandling his finances, he went from boom to near bust. Driven to do whatever he could to restore the cash flow for his family, he found himself reluctantly making lecture tours, reading from his own works, giving recitations, and probably speaking of literary matters. He traveled wherever there might be a remunerative audience for his literary presence, and he seemingly had a keen sense of his audience. Understandably, the theme of money was of considerable significance in his thinking and writing—recall the iconic Zero Mostel's "If I Were a Rich Man" number in the enormously successful 1960s stage musical *Fiddler on the Roof*. (More information on this adaptation of Sholem Aleichem's stories is given in the entry on *Tevye's Daughters* in the present volume.)

One more literary comparison with Sholem Aleichem may be mentioned, although the parallel is not quite as close as that with Mark Twain. He has been compared to Charles Dickens, who, according to the Sholem Aleichem expert Dan Miron, was "his favorite European author." Each adopted the familiar formula of "make them laugh, make them cry." Comic scenes plus a cluster of caricatures plus melodrama—the result: comic relief.

Sholem Aleichem came to the United States first in 1906. He settled in New York City, where he wrote for Yiddish journals and had two plays produced in the Yiddish theater. He also spent the last two years of his life in New York and was buried in Brooklyn. His time in New York was deeply disappointing to him, however, primarily because he did not "go over" to the extent he had hoped for, even though he had considerable popular recognition and was not only a prolific writer but a deeply committed and persevering one. He was simply not taken up by people of influence and power, which would have given him a basis for settling permanently with his family in the United States. This resulted in his traveling around eastern Europe, seeking more favorable conditions for promoting his stories and plays, as well as his newspaper writing. A certain amount of his writing was for a much more select audience: Yiddish and Russian readers, mostly in Europe, but some in New York as well, of the feuilletons—a European newspaper section containing literature and related pieces. Versatile writer that he was (stories, novels, plays, etc.), Sholem Aleichem had long contributed these short feuilleton pieces to the Russian Yiddish press.

After the outbreak of World War I, he managed to return to the United States with his family, for the last time. But his feuilleton audience dwindled and then disappeared. Other audiences were dwindling or becoming unavailable. His books were no longer selling, and things looked increasingly grim. Desperate for financial survival and in ill health, he resumed his lecture tours, but he broke under the strain and died in May 1916. He was buried in Brooklyn, in Mount Carmel Cemetery.

Since the greater part of Sholem Aleichem's writing is in obscure Yiddish and Hebrew publications, the interested reader may choose English translations. Among the titles Dan Miron provides are *Adventures of Mottel the Cantor's Son; Collected Stories of Sholom Aleichem: vol. 1: The Old Country, vol. 2: Tevye's Daughters; The Great Fair; Inside Kasrilevke; Old Country Tales; Selected Stories; Stories and Satires; Wandering Star;* and *Sholom Aleichem Panorama.*

Bibliography

Butwin, Frances. Foreword to *The Old Country,* by Sholom Aleichem. New York, 1946.
Miron, Dan. "Sholom Aleichem." In *Encyclopaedia Judaica.* Vol. 14. CD-ROM. Jerusalem: Keter.
                                    —Samuel I. Bellman

Allen, Woody (1935–)

Woody Allen was born Allan Stewart Konigsberg to Orthodox Jewish parents on December 1, 1935, in the Bronx section of New York City, a city that is the setting for many of his works. Both a dramatic and comic writer, Allen is a prolific artist who has seen critical and commercial success during his long and influential career as a writer, director, and actor. At times criticized for his uncomplimentary treatment of Jewish characters, he is best known for his quirky stage and screen persona as an unlucky-in-love, quick-witted neurotic.

Konigsberg became "Woody Allen" when he embarked on his comic career, submitting jokes under the pseudonym to New York newspapers in 1952. He continued his comedy writing throughout high school and first performed stand-up, though not his own material, in 1952 at the Young Israel social club. Even before graduating from high school, Allen wrote jokes for comedian David Alber for $20 a week.

After being expelled from both New York University and City College of New York for low grades and poor attendance, Allen began working for NBC's Writer's Development Program in 1955. After a short stay in Hollywood writing for the *Colgate Comedy Hour,* Allen returned to New York in 1956 with his new wife, Harlene Rosen. In New York, Allen wrote for TV comedies like *Stanley,*

The Pat Boone-Chevy Show, and *Sid Caesar's Chevy Show,* the last of which received an Emmy Award nomination and a Sylvania Award.

One of the most important developments in Allen's career occurred in 1958 when he began his professional relationship with Jack Rollins and Charles Joffe, the management team that first helped Allen develop as a performer and then later produced his films. Allen continued performing stand-up at clubs in New York before transitioning to performing on television in the early sixties, appearing on shows such as *The Ed Sullivan Show, The Steve Allen Show,* and *Candid Camera.* Allen and Rosen divorced in 1962. His unflattering treatment of her in his comedy routine led Rosen to file a lawsuit against Allen and NBC in 1967. The suit was settled out of court.

By 1964, Allen was a popular and well-paid comic when he was hired to write the screenplay for *What's New, Pussycat?* (1965), a box office success that secured his reputation as a marketable comedian. Allen married Louise Lasser in 1966, but was divorced in 1969, the same year his first film over which he had artistic control, *Take the Money and Run* (1969), was released. Allen continued to write, direct, and act in bold and bawdy comedies such as *Bananas* (1971) and *Everything You Always Wanted to Know About Sex* (*But Were Afraid to Ask)* (1972)—a series of skits based on the popular book of the same title.

Allen became more experimental, making films containing darker themes, as in *Interiors* (1978), *Manhattan* (1979), and *Stardust Memories* (1980)—a black-and-white film with a highly disjointed narrative structure in which Allen plays Sandy Bates, a screenwriter plagued by celebrity, neuroses, and destructive relationships. The film concludes with the characters exiting a movie theater in which they have just watched their own movie, giving a sense of hyper-reality and anticlimax.

Annie Hall (1977), one of Allen's most notable and important films, has become an American classic about a doomed love affair between Annie (Diane Keaton) and Alvy Singer (Allen). He used atypical, innovative narrative techniques such as flashbacks and addressing the camera, making this an influential film for other filmmakers. Although the relationship between Annie and Alvy is dysfunctional, *Annie Hall* was above and beyond functional for the critics. The film won Allen the New York Film Critics Award for Best Director and Best Screenplay, as well as the National Society of Film Critics Screenwriting Award. Also for *Annie Hall*, Allen was nominated for an Academy Award for Best Actor and won Academy Awards for Best Director, Best Screenplay Directly for the Screen (with cowriter Marshall Brickman), and Best Picture. These Oscars were not to be the last for Allen, who has been nominated 15 times in total.

Allen and Keaton, romantically linked until 1970, worked together on other films: the film version of Allen's play *Play It Again, Sam* in 1972, *Sleeper* (1973), and *Love and Death* (1975). They later reunited in 1993 for *Manhattan Murder Mystery*. Allen had other successful, long-lasting working relationships with actresses. Mia Farrow, whom Allen met in 1979 and was romantically connected with (though never married to) until 1992, acted in 13 of his films, including *The Purple Rose of Cairo* (1985), *Hannah and Her Sisters* (1986), *Crimes and Misdemeanors* (1989), and *Husbands and Wives* (1992). It was while filming this last film that Farrow discovered Allen was having an affair with Farrow's 21-year-old adopted daughter, Soon-Yi Previn, whom he later married in 1997. Allen's films have been more comedic in recent years, with *Mighty Aphrodite* (1995) and *The Curse of the Jade Scorpion* (2001). Most recently, Allen wrote and directed the drama *Match Point* (2005). Allen currently lives in New York City with Previn.

The diversity of projects Allen has undertaken shows his versatility as an artist. In addition to having plays like *From A to Z* (1960), *Don't Drink the Water* (1966), and *Play It Again, Sam* (1969) produced on Broadway, Allen recorded three comic albums, *Woody Allen* (1964), *Woody Allen, Volume 2* (1965), and *The Third Woody Allen Album* (1968), the first of which garnered him a Grammy nomination. Additionally, Allen has published short stories in publications like the *New Yorker* and the *New York Times Magazine* and has written three books, *Getting Even* (1971), *Without Feathers* (1975), and *SIDE EFFECTS* (1980). Allen's prominent and reoccurring themes—regardless of genre—include death, love and passion, familial relationships, and Jewish cultural identity.

Bibliography

Lax, Eric. *Woody Allen: A Biography.* Cambridge, Mass.: Da Capo Press, 2000.

Schwartz, Richard A. *Woody, From Antz to Zelig: A Reference Guide to Woody Allen's Creative Work, 1964–1998.* Westport, Conn.: Greenwood Press, 2000.

Spignesi, Stephen J. *The Woody Allen Companion.* Kansas City, Mo.: Andrews and McMeel, 1992.

—**Rachel Mayrer**

The Amazing Adventures of Kavalier and Clay **Michael Chabon** (2000)

This novel based on the historical figures Jerry Siegel and Joe Shuster, the creators of Superman, features two Jewish cousins who help to create the comic book industry. The book is dense in detailed portraits of an entire generation of Greenwich Village artists, notables, eccentrics, bohemians, crooks, carnival characters, jazz musicians, big band era night clubs, early radio personalities, and pulp fiction writers, of the 1940s, all recounted by the elusive third-person narrator (perhaps Josef and Sammy's son). Against this rich texture of American pop culture MICHAEL CHABON recounts this story about two Jewish adolescents living the American dream and the Holocaust. The freedom of polyglot, buoyant 1940s American culture is juxtaposed with images of failed escapes by an embattled European Jewry.

Josef, the Prague cousin, already an *Ausbrecher,* or escape artist, has escaped to New York in a coffin containing the magical golem fashioned by a 16th-century rabbi to protect the Jews from anti-Semitism, thus establishing the book's overriding motif of disappearing acts and daring hoaxes. New York City is at the beginning of the comic book craze, and together with his American-born cousin, Sammy, an escapee from childhood polio, he creates a superhero, the Escapist, who fights Nazis. Summoned out of language and cartoon art in answer to the Holocaust, just like the Kabbalistic 16th-century golem, the Escapist reveals Josef's obsession with freeing his younger brother from Prague. The narrative provides a sensitive picture of adolescent crises and survivor guilt as the two cousins become wealthy, fail to rescue the brother, and encounter adult reality. Josef subsequently plunges into grief and ends up on a military assignment to the Antarctic, where he progressively loses faith in history. His steady erasure from history and his final unbelonging is demonstrated by his escalating losses: his city, Bernard Kornblum, mother, father, brother, grandfather, friends, foes, lover, son, and cousin. Out of love for them all Joe Shuster, the American-born gay cousin, marries Josef's lover and raises Josef's son.

Chabon's exploration of homosexual love and New York's queer demimonde of the 1940s has been criticized as distracting and too lengthy, despite the fact that it completes Chabon's brilliant chronicling of the age. His exploration of the uniquely American relationship between high art and pop culture is done in stylish, lush prose as the book mimics the style of comic book adventure. However, beneath the poignant characterization and exquisitely rendered tableaux covering all of Brooklyn and New York, Chabon invokes the paranoia and nightmare of broken history as the appalling mystery of the Holocaust looms over everything. *Kavalier and Clay* won the 2001 Pulitzer Prize for fiction and a nomination for the National Book Critics Circle Award.

Bibliography

Behlman, Lee. "The Escapist: Fantasy, Folklore, and the Pleasures of the Comic Book in Recent Jewish American Holocaust Fiction." *Shofar: An Interdisciplinary Journal of Jewish Studies* 22, no. 3 (Spring 2004): 56–71.

Maliszewski, Paul. "Lie, Memory: Michael Chabon's Own Private Holocaust." *BookForum: The Review for Art, Fiction, & Culture* 12, no. 1 (April–May 2005): 4–8.

—Gloria L. Cronin

American Pastoral   Philip Roth   (1997)

With the publication of *American Pastoral* in 1997, PHILIP ROTH moved away from fictional mirror games of self-reflexivity (found in such works as *The COUNTERLIFE, Deception,* and *Operation Shylock*) to an examination of the larger American historical landscape. He did so through the use of Nathan Zuckerman, the artist-hero of such foundational novels as *My Life as a Man, The Ghost Writer, The Anatomy Lesson,* and *The Counterlife.* Over a series of three novels called the American Trilogy—*American Pastoral, I Married a Communist* (1998), and *The HUMAN STAIN* (2000)—Roth explored many of the events that have defined post–World War II America, from the McCarthyite 1950s to the Monica Lewinski–based political witch hunt of the 1990s. Individually, each book is a demonstration of how individuals negotiate their lives in the face of historical forces beyond their control. The American Trilogy is perhaps Roth's most ambitious literary effort, and *American Pastoral* in particular is often cited as Roth's greatest work.

All three novels show how an individual becomes, in the words of the author, "history's hostage" to the various economic, ethnic, and political determinants into which he is born. *American Pastoral*'s protagonist is Seymour "Swede" Levov, a former high school athlete idolized by the Jews of his Weequahic, New Jersey, neighborhood. He represents to his community an entry into the successful and assimilated world of white-bread, gentile America. Nicknamed for his notable Nordic features, the Swede spends much of the narrative trying to live a Norman Rockwellesque dream. He marries a former Miss New Jersey, inherits his father's lucrative glove-making business, and takes up residence in bucolic Old Rimrock, New Jersey. However, his attempts to secure a "pastoral" life without complications are undermined by his malcontented teenage daughter, ironically named Merry, who falls under the sway of anti–Vietnam War radicals. She detonates a bomb in their small community's local post office and as a result kills the town's beloved doctor. Not only do her violent actions bring the war to the doorsteps of peaceful

Old Rimrock, but they set into motion the ultimate downfall of the Levov family. Throughout most of *American Pastoral*, the Swede desperately tries to make sense of Merry's actions and keep his family from disintegrating. As the novel reveals, the Swede is ill-equipped to carry out these tasks, and through this incompetence, Roth is able to reveal the unsteady and chaotic world underlying its placid facade.

What makes *American Pastoral* a significant work within Roth's oeuvre is not so much the story of Swede Levov as it is the manner in which his story is told. The events are narrated by Nathan Zuckerman, the once provocative and volatile novelist, now an aging recluse, impotent and incontinent due to an earlier bout with prostate cancer. He gives life to the Swede by pulling together what are assumed to be historical facts, while at the same time infusing into his narrative various speculations or reimaginings of his own. As a result, the story of the Swede—or at least, the story of the Swede to which the reader is privy—is an unsteady mixture of fact and (probable) fiction. In *American Pastoral,* a novel about the necessity for understanding a person's life, it becomes clear that Zuckerman cannot possibly know the underlying secrets of Swede Levov. In fact, not knowing is a central theme of this novel. But instead of lapsing into nihilism, Roth uses the absence of knowledge as an affirmation (albeit a qualified one) of life. As Zuckerman states in *American Pastoral*, "getting people right is not what living is all about anyway. It's getting them wrong that is living . . . That's how we know we're alive: we're wrong."

In reimagining, or "making up," much of the Swede's life, Zuckerman reveals the events in a highly fragmented manner. His disjunctive chronology and speculative fictions are significant in that they underscore the inextricable links between memory and narrative. In *American Pastoral* the emphasis is on storytelling and the ways in which narratives—and identities—are constructed. As a result, the novel is not only a chronicle of an individual "held hostage" by the forces of history, but the story of Zuckerman himself as narrating subject. Or to put it another way, through his efforts as a storyteller—the way he structures the events, what he chooses to put in and leave out, how much he "makes up" and intermingles with "fact"—Nathan Zuckerman reveals more about himself than he does the life of Swede Levov. Read from this perspective, *American Pastoral* is not only a gripping account of postwar America, but also a telling narrative exercise in "reconstructing" the subject.

Bibliography

Gentry, Marshall Bruce. "Newark Maid Feminism in Philip Roth's *American Pastoral.*" *Shofar* 19, no. 1 (Fall 2000): 74–83.

MacArthur, Kathleen L. "Shattering the American Pastoral: Philip Roth's Vision of Trauma and the American Dream." *Studies in American Jewish Literature* 23 (2004): 15–26.

Parrish, Timothy L. "The End of Identity: Philip Roth's *American Pastoral.*" *Shofar* 19, no. 1 (Fall 2000): 84–99.

Royal, Derek Parker. "Fictional Realms of Possibility: Reimagining the Ethnic Subject in Philip Roth's *American Pastoral.*" *Studies in American Jewish Literature* 20 (2001): 1–16.

Stanley, Sandra Kumamoto. "Mourning the 'Greatest Generation': Myth and History in Philip Roth's *American Pastoral. Twentieth-Century Literature* 51, no. 1 (2005): 1–24.

—Derek Parker Royal

Antin, Mary (1881–1949)

"I was born, I have lived, and I have been made over," says Mary Antin in the introduction to her autobiography, *The Promised Land.* Referring to her emigration from Russia to the United States, she says that she "began life in the Middle Ages, and here am I still, your contemporary in the twentieth century, thrilling with your latest thought." She was born in Plotzk, Russia, in 1881 and immigrated with her parents and siblings to Boston in 1894. Even in Russia, where education for Jewish girls was limited, Antin's father determined that he would try to provide as much education for his children as he could. When the family moved to Boston, Mary entered school while her older sister went to work to help support the family. Mary Antin amazed her teachers with her enthusiastic attitude and hard work; she learned English quickly and established a lifelong friendship with one of her teachers, Mary S. Dillingham.

Thanks to the efforts of Dillingham, one of Antin's first essays was published in the magazine *Primary Education.* Soon she began writing poetry for newspapers and aspired to becoming a writer. While attending the Boston Latin School for Girls, Antin received encouragement in her studies from a number of people, including Edward Everett Hale, who invited her to his home to use his library. Hattie Hecht, a prominent Jewish philanthropist in Boston, became her mentor.

Antin had written in Yiddish of her experiences in Russia and of the family's immigration to America. Hecht introduced her to Rabbi Solomon Schindler, a Reform rabbi, who helped her translate her Yiddish notes to write her first book, *From Plotzk to Boston.* Hecht then introduced Antin to Phillip Cowan, publisher of American Hebrew. Cowan published portions of the book, and he and his wife persuaded ISRAEL ZANGWILL, the well-known novelist who would later write *The Melting Pot,* a play about the immigration experience, to write the introduction to *From Plotzk to Boston.* The book was published in 1899; at that time Antin had lived in America for only five years.

Mary Antin continued to attend the Boston Latin School for Girls, preparing to enter Radcliffe College after graduation. She attended programs at Hale House, the settlement house that Edward Everett Hale had founded, and through the natural history club that she joined as a respite from literary pursuits, she met Amadeus William Grabau, a German-American graduate student at Harvard University. Grabau, 10 years older than Antin, was the son and grandson of Lutheran pastors. They married in 1901, and Grabau began working at Columbia University while Antin attended classes at Barnard College. Her friendship with the Cowans continued, and through them she met Josephine Lazarus, sister of the well-known Emma, whose poem "The New Colossus" is inscribed on the Statue of Liberty. EMMA LAZARUS had rejected

Judaism in favor of transcendentalism, and Josephine introduced these ideas to Antin, who would also abandon Jewish traditions. In 1907 Antin's only child, Josephine Esther, was born and named after her mentor, Josephine Lazarus, and her mother, Esther Weltman Antin.

Josephine Lazarus had encouraged Antin to write her autobiography for some time, but it was not until after Lazarus's death in 1910 that she began writing the book that would become *The Promised Land.* This book included some of the same material as *From Plotzk to Boston,* but concentrated more on Antin's American educational experiences. Excerpts from *The Promised Land* were published by *Atlantic Monthly* in 1911 and 1912. When it was published in 1912, *The Promised Land* became a tremendous success, and by 1949, the year of Antin's death, it had gone through 33 printings and sold about 84,000 copies. As a result of the notoriety following the publication of this book, Antin was asked to lecture for the Progressive Party by Theodore Roosevelt, and she continued to give lectures around the country.

The Promised Land begins with a description of the lifestyle of the Antin family in Polotzk, Russia, where Jews lived in fear of pogroms where "stupid peasants," believing that Jews murdered Christian children, would "fill themselves with vodka, and set out to kill the Jews" and Jewish boys of seven or eight were "kidnapped by the Czar's agents and brought up in Gentile families until they were old enough to enter the army." After financial setbacks, Antin's father decided to seek a better life in America and sent for his family three years later. When she arrived in Boston, Mary learned that in America she could be "free to fashion my own life, and should dream my dreams in English phrases." The education she received in the public schools and the people she met in America made Antin's dreams a reality.

In 1914 Antin published another book, *They Who Knock at Our Gates,* in which she discussed the victimization of immigrants and urged readers to support open immigration policies at a time when public sentiment was turning against immigrants. While Antin was lecturing for the Allies during World War I, her husband supported the Germans. Tormented by ideological differences, the couple separated. Grabau was dismissed from his position at Columbia University and took a new job as China Foundation Research Professor at the National University in Peking and chief paleontologist of the Chinese Geological Survey. After the breakup of her marriage, Antin suffered from a condition she refers to as "psychoneurosis," which persisted for the rest of her life.

Although she continued to correspond with her editors and other writers, and published a few magazine articles, Mary Antin never wrote another book. In her later years she became interested in health and spirituality, spending time at the Gould Farm in the Adirondack Mountains, where she sought comfort in the philosophical ideas of William and Agnes Gould. She also studied Christianity in an effort to understand better the Goulds' version of spirituality. She died in 1949, never returning to her Jewish roots.

Bibliography

Guttmann, Allen. "The Rise of a Lucky Few: Mary Antin and Abraham Cahan." In *The Jewish Writer in America: Assimilation and the Crisis of Identity*. New York: Oxford University Press, 1971.

Rubin, Steven J. "Style and Meaning in Mary Antin's *The Promised Land*: A Reevaluation." *Studies in American Jewish Literature* 5 (1986): 29–34.

Tuerk, Richard. "Assimilation in Jewish-American Autobiography: Mary Antin and Ludwig Lewisohn." *A/B: Auto/Biography Studies* 3, no. 2 (Summer 1987): 26–33.

—Rosalind Benjet

Anya Susan Fromberg Schaeffer (1974)

Anya tells the fictional story of Anya Savikin. The audience sees, with SUSAN FROMBERG SCHAEFFER's cinematic imagery, Anya's childhood in Poland, her experiences in medical school, her marriage, her personal horror at the Holocaust, and its effects on the rest of her life. The setting is as much a character in the book as Anya's family and close friends. The happy, paradisiacal Poland of Anya's childhood and young adult life is the first casualty. Her father is her first family member to die and the rest follow one by one as Anya is forced to live in the Vilna ghetto and then in the Kaiserwald labor camp—until she is left with only her daughter Ninka. After escaping the labor camp, Anya flees Poland with her daughter to find sanctuary in the United States. As the reader discovers, the novel is not merely a fictionalized account of Anya and the Holocaust, but a contextualization of the war and its enduring consequences.

The book is significant because it is one of the first fictions that directly depict the Holocaust. After the war, there was a stigma against fictional representations of the Holocaust for moral and social reasons—mainly an apprehension of generalizing the experience and thus desensitizing the audience. *Anya* as a creative work refutes this fear and becomes a powerful illustration of the Holocaust because the narration is holistic. Schaeffer, through Anya, shows how the war murdered a way of life and continues to affect the survivors and their posterity.

This holistic view was important to Schaeffer because she knew it was significant to the survivors. She built Anya's story through personal interviews with people who lived in Europe and survived the war. In an essay on the novel, Schaeffer writes that she was surprised to find she was close to so many survivors because they never talked about their experiences. Once asked, they were willing to share their stories but they would not discuss their lives *before* the war. The more Schaeffer struggled to learn about their lives before the Holocaust, the more she realized the factor it played in the Holocaust experience. Accordingly, the first quarter of the book illustrates Anya's childhood, thus providing a contrast for the final chapters, in which the reader realizes how much was really lost.

There is a distinct consciousness of storytelling throughout the novel. Schaeffer is telling a composite story of true events through a fictional character. Anya is telling her "true" story through memories. Anya does not always remember everything, and new memories flash into her mind after the war. Thus, readers of the novel experience remembered events with Anya, both psychological and physical, as they would their own memories. The idea of truth told through fiction is also mirrored in the secular Russian folktales Schaeffer embeds in the text. Anya's mother tells them. Anya's father tells them. Anya retells them to the audience and to her own family and friends. The stories tell truths although they are only folktales, just as Schaeffer's story of Anya is true even though it is fiction.

A tension between human independence and dependence on God also exists throughout the book. Anya's father is an atheist but described as "a saint," while her mother, who is described as "human," is religious. Contrastingly, her mother believes in personal responsibility while her father believes in fate. Before the war Anya never considers the existence of God. She comes to believe in a superpower because she survives. She attributes her survival to a combination of her own determination to live and to this fate. Interestingly, this confidence in a superpower never causes her to question why the Holocaust happens. She simply comes to believe that she was meant to survive. Why she is chosen to survive is a question she struggles with throughout the telling of her story.

Family plays a central role in the plot. Family is the reason Anya wants to live—specifically to save her daughter Ninka. Ninka represents all of Anya's memories. When Anya realizes she does not know what happened to the treasured family photo albums, she looks at Ninka and sees all of the memories living in her. The continuation of family is her reason for living. Even in her old age, Anya obsesses over her grandchildren and their safety. It deeply saddens her that she cannot raise her family as she was raised because that world does not exist anymore. Although Anya constantly questions whether it was worth it to survive the Holocaust, she always comes back to her family as the meaning in her survival.

Bibliography
Berger, Alan L. "Bearing Witness: Second Generation Literature of the 'Shoah.'" *Modern Judaism* 10, no. 1 (1990): 43–63.
Brauner, David. "Breaking the Silences: Jewish-American Women Writing the Holocaust." *Yearbook of English Studies* 31 (2001): 24–38.
Schaeffer, Susan Fromberg. "The Writer on Her Work." In *Anya*. New York: W.W. Norton, 2004.

—Emily Dyer

The Apprenticeship of Duddy Kravitz
Mordecai Richler (1959)

Duddy Kravitz is MORDECAI RICHLER's critical commentary on many interwoven themes: anti-Semitism, the consequences of segregation, Jewish alienation, materialism's debasing potential, the damaging outcomes of sexual self-gratification, and the insanity that surrounds victimizing and victimization. Indeed, the novel's protagonist suffers a nervous breakdown because of the ethical consequences of his duplicitous motivations. This novel, lauded for its comedic dimensions, must also be understood as serious social commentary.

Duddy Kravitz is a character based on an actual person, Eli Weinstein, actually nicknamed Duddy (Posner 37). And the experiences, neighborhoods, and concerns in the novel stem directly from Richler's youthful experiences on St. Urban Street in the poor section of Montreal, Canada. The Fletcher Field High School of the novel and the high school's student body are direct reflections of Richler's experiences at Baron Byng—a high school that was "96 per cent Jewish" with "a potpourri of problem teachers and aspiring kids whose parents [were] immigrants, who . . . decided that education [was] the avenue to prosperity. . . . The interesting thing is that Baron Byng graduated some of the most notorious criminals, some of the most notorious scientists, one of the most notorious writers, which was Mordecai, and some of the greatest athletes in Montreal" (Posner 30–31).

Duddy shares Mordecai's reputation for being "a prankster who enjoyed putting people down" (Posner 34). A close classmate of Richler's, Sid Kastner, says that Richler grew up in the generation following the Second World War, the Post Holocaust era, when "to be a Jew was to be a second-class citizen." However, this was also a time when Jews were becoming recognized as a people. Kastner maintains that Richler "had to prove something. So he wrote about these emerging Jewish characters in a society that was finally allowing the Jew to create something for himself and was reaching a level that could not have been achieved." Many of Richler's classmates realized their dreams through accumulating wealth in various industries. Richler did not approve. Duddy, from age 16 to 21, for example, worked any scheme available to earn enough money to buy land because his grandfather told him that a man without land was a nobody. Duddy uses people—often convincing them and himself that his intentions are good—that when he has land, everyone will be taken care of: his grandfather; his girl Friday, Yvette; and his employee, Virgil. One of his means (when he is too young for more viable options) for getting rich is to make films of bar mitzvahs. He is successful—parents want to see their children on film. But his first effort is an admixture of bizarre images masking as social commentary and Jewish ritual.

In other words, with ribald humor, Richler manages to analyze the failing moments of the Jewish "seize the day" era in Montreal—especially with regard to the failed Jewish male. In the novel, Duddy asks his uncle Benjy why he never had time for him. "Because you're a *pusherke*. A little Jew-boy on the make. Guys like you make me sick and ashamed," is Uncle Benjy's response (284). David Baile, in his book *Eros and the Jews,* concurs: Richler "works with a Jewish stereotype very different from the schlemiel: the *pusherke,* or 'pushy Jew.'" Baile proposes that Duddy is "a classic representative" of a type of male going back to the eastern European shtetl:

> Duddy is aggressive, crude, ruthlessly self-serving, and materialistic. His story is that of a reverse Horatio Alger: bad boy makes good in America. Duddy's eroticism is part and parcel of his aggressiveness, and he uses sex as a tool in his relentless attempt to make it. Duddy may be erotic, but his main interest lies elsewhere, as his contempt and exploitation of women reveals. For this reason, his seduction of the

> French Canadian, Yvette, is curiously distracted because Yvette is less a sexual conquest than a vehicle for helping him achieve his material ends: as he makes love to her next to the lake he intends to buy, he cannot help but think about his future possession. (217–218).

In fact, Duddy does not want to marry Yvette, his girl Friday. He wants to marry a rich Jewish princess. Duddy is not sexually incompetent, like many Jewish male characters described by prominent Jewish novelists. But he also does not fulfill any healthy Kabbalistic ideal.

By all accounts, *The Apprenticeship of Duddy Kravitz* was Richler's breakthrough novel. The *Washington Times* announced that with its publication it was "time to recognize Mr. Richler as one of North America's most powerful novelists." The popularity of Duddy Kravitz as a character also drew Richler into the world of screenwriters. In 1975, Richler's screenplay for *The Apprenticeship of Duddy Kravitz* won the Screenwriters Guild of America award for best comedy and was also nominated for an Academy Award. Richler's adaptation of his novel to film was also nominated by the Hollywood Foreign Press Association for a Best Foreign Film Golden Globe Award in 1975. The previous year, the producer of the film, John Kemeny, won the award for Film of the Year at the Canadian Film Awards, and director Ted Kocheff won the Golden Berlin Award at the Berlin International Film Festival. This impressive list of honors indicates the international recognition of Richler as a major 20th-century literary talent. Little is known, however, about the adaptations, under Richler's direction, of the novel to the musical genre. In 1984 the Citadel Theatre in Edmonton, Canada, adapted the novel to a musical, *Duddy,* with a score by Jerry Leiber and Mike Stoller. In a 1987 musical adaptation, Alan Menken wrote the score and David Spencer the lyrics. In both the 1984 and 1987 musicals, Lonny Price played Duddy Kravitz.

Richard Dreyfuss, however, is the actor who brought Duddy Kravitz and his creator to wide public attention. Somehow, Dreyfuss was able to empathetically play Richler's mostly unlikable Duddy. Perhaps film critic Robert Ebert best explains audiences'/readers' attraction to Duddy: "*The Apprenticeship of Duddy Kravitz* is a movie that somehow manages to be breakneck and curiously touching at the same time. It's a story of ambition and greed, with a hero that will stop at almost nothing (by the movie's end, Duddy has succeeded in alienating the girl who loves him, has lost all his friends, has brought his grandfather to despair, and has paralyzed his most loyal employee). And yet we like Duddy, with a kind of exasperation, because we get some notion of the hungers that drive him, and because nobody suffers at his hands more than he does himself" (rogerebert.com).

Bibliography

Biale, David. *Eros and the Jews: From Biblical Israel to Contemporary America.* New York: Basic Books, 1992.

Ebert, Roger. "*The Apprenticeship of Duddy Kravitz.*" Review January 1, 1974. Available online. URL: http://rogerebert.suntimes.com/apps/pbcs.dll/articl?AID=19740101/REVIEW/40101035/17/2008. Accessed July 1, 2008.

Posner, Michael. *The Last Honest Man: Mordecai Richler.* Toronto: McClelland & Stewart Ltd., 2004.

Richler, Mordecai. *The Apprenticeship of Duddy Kravitz.* New York: Pocket Books, 1959.

—**Suzanne Evertsen Lundquist**

The Armies of the Night
Norman Mailer (1968)

NORMAN MAILER's *The Armies of the Night* is one of the most influential works of the New Journalism of the 1960s, a movement in which reporters abandoned the pretense of objectivity toward their subjects and gave subjective responses or even participated in the events they reported. In the New Journalism, also known as "the nonfiction novel," fact and fiction merged as journalists adopted the techniques of novelists while novelists adopted the techniques of journalism to create a new genre.

The Armies of the Night is an autobiographical work written in the third person about a comic hero with the author's name, Norman Mailer. Mailer's 20-year experiment with form—from omniscient to first-person narration, to essays and reportage, to self-interviews—led to this book, in whose third-person narration and formal tone he found a congenial solution to the problem of presenting himself in print without seeming too aggressive or too egotistical. He harnessed his aggression and ambivalence in a form and style that yielded maximum dividends.

Book One, "History as a Novel: The Steps of the Pentagon," recounts the events surrounding Mailer's arrest and imprisonment stemming from his participation in an anti–Vietnam War march on the Pentagon in 1967. The far shorter Book Two, "The Novel as History: The Battle of the Pentagon," tells the story of the organization of the march and what took place during the march and the long day and night when a group of protestors sat in on the steps of the Pentagon and defied the military until they were arrested and removed. Although the first reads more like fiction and the second more like journalism, there are elements of fact and fiction in both books, and the stories are clearly parallel. If the first book is Mailer's personal rite of passage as a middle-aged Jewish man, in which he shows his courage by protesting the war, getting arrested, and spending a night in jail, then Book Two is about the collective rite of passage of the largely young protesters. Taken together, the two stories take the pulse of a divided nation at a crucial time in recent American history.

Mailer's attitude toward himself as hero is wry and often self-deflating. Mailer as comic hero of Book One resembles in part his own antihero, the Jewish schlemiel Sam Slovoda in his short story "The Man Who Studied Yoga." The comedy in both works depends upon the disparity between the hero's grandiose visions and the petty realities of his life. And in both works the narrator contemplates the hero's foibles and neuroses with detached affection and ironic amusement.

But Mailer as hero of *The Armies of the Night* has another side he calls "the Beast." This alter ego is the antithesis of Sam, who is humane, pacifistic, and Jewish. Instead, he more closely resembles Sergius, the gentile narrator in Mailer's story "The Time of Her Time." As the critic Richard Levine argues, "Sergius, the Cossack in Mailer, fearlessly enters the fray, while Sam, the Jew, watches from the sidelines in terror." Mailer tends to see the Jewish side of himself as unmanly, a weak momma's boy. In *The Armies of the Night* he notes that this Jewish Mailer is too modest for his taste, "and he hated this because modesty was an old family relative, he had been born to a modest family, had been a modest boy, a modest young man, and he hated that, he loved the pride and the arrogance and the egocentricity he had gathered over the years." One senses in *The Armies of the Night* how much Mailer has attempted to remake his image over the years, to suppress what he views as his loathsomely weak side—Sam Slovoda, the Jewish intellectual—and defend against it through aggressive action and shameless exhibitionism, qualities he and many other Americans mistakenly equate with manhood. The modest, gentle Jewish man who is also part of him he sees as "a fatal taint." As he writes, "The trouble with being gentle is that one has no defense against shame."

The comedy in *The Armies of the Night* helps to balance the aggressiveness of Mailer's attack on himself, on liberal academics, and on the middle class. Mailer comes across as a heroic schlemiel, urinating on the floor in a darkened men's room, making a broken-field run in a three-piece suit to get himself arrested, exchanging insults with a Nazi in a police van ("Dirty Jew." "Kraut pig."), and being released from prison through the skill of a clever Jewish lawyer who impresses the WASP judge. In contrast to Mailer as Jewish schlemiel is the heroic dignity of the poet Robert Lowell, who represents for Mailer the conscience of WASP America.

The courtroom battle between Mailer's lawyer Hirschkop and the judge, Commissioner Scaife, is a fine comic duel of legal wits that Mailer depicts as "the natural face-off between a tough Jew and a well-made son of Virginia gentry." When Hirschkop wears Scaife down with a series of clever arguments and counterarguments and finally gets his client released on bail despite the judge's initial refusal to set bail, the tight-lipped Scaife smiles in admiration, "as if when all was said there was no lawyer like a good Jewish lawyer."

In a final comic irony, after his release he makes a solemn speech to the reporters, trying to appeal to the Christian conscience of the American people, saying, "Today is Sunday, and while I am not a Christian, I happen to be married to one." And he explains that he was protesting the war and was willing to be arrested because "You see, dear fellow Americans, it is Sunday, and we are burning the body and blood of Christ in Vietnam." But when Mailer reads the account of his speech in the *Washington Post,* he finds it undercut by the final sentence: "Mailer is a Jew." The *Post* reporter subtly suggests that a Jew has no business preaching a sermon telling his fellow Americans that they are acting un-Christian.

The march on the Pentagon was an inconclusive, ambiguous event, not a turning point in national history. If it is recalled today, it is largely because Norman Mailer was there and chose to write about it. He does succeed, nevertheless, in capturing and making comprehensible the drift of American history in the 1960s and the behavior of an individual caught up in a crucial event of a mass movement.

Mailer applied similar novelistic techniques in many later works, including his reports on the 1968 presidential conventions in *Miami and the Siege of Chicago* (1968) and on man's landing on the moon in *Of a Fire on the Moon* (1970). But these books are not as dramatically compelling as *The Armies of the Night* because Mailer was more of a reporter than an active participant in these events; readers are deprived of the focus on the adventures of a comic hero to unify the action and hold interest.

Bibliography

Humm, Peter. "Reading the Lines: Television and New Fiction." In *Re-Reading English.* New York: Methuen, 1982.

Macilwee, Michael. "Saul Bellow and Norman Mailer." *Saul Bellow Journal* 19, no. 1 (Winter 2003): 3–22.

—**Andrew Gordon**

Arrogant Beggar Anzia Yezierska (1927)

Poverty-stricken but optimistic, Adele Lidner, the second-generation Jewish-American protagonist of ANZIA YEZIERSKA's *Arrogant Beggar,* enters a charity home expecting to find a place to capitalize on her unique potential. Instead, she finds herself capitalized on. As time reveals, the affluent, white, female proprietors running this "home" view Adele as a business venture in which they hope, mainly through food-related experiences, to fashion her into a subservient, useful commodity. Some may think this plot—that of a clever, Jewish-American youngster fighting for a chance to be successful—has an all too familiar taste to it.

As Yezierska explained, "Critics have said that I have but one story to tell and that I tell that one story in different ways each time I write. That is true. My one story is hunger. Hunger driven by loneliness. . . . [For w]hat is at the root of economics, sociology, literature, and all art but man's bread hunger and man's love hunger?" ("Mostly About Myself," 136). Yezierska knew that critics often judged her work as watered down stories of "the usual"—tales of the starving immigrant hungering for nourishment of the heart, body, and mind and a chance to prove his or her significance. Although as she herself implies, her work may not be a buffet, it *is* a generous serving of the staple of human experience.

Arrogant Beggar is a story of pointedly subversive "love hunger," wherein the young woman ultimately shuns a well-off, respected American capitalist in favor of a poor, immigrant musician—one who is quite content with her decision to become his wife but remain a businesswoman. At first sight of Arthur Hellman, her benefactress's handsome, cultivated son, Adele thinks she is in love and believes that if only he would return her feelings, her success would be complete. The dashing and well-intentioned but shallow young man slights her one moment and repents the next, even tracking her down when she flees from the home. While he plays at being a gallant savior and nursemaid, ready to rescue her from the common life of squalor, Arthur is not exactly in love with her. Yezierska therefore subverts the typical romances of the day because her protagonist rejects the seemingly perfect opportunity to marry into the American dream. Adele realizes that this man is less in love with her than he is in love with the idea of possessing such a rebellious, "exotic" woman. While this book ends with a marriage like other female-authored novels of the day, Adele chooses a rather unlikely suitor by society's standards. She falls for a destitute yet talented Polish immigrant, Jean Rachmansky, who has grown tired of being Arthur's musical showpiece of sorts. Notably, after they marry, Jean does not insist that she give up her work in the restaurant.

Yezierska also explores "bread hunger," staging a culinary revolt against the social prejudice and sham charity of that era. Katherine Stubbs writes in her introduction that this novel is "designed to dismantle a hallowed institution of American philanthropy." What Stubbs and most critics overlook is that the story is not just about the fact that these women practice artificial charity, it is the *way* in which they go about structuring this selfish philanthropy—and its recipients. The home's philanthropists adopt "scientific," modern food narratives that markedly alienate the workers from their individuality and independence, reducing them to publicity-garnering commodities. Young Adele is thrown into a movement better known as domestic science. The girls at the home are fed the same cheap meals time and again while the headmistress dines on spring lamb and other tasty fare. They are put on display as merchandise, cookie-cut products of "properly" scientific charity. The domestic students are taught to cook only mainstream food and to clean the dishes, kitchen, and themselves in a carefully prescribed manner.

Once Adele realizes that Mrs. Hellman regards her as repulsively inferior, Adele flees in shame—even rejecting her son Arthur, whose attentions could have signified her authenticity as an American. Scrambling to find work, Adele ends up at a greasy spoon, where she meets Muhmenkah, a timeworn old woman with an endless reservoir of love for others. Notably, food is a major component of Muhmenkah's angelic charity. Just as Adele begins to reclaim her individuality, though, her aged friend dies.

Ultimately, Adele's recollection of her friend's nurturing spirit inspires her to begin a daring culinary resistance—to fight food with food. For days, she labors to convert the old woman's flat into Muhmenkah's Coffee Shop. Here, Adele creates the opposite atmosphere from the Hellman Home; she generates a space where physical, spiritual, and intellectual nourishment is plentiful and where all are welcome and equal. Trusting in the goodness of others, she lets people pay whatever they can afford or think is fair. Unlike the home, her café has no set menu and no type of cuisine is deemed off-limits. Adele builds a very unbusinesslike business, free from culinary racism and the commodification and alienation of her individual skills. Clearly, Adele operates a salon where all people and their gifts are welcome. A special musical performance by Jean attracts a wide assortment of people: "Students, plumbers, salesmen, tailors. Slim stenographers and school teachers side by side with shawled *yentehs* and gray-bearded old men" (144). And so it appears that beggars can, after all, be choosers.

Bibliography

Drucker, Sally Ann. "Yiddish, Yidgin, and Yezierska." *Yiddish* 6, no. 4 (1987): 99–113.

Schoen, Carol B. *Anzia Yezierska*. Boston: Twayne, 1982.

—Sarah Bylund

Asch, Sholem (1880–1957)

Sholem Asch, the most popular and important Yiddish writer in the first half of the 20th century, was born to a Hasidic family in the shtetl of Kutno, Poland (then a part of the Russian Empire). He received a traditional Jewish education while he secretly taught himself German. Encouraged by his mentor Yitskhok Leybush Peretz, Asch settled in Warsaw in 1900. His prodigious body of work, encompassing stories, novellas, dramas, poetry, novels, and essays, presents a history of Jewish life. He was a featured writer for the Warsaw *Haynt* and the New York *Forverts*. In 1920 Asch became a U.S. citizen, although he continued to move around all his life, and he immigrated to Israel in 1956. He was the first Yiddish writer to see his works widely translated and also become best sellers in English. He died in London in 1957.

Asch first charmed his Yiddish-reading audience with his idyllic, lyrical depictions of shtetl life, notably in *Dos shtetl* (1904) and *Reb Shloyme nogid* (*Wealthy Shloyme*, 1913). He soon ventured into works broader in scope. His drama *Got fun nekome*, 1907 (*God of Vengeance*, 1918), takes place in a Jewish brothel. Yankl, the proprietor, purchases a Torah scroll, hoping this will ensure his daughter's purity. Instead, she falls in love with one of the prostitutes and runs away with her. Asch tenderly describes the affection between the young lesbians; this subject became a problem only when the drama was produced in English on Broadway in New York in 1923, where the cast was arrested and fined. Asch also portrayed the Jewish underworld of pimps, thieves, and whores in his wildly popular *Motke ganiv* (1916), written first as a novel, then a play.

His literary works expanded to become international in concern. Asch saw himself as an artist belonging to both the Jewish world and global literature. He explored Old Testament topics in several works, as in his novel *Moyshe* (*Moses*, 1951). He wrote about the hardships in building up Palestine, especially in *Dos gezang fun tol*, 1938 (*Song of the Valley*, 1939). Asch's first best seller in the United States in English translation was the trilogy *Farn mabl* (1929–31; *Three Cities*, 1933), a grandiose account of Jewish life between 1910 and 1920 in St. Petersburg (Russia), Warsaw, and Moscow.

Asch had always been fascinated by the subject of faith, and particularly in its extremes of messianism and martyrdom. *Kiddush haShem* (1919) was one of the first historical novels in Yiddish literature. It deals with responses of faith to Bogdan Chmielnicki's slaughter of more than 100,000 Jews in Ukraine in the 17th century. The holy Jewish tailor selling "faith" is one of Asch's most significant symbolic figures. *Di kishufmakherin fun kastilien* (*The Witch of Castile*, 1921), set in Rome during the Spanish Inquisition, features many Jewish martyrs dying horribly. In the novel

Der tilim yid (*Psalm Jew,* 1934), Yekhiel is a saintly rebbe. Asch's most exalted character, however, is Yeshua, messiah and martyr of *Der man fun natseres* (*The NAZARENE,* 1939). This novel, absolutely Jewish in theme and treatment, was followed by *The Apostle* (1943), featuring Paul of Tarsus, and then by *Mary* (1949). These works were critically acclaimed and were best sellers in English translation. However, they were bitterly attacked by the editor of *Forverts,* ABRAHAM CAHAN. Asch also published Holocaust stories, later gathered and published in his collection *Der brenendiker dorn* (*Burning Bush,* 1946).

Some of his best works were about Jews in America, including *Amerikaner dertseylungen* (*American Stories,* 1918), *Onkl mozes,* 1918 (*Uncle Moses,* 1920), *Di muter,* 1919 (*Mother,* 1930), *Toyt-urteyl* (*Death Sentence,* 1924), *Chaim Leyderer's tsurik-kumen,* 1927 (*Chaim Leyderer's Return,* 1938), and *Grosman un zun* (*Grosman and Son,* 1954). *Uncle Moses* is a novel dealing with the Jewish-American immigrant experience, the socioeconomic realities of the American dream, the rise of labor unions, political corruption, conflicts between socialism and capitalism, and between tradition and newer American ways of life. It explores love, focusing on the relationship between wealth and happiness. *Uncle Moses* was made into a "talkie" film, codirected by and starring Maurice Schwartz, in 1932. *Ist River* (*East River,* 1946), however, is one of the greatest American novels. Here Asch vividly depicts the quintessential American melting pot on Manhattan's Lower East Side, and highlights the relationship between Jews and non-Jews in this so-called land of equality and opportunity. Always praising America for its freedoms, Asch's crippled scholar Nathan Davidowsky asserts that America has "the highest moral order yet achieved in the world."

Sholem Asch had an enormous influence on later Jewish-American writers. In his masterpiece *East River,* Moshe Wolf Davidowsky suffers shame when his son Irving jilts Rachel, daughter of his dying friend, and marries Irish-American Mary McCarthy instead. Yet he learns to embrace his Catholic daughter-in-law and grandchild. This acceptance, although denounced by devout Jews who were traumatized by the Holocaust, was unprecedented in Yiddish literature. It could only happen in America. There are traces of Asch's direct influence on I. B. Singer, Bernard Malamud, and others. Asch was one of the first to tell the story of immigrants and others pursuing the American dream, whether religious or secular, rich or poor, Jew or non-Jew.

Asch was elected honorary president of the Yiddish PEN Club in 1932. He was awarded the Polonia Restituta in 1932. In 1933 he was nominated for the Nobel Prize, as he was again a decade later. By 1936 the author was listed in the *New York Times* as one of the "World's Ten Greatest Living Jews." The following year, he received an honorary Doctor of Hebrew Letters from the Jewish Theological Seminary in New York. His *East River* won the Anisfield-Wolf Award in 1946 for its treatment of "racial relations." The Shalom Asch Museum is located in Bat-Yam, Israel.

Bibliography
Fischthal, Hannah Berliner. "Uncle Moses." *When Joseph Met Molly: A Reader on Yiddish Film.* Edited by Sylvia Paskin. Nottingham, U.K.: Five Leaves, 1999.

———. "Sholem Asch and the Shift in His Reputation: 'The Nazarene' as Culprit or Victim?" Ph.D. diss., City University of New York, 1994.

Siegel, Ben. *The Controversial Sholem Asch: An Introduction to his Fiction.* Bowling Green, Ohio: Bowling Green University Popular Press, 1976.

Stahl, Nanette, ed. *Sholem Asch Reconsidered.* New Haven, Conn.: Beinecke, 2004.

—Hannah Berliner Fischthal

Asimov, Isaac (1920–1992)

Asimov became one of the most prolific writers of the 20th century, producing works in nearly every literary genre. He began life as a Russian Jew who immigrated at age three to Brooklyn, New York. His father, Judah, a candy store owner, was concerned that his son's interest in the science fiction magazines on the store's newsstands would hinder the boy's intellectual development, but the boy eventually gained his father's permission to read the publications and immediately became hooked on science fiction and adventure stories, which he began to write shortly thereafter. Despite his initial antagonism, in 1938 Judah encouraged the 17-year-old Isaac to take his short story "Cosmic Corkscrew" in person to John W. Campbell, editor of *Astounding Science Fiction,* the genre's most popular magazine, for publication. Though the story wasn't initially accepted, Asimov began a longtime association with Campbell, himself a well known sci-fi writer who also mentored other prominent science fiction authors of the time, including Robert Heinlein and Arthur C. Clarke.

Asimov went on to write many short stories that would forever change science fiction literature. In the forties, he began a series of short stories influenced by Edward Gibbon's *Decline and Fall of the Roman Empire* that would eventually be collected into the hugely successful and influential Foundation series, published as the trilogy *Foundation* (1951), *Foundation and Empire* (1952), and *Second Foundation* (1953). The novels told a multigenerational story about a foundation established to protect the history and technology of the Galactic Empire, because Hari Seldon, a "psychohistorian" (a fictional branch of science concerned with telling the future), deduces that the deteriorating empire is gradually sliding toward collapse. Asimov's grandiose plot devices such as interstellar governments and political intrigue, renegade leaders and multigenerational storylines, science that seems mystical and unbelievable to the uneducated, futuristic socioreligious cultural themes, and the collapse and rebirth of civilizations on a galactic scale have become staples of science fiction literature, influencing the works of the genre's major authors, including Frank Herbert's "Dune" series, Gene Roddenberry's "Star Trek," George Lucas's "Star Wars" saga, and Orson Scott Card's "Ender" and "Memory of Earth" series. Asimov eventually continued the "Foundation" series with *Foundation's Edge* (1982), *Foundation and Earth* (1986), *Prelude to Foundation* (1988), and *Forward the Foundation* (1993), the last novel he wrote before his death.

In 1950 Asimov's other most influential work, *I, Robot,* a collection of short stories, was published. It not only introduced Asimov's invented words "robotics" and "positronic" (a fictional word still used in sci-fi), but also introduced "the Three Laws of Robotics," which control how robots should be programmed to serve humanity the best. The laws immediately changed the way robot stories were written and even paved the way for the dystopian robot worlds of future science fiction, including *The Terminator* and *The Matrix* movies. Asimov's robot stories explore philosophical concepts that now permeate science fiction; in particular, the story "Bicentennial Man," about a robot whose owners encourage him to develop his agency, examines esoteric questions concerning the development of the self and the meaning of the soul. Despite his own avowed atheism (which softened toward agnosticism later in life), these stories more than any other demonstrate Asimov's Jewish background as he confronts traditional religious questions disguised in a sci-fi gloss. In later stories Asimov wove the "Robot" stories into his "Foundation" series, combining his two great contributions to the genre into one holistic vision.

Though Asimov's best-known works and most lasting influence are in science fiction, he was not content with limiting himself to a single field. He wrote books in nearly every genre of literature, including humor, with the tongue-in-cheek *The Sensuous, Dirty Old Man,* under the pseudonym "Dr. A" (1971); several mysteries, among which was *The Black Widowers* series (1984–90); and fantasy, in *Azazel* (1988), and the "Final Fantasy" series published after his death in 1995.

Asimov's academic studies were not literary, but scientific (a Columbia University Ph.D. in biochemistry in 1948), and he spent most of his career teaching at the prestigious Boston University School of Medicine (1949–92). Self-educated in various fields, he published several nonfiction works. A medical textbook, *Biochemistry and the Human Metabolism,* coauthored in the fifties, stands among many publications on science and nature, including his best-known science books, *The Realm of Numbers* (1959), *The Intelligent Man's Guide to Science* (1960), and *The Genetic Code* (1963). He authored several critical literary collections, including *Asimov's Guide to Shakespeare* (1970) and *Asimov's Guide to the Bible* (1968), as well as annotated versions of Byron's *Don Juan,* Milton's *Paradise Lost,* Swift's *Gulliver's Travels* and the productions of Gilbert and Sullivan. He was also a proficient essayist whose works were collected in such publications as *The Roving Mind* (1983), and he wrote an ongoing column about science and other things in the *Magazine of Fantasy and Science Fiction* (1962–90). His several autobiographies include *In Memory Yet Green* (1979) and the posthumous *I, Asimov* (1994), and in 1995, his brother Stanley Asimov published *Yours, Isaac Asimov,* a collection of the author's letters, which demonstrated that, like many great writers, Asimov was also a voluminous correspondent.

Many anthologies and collections, as well as several commemoratory works by other authors, appeared in the years preceding and following Asimov's death in 1992. It was later revealed that the author had died from complications due to AIDS, which he contracted during a blood transfusion received while undergoing triple-bypass surgery in 1983.

Isaac Asimov is the only known writer to have written in nearly every genre of literature, the only exception being philosophy. However, especially considering the philosophical implications and themes of so many of his stories, he may be counted as the most versatile writer of the 20th century.

Bibliography
Freedman, Carl, ed. *Conversations with Isaac Asimov.* Jackson: University of Mississippi Press, 2005.
—**Jacob Robertson**

The Assistant Bernard Malamud (1957)

The Assistant, BERNARD MALAMUD's second novel (after *The NATURAL*), is the story of poor immigrant grocer Morris Bober, age 60, his wife, Ida, their 23-year-old unmarried daughter, Helen, and Frank Alpine, who becomes the Bobers' assistant. After robbing the grocery with an anti-Semitic partner who pistol-whips the penniless old Morris, Frank returns to the store offering his services as a clerk. When Morris declines because the store, in a poor neighborhood, barely subsists, Frank secretly begins living in the Bobers' basement, stealing rolls and milk to survive. He is discovered in time to rescue a passed-out Bober as he tries to drag heavy cases of milk bottles into the store. Frank repeatedly saves Morris's life and eventually takes the grocer's place in the store. Business improves as the anti-Semitic neighborhood will buy from a gentile rather than a Jew, but Frank still steals daily from the cash register. He lives above the store with Italians who rent from the Bobers and falls in love with Helen. Their courtship is conducted largely in a library, where they give each other personally significant books—*The Life of St. Francis of Assisi,* the Bible, *Madame Bovary,* and *Crime and Punishment,* among others. Gradually, Helen falls in love with the Italian Frank, spurning neighborhood Jewish suitors. She wants to go to college full time but must work to help support her family. One evening Helen is attacked by Frank's violent accomplice in the earlier robbery, Ward Minogue, who is also the police detective's reprobate son. Frank hears Helen's screams and rescues her from the would-be rapist, nearly killing him, but rapes her himself. Guilt-ridden, Frank dearly wants her forgiveness and plans to send her to college. That winter, after Morris dies from his second bout with pneumonia, Frank takes the grocer's place behind the counter, gets circumcised, and converts to Judaism after Passover.

The Assistant is a benchmark in Malamud's fiction, initiating many of the themes developed in his later works. It also continues the premise that life behind a counter is a prison, begun in the 1943 short story, "The Grocery Store." *The Assistant* expands this metaphor to include the meaning of suffering, the possibility for redemption, and the ethical meaning of being a Jew. The novel is also a metaphor of the Holocaust, as the story's vicious anti-Semitism is executed by a Pole, a German, and an Italian who are responsible for Morris's failed business. In addition, one of the neighborhood's three Jewish families perishes in a fire, representing the one-third of world Jewry destroyed by the three Axis powers (Germany, Italy, and Japan).

In this book Malamud combines the life and lore of St. Francis of Assisi in the character of Frank Alpine (the assistant), Martin Buber's *I and Thou* in the character and dialog of Morris Bober, Dostoyevsky's *Crime and Punishment,* and four father-son relationships reminiscent of the Passover Seder's four questioning sons. The numerous parallels between St. Francis and Frank run from their profligate youths to redemption through poverty to their connections with bird (freedom) imagery, fire rescues, and self-inflicted stigmata. Malamud fuses the Catholic St. Francis with Martin Buber's book on human beings' relationship with God to redefine Judaism in ethical humanistic terms. Frank asks Morris whether he considers himself a Jew, since he eats ham. Morris answers that being a Jew means following the law, "This means to do what is right, to be honest, to be good. This means to other people." Consequently, when Frank asks Morris what he suffers for, the old man responds, "I suffer for you." Slowly, Frank's anti-Semitic objectification of Morris in an "I-it" relationship evolves into a humanistic "I-Thou" bond.

Similarly, the bird imagery associated with St. Francis is used throughout the novel to represent Jews. Even Frank's painful circumcision is a Jewish version of St. Francis's self-inflicted stigmata, wounds supposed to represent the wounds of Christ. The book's *Crime and Punishment* analog also reinforces the way to redemption through human love, although Helen is not quite the virgin prostitute, Sonya. In a more Judaic context, Malamud's four pairs of fathers and sons emphasize the need for legacy and transmission of values from one generation to the next. In place of Morris's late son, Ephraim, Frank Alpine continues Bober's work as a father (for he puts Helen through college) and as a Jew who suffers behind the counter and lives for the law.

Bibliography
Leer, Norman. "The Double Theme in Malamud's *The Assistant*: Dostoevsky with Irony." *Mosaic* 4, no. 3 (Spring 1971): 89–102.
Stern, David. "Malamud: Seen and Unseen." In *The Magic Worlds of Bernard Malamud.* Albany: State University of New York Press, 2001.
—Eileen H. Watts

The Autobiography of Alice B. Toklas
Gertrude Stein (1933)

Until *The Autobiography of Alice B. Toklas* was published in 1933 by the *Atlantic Monthly* and Harcourt Brace, GERTRUDE STEIN was a largely self-published and unknown author. The experimental work that she had managed to distribute to the public thus far had met with sharp criticism and even ridicule. But, *The Autobiography* marked a distinct, if momentary, departure from Stein's typically cryptic style: it was easy reading and well received.

Despite its title, the book is not Toklas's autobiography but Stein's, though she writes it from Toklas's perspective and in her voice. Stein does not reveal the book's authorship until the last page. *The Autobiography* dwells on Stein's life in the United States and, most significantly, both women's life together in Paris. Parts of it are set in the bohemian Montmartre section of Paris before and after World War I. The book also documents the stream of famous personalities that frequented Stein's famous "salon" at 27, rue de Fleurus. These included American authors Sherwood Anderson, Ernest Hemingway, F. Scott Fitzgerald, Spanish painter Pablo Picasso, and French artists Henry Matisse and Paul Cézanne. The narrator describes Stein conversing with these geniuses while Toklas entertained their wives. Toklas herself was Stein's "wife," but mention of their romantic relationship is conspicuously absent in *The Autobiography,* evidence of how unaccepted lesbianism was in the early 20th century.

Though *The Autobiography* is one of the most understandable of Stein's works, it is not altogether conventional due to its unique narrative style—an autobiography written by a different person. This narrative fact has caused many critics to label the work postmodern, or at least anticipatory of postmodern autobiographical forms, which attempt to decenter the subject of the text (in this case, the author) by portraying his or her identity as subjective and fragmented. Stein reveals the performative nature of identity by speaking through Toklas. *The Autobiography* is also circular and unbounded: The last page loops back to the origins of the project (Johnston 590), suggesting that the book be read again in light of the revelation that Stein has written it. Simultaneously, the ending surpasses typical narrative boundaries by exposing the world outside of the text. This, along with the narrator's habit of skipping back and forth in time, demonstrates Stein's interest in escaping traditional, time-bound structures. Though *The Autobiography*'s sentences do not follow Stein's usual repetitive patterns, many of the book's events are mentioned multiple times (Lenart-Cheng 127), reinforcing the notion that Stein employed a more subtle but nonetheless characteristic method of writing this best seller.

One critic has argued that *The Autobiography* follows many of the same conventions as commercials and that the book primarily served to "sell" Stein's personality and work to the public (Lenart-Cheng). Regardless of whether this was Stein's intention, the book definitely defined her as a celebrity for the first time, and she was received warmly in the United States after its publication. Stein was ambivalent about her new-found fame since she did not consider *The Autobiography* to be one of her best works, but the image it paints of the intelligent, witty author and patron of the arts remains important.

Bibliography

Breslin, James E. "Gertrude Stein and the Problems of Autobiography." *Georgia Review* 33, no. 4 (Winter 1979): 901–913.

Johnston, Georgia. "Narratologies of Pleasure: Gertrude Stein's *The Autobiography of Alice B. Toklas.*" *Modern Fiction Studies* 42, no. 3 (1996): 590–606.

Lenart-Cheng, Helga. "Autobiography as Advertisement: Why Do Gertrude Stein's Sentences Get Under Our Skin?" *New Literary History* 34, no. 1 (Winter 2003): 117–133.

—Rachel Ligairi

B

Barney's Version **Mordecai Richler** (1998)

MORDECAI RICHLER's *Barney's Version* is a variation on the theme of the self-deprecating Jewish-American male—a male preoccupied/struggling with sex, marital relationships, self-gratification, pscyhoanalysis, intellectual or financial success, and, as a result, personal alienation. "To come clean," says Barney, "I'm starting on this shambles that is the true story of my wasted life . . . as a riposte to the scurrilous charges Terry Melver has made in his forthcoming autobiography: about me, my three wives, a.k.a. Barney Panofsky's troika, the nature of my friendship with Boogie, and, of course, the scandal I will carry to my grave like a humpback" (3). At age 67, and recently diagnosed with Alzheimer's disease, Barney attempts to interpret, even justify, his life experiences. He leaves the corrections for the inaccuracies in his autobiography to Michael, his oldest son—corrections that appear as footnotes throughout the novel. Michael, however, can only correct factual details—dates, author's names, the actual places of events, or he can add brief familial commentaries as well as the afterword. Michael cannot correct the gaps between Barney's interpretation of events and what actually occurred, especially with regard to whether his father murdered his best friend, Bernard (Boogie) Moscovitch, the crime, *the* "scandal," for which Barney is acquitted (because there is no body).

As a narrator, Barney is unreliable. The novel spans 46 years of Barney's life and is divided into chapters named after "the troika," his three wives. Chapter titles also include the duration of Barney's "official" relationship with each wife: Clara (1950–52). The (never named) Second Mrs. Panofsky (1958–60), and Miriam, his heart's desire (1960–   ).

Early in the novel, Barney's friend Hymie Mintzbaum encourages him to see a Jungian analyst. Hymie has moved from working with a Reichian analyst to a Jungian one and suggests that Barney do the same (36). According to Mark Shechner, Wilhelm Reich taught: "Neither the death instinct nor the superego nor the innate aggression of the species nor alienation but 'the social suppression of genital love' is the bacillus of totalitarianism" (93). Barney does not suppress genital love; he just does not know how to achieve it. Barney's malady is not as severe as Alexander Portnoy's—a complaint defined as: "A disorder in which strongly-felt ethical and altruistic impulses are perpetually warring with extreme sexual longings, often of a perverse nature" (*PORTNOY'S COMPLAINT* 1). "My problem is," writes Barney, "I am unable to get to the bottom of things. I don't mind not understanding other people's motives . . . but why don't I understand why *I* do things?" (96).

Barney needs to understand his tendencies to be socially inappropriate, even crass and rude.

Barney has an acerbic wit born of his critically refined intelligence as well as his failure to achieve the kind of success Terry McIver attains. He also needs to grasp why his marriages fail. But he does not "hold with shamans, witch doctors, or psychiatrists." He prefers "Shakespeare, Tolstoy, or even Dickens," to various psychoanalytical approaches to helping individuals achieve mental health. He believes that great authors "understood more about the human condition than ever occurred" to psychotherapists. "You overrated bunch of charlatans deal with the grammar of human problems, and the writers I've mentioned with the essence," claims Barney (336–337). Rather than "munch" a few pills "twice a day for paranoia" or a pill "before meals for schizophrenia," Barney takes "single malts and Montecristos for everything" (337). Throughout the novel, Barney spends considerable time self-medicating, along with his "friends," at clubs, restaurants, and drinking establishments in Paris, London, and Montreal.

Barney admits that while living in Paris, he "slipped into" his relationship with the first Mrs. Panofsky (48). He "was nutty Clara's keeper" (50) Clara Chambers, a neurotic "dirty talking" yet renowned poet and painter, went to Barney's apartment one night when she was not feeling well and did not leave until her death. A pregnancy and stillborn birth fills the space between. After the birth, the doctor tells Barney that Clara is a "healthy young woman" and "would certainly be able to bear other children." He tells Barney these things because, he says, "I take it you are the father." Barney responds, "Yes." To which the Dr. answers: "In that case . . . you must be an albino" (101). Barney's black friend, Cedric Richardson, is the father—a fact that estranges Barney from Clara. It is not until after her suicide that Barney finds out Clara's real name: Clara Charnofsky. Clara, he discovers, was a tormented, sexually abused, neurotic yet perversely talented Jewish woman from a dysfunctional family. Clara, readers realize, seems to have found the only stability in her life with Barney. Nevertheless, Barney surrenders his rights to Clara's poetry and paintings

to a representative of the Charnofsky family—a legacy that ensures considerable wealth.

Barney marries the Second Mrs. Panofsky for no other reason than that he is a wealthy man "in want of a wife" (an unacknowledged crib from Jane Austen) (161), and she is a Jewish princess. At the party immediately following the wedding ceremony, Barney spies the third Mrs. Panofsky, Miriam Greenberg. The evening is a comic romp: Barney circling the bar time and again to find out the score of a hockey game ("Final Score. Canadiens 5, Toronto 3"), his declaration to Boogie that "For the first time in my life I am truly, seriously, irretrievably in love" (not with his wife, however, who overhears the comment and thinks Barney is speaking about her), and his audacious pursuit of the flattered yet incredulous Miriam (182). During their very brief marriage, Barney is finally able to find a reason to divorce the Second Mrs. Panofsky: He finds her in bed with Boogie Moscovitch. Barney writes of this event: ". . . lo and behold, there they were, my wife and best friend, snug in bed. I couldn't believe my good luck" (248). He admits to Boogie, "I want you to agree to be a co-respondent in my divorce" (252).

Barney is both angry with Boogie and relieved to find him in bed with his wife—even though this means that Barney, once again, plays the cuckold. Boogie is one of the pillars of Barney's identity as a philanthropist. Barney writes: "Alfred Kazin once wrote of Saul Bellow that even when he was still young and unknown, he already had the aura about him of a man destined for greatness. I felt the same about Boogie, who was uncommonly generous at the time to other young writers [early 1950s], it being understood that he was superior to any of them" (9). In retrospect, Barney writes: "I wasn't going to allow Boogie, even given his drugged-out state on the lake, that once soaring talent addled beyond repair, would take off forever just to get back at me. More likely we were to blame for his self-destruction, having anointed him, when we were young and foolish, as the only one of our bunch destined for greatness" (341). Over Boogie's lifetime, Barney continually bails him out in the hope that Boogie's great novel will be forthcoming. However, as noted, Boogie is literary, brilliant, a drug addict, and a drunk. He shows up at Barney's cabin to "dry out" yet another time. And rather than deal with his betrayal of Barney, Boogie chooses to go for a swim—a swim from which Boogie never comes back, hence the murder charge.

Barney writes of his marriage to the third Mrs. Panofsky: "until I cheated, I was blessed with a sanctuary. Miriam. Our children. Our home. Where I was never required to be deceitful" (306). Happily married to Miriam for 31 years, Barney is not aware of how his marriage has been experienced by his wife. She tells him, shortly before their divorce, "Barney, I'm weary of pleasing everybody. You. The children. Your friends. You've been making all the decisions for me ever since we married. I'd like to make some decisions of my own, good or bad, before I'm too old" (309). Miriam wants to go back to school, to work for the Canadian Broadcasting Company as a radio journalist, to expand her multiple capacities as a refined Jewish intellectual. And yet Barney does not see her needs because he is a millionaire with enough money to supply his wife with every necessity—for travel, clothes, elegant elitist experiences. And yet Miriam wants to create rather than consume experiences. Early in their relationship, Miriam tells Barney: "You're devouring me" (36). Enter, the final male to take away another of Barney's wives' affections: university professor Blair Hopper. In the midst of Barney's difficulties with Miriam's needs to become someone in her own right, Barney is left to his own devices: drinking away his problems. During one particular binge, Barney cheats on Miriam—an act that results in her more suitable marriage to Blair.

Barney's Version is a rich, philosophically and culturally dense novel. Barney's financial success as the owner of Totally Unnecessary Production Ltd. allows him to leave an abundant inheritance to those closest to him. However, the legacy of this novel might be the carefully crafted recognition of what makes human beings truly wealthy: "Live joyfully with thy wife [and children] whom thou lovest all the days of the life of thy vanity . . . for that is thy portion in this life . . . (Ecclesiastes 9: 9). Certainly, before Barney completely loses his memories, he desires something of biblical proportions for his children: Michael, Saul, and Kate (who always believed in her father's innocence): "Oh my oh my, if I were an angel of the Lord, I would mark the doors of each of my children's home with an X, so that plague and misfortune will pass over them. Alas, I lack the qualifications" (344).

Bibliography

Richler, Mordecai. *Barney's Version.* New York: Pocket Books, 1997.
Roth, Philip. *Portnoy's Complaint.* New York: Bantam Books, 1972.
Shechner, Mark. *After the Revolution: Studies in the Contemporary Jewish Imagination.* Bloomington: Indiana University Press, 1987.

—Suzanne Evertsen Lundquist

Bellow, Saul (1915–2005)

Lachine, Montreal, Canada, where Saul Bellow was born on June 10, 1915, to Abraham (Abram) and Lescha (Liza) Belo, was a colorful, working-class town on the outskirts of Montreal and home to Ukrainians, Russians, Italians, Greeks, Hungarians, and Poles. His Jewish immigrant parents had arrived from St. Petersburg, Russia, in 1913. In 1918 the family moved to St. Dominique Street, Montreal, also a slum neighborhood of mostly Jewish immigrants. Saul's bookishness and his six months in the tuberculosis ward at the Royal Victoria Hospital in Mount Royal Park permanently estranged him from his father and brothers. This, coupled with the ravages of the 1918 influenza epidemic, established a fictional obsession with the plight of a dreamer emotionally isolated within his own family, unable to maintain relationships with women, and obsessed with death. In 1924 the family moved to the immigrant tenements of Humboldt Park, Chicago, where in the 1920s everyone spoke an idiomatic immigrant English enhanced by Yiddish, Hebrew, Russian, and other European languages. The surrounding neighborhoods with their relief associations, famous Chicago mafia criminals, and local characters would repeatedly resurface in his fiction. In February 1933 Liza died at home, leaving the adolescent Bellow bereft. Determined to become a writer and already interested in leftist politics, Bellow entered the University of Chicago in 1934. He graduated in 1937 from Northwestern University. He married Anita Goshkin just before Christmas. From 1938 to 1939 he worked on the WPA project and the *Synopticon* for the "Great Books" series.

During the 1940s Bellow was fascinated with 19th-century Russian writers, Freud, French existentialism, and the already too famous Hemingway. Hemingway's masculine adventure tales, stoic masculinity, and dominant mood of despair repulsed the upbeat and ambitiously competitive Bellow. *Dangling Man* (1944) features Joseph, a would-be intellectual seeking spiritual enlightenment in his own room while he studies Enlightenment thinkers. He cheats on his wife, Eva, insults friends and family, becomes increasingly paranoid, and finally admits that his perspectives have all ended in four walls. *Dangling Man* features typically existentialist themes concerning individual freedom, moral responsibility, the impossibility of transcendence, and the social contract. *The Victim* (1947) reflects the alienating, anti-Semitic atmosphere of post-Holocaust Jewish America. Paranoid protagonist Asa Leventhal spends a long, hot summer fending off his WASP nemesis, Kirby Albee, and caring for his brother's family.

From 1948 to 1950 Bellow lived in post–World War II Paris and began work on *The Adventures of Augie March*, published in 1953. Augie is a first-generation Jewish-American *pícaro* and American optimist journeying through a depression-era Chicago reminiscent of Bellow's youth. In it Bellow found his uniquely Chicagoan voice and the antimodernist philosophical approach that would shape the rest of his writings. In 1952 he received the National Institute of Arts and Letters Award and became the Creative Writing Fellow at Princeton University. Between 1949 and 1954 several of his short stories began to appear, and in 1954 he received the Ford Foundation Grant.

In 1955 Bellow embarked on a lecture tour of Europe to recuperate from his first failed marriage—in all there would be five marriages, which produced four children. Not surprisingly, *Seize the Day* (1956), written in the midst of his second marriage, features Tommy Wilhelm, a spurned son and husband who opts for emotional empathy instead of capitalist America. When *Henderson the Rain King* appeared in 1959, Bellow's father had already died in 1955, several friends had betrayed him, his house was under constant repair, his new marriage was in trouble, his longtime friend, writer Isaac Rosenfeld, had died, his trusted Viking Press publisher and friend, Ben Huebsch, had died, and friend Delmore Schwartz was very close to the end of his life. Writing *Henderson the Rain King* was clearly an escape from this decade of overwhelming loss. Set in some Africa of the soul, it is a parody of the colonial adventure story, Hemingwayesque existentialism, and literary modernism.

The traumas of Bellow's marriage to Susan Glassman and his subsequent cuckolding and divorce are all featured in *Herzog* (1964), his acknowledged masterwork. It takes the form of an epistolary novel in which the embattled Herzog, a victimized divorcé and failed academic, realizes his great magnum opus on romanticism will never be finished. He writes endless letters to Nietzsche, Heidegger, Freud, Dewey, Whitehead, and others attacking the modern physical and social sciences, including Darwinism and Freudianism. In 1965 he received the James L. Dow Award, the Fomentor Award, the National Book Award, and the International Prize, which finally secured Bellow's international reputation. However, his play, *The Last Analysis,* closed after only two weeks on Broadway. In 1967 he had made an important trip to Israel to report firsthand on the Six Day War for *Newsday Magazine.* In 1968 *Mosby's Memoirs and Other Stories* appeared, he divorced Glassman, and he won both the French Croix de Chevalier des Arts et Lettres and the B' Nai Brith Award.

By the 1970s it seemed the old comic spirit deserted him. He was booed off the stage at San Francisco State College by student radicals signaling their contempt for established intellectuals, and made his stinging denunciation of 1960s youth culture in MR. SAMMLER'S PLANET, (1970). It won the National Book Award in 1971. Mr. Sammler is an emotionally damaged Holocaust survivor whose Anglophile education and his near-death experiences during the Holocaust have rendered him emotionally disengaged. He despises hippie-era New York and most of his relatives, but now he knows that he must learn to love. Many critics took serious umbrage at Bellow's racist stereotyping of the black pickpocket who so famously exposes himself to the elderly Jew. Both *Mr. Sammler's Planet* (1970) and HUMBOLDT'S GIFT (1975) register Bellow's interest in transcendental experience, and in anthroposophists Rudolph Steiner and Owen Barfield. In 1974 Bellow began discussions on anthroposophy with his new mentor, Professor Le May. *Humboldt's Gift* registers Bellow's interest in anthroposophy and his belief that the modern condition has depleted the inner life of the artist, killed poetic sensibility, bankrupted Western humanism, and diminished the private life. In Humboldt von Fleisher he memorializes his friends Delmore Schwartz and Isaac Rosenfeld, and records the angst of his most recent divorce. The central protagonist, Charlie Citrine, a Chicagoan with a taste for gangland excitement and pneumatic young women, now tries to recoup the poetic gift he has all but squandered. *To Jerusalem and Back: A Personal Account* (1976), Bellow's documentary account of his recent trip to Israel, was poorly received. It combines interviews, a chronology of his stay, fictional stories, reported conversations, travelogue, and pieces of essays and public addresses. In 1974, while visiting Bucharest with his Romanian wife, Alexandra, he began work on *The Dean's December,* a tale of two cities, Bucharest and Chicago, in which cultural degradation and the growing inaccessibility of truth are far advanced. As Corde tries to read the signs of a Platonic home-world beyond a nightmarish daily experience of both worlds, he comes to despise the artificiality of academic and media-based views of history. This book was generally greeted with disappointment. "A Silver Dish" (1978), a funny and

moving story of a sharpster father and a naive son, is one of his best-loved short stories.

In 1984 *Him with His Foot in His Mouth,* a volume of short stories, appeared, followed in 1987 by MORE DIE OF HEARTBREAK. The latter is a Prufrockian lament full of misogynous love lore, botched loves, fatal forays into the danger zones of sex and romance, farcical retreats, and crackpot sexual philosophizing. In 1989 two paperback novellas, *A Theft* and *The Bellarosa Connection,* appeared. *A Theft,* featuring Bellow's first female protagonist, is a comic opera on the hijinks of Clara Velde and her lover Ithiel Regler. Clara, who has been raised on old-time Midwestern religious values and plunged into the urban world of contemporary marriage and business, is now four times divorced and still involved with her only true love, Regler, whom she now knows will never marry her. It revisits the old Bellowian themes such as the Hawthornian theft of the human heart, the lure of the intellect, the classic evasions of the male lover, the social chaos of "Gogmagogsville," the seeming impossibility of higher synthesis, the human comedy of sexual desire, the failure of psychiatry, boredom, power politics, the chaotic nuisance of ethnic others, the absence of civilized spaces, and the diminished status of the individual. Bellow's demythologization of romantic love in "Gogmagogsville" once again hinges on the ironic portrayal of an intellectual male protagonist torn between desire for ultimate union with the female and pursuit of the rational intellect. *The Bellarosa Connection* (1989) features an unnamed narrator, a memory freak, trying desperately to recapture a lost opportunity for a relationship with the authentic and mysterious Sorella Fonstein and her Holocaust survivor husband, Harry. Both died several months earlier and he now knows that he has lived more through memory than through actual relationships.

Bellow's collected essays appeared under the title *It All Adds Up* (1994), followed by another novella, *The Actual* (1997). The latter tells the familiar Bellow story of an old adolescent love reclaimed in late middle age. The worldly and clever Harry Trellman, an intellectual social observer and ambassador of the arts, is invited to "notice" on behalf of Sigmund Adletsky. Harry will be his brain trust, while Adletsky will discern the nature of Harry's great unrequited adolescent love, Amy Wustrin, and bring the now aged pair together. The plot turns on one of Bellow's favorite Platonic themes, the existence of one's soul mate or "actual."

The last book, *RAVELSTEIN* (2000), was written ostensibly as a memorial to the late Allan Bloom of the University of Chicago, and as a tribute to Bellow's latest wife, Janis Freedman. Chick (Bellow), through Ravelstein (Bloom), finally understands the origins of his own Jewish voice, moral anxiety, and immigrant legacy. Rife with Catskill comedian gags, meditations on Platonic idealism, and a preoccupation with death, it also features Rosamund (Janis Freedman), who saves Chick's (Bellow's) life after a nearly fatal episode of food poisoning. Bellow's death in April 2005, in Brookline, Massachusetts, has left readers and critics curious to see if yet other manuscripts appear posthumously. Bellow is now ranked among the greatest of 20th-century American writers.

Bibliography

Atlas, James. *Bellow*. New York: Random House, 2000; London: Faber & Faber, 2001; New York: Modern Library, 2002.

Cronin, Gloria L. *A Room of His Own: In Search of the Feminine in the Novels of Saul Bellow. Judaic Traditions in Literature, Music & Art.* Syracuse, N.Y.: Syracuse University Press, 2000.

—Gloria L. Cronin

Berriault, Gina (1926–1999)

Gina Berriault was born Arline Shandeling in Long Beach, California, on January 1, 1926, the third child of working-class Jewish immigrants from Lithuania and Latvia. An early reader, she took solace in the fact that poor children like herself could be the subject of literature. Her father, in youth a marble cutter, then later a writer and ad solicitor for trade journals, died when she was in her teens, and she took over his work to help support the family. Through much of her adult life, mainly in the Bay Area, Berriault worked at low-wage and temporary jobs; with little or no formal education beyond high school, she was a largely self-taught writer. She married J. V. Berriault, a musician, but later divorced; they had one child, Julie Elena, whom Berriault was raising on her own by 1962. In 1963 she lived and wrote in Mexico City on a fellowship from the Centro Mexicano de Escritores; in 1966 she held an appointment as a scholar at the Radcliffe Institute of Harvard University. She won a National Endowment for the Arts grant and both Guggenheim and Ingram-Merrill Fellowships. She taught briefly at the Iowa Writers Workshop and for several years at San Francisco State College, and lived for many years with the writer Leonard Gardner. She lived her last years in her daughter's apartment in Sausalito, and died after a short illness in Marin General Hospital on July 15, 1999.

Berriault's first published story, "Return of the Griffins," signed "A. E. Shandeling," appeared as the lead story in the spring 1948 issue of the prestigious magazine *Story* (vol. 32, no. 128) and was anthologized in *Story: The Fiction of the Forties* (1949). Others soon followed, signed "Gina Berriault," and several won awards and publication in *Best American Short Stories* and the O. Henry *Prize Stories*. A set of seven, *The Houses of the City*, appeared in Scribner's multiauthor collection *Short Story 1* (1958).

Berriault did "not wish to be thought of as a Jewish writer or a feminist writer or as a California writer or as a leftwing writer or categorized by any interpretation." Her deepest literary affinities lay with great Russian and French writers. Philosophically, her work calls to mind the thought of the Lithuanian-born Jewish philosopher Emmanuel Levinas (whom she had not read) in its acute tension between eros and ethics, its concern with the face of the other as accusing the self's arbitrary freedom and commanding justice for the widow, the orphan, and the stranger.

Thus in the title story of Berriault's first major collection, *The Mistress and Other Stories* (1965), a woman meets the teenaged son of a former lover, tells him of the affair, then sees "a child's accusing eyes" as he recalls his mother "used to cry" when he was six. He leaves her "seeing the face of his mother weeping black, bitter tears." *The Mistress* reprinted five stories from the 1958 gathering and added 10 new ones, including the prize-winning "The Stone Boy," from which Berriault later wrote the screenplay for a film of the same title, produced in 1984 and starring Robert Duvall and Glenn Close.

The Infinite Passion of Expectation: Twenty-Five Stories (1982) added nine new stories and restored one from the 1958 set. Berriault so persistently and meticulously revised her fiction that many of her stories appeared in two or more versions. Three of her four novels likewise underwent revision for later reissue, as she combined or condensed chapters and cut and recast sentences in pursuit of an austere precision, economy, and elegance that she admired in great European short novels.

The Descent (1960, 1986), is a cold war fantasy/satire about a benign Midwestern history professor appointed secretary for humanity in a nation stockpiling nuclear bombs and digging fallout shelters. At the end, Arnold Elkins trundles wet concrete deep in a pit "filled with the sounds of persevering chaos," from which (in a negative echo of the last lines of Dante's *Inferno*) he cannot see "the night sky and its stars."

In *Conference of Victims* (1962, 1985, 1998), a congressional candidate commits suicide on the eve of an election because his affair with a teenage girl has been discovered. His older sister, younger brother, and lover all face what Albert Camus called the "one truly serious philosophical problem": suicide, or how to find "a reason to stay on this earth." A sort of literary "impossible object" with an implausible premise, an implausible structure (successive chapters from seldom convergent points of view, spread over several years in the 1950s), and, in the stolid Naomi Costigan, an implausible heroine, the novel achieves a modest and movingly human beauty.

Berriault's third novel, *The Son* (1966, 1985, 1998), set in northern California from the late thirties to the mid-fifties, follows the erotic career of Vivian Carpentier, a woman who futilely seeks validation in her relationships with men—three marriages and several affairs, culminating in her tragic seduction of her 16-year-old son,

"obliterating the holy separateness she had given him at birth."

The LIGHTS OF EARTH (1984, 1997) is autobiographical in some of the history and situation of its heroine, a writer named Ilona Lewis, and in its "attempt," in Berriault's words, "to redeem and forgive [her]self." When her newly famous lover leaves her for another woman, Ilona suffers not only erotic loss but also self-accusation for having abandoned her brother 20 years before. Still, though now "forsaken" herself, no longer "blessed," Ilona retains the capacity to bless her daughter, and near the end she ponders how "The lights of earth are all the beings who draw you out from the dark, and are they everyone in your life?"

Berriault's summative collection brought her work more of the rich recognition it had long deserved: *WOMEN IN THEIR BEDS* (1996, 1997) won not only awards in California from the Bay Area Book Critics and the Commonwealth Club, but also the National Book Critics Circle and PEN/Faulkner awards, and a Rea Award for lifetime achievement in the short story. Shortly before her death, she finished writing and illustrating *The Great Petrowski* (2000), a fable about a parrot who learns to sing grand opera and seeks to use his music to save the Amazon rain forest, his first home. *The Tea Ceremony: The Uncollected Writings* (2003) gathered some early and late stories as well as some of Berriault's best literary journalism.

Gina Berriault did not claim to speak for or to a Jewish community. Only a few of her characters are explicitly Jewish—the sisters in the late autobiographical story "Stolen Pleasures," the aged and dying actor Max Laurie in *The Son* (the one man Vivian loves beyond self-regard), perhaps Ilona Lewis, and definitely Marie in "The Light at Birth" (which closes the last two collections): A writer-teacher in retreat in a seacoast house with a German woman and her aged and dying mother, Marie slowly overcomes her fearful habit of mistaking "strangers for the enemy." Berriault's protagonists may be small boys or old women, married couples or lovers, parents or children, siblings or friends, poor or affluent, artistic or inarticulate; but whoever they are, however comfortable or deprived their status, Berriault discovers the human "out-sider" or "refugee" in each one, exiled in a "tragic world" and "alone with the enemy of us all," our "unknowing of one another."

Bibliography

Boken, Julia B. "Gina Berriault." In *American Short Story Writers Since World War II.* Detroit: Thomson Gale, 1993.

Hamilton, Carole L. "Reading between the Lines of Gina Berriault's 'The Stone Boy.'" In *Short Stories in the Classroom,* edited by Carole L. Hamilton and Peter Kratzke. Urbana, Ill.: NCTE, 1999.

—B. W. Jorgensen

"Big Blonde" Dorothy Parker (1929)

Originally published in *Bookman Magazine* in February 1929, then collected in *Laments for the Living* in 1930, "Big Blonde" is an earnest short story about the plight of an aging party girl. The tale of the protagonist, Hazel Morse, is told via succinct, revealing paragraphs. Morse's life is not simply one composed of love, marriage, domesticity, and the clichéd happily-ever-after ending. Instead, it is made up of the bleak realization that she is dependent on the various men who come into and out of her life—for the purpose of love, companionship, money, and self-esteem. What makes the work all the more sad are the parallels it has with DOROTHY PARKER's own life—her failed romances, her bouts with alcoholism and depression, and her desire for death. "Big Blonde" embraces the darkness that lingered in Parker in the late 1920s and confesses her despair, despite many literary success, any number of friendships, and romantic involvements.

Hazel Morse is a matter-of-fact woman rarely excited about the different things life has to offer. She accepts without question how she should be occupying her time, and with whom she should be occupying it. Men are attracted to her from the start because she is a good sport, and "men liked a good sport" (Parker 187). This frame of mind, though, is what ultimately leads to her misery. Nearing 30, she decides she should marry. Six weeks after meeting him, Hazel marries Herbie

Morse and allows herself to fall passionately in love with the idea of being a bride. From the start, their relationship is not one built around romance and a traditional courtship; instead, Hazel is first attracted to him because "she was enormously amused at his fast, slurred sentences, his interpolations of apt phrases from vaudeville acts and comic strips; she thrilled at the feel of his lean arm tucked firm beneath the sleeve of her coat; she wanted to touch the wet, flat surface of his hair" (Parker 188). Eager to enter into the security (and, as Herbie would later see it, complacency) of marriage, Hazel relinquishes being a "good sport" all the time, instead choosing to surrender to bouts of depression, whimsy, tears, and self-pity. The one thing she does not count on is that no one wants to be around a plump 30-something woman continually filled with anguish.

Eventually, though she never relied on it before marrying, Hazel begins to drink: "Herbie pressed it on her. He was glad to see her drink. They both felt it might restore her high spirits" (Parker 192). Despite her willingness to do whatever might please her husband, Hazel is finally abandoned. This scenario is repeated time and again by the future lovers that grace her doorstep. Some offer money, some entertainment, but none stirs in her a lasting impression or the desire for an enduring relationship. The men come and go, and though Hazel is happy enough when they are near, she is unaffected when they depart.

In time, Hazel, tired of consistently pretending to be gay and amusing, grows increasingly exhausted with people and with life, and opts to end her days. Much like the speaker in Parker's poem "RÉSUMÉ," she contemplates various methods of committing suicide, including jumping from a height, shooting or gassing herself, slitting her wrists, and taking poison. Like Parker, she ingests two bottles of the sedative veronal in the hope that she will not awake from the dose, but the attempt fails. Even when she tries to discontinue her unhappy existence, she is met with disappointment. Much like Parker, Hazel is a survivor against her own wishes. She outlasts a broken marriage, countless insincere lovers, and sleeping pills only to live another day.

"Big Blonde" offers a glimpse into the disappointment one woman (and quite possibly, many women in the late 1920s) felt. A futility and uselessness overshadows any attempts at autonomy and independence. Women, despite their newfound right to vote and various jobs in the workforce, still leaned on men and expected to be cared and provided for. Hazel Morse teaches the moral that, though that may have been the trend for her day, there was little joy in it, and in fact, such expectations led women to feel empty and unfulfilled.

Bibliography

Keats, John. *You Might As Well Live.* New York: Simon & Schuster, 1970.

Kinney, Arthur. "The Other Dorothy Parkers." In *The Critical Waltz: Essays on the Work of Dorothy Parker.* Madison, N.J.: Fairleigh Dickinson University Press, 2005.

Parker, Dorothy. "Big Blonde." In *The Portable Dorothy Parker.* New York: Viking Press, 1973.

—Kathena H. DeGrassi

Billy Bathgate   E. L. Doctorow (1989)

In his seventh novel, *Billy Bathgate,* E. L. DOCTOROW melds fiction and fact into seamless narrative, a technique also used in his previous books *Welcome to Hard Times* (1960), *The BOOK OF DANIEL* (1971), *RAGTIME* (1975), *Loon Lake* (1980), and *World's Fair* (1985). *Billy Bathgate* tells the story of a teenage boy, a fictional character associated with the real-life Dutch Schultz gang in Depression-era New York City. While the book focuses on the life of the fictional protagonist, most of the events Billy is either privy to or involved with actually happened. Also, most of the people with whom Billy interacts lived and worked in the Schultz gang. Although the novel takes place against a historical backdrop, the story belongs to Billy, who lives with the gang, learns their trades, and reads of their exploits in the local papers. By using the fictional Billy to tell the story of the gang's demise, Doctorow provides details of events not given in newspaper stories, court records, and other historical documents and in the process challenges the "reader's preconceived notions about the validity of what has been too readily named historical 'truth'" (Henry 33). For example, readers see how Schultz, born Arthur Flegenheimer, secures a not-guilty verdict in his trial in Onondaga, New York, by ingratiating himself into the economically desperate community and converting from Judaism to Catholicism. Schultz's initiation into the Catholic Church, replete with Al Capone as his character witness, is not popular with all of the gang members, most of whom are Jewish. Billy explains Schultz's departure from the faith of his family as a business move with Schultz appropriating the Catholic Church to fit his own needs.

Written as a first-person memoir, Billy's story is told in the street language of a gangster, marked by run-on sentences and loose punctuation. At the beginning of the novel, Billy is officially "initiated" into the gang as witness to the murder of Bo Weinberg, a crony of Schultz who in real life mysteriously disappeared and was thought to have been drowned in the sea wearing a pair of cement shoes. While the first scene of the book marks Billy's official acceptance into the gang, we soon find out that he was first noticed by Schultz while juggling for a group of boys loitering outside a Bronx warehouse used by the gang. Juggling is a dominant theme in this novel as Billy juggles his commitments to his new gang family with those to his mother, a perpetually grieving woman who was abandoned by Billy's Jewish father while the boy was young. We are told that Billy's mother, Mary Behan, is an Irish Catholic who maintains a candlelight vigil for Billy's missing father and takes comfort in going upstairs and sitting with the women at the synagogue. Billy also juggles his loyalty between Schultz and Berman, a member of Schultz's gang, and between the men and Drew Preston, Bo Weinberg's former lover who, after Weinberg's death, becomes Schultz's moll. In addition, Billy juggles his identity as errand boy for the gang while giving the impression of being a law-abiding citizen so he can spy for the organization. Through Billy's eyes and sensitivity, the violent world of the gang is given a humanity not often associated with gangsters.

Just as Doctorow illustrates that a fine line exists between fictional narratives and historical accounts, he shows that there is an equally fine line between legitimate and illegitimate business. By creating a likable and sympathetic underworld protagonist, Doctorow shows why crime was and continues to be an attractive route out of the immigrant ghetto. During his apprenticeship with the gang, Billy is often told that he is being groomed as the next generation of gangster and, as such, is taught the various trades that ensure the organization functions smoothly. From Lulu Rosenkrantz and Irving, Schultz's right hand man, Billy learns how to care for and fire a gun while Otto "Abadabba" Berman teaches him about the numbers racket and the intellectual aspects of organized crime. While Schultz brings Billy into the fold, it is Berman who gives him the business skills the adult Billy uses to manage his business—a legitimate company he establishes using Schultz's fortune, once thought by mainstream history to have been lost.

Bibliography

Baba, Minako. "The Young Gangster as Mythic American Hero: E. L. Doctorow's *Billy Bathgate*." *MELUS* 18, no. 2 (Summer 1993): 33–46.

Heber, Janice Stewart. "The X-Factor in E. L. Doctorow's *Billy Bathgate*: Powerless Women and History as Myth." *Modern Language Studies* 22, no. 4 (Autumn 1992): 33–41.

Henry, Matthew A. "Problematized Narratives: History as Fiction in E. L. Doctorow's *Billy Bathgate*." *Critique* 39, no. 1 (Fall 1997): 32–41.

—Rebecca Kuhn

Bitton-Jackson, Livia (1931–   )

Livia Bitton-Jackson, born Elli Livia Friedman in Czechoslovakia, published her first book, *Elli: Coming of Age in the Holocaust*, in 1980, 29 years after immigrating to the United States. Written at the urging of her husband, *Elli* is a graphic memoir that recounts Bitton-Jackson's journey from her small Czech village into the Holocaust. *Elli*, which won the Christopher Award, the Eleanor Roosevelt Humanitarian Award, and the Jewish Heritage Award, tells of Bitton-Jackson's separation from her father and then of her incarceration in the German camps of Auschwitz, Płaszów, Augsburg, and Mühldorf. Even though as a 14 year old she would normally have been sent to the gas chambers, her blond hair and light complexion caused the guards to pity her and let her live.

Despite periods of respite when she was at Augsburg work camp, she suffered such torturous conditions that at the age of 14 she was mistaken for a 60-year old woman. Abused and starved, Bitton-Jackson and the remains of her family were finally liberated in 1945. She completed her high school education in a displaced persons camp and arrived in America in 1951.

Bitton-Jackson received a B.A. from Brooklyn College, City University of New York, and a Ph.D. in Hebrew culture and Jewish history from New York University. She has been a professor of history at the City University of New York since 1980.

In 1997 Livia Bitton-Jackson rewrote *Elli: Coming of Age in the Holocaust* for a young adult audience and called it *I Have Lived a Thousand Years: Growing Up in the Holocaust*. She explores not only the inhumanity and atrocity of the Holocaust, but also the sacrifices and kindnesses that were found even in the concentration camps, making her story as sweet as it is tragic. In 1999 she published the sequel: *My Bridges of Hope: Searching for Life and Love after Auschwitz*. In this memoir Bitton-Jackson tells of her time in the displaced persons camp as she dealt with the ordinary turbulent feelings of a teenager, complicated by her earlier trauma. She describes her experiences running a Jewish school, helping Jews escape to Palestine, and rescuing orphans from riots. Through her memoir she shows how a young lost girl finds an identity for her self as a young Jewish woman.

Not limiting herself to memoirs, Bitton Jackson has used her scholarly writing to examine further the identity of Jewish women. Her works include *A Decade of Zionism in Hungary, the Formative Years: The Post–World War I Period: 1918–1928* (as Livia Elvira Bitton, 1968), *The Jewess As a Fictional Sex Symbol* (1973), *Biblical Names of Literary Jewesses* (originally a speech, 1973), and *Madonna or Courtesan: The Jewish Woman in Christian Literature* (1982).

Her book *Madonna or Courtesan: The Jewish Woman in Christian Literature* focuses on the imagery of the Jewess in Greek, German, Russian, and French literature. Critics claim that the originality in the book lies not in the illumination of the paradox between the literary portrayal of Jews and the historical facts, but in the author's focus on Jewish women. Bitton-Jackson's book states that while Jewish men were portrayed as wicked tricksters, the Jewess is described as either a redeemer or a seducer, and is more often a victim than a predator. The Jewess, not the Jewish man, is more likely to counter the negative image of the greedy, traitorous cowardly Jew. Bitton-Jackson explains that the reason for this literary portrayal of Jewish women lies in the connection of the Jewess to a female biblical prototype that combines virtue and seduction into one feminine persona.

For her powerful portrayals and explorations of Jewish women, Livia Bitton-Jackson has received many awards, including Long Island University's outstanding teacher award, 1967; New York University Founder's Day award, for highest bracket of scholastic preferment, 1969; a Christopher award, 1981, for *Elli: Coming of Age in the Holocaust*; The United Jewish Appeal Eleanor Roosevelt humanitarian award; and The Jewish Teachers Union Jewish heritage award, both in 1982, for *Elli: Coming of Age in the Holocaust*.

Livia Bitton-Jackson lives with her husband, children, and grandchildren in Israel.

Bibliography

Jackson, Livia Bitton. *Elli: Coming of Age in the Holocaust.* New York: Times Books, 1980.
———. *I have Lived a Thousand Years: Growing Up in the Holocaust.* New York: Simon & Schuster Books for Young Readers, 1997.

—Anna Lewis

A Blessing on the Moon
Joseph Skibell (1997)

Joseph Skibell's debut novel about the Holocaust is a veritable tour de force of the Jewish imagination, magical realism, and the postmodern temper of the times. One of a gradually emerging genre of third-generation works—those written by grandchildren of Holocaust survivors—Skibell's book, unlike the memoirs of Daniel Mendelsohn (*The Lost,* 2006) and Andrea Simon (*Bashert,* 2002), is noteworthy for its utilization of motifs from Jewish folklore and fables in coming to grips with his Holocaust legacy. Skibell's novel is both a response to the massive evil of the Shoah and to the fact that he was raised in a family that refrained from speaking about the murder of 18 members of his grandfather's immediate relations. Originating as a play, *A Blessing on the Moon* then became an award-winning short story and, finally, a novel.

The novel opens with the murder of its protagonist, Chaim Skibelski, a pious Jewish businessman shot to death by the Germans in a Polish village. Rather than resting in peace in the next world (*Olam haBa'ah*), Chaim—Hebrew for "life"—embarks on a series of journeys: to his own home now occupied by gentile Poles, to the mass grave containing the corpses of his Jewish friends, to a mysterious hotel that caters to the dead Jews, and tends to the raising of the moon (with the help of Zalman and Kalman), which, according to legend, has been pulled from the sky by two quarreling Hasidim. He is accompanied on his journeys by a talking crow who in fact is the ghost of his murdered rabbi. Chaim also encounters the severed head of the German soldier who shot him on the novel's opening page.

Throughout the novel, despite or perhaps because of the utter physical and metaphysical wreckage caused by the Holocaust, there is a constant tension between the physical destruction of the Jewish people and their theological beliefs, on the one hand, and, on the other hand, the traditional possibility of redemption. A good deal of the religious and messianic energy is reflected in its title. The cyclical appearance of the New Moon is seen as an occasion for giving thanks to God. "Sanctification of the Moon" (*Kiddush Levanah*) is also associated with messianic hope. The prayer stresses renewal in the world of nature and, by implication, symbolizes Israel's renewal as well. The dreadful fate of the Jewish people in the Holocaust has caused the moon to fall. The fact that Chaim has been able, through Skibell's use of magical realism, to effect its rise indicates that redemption of the Jewish people is still possible.

A Blessing on the Moon also raises a significant moral question: What is the role of forgiveness in relationship to the Holocaust? Chaim's "dialogue" with the severed head of the German soldier who murdered him includes his response to the head's plea for forgiveness: "Little head when you killed me you took everything. My home, my wife, my children. Must you now have my forgiveness as well?" While not directly responding to this issue, Skibell articulates his belief that everything that happens to the Jewish people is a blessing, good or bad. In monotheism God is the source of everything. While this contention evades the nuance and variety of post-Holocaust discussion of the possibility of forgivenenss—especially as it is raised in Simon Wiesenthal's stunning work *The Sunflower*—Skibell is on firmer grounds when he asserts his hope that his novel "is a book of blessing."

Skibell's novel incorporates elements of some of the great 20th-century Jewish writers. The talking crow who guides Chaim on his postmortem earthly sojourn is reminiscent of Bernard Malamud's short story "The Jewbird." Furthermore, the book's fascination with invisible ghosts who nevertheless have an earthly impact recalls many of Isaac Bashevis Singer's short stories. Skibell's novel evokes the lost world of eastern European Judaism that was permeated by a love of Torah and tradition, no less than an intimate familiarity with tales that featured ghosts and conversations with the dead. Dealing with the grizzly and surreal world of the Holocaust, *A Blessing on the Moon* reveals that perhaps the only way to begin adequately to respond to the outrage of hatred against Jews is by reverting to legends and tales that defy the murdering actions of tyrants and the world's indifference by continuing to offer hope for a redemptive future.

A Blessing on the Moon has received widespread critical acclaim. The novel, which has been translated into a half-dozen languages, won the American Academy of Arts and Letters's Richard and Hinda Rosenthal Foundation Award and the Turner Prize for First Fiction from the Texas Institute of Letters. Furthermore, Skibell's novel was a Book of the Month Club selection and named one of the year's best by *Publisher's Weekly, Le Monde,* and Amazon.com. The author's second novel, *The English Disease* (2003), won the Jesse H. Jones award from the Texas Institute of Letters.

Bibliography
Kersell, Nancy D. "Phantoms Past and Present in Holocaust Fiction." *Kentucky Philological Review* 14 (March 1999): 16–20.
Skibell, Joseph. "In the Invisible Courtyards of Chaim Skibelski," *New York Times Sophisticated Traveler Magazine,* 8 November 1998.
—Alan L. Berger

The Book of Daniel   E. L. Doctorow   (1971)

E. L. DOCTOROW's third novel opens with three epigraphs: the first from the biblical book of Daniel describing the pomp and circumstance that signaled the people's worship of Nebuchadnezzar's golden idol; the second from Walt Whitman's "Song of Myself," describing marches being played not only for the victors, but also for the dead and the conquered; the third from ALLEN GINSBERG's "America," declaring that everything personal had been given and that nothing remained, concluding with this admonition to the country—"Go fuck yourself with your atom bomb." These three epigraphs function as insightful introductions to the novel, glossing three important aspects of the text. The first involves the parallels between the biblical, dream-interpreting Daniel, with his idol worship–refusing kinsmen Shadrach, Meshach, and Abednego, and Doctorow's activist protagonist Daniel. Both Daniels are required to read the "writing on the wall" of their respective times and to refuse to bow down in worship before the powers-that-be or the idols they've erected. The second involves an evocation of America's quintessential 19th-century poet and his personal poetic response to the Civil War, that bloody conflict of a nation divided against itself. Whitman, as the poetic embodiment of America's Everyman, must celebrate for the whole divided nation, not just for the victorious North. So too must Daniel, himself in the midst of the revolutions of the sixties, resurrect and celebrate the earlier socialist activists from whom he has literally and figuratively sprung. The third involves a parallel evocation of the contemporary American poet who has inherited Whitman's poetic mission most fully, Allen Ginsberg, who, like Whitman, celebrated and berated virtually every aspect of American culture, albeit with much more colloquial directness and sexual candor. In the novel, set in 1967, Daniel narrates his own version of the personal and political past of the country just over 10 years after Ginsberg wrote "America." Both texts create a particular vision of history as fiction, a function of who writes for what purpose.

Grounded loosely on events surrounding the Julius and Ethel Rosenberg trial and execution for espionage, *The Book of Daniel* tells the story of the son of fictional Rosenbergs, Paul and Rochelle Isaacson, and his quest to determine the reasons why his parents sacrificed their own lives and their children's childhoods as political martyrs. This quest, rather than attacking the very foundations of the system, revolves more around Daniel's search for self-identity in a time when activism seems to have eclipsed the pathetic attempts of his parents and their lawyer to work within that system. Doctorow's narrative style reflects nicely the complexities of Daniel's quest with alternating first- and third-person narrative sections and embedded outlines and notes and titles for scholarly papers; letters to the editor; family correspondence; and whatever—all evocative of the style established in *The U.S.A. Trilogy* by John Dos Passos, which uses a multivoiced narrative combination to address the same themes as Doctorow does in *The Book of Daniel,* as well as in many of his other texts. This approach can be very confusing to readers who, like Daniel, must search through the text for a reading strategy that will open it up to understanding, even of the most basic kind. For example, it takes some time to figure out that Daniel and his sister, Susan, have two surnames, Lewin and Isaacson, the first for the couple, Robert and Lise Lewin, who adopt them

after their parents' deaths, and the second for their biological parents. The novel opens with Daniel, his wife, Phyllis, and their eight-month-old son, Paul, hitchhiking to visit Susan, who has been committed to the Worchester State Hospital after a suicide attempt in a public toilet. Some 14 years after their parents' execution, it is very clear that both Daniel and Susan have, as they say, issues to resolve. Daniel matches Susan's self-destructive impulse with his impulse to demean and mortify Phyllis, who, according to Daniel, bases all her actions on political principles. Obviously, the politics Daniel practices on her are sexual.

Divided into four books—"Memorial Day," "Halloween," "Starfish," and "Christmas"—the novel orders itself according to a chronology and rationale of its own device, emphasizing again the fictional construction of history and narration's complicated nature. Although the unfolding of Daniel's narrative cannot be random, its rationale does not reveal itself easily as episodes from the past are presented, especially in Daniel's mind, within contexts where the connections are not always clear. Thus, Daniel's intense effort to get to the very bottom of things must be doomed to failure because everything always remains in a state of flux, especially memory, his most consistent window to the past. It's no wonder that the novel concludes with three possible endings.

Bibliography

Culp, Mildred Louise. "E. L. Doctorow." In *Twentieth-Century American-Jewish Fiction Writers.* Detroit: Gale, 1984.

Rapf, Joanna E. "Sidney Lumet and the Politics of the Left: The Centrality of Daniel." *Literature Film Quarterly* 31, no. 2 (2003): 148–155.

Stark, John. "Alienation and Analysis in Doctorow's *The Book of Daniel.*" *Critique* 16, no. 3 (1975): 101–110.

—Phillip A. Snyder

Bread Givers   Anzia Yezierska (1925)

Published in 1925, *Bread Givers,* Anzia Yezierska's most popular novel, is a story about the successful integration into American society of a Jewish woman immigrant. Simplistically seen by many as the struggle between a father who cannot let go of the old Jewish ways and a daughter who buys into the values and mores of her newly adopted country, "*die goldene medine,*" the golden land, as they called America, the novel surprises the modern reader with its depth and clarity of vision.

Yezierska uses a first-person narrator who speaks with a great deal of emotional intensity. The narrator uses a Yiddish-English dialect, which can obscure the fact that she crafted the story deliberately and carefully. Readers unfamiliar with Yezierska's craftsmanship run the risk of focusing solely on how the story relates to episodes in her life, rather than on Yezierska's colorful characters, her wonderful imagery, and the clever use of language and traditional Jewish humor. *Bread Givers* is not strictly autobiographical; it is the fine product of an artist's sophisticated work. In this novel, Yezierska fuses aspects of realism and romanticism, ultimately frustrating attempts to categorize it.

Born in a Polish shtetl near the border with Russia, Yezierska experienced life in the European ghetto firsthand. At the age of 15, she exchanged the squalor of the mud hut in Poland for the dirt and poverty of the tenement on New York's Lower East Side. Yezierska and her family, as she describes in her novel *Bread Givers,* dared to dream of a better life in a wonderful place called America. They left the old country knowing nothing about the real America. They traveled to a place where "the streets were paved with gold," as the heroine's father says in the novel, a place where summer never ended, where they could shed the objects of their shabby existence and live as Jews without persecution. The characters of *Bread Givers* followed a dream, a fiction conjured up by poor Jews who could no longer endure the violence, the pogroms, the seemingly endless discrimination, or the poverty.

In *Bread Givers,* Yezierska also portrays the America she experienced as an immigrant: a harsh, alien, and frightening land. The heroine's mother needs to work at menial jobs to support the family. The daughters too go out to work as maids and in sweatshops. Their life is difficult and their work unrewarding.

Structured on two intersecting coordinates, immigration and acculturation, the novel focuses on the father-daughter relationship, which is hurled against a new set of complex codes and subjected to growing turmoil and change. By adopting this narrative strategy, Yezierska compels the reader who may be unfamiliar with traditional Jewish culture or the struggle of Jewish immigrants to take a new look at both Jewish and American history. A powerful Jewish-American novel, *Bread Givers* helps the reader reflect on what the heroine had to give up to become Americanized—family and culture. This may not be readily apparent, given the heroine's economic and status gains from the process.

Bread Givers immerses the reader in the ghetto experience and explores the heroine's feelings of loss and alienation. Although most readers today come from very different backgrounds from that of her characters, the novel seems to resonate with the new immigrants, ghetto youth, working-class employees, and women. Contemporary audiences, particularly female readers, respond especially to the immigrant waif characters as women who forged cultural and economic identities by their own strength, energy, and perseverance.

Yezierska's novel offers a fine model for successful acculturation by showing how a woman pursues the American Dream while at the same time holding on to her Jewish tradition. As Sara, the daughter, asks the father to come and live with her in her home, symbolically, she indeed "makes room" for tradition in her own Americanized home. With this ending, *Bread Giver* takes its place among other fine works that chronicle immigrant Jewish life. Like *The Promised Land* by Mary Antin, *Yekl* by Abraham Cahan, *Jews Without Money* by Michael Gold, and "Tell Me a Riddle" by Tillie Olsen, *Bread Givers* is a quintessentially Jewish-American story.

Bibliography
Henriksen, Louise Levitas. "Afterword." In *The Open Cage: An Anzia Yezierska Collection.* New York: Persea Books, 1979.

Kessler-Harris, Alice. "Introduction." In *The Open Cage: An Anzia Yezierska Collection*. New York: Persea Books, 1979.

Pratt, Norma Fain. "Culture and Radical Politics: Yiddish Women Writers, 1890–1940." *American Jewish History* 70, no. 1 (September 1980): 68–90.

—Gila Safran Naveh

Broner, E. M. (1930–)

Esther Masserman Broner was born in 1930 in Detroit, Michigan, the daughter of Paul Masserman, a noted Jewish historian and journalist, and Beatrice Weckstein Masserman, an actress in the Yiddish theater in Poland. Her background endowed her with a commitment to drama, love of storytelling, and sense of social activism. She attended Wayne State University, where she received a B.A. in 1950 and an M.A. in 1962. She received a Ph.D in 1978 from Union Graduate School in New York City. She is professor emerita at Wayne State University, where she taught creative writing, playwriting, women's studies, and American, Israeli, and contemporary Jewish literature. She also was a visiting professor at Haifa University and Hebrew University in Israel.

The author of 10 plays, novels, short stories, memoirs, and Jewish women's liturgical texts, she began her career as a playwright with *Summer Is a Foreign Land* (1966); continued publishing plays including *The Body Parts of Margaret Fuller,* which had its New York debut at Playwrights Horizon in 1976; and, most recently, saw her musical, *Higginson: An American Life,* performed at the Michigan Opera Company (2005).

Broner has devoted her life to creating feminist works that render visible the everyday lives and voices of women, expand the vision of women's experiences, and challenge patriarchal texts, institutions, and values. Her fiction explores women's gender roles, particularly their subordinate place in Jewish religion and tradition. To borrow a phrase from Virginia Woolf that serves as the epigram to *Her Mothers,* Broner "thinks back through her mothers," to foreground women's experience, knowledge, and motifs of self-enfranchisement as she reenvisions approaches to Jewish ritual, ceremony, and practice. In so doing, she builds a more expansive view of women's capabilities, history, knowledge, community, and traditions.

Her Mothers (1975) traces the coming-of-age journeys and choices of a group of representative female protagonists as they move from high school to old age. The central figure, Beatrix Palmer, engages in a spiritual pilgrimage to find herself and her lost daughter, Lena, and, in the process, she authors three works; encounters her biblical, literary, and political precursors (i.e., Margaret Fuller, Emily Dickinson, and Charlotte Forten); and, finally, emerges whole in her old-age reunion with her daughter in Florida. The reiterated motif in the novel—"I'm pregnant with a baby girl . . ."—suggests the need for women psychically, emotionally, and spiritually to give birth to themselves as well as face "unafraid" a sexist world. The novel moves in a nonlinear manner, includes biblical and literary references and allusions, and uses poetic language (metaphor and repetition) to integrate the different fragments of the work.

A WEAVE OF WOMEN (1978), Broner's masterpiece, praised by critics as a classic feminist work, weaves together stories of 12 different women—American, English, German, Israeli, Jewish, and non-Jewish—and three wayward girls, living together in a stone house in East Jerusalem in the 1970s. Influenced by her stay in Israel, Broner depicts the women's struggle as they strive for autonomy, self-realization, and a more just society. The novel focuses on their relationships with men, their confrontation with forms of sexual oppression (violence, abuse, and discrimination), and other complex issues in the Israeli-Arab world. The novel, a collage of voices, perspectives, and images, moves in a fragmented yet cyclic fashion as it embodies a pattern of birth, life, death, and rebirth for the women. The sensuous, poetic, and lyrical text also includes reinterpretations of Jewish holidays, traditions, and prayers, as well as new rituals to commemorate aspects of women's lives. Critics applaud the novel for its technical innovations, as well as its fusion of social, political, and spiritual concerns.

After these novels, Broner worked on two autobiographically inspired works, written after the death of her father (*Mornings and Mourning: A Kaddish Journal* [1994]) and her mother (*Ghost Stories* [1994]). While *Her Mothers* begins with the quest for the daughter, *Ghost Stories* centers on a daughter's desire to understand and connect with the spirit of her deceased mother. The novel, constructed as a series of stories, depicts the shifting relationships of the mother and daughter and the dialogue between them. As Jeffrey Ann Goudie comments, "Her rendering of the push-pull dynamic of the mother-daughter relationship certainly rings with real life, keenly observed and distilled" (34).

Broner's most recent works reenvision Jewish religious ritual through a feminist lens. With another of the founding members of the Women's Seder, Nomi Nimrod, (started in 1976 with Bella Abzug, Phyllis Chesler, Gloria Steinem, GRACE PALEY, and others), Broner cowrote the *Women's Haggadah,* first published in *Ms.* magazine in 1977. In *The Telling* (1993), Broner relates the history of the seder, placing each year's holiday in its appropriate historic and cultural context. Most recently, she authored *Bringing Home the Light: A Jewish Woman's Handbook of Ritual* (1999), which includes ceremonies for holidays, specific reinterpretations of prayers, and new rituals for women's experience and concerns such as a healing circle for women with breast cancer.

Her awards include a National Endowment for the Arts fellowship in literature (1980, 1981), an O'Henry Award (second prize in 1968 for "New Nobility"), and First Prize in the Bicentennial Playwriting Contest in 1976 for *The Body Parts of Margaret Fuller.* In 1983 Broner received a Wonder Woman Foundation Award "for courage in changing custom with ceremony."

In her introduction to *Weave of Women,* Marilyn French praises Broner for her efforts to enlarge the concept of the "Jewish novel" to express the concerns of women and for her "deep examinations of the effects of the Jewish tradition on women"(xi).

Bibliography
French, Marilyn. "Introduction." In *Weave of Women* by E. M. Broner. Bloomington: Indiana University Press, 1985.
Goudie, Jeffrey Ann. Review of *Ghost Stories. The Women's Review of Books* 12, nos. 10–11 (July 1995): 34.

—Jan Schmidt

Bukiet, Melvin Jules (1953–   )

As a child of Holocaust survivors, Melvin Jules Bukiet explores the unspeakable horror of that singular moment in human history with unsentimental veracity and a sardonic eye that spares no one. A member of the "second generation," a novelist, and a literary critic living in New York City, Bukiet represents a new direction in Jewish-American literature that promises to make the next decades at least as interesting and rich as the ones that gave us Bellow, Malamud, Roth, Singer, and Ozick.

Bukiet graduated cum laude from Sarah Lawrence College in Bronxville, New York. He continued his formal education at Columbia University, where he took a master in fine arts. From 1988 to 1993 Bukiet taught writing for The Writer's Voice. He later served as the fiction editor of the well-known *Tikkun* magazine. Since 1993 he has been a faculty member of Sarah Lawrence College, where he focuses mainly on teaching creative writing.

Since the eighties Bukiet has written essays and op-eds for virtually all major papers and journals in the United States, including the *Washington Post, Boston Globe, Los Angeles Times, Baltimore Sun, New York Times, Forward, Philadelphia Inquirer, San Francisco Chronicle, Chicago Tribune, Tikkun,* and the *Chronicle of Higher Education.* One can read his work in Polish, German, Italian, Czech, Brazilian, or Israeli journals as well. Too numerous to mention, his titles include "Machers and Mourners" (*Tikkun* 1997), "Authenticity and Marginality: Conversation with Cynthia Ozick and Illan Staven" (*Jewish Quarterly* 1999), "Hope against Hope" (*New York Times* 2001), "Jews as Metaphors" (*Forward* 2003), and "Custom and Law" (*American Scholar*

2005). To this work, he brings insightfulness and a true writer's instinct.

Bukiet is the author of a number of outstanding novels, including *Sandman's Dust* (1985), *While the Messiah Tarries* (1995), *After* (1996), *Signs and Wonders* (1999), *Strange Fire* (2001), and *A Faker's Dozen* (2003). He edited the collections *Neurotica: Jewish Writers on Sex* (1999), and *Nothing Makes You Free: Writings by Descendants of Jewish Holocaust Survivors"* (2002). Bukiet's works have been translated into a half-dozen languages, and he has won the Edward Lewis Wallant award (1993) and the Pushcart Prize (1998), as well as many other prizes and honors.

Bukiet came to wide attention with *Stories of an Imaginary Childhood* (1992), a collection set in Proszowice, Poland, about Jews blissfully unaware of the impending catastrophe. Bukiet re-creates a world on the brink of the abyss with no news from the public realm that may serve as a warning to the victims, nor is the victims' impending doom presented as part of a European catastrophe. Bukiet's unnamed narrator introduces himself in a language that seems at once altogether fresh and hauntingly familiar: "Show me a Jewish home without a prodigy and I'll show you an orphanage." Bukiet brings a moral passion and an unstinting craft to a subject that often reduces others to silence.

If in *Stories of an Imaginary Childhood* Bukiet gives the reader a taste of Jewish life just before the Holocaust, his irreverent 1996 black comedy, *After,* imagines what life must have been like for the Jews who survived the death camps. This work is a Jewish testimony of the first order. As he puts it, in an expression of the new sensibility in perhaps its purest form, "In the beginning was Auschwitz." Yet Bukiet does not write about the Holocaust directly. There are no scenes of selection, no gas chambers, and no mass graves. Instead, his fiction explores the long shadow of the Shoah. His novel opens at the moment the camps are liberated and follows a group of survivors as they scheme their way through a destroyed and thoroughly chaotic landscape. Bukiet allows his characters the full range of humanity, from the noble to the base, and in the process his vision will surely offend those who have wrapped the subject in such veils of piety that only sanitized portrayals are acceptable. If Bukiet's work is significantly darker than that of his literary progenitors, it is because the older writer, at least, could recollect the world before the cataclysm. For the second generation, however, there is only "After," a word that makes one shiver even as it perplexes. *After* drives home its point by assaulting our sense of the tasteful, challenging the notion that decorum could be the same thing "after" as it had been before. *After* is Bukiet's shattered-teeth smile, a smile that, like Franz Kafka's humor, comes after despair.

Bukiet is currently working on two novels, one of which, reportedly entitled "The Unacknowledged Legislator," is a moral thriller set in Washington, D.C.; the title is inspired by Shelley. The protagonist is the poet laureate of the United States. *Manhattan Rhapsody* is a multigenerational story narrated by Manhattan island. *Scribblers on the Roof,* a work he coedited with David Roskies, appeared in 2006.

To categorize Bukiet's work with its many shades of magic realism and steely sarcasm, one may wish to reread his essay "Mourners and Machers." There are those who only mourn, he says, and there are those who are machers, creators of fine fiction and dreams. Bukiet's powerful prose thus far compels us to invent a new term: he is a "mournmacher."

Bibliography
Hoffman, Eva. "After Such Knowledge: Memory, History, and the Aftermath of the Holocaust." *Kirkus Reviews,* 15 November 2003.
Graeber, Laurel. "New and Noteworthy Paperbacks." *New York Times,* 22 February 1998, sec. 7, p. 7.

—**Gila Safran Naveh**

Cahan, Abraham (1860–1951)

Abraham Cahan had a threefold career as an out-spoken proponent of socialism and organized labor, a leading Yiddish journalist and editor, and an author of English fiction and social commentary. He was 21 when he fled Russia to come to the United States, where he began to teach himself English. His native language was Yiddish, and he learned Hebrew as a boy, but even then he yearned for the secular education that a knowledge of Russian could bring. During his training in Vilna to teach in a government school, writings on revolutionary socialism came to his attention, and Cahan became acquainted with members of the underground movement. This led to his being observed by Czar Alexander III's police soon after he received his credentials and commenced his duties as a provincial teacher in 1881. Because he knew that such observation was often followed by imprisonment, he fled at night and made a dangerous journey to safety that led him to England, where he purchased his bilingual dictionary, from which he learned English, and then to America. In New York on June 8, 1882, Cahan was formally admitted as an immigrant, having gained a halting knowledge of English on the transatlantic crossing.

Within a decade after his arrival in New York, Cahan was already publishing newspaper articles in his adopted language, translating English writings for the Yiddish press, and reading the most sophisticated American literary works of the period, including those of Howells and James. After reading Cahan's first story in English, "A Providential Match," Howells recognized that it opened the door to a new setting for American realism: the unfamiliar—and to most Americans, unknown—world of the burgeoning Jewish ghetto. He suggested that Cahan continue setting his fiction among the Yiddish-speaking immigrants of New York's Lower East Side and elsewhere in the city, areas Cahan knew well and could present with the truth of life. Howells persuaded D. Appleton & Co. to publish Cahan's first novel, *Yekl*, the following year and reviewed it enthusiastically in the New York *World* under a title that thrilled Cahan: "The Great Novelist Hails Abraham Cahan, the Author of 'Yekl,' as a New Star of Realism, and Says that He and Stephen Crane Have Drawn the Truest Pictures of East Side Life" (26 July 1896: 18). In 1898 he brought out *The Imported Bridegroom, and Other Stories of the New York Ghetto*, a collection of his stories published over the past three years in the *Atlantic*, *Cosmopolitan*, and other national magazines; it, too, was warmly greeted by Howells. For the next two decades Cahan continued to publish realistic fiction in English.

As cofounder of the Jewish daily *Forward* in 1897 and its editor for 50 years, Cahan strived to Americanize his east-European, Yiddish-speaking compatriots by teaching them in their own language how to take advantage of opportunity in the New World. In its early decades, the *Forward* was a strong voice for socialism and organized labor when socialist factions fought internecine newspaper wars with theorists of one stripe battling those of another. Cahan argued that the socialists were defeating their own purpose and insisted that the *Forward* disregard the hyperintellectualized world of theory that most readers could not understand anyway. Instead, his paper dealt with practical issues so as to teach them what he thought they should know about American life and history as well as more generally about science, literature, and the arts because most of his readers were uneducated in such worldly matters.

Because he disagreed on aims and methods with others on the editorial staff, Cahan left the *Forward* for four years (1897–1901) to write for the New York *Commercial Advertiser* under its city editor, Lincoln Steffens. Shortly after leaving the *Advertiser,* he resumed editorship of the *Forward* and led it to become the world's preeminent Yiddish newspaper in terms of circulation and influence. As both a socialist and a fiction writer he remained persistently a realist. Although he wrote no more short stories in English after 1901, he published three extended works in the next 16 years.

A massacre of Jews in Chişinău (in present-day Moldova) early in 1903 motivated him to write *The White Terror and the Red* (1905), a powerful yet underrated novel set in prerevolutionary Russia that highlights the pervasive anti-Semitism there in the government, amid the people, and among the radicals. Although it describes events shortly before and after the assassination of Alexander II in 1881, the climactic slaughter and destruction of the Jewish community in Miroslav appears to be patterned on the Chişinău massacre and other recent pogroms in Russia.

Eight years later, in four issues of *McClure's Magazine*, Cahan serialized a preliminary version of his major novel, *The Autobiography of an American Jew,* with "The Rise of David Levinsky" as its subtitle (April–July 1912). In 1917 Harper and Brothers published *The Rise of David Levinsky* in its final form, a novel in which Cahan included much of his own experience as an immigrant Jew in New York City. He drew especially on his affiliation with socialism, the labor movement, and, by extension, American business, notably the garment trade with its diverse facets, from production, financing, and sales, to the dubious ethical practices among those and other parts of the industry. The title alone suggests the strong influence of Howells, although the parallel with *The Rise of Silas Lapham* (1885) is ironic because, unlike Lapham, Levinsky is an alienated capitalist who retains his wealth but has little to show for it—no love, no real friendship, no deep Jewish values.

All told, Ab Cahan, as he liked to identify himself, had a highly distinguished career, particularly as a journalist and editor, whose influence among millions of his constituents was no less than Howells's among his own—and probably little overlap existed among their readers. Yet his fiction warrants continuing attention for more than its place in literary history because it presents in a realistic mode "the true poetry of modern life" for which he aimed. *The Rise of David Levinsky* remains unsurpassed for its graphic portrayal of human strength and frailty among the exploiters and exploited in the heavily Jewish garment district of New York's Lower East Side in the late 19th and early 20th centuries.

Bibliography

Cahan, Abraham. *The Education of Abraham Cahan.* Vols. 1 and 2 of *Bleter fun mayn lebn.* Translated by Leon Stein, Abraham B. Conan, and Lynn Davidson. Introduction by Leon Stein. Philadelphia: Jewish Publication Society of America, 1969.

Chametzky, Jules. *From the Ghetto: The Fiction of Abraham Cahan.* Amherst: University of Massachusetts Press, 1977.

Marovitz, Sanford E. *Abraham Cahan.* New York: Twayne, 1996.

Sanders, Ronald. *The Downtown Jews: Portraits of an Immigrant Generation.* New York: Harper & Row, 1969.

—**Sanford E. Marovitz**

Calisher, Hortense (1911–)

Hortense Calisher is first and foremost a chronicler of New York and the 20th-century urban experience. She wrote in 1958: "Nobody can appropriate a great city. Every citizen tries to, in as many ways as that city has streets. New York and I have been together since I was born. I own tone poems of its sounds, playable on no earthly cassette of present design. My brain is scrawled with its old byways, which if streets have sexes, must have several times shifted roles. What's more, I tremor—happily, in most cases—toward their next transformation. Because I know I have to. I know the rules . . . And no one is ever going to make me into a sunbelt girl. Over the years when my children and I live on many rural roads, the Hudson River road that leads to my city will be the one I understand the best. It leads to the smell of good newsprint, hot, used libraries, hands dirty with art, and to that complicated skyline under which I can slouch easy. It leads to my hometown, where the pavement has my stamp on it" (*New York Times*, 28 April 1958).

Though Hortense Calisher has set many of her books in other cities of the world, it is New York that has inspired her best fiction. Calisher was born in New York City to Joseph Henry and Hedvig Lechstern, and, despite her sheltered and highly supervised childhood, grew up an accutely observant child of the city streets. She was intimate with the mixed-race neighborhoods that bounded her West Side apartment from which she walked 12 long blocks to PS 46 at 150th Street and Amsterdam Avenue. She describes familiarly these early desegregated districts composed of many black and white families and has cited diversity as the defining element of the 20th century. It was her habit to take detailed mental notes of her surroundings and commit them to her visual memory. This habit, plus the legacy of her father's southern-style storytelling characterized her work. From her father, Calisher learned the rhythms, style, color, and anecdotal content of storytelling.

Her parents' New York household, typically a place of southern hospitality, was usually filled to capacity with down-on-their-luck aunts, uncles, and cousins. Her father's numerous southern-born relatives, with whom she would later stay and write about, were ready material for fiction. Ultimately, however, Joseph Henry's crazy generosity caused the family a financial failure from which they did not recover. Calisher recalls her hated job at Macy's, where she worked to finance her first year at college. Her fine education at Hunter College High School stood her in good stead for entry to Barnard College, from which she was awarded an A.B. degree in 1932. She married Curtis Harnack in 1959, and together the couple raised two children, Bennet Hughes and Peter Heffelfinger, by Calisher's previous marriage to Heaton Benett Heffelfinger in 1935.

From 1957 to 1986 Calisher was a lecturer at numerous prestigious schools, such as the University of Iowa, Stanford, Brandeis, Bennington, and Brown. She also lectured widely in several of the former Eastern bloc countries, as well as in the Republic of China. Speaking of her teaching experiences in an essay entitled "Authors in the Classroom," she notes: "I enjoy teaching, if you have good students, you can't help it. I'm very grateful that I'm not shut away from young people. I see many of my contemporaries who don't have this experience, and its quite shocking to see what they turn into" (*Washington Post*).

Hortense Calisher's short stories began to appear in the *New Yorker* in 1948, with even the earliest material speaking to female coming-of-age issues, the evolution of great cities, and the generational evolution of families. Her numerous novels include *False Entry* (1961), *Textures of Life* (1962), *The New Yorkers* (1969), *Journal from Ellipsia* (1965), *Queenie* (1971), *Standard Dreaming* (1972), *Eagle Eye* (1973), *On Keeping Women* (1977), *Mysteries of Motion* (1984), and *The Bobby-Soxer* (1986, for which she received the Kafka Prize from the University of Rochester in 1987). Her novel *Age* (1987) was published under the pseudonym Jack Fenno. Other novels include *The Small Bang* (1992), *In the Palace of the Movie-King* (1994), and *In the Slammer*, written with Carol Smith (1997). Her novellas include *The Railway Police* (1996) and *The Last Trolley Ride* (1966). Her short stories include "The Absence of Angels" (1951), "Tale for the Mirror"(1962), "Extreme Magic" (1963), "Saratoga Hot" (1985), and *Collected Stories* (1975). Addressing the short story form in the *New York Times* (10 June 1984), Calisher wrote: "The short story comes completely enclosed, not as a completed thing, but as an outline for a completed thing, so that I can hold it in my head and write towards the end."

In 1972 her autobiography *Herself* was published. Calisher has also written a memoir entitled *Kissing Cousins* (1988) and contributed numerous essays and articles to such publications as *American Scholar,* the *New York Times, Harper's, Yale Review,* and the *New Criterion.*

Among the many awards she has received are a Guggenheim Fellowship, in 1952, and the Department of State's American Specialist grantee to Southeast Asia, 1958. She was awarded the Academy of Arts and Letters Award in 1967, the National Council Award in 1967, and the Lifetime Achievement Award of the National Endowment for the Arts in 1989.

Calisher's style often contains confusing punctuation and syntax and complex subplots. Her works are informed by memory and contain lush language and evocative scenes. Her writing has been described as postfeminist and heavily autobiographical and is compared to the work of Edith Wharton and Marcel Proust. The general effect of Calisher's work is lyrical, romantic, sometimes unconvincing in her experiments in point of view, and always Dickensian in its creativity. Despite the numerous settings of her many works, New Yorkers, and particularly New York Jews, are to Hortense Calisher what London was to Charles Dickens and Dublin and its Roman Catholics to James Joyce. Calisher's fiction is notable for its geographic clarity, its breadth of detail, its family sagas, wit, sexual candor, urban realism, historical memory, comedy of manners, Jewish customs, complex syntax and experimental punctuation, and lush prose. The books abound in evocatively recalled interiors, street scenes, conversations, and colorful characters.

SUNDAY JEWS, perhaps her quintessential book, is a semiautobiographical Jewish family saga written in a neorealist style reminiscent of Jane Austen and Henry James. Elegiac and tragicomic in tone, it is a complex historical and anthropological account of 20th-century New York Jewish social history. Peter Duffey, a lapsed Catholic, has married Zipporah Zangwill, an assimilated Jewish woman. Now he wonders "In the thicket of opinion, confusion, diffusion, and downright exclusion that is now our America, how will we interface them, our kids?" (292). Through the narrative recounting of family folklore, a murder, affairs, divorces, scandals, and myriad family secrets emerge. While *Sunday Jews* describes Jewish kibbutzim who were lazy or who went to Tel Aviv to be shopkeepers, *Sunday Jews* also describes those who gather at Zipporah and Peter's famous Sunday afternoons. The reader is left to judge whether these assimilated American "Sunday Jews" bear the burden of the clan and the larger human family. Critics continue to call the novel Calisher's best work and praise its lyrical prose, compassionate meditations, moral depth, and sparkling intelligence.

Bibliography

Calisher, Hortense. "Authors in the Classroom." The *Washington Post,* 17 July 1997, p. R108.

———. Byline. *New York Times,* 28 April 1958.

———. Byline. *New York Times,* 10 June 1984.

Hahn, Emily. "In Appreciation of Hortense Calisher." *Wisconsin Studies in Contemporary Literature* 6, no. 2 (Summer 1965): 243–249.

Snodgrass, Kathleen. "Hortense Calisher." In *American Short Story Writers Since WWII: Second Series,* edited by Patrick Meanor, 89–97. Detroit: Thomson-Gale, 2000.

—Gloria L. Cronin

Call It Sleep Henry Roth (1934)

Call It Sleep, HENRY ROTH's first—and for many years his only—published novel, was well received when it debuted in 1934, though it sold fewer than 2,000 copies during its first run. The *Herald Tribune* declared that Roth provided "the most accurate and profound study of an American slum childhood that has yet appeared." The *New York Times* compared Roth's treatment of New York's

Lower East Side with the Irish-American writer James T. Farrell's treatment of the Chicago Irish. The *New York Sun* declared Roth "a brilliant disciple of James Joyce." Indeed, even with its minimal readership, the novel remained a favorite of critics and writers such as Alfred Kazin and Leslie Fiedler. In 1960 *Call It Sleep* came out in a smaller hardcover edition, and in 1964 it came out in a paperback edition. Irving Howe, in response to this edition, wrote an enthusiastic review for the cover of the *Times Book Review.* The novel became a best seller and was soon established as a masterpiece of American literature.

Call It Sleep revolves around the story of David Schearl, his intimate relationship with his mother, Genya, and his often violent and tortured relationship with his father, Albert Schearl. The novel is highly autobiographical and shadows Roth's own move to America from Galicia in 1907, when the one-year-old Roth and his mother followed his father to New York. Like Genya Schearl, Roth's mother was pressured to marry his father after scandalously falling in love with a gentile. Chaim Roth, similar to Roth's characterization of Albert Schearl, was quick to anger and violence, often beating his son and otherwise tormenting those closest to him.

Roth's characterization of the Schearl family, in which he depicts the struggles of a young, Yiddish-speaking family, is not only a study of immigrant life and immigrant communities; he also explores the physical and emotional boundaries that define a particular family. The primary tension of the novel's first section, repeated throughout the text, is a product of the purity of David's love for his mother and the ominous overtones of his first sexual experience, where a handicapped girl, the older sister of a playmate, both asks him and makes him repeat: "Yuh wanna play bad?" After this incident, David becomes self-conscious about his body around his mother, and aware of her softness, her sweetness. Men such as his father, and his father's friend, Mr. Luter, threaten him because of the access they have to his mother, an access that he is aware of even if denied.

Physical exchanges, whether they are the beatings or dark looks from his father, or his mother's caresses and kisses, are imbued with the sense of "playing bad." Nowhere is this more evident than in the events leading up to and including the novel's climax, which begins with David's lingering embrace of his near-naked mother, and ends with his father accusing him of being another man's son. Indeed, readers differ on the veracity of this point, some agreeing with Albert that Genya's hasty marriage to him was precipitated by her pregnancy, and others viewing Genya as too upright and transparent to be implicated in such a vast web of lies. Albert's own past also comes back to haunt him at this time: Genya confesses for the first time that Albert's mother told her, on the eve of their marriage, that after a protracted argument with his father, Albert watched a bull gore him to death and failed to help him. As *Call It Sleep* builds to its climax, Genya claims not to believe the accusation. But at the crucial moment, she pushes her son out of the apartment to save him from his father's wrath.

In fact, readers will never know definitively about Genya's or Albert's past, or about which version of the truth is the actual truth. It is precisely this kind of ambiguity that Roth excels at and to which he devotes himself. As the title of the novel suggests, one can call it—the past, the present, the condition of being—one can call it many things. In the final lines, the narrator struggles to define "it," calling it feeling, or calling it triumph, or calling it acquiescence. Finally, though, he settles on calling it sleep, with all the sense of the unknown and the unconscious such a word conveys.

Bibliography
Kellman, Steven G. *Redemption: The Life of Henry Roth.* New York: W.W. Norton, 2005.
Rosen, Jonathan. "Writer, Interrupted: The Resurrection of Henry Roth." *New Yorker,* 1 August 2005, 74–79.

—Jessica Lang

The Catcher in the Rye J. D. Salinger (1951)
Despite the fact that J. D. SALINGER wrote dozens of stories, *The Catcher in the Rye,* his only novel,

remains his best-known and enduring work. Developed through much of the forties in short stories he wrote for *The New Yorker* that introduced the semiautobiographical character of Holden Caulfield, who narrates the novel, *Catcher* is a coming-of-age story relating the events of Holden's excursion into New York City after his expulsion from fictional Pency Prep School just before Christmas break. The novel's authentic use of adolescent language and subject matter, its often humorous, unreliable narrator, and its depiction of "teen angst" and of the adult world as seen through the eyes of its young protagonist, make it the prototype of today's teen novel, and a staple of high school curricula nationwide. But, the very language, style, and subject matter that have made Holden so real and appealing to young audiences are also what make *Catcher* one of the most criticized and frequently banned books in the history of American literature.

Holden's psychological journey mimics those of mythological heroes, particularly the Buddha (evidence of Salinger's growing interest in Eastern philosophy). Wealthy, on the brink of adulthood, desperately in search of an adult mentor, but simultaneously repelled by the "phoniness" of the adult world around him, represented by the superficiality of his interactions with others, and personified by his older brother, D.B., who prostitutes his writing talent as a Hollywood screenwriter, Holden experiences a series of crises involving sexuality, wealth, sickness, aging, and death, which highlight his disillusionment and build toward a climactic moment of "enlightenment." The last pure things in the world, he imagines, are children, like his younger brother, Allie, who died of leukemia at 11, and whom Holden sees as safe in death, from the death of the soul that comes with adulthood. He decides that instead of running away, he must return home with his little sister, Phoebe, as a kind of savior. He imagines himself catching children who run toward the cliff from a nearby field of rye, keeping them from falling, an image he gleans mistakenly from a line in Robert Burns's "Comin' Thro' the Rye," which he thinks reads "When a body *catch* a body comin' thro' the rye,"

but, as Phoebe corrects him, actually says "When a body *meet* a body . . ." Ultimately, Holden's inability to reconcile with his disillusionment leads to an emotional breakdown.

Ironically, the very things that readers dislike about Holden are the very things that make him so endearingly memorable: He is an unreliable narrator whose stream-of-consciousness narrative sharply criticizes all artificiality, hypocrisy, and materialism that he witnesses, despite the fact that he, hypocritically, manifests the very characteristics that he so despises in others. He tries to come across as cool and in control, yet inside he is a quivering child, motivated more by his own fear and uncertainty than by any nobleness of character. Significantly, Holden regularly dons a red hunting cap, which acts as a kind of ritualistic mask that he uses to create a more confident, extroversive—and false—alter ego and gives him the power to say and do things he wouldn't otherwise. By creating a teen character with such a genuine and authentic voice, Salinger created, in Holden, an iconic, archetypal literary figure, securing *The Catcher in the Rye*'s place in the literary canon.

Bibliography

Alexander, Paul. *Salinger: A Biography*. Los Angeles: Renaissance Books, 1999.

Kotzen, Kip, and Thomas Beller, ed. *With Love and Squalor: 14 Writers Respond to the Work of J. D. Salinger*. New York: Broadway Books, 2001.

Rosen, Gerald. *Zen in the Art of J. D. Salinger*. Berkley, Calif.: Creative Arts Book Company, 1977.

—**Jacob Robertson**

Catch-22   Joseph Heller   (1961)

Catch-22 is a brilliant, absurd, bitterly funny dramatization of the madness of war. Set in Pianosa, an island in the Mediterranean Sea, the novel describes the travails of Captain John Yossarian, an American bombardier whose squadron is based in Pianosa during World War II. Surrounded by power mongers, suck-ups, imbeciles, and ne'er-do-wells, Yossarian is a rational man living in an irrational world, and he is forced to behave absurdly to survive.

Although *Catch-22* has a loose chronological progression, it is structured by repetition compulsion rather than linearity. Many of the novel's chapters are flashback portraits of Yossarian's adversaries, and the book repeatedly attempts to fold history back upon itself, revisiting past events in a vain attempt to massage madness into sanity. In particular, the death of Snowden—whose guts spill out like a grim message from God—reverberates throughout the narrative, clear evidence of psychological trauma.

Yossarian's adversaries include not merely the Germans who hurl flack at his plane, but also his military superiors, each of whom is defined by a comic malignancy: Lieutenant Scheisskopf, who is obsessed with military parades; Captain Black, who inaugurates the Glorious Loyalty Oath Crusade; Colonel Cathcart, who keeps raising the number of missions his men must fly; Generals Peckem and Dreedle; and a whole host of other officers, MPs, and CID agents—two of whom are engaged in a relentless pursuit of the perpetually vanishing Washington Irving.

Behind the military bureaucracy lurks the military-industrial complex, and in addition to being bedeviled by his military superiors, Yossarian is perpetually flanked—and outflanked—by the complex's agents provocateurs: ex-PFC Wintergreen, who runs the war from his clerk's desk, and Milo Minderbinder, who turns war profiteering into an art form. Equal parts idealism, greed, and patriotic cant, Minderbinder is anxious to put the war on a businesslike footing. He establishes a syndicate, even going so far as to distribute shares, which allows him to sell food to the military at huge profits. He forms his own private army, which he hires out to the highest bidder. And in a stirring attempt to privatize the war, he bombs and strafes his own base to fulfill a contract with his German clients and rationalizes the action by equating the welfare of the country with that of the syndicate.

Behind both the military and its profiteers is Catch-22. Catch-22 is the hidden loophole in every law, the loophole that allows institutions to maintain control over individuals even—and especially—when claiming to renounce that control. Because of Catch-22, cruelty flourishes, the innocent are victimized, and Yossarian is condemned to fly an endless string of missions. And because of Catch-22, the world has become a charnel house of broken lives. Even Rome—the eternal city—makes Yossarian recoil in sickness and dread.

Recognizing that much of the world seems bent on his destruction, Yossarian does what any reasonable man would do. He sabotages equipment, fakes illnesses, goes AWOL, and nearly sanctions the murder of his commanding officer. And when his refusal to fly more missions is thwarted by Catch-22, he makes a break for Sweden, with Orr, his lodestar, Nately's whore, his spur. And though the end of *Catch-22* is artistically unsatisfactory, Yossarian's mad dash for freedom became a rallying cry for a generation traumatized by the Vietnam War: "YOSSARIAN LIVES."

Bibliography

Bertonneau, Thomas F. "The Mind Bound Round:" Language and Reality in Heller's *Catch-22*. *Studies in American Jewish Literature* 15 (1996): 29–41.

Woodson, Jon. *A Study of Joseph Heller's* Catch-22: *Going Around Twice*. New York: Peter Lang, 2001.

—**Daniel K. Muhlestein**

Chabon, Michael (1963–   )

Michael Chabon, one of the most prolific and dazzling of the current generation of Jewish-American writers, has been described as a brilliant fantasist who creates richly imagined universes. His work is often counterfactual, rich in mythic paradigms, resonant with Jewish historical content, and indebted to *Yiddishkeit*. Chabon's recurring themes involve cultural nostalgia, friendship, male coming-of-age issues, the travails of the artist, loss of innocence, Jewish history, Jewish religion, Zionism, Nazi Germany, and the Holocaust. Abandonment, divorce, gay issues, parenthood, and an amazing variety of male/male relationships are also a steady feature of his work. By now he has been regularly compared to such literary masters as Vladimir Nabokov, John Cheever, and John Updike for his brilliant prose style. In elegant, rich, allusive, and highly metaphorical language, he addresses the age-old American literary themes of the American dream, survival, transformation, and spiritual transcendence.

Chabon was born in Georgetown, Washington, D.C., and spent his young childhood mostly in diverse suburban Maryland. Devastated by the departure of his pediatrician-lawyer father and his parents' subsequent divorce, he developed a fascination with the comic book era of his father's Brooklyn childhood. At age 10 Chabon began buying comic books, and he later started the Columbia Comic Book Club, renting a club room in a local community center, and even created a newsletter. Robert Louis Stevenson's *Treasure Island* held similar fascination for him and reverberates through most of the fiction. Though at age 16 Chabon abruptly stopped reading comic books and sold his large collection, they have remained a lifelong interest.

Chabon received a B.A. in English from the University of Pittsburgh in 1984. He graduated from the University of California, Irvine, with an M.F.A. in creative writing in 1987, the same year that he married poet Lollie Groth. The couple would divorce in 1991. His publishing career began when his M.F.A. adviser, Donald Heiney, sent the manuscript of *The Mysteries of Pittsburgh* (1988) to a literary agent, Mary Evans, who promptly sold it to William Morrow Publishers for the remarkable sum of $155,000. The novel established Chabon as a bestselling author at age 24. The work's 23 chapters mythologize Pittsburgh as an Edenic world, and it is structured around the Arthurian Grail quest. A coming-of-age narrative, it features the sexual and spiritual transformations of its bisexual hero, Art Bechstein, as well as the lost worlds of childhood and adolescence, and much Freudian family angst.

After the appearance of *The Mysteries of Pittsburgh* and *A Model World and Other Stories* (1991), Chabon worked for several frustrating years on a novel entitled "Fountain City," and was finally forced to drop it when it failed to coalesce. Set in Paris and Florida, it grew to 1,500 pages, some of

which was later salvaged for the highly successful *Wonder Boys* (1995). In this coming-of-age, picaresque autobiographical novel, Chabon reveals much writerly misery over not being able to finish his previous novel. The book resounds with the abuse of alcohol, drugs, and generally self-destructive behaviors. It was made into a well-received movie in 2000. *Werewolves in Their Youth* (2000), a collection of short stories, came next, followed by the much-acclaimed *KAVALIER AND CLAY* (2000). This novel established Chabon as a major literary talent and garnered the writer the Pulitzer Prize in 2001. Based on two historical figures, Jerry Siegel and Joe Shuster, the creators of the 1938 Superman comic books, *Kavalier and Klay* is a fondly created rendering of Chabon's father's Brooklyn, with its high art and pop culture, and also depicts the lives of increasingly embattled European Jews. It tells the story of the development and training of Joseph Kavalier, a European *Ausbrecher* (a Houdini-like escape artist), and his American cousin Sammy Clay, who is a victim of polio. Together, the two teenagers create an amazing comic book series named *The Escapist,* featuring an eponymous Superman-type character who fights Nazis, and a resurrected 16th-century golem. The Escapist fights oppression and crime in an effort to bring about liberation and freedom. Ultimately, however, the epic bears dark witness to paranoia, broken history, and the continuing nightmare of the Holocaust. Underlying the story is a trenchant and historically accurate account of the historical abuse of American writers by major publishing houses. Both bildungsroman and *Künstlerroman,* the novel is a magical realist work asserting the transformational power of art and the human imagination to counter spiritual death and broken history. Both flawed characters, Joseph and Sammy finally escape history to find their direction. Joe Kavalier will eventually return to claim his son and lover, while Sammy Clay will finally embrace his homosexuality and leave New York. Meantime, their respective artistic gifts have become a shared personal gift for evading and transcending a meaningless world.

Summerland (2002) is a fantasy novel for young readers and has been seen as Chabon's answer to the Harry Potter phenomenon. In this story informed by Americana, however, the hero journey is based on Native American and Norse mythology. Built into its American baseball and Coyote mythos are magical creatures, parallel universes, and magic portals. Rich in fantasy and set in yet another dead world, it also presents a hero whose transformation and transcendence are facilitated by true friendship and loyal helpers in the face of a darkening universe.

This novel was quickly followed by the much darker The FINAL SOLUTION (2004), which resurrects the brilliant and quirky Sherlock Holmes, who is still practicing his investigative skills during World War II. Gentlemen of the Road (2007) is set in the Middle Ages and reflects Chabon's fascination with The Arabian Nights, Scheherazade, Alexandre Dumas, and Fritz Lieber. Set in the Caucasus Mountains circa A.D. 950, the height of the Khazar Empire, it narrates the adventurous and violent life on the road among a company of thieves, adventurers, con men and cutthroats.

THE YIDDISH POLICEMEN'S UNION (2007) recounts a counterfactual history of the imagined fall of the state of Israel in 1948. In this novel Chabon's Jews encounter yet another leg in their unending historical disapora and end up in Sitka, Alaska. By secular means, it appears, the Messiah's coming must now be hastened. The language is dense in faux or mock Yiddish expressions, messianic yearnings, and dense biblical allusions. This mythic rendering of Jewish history takes the form of a parable and is clearly a response to PHILIP ROTH's THE PLOT AGAINST AMERICA. With its hard-boiled detective fiction formula so famously exemplified by Raymond Chandler and Dashiell Hammett, it is also a paradoxical parable of the failure of the Jews to deliver a messiah. Its zany characters echo their counterparts within the Yiddish literary tradition, while the work centers itself ethically, literally, and mythically in the Holocaust. The Yiddish Policemen's Union received favorable reviews and was named a Notable Book by the American Library Association. Columbia Pictures immediately bought the movie rights.

In 1993 Chabon married Ayelet Waldman, an Israeli-born and U.S.-raised lawyer who is now a successful novelist in her own right. The couple lives in Berkeley, California, with their four children. Chabon frequently describes their working life as typically suburban and middle-class. He writes from 10 A.M. to 3 P.M., Sunday through Thursday, attempting to produce 1,000 words per day. He also lectures on writing and the traditions of Jewish-American literature and remains interested in genre fiction, trickster literature, children's literature, screen plays, comics, newspaper serials, and film scripts.

Bibliography

Binelli, Mark, and Bryce Duffy. "The Amazing Story of the Comic Book Nerd Who Won the Pulitzer Prize for Fiction." Rolling Stone, 27 September 2001.

Leonard, John. "Meshuga, Alaska." New York Times Review of Books, 14 June 2007.

Meanor, Patrick. "Michael Chabon." In Dictionary of Literary Biography: American Novelists Since World War II, Seventh Series. Vol. 278, edited by James R. and Wanda H. Giles, 81–90. Detroit, Mich.: Gale, 2003.

Safier, Rachel. "On the Mommy Track." The Jerusalem Report, 15 May 2006.

—Gloria L. Cronin

Charyn, Jerome (1937–)

Jerome Charyn was born in 1937 in New York City. He came of age in the Bronx, where he absorbed a lifelong interest in comic books, crime stories, and the movies. Educated at Columbia College of Columbia University and graduating cum laude, Charyn went directly from college to work on his writing career. As he explains in a self-penned biography, "While friends of mine went on to graduate school, I worked as a playground director, trying to learn the strange—almost invisible—craft of a writer." Still, in spite of a successful—and highly prolific—career as a fiction writer, Charyn has worked as an educator in a variety of systems, and has taught at a wide range of institutions, from the

New York City public schools to Princeton and Stanford. He is currently professor of film studies at the American University of Paris. Charyn's professional output has been just as diverse: Having published 33 books of fiction, he has also published nonfiction texts on a variety of topics and a series of memoirs and has contributed to a number of notable publications.

Charyn's first novel, ONCE UPON A DROSHKY, was published in 1964, when the author was 26 years old. Much of his early work, including this novel, has been described by one critic as a New York Jewish version of "Dickensian geniality and comic life." Accordingly, the novel's prose is often composed in Yiddish and, in terms of both structure and content, bears the influence of Jewish fairy tales. It is a book that draws heavily on Charyn's experiences as a child in the Bronx, and is perhaps his most cleanly articulated expression of the tension between figures representing the Jewish tradition and those of a more typically American mold. Charyn's next two books—*On a Darkening Green* and *The Man Who Grew Younger*—explore similar terrain, being largely concerned with the different avenues of Jewish-American life in New York City. And yet while these early texts employ a more standard approach to structure and content, they contain creeping hints of the fantastic themes and formal experiments that came to characterize his later work. Perhaps the first fully formed manifestation of such was 1971's *Eisenhower, My Eisenhower*, a book that defied the standards of the conventional novel with its mystical overtones and its antirealist tale of an urban American war between a race of Gypsies called the Azazians and the dominant cultural group, the Anglos. Charyn instructively referred to this as "my first book, really," and the novel's far-flung premise and unique structure are characteristic of much of his subsequent work.

Charyn is most popularly recognized as a detective writer who reinvents the genre's archetypes. His crime fiction is perhaps best represented by the Isaac Sidel Quartet, a series of books that includes *Blue Eyes* (1975), *Marilyn the Wild* (1976), *The Education of Patrick Silver* (1976), and *Secret Isaac* (1978). These books follow the career of New York City detective Isaac Sidel, his battles with the Guzzman crime syndicate, and the lasting effects of the death of his son, Manfred Coen. Throughout the series, Charyn inverted the detective story by adding more complex psychological dimensions, employing a dense, Joycean approach to narrative, and allowing the detective a healthy relationship with the absurd.

Charyn's most recent fiction has been among his best received. In 1997 he published a fictionalized memoir based on the life of his mother titled *Dark Lady from Belorusse*. This was the beginning of a trilogy that included 2000's *Black Swan* and 2002's *Bronx Boy*, both of which explore adolescent life in the East Bronx of the 1940s, using Charyn's own life as a backbone and taking liberties with some of the more fantastic details. The 1999 novel *Captain Kidd*, described on the cover as "A Tragi-comedy of War and Peace," examines the exploits of a captain in General Patton's Third Army Corps who finds himself tangled up in both the military and organized crime. *The Green Lantern: A Romance of Stalinist Russia* (2004) was released to critical plaudits, which included a nomination for the PEN/Faulkner award. The book follows the rise of a poor Shakespearean actor in Stalinist Russia, his romance with an acclaimed actress, and the artists' relationship with Stalin himself and his regime.

The subjects of Charyn's nonfiction mirror his fictional interests in many significant ways. These include studies of New York City and its culture (*Metropolis: New York as Myth, Marketplace, and Magical Land* [1986] and *Gangsters and Gold Diggers: Old New York, the Jazz Age, and the Birth of Broadway* [2003]), Hollywood and movies (*Movieland: Hollywood and the Great American Dream Culture* [1989] and *Raised by Wolves: The Turbulent Art and Times of Quentin Tarantino* [2006]), and artists in Russia (*Savage Shorthand: The Life and Death of Isaac Babel* [2005]). He also published a piece of juvenile fiction, 1993's *Back to Bataan*, and has written for the *New York Times* and the *New York Times Book Review*.

Charyn's work often reflects the parameters of what the author himself describes as "an imagination that leap[s] from one form of chaos to another." A 1990 article for *The Review of Contemporary Fiction* cited the influence of George Herriman's Krazy Kat cartoons of the early 20th century. Like Herriman's work, Charyn's novels tend to seek out a space that transcends the grammar of the medium, a space infused with surrealism and subversive playfulness. It is through this lens that his work should be examined. As Charyn explained in the same interview, his efforts are frustrated when readers make "realistic demands on works that aren't meant to be realistic." Interestingly enough, Charyn's output seems to have been received with greater enthusiasm in Europe, and his novels have been translated into 12 languages.

Although U.S. critics have at times been baffled by Charyn's approach to fiction, he has emerged as an eminently important American writer, whose antirealist innovations have attempted to bend the borders of the conventional novel and whose works have always been anything but predictable.

Bibliography

Woolf, Mike. "Exploding the Genre: The Crime Fiction of Jerome Charyn." In *American Crime Fiction: Studies in the Genre.* New York: St. Martin's Press, 1988.
———. "Charyn in the 1960s: Among the Jews." *Review of Contemporary Fiction* 12, no. 2 (Summer 1992): 143–151.

—Ben Child

The Chosen Chaim Potok (1967)

CHAIM POTOK's *The Chosen* is a novel about Orthodox and Hasidic Jews living in Brooklyn toward the end of World War II. A close reading of the text reveals it to be a novel about two kinds of orthodoxy, two subcultures confronting each other. It is also a kind of love story, about Danny and Reuven, not another angst-ridden novel about alienation.

In *The Chosen*, set in the urban Crown Heights and Williamsburg sections of Brooklyn, a baseball game between an Orthodox team and a Hasidic team brings together Danny Saunders, son of the Hasidic Rebbe (and thus heir to his father's position), and Reuven Malter, son of a Zionist activist modern Orthodox talmudic textual scholar. Danny, elevating the game to a holy war, purposely hits Reuven with a ball, sending him to the hospital. At the hospital, Danny visits Reuven and makes amends. They become friends, which is frowned on by the Rebbe, who, believing that there is a danger that his son's soul might be dominated by his brilliant mind, decides to interact with him only in silence. In this way he seeks to foster the values of heart and soul.

Mr. Malter, viewed by the Hasidim as a rationalist and not a true believer, fuses the best secular learning with the best in talmudic scholarship. As the relationship between Danny and Reuven ripens, Danny decides to become a psychologist, abdicating his role as his father's heir, while Reuven decides to become a rabbi, to whom symbolic logic, math, and secular philosophy would help fuse the sacred and the secular. Each combines two cultures and each reflects his and Potok's own attempts as a *zwischenmensch* (a between person) to explore the role of Judaism in a secular society. Danny's decision at the end to become a psychologist combines the insights of Freud and talmudic study. Reuven, on the other hand, will be a rabbi, a righteous occupation that includes scientific talmudic interpretation, anathema to Danny's Hasidic family.

In writing *The Chosen*, Potok discovered a cultural dynamic, a "culture war." Within the overarching culture of Western secular humanism, what Peter Gay called "modern paganism," there is a whole spectrum of subcultures in which he found a core-to-core cultural confrontation. Attempting to track elements of this confrontation, such as Danny confronting the rigidity of his Hasidic upbringing with Freudian psychoanalytic theory, Potok isolated the constant struggle between one's own traditional Jewish background and the larger world he longed to embrace.

Born in 1929 in the Bronx to Hasidic parents, Potok grew up in an Orthodox Jewish family in an Orthodox Jewish neighborhood. Attending a cheder, a primary Jewish parochial school, his interest in and talent for painting came to the fore when one summer his Yeshiva inexplicably hired an artist to give a course in painting to the children.

That was his first step into the world of Western art. In his childhood what Joyce was to Jesuits, painting was to Talmud. Deep into the study of Torah and Talmud, he began a journey that would illuminate the conflict between Jewish tradition and the secular Western world.

The Chosen poses two questions: How can one live as an observant Jew in a secular society, and to what degree can one hold to the tradition of Orthodox separateness in a secular society? In *The Chosen,* Danny and Reuven represent the two poles within Orthodox Judaism. In that space are the tensions Potok explored. As a writer, as a rabbi, as a scholar, he was trying to understand and explain the forces that are manifest as Judaism, traditional and modern, comes in contact with the modern, secular world.

Bibliography

Abramson, Edward. *Chaim Potok.* Boston: Twayne, 1986.

Nissenson, Hugh. Review of *The Chosen, New York Times Book Review,* 7 May 1967.

Walden, Daniel, ed. *Conversations with Chaim Potok.* Oxford: University Press of Mississippi, 2001.

—Daniel Walden

Cohen, Arthur Allen (1928–1986)

Arthur A. Cohen was an original thinker and award-winning novelist of great intellectual virtuosity. Trained as a philosopher and a theologian, he came late to the writing of fiction. Consequently, his novels are suffused with theological erudition while exploring the meaning of history, the nature of faith, and the possibility of redemption. Born in New York, Cohen received a B.A. (1946) and M.A. (1949) degree from the University of Chicago, doing additional graduate work at the Jewish Theological Seminary of America in New York City. The author of six novels, Cohen, who was also an art historian, wrote 11 scholarly books and edited or coedited seven others. An astute publisher, he cofounded Noonday Press, established and was president of Meridian Books, and held executive positions at several major publishing houses. He and his wife, Elaine Firstenberg Lustig, an artist, founded Ex Libris, a rare book company. The Cohens have one daughter.

Cohen was deeply committed to the life of Jewish scholarship, and his work can be viewed as an attempt to articulate a meaningful Jewish theology. While a graduate student at Chicago, however, he experienced a crisis of faith and considered converting to Christianity. Under the tutelage of Rabbi Milton Steinberg, the towering Jewish spiritual figure of the time, Cohen reimmersed himself in Judaism and its texts and subsequently published an autobiographical essay "Why I Choose To Be a Jew" (April 1959). Among Cohen's distinguished theological writings *The Natural and the Supernatural Jew* (1963), *The Myth of the Judeo-Christian Tradition* (1970), and *The Tremendum: A Theological Interpretation of the Holocaust* (1981) remain significant scholarly resources.

Cohen wore many hats including involvement in academe. He was a visiting lecturer at both Brown University (1972) and the Jewish Institute of Religion (1977). Moreover, in 1979 the author was the Tisch lecturer in Judaic theology at Brown. He was a member of the Advisory Board of Brandeis University's Institute for Advanced Judaic Studies and served as consultant to the "Religion and the Free Society" project of the Fund for the Republic. Cohen was on the Board of the PEN American Center and chaired the board at Yiddish Scientific Institute (YIVO) Institute for Jewish research.

Arthur Cohen's language was elegant and highly sophisticated. Consequently, his works were not always readily accessible, although they were always insightful. A Jewish theologian of culture, Cohen was deeply impressed by a statement of Franz Rosenzweig, an early 20th-century Jewish philosopher who also nearly converted to Christianity: "We have to smuggle Jewish ideas into general culture" (Cole 34). Consequently, the author writes with great insight about the implications of Jewish history and its theological concepts and their wider implications. Cohen the novelist opines that fiction "should smuggle something special into it. My novels are all tales plus something else" (Cole 35). This something else involves issues of identity, authenticity, Messianism, morality, and a spiritual journey.

Of Cohen's six novels, four deal directly with Judaism: *The Carpenter Years* (1967), *In the Days of Simon Stern* (1973), *A Hero in His Time* (1976), and *An Admirable Woman* (1983). The other two, *Acts of Theft* (1980) and the posthumously published *Artists & Enemies: Three Novellas* (1987), deal with the world of art, although it may be argued that even these novels engage a Jewish theme in dealing with the prohibition against making graven images. Cohen's first novel deals with the difficulties of being a Jew in Christian America. The title refers to "the carpenter years of Jesus," the time that is of greatest interest to Morris Edelman, the novel's protagonist. Edelman converts to Christianity, changing his name to Edgar Morris and taking a position as director of a YMCA. Danny, his estranged son, finds him and berates his father for abandoning Judaism.

Cohen addresses the theological implications of the Holocaust in his sprawling and richly textured *In the Days of Simon Stern,* which draws extensively on Jewish myth and mysticism. The novel's protagonist, Simon Stern, is an American millionaire and secular messiah who rescues a remnant of Holocaust survivors. Blind Nathan of Gaza, a seer, announced Simon's identity as Messiah. Simon plans to ensconce them in a building, modeled on the Temple in Jerusalem. This third Temple is, however, fated—like its two predecessors in antiquity—to be destroyed. At novel's end, Nathan foretells of Simon continuing struggles to achieve redemption for the Jewish people and, by implication, underscores that redemption is an open-ended process for all of humanity.

The author turns his attention from religion to politics in *A Hero in His Time.* Written shortly after Cohen published his historical study of the persecuted Soviet Jewish poet Osip Mandelstam, the novel tells the tale of Yuri Maximovich Isakovsky, a minor Jewish poet in the Soviet Union. Isakovsky is unexpectedly chosen to attend a poetry conference in New York City, where he is to read a poem given him by the authorities. Unbeknown to the poet, the poem is in fact a coded message to a KGB agent. Isakovsky rewrites the poem, not for political reasons but because it's aesthetically offensive. In the process he obliterates the coded message. Isakovsky refuses to defect, however, believing that his poetic soul is nurtured by his homeland. Cohen's novel, by turns comic and serious, means to underscore that art is more powerful than military or ideological weapons.

An Admirable Woman purports to be a memoir of Erika Margaret Hertz, a German-Jewish refugee who becomes part of the community of exiled German intellectuals gathered on New York City's West Side. Erika becomes a major force on the American and international scene. The novel is based on the distinctive life of Hannah Arendt, the political philosopher and friend of the author. In this work, which Cohen writes in a female voice, the author explores the possible meanings of the word *admirable* which has been applied to the intellectually gifted Erika, while exploring the role of the intellectual in society.

Among Arthur Cohen's literary awards are the Edward Lewis Wallant prize for *In the Days of Simon Stern* (1973), and the Jewish Book Council National Jewish Book Award in Fiction (1984) and William and Janice Epstein Award for a Book of Jewish Fiction (1985), both for *An Admirable Woman.* Cohen also received the George Wittenborn Memorial Award (1986) for *Herbert Bayer: The Complete Works.* His *A People Apart: Hasidism in America* was nominated for a National Book Award in 1972.

Bibliography

Cohen, Arthur Allen. "Why I Choose to Be a Jew." *Harper's Magazine,* April 1959, 61–66.

Cole, Diane. "Profession: Renaissance Man: Arthur A. Cohen." *Present Tense* 9 (Fall 1981): 32–35.

—**Alan L. Berger**

Cohen, Sarah Blacher (1936–   )

Sarah Blacher Cohen, a Jewish-American playwright, critic, editor, and professor, balances successfully her dual roles of critic and playwright.

Recently, Cohen has begun to address the challenges of growing up disabled; her most powerful works manage to transform her own disability into an opportunity for self-discovery.

In the "Economy" section of *Walden*, Henry David Thoreau famously opined: "I have travelled a good deal in Concord." In a recent interview Cohen, paraphrasing Thoreau, says:

> I have traveled much in Albany. Now that I have a harder time getting around I must recreate the world around me within my own home in Albany and within my own imagination through my plays and my writing on Jewish American literature. As a result of my recent illnesses I now need oxygen to help me breathe; this has forced me to be careful of each word that I use, both in my critical and creative writing as well as in daily conversation with family and friends. Realizing I have a limited number of words to use in a day—I want to make certain I use the right ones. Words are precious and not to be squandered. (Interview)

Despite the seriousness of Cohen's works, both critical and dramatic, she always manages to combine her complex Jewish faith with a certain dark humor. This humor is always apparent in her character's dialogue, as well as in Cohen's own conversations. Speaking of her youth, Cohen sardonically recalls: "I couldn't run fast, but I could think fast." From her earlier career as an academic scholar focusing on the work of Saul Bellow and other Jewish-American writers, to her more recent successes as a playwright with a national reputation, Cohen presents her audiences with a humorous literary journey.

Cohen is the youngest daughter of Mary and Louis Blacher, Yiddish-speaking immigrants from Minsk (present-day Belarus). Louis was a junk dealer in rural Appleton, Wisconsin, and Cohen is currently completing a memoir titled *Junk-Dealer's Daughter*, based on her distinctive, Midwest Jewish-American childhood. Reminiscing about her youth, Cohen reveals a major theme of her dramatic work:

> My mom didn't want me to have a big voice, to have *chutzpah;* she wanted me to be *'adel,'* genteel and quiet. If I spoke up she was upset. She raised the Cohen girls to defer to authority. I challenged authority and gained independence from my mother through my big voice. Looking at my disability my mother would tell me I couldn't do things physically; in contrast my father encouraged me to do whatever I wanted. These days, with my tracheotomy 'my loudest voice' has become transformed into a baritone, but I still speak loudly and defy authority through my playwriting. (Interview)

From the beginning of her dramatic career, Cohen has been drawn to write about women with loud voices. The resulting dual themes of empowering women and giving voice to the voiceless occupy a prominent position in Cohen's work both on and off the stage.

Cohen began her career as a literary scholar with her well-received *Saul Bellow's Enigmatic Laughter,* published in 1974. Since that first volume Cohen has written and edited nearly half a dozen other books, including *Comic Relief: Humor in Contemporary American Literature, Jewish Wry: Essays on Jewish Humor, Cynthia Ozick's Comic Art,* and *Making a Scene: The Contemporary Drama of Jewish-American Women.*

After having written several highly regarded critical studies, it appeared as if Cohen's career was destined for the academy and not the stage. Despite her many accomplishments as a professor of English at the University of Albany, SUNY, Cohen's work has recently taken a less academic turn. In the last few decades, Cohen has followed Cynthia Ozick's advice and transformed herself into an increasingly visible and influential playwright. In her foreword to her 1983 collection of essays *Art and Ardor,* Ozick says about Cohen: "I have a conscientious and responsible friend, a professor and a scholar, and also a reputable literary critic; in her heart she is a secret playwright. She wants to make things up: characters, settings, dialogues, plots.... She will not permit herself a descent, however alluring, into the region of the trivial. She is a writer of essays" (ix). Six years later, in 1989, Cohen made that "descent" with her first drama, *The Ladies Locker Room.*

Before creating this autobiographical play, Cohen played the midwife in the off-Broadway play *Schlemiel the First.* Since then Cohen has cowritten plays of increasing range and humor. *Sophie, Totie and Belle,* a musical about "unkosher" Jewish comediennes, was first produced in 1992 before moving to Off-Broadway in 2000. In 1994 Cohen staged *Molly Picon's Return Engagement,* a dynamic musical about the most vibrant Yiddish singer of her time. *Henrietta Szold: Woman of Valor,* sponsored by the New York State Writers Institute, is a rousing tribute to the courageous founder of Israel's Hadassah Hospital. It was first staged in 2000. *Danny Kaye: Supreme Court Jester,* a musical about America's mid-20th-century ambassador of good wit, had its world premier in 2001.

Cohen's current book project is *Shared Stages: The Drama of Blacks and Jews,* which contains her coauthored play, *Soul Sisters,* a multicultural musical celebrating the relationship between African-American and Jewish women during the civil rights era. This book seeks to combine both of Cohen's loves: scholarly and dramatic writing. Cohen's most recent dramatic premiere is *American Klezmer,* a musical comedy about a Jewish woman who, having emigrated from Russia in 1910, wants to sing on the stage, but is not allowed to by her Orthodox parents, who are concerned about *kol isha,* the traditional prohibition of women singing before men in a public setting. The themes that have animated Cohen's scholarship and dramatic writing are glimpsed here once again: the conflict of art and religion, modernity and tradition. Through all these conflicts can be heard the loud voice of Cohen's female characters breaking boundaries.

Cohen is also currently finishing a new play, a comedy titled *The Caregivers,* about the idiosyncratic cadre of women nurses who have been taking care of her during her recent illnesses—all of which are related to her degenerative condition. Speaking about her work that outspokenly deals with disability, Cohen says:

My attitude towards disability has changed considerably. Early in my career as a playwright in *The Ladies Locker Room* I felt guilty about speaking about my private life and my disability. Now I find that I am in demand, I feel in a perverse way that my disability has turned me into the chosen kid on the block; I am no longer someone to be mocked and pitied. I've also become more militant about disability: instead of being the passive victim of my disability, now I am the triumphant victor who can talk about disability and champion the cause of those disabled people who have yet to find their large voice. (Interview)

Concerning her many female characters who possess the "loud voice" Cohen admires, she writes:

As an untamed playwright, I have employed gleeful abandon to make these unorthodox ladies into *vilde chayes* (wild beasts), leaping over the boundaries of Jewish respectability. Yet I have not alienated audiences with their breaches of decency. Rather than offending sensibilities, their big mouths have created an enduring tumult, and their innovative *schmutz* (filth) has left an indelible mark. Meanwhile, as playwright, I am in the process of creating other obstreperous sisters to disturb the peace. ("From Critic to Playwright" 203)

In her transformation from critic to playwright, Cohen overcomes years of "dramatic silence." As she continues to write plays of increasing depth, each suffused with her biographical challenges, Cohen inscribes that "indelible mark" on readers and theatergoers alike.

Bibliography
Cappell, Ezra. Interview with Sarah Blacher Cohen, July 26, 2006. Albany, N.Y.
Cohen, Sarah Blacher. "From Critic to Playwright: Fleshing Out Jewish Women in Contemporary Drama." In *Talking Back: Images of Jewish Women in American Popular Culture,* edited by

Joyce Antler. Hanover, N.H.: Brandeis University Press, 1998.

—Ezra Cappell

Collected Early Poems 1950–1970
Adrienne Rich (1993)

The recognition of the power of poetry to effect change and chronicle the process of revolution is a key component of the contribution to American literature made by poet ADRIENNE RICH. Published in 1993, her *Collected Early Poems 1950–1970* reflects the fundamental changes at the heart of Rich's literary development and her movement from the safety of traditional formalism to the uncharted territory of feminist poetics. Rich's early work arose from the encouragement of her father, a doctor and professor at Johns Hopkins University. Rich, born in 1929 in Baltimore, Maryland, graduated from Radcliffe, winning the prestigious Yale Younger Poets Prize for her first book, *A Change of World*. Poems such as "Aunt Jennifer's Tigers," "Boundary," and "At a Bach Concert," reprinted in both the *Collected Early Poems* and *The Fact of a Doorframe* (1984), earned the praise of W. H. Auden, the judge for the award, and other members of what Rich later viewed as the literary canon of white male power and patriarchy. From a contemporary perspective, Auden's preface to the book typifies the dismissal of the female voice against which Rich and others of her generation fought. At the time, however, the preface only served to praise Rich's technical expertise, finely tuned structure, and acceptably feminine emotional restraint. In "Aunt Jennifer's Tigers," Rich tells us that "The massive weight of Uncle's wedding band/ Sits heavily upon Aunt Jennifer's hand" (lines 7–8). The haunting aloneness reflected in "An Unsaid Word" reminds the modern reader, aware of Rich's later feminism, of what the poet will later call into question as compulsory heterosexuality. Though "Storm Warnings" describes in lyrical language the gathering of a literal storm, a reader approaching Rich's poetry in the 1993 collection would undoubtedly find metaphorical meaning in the lines: "Between foreseeing and averting change/ Lies all the mastery of the elements" (lines 15–16).

The poems contained in the *Collected Early Poems* illustrate Rich's struggle to synthesize her life as an artist with traditional female roles and her formulating identity as a political activist and radically feminist lesbian. Published in 1993, 20 years after the appearance of her groundbreaking and critically acclaimed *Diving into the Wreck,* the *Collected Early Poems* allows the reader to view the earlier works through the historical lens of cultural and political change. In "Living in Sin," reprinted from the 1955 *The Diamond Cutters,* the message becomes even more powerful and significant to the modern reader with contextual awareness of Rich's later criticism of the traditional institution of heterosexual marriage.

In 1956 Rich began dating each of her poems, to place them in historical context with changes in the cultural climate and her own personal revolution of freedom and identity. Rich believed in the power of language that is connected to the existence and perpetuation of institutions of male privilege, including the literary world. In the title essay of her 1986 *Blood, Bread and Poetry,* Rich says, "There is the falsely mystical view of art that assumes a kind of supernatural inspiration, a possession by universal forces unrelated to questions of power and privilege." Poems in the *Collected Early Poems,* reprinted from earlier volumes, reveal the intimate relationship between Rich's role as a woman and her emergence as one of the keystone figures of 20th-century feminist literature. SNAPSHOTS OF A DAUGHTER-IN-LAW appeared in 1963, and was poorly received critically; Rich was beginning to move away from her earlier formalism and emotional restraint as she struggled with her own emerging identity. In "A Marriage in the Sixties," also included in the *Collected Early Poems,* we sense the poet's growing dissatisfaction with the roles of women in the shadow of patriarchy. In 1962 Rich wrote in "To Judith, Taking Leave" about the meeting of two women: "as two eyes in one brow/ receiving at one moment/ the rainbow of the world" (lines 86–88). Though the poet would not come out as a lesbian until more than a decade later, a 1993 reader of the 1962 poem in the *Collected Early Poems* might hear the voice of the feminist theorist and activist who would later write the seminal essay "Compulsory Heterosexuality and Lesbian Existence" (1980). Poems included in the *Collected Early Works* from Rich's fourth volume, *Necessities of Life* (1966), including the title poem, reflect her reaction to the rejection of *Snapshots*. Works such as "In the Woods," "The Corpse Plant," and "Halfway" resonate with decay and death. As always, Rich's work as a poet merges with the changing landscape of contemporary culture and her own personal struggles.

Rich moved to New York City in 1966, where she became involved in a program working with low-income minority college students, fueling her passion for decoding and dismantling the institutional oppression associated with language. She also became involved in peace activism and the fledgling women's movement. Poems appearing in *Collected Early Poems* from her 1969 *Leaflets* reflect this focus on change and revolution. Several of these poems, including "Jerusalem" and "There Are Such Springlike Nights," reflect the poet's respect for her Jewish heritage and her understanding of common experiences of oppression.

The poetry of Adrienne Rich, even in her earlier, more stylistically traditional work, speaks to the pain and uncertainty that led to her later transformation into a powerful feminist writer and theorist. The fact that these early poems were republished in 1993 as part of a collection of works highlights the significance of Rich's contribution to American literature.

Bibliography

Baym, Nina, ed. *Norton Anthology of American Literature,* 5th ed. New York: W.W. Norton, 1998.

Rothschild, Matthew. "Interview with Adrienne Rich." *The Progressive.* Available online. URL: http://www.progressive.org/rothrich9401.htm. Accessed Jan. 6, 2007.

—**Ginna Wilkerson**

The Counterlife Philip Roth (1986)

The Counterlife is the 30th novel by Jewish-American writer PHILIP ROTH. The novel was awarded the 1987 National Book Critics Circle Award and the Present Tense/Joel H. Cavior Literary Award. The book is widely regarded as one of Roth's most ambitious, elegant, and deeply Jewish works, with shifts both in technique and focus from his earlier fiction. Despite these departures, *The Counterlife* revisits many of Roth's trademark themes, including the nature of both Jewish and human identity, sexual expression and male/female relationships, truth and fiction, family support and suppression. It also returns to the writer's alter ego Nathan Zuckerman, introduced at later stages of his life in *The Ghost Writer* (1979), *The Anatomy Lesson* (1983), and *Zuckerman Unbound* (1981), as well as in the novella *The Prague Orgy* (1985). Later in Roth's career, he was to return again to Zuckerman, in his so-called American trilogy (including *AMERICAN PASTORAL*) and *Exit Ghost.*

Unlike Roth's earlier fiction, as well as that of most Jewish-American literature up to that point, a significant portion of the novel is set in Israel, whether at Jerusalem's Western Wall, a Tel Aviv cafe, or an extremist enclave in the West Bank. What is more, some of the book's most compelling characters are Israeli, such as the Kahane-like firebrand Mordechai Lippman and the cynical intellectual Shuki Elchanan. These settings and characters contribute to the novel's central debate regarding the Jewish Question—the centuries-long discussion of relations between Jews and non-Jews—as well as a play on the question "What is a Jew?" that underpins the Israeli Law of Return granting Jews automatic citizenship. *The Counterlife* is, moreover, an exploration of the relationship between Jews of the Diaspora (particularly those of the United States) and Israeli Jews.

The book's five sections recall the Torah. Indeed, the novel echoes several Biblical themes, including a journey of 40 years (the main characters are in their early-to-mid-40s) characterized by an evolution of Jewish identity, as well as an examination of the behaviors that a Jewish life comprises.

Whereas the Bible approaches these matters with certainty, *The Counterlife* assiduously sticks to questions. The plot centers around two Jewish brothers, Nathan Zuckerman, the family black sheep, a middle-aged novelist with a career nearly identical to that of Roth himself—including, significantly, the authorship of an infamous book that embarrassed both his family and a good deal of his people—and his younger brother Henry, a successful New Jersey dentist. The sections, which all take place in 1978, restate the book's central debate in different terms. In the first, titled "Basel," philandering Henry dies in New Jersey after undergoing risky cardiac surgery as an alternative to impotence-inducing medication. In the second section, the longest of the book, "Judea," rather than dying after surgery, Henry abruptly moves to a right-wing settlement in Israel. In section three, "Aloft," the exact center of the book, Nathan is on a flight to the United States from Israel, where he had unsuccessfully tried to convince his brother to return home, when the plane is nearly hijacked by a deranged fan he met in Jerusalem. "Gloucestershire," section four, takes place at and following the funeral of Nathan/Henry, who is now dead from bypass surgery. *The Counterlife* ends with "Christendom," in which Nathan's marriage to his former English lover Maria—the name of Henry's former Swiss lover in the first section—is threatened after Nathan encounters anti-Semitic attitudes and behavior in Britain.

The book's title refers to the multiplicity of alternate lives, or selves, that Roth demonstrates as options—especially, but not solely, with respect to Jews. This theme is reflected in the book's structure, with stories within stories within stories and plotlines that, like a Mobius strip, circle in and around each other in a nonlinear, contradictory fashion. This presentation of narratives from a subjunctive, "what if" perspective has led to numerous comparisons to the novels of postmodernists such as John Barth and Robert Coover. In this way, the title *counterlife* also reflects the postmodern term *Countertext*, as the book takes on the deconstructive project of examining the interplay of alterative texts, while refusing to privilege any.

Tellingly, the 20th-century debate between assimilation and pluralism that evolved from intellectual responses to the Jewish question is a hallmark of postmodernism. The novel's style therefore mirrors the ongoing struggle for self-definition on the part of the Jews and of Israel. What is more, Roth undertakes a discussion of self-as-performance, a further volley in his ongoing argument against the existence of authentic identity, be it personal or tribal.

With its mixture of texts and fictional realities, *The Counterlife* serves as a transition for Roth into a deeper examination of his familiar territory of autobiography and fiction, self and other, and narrative authority. Though he employed alter egos in this and previous books, in his next four his doppelgänger is, in fact, named Philip Roth, blurring the lines between truth and fiction more than ever. Of these works, only one, *Deception* (1990), was billed as fiction.

This now-you-see-me-now-you-don't approach underscores another Roth trademark. The sense of play that characterizes much of his fiction is still very much in evidence in *The Counterlife*, be it in the form of satire, black humor, comic irony, or shtick. Roth further develops humor by derailing conventional expectations of plot and character, as with the metafictional technique of having a character threaten to leave the book. Little wonder that he has Zuckerman refer to humankind as *Homo ludens*, the playful animal.

The novel concludes on an eminently hopeful note, transforming an emphasis on the phallus as object of sexual gratification and self-obsession that opened the book into a recognition of circumcision as the connecting thread among Jews throughout history and geography. Thus while *The Counterlife* does not offer definitive answers to the Jewish question or to Jewish questions, it more than underscores the seriousness of its author's concern.

Bibliography
Cooper, Alan. *Philip Roth and the Jews.* Albany: SUNY Press, 1991.

Royal, Derek Parker. "Postmodern Jewish Identity in Philip Roth's *The Counterlife.*" *Modern Fiction Studies* 48, no. 2 (Summer 2002): 422–443.

Safer, Elaine B. *Mocking the Age: The Later Novels of Philip Roth.* Albany: SUNY Press, 1996.

—Caren S. Neile

The Crucible Arthur Miller (1953)

The Crucible and *DEATH OF A SALESMAN* are ARTHUR MILLER's most often produced plays. Miller, suggesting the political and social significance of *The Crucible,* remarked that "if I hadn't written *The Crucible,* that period would be unregistered in our literature on any popular level" (Navasky 199–206). Moreover, it continues to be the work he "feels proudest of because I made something lasting out of a violent but brief turmoil." That turmoil was the rise of McCarthyism and the House Un-American Activities (HUAC) hearings of the 1950s.

Miller's interpretation of two odious periods, the 1692 Salem Witchcraft Trials and their parallel in the anticommunist hysteria of the 1950s, originally ran for only 197 performances on Broadway, but has become a classic because of its incisive critique of these linked political events.

John Proctor, who challenges the autocratic authority to coerce others through terror, "sees no light of God" in Reverend Parris's actions, his fire and brimstone threats, and his addiction to materialism. Abigail, reflecting on what she sees as her seduction by John Proctor, exclaims that her eyes had been opened by the experience, that "I never knew the lying lesions I was taught by all these Christian women with their covenanted men!" Reacting to the threats of the theocracy, she asks "And now you bid me to tear the light out of my eyes?" The fire of her passion was the crucible in which she evolved from ignorance to experience.

Through it all, wise old Rebecca Nurse, seeing the girls claiming frenziedly that they had seen "so-and-so" with the Devil, tries calmly to explain that she had seen children's games before, that the girls were going through their "silly seasons, and when it comes on them they will run the Devil bow-legged keeping up with their mischief." However, the issue goes much farther, and John Proctor and Giles Corey, facing death, refuse to name names, as Miller and Lillian Hellman and others refused to name names when called before the House Un-American Activities Committee.

The point of the play, the real theme, as Miller has written, is "the handing over of the conscience to another, be it women, the state, or a town, and the realization that with conscience goes the person, the soul immortal, and the name" (*Collected Plays,* 47). John's wife, Elizabeth, speaking of John's refusal to hand over his conscience, says "He have his goodness now."

In the preface to the first published edition, Miller described his play as revealing "the essential nature of one of the strangest and most awful chapters in human history," a remark intended to direct the reader to the 1692 witch hunts. But in a remark 50 years later (Gottfried 221), Miller's slip of the tongue, in print, revealed his original impulse. Referring to John Proctor, he described him as "a leader of sorts, a moral example, perhaps for others, so he's letting down a lot of people if he should accede to the committee." Needless to say there is no committee in *The Crucible.* He meant to say "the inquisition."

Miller's individual significance resides in his moral force and his confirmed sense of justice. In *The Crucible,* the guilt of John Proctor and the working out of that guilt are the center of the play. A confirmed antifascist from his University of Michigan days, seeking to identify with humankind, rather than one small fraction of it, Arthur Miller wrote *The Crucible* because he couldn't abide the interference of others in his work, because he felt violated by HUAC, and because as a Jew he wrote the anxiety ordinary Jewish people were feeling at a very strange and threatening period in American history.

Bibliography
Bigsby, Christopher. *The Cambridge Companion to Arthur Miller.* Cambridge, New York: Cambridge University Press, 1997.

Brater, Enoch, ed. *Arthur Miller's America: Theatre and Culture in a Time of Change.* Ann Arbor: University of Michigan Press, 2005.

Gottfried, Martin. *Arthur Miller, His Life and Work.* Cambridge, Mass.: DaCapo Press, 2003.

Miller, Arthur. *Collected Plays.* New York: Viking Press, 1957, 1981.

Navasky, Victor. *Naming Names.* New York: Viking Press, 1980.

—**Daniel Walden**

The Day of the Locust
Nathanael West (1939)

Amid the turmoil of the Great Depression and well into its aftermath, California—and Hollywood in particular—became an irresistible symbol to writers and artists of the opulence, falsity, and aggression of American society. A sort of "unplace," a space where people lived but did not necessarily identify as natives, Hollywood seemed to represent the growing restlessness and alienation brought on by economic crisis, sustained by enduring poverty, and compounded by increasing greed, materialism, and social ambition. NATHANAEL WEST—born Nathaniel Wallenstein Weinstein—was one of a host of authors to explore the contradictions that riddled Hollywood's social hierarchy, but perhaps the only one to exploit the masquerade to such sardonic, incisive effect. Born in New York to upper-middle-class Jewish immigrants, West seemed always able to view American society at a remove, to apply his idiosyncratic artistic talent and acerbic wit in depictions of lives betrayed by entertainment and the hollow promise of materialism.

Never an assiduous student, West relied on his craftiness rather than intellect to gain admittance to a series of schools, finally securing a job as a hotel manager. This job—obtained chiefly through the social connections of his then-impoverished family—allowed West to remain afloat financially even as the world around him crumpled under economic and emotional strain. Although West associated with various coteries of surrealists and erudite authors, he drew his artistic inspiration from the bedraggled masses brought low by the ravages of the Depression. Among beggars, vagrants, prostitutes, and frauds, West found characters that seemed to him to offset the more popular narratives of Hollywood glamour or rags-to-riches Americanism with the realism of the bleak—and often grotesque—underbelly of commodity culture.

Critics often read West's gifts as an illustrator and caricaturist, as well as his disillusioning stint as a screenwriter in Hollywood (where he lived just off Hollywood Boulevard), into Tod Hackett, the protagonist of West's fourth and final novel, *The Day of the Locust.* And undoubtedly, West's proximity to the masses that made up the structure of a thinly veneered pyramid on which perched the elite of Hollywood's golden era gave him a sense of the underrepresented—and yet infinitely more representative—characters who play out the novel's bizarre conflation of fun (which Theodor Adorno defines as a manufactured attempt at genuine pleasure), entertainment, and violence.

To construct this interplay, West relies on a cast of grotesques. Tod, a Yale-educated artist, comes to Hollywood as a costume and set designer for National Films, where he is befriended by Honest Abe Kusich, a bookkeeping dwarf. Subsequently, he meets Faye Greener, a crass starlet who makes up in solipsism and wantonness what she lacks in talent; he begins to lust after Faye and, in an effort to get close to her, strikes up a relationship with her father, Harry Greener, a former vaudevillian clown who keeps up his character despite his inability to secure a career as a performer in Hollywood. Harry falls ill at the home of Homer Simpson, a hotel bookkeeper from Iowa who tries to maintain in California a banal quotidian routine in lieu of meaningful relationships. When Harry dies, Faye moves in with Homer, yet maintains a relationship with her handsome, violent, and vacuous boyfriend, Earle. Finally, Homer—broken and betrayed by his experience in California—determines to return to Iowa.

In the novel's final scene, Tod wanders downtown to find Homer sitting amid a crowd waiting for a movie premier to begin; the scene erupts in chaos and violence when Homer finally responds to the taunts of a boy and, as he stomps on the boy's back, the crowd falls on Homer. Tod, rescued from the crowd by a police officer, sits in the back of the police car and screams along with the siren: In the novel's final moment of rupture, Tod, never able to distinguish Hollywood's mechanical reproductions from genuine experience, actually becomes the experience himself. After surrounding himself with—and creating—the "cardboard food in front of a cellophane waterfall" and the "small pond with large celluloid swans floating on it" (126), Tod reaches the point at which the simulated world of the movie sets comes to represent and then supersede the real world and authentic experience for himself and the actors he associates with. And, West seems to suggest, this replacement of the genuine with the artificial, this unfulfilling relationship to facade and commodities, ultimately gives way to disillusionment, disgust, and spastic violence.

In one sense, Homer functions as the novel's most pathetic character, a spineless, solicitous figure who tolerates Faye's infidelity and domination of him with a sort of apathetic passivity, one of many indications of a consciousness so evacuated that he fails to register even pain and betrayal. He is, however, only one of the novel's myriad characters to accept entertainment, sexuality, and performance as a substitute for personal fulfillment or authentic emotion and interaction. In light of these characters, it becomes significant that West's original title for the novel was *The Cheated*, since the novel probes the great betrayal of American modernity: Characters invest in kitsch, pretense, and hope of professional and social advancement, only to be ultimately cheated by false promises of easy success, instant gratification, and manufactured scenery and experience masquerading as the real.

Bibliography

Bordewyk, Gordon. "Nathanael West and *Seize the Day*." In *Critical Essays on Nathanael West*. New York: Hall, 1994.

Greenberg, Jonathan. "Nathanael West and the Mystery of Feeling." *Modern Fiction Studies* 52, no. 3 (Fall 2006): 588–612.

—Mary Kathleen Eyring

Death of a Salesman Arthur Miller (1949)

Death of a Salesman is one of the most famous plays written and produced in America at the end of the modern period. It is the family tragedy of an aging, failed Brooklyn salesman who returns home at the end of the week too worn out to go again on his New England road trip. He quarrels with his wife, rails against his sons, regrets his lost youth, and complains that the house, which is almost paid off, has lost all of its yard and flower gardens to the surrounding tall, ugly apartment buildings. The play steadily reveals Willy's delusional mind as he relives scenes from the past, enacts mental retreats from the present, and, after totally withdrawing from reality, drives off in his car to kill himself.

It is a play in which all of the characters are lost to the corruption in modern business, urbanization, father-son conflicts, and the general failure of the American dream. The play received immediate recognition because of its fine stagecraft, serious social issues, and modern definitions of tragedy. Influenced by the earlier experimental works of the Norwegian playwright Henrik Ibsen and the Swedish playwright August Strindberg, it is distinguished by its finely crafted plot, clever foreshadowing, effective irony, and dense symbolism. While it observes the traditional unities of action, place, and time, its experimental flashbacks allow for much fluidity. Though it is set in Willy Loman's house and takes place within a brief period of two to three days, flashbacks shift the audience freely from place to place and time period to time period. Asides effectively reveal the inner psychological tensions that drive Willy Loman to self-destruction. The original set was designed for freedom of movement, and the atmosphere of the play was established with innovative lighting and background music that also clarify the time and place transitions. A haunting flute melody establishes the changes of mood. The action consists of the inner workings of Willy Loman's mind, as well as those of wife, Linda, and sons, Biff and Happy.

Critics of the day were very impressed with AR-THUR MILLER's use of such expressionist methods and with his technical skills, stage innovations, and concentration on psychological aspects of character. What made this play part of the late modern moment was its substitution of an antihero for the usual exceptional hero of classical tragedy. Instead of the audience being stirred by human greatness and nobility, Miller engages them in identification with the plight of an ordinary man who just wants to be liked and prosperous, who nevertheless faces enormous odds in his effort to reach his simple vision. Like most of his type, he is neither very bright nor given to much introspection. Willy Loman is defeated by a combination of his own flaws and the social environment that surrounds him, and his tragic status derives from his undeviating commitment to this vision, however shallow and flawed it might be.

Miller was no doubt influenced by his own upbringing in a struggling Jewish immigrant family in Brooklyn during the Great Depression and by the years he spent working in warehouses and dockyards while the dream of a college education continued to elude him. Willy has all of Miller's social awareness, as well as the sad sight of the lovely rural gardens of his youth being swallowed up by towering apartment houses.

Death of a Salesman reveals many of Miller's recurring social concerns: workplace overemphasis of surface charm, the overvaluing of muscular sports at the expense of strenuous trades like salesmanship, the spiritual enervation of the workplace, the plight of aging employees, the moral consequences of the creeping dishonesty inherent in "getting ahead," ruthless competition, smugness, and narrowmindedness. He was concerned that Americans were losing sight of their responsibilities to the larger social group.

Some critics thought he was too hard on business, that his language was too flat, that he was negative about America, and that his common-man heroes were meanly bourgeois. Others criticized his dramatic techniques as derivative. It is true that Henrik Ibsen, August Strindberg, Eugene O'Neill, Clifford Odets, Robert Sherwood, and Maxwell Anderson had secured many of these modern dramatic formulas before him. But Miller's efforts were immediately hailed as very significant. *Death of a Salesman* won the Pulitzer Prize for the 1948–49 theatrical season, as well as the New York Drama Critics Circle Award, the Antoinette Perry Award, the Theatre Club Award, and the Front Page Award. The production chronology reveals the thousands of times this play has been staged since its original appearance in 1948. The discography, videography, and filmography are also remarkably extensive. The play itself established Miller as a major American playwright, and the character of Willy Loman remains firmly entrenched in American culture and American literary history.

Bibliography

Burgard, Peter J. "Two Parts Ibsen, One Part American Dream: On Derivation and Originality in Arthur Miller's *Death of a Salesman.*" *Orbis Litterarum: International Review of Literary Studies* 43, no. 4 (1988): 336–353.

Miller, Arthur. *Death of a Salesman: Revised Edition* (Viking Critical Library). New York: Penguin, 1996.

Vogel, Dan. "From Milkman to Salesman: Glimpses of the Galut." *Studies in American Jewish Literature* 10, no. 2 (Fall 1991): 172–178.

—Gloria L. Cronin

Doctorow, E. L. (1931–   )

Edgar Laurence Doctorow is one of America's most respected contemporary novelists. He was born January 6, 1931, in New York City, the son of David Richard Doctorow and Rose Levine Doctorow (later Rose Doctorow Buck). Both parents were children of Russian-Jewish immigrants. Doctorow decided early that writing would be his vocation, but he was uncertain as to what form this interest would take. From the Bronx High School of Science he moved on to Ohio's Kenyon College to study with poet John Crowe Ransom. During his four years at Kenyon, however, he did little writing, as his focus had shifted from literature to philosophy and acting.

Doctorow took a B.A. degree in 1952, and for the next year he did graduate work at New York's Columbia University in English drama and in playwriting, acting, and directing. He married Helen Esther Setzer on August 20, 1954, and they had three children: Jenny, Caroline, and Richard. After a series of jobs for which he had little taste, he became, in the late 1950s, a script reader for Columbia Pictures Industries in New York. Here he suffered through what he termed "one lousy Western after another." He finally reasoned that he could "lie in a much more interesting way" than the writers of the scripts he was evaluating. To prove his point, he wrote a short story that soon evolved into the opening chapter of *Welcome to Hard Times* (1960), his first novel.

Centered in a Dakota mining camp, this early work formulated the theme basic to all his subsequent writings: the difficulty of separating history from fiction, appearance from reality—that is, of grasping and conveying reality or truth in imaginative terms. Here and in subsequent novels, Doctorow set himself to rewriting earlier periods in American history by altering their significant events and exposing the true characters and personalities of their famous public figures. This first novel garnered a few favorable reviews but little public attention.

In 1966 Doctorow brought out his most unusual novel, *Big as Life*. This second effort garnered only three reviews and few readers. Its basic plot details are mind-boggling: A gigantic nude man and woman materialize one day in New York harbor. Each is 2,000 feet high. The general panic is intensified by inept city and national leaders and the military, and by a science establishment interested primarily in accumulating data. Doctorow's point is clear: So bogged down in bureaucratic inefficiency and self-interest is modern society that it is unable to resolve any problem that exceeds the ordinary. Later Doctorow would dismiss this book as his worst writing.

In 1969 Doctorow accepted a one-year appointment as writer in residence at the University of California at Irvine. He quickly discovered that he liked teaching, and in 1971 he left publishing to join the Sarah Lawrence College faculty. The following year he received a Guggenheim Fellowship. Also in 1971 he brought out his first major novel, *The BOOK OF DANIEL*. Clearly based on the notorious Rosenberg case, this novel has as its central figure Daniel Lewin, a 27-year-old graduate student at Columbia. He and his younger sister, Susan, are the children of Bronx Jews named Isaacson, who were executed at Sing Sing Prison in the early 1950s for conspiring to steal atomic secrets for the Soviet Union. Critics credited Doctorow with having written the best political novel of our time, claiming he had caught the quintessence of the 1960s political turmoil.

In 1975 Doctorow published his fourth novel, *RAGTIME*, which brought him not only more critical accolades but also his first popular success. Doctorow was here strongly influenced by his love of film, of the "cinematic" way of telling a story. Rejecting realism's "transition" narratives of the 19th-century novel, he opted instead for the discontinuity, the shifts in scene, tense, voice, and speakers that shape the structures of both television and movie scenarios. In *Ragtime* Doctorow centers on the Progressive period between 1900 and World War I. Those years saw the creation of the auto assembly line and the Model T Ford, moving pictures, and ragtime music—most notably in Scott Joplin's rags. They witnessed also the growth of professional baseball and the constant arrivals of "rag ships" laden with eastern European immigrants. Expanding on the varied uses of historical figures by fiction writers as different as William Thackeray in *Henry Esmond* and John Dos Passos in *USA,* Doctorow intermingles in *Ragtime* a cluster of that era's significant individuals with three fictional families. Thus he blends fact and fiction to create what some critics soon termed "faction."

In 1979 Doctorow tried his hand at a play, *Drinks Before Dinner: A Play.* The few reviewers who bothered to acknowledge it agreed the work was not a success. Doctorow provided grist for the negative reviews by explaining in his introduction his rejection of the drama of character and action in favor of a play of language and ideas. He also published *Loon Lake* (1980), a novel set in 1936, the heart of the Depression. It is essentially a dual narrative that follows two working-class youths striving for their own conceptions of the American dream whose paths cross on the estate of a powerful capitalist.

In 1982, after numerous appointments at other American universities, Doctorow settled into a steady teaching position at New York University as the Glucksman Professor of English and American Letters, a position he holds to this day. In 1984 he published his sixth book, *Lives of the Poets,* made up of six short stories and a novella. Highly experimental, its reviews were even more mixed than previous ones. (Two stories foreshadow the later novels *World's Fair* and *The Waterworks.*) For those who liked the book, *Lives of the Poets* offered bold, satiric views of failed marriages, middle-aged crises of confidence, and New York literary society.

The next year Doctorow published his most directly autobiographical work, *World's Fair* (1985), an offbeat mix of novel and memoir. It is a nostalgic view of life in New York during the Depression, as experienced by a boy who recounts his first nine years and ends his account with his 1939 visit to the World's Fair in Flushing Meadow, New York.

The boy's first name is Edgar—as is Doctorow's—and he, too, grows up in the Bronx. Edgar's recollections are interrupted from time to time by his mother, older brother, and aunt. While acutely aware of worldly events, young Edgar focuses on the family living room, radio and movie serials, the schoolyard and neighborhood park, and the nearby street corner where a pushcart vendor serves up deliciously hot sweet potatoes.

Four years after *World's Fair,* Doctorow published *BILLY BATHGATE* (1989), a vividly detailed chronicle of a 15-year-old boy's journey from childhood to adulthood, a trek marked by encounters with hustlers and killers. Young Billy has replaced his family name with that of the street on which he lives. He is a rough, tough high-school dropout with a talent for juggling and living by his wits in the Bronx. With this his eighth novel, Doctorow received an almost unqualified critical success. He continued probing American society's dark side in *The Waterworks* (1994). His ninth novel is narrated in retrospective old age by McIlvaine (no first name given), a quick-witted but lapsed Presbyterian and former city editor of the *New York Evening Telegraph.* The action year is 1871, when the corruptions of the Grant administration are known to all, and Boss Tweed runs the city's political machine. Graft, greed, and crime prevail.

Doctorow set himself his most difficult task in his next novel, *City of God* (2000). He here explores nothing less than the nature and problems of religious faith at the end of a technologically and scientifically advanced 20th century of blood and violence. Falling back on a structural device he used in *The Lives of the Poets,* Doctorow has the entire novel come from the notebooks of a writer—here called Everett. The writer's last name is never revealed, but the few personal details of his life parallel those of Doctorow himself. Seeking material for a new novel, Everett stumbles onto a newspaper story of a huge cross stolen from St. Timothy's Episcopal Church in New York's East Village that has reappeared on the roof of the Synagogue of Evolutionary Judaism. Everett meets and recounts the intellectual and emotional interplay of the church's Rev. Thomas Pemberton and the synagogue's Rabbi Joshua Gruen and his wife, the beautiful Rabbi Sarah. The novel's fragmented sections also include bits of social commentary and song, as well as a back-plot Holocaust tale.

His latest novel, *THE MARCH* (2005), is a fast-moving cinematic account of Union general William Tecumseh Sherman's bloody 60-mile push through Georgia and the Carolinas during the Civil War. As in *Ragtime,* Doctorow's historical and fictional characters intermingle in varied, unexpected ways. Like Faulkner, whose presence is felt throughout the narrative, Doctorow presents several figures whose origins go back to his earlier works. Obvious examples are his freed slave Coalhouse Walker, who proves to be the father of the same-named musician-turned-terrorist in *Ragtime,* and his Doctor Wrede Sartorious, who plays a major role in *The Waterworks,* and clearly echoes Faulkner's Sartoris family name.

As of this writing, Doctorow has published 10 novels, one drama, two volumes of short stories (*Lives of the Poets* and *Sweet Land Stories,* 2004), screenplays for two of his own novels, the text for a book of American photographs, and a collection of essays (*Reporting the Universe,* 2003). His work has been translated into more than 20 languages, and four of his novels (*Welcome to Hard Times, The Book of Daniel, Ragtime,* and *Billy Bathgate*) have been made into films, and the musical version of *Ragtime* has been an acclaimed success in America and abroad. These and the other honors and awards he has won for his work have established E. L. Doctorow as a formidable presence in contemporary American literature and the arts.

Bibliography

Bloom, Harold, ed. *E. L. Doctorow.* Philadelphia: Chelsea House, 2002.

Harter, Carol, and James R. Thompson. *E. L. Doctorow.* Boston: Twayne, 1990.

Morris, Christopher, ed. *Conversations with E. L. Doctorow.* Jackson: University Press of Mississippi, 1999.

Siegel, Ben, ed. *Critical Essays on E. L. Doctorow.* New York: G.K. Hall, 2000.

—**Ben Siegel**

Elijah Visible: Stories
Thane Rosenbaum (1996)

The Holocaust continues to haunt those born in its aftermath. Ghosts inhabit the literary universe of THANE ROSENBAUM, floating in and out of his consciousness and his narratives. The nine stories of *Elijah Visible* (winner of the Edward Lewis Wallant Award) convey the traumatic memories and deep pain that Thane Rosenbaum, like other descendants of survivors, has inherited.

Adam Posner, the protagonist throughout the tales, assumes a multifaceted identity as lawyer, college professor, and artist. He also appears in different stages and ages of his life, beginning as a lawyer stuck in an elevator that triggers off the terror of being crammed into a cattle car ("Cattle Car Complex"), and concluding with Adam as a five-year-old in "The Little Blue Snowman of Washington Heights." In between he is portrayed as a nine-year-old, a 13-year-old, a 16-year-old, though not in chronological order. Some stories represent Adam as both child and adult ("Bingo by the Bungalow" and "Lost, in a Sense").

What remains consistent is Adam's identity as the son of Holocaust survivors. Surrounded by the silence and secrecy of parents who seek to protect him from the burden of memory, he is nevertheless haunted by their concentration camp nightmares and their screams at night. He also has not recovered from their early deaths. The deteriorating health of his parents is often evoked: his mother dying from cancer in a hospital room ("The Pants in the Family"), or saying his own kind of kaddish for his mother ("Romancing the Yohrzeit Light"). Disabled by a heart condition, his father succumbs a few months after his wife. Adam, like Rosenbaum, is 20 years old, a college sophomore, when he loses both parents as recounted in "The Rabbi Double Faults."

The principal theme throughout is the legacy his parents have transmitted, the ghosts and "psychic demons" that make their presence felt. Two stories, in particular, demonstrate Adam's attempt to face these phantoms who are tormenting him. In "An Act of Defiance" Adam teaches a college course on the Holocaust, immersing himself in books, as well as filling the gaps in his memory by forging his own "long series of mangled family portraits, constructed by me, for me. . . . I had created my own ghosts from memories that were not mine." He salvages his parents' past by revising and reinventing their stories.

Adam's image of the Holocaust survivor, based on fantasies, is transformed into a myth deconstructed when the confrontation between the real and the imaginary occurs. This lies at the core of the narrative. Adam finally encounters a living ghost, his father's sprightly, pleasure-seeking 80-year-old brother, Uncle Haskell, a survivor from Belgium whose mission is to rid Adam of the specters imprisoning him. By his very example, Haskell seems to succeed in demystifying his nephew's image of the survivor. Adam also learns about his father as resistance fighter and about family members who perished—the history his parents had refused him. The pain will not disappear but the ghosts have become more real, more human.

In the title story, another living ghost intrudes on the present. Cousin Artur from Belgium, an Auschwitz survivor, writes to Adam's cousins that he is coming to unearth family memories. Adam alone craves knowledge; the cousins avoid, deny, and reject their past. Rosenbaum exposes the collapse of communication between generations, and shows how members of the same generation have conflicting responses to the Holocaust. By writing about his ghosts—by making the invisible visible—Rosenbaum confronts them, dialogues with them, and ultimately recalls the absent ones back to life.

Bibliography

Aarons, Victoria. "The Legacy of the Disinherited: Thane Rosenbaum's Holocaust Fiction." In *What Happened to Abraham? Reinventing the Covenant in American Jewish Fiction.* Newark: University of Delaware Press, 2005.

Berger, Alan L. "Mourning, Rage, and Redemption: Representing the Holocaust: The Work of Thane Rosenbaum." *Studies in Jewish American Literature* 19 (2000): 6–15.

—Ellen S. Fine

Elman, Richard (1934–1997)

Contrary to a popular mistake of identity, Richard Elman is not the same person as Richard Ellmann, who lived at the same time, studied in the same field, and became famous for his award-winning biographies of literary figures such as James Joyce. Richard Elman was a university professor and a radio man, in addition to numerous other occupations. His most treasured occupation, however, was novelist.

Richard Elman was born in Brooklyn, New York, in 1934. He graduated from Syracuse University in 1955 and received a master's degree from Stanford University in 1957. After a brief stint in the U.S. Army he worked as a freelance writer and radio journalist and, from 1960 to 1963, worked as the director of public affairs and drama and literature for WBAI-Pacifica. He began his academic career as a lecturer in literature at Bennington College, Vermont, from 1967 to 1968. At the conclusion of that appointment he took a position at New York's Columbia University, where he taught until 1975. He then began a touring career as visiting professor of creative writing that lasted until his death in 1997. The universities at which he taught during this time included one State University of New York (Stony Brook), Michigan, Arizona, Pennsylvania, Wichita State, Notre Dame, and Tennessee.

Elman began his career as a creative writer shortly after he completed his military service. His first novel, *A Coat for the Czar,* was published in 1959. Although he continued to work in radio for several years after the novel's publication, the experience convinced him that his true vocation was that of full-time author. His next work was the nonfiction *The Poorhouse State: The American Way of Life on Public Assistance,* published in 1966. In this text Elman documents his visits to disadvantaged members of the "Poorhouse State" living in New York City. He details the clash between the "Poorhouse State" and the "Welfare State," and begins to articulate the leftist politics that would shape his later fiction. These ideals would play out in three of his works, all centered around a Jewish family from Hungary: *The Twenty-Eighth Day of Ehul* (1967), *Lilo's Diary* (1968), and *The Reckoning* (1969). It is also around this time that he met President Lyndon B. Johnson and, shortly thereafter, joined in protests against American involvement in the Vietnam War.

Of the more than 20 books and three volumes of poetry that Elman published, two stand out in importance to the literary community. The first is *Tar Beach,* published in 1991. It details the coming-of-age of an eight-year-old boy growing up in Brooklyn after World War II. The second is *Cathedral-Tree-Train,* a long poem that functions as a memoir or oration of past artistic heroes including jazz musicians and abstract expressionists. Pat Monaghan of *Booklist* writes that the section detailing and contemplating the suicide of a young painter "questions the reasons for this waste of life and talent. Like an archeologist, he excavates his memories, examining them for clues to understanding. That he does not, at last, understand seems the truest thing in these poems."

Ironically, Elman's work that has received the most critical attention is not actually fiction or poetry. Rather, it is his memoir, *Namedropping: Mostly Literary Memoirs*. In it he details his interaction with those he considers his "teachers" and "dear mentors," most of whom are members of the contemporary American writing community. Of Elman's both humorous and painful recollections, the *New York Times Book Review* said, "Elman had what Keats called negative capability—the ability to enter into other people's moral natures while suspending moral judgment—in abundance." Since most of Elman's works are now out of print, this memoir may prove crucial for keeping his memory alive.

Bibliography

Elman, Richard. *Namedropping: Mostly Literary Memoirs*. Albany: SUNY Press, 1998.

———. *The Poorhouse State: The American Way of Life on Public Assistance*. New York: Pantheon Books, 1966.

Monaghan, Pat. *Review of Namedropping: Mostly Literary Memoirs, Booklist*. Available online. URL: http://literati.net/Elman/ElmanReviews.htm.

Siegel, Lee. "Review of *Namedropping*." *New York Times Book Review* (August 23, 1998), 11–13.

—**Brian Wall**

Englander, Nathan (1970–)

Nathan Englander's work echoes the major Jewish writers (living and deceased) in a way that assimilates their insights and articulates its own voice. He graduated from the Iowa Writers Workshop, published stories in prestigious magazines (the *New Yorker*, for example), and won the coveted Pushcart Prize. A splash accompanied the publication of his first major work.

His first book, *For the Relief of Unbearable Urges* (New York: Albert Knopf), appeared in April of 1999. Many years passed before the publication of his second. In the meantime, critics became skeptical, wondering whether he was yet another American writer whose early publications dazzle but who, for whatever reason, never publishes a significant work again. The reception of his second novel, *The Ministry of Special Cases* (2007), has begun to dispell such concerns.

Whether he ends up writing two books or 27, Englander's importance as a writer appears to be guaranteed. He speaks with a powerful, unique, and compelling voice that articulates Judaism from within the Orthodox community and thereby accomplishes something extraordinary: He transgresses the American Orthodox rejection of intercourse with outsiders.

The nine stories of his first collection constitute an anatomy of Jewish life during the Holocaust, in its immediate aftermath in suburban America, and in a Jerusalem contemporary with the book's composition. His themes range from the deportation of Jews from eastern European shtetls to Joseph Stalin's murder of Yiddish writers in 1952, to domestic and social violence in Jewish life in the affluent community of Bridgelawn, to writing amid the hail of terrorist bombings in Jerusalem cafes.

Thwarting the precariousness and self-destructiveness of such surroundings, Englander poses a new and astounding question: Did we die during the night? To the incessant postwar refrain "God died at Auschwitz," he offers a curious hopefulness. Perhaps it is not God who died at Auschwitz but us. Perhaps the Diasporic Jewishness in which we have been living for some 2,000 years (since the Second Temple), one that has progressively lost its connection to the founding horror of the catastrophic collapse of Jerusalem in 586 B.C.E. (from which the text-centered religion itself developed) has somehow altered, and after the Holocaust we can begin to regain our bearings within the real strength of a tradition that has survived from antiquity to the present day (amid so many failures), one example of which is its classical literature.

For Englander this gesture is not at all redemptive. When the news of the death camps first surfaced, Christians hugged their local Jewish victims, sobbing that these poor Jews had to learn the hard way what enlightened Christians already knew—that Jesus died for our sins—thus denying Judaism once again even in the act of embracing it. Later, secular Zionists derived hope from the Holocaust as enabling in part the founding of the state of Israel where the call of "Never Again" (from the ancient hilltop fortification of Masada) could again become the battle cry of the young settlers. In a series of books with titles like *Admitting the Holocaust* and *Perpetuating the Holocaust,* Lawrence Langer has shown convincingly the potential for an ironic and secret complicity of all such memorialization attempts with the very horror they so fervently combat.

Englander's book rejects the idea that the Holocaust is a good thing. On the other hand, he does see in it the end of theodicy, the explosive terminus of a conception of God and Judaism positing a core of human decency and reason behind all disaster upon which we may always depend, a conception vigorously revived in the past two hundred years by Enlightenment thinkers. Disaster has never not been part of the scriptures, he tells us; scripture is never not "the writing of the disaster" (Blanchot's phrase). If we forgot that, and convinced ourselves we could live together in harmony and mutual respect, the Holocaust pulled the rug out from any rational one-to-one correspondence of the divine world with the human in which one fantasized a moral equivalency of truth, justice, and democracy on the world political stage. Detailing midrashically the aberrations of modern Jewish orthodoxy, Englander's book reinstates the necessity of Judaism and Jewish writing as an active thinking out of the political and ethical in modern secular and religious contexts.

Born in New York within an Orthodox Jewish community in 1970, and living between New York and Jerusalem (when he arrived in Israel for a recent visit, and the Tel Aviv passport clerk inquired about his long absence, he is reputed to have replied "I became Israeli. So I left for New York"), Englander notes that the religious community in which he grew up limited engagement of such ideas. But his work explores these ideas for us, not unlike that of thinkers such as Martin Buber, Emil Fackenheim, and Emmanuel Levinas. This seems an astounding and enduring achievement, one that should secure for him first rank status in Jewish American fictional letters.

Bibliography
Behlman, Lee. "The Escapist: Fantasy, Folklore, and the Pleasures of the Comic Book in Recent Jewish American Holocaust Fiction." *Shofar* 22, no. 3 (Spring 2004): 56–71.

Meyer, Adam. "Putting the 'Jewish' Back in 'Jewish American Fiction': A Look at Jewish American Fiction from 1977 to 2002 and an Allegorical Reading of Nathan Englander's 'The Gilgul of Park Avenue.'" *Shofar* 22, no. 3 (Spring 2004): 104–120.

—Sandor Goodhart

Epstein, Helen (1947–)

Helen Epstein, born in Prague in what was then Czechoslovakia, is a journalist and writer of literary nonfiction whose main concern is with family history, trauma transmission, and memoir. She was educated at Hunter College High School in New York City and received an undergraduate degree from the Hebrew University, where she studied musicology, in 1970. One year later she obtained a master's degree in journalism from Columbia University. Her journalism career began in 1968 when, still an undergraduate, she was caught up in the Soviet invasion of her homeland. Epstein is the oldest of three children and the only daughter of Franzi (née Rabinek) and Kurt Epstein. Her parents were both Holocaust survivors. Kurt Epstein played on Czechoslovakia's Olympic water polo team, and his multilingual wife was a dressmaker. Although the Holocaust was rarely discussed when

Helen was growing up, it left an indelible imprint on her life and work.

Like her mother, Epstein speaks several languages. She taught for 12 years at New York University, becoming the first tenured woman in its journalism school. Her journalistic pieces have appeared in a variety of venues including the Sunday *New York Times Magazine, McCalls, Ms.,* and *Midstream.* She is the author of six books: *Children of the Holocaust: Conversations with Sons and Daughters of Survivors* was translated into French, German, Italian, Czech, Swedish, and Japanese; *Joe Papp: An American Life* profiles the life of the theater impresario; *Music Talks* paints portraits of various musicians; *The Companies She Keeps* is a portrayal of Tina Packer, Shakespeare & Company's founder; *Under a Cruel Star* is the memoir of survivor Heda Kovaly, which Epstein translated from Czech; and *Where She Came From: A Daughter's Search for her Mother's History* is simultaneously a family memoir and a social history of Jews in Czech lands.

Children of the Holocaust is a pioneering work that reveals the psychological and sociological impact of the Holocaust on survivors' children who are "an invisible, silent family scattered about the world." Epstein interviewed these family members in North and South America and Israel. She found that the second generation was united by their inheritance of trauma and Holocaust imagery; for example, she herself analogizes the subway to a "train of cattle cars headed to Poland." Further, Epstein's book not only brought to public attention the existence of the second generation but made possible an informed discussion about its role in bearing witness, not to the Holocaust per se, but to the experience of growing up in survivor households. In Epstein's case she recalls that her parents believed that because of the Holocaust there was no God. Her mother suffered periodic fits of depression bordering on the suicidal, and Helen was acutely aware that her parents were not like other Americans.

Where She Came From is an exquisite work tracing the lives of three generations of secular Czech women: Epstein's great-grandmother Theresa, her grandmother Pepi, and her mother Franci. Long before the advent of the 20th-century womens liberation movement, Epstein's maternal ancestors had been independent women. Her grandmother owned a salon and initiated divorce proceedings against her husband, a convert from Judaism. Based on Franci's 12-page family history, Epstein's own book enabled her to get to know better her deceased family members, especially her mother, even after Franci's death. Writing the book, Helen became an archaeologist of Jewish memory and history. Moreover, like Julie Salamon and Art Spiegelman, she undertakes a pilgrimage to her parental birthplace the better to understand both her Holocaust legacy and her own Jewish identity.

Seeking to stitch together the many fragments of her mother's stories, Epstein employs an image taken from Franci's dressmaking workroom. The women in the workroom "swept up and threw out threads and scraps of cloth." Helen, in contrast, reports that she "collected scraps of stories, hoarding them, mulling them over." Epstein muses on the difference between her mother's skillful dressmaking and the large gaps in her Holocaust stories: "My mother would never have made a dress the way she told [Holocaust] stories." The parts of Franci's past never fit together.

Children of the Holocaust, Joe Papp, and *Where She Came From* were all *New York Times* Notable Books of the Year. Epstein's books have been well reviewed in leading publications such as the *New York Times.* Furthermore, she is a sought-after speaker and is associated both with Harvard University's Center for European Studies and Charles University's Prague Seminars. Epstein's voice is heard not only on second-generation holocaust matters, but also on cultural and societal matters.

Bibliography

Alphen, Ernst van. "Second-Generation Testimony, Transmission of Trauma, and Postmemory." *Poetics Today* 27, no. 2 (Summer 2006): 473–488.

Burstein, Janet. "Traumatic Memory and American Jewish Writers: One Generation after the Holocaust." *Yiddish* 11, no. 3–4 (1999): 188–197.

—Alan L. Berger

Erik Dorn BEN HECHT (1921)

Erik Dorn, BEN HECHT's first published novel, made his reputation as a writer. Drawn from two shocking unpublished manuscripts, "Moise" and "Grimaces," this book, despite editorial precensoring, still shocked many readers and contributed significantly to Hecht's reputation as a suggestive, even erotic writer. Saul Bellow credited Hecht and *Erik Dorn* with convincing him that literature could be made out of the gritty realism of Chicago's streets and backyards.

In the book, Hecht's painful personal life and embitterment at the stupid world he found himself in took shape in his fictional alter ego, Erik Dorn. Thus was born the prototypical and much-written-about "Hechtian man" of many of Hecht's subsequent novels. The story is structured around a love triangle in which the various relationships fail, at least in part because of their dreadful urban pathology. The main focus, however, is the psychoanalysis of Erik Dorn, a man who now speaks mostly in epigrams because he no longer finds meaning in anything. Out of touch with his emotions, this newspaperman has become jaded by his microcosmic exposure to a raw and ugly Chicago now dominated by engineers, scientists, and businessmen. Thus thwarted in his artistic brilliance, he becomes a psychotic who tosses out epigrams to cover his lack of engagement with life. When his marriage to the boring Anna is worn out through sheer neglect, he begins a relationship with Rachel, a magazine artist. Unlike Rachel, Anna now knows that Dorn's immense linguistic facility is a mask for his emptiness and disengagement. For Erik Dorn life is theater, a mere game. When Rachel is attracted to Hazlitt, a serious, prosaic, and literal-minded young lawyer, Dorn ruins their romantic chances. Then, as he grows tired of Rachel's own authenticity and ability to see through him, he takes out his jealous resentments on Lockwood, a 45-year-old author of four novels about the Midwest. When Rachel finally escapes Dorn's increasing instability by moving to New York, Dorn moves to wartime Berlin as a foreign correspondent.

One of Hecht's brilliant achievements in this book is the exaggerated and macabre depiction of wartime Berlin, which he achieves through exotic imagery and expressionist techniques. In one episode, for instance, Dorn climbs a tree to witness firsthand hundreds of people being machine-gunned in a massacre in the Moabit Prison. In Hecht's accounting, Erik Dorn's Berlin is a fittingly bizarre place for his next two relationships and his ultimate meltdown. He becomes allied with double agent Karl von Stimmes, a real cynic, and falls in love with the passionate Mathilde, who is continuously invested in romantic causes. Dorn's final prostitution of himself as a journalist comes when he helps these two smuggle money to Munich to buy arms for an insurrection. His only defense is that he is simply a man without convictions or sentiments. Back in the States, Anna marries Eddy Meredith, and Rachel takes up with a radical artist named Emil Telse. However, Hazlitt, Dorn's old rival for Rachel's love, turns up in Berlin as an American army officer and accuses Dorn of destroying his relationship with Rachel. When Dorn shoots him dead, it is clear that this violent gesture proceeds not from any kind of passion on his part but from the desperate attempt to recover passion.

Unlike the central protagonists of the majority of bourgeois utopian American novels, the protagonist makes no psychological progress at all during the course of this novel and can only be declared an anti-utopian character. William MacAdams has called him "a Michigan Avenue Nietzsche come down off the mountain" (59). Critics have generally agreed that *Erik Dorn,* a tour de force of irony and disillusionment, was Ben Hecht's best novel and best prose. It became widely read only when it was republished by the University of Chicago Press in 1963 as part of its Chicago Renaissance series. In the otherwise laudatory "Introduction" to this reprinted volume, Nelson Algren concluded that Hecht had peaked too early with *Erik Dorn,* and simply had run out of literary gas. Ten years after his death in 1964, this volume was the only one of his books still in print.

Bibliography

Fetherling, Doug. *The Five Lives of Ben Hecht.* Toronto, Canada: Lester and Orpen Limited, 1977.

MacAdams, William. *Ben Hecht: The Man Behind the Legend.* New York: Scribner, 1990.

—Gloria L. Cronin

Everyman Philip Roth (2006)

PHILIP ROTH's novel *Everyman* focuses on issues associated with illness, aging, and death. The author's preoccupation with the body's decay and mortality is partially, but not solely, due to Roth's own experiences with illnesses and age. The 73-year-old author, himself a survivor of a number of surgeries, including quintuple bypass and back and knee operations, dealt with the "medical history of the male body" and its inseparability from a man's overall biography in a number of his earlier writings, PATRIMONY, SABBATH'S THEATER, and *The Dying Animal,* among them. In these novels, he has done so within the context of the other artistic themes he has explored in the course of his literary career. In *Everyman,* however, the nameless protagonist's medical biography becomes "identical" with his personal biography, and the close focus on the body's decomposition insists the reader pay attention to parallel processes of disintegration that take place in the realms of interpersonal and professional relationships: those between parents and a son, a husband and his spouses, a father and his children, a brother and his sibling, an advertising agency's artistic director and his colleagues and friends, an artist and his disciples. The exploration of the tensions generated by these categories that constitute the rich and complicated tapestry of human existence gives rise to a powerful and self-propelling narrative of a man's need to account for both his past deeds and the moral and ethical choices that informed his behavior and decisions as he faces death.

What makes this particular main character's journey of self-examination, self-understanding, introspection, and honest stock-taking so poignant and memorable is that the unraveling of the protagonist's life story and his experiences with death are played out against the background and in the aftermath of a major traumatic event in the history of his country—the brutal attack on the World Trade Center on September 11, 2001. This catastrophe made many citizens embark on a process of self-reflection and question their life's direction, reexamine their value system, and reevaluate their priorities. Facing a major operation fraught with uncertainty, his sense of security seriously undermined by the unpredictable nature of world events that brutally intrude in private lives, *Everyman*'s protagonist finds it imperative, as the novel seems to suggest everyone should, to engage in a *Heshbon Hanefesh,* an account of one's soul and deeds. We have the capacity to make our own reality; once it is made, however, "there is no remaking of reality," a fact of life, the novel insists, one must accept.

Roth's novel derives its title from a 15th-century morality play. Unlike the protagonist of this frighteningly didactic allegorical tale, who, upon encountering Death, acknowledges his sinful earthly existence and pleads for a chance to repent and face his death with Christian humility in an attempt to earn his place in heaven, the main character in Philip Roth's novel does not torture himself with issues of the afterlife. He is more concerned and genuinely pained by the untimely predicament of his pending demise and, as he surveys his life, he comes to the agonizing but ultimately inevitable realization that he cannot "have it all over again." Like its medieval predecessor, Roth's novel is informed by one of the strongest and most potent lines uttered, as Roth puts it, "between the death of Chaucer and the birth of Shakespeare," spoken by the protagonist of the morality play: "Oh, death, thou comest when I had thee least in mind." Unlike the play, Roth's *Everyman* is not a recipe for salvation but, rather, a meditation on the meaning of life and the intended and unintended consequences of one's actions.

Bibliography

Banville, John. "Grave Thoughts from a Master: A Blank Style Masks the Magical Craft of the Novelist," *Guardian* (London), 29 April 2006, p. 7.
McGrath, Charles. "Roth, Haunted by Illness, Feels Fine," *New York Times,* 25 April 2006, p. E1.

—Asher Z. Milbauer

Everything Is Illuminated
Jonathan Safran Foer (2002)

Everything Is Illuminated, JONATHAN SAFRAN FOER's debut novel, received high praise upon its publication in 2002. Enthusiastically heralded by Joyce Carol Oates (Foer's mentor at Princeton University), John Updike, and Salman Rushdie, the novel was described by *The Times* of London as "a work of genius." Foer, who was just 25 years old at the time, was praised as "one of the best young novelists around" who had "staked his claim for literary greatness." The book went on to receive the National Jewish Book Award and the Guardian First Book Award. In 2005 the book was adapted into a film starring Elijah Wood. Critics, however, have accused Foer of being pretentious, gimmicky, and derivative. Harry Siegel of the *New York Press* went as far as calling him a "fraud and a hack" who exploits tragedies for personal gain.

Everything Is Illuminated tells the story of young American writer Jonathan Safran Foer who travels to eastern Europe with an old photograph in hand in search of Augustine, the woman he believes saved his grandfather from the Germans during World War II. Accompanying Jonathan on his journey (and conarrating the story) is Alex, a young Ukrainian who speaks a "sublimely butchered English" and has an affinity for American pop culture. Also joining the trip are Alex's grandfather (also named Alex), a "blind" old man haunted by his memories of the war, and the family dog, Sammy Davis, Junior, Junior, affectionately referred to as the "seeing-eye bitch" for his services as a "guide." Intertwined with Jonathan's contemporary quest is the event-filled story of Jonathan's ancestors and their fellow villagers in the shtetl of Trachimbrod. Combining history and folklore, Foer shows the evolution of this community from its unlikely beginning in 1791 to World War II in 1942, when the Germans invade Ukraine. The novel culminates when Jonathan, Alex, and his grandfather find the lone survivor of Trachimbrod, an old woman (initially mistaken for Augustine) who helps connect the past with the present. She has kept in boxes all the remains of the now desolate village—family heirlooms, jewelry, combs, diaries. After leading the travelers to a monument signify-ing the 1,204 Trachimbroders who were killed in the war, she gives Jonathan a box marked IN CASE, as well as a surviving wedding ring. "The ring does not exist for you," she tells Jonathan, as she places it on his finger. "You exist for the ring. The ring is not in case of you. You are in case of the ring."

Foer approaches his subject with humor and pathos. He uses an innovative narrative structure, blending past and present stories into a rhythmic, fablelike journey. The novel's title is derived from a quote from Milan Kundera's novel *The Unbearable Lightness of Being*: "In the sunset of dissolution, everything is illuminated in the aura of nostalgia, even the guillotine." The quote highlights one of Foer's major themes in *Everything Is Illuminated*: the process of recovering the past by re-creating it. For Jonathan this is the only way even to begin to comprehend something as tragic as the Holocaust. His journey back to his roots and his subsequent personal reflections and correspondence with Alex help Jonathan to delve deeply into the heart of his heritage and identity. The novel is ultimately about searching and connecting—in spite of changes in time, place, and culture. Illumination comes literally in the book from making love, a connection that creates light visible from far away according to the folklore of Trachimbrod. Similarly, a sort of spiritual illumination comes in the end as characters once mutually foreign come to see and understand each other for who they are.

Bibliography
Feuer, Menachem. "Almost Friends: Post-Holocaust Comedy, Tragedy, and Friendship in Jonathan Safran Foer's *Everything Is Illuminated*." *Shofar* 25, no. 2 (Winter 2007): 24–48.

Gessen, Keith. "Horror Tour." *New York Review of Books* 52, no. 14 (September 22, 2005): 68–72.
                                                    —Joe Vogel

Eve's Apple Jonathan Rosen (1997)

In *Eve's Apple,* JONATHAN ROSEN uses food and anorexia as powerful metaphorical tools to explore spiritual and physical identity in late 1980s America. The novel portrays an iconic postmodern couple, Joseph Zimmerman and Ruth Simon, struggling to escape 5,000 years of Judeo-Christian body myths that flourish in 1980s America.

Joseph, the young Jewish protagonist/narrator, is obsessed with his culture's fear of, and animosity toward, the human body. This obsession is kindled by his relationship with his beautiful, intelligent Jewish girlfriend, Ruth, who suffers from serious eating disorders. What makes Rosen's critique even more interesting is that Joseph becomes "a binge reader," "gorging [him]self on the horrific history of women and food" in hopes of "saving" Ruth from herself.

Slowly, however, Joseph realizes that he will never find victory because, as Flek—the book's zany sage figure—tells Joseph, "You could spend the rest of your life reading and never come to the end." As Rosen comments via Flek, "the body is our one great book," "our true Bible," but "unfortunately it is written in a language we no longer understand." Rosen implies that our bodies are metaphorically inscribed with narratives that give rise to what might be termed a bodily confusion of absence. Rosen exposes Christianity's gradual embrace of the Platonic separation of mind, spirit, and body as Joseph realizes that Ruth's anorexia is caused, in part, by her quest for purity or sainthood, which she believes is threatened by bodily demands.

Eve's Apple suggests that, to clear a space for reinventing how we view our bodies, Western culture must be uncovered and reevaluated. Yet Rosen is by no means suggesting that it is advisable or even possible to uncover, salvage, or rewrite every single chapter and footnote of our fragmented bodily histories. He instead seeks to deconstruct modernity's pursuit of disembodied, transcendent truth and spirituality—an idealistic tradition stretching back to Plato and even farther to Adam and Eve.

Midway through the novel, Ruth tests Joseph's loyalty by offhandedly remarking, "I should have told him [my father] I'm pregnant and seen how he reacted." Even though she is far too thin even to menstruate, Ruth convinces Joseph that her phantom pregnancy is real. Without even considering that a woman who "feared physical expansion" might want to carry a child, Joseph assumes that she will have an abortion. Ruth continues the charade to punish Joseph—and herself. She donates blood (after lying about her weight), faints, returns home pale and weak, and mourns her imaginary child in Joseph's arms.

When Ruth's father unexpectedly offers her a free six-week trip to France, Ruth is thrilled. But in France, bereft of her watchful "knight," she descends into severe anorexia. While she is gone, Joseph takes refuge in the arms of a coworker, whose appetites for food and sex astound him. Upon Ruth's return, Joseph (hypocritically) accuses Ruth of being unfaithful and is coldly blasé about her imaginary abortion.

Ruth explains that although she was never pregnant, Joseph had killed her fantasy of being willingly "full and fertile" and so she "wanted [him] to think that [he had] really killed something." Proudly, she removes her clothing so he can see how thin she is. Before throwing on some clothes and fleeing, Ruth fractures Joseph's masculine pride: "I thought you wanted me to get better, but that's not true, is it? You like me this way."

Rosen implies that both men and women must commit to rewriting their bodies' narratives of masculinity and femininity if they are to author a mutually beneficial volume of flesh-and-soul narratives. Joseph eventually learns that he is part of the problem. He had attempted to categorize the reasons for Ruth's illness in order to set himself up as her gallant rescuer. Only when Joseph realizes that he has constructed her as a disembodied feminine subject of his own masculinity does hope appear on the horizon for them both. Bit by bit, they begin to reformulate their relationship, their future, and new texts of masculinity and femininity.

Bibliography

Kravitz, Bennett. "The Culture of Disease or the Disease of culture in *Motherless Brooklyn* and *Eve's Apple*." *Journal of American Culture* 26, no. 2 (June 2003): 171–179.

Sol, Adam. "'Were it not for the Yetzer Hara:' Eating, Knowledge, and the Physical in Jonathan Rosen's *Eve's Apple*." *Shofar* 22, no. 3 (Spring 2004): 95–103.

—Sarah Bylund

Exodus Leon Uris (1958)

Exodus may stand as the best work by Jewish-American novelist LEON URIS. Given that Uris penned countless best sellers and several Hollywood blockbusters, having any one of his works stand out in a substantial way, as *Exodus* does, is remarkable.

The novel's title comes from the 1947 ship, *Exodus*, which attempted to transport Jewish emigrants from France to Palestine. In the novel the ship departs from Cyprus for Palestine, but the circumstances (Jewish refugees fleeing post–World War II) were quite similar.

Uris wrote *Exodus* after a two-year period of intensive research about the founding of the state of Israel, which is central to the novel. During this research, Uris traveled roughly 50,000 miles (12,000 in Israel alone), read over 300 books on the topic, shot over 1,000 photos, and conducted hundreds of interviews.

At just over 600 pages, *Exodus* is a massive novel, and, as such, tracks far more than merely the transporting of Jewish emigrants from Cyprus to Palestine. After the novel's protagonist, Ari Ben Canaan, has transported Jews into Palestine, the focus becomes his constant battle to protect them from the retribution of angry Arabs.

Uris makes the usually arduous task of following a historical drama—which exhibits his extensive research—easier by giving readers (mostly) likable characters to follow. First, there is Ari, the mastermind behind the *Exodus*'s escape. Once in Palestine, he remains a central figure in the Israeli freedom movement, which is the central story line in the novel. In fact, most of *Exodus* is concerned with the violence and hatred of Arabs toward Jews and vice versa, which is being particularly agitated by the British in Israel and the rest of the Middle East.

The central American figure is Katherine "Kitty" Fremont, an American nurse working overseas after the death of her husband and daughter. She is hesitant to join Ari's resistance movement, but once she meets Karen Hansen Clement, she can no longer sit idly by; she is drawn into the movement and begins taking care of the children of the *Exodus*. Karen Hansen Clement is a German-Jewish teenage girl who has been directly affected by the war and the postwar displacement. Most of her family was killed, except her shell-shocked father, who is unable to recognize Karen. Thus she moves from one adopted family to another. Bruce Sutherland is the main British military figure in the novel, although his role is substantially smaller than those of the other characters. Unlike most of the other British officers depicted, Sutherland shows compassion, perhaps because his own mother was Jewish. One more major character is the Jewish youth Dov Landau, who has lost his entire family in the Holocaust. He and Karen are good friends and emerging lovers, yet Dov is a loose cannon bent on revenge and joins the Maccabees, a Jewish terrorist organization.

This sets the stage for each of these characters' post-*Exodus* lives in Palestine, where, in between dispersing each character's backstory, Uris weaves in the kind of human drama that made him such a formidable screenwriter. Yet despite *Exodus*'s Hollywood moments, the novel is still a remarkable feat that seamlessly intertwines factual research with character and plot development. Once they are in Palestine, the lives of each character are marred by the violence between Jews and Arabs. Although Dov, Kitty, Sutherland, and Ari ultimately end up in the clear, Karen pays dearly with her death at the hands of terrorists, marring the otherwise relatively optimistic ending. Dov—who has by the novel's end become a major in the army of Israel—continues to work for the state of Israel in Karen's honor. Meanwhile, the love affair between Ari and Kitty, which has been festering and troubled since the novel's first quarter, reaches a melancholy point when both sadly understand each other's position and realize that neither is likely to accept the other completely. For instance, Kitty remains uneasy about Ari's feelings toward death, which are vacant and emotionless, but understands his unwavering dedication to Israel. Ari sees in Kitty a woman of equal worth and ability as his murdered fiancée, Dafna, yet he has likely lost the ability to love so freely again. Finally, Sutherland remains in Palestine, as a good friend and surrogate father figure to Ari, Kitty, Dov, and, before her death, Karen.

The setting of *Exodus* is rife with melodrama between lovers, friends, and enemies, yet looked at alongside the meticulous research Uris performed, one cannot help but see this novel as a magnificent accomplishment. It impressively serves as both a fantastic historical document and a classic, Hollywood-style epic.

Bibliography

Gonshak, Henry. "'Rambowitz' versus the 'Schlemiel' in Leon Uris' *Exodus*." *Journal of American Culture* 22, no. 1 (Spring 1999): 9–16.

Weissbrod, Rachel. "*Exodus* as a Zionist Melodrama." *Israel Studies* 4, no. 1 (Spring 1999): 129–152.

—Holli G. Levitsky

Extremely Loud and Incredibly Close
Jonathan Safran Foer (2005)

Like his first novel, EVERYTHING IS ILLUMINATED, JONATHAN SAFRAN FOER's second novel, *Extremely Loud and Incredibly Close,* was an enthusiastically received best seller. This work immediately stands out from traditional literature because of its unconventional narrative voice and its use of visual materials as part of the story. The book's first page has the nine-year old narrator, Oskar Schell, musing about the possibilities of training his anus to enunciate during flatulation. Oskar's narration blends a precocious intellect and a maturity contingent on the loss of his father with the naïveté of a nine-year-old idealist. The sentimental passages in the book (which are many) are somehow admissible, perhaps because of the ever-present backdrop of September 11, 2001, when Oskar lost his father.

The book's visual element consists of images as diverse as a picture of the theoretical physicist Stephen Hawking, a page of handwriting samples from a store that sells pens, a page with red handwritten notations and marginalia, several pages where the lines get closer and closer together until they overlap and the text is illegible, and a series of pictures of a man falling from the World Trade Center in reverse order. Speaking of his choice to include the visual element in his novel, Foer says, "if I was a painter, and I put text into one of my paintings, nobody would ask me why I did that . . . but when you put a picture in a book it does seem to beg a lot of questions. Why did I do it? I did it because it felt right" (Interview, November 21, 2006).

Foer has been both praised and criticized for the book's treatment of the September 11 attacks on the World Trade Center buildings in New York City. One critic, accusing Foer of using that subject to lend importance to his own writing, called him "not just a bad author . . . [but] a vile one . . . in a calculated move, he threw in 9/11 to make things important, to get paid" (Harry Siegel, quoted in Hamer). On the other hand, Foer himself relates that "some of the kindest responses" to the book were from the families of September 11 victims (Interview, November 21, 2006). *Extremely Loud and Incredibly Close* is one of the first works to engage the subject of the terrorist attacks so directly. Speaking of his choice to write about that subject, Foer said that "it just felt unavoidable . . . To me, the question isn't 'Why'd you write about it?' but rather, 'Why hasn't everyone been writing about it?'" (Interview, November 21, 2006).

The book is the story of Oskar's attempts to reconcile himself with his father's absence and with the manner of his death. The plot follows Oskar on a treasure hunt for clues about his father's activities before his death. When Oskar finds a strange vase containing a key and the word *Black* in his father's closet, he determines to contact every person with the last name Black in New York City until he finds the one who can tell him the purpose of the key. Oskar's ability to earn the trust of the various Blacks leads to the disclosure of some of these peoples' most intimate life events. The result is a heartwarming/heartbreaking collage of life experiences and an irony that operates on the tension between what the reader and the Blacks know and what the nine-year-old Oskar does not. The reader can share the excitement of the search for clues about the key with Oskar while knowing all along that the conclusion is not going to yield the dramatic, world-changing result Oskar hopes for.

Foer's first novel, *Everything Is Illuminated,* told the story of a young man in search of knowledge about his grandfather's experience with the Holocaust. Unlike the first novel, *Extremely Loud* doesn't center on a Jewish theme or contain a Jewish protagonist. In one statement, Foer suggests that the book with the Jewish theme was the more anomalous of his two works: "I had no identification with my Jewish roots, and no desire to identify with them, and then I wrote this book" (Interview, November 21, 2006). In another, he says that *Everything Is Illuminated* might be more characteristic of what he really wants to do: "A large part of me just wants to continue what I wrote with the first book, to follow my grandparents further, follow my parents to America, come to my childhood. If

that were my life's project . . . I would feel like I was doing what I set out to do" (Interview, October 28, 2006). When asked in the same interview about his feelings for *Extremely Loud and Incredibly Close,* Foer said "I'm proud of the book. And at the same time I kind of wish I hadn't written it."

Bibliography
Donnelly, Pat. "Not Yet 30, but Feeling Older," *Gazette,* 28 October 2006, p. J6.

Hamer, Katharine. "The Price of Fame: Cheap," *Vancouver Sun,* 18 November 2006, p. C11.

Singer, Elliot, and David Wittenberg. "Cornell Sun Interviews Best-Selling Novelist," *Cornell Sun,* 21 November 2006.

—Andrew Schultz

The Family Moskat
Isaac Bashevis Singer (1950)

The Family Moskat was the first book I. B. SINGER wrote in the United States. It appeared serially for three years in the Jewish daily periodical *Forward* before it was translated from Yiddish and published in English. Singer began work on *The Family Moskat* in 1945, a decade after the publication of his last work, *Satan in Goray.* The many similarities between *The Family Moskat* and the novel *The Brothers Ashkenazi,* written by Singer's elder brother Israel Joshua Singer, and the fact that Singer began work on *Moskat* the year after Israel Joshua's untimely death, have led some critics to classify the work as an outgrowth of that event.

Critics have noted the debt *The Family Moskat* owes to an earlier genre of novels written in the 19th century, which Lawrence S. Friedman calls the "massive family chronicle" (76), exemplified best by the works of the novelist Thomas Mann. The Jewish conception of the family as the dominant unit in and most representative unit of society figures in the form of these novels, which follow the fortunes of a Jewish family through several generations. Singer uses the Jewish family as a representative of the Jewish community as a whole to comment on the issues and forces that threatened the community, issues such as anti-Semitism and assimilation. The size of the narrative, which follows a number of characters and plotlines, is also reminiscent of the most famous serialized novels, the mainstream Victorian novel popularized by Charles Dickens.

The novel begins with Meshulam Moskat, the aged and orthodox head of the Moskat family. The family's decay is emblemized in his increasing decrepitude. Meshulam's grandchildren, the generation that experiences the Holocaust as adults, have assimilated, retaining only fragments of their Jewish heritage in their secularized identities. The Moskat family takes a backseat to other characters in the later narrative, especially to Asa Heschel, an assimilated Jew whose disenchantment with the secular world forms a critique of the decision to assimilate. The realization that the Nazi German exterminators make no distinction between assimilated and orthodox Jews raises the question of whether true assimilation is even possible. The novel ends with the German invasion of Poland in September 1939. Several pages of Singer's original Yiddish version are omitted from the English translation, which ends with the bitter reflection that the only redemption for Jews is death. The original Yiddish version's ending moved beyond that reflection to a guardedly hopeful albeit didactic one, in which a small group of Jews escape the Polish capital, Warsaw, and examine the possibility of a return to traditional and religious Jewish identity.

Asa Heschel's malaise in the secular world comes as he, like other protagonists in Singer's fiction, "flails about in a futile search for happiness with-out God" (Friedman 89–90). Friedman identifies Zionism and communism as the two most common secular movements that Jews in *The Family Moskat* use to fill the space created by their departure from Jewish orthodoxy. He also identifies the principles that make these surrogates unacceptable to Asa, who is unable to invest fully in either of them. The brutal behavior of the communists turns him away from communism. Zionism, the secular movement that pushed for the establishment of a Jewish state in Palestine, is also unacceptable; Asa's grandfather, a rabbi, points out the inconsistency behind that program, asking why a people that insisted on rejecting God should be so zealous about returning to the land that God promised them. Singer's characters ultimately fail to fill the space meaningfully that opened when they removed Judaism from their lives—as Asa observes, "they had lost God and had not won the world" (491). Asa himself is described by his first wife as "one of those who must serve God or die. He had forsaken God, and because of this he was dead" (Schulz 86). In this, Asa represents all of Jewry. His inability to find a happy place in the world ends in this malaise that ultimately asks the question whether Jews can cease to be Jews, and whether any happiness can exist for those who try.

Although some critics feel that Singer's later writing is his best, all agree that *The Family Moskat* is an important work, and most agree that it is a good one. Some fault the book for its unflattering portrayal of Jews, and argue that Singer unjustly focuses on the ugly and grotesque parts of Jewish life. Martin Hindus, writing in 1965, when the book was reprinted in a new edition, argued that *The Family Moskat* was part of a body of "solid and substantial work" that would ensure I. B. Singer a place in the literary memory.

Bibliography

Alexander, Edward. *Isaac Bashevis Singer*. Boston: Twayne, 1980.

Friedman, Lawrence S. *Understanding Isaac Bashevis Singer*. Columbia: University of South Carolina Press, 1988.

Schulz, Max F. "The Family Chronicle as a Paradigm of History." In *The Achievement of Isaac Bashevis Singer*, edited by Marcia Allentuck. Carbondale and Edwardsville: Southern Illinois University Press, 1969.

—Andrew Schultz

Fanny: Being the True History of the Adventures of Fanny Hackabout-Jones
Erica Jong (1980)

A parody of the 18th-century picaresque novel, *Fanny: Being the True History of the Adventures of Fanny Hackabout-Jones* demonstrates ERICA JONG's impressive command of 18th-century literary techniques and showcases her ability to infuse satire with lyrical energy and a deep sense of feminist entitlement. With *Fanny*, Jong successfully brings generations of women writers into dialogue with literary greats such as Daniel Defoe, Samuel Richardson, Henry Fielding, and Lawrence Sterne by adapting their 18th-century literary styles and ambitiously incorporating all her themes of womanhood into the story of Fanny. But while the novel speaks from the reality of 18th-century English life and history, it also addresses contemporary issue, particularly in their relevance to the struggles and aspirations of women throughout the centuries leading up to the present. The novel imagines a female counterpart to the literary giants of the 18th century and is aggressively rewritten to include Jong's own uncertainty with regard to the capacity for such male writers to reflect the female experience accurately.

In keeping with Jong's purposeful response to the tradition of 18th-century male writers, she takes the name for her illustrious heroine from John Cleland's *Fanny Hill*. Jong's story of Fanny commences as she is discovered upon the doorstep of an immense house in Wiltshire, where she becomes a woman under the care of Lord and Lady Bellars. The story is told through diary entries that Fanny has composed for her daughter, Belinda, in which we learn that Fanny runs away to London to "seek her fortune." While on this journey, she interacts with highwaymen, a madam, witches, famous notables of the day (such as Jonathan Swift), pirates, and various other characters. Jong is at her literary finest with this story, and the novel is an endless succession of humorous incidents that are often bawdy but always witty and intelligent. In addition to the many details of Fanny's adventures, the numerous diary entries that Fanny's story comprises contain precisely detailed depictions of the world of 18th-century England, Africa, and the Caribbean as the heroine embarks on journeys through pirate ships, brothels, masked balls, witches' covens, country houses, and anywhere else one can imagine that a daring young heroine might venture.

Although the novel is written in the language of the 18th century and explores the life of a woman of that period—a time when women endured different, if not greater difficulties and oppressions than contemporary women—*Fanny* is written from the perspective of a 20th-century woman who, while grateful for the advances in the women's rights arena, is also acutely aware that there is still much work to be done. Fanny's journey toward a meaningful existence in 18th-century society is not unlike the contemporary woman's desire for liberation and self-consciousness. In keeping with typical bildungsroman novels, *Fanny* charts the growth and development of its heroine within the context of a defined 18th-century social order. The growth process that the heroine undergoes is at its center a quest story that tracks Fanny's search for meaningful existence within her society. This is not to say, however, that Fanny always does everything by the book—quite the contrary. In fact, she leads a rather roguish existence that has led some critics to examine the story as one that toys with utopian and dystopian themes as Fanny forms a familial community with other roguelike characters.

Fanny is very much the story of a young woman whose desires and characteristics often clash with social expectations. She is stunningly beautiful as well as remarkably intelligent, and is baffled that she is expected to remain home and devote her energies to needlepoint, pastry making, and dancing. She is well read, and much more excited by the idea of devouring the books of Swift and Pope, Shakespeare and Milton—not to mention the prospect of an erotic encounter with Pope and any other heterosexual male on whom she sets her sights. Fanny is as sexually uninhibited as she is sharp and witty, and the tales she recounts to her daughter through diary entries are bursting with instances of both the erotic and the intellectual. But while many of the adventures are wildly humorous, Fanny also recounts traumatic experiences such as watching her female friends be murdered, being raped by her stepfather, and the kidnapping of her infant daughter. Incidents such as these balance out the novel's humor in a manner that reminds us that she is a woman oppressed by the cultural restraints of her time, yet her self-reliance in the face of adversity allows her ultimately to remain heroic.

While *Fanny* has no Jewish characters or themes, one critic has argued that the novel is in fact part of a Jewish tradition in fiction based on certain motifs that are traditionally Jewish such as victimization, wandering and rootlessness, and humor. This is not, however, the general consensus regarding the novel, as it is not typically viewed as a particularly Jewish book, nor did Jong intend it to be viewed as such. In the afterword, Jong admits that Fanny is not necessarily an emblematic 18th-century woman, and recognizes that her "consciousness is modern"—much like Jong's insistence that in every age there are people whose consciousness transcends the limitations of their own era. It is likely that this is the very reason that *Fanny* appeals to us today.

Bibliography
Scott, Robert F. "'Sweets' and 'Bitters': *Fanny* and the Feminization of the Eighteenth-Century Novel." *Midwest Quarterly* 42, no. 1 (Autumn 2000): 81–93.
Templin, Charlotte, ed. *Conversations with Erica Jong.* Jackson: University of Mississippi Press, 2002.
                                          —**Monica Osborne**

Fast, Howard Melvin (1914–2003)
Howard Fast was a man of multiple careers, and passionate about all of them. As a prolific author of historical novels, Fast was recognized for his

new outlooks on history (especially American), and for his ability to carry an action scene. But as a child of the Great Depression (having spent time riding the rails as a teenager), and as an ardent member of the Communist Party (1943–56), Fast was, and always remained, a visionary whose idealism infused his novels, often bringing him criticism for his stock characters, sentimentality, and at times outright propaganda. Fast's first novel, *Two Valleys* (1933), written when he was only 18, set the style of historical novel for which Fast became famous, including the image of the expansive, new "frontier," full of possibilities and peopled with bold (and often oppressed) heroes strong enough to create a brave new world. In *The Unvanquished* (1942), the story of George Washington and the retreat from New York in 1776, Fast bucked the then-current trend to revise down the great men of American history (if anything, Fast's tendency was to treat his heroic characters with ingenuous sentimentality). But Fast was not a hagiographer of American history (*Citizen Tom Paine* [1943] probably goes further than most of Fast's novels to paint a character, warts and all), for while he praised the Founding Fathers, he also highlighted and championed the plight of those who had been left outside the ideals of American democracy, as in *The Last Frontier* (1941), the story of the 1878 retreat of the Cheyenne from Oklahoma to Montana, or *Freedom Road* (1944), set in Reconstruction-era South Carolina.

In order for Fast to be so prolific, he had to make concessions. Many reviewers, while enjoying and praising his novels, wished they were not so superficial, so easy with poetic license. But being concerned with and for the masses, Fast wrote to educate the general public in the lessons of history. Consequently, it is not surprising that reviewers consistently complained that his novels too often came off like didactic tracts. By the time he wrote his most famous novel, *Spartacus* (1951), the story of the slave revolts that plagued Rome, Fast was as (in)famous for being a communist as for being a novelist (even *Citizen Tom Paine* had been removed from the shelves of New York City libraries [Meyer 87]), and the reception of *Spartacus* suffered for it

(rejected by the major houses, it had to be privately published). The novel was dismissed as being just another of Fast's political pamphlets in disguise. Ultimately, Fast's archetypal story is that of utopia, a dream separated into three stages: Pre-Communist, Communist, and Judaic. In the Pre-Communist phase, Fast looked to the American experiment (e.g., *Citizen Tom Paine*) and the promise of democracy; communism sharpened the focus on slavery and revolution (*Spartacus*); and after his break with the Communist Party, Fast's dream of utopia turned to the Jewish tradition (*Moses, Prince of Egypt* [1958]). Summed up by Walter B. Rideout, "[T]he conception basic to most of [Fast's] work is a dialectic of revolutionary development whereby certain past events are viewed as acts in the extended drama of mankind's struggle toward a classless society" (275). On the other hand, no topic was so pedestrian that Fast could not turn it into an historical novel or nonfiction adventure, witness his *Lord Baden-Powell of the Boy Scouts* (1941).

Writing under the pseudonym E. V. Cunningham, Fast launched a simultaneous career as a romance writer, beginning with the detective novel *Sylvia* (1960), and followed by a succession of (at least 11) similar novels with women's names as titles: *Phyllis* (1962), *Alice* (1963), *Shirley* (1964), *Lydia* (1964), and so on. And with one of these E. V. Cunningham novels, *Samantha* (1967), later retitled *The Case of the Angry Actress*, Fast launched his Masao Masuto mysteries about a capable Japanese detective, with six volumes to follow. Not surprisingly, many reviewers were not fooled, easily spotting Fast's handiwork behind E. V. Cunningham.

Fast's career in the Communist Party was as prolific and problematic as was his career in literature; in fact, the two went hand in hand:

[f]rom 1943 until 1956, while Fast was a Party member, the Party and indeed the world movement lionized him. It was during this period that the vast circulation of his books occurred. In his popular historical novels—*Citizen Tom Paine, Freedom Road, The American* (about John Peter Altgeld), *The Last Frontier,* and *Spartacus*—protagonists from the oppressed

classes . . . dramatized the class struggle, with its tragic setbacks yet somehow certain ultimate victory. . . . [Fast] was ranked together with Paul Robeson and W. E. B. Du Bois. . . . Pablo Picasso kissed him on the mouth and offered him any painting he chose. Later, Pablo Neruda wrote a poem to him. In 1954, he received the Stalin Peace Prize. (Meyer 87)

In 1950 Fast was jailed for three months for refusing to reveal to the House Committee on Un-American Activities the names of the 30,000 donors to the Joint Anti-Fascist Refugee Committee (a relief organization for refugees from the Spanish Civil War, a list that included donors from Eleanor Roosevelt to Lucille Ball). In 1952 Fast ran for Congress as the American Labor Party candidate. But Fast's idealism collided with the reality of 1950s Soviet communism, and in 1956 he resigned from the Communist Party, issuing his story and mea culpa in *The Naked God* (1957). With the collapse of communist states in the late 1980s, Fast seemed compelled or freed to defend the ideology he had denounced 30 years earlier, and he issued *Being Red* (1990), a revision/retraction of his earlier memoir of his communist affiliation, *The Naked God*. "*The Naked God* served as a questionable passport used to gain reentry into the capitalist publishing world," while "*Being Red* is the autobiography of an old man who wants to be remembered as a man of the left" (Meyer 89).

Fast never regained the literary success he enjoyed when embroiled in and inspired by politics during the 1940s and 1950s. In 1974 he moved to California and worked on film and television scripts, including episodes of the miniseries *How the West Was Won* (1978), then in 1977 he published *The Immigrants,* the first novel of a successful six-volume series chronicling the life of a San Francisco family. Fast enjoyed a successful collaboration with actor Richard Thomas in producing the stage version of his earlier novel *Citizen Tom Paine: A Play in Two Acts* (1986). Still, Fast's earlier work has left an amazing (if not fully recognized) legacy. Gerald Meyer, writing in *Science & Society,* 10 years before Fast's death, summed up his prolific career:

his corpus includes more than 80 books, including 50 novels, ten plays, and 20 books of nonfiction. Worldwide sales of his novels have exceeded 80 million. His writings have been translated into 82 languages and many observers—including Fast—insist that he may be the most widely read writer of the 20th century. (86)

Bibliography
Meyer, Gerald. "Howard Fast: An American Leftist Reinterprets His Life." *Science & Society* 57, no. 1 (Spring 1993): 86–91.
Rideout, Walter B. "The Long Retreat." In *The Radical Novel in the United States: Some Interrelations of Literature and Society.* Cambridge, Mass.: Harvard University Press, 1956.

—**Robert S. Means**

Fathers: a Novel in the Form of a Memoir
Herbert Gold (1967)

Later reprinted as simply *Fathers,* HERBERT GOLD's fictionalized flashback autobiography spans from Russia in the 1800s, to New York City in the 1920s, to Cleveland during the Great Depression, and finally to San Francisco in the 1960s. Gold's father, rebelling against the tradition of his Ukrainian village and family, comes to America at age 13, just after his bar mitzvah. Arriving in New York City, around 1911, he takes the name Sam Gold (to ally himself with the pavement of the streets in America). He works at odd jobs, rolls cigars for six years, brings his two brothers and sister to America (they also take the name Gold, but with varying degrees of success), obtains the initial trappings of American capitalist wealth (a gold tooth and green shoes) and whistles his way back to the old country, from where he hopes to convince his parents to emigrate. Unfortunately, his parents are caught in a pogrom in 1914 at the outbreak of the Great War before Sam can bring them to America. The old village of Kamenets-Podolsk is destroyed, and only Sam's grandfather survives.

Sam moves the family (himself and his brothers and sister) to Canton, Ohio, and then to Cleveland.

He opens a grocery store in Cleveland, cuts a figure as a successful-roguish-Jewish-immigrant-man-about-town, and marries in October 1923. He and his wife, Frieda, have four sons (Herbert Gold, the narrator, is the oldest). Sam is successful in his grocery store business, and he carves out a niche for himself and his family in spite of the Great Depression, and in spite of having to deal with the "Cossacks" of this new country: gangsters and police (both demanding protection payoffs), thieving employees, kleptomaniac customers, anti-Semitic farmers, and union racketeers (like another Ukrainian-Jewish immigrant, Shloimi Spitz, who weaves in and out of Sam's life).

Young Herb rejects the grocery business that his father and mother have built and pines for a wealthy, all-American girl who rejects him. Here Herb discovers his Jewish identity. He serves in the U.S. Army in World War II and returns home to become a professional student on the GI Bill. Herb marries, has two daughters, and teaches. He and his wife grow apart and divorce. Meanwhile Sam has sold the grocery store and become a real estate speculator. Now approaching 80, he is still a risk-taking opportunist, and along with Frieda visits Herb, a writer living in San Francisco, on their way to Hawaii.

Introducing the book in 1967, Herbert Gold said, "this is a book I have been writing all my life," and several chapters had been published previously as short stories. It is also important to remember that this novel is "in the form of a memoir," using real names and being set in real places, but, as Gold himself has admitted, it is not an autobiography, rather the way things *might* have happened. That understood, most chapters of the book are vignettes from narrator Gold's childhood in the Great Depression: the episode when his mother drives the car into the Cuyahoga River; when grocery store employee Caruso steals the store truck for a cross-state joy ride; his father's affair with a store employee; Sunday mornings at the all-male, other-world of the steaming Russian baths; and his father's fight with the anti-Semitic farmer Al Flavin.

A major theme of the book is movement—the necessity for a man to seek greener pastures, other opportunities in America: Sam moves west from Ukraine, to New York, to Cleveland, to San Francisco (to visit his son), and to Hawaii (to see the limits of the United States).

The other major theme is the inescapable, intermingling past, exemplified symbolically as father visits son in his San Francisco apartment on "Russian Hill." In the final chapter, appropriately titled "Epilogue and Beginning," Gold takes the thread back to the beginning and returns to the 1830s in the village of Kamenets-Podolsk to tell the story of his father's grandfather, the sole survivor of the 1914 pogrom, and to explore the legacy of "The Crippler"—who "saved" Jewish boys from the death of Russian uncleanness in the czar's army by intentionally mutilating them. After the shock of this final chapter, Gold's moral is clear: That despite the generational schisms, we are all bound by the shared wounds (some accidental, some inflicted with the best intentions) that reach from father to son; we are all crippled and saved by the same stroke of our shared fate. But on reflection, it is difficult to make such straight connections. In light of what awaited him had he stayed in Ukraine, Sam's flight to and success in America is heroic and ennobling; however, it is difficult to make the leap that the desperation and cruelty of the Crippler episode is equaled by Herb's late-20th-century angst for self-actualization.

Bibliography

Smith, Larry. "Herbert Gold: Belief and Craft." *Ohioana Quarterly* 21 (1978): 148–156.

Wohlgelernter, Maurice. "Herbert Gold: A Boy of Early Autumn." *Studies in American Jewish Literature* 10, no. 2 (Fall 1991): 136–171.

—Robert S. Means

Fear of Flying Erica Jong (1973)

With its strong female narrative voice and brazen unveiling of women's erotic desires, ERICA JONG's *Fear of Flying* is a literary icon of the 1970s sexual revolution. Also epitomizing the women's liberation movement of the same period, the novel was embraced by a multitude of women,

perhaps particularly by women who considered themselves to be in unfulfilled marriages and relationships with men. Much like a literal fear of flying, Jong's story draws from an acute sense of helplessness—the sense that one is trapped in or by something that cannot be controlled.

For Isadora Wing, Jong's witty narrator and heroine, by what exactly she is controlled and trapped is often ambiguous. On one level she is ensnared indefinitely by the social constraints placed on women as well as by the institution of marriage, in this case to Bennett Wing, Isadora's second husband. On another level, she is trapped by her own body and the erotic desires that accompany the sole ownership of a living, breathing female body. With its blunt treatment of women's sexual cravings, this novel aspires to strike a balance between the body and the mind, the erotic and the intellectual. Often this results in a transgression of sexual norms as Isadora moves toward achieving a sense of liberation that, for her, can be achieved only by obliterating the boundaries—social, sexual, marital—that threaten to asphyxiate her.

The novel opens on an airplane crowded with psychiatrists on their way to Vienna for a psychoanalytic congress celebrating Sigmund Freud. Isadora, who has agreed to accompany her psychiatrist husband as well as write a satirical piece about the convention for a new magazine, ruminates about her literal fear of flying as she simultaneously examines the breakdown of her five-year marriage. Ironically, the transatlantic journey marks the beginning of a voyage away from her emotionless husband and toward an exuberant process of self-discovery that is very much about the body's desire for sex and the mind's yearning for freedom and liberation. Whether this means liberation from the social constraints of marriage or from the impulsive desires of her physical body is often ambiguous. Isadora's adventures begin as she meets Dr. Adrian Goodlove, an unrestrained analyst with whom she quickly develops a sexual relationship and experiences her first "zipless fuck," the phrase that Isadora has coined to suggest her recurring fantasy of a sexual rendezvous with a man she knows very little about—indeed the first prerequisite

to the "zipless fuck" is a purposeful disinterest in the personal life of the man with whom she interacts. The problem, however, is that the "zipless fuck" ideal is quite simply only an ideal, and while Isadora fantasizes about its many manifestations and imagines that it is a necessary and thrilling part of the journey to selfhood, it is impossible to maintain her fascination with the particular man who inevitably reveals to her the banal details of his life, rendering him just another ordinary man with whom it is impossible to maintain a passionate and gratifying sexual relationship.

To be sure, it is passion that Isadora believes she is after, and it is with exuberance, albeit waveringly, that she attempts to flee from the monotony of her five-year marriage and into the willing arms of Dr. Goodlove. Ironically, however, love of the doctor is not the stuff of which fantasies are made, and Isadora comes to the stark realization that, while the "zipless fuck" may be a way of staunchly articulating her liberation, it does not always result in the most satisfying sexual encounter. The result is not, however, altogether bleak—Isadora's misadventures help cultivate a greater, though never fully realized, awareness of herself as both a woman and an artist, for Isadora is a composer of erotic poetry in addition to being a writer of magazine articles. Moreover, there is a sense that although Isadora ultimately views the "zipless fuck" in a manner that is much less idealistic, she does not regret such encounters and instead understands that the difficulty of looking back on them is the price she must pay for the bliss of the moment.

While the erotic, and to a lesser degree, the artistic, take center stage in this novel, Jewishness is a thematic presence that hovers about emphatically but is never explored. Isadora is acutely aware of her Jewish identity, perhaps even more so as she ventures to a place with a name that serves as a reminder of the cruel persecution of Jews that occurred only a few decades earlier. The Jewish aspect of Isadora's identity is perhaps the one facet of herself with which she is most uncomfortable. A tentative uneasiness underscores her sarcastic jokes about her Jewish history. Furthermore, it is Isadora's Jewishness, her Jewish "look," that becomes so

alluring to Dr. Goodlove, and her awareness of his anti-Semitism peaks with his confession that he is captivated by Jewish women. When her Jewishness intersects with the erotic, Isadora is equally uncomfortable with the perverse objectification and appreciative of the momentary power it affords her. This ambivalence is nonetheless overshadowed by the candor with which Jong approaches women's sexuality. And while the emergence of such honesty ignited impassioned debate with the publication of this novel, the exuberance that tinges every word of the book is not constrained by the question of what people think—and perhaps this is how Isadora, and Jong, lose their fear of flying.

Bibliography
Butler, Robert J. "The Woman Writer as American Picaro: Open Journeying in Erica Jong's *Fear of Flying.*" *The Centennial Review* 31, no. 3 (Summer 1987): 306–318.
Nitzsche, Jane Chance. "'Isadora Icarus:' The Mythic Unity of Erica Jong's *Fear of Flying.*" *Rice University Studies* 64, no. 1 (1978): 89–100.

—Monica Osborne

Ferber, Edna (1885–1968)

Throughout her prolific career Pulitzer Prize–winning author Edna Ferber told the story of America. Ferber was born in Kalamazoo, Michigan, on August 15, 1885, the first child of a second-generation American mother and Hungarian immigrant father. When Ferber was 12 her family relocated to Appleton, Wisconsin, where her father owned and operated a general store.

Ferber began her writing career as editor of her high school newspaper, the *Ryan Clarion.* After graduating high school in 1902 she was unable to pursue her dream of attending college at Northwestern University because of her family's financial restrictions. Instead, she took a reporting job at the *Appleton Daily Crescent,* where she earned $3.00 per week and later she went on to write for the *Milwaukee Journal.* She later credited much of her writing ability to her early career as a reporter.

In 1910 *Everybody's Magazine* published Ferber's first short story, "The Homely Heroine." Her novel, *Dawn O'Hara, The Girl Who Laughed,* the story of a young independent newspaper woman, followed in 1911. Shortly thereafter Ferber gained national recognition when her series of stories about a fictional traveling saleswoman, Emma McChesney, began to appear in popular magazines. Ferber's first play, *Our Mrs. McChesney,* based on the series, debuted on Broadway in 1915, with the renowned actress Ethel Barrymore in the lead role. In her many novels Ferber's heroines are assertive and successful, and in real life Ferber was an independent woman who defied societal conventions of the day, including never marrying.

Among Ferber's published works are two autobiographies, *A Peculiar Treasure* (1939) and *A Kind of Magic* (1963), 13 novels, eight plays, and several collections of short stories. Her works provided glimpses into the diverse landscape of American life, focusing on middle- and lower-class characters. Ideas from many of her novels came from bits of conversations she overheard that interested her.

Ferber would go to great lengths for her craft, frequently traveling to research the background for novels set in Texas (*Giant*), Oklahoma (*Cimarron*), Connecticut (*American Beauty*), New York State (*Saratoga Trunk*), and Alaska (*Ice Palace*). She made five separate research trips to Alaska alone during the process of writing *Ice Palace,* which was published in 1958. The book provided readers with an insider's perspective into the region, and she was credited by some for having contributed substantially to Alaska becoming the 49th state in 1958.

Throughout her career several of her works were adapted to stage and screen, including *Giant Saratoga Trunk,* and *Showboat* (1926), which was made into a Broadway musical and produced in three subsequent film versions (1929, 1936, and 1951). *So Big,* the story of a widow raising her only son in early 20th-century Chicago, sold more than 300,000 copies, earned Ferber the Pulitzer Prize in 1925, and was adapted for the screen.

Bibliography

"Edna Ferber Is Eulogized Here as Champion of Great Causes," *New York Times,* 19 April 1968, p. 47.

"Edna Ferber, Novelist, 82 Dies," *New York Times,* 17 April 1968, p. 1.

—Jacqueline May

Fiedler, Leslie (1917–2003)

Leslie Fiedler was born Eliezer Aaron in 1917, the year of the Russian Revolution. Radicalism was a family heritage. His grandfather, Lieb Rosenstrauch from Galicia, had settled in Newark, New Jersey. He was a leather worker, a union organizer, and an antireligious closet intellectual who inclined to revolutionary socialism. Leslie remembered him most for his warmth and strength, as well as for his amazing ability to tell fairytales. His grandmother, Perl, was initially illiterate, and finally went to school after her children were raised. These two grandparents were his primary "parents." His mother and father, Lillian Rosenstruch and Jack (Jacob) Fiedler, were less influential. Jacob, a self-hating Jew, was anticommunist and puritanical. Leslie hated his father's anti-Semitism and that of his community. His childhood years were marked by the anti-Semitism of the local Protestants and Catholics. At Southside Avenue School 95 percent of the students were Jewish, while all the teachers were suburban non-Jewish women who deplored his accent. On reflection, he thought of Newark with despair and disgust for its racism and anti-Semitism, but also realized he had enjoyed there the resources of a fine museum and a great public library. The Third Ward of Newark was a largely black neighborhood where blacks and Jews walked on separate sides of the street and always in packs. It was here he learned about racism in America, a frequent theme in his books.

Leslie soon became a Stalinist, thus estranging himself from his conservative father. When Stalin's atrocities surfaced, Leslie became a Trotskyite and joined the Young Communist League, only to abandon that after Trotsky's violence was revealed. A committed cultural avant-gardist, he grew up in reaction to the politics of the cold war era. Owing to the politics that he endorsed in high school, he failed to gain enthusiastic letters of recommendation and was thus refused entry to eastern Ivy League schools. He finally went to the University of Wisconsin in 1934. He earned a B.A. from New York University in 1938, an M.A. from the University of Wisconsin in 1939, and a Ph.D. in 1941. He married Margaret Shipley in 1940. In 1942 he enlisted in the U.S. naval reserve and was discharged in 1946 after performing translation duties. During the 1940s and 1950s, he came to the attention of the literary establishment by publishing in many journals and by being named in 1956 as the *Kenyon Review* fellow in criticism. His most famous critical essay, "Come Back to the Raft Ag'in, Huck Honey," suggesting the homoerotic and racial underpinnings of the American literary tradition, sent shock waves through the literary critical establishment when it appeared in 1948. He was Fulbright lecturer in Rome and Bologna from 1951 to 1953, after which he published *An End to Innocence* (1955). He was the Christian Gauss lecturer at Princeton in 1956. *Love and Death in the American Novel* appeared in 1960 (revised 1966); it significantly changed the way literary critics read the then canon of American literature. In 1960 the equally famous *No! in Thunder: Essays on Myth and Literature* (1960) appeared. It attacked the American literary critical establishment for being too clinically detached and too ill equipped to examine the moral and political dimensions of content, form, and style in literature. For Fiedler, to engage in art and intellectual life was moral combat. Works of art must fulfill their essential moral obligation. Because of this reasoning he led the attack on Myth Criticism and on New Criticism during the turbulent decades of the 1960s and 1970s. Earlier than most, he joyously predicted the death of modernism and was one of the first critics to employ the term *postmodern.* Fiedler also published fiction, including the novellas collected in *The Last Jew in America* (1966).

In 1967 after six weeks of police surveillance, Fiedler's home was searched on the last day of a warrant. He was arrested and later found guilty of possession of marijuana and hashish. There was no direct evidence connecting him to these drugs, and Marsha Van der Voort later confessed to planting it just minutes before the raid. But the charges were not reversed until 1972, and the ensuing scandal was extremely damaging. He wrote about the experience in *Being Busted* (1969) and dedicated the book to his grandson. In 1973 he divorced Margaret A. Shipley, whom he had married in 1939. The couple had six children: Kurt Fiedler (b. 1941), Eric Ellery Fiedler (b. 1942), Michael (b. 1947), Debbie (b. 1949), Jenny (b. 1952), and Miriam (b. 1955). That same year he married Sally Smith Anderson, and with her raised two stepsons. During this decade several more works appeared: *Messengers Will Come No More* (1974), *In Dreams Awake* (1976), *Freaks: Myths and Images of the Secret Self* (1978), and *The Inadvertant Epic* (1978). By now he was a media figure who appeared on television shows and at Hollywood parties. In the late 1970s and early 1980s he ventured into pop culture criticism, and in 1983 he wrote a critical work on science fiction, *Olaf Stapelton: A Man Divided*. In 1988 he was elected to the American Academy of Arts and Letters, and in 1989 received the Chancellor Charles P. Norton medal. During the 1990s he wrote very little, but in 1993 he was awarded the National Critics Circle Ivan Sandrof Lifetime Achievement Award. In 1997 he was again honored, this time by the National Book Critics Circle. He died just one month before his 86th birthday, on January 29, 2003.

Leslie Fiedler's legacy among intellectuals and English professors is that of a major gadfly who shed his middle-class upbringing to present himself as a disreputable bohemian Jew, disruptive, political, and always radical. His radical grandfather and his coming-of-age during the early years of the cold war shaped his politics. He quickly became the controversial darling of the 1960s campus youth culture and forever altered the then class bound and racially bound literary conversation in American letters. He was among the first to eagerly proclaim the death of modernism and the birth of postmodernism. He was also among the first to engage in race, class, gender, and queer cultural commentary. Even though his career as

critic and writer was ultimately uneven, in part due to his provocative political activism and his use of drugs and alcohol, he was nevertheless a critical literary celebrity who broke the back of formalist literary criticism and detached analysis in the academy. In his day he was called Falstaffian, egomaniacal, vulgar, noisy, and ill mannered. His perpetual rage at the American bourgeoisie and at class and race inequities of 20th-century American culture was a consistent component in both his fiction and his criticism.

Bibliography
Kellerman, S. G., and Irving Malin, eds. *Leslie Fiedler and American Culture.* Newark: University of Delaware Press, 1991.
Winchell, Mark Roydon. *Leslie Fiedler.* Boston: Twayne, 1985.
———. *"Too Good to Be True:" The Life and Work of Leslie Fiedler.* Columbia: University of Missouri Press, 2002.

—Gloria L. Cronin

The Final Solution: A Story of Detection
Michael Chabon (2004)

MICHAEL CHABON pays homage to the detective story tradition with this novella that followed the critical success of his Pulitzer Prize–winning novel *The AMAZING ADVENTURES OF KAVALIER & CLAY.* Even as it honors the work of such predecessors as Edgar Allan Poe and, especially, Arthur Conan Doyle, however, this 131-page volume also speaks to Chabon's view of how fiction works and what might be required of readers to have any story—mystery or otherwise—reach its full potential.

The story itself finds an aged detective, who is never named but who bears the unmistakable characteristics of the great Sherlock Holmes himself, forced to leave behind his hobby as a doddering beekeeper to solve the murder of a lodger at a nearby inn. At the same time, the detective seeks to solve the disappearance of a mysterious African gray parrot, the erstwhile companion to a nine-year-old mute Jewish boy who has fled to England as a refugee from the Nazi menace.

The bird itself is a curiosity; indeed, the detective purports to be interested primarily in finding the bird, and comments that if he solves the murder along the way, then it will be all the better for the police. The bird spouts Goethe and Schiller, but, most important, recites long sequences of numbers in German. What are these numbers? Are they Nazi codes? Are they numbers to some Swiss bank account? Increasingly, it becomes obvious that the bird was the occasion for the murder, and that a variety of different parties are interested in possessing the bird and decoding the secret ciphers.

In a startling move, Chabon spends much of one of the final passages inside the bird's mind, privy to the bird's memories of its different owners. At no point do we ever learn the secret of the ciphers—that is the bird's and the bird's alone—but only that the bird thinks of the sequence of numbers as "the train song." When the bird is successfully retrieved by the detective and returned to its beloved Jewish boy, the mystery ends, having never been truly solved. Thus Chabon's homage to the detective genre that he loved growing up ends by frustrating the very genre conventions that it sought to honor, allowing Chabon's novella to be a postmodern twist on the well-established Victorian genre.

Deborah Friedell has pointed out that "The Final Solution" is an allusion to the infamous Sherlock Holmes story "The Final Problem," in which Sherlock Holmes allegedly died after being swept over the Reichenbach Falls (only to have Holmes brought back for subsequent stories after a huge public outcry at the character's supposed death). But Friedell also notes that "the Holocaust reference is transparent," and it would seem that the bird's "train song" number sequence would also reference the sequences of boxcars that carried millions of Jewish men, women, and children to their deaths. Inasmuch as Chabon states in an interview published in *The Final Solution*'s afterword that he admires Arthur Conan Doyle for being "in touch with powerful, painful, deep stuff," it would seem appropriate that the Holocaust be the largest unsolved mystery looming behind the entire novella. Not even Sherlock Holmes can solve such

dark forces in the 1944 time frame of the novella. It would appear that in Chabon's world, the famed Holmesian economy of perception—that is, that Sherlock Holmes knows everything and misses nothing—is either so dulled by age and the trivialities of beekeeping, or has grown so indifferent to what seems to be the distant and abstract plight of the Jews in continental Europe, that the traditional detective story has little if nothing final to decipher in the Germans' Final Solution. That Holmes holds a tender spot in his aged heart for the needs of the nine-year-old Jewish boy who has lost his beloved parrot is, one would suppose, the best that we can hope for the famed detective to offer.

Most critical responses to this novella were positive, focusing on Chabon's power to immerse the reader within the mystery novel genre, his wonderful detail, and his warm-mannered prose. Almost all critics and reviewers speak of his breathtaking prose effects, poise, power, and elegiac atmosphere. Along with the praise of his sheer literary beauty and economy, most saw this as another Chabon genre exercise done in a minor key.

Bibliography

Friedell, Deborah. "Bird of the Baskervilles." *New York Times*. Available online. URL: http://www.nytimes.com/2004/11/14/books/review/14FRIEDEL.html?ex=1169096400<0x002 6>en=890f7b4977a 9299c&ei=5070. Accessed November 14, 2004.

—Trenton Hickman

Foer, Jonathan Safran (1977–   )

Jonathan Safran Foer is a Brooklyn-based author of the novels EVERYTHING IS ILLUMINATED (2002) and EXTREMELY LOUD AND INCREDIBLY CLOSE (2005). He is the middle of three sons; his two brothers are also involved in editing and writing. The Safran family originated in Ukraine, where many perished in the Holocaust, a major subject in Foer's fiction. Foer was born and raised in the Washington, D.C., area, and was educated at Georgetown Day School. Later, at Princeton University he studied philosophy, literature, and creative writing. In 2004 Foer married Nicole Krauss, author of the novels *Man*

Walks into a Room (2002) and *The History of Love* (2005), and the couple welcomed their first child, a son, Sasha, in 2006.

Foer's arrival on the literary scene owes much to the remarkable mentoring of teachers Joyce Carol Oates, Russell Banks, and Jeffrey Eugenides. He is best known for his novels but has also published several short stories. His first literary project was an edited anthology entitled *A Convergence of Birds: Original Fiction and Poetry Inspired by the Work of Joseph Cornell* (2001), which contained his story "If the Aging Magician Should Begin to Believe." The anthology was completed while Foer was still at Princeton. The story "The Very Rigid Search" from *Everything Is Illuminated* first appeared in *The New Yorker* in June of 2001. In 2002 "A Primer for the Punctuation of Heart Disease" appeared in *The New Yorker* and "About the Typefaces Not Used in This Edition" appeared in *The Guardian*. The story "Room after Room" was included in *Best of Young American Novelists 2* in the journal *Granta* in 2007.

Everything Is Illuminated launched Foer into overnight literary eminence. It came out of what Foer has described as an ill-conceived, mostly farcical 1999 trip to Ukraine to research the life of his grandfather Safran. Much of the novel's humor and poignancy develops out of those portions purportedly written by the young Ukranian narrator, Alex, an appealing and zany operator in a family tour business which exploits naive American Jews trying to trace their family history and genealogy in Ukraine. The supposedly collaborative account Alex and Jonathan create together features Alex's hilariously tortured English, whose dictionary-derived syntax and tortured word choices provide much of the book's charm and humor. Beyond this, Foer examines an American's bewildering attempts to plumb the history of the Holocaust and an eastern European family. Steadily the book reveals the painful denials and layers of subterfuge of the Holocaust generation, and the suffering of the postwar Americans and Ukrainians, with their family dysfunctions, ethical responsibilities, and ignorance. *Everything Is Illuminated,* which developed out of Foer's thesis at Princeton, won the senior thesis creative writing prize. The book

received both wildly enthusiastic and wildly critical reviews, some commenting on its highly creative, eccentric, brilliance, and hilarious humor. *Publisher's Weekly* called the novel the work of a "demented genius"—the word demented also appeared in Francine Prose's *New York Times* book review. Other critics dismissed it as a catalog of derivative modernist and postmodernist literary tricks, a nuisance to wade through, and ultimately a pretentious failure. The book is now garnering more moderate literary critical responses. By now the book has been translated into 30 languages, and has earned Foer such awards as the Guardian First Book Prize, and the New York Public Library Young Lions Prize, and the *Los Angeles Times* Book of the Year award. Foer has also been named in *Rolling Stone*'s "People of the Year," and *Esquire*'s "Best and Brightest," and won the National Jewish Book Award. Liev Schreiber's film based on *Everything Is Illuminated* appeared in 2005.

Foer's second novel, *Extremely Loud and Incredibly Close* (2005), also received accolades. The word *stunning* echoes through the reviews. Most reviewers recognized his concentration on suffering, history, human rights abuses, and memory. *Extremely Loud and Incredibly Close* features protagonist Oskar Schell, a nine-year old atheist mourning the death of his father in the September 11, 2001, tragedy. The book features a grab bag of modern and early postmodern experimental devices, such as pastiche and magical realism. It employs Yiddish vocabulary, photographs, pictures of door knobs and keyholes, blank pages, typography of various kinds, letters, flip book pages, and the like. While some critics describe these devices as irritating, fraudulent, silly, mannered, pretentious, melodramatic, and demanding, others marvel at Foer's willingness to place such tremendous demands on his readers and comment on his brilliance, humor, compassion, psychological insight, and sheer inventiveness.

Foer has also published a variety of nonfiction op-ed pieces for the *New York Times,* and even a libretto for an opera. Though nervous about being pegged as a Jewish-American writer, Foer admits that he is grateful to have such a rich Jewish heritage. Currently, he teaches creative writing as a visiting professor at Yale University. Foer has been a vegetarian from age 10, and is also an animal-rights activist. "If This Is Kosher," a video protesting the animal abuses at AgriProcessors Inc., appeared in 2006, targeting the largest glatt kosher slaughterhouse in the American kosher butchery industry.

Bibliography

Birnbaum, Robert. "Author of *Everything Is Illuminated* Talks with Robert Birnbaum." *Identity Theory* 26 May 2003.

Burkeman, Oliver. "Voyage of Discovery." *The Guardian* 4 December 2002.

Siegel, Harry. "Extremely Cloying and Incredibly False: Why the Author of *Everything Is Illuminated* is a Fraud and Hack." *New York Press* 13 April 2005.

Updike, John. "Mixed Messages." *The New Yorker* 14 March 2005.

—**Gloria L. Cronin**

The Forgotten   Elie Wiesel (1992)

The Forgotten (*L'Oublie*, 1989) focuses on ELIE WIESEL's commitment to preserving the memory of the Holocaust and how that memory is to be transmitted to the second and future generations. This haunting tale begins and ends with the prayer of Elhanan Rosenbaum (whose first name means "merciful God"), a Holocaust survivor and widower afflicted with Alzheimer's disease. Elhanan has a twofold task; he must transmit his memory to his son Malkiel ("God is my king"), and he feels the need to ensure that God, the source of memory, also remembers the Holocaust. The novel is set primarily in America, although certain events occur in pre- and postwar Europe as well as in Israel. Unlike his earlier second-generation works, *The Oath* (1973), *The Testament* (1981), and *The Fifth Son* (1985), *The Forgotten* is Wiesel's most nuanced portrait of the representation of second-generation Holocaust memory.

Wiesel's novel explicitly asks whether memory, like blood, can be transfused. His response reveals both the similarities and the differences between survivors and the second generation. On the one hand, growing up in a survivor household means that the second generation has intimate knowledge of the impact of the survivor's continuing survival. Psychologically, the second generation exhibits what Marianne Hirsch terms "postmemory," which results from "generational distance" but "deep personal connection" to a traumatic event in the life of a close relative. This type of memory requires an "imaginative investment and creation" (22–23). On the other hand, however, while Malkiel can bear witness for Elhanan, he also muses, "Forgive me, Father. There is no such thing as a memory transfusion. Yours will never become mine."

The Forgotten explores the sinuous relationship between survivor and second-generation memory by focusing on two fundamental themes: the father-son relationship, and second-generation memory rituals (Berger). The father-son relationship, first articulated in Wiesel's classic memoir *NIGHT*, emphasizes that a son's duty is to continue his father's tale. *The Forgotten* describes a warm and loving father-son relationship in which the two study Talmud and spend Jewish holidays together. To continue Elhanan's tale, Malkiel makes a pilgrimage to Feherfalu (White Village), his father's Romanian birthplace.

There he meets the village's only two remaining Jews, Herschel the gravedigger and Ephraim. The gravedigger relates the tale of Malkiel's grandfather's martyrdom during the Holocaust. Furthermore, he tells of the Great Reunion, a gathering of long-dead pious rabbis who meet at the village cemetery to discuss ways to assist the mortally threatened Jews. Blind Ephraim, who embodies memory, instructs Malkiel on the possibility and limitation of postmemory. In a scene reminiscent of Michaelangelo's *The Creation of Adam*, Ephraim's breath "enters Malkiel's nostrils." Yet, he tells the American pilgrim, "feel the chill of my hand (and) go home." Consequently, "memory is both bond and barrier" (Berger).

The Forgotten raises the issue of the fate of Holocaust memory in a world without survivors. Moreover, for Wiesel literature and prayer form a seamless web. Elhanan prays to God, "You well know, You, source of memory, that to forget is to abandon, to forget is to repudiate. Do not abandon me, God of my fathers, for I have never repudiated You." Wiesel's post-Holocaust prayer implores God to listen to his people, thus reversing the classic pattern of the Shema Israel prayer that enjoins the Jewish people to hear (listen to) God. Wiesel ends his novel, however, on an ambiguous note. While Malkiel continues to learn as much as he can about his father and the Holocaust, Elhanan's last words are cut off in midsentence.

Wiesel's novel was well received. The author was invited to address a conference of physicians who treat Alzheimers disease. Moreover, critics praised the work for its sympathetic portrayal of both survivors and their children. *The Forgotten* is also Wiesel's response to a world in which memory of the Holocaust is threatened by indifference and trivialization.

Bibliography

Berger, Alan L. "Transfusing Memory: Second-Generation Postmemory in Elie Wiesel's *The Forgotten.*" *Obliged by Memory: Literature, Religion, Ethics: A Collection of Essays Honoring Elie Wiesel's Seventieth Birthday.* Edited by Steven T. Katz and Alan Rosen. Syracuse, N.Y.: Syracuse University Press, 2006.

Hirsch, Marianne. *Family Frames: Photography, Narrative, and Postmemory.* Cambridge, Mass: Harvard University Press, 1997.

—Alan L. Berger

For the Relief of Unbearable Urges
Nathan Englander (1999)

NATHAN ENGLANDER's book presents a novelistic anatomy of post-Holocaust Jewish life. Nine stories comprise three groups. Stories three through eight examine postwar American orthodoxy, two initial stories suggest its origins, and the final story glimpses contemporary circumstances in which the collection was composed.

Six stories are paired and concentric. "Reb Kringle" and "The Gilgul of Park Avenue" concern identity. A Jewish janitor playing Santa Claus

for Christians resigns after encountering a Jewish child; an uptown Christian discovering Judaism in a New York taxicab discovers as well a failing marriage. "The Wig" and "The Last One Way" probe beauty and aging. An aging wig maker, beautifying herself with acquired natural hair, is blackmailed by her male source; a woman who wants out of an unhappy marriage is refused a divorce by her roughed-up husband. "Reunion" and the title story, "For the Relief of Unbearable Urges," describe marital difficulties. A resident of a posh suburban community who would engineer a reconciliation between warring family members promotes a pushing match between the rabbi and his estranged brother; an attentive husband, insane with desire for a reluctant wife, securing (through his rabbi) the services of a prostitute, reverses the terms of the marital disharmony without improving them.

Two other stories correspond—the first and last. Both are concerned with writing and violence. In "The Twenty-seventh Man," Stalin murders a generation of Yiddish writers, and "In This Way We Are Wise" follows the aftermath of terrorist bombings through the eyes of American-born narrator—"Nathan"—living in Israel. In both, writing results. One prisoner who is not a writer—but mistakenly rounded up with them—learns to compose midrash (a certain type of scriptural interpretive commentary) within this illustrious company. And the insights governing this book emerge in Jerusalem amid the hail of gunfire.

One tale catapults out of order. "The Tumblers" recounts a deportation in which some Jews board the wrong end of the transport and, mistaken for "acrobats," tour Europe in a traveling circus. Rumors abound about the "magic of the disappearing Jews," and at the story's conclusion, they are interrupted by an SS officer who applauds their "Jewish ballet." Standing before the footlights separating them from their would-be executioners, they consciously accept roles that parody their former selves, enacting the drama the Kommandant has assigned them rather than become his victims.

That moment reflects the challenge of the book at large: What if we died during the night? What if contemporary Judaism parodies older forms? To the external assault (and baring the unbearable), Englander adds the grim consideration of other ways the "magic of the disappearing Jews" has been effectuated.

Bibliography

Behlman, Lee. "The Escapist: Fantasy, Folklore, and the Pleasures of the Comic Book in Recent Jewish American Holocaust Fiction." *Shofar* 22, no. 3 (Spring 2004): 56–71.

Solomon, Deborah. "The Fabulist," *New York Times Magazine,* 8 April 2007, p. 18.

—Sandor Goodhart

Fuchs, Daniel (1909–1993)

The emergence of SAUL BELLOW, BERNARD MALAMUD, and PHILIP ROTH in the years after World War II spurred interest in earlier Jewish novelists, especially those who had established themselves in the 1930s. During that troubled decade, America's first native Jewish generation found its voice in young writers like BEN HECHT, LUDWIG LEWISOHN, HENRY ROTH, MEYER LEVIN, and Daniel Fuchs. These gave the Jewish novel its dominant contour and characters, while their composite portrait of the urban ghetto added a vital dimension to American fiction.

No Depression writer conveyed ghetto life more effectively than Daniel Fuchs, a young high school teacher who produced three novels in four years, called the *Williamsburg Trilogy*. His *Summer in Williamsburg* (1934) appeared when Fuchs was 24, and it was followed by *Homage to Blenholt* (1936) and *Low Company* (1937). Going against the grain of most of that decade's fiction, Fuchs focused on private neuroses rather than public disorders; in fact, he rarely touched on politics—and then only to laugh. Even sex provided his characters with less motivation than did the obsessive desires for dignity, success, and money. To augment his salary as a permanent substitute teacher, Fuchs, when still in his twenties, began publishing stories in *Collier's,* the *Saturday Evening Post,* and *The New Yorker.* One *Collier* story caught the attention of Hollywood, and Fuchs headed to the West Coast

for a lengthy career as a screenwriter. His screenplay for Elia Kazan's *Panic in the Streets* (1950) won high praise, and his script for *Love Me or Leave Me* (1955) earned him an Academy Award.

But Daniel Fuchs is best remembered for his *Williamsburg Trilogy*. All three novels are summer narratives. Life then is more exposed, emotions more volatile, uncertainty more evident. Fuchs's little people are not symbols or folk heroes enacting tribal myths; they are clamoring, sweating, lower-middle-class Jews who have inched from Ellis Island to Brooklyn across the East River's Williamsburg Bridge. Now locked into stifling little rooms, they are torn between Judaism's high principles and Jewish life's low facts. Most are natural losers attaining only anxiety and pain. In *Summer in Williamsburg,* Fuchs catches the cosmic absurdity of their lives. Rejecting a linear narrative for a mélange of contrapuntal scenes, he explores the moral choices confronting a dozen Ripple Street eccentrics during eight sweltering, explosive weeks. He centers most clearly on a young would-be writer, Philip Hayman, his family, and friends. For Philip, at 20, the summer is a time of choice and exploration. For several of his neighbors it proves life's end.

Even as a new novelist Fuchs opted for cinematic narrative. But to avoid undue literary influence, he derived his structure less from John Dos Passos's "Camera Eye" than from actual film-editing techniques. Leaning heavily on dialogue, gesture, and setting, he bridged his imagistic scenes by a quick dissolve at points of greatest stress. Such mechanical cross patching has its dangers: a sense of incompletion, fragmentary profiles rather than rounded portraits, characters abandoned with emotions exposed not explained, actions left dangling in mid-gesture. Yet his resolve to look anew at people and events too often glazed by familiarity and sentiment enables Fuchs to infuse *Summer in Williamsburg* with a self-sustaining vitality. It remains a hard, convincing montage of a Brooklyn summer.

His *Homage to Blenholt* is an even more mocking commentary on the American dream. Here again, amid the airless redbrick tenements, are self-pitying little people shouting, slamming doors, overflowing kitchen and flat to cover fire escape, sidewalk, and alley. Gleaning dreams from movies and tabloids, they suffer from barren delusions, bad luck, and crushing conditions. The sad-funny narrative is spun of two hectic days in the lives of three young misfits—Max Balkan, Mendel Munves, and Coblenz—who, striving mightily to enrich their lives, only make them more frantic, comic, and pitiable. Yet each, by accepting without whining his inevitable fate, attains a measure of dignity. In Depression America few can expect much more.

Not surprisingly, *Homage to Blenholt* evoked charges of cynicism, but Fuchs's cynicism was that of the committed moralist or frustrated idealist who doubted our ability to control our destiny. Life seemed to him a cosmic burlesque comprised equally of the tragic and the comic, the sublime and the ridiculous. With an eye for every reflex and ambiguity, an ear for every sigh, Fuchs shaped nuance, slang, and gesture into telling revelations of character; in the process, he deftly fused Yiddish-English and Brooklyn patois into a vernacular as idiomatic as Hemingway's, as native as Faulkner's or O'Hara's.

His *Low Company* is the most somber and violent of the novels. It is also the best constructed, with plotting tighter, incidents more revealing, and characters more fully realized. Intensifying his caricatures, Fuchs moves from sour humor to greed and brutality, and from Williamsburg to Brooklyn's soggy fringe. Neptune Beach (a composite of Brighton Beach and Coney Island) is a marginal world of squalid beach cottages, sand, weeds, and flimsy boardwalk gaiety. Sun-soaked concession stands hide a struggling, embittered world verging on violence and disaster. Its human flotsam have been cast upon the sands by an inability to cope with city complexities. Maimed, brutalized, rejected, the Neptuners here spend three days messing up their lives. Most damaged is Shubunka, the ugly brothel operator; a childhood fall had bent both legs, heightened his apelike appearance, and rendered him a lonely grotesque. Intelligent, sensitive, and gentle, he arouses in those about him disgust and suspicion. Yet in the confused reader he evokes not only compassion but also guilt for misplaced sympathy. Shubunka at least recognizes his own evil, the peculiar justice of his pathetic fate, and his need for atonement.

Thus Fuchs touches notes long sounded by tragic poets, naturalists, and existentialists: The individual discovers little from experience but to exist and endure. He learns that all prayers are to a God indifferent to individual loss and collapse. Before such cosmic indifference, Fuchs implies, we can rely only on what we can grab, steal, or find. Fuchs himself neither condemns nor judges. Time did not change Fuchs's views. His long-awaited fourth novel, *West of the Rockies* (1971), proved a vigorous but formless distillation of three decades of accumulated movieland impressions. But despite the California locale, his scurrying hyperactives seem as scarred and self-pitying as their older New York cousins. Caught up in the same savage ritual (the need to "make it"), they are propelled by similar anxieties and compulsions. Each is a survivor, with a proved ability to claw a limited victory from any defeat. Yet for all its vivid, quick-paced truths, *West of the Rockies* was not vintage Fuchs. He wrote it as a screenplay, but when it failed to sell, he turned it into a short novel (166 pages), with thoughts and deeds summarized rather than acted out.

In 1979 he brought out *The Apathetic Bookie Joint,* a collection of previously published stories and essays. His admirers refuse to let him be forgotten. In 2005, another selection of his stories and essays appeared as *The Golden West: Hollywood Stories by Daniel Fuchs,* with an introduction by John Updike (Black Sparrow Press/David R. Godine).

Bibliography

Fuchs, Daniel. *The Apathetic Bookie Joint.* New York: Methuen, 1979.

Krafchick, Marcelline. *World Without Heroes: The Brooklyn Novels of Daniel Fuchs.* Rutherford, N.J.: Fairleigh Dickinson University Press, 1988.

Miller, Gabriel. *Daniel Fuchs.* Boston: Twayne, 1979.

—**Ben Siegel**

Fugitive Pieces Anne Michaels (1996)

Fugitive Pieces (1996), ANNE MICHAELS's first novel, brought her numerous awards and international acclaim. Within the first two years of publication, Michaels won 10 literary awards for the novel—including the Guardian Fiction Award and the Orange Prize for Fiction in the United Kingdom, and the Lannan Literary Award for Fiction in the United States. In 2001 *Fugitive Pieces* also won the Acerbi Prize in Italy. To date, publishers in 30 countries have secured sales rights for this novel—in Europe, Asia, the Middle East, and the former Soviet Union. Michaels spent 10 years writing *Fugitive Pieces,* which is based on research into numerous fields of natural and human history—especially with regard to the effect of the Holocaust on perpetrators, victims, and witnesses. All were degraded by this event, which brought the entire human project into doubt. And yet the primary narrator of the novel, Jakob Beer, contends: "We look for the spirit precisely in the place of greatest degradation. It's from there that the new Adam must raise himself, must begin again" (167).

Jakob also insists that "Nazi policy was beyond racism, it was anti-matter, for Jews were not considered human" but "referred to" as *"figuren"* or *"stücke."* "Humans were not being gassed, only 'figuren,' so ethics weren't being violated" (165). The corporeality of Michaels's theory of regeneration is complex and paradoxical—showing how light (healing) is both a particle (matter, or of the body) and a wave (motion through time). Introduction to this duality begins with the title: Fugitive—transitory, fleeing away from prosecution or harm, changing—and Pieces—fragments, parts of something broken, falling apart emotionally, to mend or join together, and artistic expressions. Jakob asks: "What does the body make us believe? That we are never ourselves until we contain two souls. For years corporeality made me believe in death. Now, inside Michaela yet watching her, death for the first time makes me believe in the body" (189). From years of yearning for his sister, Jakob also learns "*that to remain with the dead is to abandon them*" (170).

Fugitive Pieces is structured in three parts: a one-page introduction announcing the 1993 deaths of the renowned poet Jakob Beer (age 60) and his second wife, Michaela, and two major sections designated Part I and II. Part one is Jakob's memoir, written shortly before his death. Part II is the narrative of a man named Ben. It describes the circumstances through which he is led to discover Jakob's memoir. Both Jakob and Ben are Jewish—Jakob a Polish survivor of the Holocaust and Ben the son of Holocaust survivors. Jakob's memoir begins with the murder of his parents and the unknown fate of his sister, Bella. To escape a similar end at the hands of German soldiers, the young Jakob hides in the bogs of an ancient buried city, Buskupin. Athos Roussos, a Greek geologist excavating Buskupin, lifts Jakob from the bog and smuggles him to his home on the Greek island of Zakynthos. There, Athos "slowly" (144) replaces parts of Jakob with his cosmology by teaching Jakob how to do an archaeology of physical (paleobotany, geology, geography—both terra incognita and cognita) and human history (languages, the humanities, biography, history). Through Athos, Jakob learns how to peel back the strata of these fields of inquiry. Athos also becomes Jakob's *koumbaros,* his godfather, and the marriage sponsor for Jakob and his sons (14). From Athos, Jakob learns that healing is reciprocal: "If you hurt yourself," with consuming grief, Athos tells Jakob, "I will have to hurt myself. You will have proven to me my love for you is useless" (45). After Athos's death, Jakob returns Athos's love and care by compiling Athos's essays into two books and also finishing Athos's book *Bearing False Witness*—a "record of how the Nazis abused archaeology to fabricate the past" by eradicating evidence of "an advanced culture that wasn't German," like Biskupin (104).

The two major sections of the novel are divided into smaller units reminiscent of the creative periods in Genesis—part I attains to seven pieces, or wholeness, and part II attains to a fourth recreative period. Michaels's conception of reformation resembles the simultaneity of the geological theories of uniformitarianism and catastrophism—what Michaels calls the "gradual instant"

(171). Jakob's regeneration moves from "The Drowned City" (the beginning of his rebirthing, or day one) to "The Gradual Instant" (the seventh day) of his long rebirth—from bog boy to wise old man. The "catastrophe of grace" comes to Jakob when he meets and marries Michaela late in life. Condensed in Michaela are generations of faithful Kievan wives for generations of devoted husbands (178). Jakob writes: "Michaela offers her ancestors to me. I'm shocked at my hunger for her memories. Love feeds on the protein of detail, sucks fact to the marrow" (179). Echoes of the Song of Songs—the sacred marriage rite that redeems a fallen world—attend this union.

In response to reading Jakob's memoirs and four books of poetry, Ben begins his own memoir—addressed to Jakob. Although Ben's journey to wholeness remains unfinished and tentative (he betrays Naomi with Petra while staying in Jakob and Michaela's home in Athens—a betrayal that he decides to withhold from Naomi), Ben comes to the conclusion that he must give what he most needs (294). The children of Holocaust survivors have different, however grievous, journeys toward overcoming their inherited despair—a journey that requires loving and wise guides. And yet, through the dramatic immediacy of literature, Anne Michaels provides patterns for healing both survivors and children of survivors of apocalyptic events.

Bibliography
Gubar, Susan. "Empathic Identification in Anne Michaels's *Fugitive Pieces*: Masculinity and Poetry after Auschwitz." *Signs* 28, no. 1 (Fall 2002): 249–276.

Kandiyoti, Dalia. "'Our Foothold in Buried Worlds': Place in Holocaust Consciousness and Anne Michaels's *Fugitive Pieces*." *Contemporary Literature* 45, no. 2 (Summer 2004): 300–330.

—**Suzanne Evertsen Lundquist**

The Gates of the Forest Elie Wiesel (1966)

The Gates of the Forest (*Les Portes de la forêt*, 1964) is a powerful reflection on the Holocaust's theological impact, the historical effects of Christianity's "Teaching of Contempt," the meaning of friendship, and the role of love. ELIE WIESEL's fifth book and fourth novel, *Gates of the Forest* is composed not of four prayers as in *The TOWN BEYOND THE WALL,* but of four sections that represent the seasons of the year. Furthermore, the protagonist, Gavriel/Gregor, is not a victim of the camps, but a partisan living in the forest while fighting the Germans. The novel's epigraph is a Hasidic tale that describes the difference between four generations of Hasidic leaders. Wiesel concludes his retelling of the tale with another epigraph, "God made man because he loves stories." The four versions of Gavriel/Gregor's retelling of the story of his murdered comrade Leib the Lion saves his own life.

The novel begins in Europe where Gregor/Gavriel is hiding in a cave waiting, in vain, for the return of his father, who had been murdered by Germans. Gavriel ("Man of God") gives his name to a stranger—perhaps the Messiah—who discovers him hiding in the cave. The story unfolds under the sign of the murderous activities of the Shoah. Ironically, it is Clara, lover of Leib the Lion, who verifies the protagonist's tale of what happened to their murdered comrade, thereby rescuing him from their initial suspicions about his innocence. The novel concludes in America with Clara and Gregor together. Attending a *Farbrengen* (Hasidic gathering) in Williamsburg, Gavriel has a crucial theological exchange with the Lubavitcher rebbe concerning the possibility of post-Holocaust belief in God.

Wiesel explores Christianity's role in the bi-millennial teaching of contempt for Judaism, and the phenomenon of the Christian helper. Leaving the cave, Gregor goes to a nearby village where he is hidden by Maria, the old family servant. She tells the villagers that he is a deaf-mute—the son of her vanished sister Ileana, a prostitute. Eager to tell their tales to a "safe" listener, the men of the village confess their affairs with Ileana. The priest also confesses to betraying a Jewish man who refused to accept Christ. Cast as Judas in the village Passion play, Gregor is beaten by audience members. He astounds them by speaking. Recovering their composure, they begin beating him again. Wiesel, linking the fate of all Jews and abolishing spatial and temporal distinction, writes that at the same moment, officers in the "crimson fields of Galicia were shouting . . . 'Fire.' A hundred Jews, ten thousand Jews were tumbling into the ditches. He would not die alone." Gregor's life is saved by a mysterious Christian nobleman who helps him escape to the forest where he joins the partisans.

Later in Brooklyn, Gregor/Gavriel encounters the Lubavitcher rebbe. The two have a theological exchange that articulates the dynamic of post-Holocaust faith and doubt. Writing about his own real-life exchange that serves as the model for this scene, Wiesel comments, "At one point I asked him point blank, 'Rebbe, how can you believe in *Hashem* (God) after the *Khourban* (Holocaust)?' He looked at me and said, 'And how can you not believe after the *Khourban*?' Well, that was a turning point in my writing, that simple dialogue" (Abrahamson). And yet Wiesel accepts the rebbe's position not as an answer, but rather as a question.

At the novel's conclusion Wiesel makes two observations that reveal the complexity of his post-Auschwitz faith and the altered dynamic between God and humanity. It does not matter if the Messiah comes, Gavriel tells Clara. "It is because it is too late that we are commanded to hope." Moreover, "The Messiah isn't one man . . . he's all men." As long as there are men there will be a Messiah. Furthermore, after the Holocaust, God desperately needs man. Reciting the Kaddish "man returns to God his crown and scepter," in spite of Auschwitz. *The Gates of the Forest* received critical acclaim as marking Wiesel's movement toward increasing communal interaction on the part of his protagonist, as well as articulating the nuance of his evolving theological position.

Bibliography

Abrahamson, Irving, ed. *Against Silence: The Voice and Vision of Elie Wiesel.* New York: Holocaust Library, 1985.

Lambert, Carol. "Friendship in *The Gates of the Forest*: Friends as 'Ladders.'" In *Is God Man's Friend? Theodicy and Friendship in the Novels of Elie Wiesel.* New York: Peter Lang, 2006.

—**Alan L. Berger**

"The German Refugee"
Bernard Malamud (1963)

"The German Refugee" is a stunning tale of loss and the destructive power of the Holocaust. Moreover, it makes a significant contribution to refugee literature. Unlike BERNARD MALAMUD's other Holocaust-related short stories, this one focuses on the plight of refugees on the eve of the Jewish tragedy. Fleeing Germany after Kristallnacht (the night of broken glass, November 9–10, 1938), they arrive in America, cut off from their home, family, and language. All the while, the specter of Nazism haunts them. Oskar Gassner, the 50-year old protagonist, had been a critic and journalist in Berlin. In America he is to give a series of lectures. Oskar's language tutor is Martin Goldberg, a college senior who narrates the story. Goldberg has no easy task—Oskar's previous two tutors had given up on the refugee in frustration.

Oskar studies English to deliver a lecture on Walt Whitman, and a series of lectures on "The Literature of the Weimar Republic." He has great difficulty with English and sinks deeper into despair. His three refugee colleagues, a former film star, a brilliant economist, and a professor of medieval history, share the pain of exile. Emphasizing the plight of the intellectuals, Malamud underscores Nazism's rejection of reason and its intolerance for either dissent or independent thought. Yet it is the trauma of the refugees which strikes the reader. All accomplished men in their native land, the intellectuals underwent a status-reversal in America. As the former film star observed in later years, "I felt like a child, or worse, often like a moron. . . . My tongue hangs useless" (200).

Oskar, emblematic of many acculturated German Jews, embraced the liberalism and idealism of the Weimar Republic (1918–33). But he now realizes that his faith in humanity had been misplaced, telling Goldberg in heavily accented English, "I have lozt faith. In my life there has been too much illusion" (206). Oskar has managed to bring his books and some artwork to America. Yet these remnants of culture do little to assuage his depression and bitterness. Preparing for his Whitman lecture, Oskar contends that certain German poets embraced the American's feeling for *Brudermensch,* or humanity. But, he bitterly notes, "this does not grow long on German earth and is soon destroyed" (209). He is certain that his gentile wife, "in her heart, was a Jew hater," like her mother (204).

Tutor and pupil become friends, often going on long walks together. In the course of their discussions, Oskar confides that he had once attempted suicide. The refugee cursed the German language, and hated the country and its people: "They are pigs masquerading as peacogs" (203). Oskar is plagued by horrible dreams of Nazi atrocities. He tells Martin that in one such dream he had returned to Germany to visit his wife. Not finding her at home, he is directed to a cemetery where he sees a tombstone, and although it doesn't bear his wife's name, her blood is seeping out of the grave. Despite this torment, Oskar's lecture on Whitman goes well. He cites the American poet's lines dealing with human solidarity and the binding power of love. Martin notes to himself that Oskar read it as though he believed it.

Two days later Oskar commits suicide by gassing himself in the oven, leaving Martin all his possessions. Going through his friend's effects, Martin discovers a letter from the man's anti-Semitic mother-in-law. She wrote that after Oskar abandoned her daughter, and against her own mother's pleas, she was converted to Judaism "by a vengeful rabbi." Shortly thereafter, the Brown Shirts (a paramilitary organization with allegiance to Hitler) had come to round up Jews. Despite the fact that her mother waves her bronze crucifix in their faces, the men drag out Oskar's wife and the other Jews in the building. Loading them into trucks, they transported them to a small town in Poland where Frau Gasner was shot in the head. She toppled into a tank ditch with the other naked Jews, some Polish soldiers, and a handful of Gypsies.

"The German Refugee" received great critical acclaim. Its power lies in Malamud's ability to evoke the profound sense of loss that overtook the refugees. Oskar and his wife are both destroyed by the Holocaust. In describing the fate that awaited Jews and others under the murderous regime of National Socialism, Malamud seeks to awaken the moral and ethical conscience of humanity.

Bibliography
Avery, Evelyn G., ed. *The Magic Worlds of Bernard Malamud.* Albany: SUNY Press, 2001.

Kremer, S. Lillian. *Witness through the Imagination: Ozick, Elman Cohen, Potok, Singer, Epstein, Bellow, Steiner, Wallant, Malamud: Jewish-American Holocaust Literature.* Detroit: Wayne State University Press, 1989.

Malamud, Bernard. *Idiots First.* New York: Dell, 1965.

—Alan L. Berger

Gimpel the Fool and Other Stories
Isaac Bashevis Singer (1957)

In *Gimpel the Fool and Other Stories,* ISAAC BASHEVIS SINGER gives voice to his conviction that only the thinnest line separates truth from appearance, the supernatural from the natural, virtue from sin. These are 11 compassionate fables of Jews who otherwise interest no one but God, the devil, and themselves. God's concern is never certain. When he does make a belated appearance, he punishes not Satan, who is merely plying his trade, but a sinfully weak human. Satan and his minions move unimpeded through Polish forests, swamps, and shtetls, debauching the vulnerable. The shtetl, with its muddy streets, shabby houses, and cluttered prayer house, was at the core of eastern Europe's Jewish life. Rabbis, scholars, and students steeped in Talmud were its important citizens; newspapers, radios, and automobiles were nonexistent there. Shattered by Western thought, its very traces obliterated, the shtetl was removed just enough in time and space to render plausible the most mythical events or legendary figures; it was also close enough to embody reality. The real and unreal fused there convincingly.

In short, Singer's tales transcend the regional and parochial to explore our moral fiber under testing circumstances and our varied stratagems as we withstand or succumb to temptation. Most sorely tried here is Gimpel of Frampol, the town baker and recognized "fool." A lineal descendant of such famed "sainted fools" as Yoshe Kalb and Bontsha Schweig, Gimpel willingly accepts every jibe and cruel prank; he believes everything, even that which common sense rejects. Why? Well, after all, he reasons, anything is possible. Further, to accuse another of falsehood is to diminish his dignity. So when all Frampol conspires to marry him to Elka, the coarse-mouthed village slut, he agrees. When he becomes a father four months after becoming a husband, he accepts the child as "premature." Finding a man in his wife's bed, he views his discovery as a "hallucination"—such things do happen. His neighbors mock his gullibility, but Gimpel stands fast. Neither mistreatment nor trickery sours him. When his wife dies, Gimpel takes to the road. In his wanderings he hears many lies and falsehoods, yet he realizes there are no lies. "Whatever doesn't really happen," he declares, "is dreamed at night. It happens to one if it doesn't happen to another, tomorrow if not today, or a century hence if not next year." The physical world is for Gimpel but illusion and "once removed from the true world."

Gimpel is more fortunate than most of the harassed little people in the collection's other tales. Satan's legions are everywhere, waiting to pounce at first hint of frailty or slackened obedience to God. An unwary reader may find himself pulling for a charmingly adroit demon to snare his weak human prey. In "From the Diary of One Not Born," for instance, the demonic narrator's pleasure proves contagious as he reduces a proud man to begging, drives an honest woman to suicide, and returns to Hell for a hero's welcome. But Satan's pride in seducing the best individuals does not compare with his joy at corrupting an entire community. In "The Gentleman from Cracow," Frampol's browbeaten Jews (who derived such pleasure from abusing Gimpel) are easily victimized. Satan arrives in Frampol during a famine as a handsome young doctor and scatters gold among the starving. The growing lust for money gives way to baser desires, and the town bursts into flame. A new village rises from the ashes, but the shame lingers through generations. In "Joy," Singer makes it clear humanity must first be cleansed of arrogance by doubt and suffering before experiencing happiness. No one should expect God to bestow arbitrarily so rare a gift.

Bibliography

Hadda, Janet. *Isaac Bashevis Singer: A Life.* New York, Oxford: Oxford University Press, 1997.

Kresh, Paul. *Isaac Bashevis Singer: The Magician of West 86th Street.* New York: Dial Press, 1979.

—Ben Siegel

Ginsberg, Allen (1926–1997)

Irwin Allen Ginsberg, the iconic Beat poet and unofficial father of the 1960s countercultural revolution, is known as much for his poems HOWL and KADDISH as for his historic role in shaping political and popular culture. His poetry captures the materialistic and conformist values of postwar America, along with its resultant rejection by the Beat generation. Ginsberg was born into a Jewish family on June 3, 1926, in Newark, New Jersey. His father, Louis Ginsberg, was a high school teacher and published poet; his mother, Naomi Levy Ginsberg, was an active member of the U.S. Communist Party and subject to mental illness. She often brought her son along with her to party meetings, and her political radicalism as well as her extreme paranoia and eventual insanity had a tremendous impact on young Allen that shows up continually in his work. These poetic leanings took shape in high school when he discovered the poetry of Walt Whitman, who, along with William Blake, was among his chief artistic influences.

Ginsberg's metamorphosis into a poet was gradual. He initially entered Columbia University to study labor law on the urging of his father. It was there, however, that he met Lucien Carr, who introduced him to fellow student Jack Kerouac. He joined a circle of artists including William S. Burroughs and John Clellon Holmes. With the eventual arrival of Neal Cassidy, the seeds of the future Beat movement were sown. Ginsberg was fascinated with Neal, as was Kerouac, and the resultant cross-country travels he inspired helped to define the Beat generation, as later recounted in Kerouac's "Beat Bible," *On the Road.* Rejecting conventional social mores and embracing what was perceived as the more vital existence of the outsider, this group increasingly appropriated an "alternative" lifestyle: hanging out in Times Square with junkies and thieves, experimenting with drugs like Benzedrine and marijuana, and transgressing established sexual boundaries. Due to this lifestyle's inherently disruptive qualities, Ginsberg was eventually expelled from Columbia; later, because of the criminal activities of several of his friends, he was arrested. As a result, he temporarily "reformed"; he declared himself a heterosexual and started dating Helen Parker, got a conventional job as a market researcher, and even enrolled in psychoanalytic treatment. Ironically, it was in the waiting room of a psychiatric hospital where he met Carl Solomon, kindred spirit and eventual inspiration for Ginsberg's poem *Howl*. Solomon in turn introduced him to a fellow Patterson, New Jersey, poet, William Carlos Williams, who became Ginsberg's mentor. Williams's modernist poetry had a huge influence on Ginsberg's own poetic style, and under his tutelage Ginsberg embraced poetry as both career and way of life.

Wholeheartedly reembracing the Beat lifestyle, Ginsberg followed its western movement to San Francisco, the location of an emerging poetry movement dubbed the "San Francisco Renaissance." He met a number of poets who would later become associated with the Beat movement, among them Gary Snyder and Michael McClure, the latter of whom passed on to him the responsibility for a gathering of local poets. This event, which took place on October 6, 1955, became the legendary poetry reading known as "The Six Gallery Reading." Besides bringing together a number of figures from the San Francisco Renaissance, it most importantly was the first public reading of Ginsberg's poem *Howl*. Destined to become his most famous work, this poem launched Ginsberg's career and put the Beats on the map. It was published in 1956 as part of a book of poetry, HOWL AND OTHER POEMS, by fellow Beat poet Lawrence Ferlinghetti's San Francisco–based City Lights press. Its explicit language and frequent homosexual references caused quite a scandal, and the book was seized by U.S. Customs officers on charges of obscenity. The 1956 ban was later lifted by Judge Clayton W. Horn. Of course, this only guaranteed the poem's and Ginsberg's fame, and the subsequent lifting of the ban by Judge Clayton W. Horn (who declared the poem to possess "redeeming social importance") was a crucial victory for free speech. The importance of *Howl* as a work of art comes not only from that fact that it successfully captures the essence of what the Beat movement was all about, but also that it epitomizes some of Ginsberg's most important recurring themes. Using the Old Testament idolatrous god Moloch as a symbol of depravity in the name of materialistic gain, Ginsberg blames the destruction of those outside the traditional boundaries of society on the consumer-driven, conformist values of post–World War II America. He links this deterioration to the Beats in general, especially Carl Solomon, but most of all to the insanity suffered by his mother. He was to return to and deal with this latter theme in his other well-known work, *Kaddish for Naomi Ginsberg (1894–1956),* published in 1961 as a book of poetry, KADDISH AND OTHER POEMS. The title refers to the Jewish song of mourning, and the autobiographical poem is a lament of grief over her death, which helped him come to terms with it.

Ginsberg thus became a key figure in the emerging Beat culture. Although he never claimed to be its leader, he certainly is remembered as its chief poet. Friendship with Ginsberg became a standard for identification as a Beat. Ginsberg was also a pivotal figure in enacting the transformation from the relatively confined Beat movement of the 1950s to the widespread countercultural revolution of the 1960s. He became its unofficial leader and iconic figurehead; the list of key events he participated in is staggering. He was the actual person who coined the emblematic hippie term "flower power." His tireless crusade against the era's domineering social values earned him the status of a revolutionary figure, along with the wrath of the U.S. government. He was a key participant in protests against the Vietnam War, and along with William S. Burroughs joined in the antiwar protests at the 1968 Democratic National Convention in Chicago. Earlier, at a 1965 protest on the Oakland-Berkeley city line, he played an important role as peacemaker by reconciling the disruptive California chapter of Sonny Barger's Hell's Angels motorcycle gang with the San Francisco hippies. He sought to overturn society's rigid moral standards against drugs, which he viewed as potent tools of enlightenment, helping Timothy Leary to publicize and promote LSD and turning on many of his friends to this hallucinogen. To Ginsberg, the revolution they fought for was political as well as spiritual; for instance, at the infamous 1967 San Francisco "Be-In," along with Gary Snyder and Michael McClure, he led the crowd in chanting the sacred Hindu syllable om. His influence was not confined to the United States alone; he was kicked out of both Cuba and Czechoslovakia for his ideas, the legacy of which influenced future revolutionary figures like the Czechoslovak Václac Havel. His 1965 reading with several other Beats at Prince Albert Hall in London essentially launched the underground scene there; based at the UFO Club, it saw the emergence of culturally iconic bands like Pink Floyd. His influence on popular culture also extended to his good friend Bob Dylan, who claimed Ginsberg was one of the few literary figures he could stand. Nor did his potency sink as the turbulent 1960s waned. In the early 1980s, for example, he participated in the punk rock movement, appearing on the Clash's *Combat Rock* album and performing with them on stage. He continued to be an active figure in politics and culture until his death near the end of the century.

Ginsberg's work, both political and artistic, was marked by a constant streak of spiritualism. His true spiritual awakening occurred at 1948 in his Harlem loft, when he claimed that William Blake appeared to him in a vision, causing him to tell family and friends that he had found God. A visionary, prophetic poet himself, Blake had a major spiritual and artistic impact on Ginsberg's work. Although raised in an agnostic household, his Jewish roots were important to him; references to it in his work are common, and it contributed heavy thematic influences to *Howl* and *Kaddish*. Another fundamental contribution to his work, as well as on his life, was Zen Buddhism. Ginsberg traveled through India in the early 1960s, and by chance coincidence in 1970 met Chongyam Trungpa Rinpoche, a Tibetan Buddhist meditation master of the Vajrayana school, when they both tried to catch the same New York City taxi. He became a lifelong friend and personal guru to Ginsberg.

Later, and together with poet Anne Waldman, Ginsberg established a poetry school, the Jack Kerouac School of Disembodied Poetics at Trungpa's Naropa Institute in Boulder, Colorado. Ginsberg is remembered during his later years in large part by his mixing of songs, chants, and other spiritual elements into his public readings.

Ginsberg continued to write and perform poetry for the remainder of his life. The work of his later years, although eclipsed by some of his earlier achievements, continued to garner acclaim. He won the National Book Award in 1974 for his book of poetry, *The Fall of America*. In 1993 he was awarded the medal of Chevalier des Arts et des Lettres (the Order of Arts and Letters) by the French minister of culture. His commitment to active community involvement was unceasing; he was a constant fixture at local readings and gatherings on New York City's Lower East Side, where he spent the remainder of his life. On April 5, 1997, at the age of 70, he died from liver cancer via complications of hepatitis.

Bibliography
Clark, Thomas. "Allen Ginsberg." In *Writers at Work—The Paris Review Interviews* 3, no. 1 (1968): 279–320.
Miles, Barry. *Ginsberg: A Biography*. London: Virgin Publishing Ltd., 2001.
Schumacher, Michael. *Dharma Lion: A Biography of Allen Ginsberg*. New York: St. Martin's Press, 1994.

—Eric Izant

Glass, Montague Marsden (1877–1934)

Montague Marsden Glass published his best-known fiction, which centered around the Jewish immigrants Abe Potash and Morris Perlmutter, at what appears retrospectively to be a particularly difficult time in the early 20th century. From the late 1800s to the 1930s, certain prominent Americans in literature, history, and art disparaged and denigrated the Jewish presence. Among them: *Puck* editor Henry Bunner, Stephen Crane, Frank Norris, Henry James, Henry Adams, Frederic Remington, and Frederick Jackson Turner. English-born Glass arrived in the United States at age 13, eventually studying and practicing law in New York City. In 1909, utilizing his legal experience, he turned writer. A major stimulus were the vibrant people he found himself observing and dealing with. Glass pioneered the lifelike depiction of immigrant American Jews competing in business and confronting personal problems, sometimes in ways that could have intensified the disparagement of Jews by anti-Semites critical of immigrants slow to use standard English forms and slow to acculturate.

Glass wrote for a number of American magazines, primarily the *Saturday Evening Post*. His works include *Potash and Perlmutter* (1910), *Abe and Mawruss* (1911), *Elkan Lubliner: American* (1912), *Worrying Won't Win* (1918), and *You Can't Learn 'Em Nothin'* (1930). The first play about Potash and Perlmutter was enormously successful in London and New York. Many have found Glass's characters amusingly likable, with their lively immigrant English, based on faulty grammar, colorful idioms, and insertion of Yiddish expressions. As a writer he seemed most at home when dealing with a folksy, temperamental duo such as Potash and Perlmutter, or Polatkin and Scheikowitz in *Elkan Lubliner: American.*

Among the interesting elements in Glass's first three works are the dynamics of operating a ladies' garment manufacturing and sales business in the early 1900s; the psychology of each of the copartners, the top-level personnel, and the customers; the sales techniques involved in getting orders; insights into ladies' fashions of the period; techniques for promoting the garments in stock; the current pay scale for certain individual employees; and the idiomatic jargon of uneducated, partially assimilated Jewish merchants and their families. But by way of contrast with these "mainstream" individuals that Glass created, there is in all three books the occasional appearance of an upscale, well-educated, well-heeled lawyer, Henry D. Feldman—expert in all legal aspects of the cloak and suit trade. Feldman held "the opinion that a liberal sprinkling of Latin phrases rendered his conversation more pleasing to his clients."

As for social consciousness, former lawyer Glass generally passed over the lowest level, "sweatshop," workers, in favor of those just below the proprietors themselves and their competitive associates. That is, the salesmen ("drummers"), cutters and assistant cutters, operators, shipping clerks, *and* office personnel such as bookkeepers and secretaries. A notable exception of sorts is the poor, disadvantaged young man, Elkan Lubliner, a refugee from Russian pogroms. Through pluck and luck, Elkan marries the love of his life, who turns out to be an unsuspecting heiress to a fortune, and soon he becomes a junior partner of the Polatkin and Scheikowitz firm. The concluding chapter of *Elkan Lubliner: American* is a gem of social satire, exposing the snobbery, exclusivity, and bad manners of the wealthiest financial group of post-immigrant Jewish society.

Glass bid farewell to his Potash and Perlmutter duo and their spirited interactions when he wrote *Worrying Won't Win* (1918), a series of dialogues on the Great War (1914–18). Aside from his short pieces, he also wrote *Can't Learn 'Em Nothin'* (1930). Some may see Glass as a forerunner of the Jewish mercantile trade genre, leading to Jerome Weidman's 1937 novel *I Can Get It for You Wholesale,* and Elick Moll's *Seidman and Son* and other stories, which came out in 1958. But Glass is really sui generis, an unfairly neglected chronicler of the New York garment trade in the early 20th century.

Bibliography
Columbia Encyclopedia. 6th ed., s.v. "Montague Marsden Glass."
"'Partners Again'—Hilarious," *New York Times,* 2 May 1922, p. 27.

—Samuel I. Bellman

God Knows Joseph Heller (1984)

The fourth of five novels written by JOSEPH HELLER, author of *CATCH-22, God Knows* is a humorous contemporary retelling of the story of King David.

When *God Knows* hit bookstores in 1984, a lot was riding on it. Heller's previous two novels, *Something Happened* (1974) and *Good as Gold*

(1979), had met with little enthusiasm. Nothing Heller had done in over 20 years had won much critical attention. His reputation was solely based on *Catch-22*. As Mordecai Richler put it: "It is one thing for him to have written one of the most celebrated of post–World War II novels and quite another to have everything that followed compared to it and found somehow wanting." Yet with the publication of *God Knows*, Heller found a change of fortune. The book sold well and was on the *New York Times* best-seller list for several weeks. To the literary world it was a success; to Heller it was a much needed comeback.

God Knows is the fictional tell-all autobiography of King David. The story opens as the aged David is looking back on the events of his life and reminiscing on what has brought him to his current position. The novel weaves through past and present as it retells, in a loosely chronological fashion, David's climactic rise to power and the struggles he encountered along the way. In the bargain readers get a fair dose of Jewish history and a series of conversations with David. Most of these conversations are aimed directly at the reader as David relates the authentic story of his life along with a wide variety of opinions. The rest of the novel is made up of dialogue between David and the characters that he encounters in his life.

Yet despite being based on a religious text, such conversations are not simply a supplement to the original. Ironically, Heller's David is anything but religious. David's speech is suffused with profanity, sarcasm, and wit. Also, David goes out of his way to distance himself from references that make him appear devout.

Still, even more than distancing himself from religion, Heller's David takes liberty from all constraints of time and place. Despite living in ancient Israel, David seems to have an omniscient sense of everything that has happened both during and after his lifetime. He speaks often about figures such as Shakespeare, Freud, Einstein, and Nietzsche. He is knowledgeable about technology such as sewing machines, chemotherapy, and telegrams. And he is aware of how his reputation has persisted through the ages.

Ultimately, the novel itself is a mix. David's quick wit and odd knowledge of all things modern make the book both humorous and light. Yet at the same time the novel has a dark side. Everyone that David is close to either dies or betrays him. The book both begins and ends with David longing for comfort and being rejected. The structure of the book is an ancient tale, but the substance is decidedly modern, and frustrates categorization.

Bibliography
Heller, Joseph. *God Knows.* New York: Knopf, 1984.
Richler, Mordecai. "He Who Laughs Last," *New York Times,* 23 September 1984, Late City Final Edition, sec. 7, p. 1.

—Jacob Wilkes

God's Grace Bernard Malamud (1982)

Parabolic in form, *God's Grace*, Bernard Malamud's last published novel, consists of six books or chapters. The protagonist of the work is Calvin Cohn, a paleologist and ex-rabbinical student who finds himself the last man on the earth after he survives an atomic holocaust while researching on the ocean floor. On returning to his abandoned ship, Cohn curses God for allowing this act to occur. In the midst of his rant, God's voice rebukes Cohn. God admits he was unaware that Cohn survived and allows him enough time to make "peace."

While drifting amid the universal flood, Cohn discovers a chimpanzee, a pet of one of his fellow scientists, among the boat's supplies. Cohn renames the chimp Buz after an old friend. The two get along well and one day Cohn connects the two wires protruding from the animal's neck. The wires belong to an artificial larynx, implanted by Buz's former owner, and allow Buz to talk. Cohn teaches Buz theology, science, and human customs. Buz is a willing student but resists Cohn's Jewish interpretation of God, falling back on his previous owner's Christian belief that God is love.

Eventually the boat drifts into an unexposed land mass and Cohn and Buz swim ashore from the sinking vessel. After creating shelter, the two eventually discover they are not alone. They are joined by two gorillas. Cohn mistakenly kills one in fear and the other, named George, watches the lessons between Cohn and Buzz.

Buz later encounters five chimpanzees, whom he promptly names, and returns with them to Cohn. They learn to speak English as a result of Buz's teaching, and form a small community. Cohn decides to set up a school in an attempt to civilize the animals and create an evolutionary breakthrough. Each of the apes, except the surly Esau, learns a specific task in cultivating or maintaining the island's food supplies.

Cohn institutes a set of rules to govern the new civilization, and all the inhabitants agree to live by them. The rules are based on a humanist view that logic governs social interactions. Cohn, perplexed with God's nature and his own relationship with him, demands that "God is God" stand over Buz's desired "God is love" on the rule board.

The sole female chimp, Mary Madelyn, becomes a source of contention. Mary desires the human relationships described by Cohn in his school, particularly Shakespeare's depiction of Juliet. When the chimp emerges into heat, she flees the advances of the other apes, much to their dismay, to remain chaste. Instead, she offers herself to Cohn, who decides to copulate with her in hopes of creating a new evolutionary leap. Mary conceives and Cohn christens the child Rebekah. Cohn muses that this new species, which he names *Homo ethicalis,* will replace the destroyed *Homo sapiens.*

The island's social structure begins to erode. Taking Mary to wife threatens Cohn's relationship with the other apes. Cohn begins to wall in his home. The appearance of eight baboons, typically lower in the food chain than chimpanzees, causes further strain as Esau kills a baboon for its meat. The killings continue as the other unhappy chimps follow Esau's lead. Eventually Buz persuades Cohn to open his cave and the other apes swarm in. They kill Rebekah, causing the distraught Mary to present herself to each of the males. Cohn responds by clipping Buz's wires and denying him speech. The act makes all the apes incapable of human language. They force Cohn

to carry a bundle of wood up the mountain where Buz sacrifices him with a stone knife. Back in the valley, the gorilla George chants Kaddish for the death of the last man.

Malamud played with the ideas in the novel for some time. In 1973 he wrote that he was reading Jane Goodall's *In the Shadow of Man.* After also reading Charles Darwin and Stephen Jay Gould, to provide the theoretical foundation that communication with chimps was possible, Malamud became convinced that the elements of the novel were workable, and by 1975 he talked about writing with apes as subjects. As he continued to work, Malamud consulted with the Stanford University Center for Advanced Study in the Behavioral Sciences for further scientific guidance.

An abundance of allusions outline many of Malamud's themes. Usually the original tales are altered and so are the forms mimicked in the text. Literary allusions include *Romeo and Juliet, Robinson Crusoe,* Abraham and Isaac, and Jacob and Esau. The books owned by Cohn after the flood are *The Works of Shakespeare,* a Pentateuch, a dictionary, and a textbook, *The Great Apes.* Also, *Tempest* references dominate the naming and arrogance assumed by Cohn in human superiority.

Critics also see the work as a response to the question of how God could allow the Holocaust, a theme running throughout Malamud's writing but climaxing in this work.

Public response to the work was mixed. The *Guardian*'s J. G. Ballard decried the work as "too preposterous to be taken on a realistic level, and too burdened by naturalistic detail to be a convincing fable." Edmund Fuller's *Wall Street Journal* piece disagreed, stating, "Malamud may have created his most lasting work."

Bibliography

Cronin, Gloria L. "The Complex Irony of Grace: A Study of Bernard Malamud's *God's Grace.*" *Studies in American Jewish Literature* 5 (1986): 119–128.

Steed, J. P. "Malamud's *God's Grace* and the Theme of Reversal: Or, Old Joke, Better Version." *Studies in American Jewish Literature* 20 (2001): 17–28.

—Eliot Wilcox

Gold, Herbert (1924–)

Herbert Gold's philosophy of writing may be summed up by a passage from FATHERS: A NOVEL IN THE FORM OF A MEMOIR (1967): "Though the writer may believe that his words can destroy his enemies—and he fears this power, too—in fact they do not kill. It is liberating to discover that shedding light is a worthier goal than murdering with words—even worthier than the intention to cause love. Like sixteen-ounce gloves, words are better suited to causing the truth to manifest itself" (241).

Born in 1924 to Russian-Jewish immigrant parents, Herbert Gold grew up in depression-era Cleveland, Ohio, worked in his father's grocery store, served in the U.S. Army Military Intelligence during World War II, and returned to earn B.A. and M.A. degrees in philosophy from Columbia University in New York. Gold has held several fellowships, including a Fulbright to the Sorbonne, Paris, and has taught at several universities, including the University of California at Berkeley, Stanford, and Harvard. After his first marriage (to Edith Durbin from 1948 to 1956) ended in divorce, Gold left the Midwest and settled in San Francisco. Excising his accomplishments and stylizing his Jewish upbringing, Gold recounts this early part of his life in a mix of fiction and autobiography in *Fathers: A Novel in the Form of a Memoir* (1967), and *Family: A Novel in the Form of a Memoir* (1981).

Gold's entry into fiction was promising, and he was heralded as a skillful chronicler of postwar society and relationships, as in his first novel, *Birth of a Hero* (1951), about a middle-age man who seeks his lost "heroism" through an affair. Gold was on time exploring the subject of civil rights in *The Prospect Before Us* (1954), about a hotel owner who champions a black guest and causes his own destruction. Gold was also praised for his extensive use of and skill with colloquialism and slang (although sometimes to excess and the alienation of the uninitiated reader). An example is the carnival jargon in *The Man Who Was Not with It* (1956), a story of morphine addiction, which is considered by some to be Gold's best novel.

Gold's two divorces influenced his writing, beginning with his portrayal of the disintegration of a marriage in *The Optimist* (1959), the title story from the short story collection *Love and Like* (1960), and his short story "Divorce as Moral Act" from the collection *Age of Happy Problems* (1962). The fallout from divorce is also a theme in *Salt* (1963), a stylized novel about the sexual exploits of two bar-hopping, 30-something New Yorkers. It was seen as the best portrayal of New York City in years. But, some critics of *Salt* saw Gold's satire beginning to slip into cliché. One critic reviewed *Fathers* (1967) unfavorably, finding its Jewish nostalgia predictable in the way that southern fiction had become predictable: tired, worn out, a formulaic bildungsroman with a protagonist that might as well have been a Unitarian as a Jew. A line from *Fathers* sums it up: "We are all sometimes slaves. And afterwards we write purple passages" (160).

In 1963 Gold moved to San Francisco (curiously, if not ironically, settling on Russian Hill). This movement from his Midwest roots to the restlessness of California is reflected in his novels, as he began to use West Coast themes in his writing. Some critics felt that Gold had come too late, that other California-bashing authors had already assassinated all the easy targets of hippie California counterculture. What Gold had tried to do with his New York images and New Yorkers, he now tried to do with California and Californians, but being a transplant, he was behind the curve and blasé, as in *The Great American Jackpot* (1969), a story of self-discovery set in 1960s San Francisco; *Swiftie the Magician* (1974), about a New York TV-movie producer lost in the California counterculture of drugs and celebrities; and *Waiting for Cordelia* (1977), about a Berkeley professor absorbed in his study of an activist prostitute.

With *Slave Trade* (1979), Gold combined a previously used theme of divorce with his academic studies and travel writing of Haiti to form a tragic story of the sex-slave trade in Haitian boys. In *He/She* (1980), Gold gave full focus to the theme of divorce in a detailed study of the breakdown of marriage, the search for freedom, and the human tendency to seek one's happiness in another person. *He/She* was well received by Gold's contemporary writers Larry McMurtry and Joyce Carol

Oates. Gold then returned to his Midwestern Jewish roots in *Family: A Novel in the Form of a Memoir* (1981), the companion to *Fathers: A Novel in the Form of a Memoir,* but with the focus now on his relationship to his mother, Frieda.

The Primus paperback editions of Gold's *Fathers: A Novel in the Form of a Memoir,* (re)titled simply *Fathers* (1991), and *Family: A Novel in the Form of a Memoir* (1991), bear a quote from Saul Bellow on the back cover: "I put Herbert Gold at the head of my small list of writers who have their own eyes and are capable of making fiction which gives pleasure." Gold has enjoyed a long writing career, winning the California Literature Medal in 1968 for *Fathers: A Novel in the Form of a Memoir,* the Commonwealth Club Award for best novel in 1982 for *Family: A Novel in the Form of a Memoir,* and the Sherwood Anderson Prize for fiction in 1989. Ultimately, however, Gold's writing has never measured up to the high expectations many critics held for him. "Potential" is a word often used in describing Gold's work, as critics seem to find aspects of his work to praise without giving his talent full recognition. Gold is seen as having achieved a near-greatness; he is often compared to and described as coming close to Salinger, Updike, Bellow, Roth, and Malamud, but is always left standing just outside their esteemed circle. Gold's own declaration on writing from *Fathers: A Novel in the Form of a Memoir* reveals the high standards he set for himself as a writer, and might well stand as his rebuttal to much of the disappointing critical appraisal: "My father, in his effort at control of the shivering void, silently hunting, had long ago sworn without words to make some abstract unity of the flesh and sense pummeling about him. I swore to try to make, perhaps with words and rhythm, something more than what the ants make in their subtle flow across the floor of the world" (250).

—Robert S. Means

Goldstein, Rebecca Newberger (1950–)

Rebecca Goldstein, in her 2005 biographical study on Kurt Gödel entitled *Incompleteness,* notes a striking similarity between her subject and his close friend, Albert Einstein: both are "political exiles, who spoke the same native tongue and found themselves strolling the improbable landscape of suburban New Jersey." This similarity connects Gödel not only to colleagues at Princeton, but also to protagonists in Goldstein's texts. The themes of exile, searching for a home, and negotiating a path between intellectual ability and emotional feeling are among those that connect Goldstein's two nonfiction studies, as well as her five novels and one collection of stories.

Born in 1950, Rebecca Newberger, one of four children, was raised in a strictly Orthodox home in White Plains, New York. Goldstein attributes her love of stories, and even her sense of heroism, both real and imagined, to her father's role as a storyteller and teacher. He served as a cantor in a local congregation and introduced her as a child to the stories of Peretz and Singer and instilled in her a recognition of the importance of history, text, and narrative.

As she recounts in her most recent work, *Betraying Spinoza* (2006), her first introduction to Spinoza occurred while attending an Orthodox yeshiva school on Manhattan's Lower East Side. That brush with a larger world instilled a desire, tinged with urgency, to "become knowledgeable" and "experience the sweet breath of real knowledge." After graduating, Goldstein earned an undergraduate degree in philosophy at Barnard College (1972), and a doctorate from Princeton University (1977). In recognizing the philosophers who most influenced her, Goldstein traces her intellectual journey from her Orthodox Jewish childhood to her current rationalist stance: Abraham, Plato, Descartes, Hume, Kant, William James, and Simone Weil.

Following graduate school, Goldstein joined the philosophy faculty at Barnard College. It was there, in 1983, two years after the birth of her older daughter, and in the wake of her father's death, that Goldstein published *The Mind-Body Problem,* the novel that would initiate her career as a writer. *The Mind-Body Problem,* Goldstein declares, was written as "a lark" in "a matter of weeks." In contrast to her work in philosophy and her commitment to logic and rational explanation, writing fiction provides her with a means to explore the puzzles and irrationality of human emotions and psychology. The symmetry and sense of a story and its narrative method come together in a seemingly random way. Goldstein's approach to writing involves using these two opposing approaches to understand the world around her.

Renee Feuer of *The Mind-Body Problem,* a philosophy graduate student at Princeton, searches for both an intellectual and an emotional home. She abandons her Orthodox Jewish background to pursue her studies, which she leaves once she marries Noam Himmel, a mathematical genius. Until both are able to recognize and value not only the pure beauty of mathematical and philosophical truths but also what it means to be true to each other, the marriage remains unfulfilling.

The Late-Summer Passion of a Woman of Mind (1989), MAZEL (1995), PROPERTIES OF LIGHT (2000), and many of the stories in *Strange Attractors* (1993) pick up the thematic ideas that Goldstein introduces in *The Mind-Body Problem.* The novels all retain important connections to academia. In spite of embracing academic achievement and creativity, Goldstein explores the idea that, to some degree, the institutionalization of ideas threatens to stifle them. In *Late-Summer Passion,* Eva Mueller, a single, beautiful, middle-aged philosophy professor surrenders to the youthful ebullience of one of her students. Recognizing her emotional strength enables her to remember her long-repressed personal history; she also recalls her more distant past, remembering her family's history and complicity in Nazi Germany.

History is also an essential narrative feature of *Mazel,* the winner of the Edward Lewis Wallant Award and the National Jewish Book Award for Fiction. Here the impending birth of Sasha's grandchild inspires her to recall her childhood in a Polish shtetl, her rebellious coming of age in Warsaw, and her journey to New York. Sasha abandons the community and practices of her parents, grandparents, and siblings but regards them with renewed respect once she understands that her granddaughter's return to traditional Jewish values is part of the legacy they both share, a legacy that is underscored by Sasha's historical narrative of self.

In 1996 the MacArthur Foundation awarded Goldstein one of their "genius grants" to enable her to devote herself exclusively to her writing. *Properties of Light,* written during the award period, also draws on the themes of exile and place. Goldstein tells readers that the intellectual outcast in her novel, Samuel Mallach, is based on the brilliant but largely marginalized Princeton physicist David Bohm. Goldstein resurrects Bohm as Mallach by giving him a devoted disciple, Justin Childs, who not only values his past work in quantum mechanics, but believes that Mallach has more physics to give to the world. Together with Mallach's daughter, Dana, the three set out to change our understanding of truth, love, and the love of truth.

The Dark Sister (1991), very different from her other novels, explores the many polarities that Goldstein addresses in all of her works. These include the relationship between the mind and the body, the presence of lightness and dark, beauty and its absence, emotional value and truth, the role of reason in the face of imagination, the effect of the past on the present, and loss and fulfillment. The novel's protagonist, Hedda, who has a deformed body but a brilliant literary imagination, finds refuge in an isolated house in Maine and begins to write her next novel. Hedda's novel, which involves multiple sets of twinlike characters, fits within Goldstein's story and its various sets of parallel characters. Ultimately, in *The Dark Sister,* as in many of her other texts, Goldstein seems to want readers to recognize that the separation between mind and body, truth and construct, reality and invention, art and science, is a razor-thin mirror of reflection.

Bibliography

Budick, Emily Miller. "Rebecca Goldstein: Jewish Visionary in Skirts." *Hollins Critic* 34, no. 2 (April 1997): 1–13.

Goldstein, Rebecca. "Dark Afterthoughts on Fiction and the Self." *Dark Clock* 1 (March 2004): 92–97.

—**Jessica Lang**

The Golems of Gotham: A Novel
Thane Rosenbaum (2002)

References to the golem date back to the Bible (Psalms 139:116) and the Talmud and continue through modern times. According to legend, the golem is a body formed out of clay and brought to life by uttering a combination of Hebrew letters and Kabbalistic mystical formulas. The most famous creator of a golem is Rabbi Yehuda Loew, the Maharal of Prague (1513–1609), who shaped a golem out of clay from the river Moldau for the purpose of saving his people from their enemies. A figure of strength but lacking the power of speech or intellect, the golem of Prague accomplished the mission of protecting the Jews. Eventually, he became too powerful, went out of control, and destroyed everything in his path. Rabbi Loew was forced to return him to inanimate matter.

The story of the golem has been a source of inspiration for writers (Gustave Meyrink, 1915), artists, playwrights (H. Leivick, 1921), and filmmakers (Paul Wegener, 1920). Like contemporary authors such as ELIE WIESEL, I. B. SINGER, and CYNTHIA OZICK, THANE ROSENBAUM, in *The Golems of Gotham,* has formulated his own interpretation of the legend. While the novel incorporates characteristics of the traditional golem, it transposes the legend onto a post-Holocaust tale that focuses on the relationship between second- and third-generation survivors Oliver Levin and his 14-year-old daughter, Ariel. Rescue and loss are dominant themes throughout the book. Ariel wants to defend her father, not against an external enemy, as with the original golem, but against "the enemy within." Oliver has not come to terms with the suicide of his parents—Holocaust survivors—and the loss of his wife, who left him when Ariel was two. A mystery writer, he also suffers from writer's block.

With mud collected from the Hudson River and playing her Klezmer violin, Ariel conjures up golems, who take the form of her grandparents. Inexperienced in kabbalistic formulas, Ariel also erroneously summons the golems of six eminent Holocaust survivor-writers who took their own lives: Primo (Levi), Paul (Celan), Jean (Améry), Jerzy (Kosinski), Piotr (Rawicz), and Tadeusz (Borowski). All eight, including Oliver's parents, resemble ghosts more than golems and the book becomes a ghost story, a fantasy imbued with comic and serious elements.

Unlike Prague's golem, these golems are playful: They glide around New York City, riding the subways and the carousel. More important, they are compassionate and strive to make New York a better place. Intellectuals, they have dialogues with each other, discussing the need to heal and whether words can change the world. Eventually, their rage at the trivialization and sanitation of the Holocaust leads them to wreak havoc on Manhattan, recalling the destruction caused by the original golem. But this is not sustained, for their principal task is to liberate Oliver; his words start flowing and he starts dealing with the losses in his life. He is pushed to know himself, where he comes from and how to "really live." Paradoxically, these writers, so articulate in their own writing, have left no suicide notes. How could they have taken their own lives after having survived the atrocities? The absence of an explanation obsesses Oliver as it does Rosenbaum. The novel asks questions rather than offering answers. It does bring to light, however, painful issues that weigh upon Rosenbaum and children of survivors: the scars of their parents, breakdown of communication, transmission of memory, the need to reimagine and restore what has been lost, to tell the tale, and above all, the moral and ethical dilemmas of post-Holocaust existence.

Bibliography

Berger, Alan L. "Myth, Mysticism, and Memory: The Holocaust in Thane Rosenbaum's *The Golems of Gotham.*" *Studies in American Jewish Literature* 24 (2005).

McNett, Gavin. "Festival of Wrath," *New York Times,* 9 January 2002, p. F21.

—Ellen S. Fine

Gone to Soldiers Marge Piercy (1987)

Although its title was probably inspired by the popular 1961 Pete Seeger protest song "Where Have All the Flowers Gone?," *Gone to Soldiers* is a

World War II novel in the epic tradition of such novels as James Jones's *From Here to Eternity* and NORMAN MAILER's *The Naked and the Dead*. Unlike those novels, however, it focuses primarily on the European theater, employs alternating narrative points of view, and concentrates particularly on Jewish characters and issues, both in America and in Europe. MARGE PIERCY obviously took the writing of this novel very seriously and personally. The novel's dedication—to her grandmother Hannah, "who was a solace to my childhood and who was a storyteller even in the English that never fit comfortably in her mouth"—underscores this personal sense of seriousness. In her "After Words" to the novel, Piercy discusses the difficulty that she, as an independent writer, experienced in completing the seven-year project and gratefully acknowledges everyone who helped her, beginning with "all the colleges and universities at which I did workshops, lectures, and everything but a fan dance." All of this suggests that, for Piercy, *Gone to Soldiers* has an aesthetic purposefulness beyond what one might find in her other work. This purposefulness, however, does not save the novel from the elements of popular marketing appeal with which she infuses it. These elements, as might be expected in a novel that Piercy must have counted on for revenue, mostly revolve around sex and romance. For example, there is something here for almost every sexual orientation, proclivity, and infidelity, which is not a problem in itself, but Piercy fails to deal with the sexuality with the same stylistic skill and insight characteristic of her other work, especially her poetry. In addition, the chapter titles are an odd mix of romance clichés, religious allusions, popular phrases, and other miscellaneous references such as: "The Crooked Desires of the Heart Fulfilled," "Flutterings," "Wither Thou Goest," "L'Chaim," "The Die Is Cast," "Lost and Found," and so forth. Thus, *Gone to Soldiers* remains an awkward hybrid of serious theme and popular execution, with more than a hint of the page-turning romance novel.

The novel's story line has four basic threads, each tied to a different family and home base: Coates (East Coast college town), Kahan (New York), Lévi-Monot (France), and Siegel (Detroit). All these familial threads revolve somehow around one another as the various characters interrelate throughout the novel as it traces this four-family diaspora. Like Faulkner's *As I Lay Dying*, *Gone to Soldiers* unfolds in sections, each with a different narrative focalization that repeats throughout the text. There are 10 different characters on whom these sections focus, each with a different number of total sections: Louise Kahan (12), Daniel Balaban (9), Jacqueline Lévi-Monot (14), Abra [Balaban] (11), Naomi [Lévi-Monot] Siegal (10), Bernice Coates (10), Jeff Coates (8), Ruthie [Siegal] Feldstein (11), Duvey Siegal (3), and Murray Feldstein (5). Jacqueline, a Jewish French Resistance fighter and concentration camp survivor who keeps up a regular journal, is the only first-person narrator. The other sections are told from a third-person limited omniscient perspective. Even with this ambitious plot and narrative approach, *Gone to Soldiers* keeps the overall narrative movement of the novel from becoming too fragmented or confusing. Louise, a romance writer publishing under the penname Annette Hollander Sinclair, is a middle-aged divorcée who becomes a war correspondent for *Colliers*. In the course of the novel, she crosses paths with virtually all the other main characters. The much younger Daniel, for example, becomes her lover in London; she meets Jacqueline in a postwar refugee camp; she has regular contact with Abra, the OSS assistant and lover of her ex-husband, Oscar; she meets with Bernice and the other women shuttle flyers as part of a story she's doing on WASPs. The other narrative threads work in much the same way. Jeff, fighting with the French Resistance under the nom de guerre of Vendôme, becomes Jacqueline's comrade in arms and lover before he dies; Abra marries Daniel at the end of the novel; Ruthie and Murray, a veteran who survived fighting in the Pacific theater, finally marry; Louise gets back with her ex-husband, who promises to give up his philandering; and Naomi goes with her older sister, Jacqueline, to work on founding the state of Israel.

In *Gone to Soldiers* Piercy explores the Jewish contributions to the war effort, even in the face of anti-Semitism, and celebrates the indomitable spirit of that community as manifested in the lives of her individual characters, whether, like Ruthie, they keep families together while working factory jobs on the home front, or, like Jacqueline, do whatever they have to do to stay alive as guerrilla fighters or concentration camp inmates.

Bibliography
Grödal, Hanne Tang. "Words, Words, Words." *Dolphin: Publications of the English Department, University of Aarhus* 18 (Spring 1990): 21–26.
Hammond, Karla. "A Conversation with Marge Piercy." *Pulp* 1, no. 1 (1978): 10–12.
—**Phillip A. Snyder**

Goodbye, Columbus and Five Short Stories
Philip Roth (1959)

Goodbye, Columbus and Five Short Stories (1959) launched Philip Roth's literary career. Saul Bellow, recognizing the 26-year old author's talent, observed that Roth seemed to appear not as a newborn "howling into the world, blind and bare" but as one already "with nails, hair, and teeth, speaking coherently." *Goodbye Columbus* won the 1960 National Book Award. In 1969 it was made into a film starring Ali MacGraw and Richard Benjamin. One of the short stories, "Defender of the Faith," won second prize in the 1960 O'Henry Short Story Contest.

Goodbye Columbus explores the dreams of Neil Klugman, a 23-year-old librarian living with his Aunt Gladys and Uncle Max in a middle-income area in Newark, New Jersey. Invited to his cousin Doris's posh Green Lane Country Club, he meets Brenda Patimkin, who lives in Short Hills, the affluent suburb west of Newark. Neil is smitten by Brenda's beauty, self-assurance, and sexual provocativeness, as well as by the ease and plenty that are part of her life. As Brenda's guest first at the country club and then at the Patimkin home, Neil enjoys a wonderful summer romance.

The novella also presents information about Neil's work in the Newark Public Library, where he always saves an edition of Gauguin reproduc-

tions for a little African-American boy who enjoys the art books in the library. The boy loves the lush pictures of Tahiti, which Neil explains is "an island in the Pacific Ocean." The boy asks, "That ain't no place you could go, is it? Like a *ree-sort*?" (37). For Neil, Brenda and Short Hills are his dream of joy. Short Hills for him is "rose-colored, like a Gauguin stream" (38).

The novella is a love story of two young people, a coming-of-age tale, and also a satire on the materialism and conformity in the American Jewish bourgeois scene. Roth exhibits "sheer playfulness and deadly seriousness" as he mocks Neil's having bought into the belief that a wealthy way of life is the achievement of the American dream. *Goodbye Columbus* attacks the 18-year-old Brenda and her nouveau riche family who—because of Ben Patimkin's successful plumbing business—moved from Newark to the affluent Short Hills. Ben encourages his two children to depend on him for a life of ease and comfort. He provides a place for son Ron in the family business and assures Brenda that he will do the same for the man she marries. Neil Klugman begins to dream of being that man.

The Patimkin family views wealth as a sign of success in American society. They are consumers: of food, sports equipment, clothes. A memorable image for the Patimkin family is their refrigerator, brimming over with all kinds of fruit, "flowing out of boxes and staining everything scarlet." He states with awe: "Fruit grew in their refrigerator and sporting goods dropped from their trees" (43). Roth describes the conspicuous consumption of the Patimkins in gross terms. At dinner their "words gurgled into mouthfuls, the syntax chopped and forgotten in heapings, spillings, and gorgings" (22). Roth mocks Neil's awe of the Patimkin family's success. For Neil, Brenda is "the King's daughter" (21). He accepts Brenda's domineering attitude and her mother's snide comments about his having a job beneath her daughter's expectation. Only at the end of the novel is Neil able to see the shallowness of the materialistic values of the Patimkins, and only then is he able to say good-bye to it all, including the image of Ron as football hero at Ohio State University, clinging to memories of the past by playing a record of "Good-bye Columbus."

Roth also uses the Patimkins to satirize the shallowness of members of the American Jewish community who have given up their Jewish identity and individuality to assimilate into American society. In his desire to be all American, Ben Patimkin has divorced the family not only from their earlier middle-class life in Newark but also from their Jewish background: "They're *goyim*, my kids," Mr. Patimkin tells Neil, "that's how much they understand" (94). In the novella, being divorced from one's background symbolizes a loss of identity and contributes to the shallow values of Brenda and her family.

Brenda breaks off the relationship with Neil because of her parents' anger when they find out that she and Neil have been intimate. Ben tells his daughter that he will purchase a coat for her: "I am willing to forgive and call Buy Gones, Buy Gones" (127). Brenda tells Neil that he cannot visit at thanksgiving: "They're still my parents. . . . They have given me everything I've wanted, haven't they?" (133–34).

Neil realizes that he cannot remain in the shallow Patimkin world. He wishes to look at his inner self, not just his outer one, and he broods over the difference between love and lust: "I was sure I had loved Brenda, though standing there, I knew I couldn't any longer" (135). Brenda, on the other hand, remains an immature, dependent woman.

The novella and *Five Short Stories* mock behavior patterns developed more fully in Roth's later novels. In "Eli the Fanatic," perhaps the most famous of the *Five Short Stories,* the Jewish suburbanites of Woodenton are upset when Leo Tzuref opens a Yeshivah in their town, fearing that the new arrivals will call attention to the fact that they, too, are Jews. The theme of assimilation is also evident in Roth's later fiction such as *I Married a Communist* (1998), AMERICAN PASTORAL (1997), and *The* HUMAN STAIN (2000).

Bibliography

Fredericksen, Brooke. "Home Is Where the Text Is: Exile, Homeland, and Jewish American Writing." *Studies in American Jewish Literature* 11, no. 1 (Spring 1992): 36–44.

Kartiganer, Donald. "Fictions of Metamorphosis: From *Goodbye, Columbus* to *Portnoy's Complaint.*" In *Reading Philip Roth.* New York: St. Martin's Press, 1988.

—Elaine B. Safer

Goodman, Allegra (1967–)

Allegra Goodman was born in Brooklyn in 1967 and spent most of the summers of her childhood in upstate New York, where she stayed with her grandparents in the ultra Orthodox community of Kaaterskill Falls. For most of her early life she was raised in the Jewish community in Honolulu, where her parents taught at the University of Hawaii. Her father was a geneticist and her mother a philosopher. She graduated from the prestigious Punahou School in Honolulu in 1985. During her school years she had the attention of both parents, who encouraged her writing by allowing her to read her work to them, thus forming her first writers group. She wrote the short story "Variant Text" before graduating from high school and saw it in print in *Commentary* during her freshman year of college.

Goodman studied as an undergraduate at Harvard University, graduating in 1989. She spent the following year in England, where she married David Goodman, who was studying mathematics at Cambridge University. Both moved to Stanford the following year, David to pursue theoretical computer science, and Allegra to pursue English literature and Shakespeare studies. At this time she began publishing the stories in *Commentary* that were ultimately collected in her first book, *Total Immersion* (1989), a *New York Times* Notable Book of the Year. By 1995 she had won the Whiting Writer's Award, her work was included in *Prize Stories*, and that year she received an O'Henry Award. During the early 1990s she steadily published fiction in the *New Yorker* and completed her next book, *The Family Markowitz* (1996). She earned a Ph.D. in English from Stanford in 1997. She received the Edward Lewis

Wallant Book Award in 1999. Her impressive list of awards includes a John Harvard scholarship, a Mellon Fellowship in the humanities, Presidential scholar in the Arts for Writing, Younger Scholars Grant, National Endowment for the Humanities, an Elizabeth Carey Agassiz scholarship, the Briggs Prize for English, and the Whiting Writers Award, carrying with it a prize of $30,000.

KAATERSKILL FALLS, her first novel, was published in August 1998. It describes, through the eyes of Elizabeth, its central protagonist, the fragile and circumscribed world of the Kirschner Orthodox in Kaaterskill Falls. It was followed in 2001 by *Paradise Park,* featuring an absurd hippie-era female religious quester and a host of pilgrims all engaged in a comic odyssey via all the organized and not-so-organized religions and isms of the post-seventies moment. It is based on the structural models of St. Augustine's *Confessions* and Chaucer's *Canterbury Tales.* What slinks its way toward Canterbury in Goodman's postmodern moment are the chaotic postmodern pilgrims of the late 20th century. Her fiction is characterized by a confident, mature, witty voice, and a developed alternate world. The satirical narrative voice always suggests an ear pitched perfectly to brilliant, zany, or witty drawing room conversations. Her humor characteristically derives from her observations of the relatively insular Jewish community. The comic tensions that run through her works arise from the constrictions of the tightly knit ethnic community, its binding ethical structures, and an individualism firmly constrained by allegiance to authority and tradition. Every protagonist experiences the rigid and even arbitrary limits placed on self-expression. Goodman believes that all art is philosophical, and she is less concerned with the epiphanic, the visible or the invisible manifestations of grace than she is with the comic human obstacles to religious experience—parochialism, the intransigence of the ordinary, the quotidian, and the stubborn fleshliness of the ordinary. Her fiction resonates with endless comic postmodern debates about class, race, otherness, power, difference, dialogue, ecology, absolute truth, transcendental pretense, the authority of the text, and world peace—in short, the conditions of the postmodern spiritual pilgrimage. The inevitable sites of these debates are the tangled byways of family psychology, kitchens, synagogues, universities, weddings, life passages, think tanks, interfaith dialogues, conferences, and even the Western Wall (Wailing Wall) in Jerusalem. She operates within the combined traditions of university-educated discourse communities, Yiddish comedy, and urbane *New Yorker* social satire. Her works are saturated in biblical allusions, postmodern philosophical constructs, Jewish theological traditions, liturgical phrases, Jewish tradition, and Jewish community. Her expressed goal as a writer is to capture the religious and spiritual dimensions of Judaism in America in the postassimilationist era. Speaking of ethnic American literature, she writes: "Ultimately all writing is ethnic writing, and all writers are ethnic writers grappling with great ambitions and a particular language and culture. . . . To make specific cultural experience an asset instead of a liability. I look at it as an old problem, and I turn to old resources—the deep Jewish tradition beneath the self-deprecating Jewish jokes, the Biblical language and the poetry welling up beneath layers of satire." Onto her crowded, noisy canvases, she projects Jewish familial disputes, temple politics, orthodoxy fights, family scandals, cross-cultural misunderstandings, a host of postmodern philosophical and gender conundrums, personal neuroses, colliding obsessions, and antic personalities.

Bibliography

Cronin, Gloria L. "Seasons of Our (Dis)Content, or Orthodox Women in Walden: Allegra Goodman's *Kaaterskill Falls.*" In *Connections and Collisons: Identities in Contemporary Jewish-American Women's Writing.* Edited by Lois Rubin. Newark: University of Delaware Press, 2005.

Halio, Jay L., and Ben Siegel, eds. "Immersions in the Postmodern: The Fiction of Allegra Goodman." In *Daughters of Valor: Contemporary Jewish-American Women Writers.* Newark: University of Delaware Press, 1998.

—**Gloria L. Cronin**

Gratz, Rebecca (1781–1869)

"Beautiful in face, aristocratic in bearing, dignified in manner, noble of soul and pure of heart" (xvii), "the leading American Jewess of her day" (v)—so David Philipson, the editor of LETTERS OF REBECCA GRATZ (1929), described Rebecca Gratz. Born in Philadelphia on March 4, 1781, Rebecca Gratz was the seventh of 12 children born to Michael and Miriam Gratz. Michael was prominent, along with his brother, Barnard, in Philadelphia business and politics. They were supporters of the American Revolution, both signing the Non-Importation Resolutions (opposing the Stamp Act) of 1765. Rebecca and her siblings "constituted what was doubtless the foremost Jewish family in their day in the United States" (Philipson xi), and of Rebecca and her four sisters, "one admirer said [they] ought to have been called not Gratzes but Graces" (Wagenknecht 3). Rebecca's older brother, Hyman, founded Gratz College in Philadelphia, and her younger brother, Benjamin, moved to Kentucky, where he became a close associate of Henry Clay and active in Kentucky politics and civic affairs.

Generous, charitable, and public spirited, Rebecca founded or participated in founding the Female Association for the Relief of Women and Children in Reduced Circumstances (1801—she was only 20 at the time), the Philadelphia Orphan Society (1815), the Hebrew Benevolent Society (1819), the Hebrew Sunday School Society (1838), and the Jewish Foster Home and Orphan Society (1855).

The portraits of Rebecca Gratz by artist Thomas Sully (1783–1872) (as reprinted in Ashton) reveal an artist in love with his subject. An early portrait of a young Rebecca casts her as a biblically dressed Jewish princess of soft, classical beauty. Later portraits portray her features as thinner, sharper, a strikingly beautiful, strikingly modern woman, strong but eminently feminine, a mix of capability and mystery. As Sully put it in his notebook: "[N]ever seen a more striking Hebraic face . . . there was about Rebecca Gratz all that princess of Blood Royal would have coveted" (Wagenknecht 6). Thomas Sully was just two years older than Rebecca Gratz. He was also flattering in his portrait of Rebecca's younger brother Benjamin. But other artist's portraits of Rebecca are undeniably plain, if not frumpy by comparison, very much proper Regency pieces.

And yet for all her beauty and charm, Rebecca Gratz never married. Publicly, she poured herself into her philanthropy, and privately, she cared for her unmarried brothers, and reared the nine orphaned children (ages three to 16) of her sister, Rachel.

In spite of all her civic work, philanthropy, and admired beauty, Gratz was essentially a private person. Yet her fame has endured largely due to her connection (fact or legend, depending on whose version one reads) with a popular literary character of her day. As Philipson says, Rebecca Gratz "is generally supposed to be the original of the famous character, Rebecca, in Sir Walter Scott's novel Ivanhoe [(1819)]" (vii)—declared by so competent a critic as Thackery to be "the sweetest character in the whole range of fiction" (xix). The story goes that Washington Irving, a close friend of the Gratz family, so impressed Scott with his description of Rebecca (then in her mid to late 30s), that Scott then created his own Rebecca character in Ivanhoe. In an alleged letter, Scott is to have written to Irving in 1819 after the publication of Ivanhoe and asked "[H]ow do you like your Rebecca? Does the Rebecca I have pictured compare well with the pattern given?" Gratz herself, when asked if she been the pattern for Scott's Rebecca, answered "[T]hey say so, my dear" (Philipson xx), and in her letters refers to Scott's Rebecca as "my namesake" (April 4, 1820). Perhaps there was also some give and take between literary character and character study, for Gratz also patterned herself after Scott's Rebecca, calling her, in her letters, "a representation of a good girl as I think human nature can reach" (May 10, 1820).

Another legend has it that, like the Rebecca of Ivanhoe, Gratz foreswore to marry the love of her life, Samuel Ewing, the son of a Christian minister. There is no mention of Ewing in any of Gratz's published letters, but at his death, she was apparently accorded (by Ewing's wife) an hour of privacy with Ewing's body, leaving three white roses and her miniature in the casket (Wagenknecht 8–9).

Rebecca Gratz died in Philadelphia on August 29 (as listed by Philipson, August 27 as listed by Wagenknecht), 1869, at the age of 88. Looking back on her own life, it was not the celebrity she gained from *Ivanhoe* that she cherished. It was her charitable work, especially the Hebrew Sunday School Society, where she helped make the textbooks, and served as president from 1838 to 1864 (resigning at age 82), that was, from accounts in her letters, her most satisfying achievement, "the crowning happiness of my life" (Wagenknecht 6).

Bibliography

Ashton, Dianne. *Rebecca Gratz: Women and Judaism in Antebellum America.* Detroit: Wayne State University Press, 1997.

Gratz, Rebecca. *Letters of Rebecca Gratz,* edited, and with an introduction and notes by Rabbi David Philipson. Philadelphia: Jewish Publication Society of America, 1929.

Wagenknecht, Edward. *Daughters of the Covenant: Portraits of Six Jewish Women.* Amherst, Mass.: University of Massachusetts Press, 1983.

—**Robert S. Means**

Hecht, Ben (1894–1964)

Benjamin (Ben) Hecht was born February 28, 1894, on the Lower East Side of New York City. His parents, Joseph and Sarah, had arrived from Minsk, Russia, in 1878, though they did not marry until 1892. Ben studied the violin, went to the Yiddish theater with his Aunt Lubi, and very briefly attended the Broome Street school. In 1899 the family moved to Chicago. In 1903 they moved again, this time to Racine, Wisconsin. In 1908 he and Peter, a younger brother, joined a circus and did a trapeze act as the Youngest Daredevils in America.

High school for Ben meant football, playing violin in a saloon orchestra, and writing rhymes for the high school yearbook. In 1910, having decided to be a writer, he moved in with his Uncle Harris and Aunt Chashe in Chicago. Although Hecht later lived in many cities, he was never again to achieve the harmony with a city that he had in Chicago.

Through a connection with a friend of his uncle's, he soon got a job with the *Chicago Daily Journal* as a picture chaser. He quickly became known as an accomplished picture thief, like today's paparazzi. A year or so later he wrote a Victorian sob story about a lady's last virtue—his editor told him it was worthless. Still unsure of himself, he began making up news stories, usually perpetrating frauds or scooping the other papers. Fortunately, Sherman Duffy, the sports editor, liked and

appreciated him and had him promoted to full-time reporter. By 1915 he had become the *Journal's* star reporter. That same year he took a job at the *Chicago Daily News* and became a member of the so-called Chicago School. Soon after, he began publishing in Margaret Anderson's *Little Review*.

In these years the Chicago Literary Renaissance was taking its first breath. Hecht's name became associated with a diverse group of writers including Francis Hackett, Kenneth Sawyer Goodman, Margery Curry, Floyd Dell, Sherwood Anderson, Maxwell Bodenheim, Margaret Anderson, Harriet Monroe, and Carl Sandburg.

The Chicago Renaissance (beginning in the 1880s and achieving a more tangible presence with the founding of Harriet Monroe's *Poetry: A Magazine of Verse* in 1912) owed its energy, glamour, publicity, and significance in large part to Ben Hecht, who epitomized the Chicago Renaissance. It was no coincidence that he and most of the important prose writers of the period from 1912 to 1925, like Sherwood Anderson, were newspapermen. Decadent naturalists, impressionistic realists, sentimental tough guys, they were described by H. L. Mencken in 1920 as the members of the "literary capital of the U.S." Hecht, looking back three decades later, recalled the scene as a "Backyard Athens."

As the writers drifted to the publishing houses and the bigger checks in the East, "the end of 1917 saw the Chicago Renaissance on the wane" (MacAdams 41). Married and deeply in debt, Hecht began a two-year stint of cranking out two stories a week for Mencken's *Smart Set*. In addition, he published five stories and three poems in the *Little Review*.

A week after the Armistice that ended World War I was signed, Hecht, several thousand dollars in debt, became the Berlin correspondent for the *News*. In spring 1918, freelancing articles for the "Book Page" in the *News*, Hecht, together with his wife, Marie, bought a house, which they furnished far beyond their means. Hecht's answer to Marie's complaining was, "My God, can't you see I'm going to be rich" (MacAdams 55). That summer, 1920, he quit the *News* and became a public relations executive who handled accounts for several of J. P. Morgan's fund drives. "Hecht did the copywriting and local organizing since he knew Chicago better than Rutledge (his boss)" (MacAdams 56).

In 1918 Hecht met Rose Caylor, who worked for the *Chicago Daily News*. Formerly Libman, Rose had changed her last name because she was also acting in plays. Hecht saw no problem with having a wife and a mistress, and the two soon became lovers. At this time, Hecht was writing his first novel, ERIK DORN. It focused on the life of a married Chicago news reporter, who, like himself, also had a mistress. Published in September 1920, it created a minor sensation. But Hecht, needing a job, now returned to the *News* to write a daily column, "1001 Afternoons in Chicago." Soon tiring of that, and convinced that he could make a living writing books and plays, he wrote *Gargoyles*, a novel about a Midwestern boor. He followed with a play, *The Egotist* (originally titled "Under False Pretenses"). In 1922 he published a novel written a few years earlier with a new title, *Fantazies Mallare*. That same year, *A Thousand and One Afternoons in Chicago* was also published. He followed with a mystery novel, *The Florentine Dagger*, in 1923.

Hecht constantly thumbed his nose at censorship. His *Erik Dorn*, seen by many as immoral, was saved by "precensorship," such as when (under protest) he altered a reference to Rachel's "breasts"

by changing the offending word to "breast" in the singular. When *Fantazies Mallare* was published in 1922, Hecht was fired from the *Daily News*. It is worth noting that between 1920 and 1924, when he finally left Chicago, Hecht wrote *Erik Dorn* (1921), *Gargoyles* (1922), *Fantazies Mallare* (1922), *The Florentine Dagger* (1923), and *Humpty Dumpty* (1924), which told the story of his boyhood in Racine, through his arrival in Chicago, his marriage, his mistress, and the breakup of his marriage. Harry Hansen, an editor at the *News*, wrote that Hecht was the "Pagliacci of the Fire Escape"; he was now being acclaimed as one of the leaders of the Chicago School and one of the most gifted novelists in America (Hansen in MacAdams 79). In all, Hecht authored more than 40 books, including *Tales of Chicago Streets* (1924), *Count Brerga* (1926), *A Jew in Love* (1931), *1001 Afternoons in New York* (1941), *A Child of the Century* (1954), *Perfidy* (1961), and *Letters from Bohemia* (1964).

Hecht's play *The Egotist* was produced in New York in 1923. He had collaborated with Kenneth Sawyer Goodman on possibly a dozen plays from 1914 to 1917. In 1917 he worked with Maxwell Bodenheim on a number of plays. Thus, when he and Charles MacArthur wrote *The Front Page*, which opened in 1928 and ran for 276 performances, it became the best-known work of both men and continues in print and in performance to this day, in film and on the stage. It was their first full-length play and their first attempt to recapture the spirit of Chicago. They modeled their characters on real people—politicians, radicals, gangsters, and the like. Indeed, Hecht had used the escape of Terrible Tommy O'Connor, a 35-year-old Irish immigrant, in supplying the story for Josef von Sternberg's film *Underworld* (1927).

In 1926, still writing stories and doing PR work, Hecht received a telegram from Helen Mankiewicz: "Will you accept three hundred per week to work for Paramount Pictures? All expenses paid. The three hundred is peanuts. Millions are to be grabbed out here and your only competition is idiots. Don't let this get around" (MacAdams 5).

In a matter of weeks Hecht and Rose were in Los Angeles. He went on to become the highest-paid scriptwriter of the time, the author of dozens of scripts—some of which he coscripted or was listed as uncredited script doctor—such as *The Front Page* (1931), *Scarface* (1932), *Twentieth Century* (1934), *Viva Villa* (1934), *Nothing Sacred* (1937), *Some Like It Hot* (1939), *Gunga Din* (1939), *Wuthering Heights* (1939), *Gone With the Wind* (1939), *His Girl Friday* (1940), *Spellbound* (1945), *Notorious* (1946), *Miracle of the Bells* (1948), *Monkey Business* (1952), *A Farewell to Arms* (1957), and *Casino Royale* (1967).

In later years Hecht continued to work productively but now with a certain degree of reflectiveness and mellowness, even melancholy. In 1947 he wrote his only work for children, *The Cat That Jumped Out of the Story.*

Child of the Century (1954) was purportedly an autobiography, or a memoir, but is actually a 950-page fictionalized autobiography. Hecht dwelt on his relatives, friends, New York, Hollywood, and Chicago, which he'd left 30 years before. Much of it was pure fantasy, a sort of recapitulation of his past novelized into a string of neat stories rather than recounted in chronological terms. "Lying is creation and fine editing," he wrote in *The Sensualists.* "When you tell truths you're sort of limited as an entertainer" (MacAdams 282). As Hecht put it in 1926, "I find an interesting tendency when writing of myself to tell pleasant lies."

At the end of his life he had become one of the greatest and best-paid screenwriters of all time. His last book, *Letters from Bohemia* (a collection of correspondence from his Chicago friends and colleagues Charles MacArthur, Maxwell Bodenheim, Sherwood Anderson, H. L. Mencken, and a few others) was published a few months after his death on April 18, 1964.

Bibliography

MacAdams, William. *Ben Hecht: The Man Behind the Legend.* New York: Scribner, 1990.
Martin, J. B. *Ben Hecht.* Ann Arbor, Mich.: UMI Research Press, 1985.

—Daniel Walden

Heidi Chronicles and Other Plays, The (Uncommon Women and Others [1977], Isn't It Romantic [1983], The Heidi Chronicles [1988])
Wendy Wasserstein (1990)

WENDY WASSERSTEIN made a career of writing about liberated, upper-class, yet frustrated women, as exemplified by her three major plays, *Uncommon Women and Others* (1977), *Isn't It Romantic* (1983), and *The Heidi Chronicles* (1988). These three were compiled in *The Heidi Chronicles and Other Plays* in 1990. Wasserstein's ability to capture the subtle nuances of realistic female characters, their conversations, and their situations in a manner that is simultaneously lighthearted and deeply earnest about the seriousness and depth of women's issues made her one of the premiere playwrights of contemporary theater.

Originally written as a one-act play for Wasserstein's graduate thesis at Yale, *Uncommon Women and Others* is set during a reunion lunch for six alumnae from Mount Holyoke College and flashes back to the 1972–73 school year to illustrate the impact of the women's movement on the women, comparing their later lives and careers with their teenage hopes. A man's voice introduces each scene, establishing the omnipresence of the male-dominated society's expectations on the young women's aspirations. The outspoken, aspiring writer Rita, whose independent rhetoric is offset by her desire to find a wealthy husband to support her as she pursues her writing, is an example of Wasserstein's common practice of weaving semiautobiographical elements into her work.

Isn't It Romantic addresses the pressing issues of marriage, children, and family in the lives of women approaching 30. The episodic story, staging conversations about the postcollegiate lives and struggles of two 28-year-old friends—frumpy Jewish writer Janie Blumberg and her beautiful, blond friend, Harriet Cornwall—was written as Wasserstein, herself, approached 30. It is notable for its prototypical use of the answering machine as a dramatic device, showing it as an important component in the lives of lonely, successful urban women, and Wasserstein uses it to introduce characters who never appear on stage, including parents, friends, and lovers, all of whom have their own set of expectations for the two women trying to realize the feminist dreams of independence and self-determination.

Originally conceived as a kind of history of second-wave feminism, *The Heidi Chronicles* is a coming-of-age story following art historian and feminist, Heidi Holland, from her teens in 1965 to single motherhood of an adopted daughter in 1989. Central to the story is the evolution of Heidi's sense of disillusionment and betrayal as her friends move away from radical feminism to find comfortable positions within the still overtly masculine cultural establishment. Ultimately, Heidi realizes that, in order to open the doors of equality for future generations of women, their own generation was forced to sacrifice a true sense of personal fulfillment, and, ultimately, abiding happiness. *The Heidi Chronicles* won several awards, including the Pulitzer Prize for Best Drama (1989) and the Tony Award for Best Play (1989).

In all of Wasserstein's plays, pop-culture references abound, helping establish the time period and cultural influences at work. Whether they are the songs from *Fiddler on the Roof* sung by Janie Blumberg's parents in *Isn't It Romantic* or the ladies listening to John Lennon's "Imagine" during a baby shower on the day of Lennon's funeral in New York City in *The Heidi Chronicles*, Wasserstein uses pop culture as a touchstone manifesting the influence of culture and community on the lives of modern women.

Bibliography
Barnett, Claudia, ed. *Wendy Wasserstein: A Casebook. Casebooks on Modern Dramatists.* New York: Garland, 1999.
Ciociola, Gail. *Wendy Wasserstein: Dramatizing Women, Their Choices and Their Boundaries.* Jefferson, N.C.: McFarland, 1998.
Wasserstein, Wendy. *The Heidi Chronicles and Other Plays.* New York: Harcourt Brace Jovanovich, 1990.

—**Jacob Levi Robertson**

Heller, Joseph (1923–1999)

Joseph Heller was born on May 1, 1923, in Coney Island, New York. The son of Russian immigrants, he grew up in a working-class neighborhood in Brooklyn. Joseph's mother, Lena, was in her late 30s when he was born, and his father, Isaac, was a bakery truck driver who suffered from chronic ulcers and died from a failed ulcer operation when Joseph was only four. Lena never remarried, and Joseph grew up with his mother and his two siblings, sister Sylvia and brother Lee—the latter of whom Joseph looked up to as a father figure (Ruderman 15–16).

The Hellers were Jewish, and both Lena and Isaac spoke Yiddish, but the family was not devout. Isaac was an agnostic, and the family observed only one Jewish holiday a year—Yom Kippur. After he graduated from Abraham Lincoln High School in 1941, Heller worked odd jobs until age 19, then he enlisted in the Army Air Corps, flying 60 combat missions in a B-25. Like many of his peers, Heller was initially eager to fly and fight. Midway through his tour, however, he flew a mission over Avignon, France, during which he momentarily believed that his plane had exploded in midair. The psychological shock of that experience made Heller terrified of flying. He completed the rest of his tour but did not fly back to America. He took a ship instead, and avoided airplane trips altogether for the next 15 years (Ruderman 17).

During his stint in the air corps, Heller kept a diary of his missions. He also wrote fiction on the side, publishing his first story—"I Don't Love You Anymore"—in *Story* magazine in fall 1945. After the war, he enrolled in the University of Southern California, transferred to New York University, and continued writing fiction, eventually selling stories to *Esquire* and the *Atlantic Monthly*. Heller later characterized his writing during this period as "*New Yorker*-type stories, stories by Jewish writers about Jewish life in Brooklyn" (Merrill 160). After graduating Phi Beta Kappa from New York University in 1948, he took a master's in American literature from Columbia University and then spent a year at Oxford University as a Fulbright Scholar, studying English literature.

Returning to America, Heller taught freshman composition at Pennsylvania State College until 1952, when he left academia for advertising, working as an adman for *Time, Look,* and *McCall's.* During the day he helped salesmen sell advertising space in the magazines. At night he began working on his first book. Initially called *Catch*-18, the novel was set during World War II but had the sociopolitical sensibility of the mid-fifties: Korea, the cold war, McCarthyism, and a country increasingly at odds with itself. Though the novel was true to the most significant aspect of Heller's own experience—his fear of dying—"*Catch*-22 wasn't," as he later explained, "really *about* World War Two. It was about American society during the Cold War, during the Korean War, and about the possibility of a Vietnam" (Merrill 160). In short, it was *M*A*S*H* before *M*A*S*H* was *M*A*S*H,* using one war as a setting within which to critique another.

It took almost a decade for Heller to write the novel, working piecemeal during evenings and weekends. And more than once he temporarily abandoned the project, until television drove him back to work: "I spent two or three hours a night on it for eight years. I gave up once and started watching television with my wife. Television drove me back to *Catch-22.* I couldn't imagine what Americans did at night when they weren't writing novels" (Merrill 163). In 1957 Heller's literary agent sent the first 250 pages of the unfinished novel to Simon and Schuster. Robert Gottlieb, a wet-behind-the-ears editorial assistant who later became president of Knopf, offered Heller a contract to publish the novel when it was finished: "I just figured if something were that good, it would eventually become a success," Gottlieb later observed (Ruderman 19). Almost half a decade later, the novel—now named *Catch-22*—was finally completed. It was published by Simon and Schuster in September 1961. The novel received mixed reviews, but aided both by an off-the-cuff comment by S. J. Perelman in an interview in the *New York Herald Tribune* and by a brilliant essay by Robert Brustein in the *New Republic, Catch-22* sold 32,000 copies the first year and became a certifiable hit when it was released in paperback in October 1962, selling well over 2 million copies that year. By the end of the decade *Catch-22* had sold more than 25 million copies, becoming—in the process—a rallying cry for a generation of Americans traumatized by the Vietnam War.

Soon after the publication of *Catch-22,* Heller returned to academic life, teaching at the University of Pennsylvania, Yale University, and—somewhat later—the City College of New York. He vigorously opposed the Vietnam War, dabbled in television and movies, and wrote a number of plays, including *We Bombed in New Haven*—which ran for 11 weeks on Broadway—*Catch-22: A Dramatization,* and *Clevinger's Trial.* He also began work on his second novel, *Something Happened,* which took more than a decade to complete and was finally published by Knopf in 1974. Subsequent books were written in a slightly more timely fashion: *Good as Gold* (1979), *GOD KNOWS* (1984), *No Laughing Matter*—coauthored with Speed Vogel—(1986), *Picture This* (1988), *Closing Time* (1994), *Portrait of an Artist, as an Old Man* (2000), and *Catch as Catch Can* (2003), the last two of which were published posthumously. Like *Catch-22,* Heller's later novels were generally best sellers that received an odd mixture of glowing and dreadful reviews—"Apparently," he once joked, "I don't write books people like a *little*" (Merrill 171). But none of them, not even *Closing Time,* the long-awaited sequel to *Catch-22,* ever quite matched the magnificent absurd splendor of his first, and still greatest, novel.

Bibliography

Merrill, Sam. "*Playboy* Interview: Joseph Heller." In *Conversations with Joseph Heller.* Edited by Adam J. Sorkin. Jackson: University Press of Mississippi, 1993.

Ruderman, Judith. *Joseph Heller.* New York: Continuum, 1991.

—Daniel K. Muhlestein

Hellman, Lillian (1905–1984)

An accomplished dramatist, screenwriter, memoirist, and political activist, Lillian Hellman produced and wrote over 10 plays, in addition to her other major contributions to 20th-century literature and film. Her work and lifestyle have emphasized social and personal responsibility, characterized by the need to "make waves" and speak out against hypocrisy and intolerance. Many have viewed Hellman's work as a key contribution to women's studies because of her portraits of powerful female figures; however, her work also reflects her multilayered identity as a Southerner, a Jew, and a woman.

Hellman was born in New Orleans to German immigrants Bernard and Julia Newhouse Hellman on June 20, 1905. She was largely influenced by the free spiritedness and humor of her father's side of the family, as opposed to the more conservative and traditional views of her mother. In addition, she had a close relationship to Sophronia, her childhood nurse, who inspired her sympathy with African Americans and surfaced as a character in several of her works.

Hellman attended college for two years (New York University from 1922 to 1924, and Columbia University in 1924). She later worked as a book reviewer for the *New York Herald Tribune* and a manuscript reader for Boni & Liveright, a position that allowed her to meet major literary figures like Ernest Hemingway, Sherwood Anderson, and Theodore Dreiser. In 1925 she married press agent Arthur Kober. During her marriage Hellman traveled in Europe (including a stint in Paris and an abortive trip to Bonn). She worked as a press agent, reviewed books, read plays, and wrote stories for the *Comet*. In 1930 she and Kober moved to Hollywood, where he became a scriptwriter while Hellman worked as a scenario reader. It was around this time that she began to cultivate a friendship with the writer Dashiell Hammett.

After divorcing Kober in 1932, Hellman moved to New York as a writing apprentice to Hammett, with whom she would have an intimate personal relationship until his death in 1961. It was Hammett who introduced her to William Roughhead's *Bad Companions*, which Hellman would later adapt into her controversial first play, *The Children's Hour* (1934).

In many ways, *The Children's Hour* set the tone and style for much of Hellman's later writing. The play tells the story of two women, Karen Wright and Martha Dobie, who run a boarding school. The women's lives are ruined when their student, Mary Tilford, tries to evade punishment by telling her grandmother that the two women have a lesbian relationship. This play, which ran for 691 performances, established Hellman's ability to employ confrontational dialogue to unearth her characters. It is a cautionary tale with a moralistic tone, exposing the dangers of hypocrisy and lies. Although the play was banned in London, Boston, and Chicago, it catapulted Hellman to fame and financial success.

Over the next 30 years, Hellman would produce over 10 plays, as well as several motion pictures. Although some of her plays bombed on stage (Hellman admits to getting sick in the aisle while watching *Days to Come* in 1936), many enjoyed high acclaim and impressively long runs. In *The Little Foxes* (1939) Hellman addresses family rifts rooted in capitalist greed and bourgeois ambitions, characterizing the rise of the middle class and its clash with Southern society and economy. Like *The Children's Hour,* the play showcases her talent for confrontations, controversial themes, and witty dialogue. The class and family rivalry of this play resurfaces in *Another Part of the Forest* (1946), a prequel to *The Little Foxes.* One of Hellman's later plays, *The Autumn Garden* (1951), also deals with family struggle, yet that play is less political and more introspective, as it depicts three generations of a family struggling with disillusionment, homosexuality, and the conflict between realism and idealism.

Both *Watch on the Rhine* (1941), which won the New York Drama Critics Circle Award, and *The Searching Wind* (1944) display Hellman's political concerns given their antifascist narratives. During the late 1940s and 1950s, Hellman also produced three adaptations, *Montserrat* (1949, based on a Roblés play), *The Lark* (1955, based on Anouilh's *L'Alouette*), and *Candide* (1956, based on Voltaire's novel). She produced her last original play in 1960, *Toys in the Attic* (also winner of the

New York Drama Critics Circle Award), exploring the themes of mortality and disillusionment with love, and her last adaptation in 1963, *My Mother, My Father and Me* (based on Burt Blechman's *How Much?*).

The 1950s were fraught with political turmoil for Hellman, as reflected in *Scoundrel Time* (1976), the last of her three memoirs. In 1952 she was subpoenaed to appear before HUAC, where she was pressured to "name names." Hellman waived her right to the Fifth Amendment and agreed to answer inquiries about herself; however, as stated in a famous letter to the chairman, she refused to implicate anyone else. Her refusal to "name names" prompted others in her position to follow suit and take a stand against McCarthyism.

Hellman's first memoir, *An Unfinished Woman* (1969), details her childhood, marriage to Kober, and relationship with Hammett. The memoir also provides a detailed account of her five-month trip to the Soviet Union, during which she visited a recently liberated concentration camp. Her second memoir, *PENTIMENTO* (1973), is more anecdotal, providing Hellman's reflections on playwriting as well as her major influences. She focuses on her life in New York, yet also provides a touching portrait of her friend Julia, who was persecuted by the Nazis. Each of her memoirs is characterized by her political views as well as her encouragement of social responsibility and human compassion.

Hellman received numerous honors during her prolific career, including the National Institute of Arts and Letters Gold Medal for Drama (1964), the National Book Award (1970), and the MacDowell Medal (1976). She was elected to the American Academy of Arts & Sciences in 1960, and she received honorary degrees from numerous colleges including Yale, New York University, and Columbia. She died of heart failure on June 30, 1984.

Bibliography

Adlam, Carol. "Anton Chekhov and Lillian Hellman: Ethics, Form and the Problem of Melodrama." In *Chekhov 2004: Chekhov Special Issues in Two Volumes. Vol. 2, Chekhov and Others.* Keele, U.K.: Keele University Students Union, 2006.

Phillips, John, and Anne Hollander. "Lillian Hellman." In *Writers at Work: The Paris Review Interviews.* New York: Viking, 1967.

Stern, Richard G. "Lillian Hellman on her Plays." *Contact* 3 (1959): 113–119.

—Lauren Cardon

Henderson the Rain King
Saul Bellow (1915–2005)

Henderson the Rain King (1959) is a wickedly funny, perpetually confusing, midlife-crisis novel about a well-heeled, emotionally adolescent WASP named Eugene Henderson. At 55, Henderson has done everything but grow up. He has lost a brother, botched school, fought in a war, married, divorced, remarried, fathered several children, and raised pigs on his ancestral estate. Through it all, Henderson is tormented by an inner voice which keeps repeating *"I want, I want, I want!"* (24) In desperation he flees Connecticut for Africa, beginning a spiritual pilgrimage that is one part Conrad, two parts Hemingway, and a dash of Cervantes.

Arriving in Africa, Henderson quarrels with his American friends, hires a native guide, and heads deep into the bush. There he comes in contact with two diametrically opposed African tribes: the Arnewi and the Wariri. The Arnewi are a gentle, cattle-loving, matriarchal tribe chock-full of *orgone,* a life force that flows through humans and nature alike. The Arnewi are suffering from drought, and their water supply has become polluted with frogs. Eager to display his Yankee ingenuity, Henderson decides to blow up the frogs with a homemade bomb. He succeeds altogether too well, destroying not only the frogs, but also both the water cistern and his friendship with the Arnewi prince, Itelo.

Henderson then flees to the land of the Wariri, a fierce, patriarchal tribe of African warriors who embody the Freudian view that society is inherently repressive and that nature and culture are antithetical. Henderson soon becomes an informal student of King Dahfu, leader of the Wariri. With Dahfu, Henderson discusses philosophy, attempts to take on the characteristics of a lioness, moves a giant statue, and loses a wager about rain, becoming—in the process—the Sungo, or rain king, second in succession to the throne. But when King Dahfu is killed while attempting to capture a male lion, Henderson runs away from his newly minted obligations, taking with him the lion cub that is said to embody the soul of his dead friend. Henderson then dismisses his native guide and leaves Africa, beginning the long journey back to America.

Henderson is both a serious quest novel and a parody of the quest novel genre, one that takes particular delight in satirizing Hemingway's safari adventures and Conrad's *Heart of Darkness*. It is a superior example of what Harold Bloom calls the anxiety of influence—the process by which a male writer attempts to make space for himself in the literary canon by simultaneously misreading and rewriting important literary precursors. *Henderson* is also a late addition to the long tradition of African travel literature exploring the tangled relationships between colonizers and colonized. The Africa to which Henderson goes in his search for spiritual enlightenment is a fictional construct rather than a historical entry, however. *Henderson* draws occasional inspiration from the travel literature of Frederick E. Forbes and John Roscoe and the African ethnography of Melville J. Herskovits. More often than not, however, Richard Burton's *A Mission to Gelele the King of Dahomey* serves as the primary source material for the novel, with Bellow inadvertently reproducing many of the colonialist racist ideologues of Burton's work. To contemporary readers *Henderson* is thus a guilty pleasure: The skill with which Bellow parodies Conrad and Hemingway is counterbalanced by the ease with which the novel slots into the colonial library.

Historically, *Henderson*'s reception has also been complicated by its helter-skelter juxtaposition of philosophy and slapstick, high seriousness and vaudevillian, earnest implausibility. The philosophical issues with which Henderson struggles are worthy of Bellow's most concentrated effort. They include Freudian personality theory, the possible truth value of Jamesian and Reichian psychology, the way in which conflicting codes of masculinity bedevil the modern Jewish-American hero,

the importance of homosocial relationships, the romantic disappointment inherent in the modern preoccupation with death, and the inability of nihilistic existentialism to humanize adequately—and thus make bearable—suffering and death. A modern sensibility wounded by the world, Henderson struggles to purge himself of modernist isms, and he searches for beauty and truth in the face of an often implacable universe. Ultimately he succeeds—or at least appears to; hence, the final image in the novel, in which Eugene Henderson runs in exaltation through the blinding whiteness of Newfoundland snow.

And yet this high seriousness is so thoroughly intermixed with castrated pigs, homemade hand grenades, transparent pantaloons, and dried cattle dung that it is hard to know quite what to make of Bellow's Bakhtinian carnival. Parody is itself parodied, philosophy sits cheek to jowl with farce, and nothing seems positively sacred or true. Even Henderson's fear of death is treated as a cosmic joke, his body becoming a giant canvas onto which are splashed the small indignities of the world: crabs, body odor, an enormous nose, a flexible sphincter. A comic American imago of gargantuan proportions, Henderson can be hard to take—and even harder to take seriously. As Reed Whittemore observed in a representative review written for the *New Republic*, "Nobody can deny that the particulars are there. . . . But the particulars are so clearly hokum that one is hardly disposed to reckon with them, except as jokes, sometimes very good jokes" (18). The final scene in *Henderson* is particularly problematic. For some critics, the novel ends too soon, before Henderson arrives back in America. For others, it ends too late, after the climactic death of King Dahfu. And in either case, the image of affirmation at the end of *Henderson* seems decidedly unearned. "The traditionally ecstatic ending of the quest novel," rightly concludes Robert F. Kiernan, "is achieved impressionistically by the considerable force of the scene's lyricism, but it is not achieved substantially" (84).

Henderson the Rain King is thus perhaps best understood as a canny double of its namesake protagonist: like him it is a gargantuan, rambling wreck of genius, as hard to put down as it is to pick up.

Bibliography

Kiernan, Robert F. *Saul Bellow.* New York: Continuum Press, 1989.

Reed, Whittemore. "Safari among the Wariri." *New Republic* 140 (March 16, 1959): 17–18.

                                        —Daniel K. Muhlestein

Herzog Saul Bellow (1964)

Herzog, a winner of both the National Book Award and the international Prix Litteraire, is a loose-jointed masterpiece about loss and longing, memory and neurosis, philosophy and betrayal. Told in retrospect, *Herzog* retraces five days in the life of Moses Herzog, a 47-year-old professor who is a part-time historian, a part-time philosopher, and a full-time philanderer. Twice divorced, Herzog is reeling from the effects of bad choices and worse wives—a combination that has driven him nearly mad. He has recently taken refuge in his Berkshire estate, a dilapidated old house he had earlier purchased in a failed attempt to build an idyllic life for himself and his second wife, Madeleine, who is now living in Chicago with Herzog's daughter and his former best friend, Valentine Gersbach, with whom Madeleine is having an affair. As he wanders through his house, Herzog reviews the events of the past week, begins to paint a piano for his daughter, and struggles to come to grips with his wife's betrayal, his friend's deception, and his own questionable state of mind. While reviewing his recent activities, Herzog analyzes the significance of his trip to Martha's Vineyard, his evening with his mistress, Ramona Donsell, his visit to the courthouse, his chat with his lawyer, his theatrical attempt to shoot Madeleine and Valentine, his day trip with his daughter, his automobile accident, and his hasty retreat to the Berkshire house in which the novel both begins and ends.

Like *Henderson the Rain King, Herzog* is a quest tale in which an overburdened protagonist searches for insight, truth, and serenity. But while Henderson's search takes the form of a physical journey into the Dark Continent, Herzog searches the recesses of his own mind, memory replacing Africa in the quest motif. Like Henderson, Herzog has a bone to pick with modern philosophy—several, in fact. *Herzog* is as much a treatise on inadequate philosophy as it is a novel about familial betrayal, with Herzog linking the latter to the former, cause to effect. Herzog's goal is to rescue humanity from a false conception of human nature, and in pursuit of that goal he goes toe to toe with Darwin, de Tocqueville, Freud, Hegel, Heidegger, Hobbes, Hume, Kant, Kierkegaard, Marx, Nietzsche, Pascal, Rousseau, Spengler, Spinoza, Tolstoy, and—in a single memorable letter—God himself. At times Herzog's preoccupation with the history of ideas threatens to suffocate the novel, but Bellow rescues *Herzog* from intellectual pretentiousness by highlighting the gap between Herzog's intellectual finesse and his hapless blunderings in the world.

Herzog is also a novel about the inescapable cost of life and memory. Time after time Herzog picks at the scabs of the past, reliving his mistakes and recounting the sins that have been committed against him. Madeleine's affair with Valentine occupies center stage, but Herzog also takes time to catalog 47 years worth of bad luck, bad choices, bad acquaintances, and inevitable loss. Of particular significance are Herzog's failures as a father, the Holocaust, and the death of Herzog's parents. Herzog once boasted that he believed in letting the dead bury their own dead. But even decades after the fact he is still devastated by the loss of his mother and father: "To haunt the past like this—to love the dead! Moses warned himself not to yield so greatly to this temptation, this peculiar weakness of his character. . . . But somehow his heart had come open at this chapter of his life and he didn't have the strength to shut it" (143). So traumatic has been the loss of his loved ones that Herzog seems obligated to attempt to write the loss both into and out of existence. His countless letters are thus more than a simple self-conscious attempt at analysis and expression. They are also examples of unconscious repetition compulsion, a form of involuntary trauma therapy in which the traumatized person attempts to textualize—

and so gain a measure of control over—the past. "I've been writing letters helter-skelter in all directions," Herzog reports. "More words. I go after reality in language. Perhaps I'd like to change it all into language" (272).

Herzog can be a difficult character to like, but he can be an even more difficult character to dislike. He is vain, narcissistic, masochistic, and misogynistic. He does not tolerate fools, but he frequently plays one himself. And yet Herzog recognizes his own weaknesses so clearly and acknowledges them so openly that readers are left little choice but to accept his self-assessment and grant him his due. No one is better at deflating Herzog's pretensions than Herzog himself, and the novel is full of declarations that begin in self-aggrandizement but end in self-deprecation. As is the case in *Seize the Day,* in *Herzog* the narrator does much of the heavy lifting for the novel's protagonist by blurring the line between narrator and protagonist so thoroughly as to give Herzog's self-assessment the appearance of credibility, even wisdom:

> Self-development, self-realization, happiness—these were the titles under which these lunacies occurred. Ah, poor fellow!—and Herzog momentarily joined the objective world in looking down on himself. He too could smile at Herzog and despise him. But there still remained the fact. *I* am Herzog. I have to *be* that man. There is no one else to do it. After smiling, he must return to his own Self and see the thing through. (66–67)

Like many of Bellow's other novels, *Herzog* ends in a way that is aesthetically pleasing but psychologically problematic. Herzog's recovery completes the trajectory of the novel, but his recovery is suspect in that it seems to be as much an expression of his finely tuned sense of drama as it is an indication of an authentic improvement in his mental health. Still, the silence with which the novel ends is a brilliant counterpoint to the hue and cry of the earlier chapters, and *Herzog,* one of Bellow's finest works, has been compared in scope to Joyce's *Ulysses.*

Bibliography
Cardon, Lauren. "*Herzog* as 'Survival Literature.'" *Saul Bellow Journal* 20, no. 2 (Fall 2004): 85–108.
Wilson, Jonathan. "*Herzog*'s Fictions of the Self." In *Saul Bellow: A Mosaic.* New York: Peter Lang, 1992.

—Daniel K. Muhlestein

Hoffman, Eva (1945–)

Born in 1945 in Kraków, Poland, Eva Hoffman immigrated to Canada at the age of 13. She later earned a Ph.D. in literature from Harvard University and became a writer and editor for the *New York Times.* She has won several awards for her writing, including the Jean Stein Award and the Guggenheim and Whiting awards.

Hoffman's best-known book, *Lost in Translation* (1989), is an autobiography that focuses on her own process of adapting to the culture of Canada and the United States as a teenage immigrant. In *Lost,* Hoffman examines the role of language in determining identity and the difficulty in determining what an American identity is. "Identity," Hoffman writes in *Lost,* is "the number one problem" in America (262). Hoffman concludes that her inability to fix an identity is what defines her: "I share with my American generation an acute sense of dislocation and an equally acute challenge of having to invent a place and identity for myself without the traditional supports . . . it is in my very uprootedness that I'm its member" (197).

Hoffman has written three nonfiction accounts of Jewish life in Poland: *Exit Into History* (1993), *Shtetl* (1997), and *After Such Knowledge* (2004), as well as a novel, *The Secret* (2001). *Exit into History* recounts Hoffman's return to Poland during the summers of 1990 and 1991. She also visits with eastern Europeans from diverse professional, economic, and social classes to examine eastern Europe after the fall of communism. She also looks at the complex current relationships between eastern Europe and its Jewish population. *Shtetl: The Life and Death of a Small Town and the World of Polish Jews* is an examination of the long history of relations between the Jewish and Catholic populations in the town of Bransk, from the 11th century to World War II. Hoffman also illustrates the class distinctions that arose within the Jewish community of Bransk.

After Such Knowledge, Hoffman's most recent book, is a collection of seven essays that look into the lives and minds of the children of Holocaust survivors, including herself. This work can be seen as a continuation of the search for identity in *Lost in Translation*; here she attempts to formulate what it means to be the child of a Holocaust survivor and how that meaning can be understood by the world at large. Hoffman also warns of the dangers of "certain kinds of exclusive ethnic and religious attachments . . . to our ancestors" in dealing with the Holocaust, preferring an "international, cross-cultural, or culturally intermingled perspective" (197). She also argues for the possibilities of new Polish-Jewish and German-Jewish relations. The final chapter of *After Such Knowledge* tackles current issues in post-9/11 America and Israel.

The Secret is Hoffman's only work of fiction and her only book not to touch upon Poland. Set in 2022, *The Secret* is the story of a clone discovering the truth of her origins. Narrated in first person, it leads the reader through the thought process as the main character comes to discover the secret of her birth. The ethical, emotional, and spiritual ramifications of human cloning, as well as the role of the complex interplay between genetics and upbringing in a person's life, are issues that loom over the narrative.

Bibliography

Krondorfer, Bjorn. "Review of *After Such Knowledge: Memory, History, and the Legacy of the Holocaust* by Eva Hoffman." *Holocaust and Genocide Studies* (October–November 2004): 291–293.

Krupnick, Mark. "Assimilation in Recent American Jewish Autobiographies." *Contemporary Literature* 34, no. 3 (1993): 457–462.

—**Aaron Keeley**

Horn, Dara (1977–   )

Dara Horn is the author, thus far, of two important Jewish-American novels, *In the Image* (2002) and *The World to Come* (2006). With these two works, Horn has established herself as one of an increasing number of young Jewish-American writers who have answered Cynthia Ozick's call for a literature grounded in specifically Jewish ideas. "I wanted to create a different style for American Jewish literature," Horn declares in an interview collected in the paperback edition of her first novel, "one more connected to the Jewish literary tradition of constant reference to ancient text."

Horn published *In the Image* at the age of 25 while she was a doctoral student of Hebrew and Yiddish literature at Harvard. (She was awarded a Ph.D. in 2006.) The debut novel earned wide and enthusiastic praise for the deft manner in which Horn explores Jewish history and texts within the context of a deeply felt coming-of-age novel. It won a number of prestigious awards, including the National Jewish Book Award for a first novel, the Reform Judaism Prize for Jewish Fiction, and the Edward Lewis Wallant Prize for the best work of Jewish-American fiction. The novel centers around a young Jewish-American heroine, Leora, whose best friend is killed while in high school. Leora is befriended by the friend's eccentric grandfather, Bill Landsmann, a war refugee who insists on showing Leora his voluminous collection of travel slides of major Jewish sites around the world. The novel unfolds as Horn interweaves the historical story of the European and immigrant experiences of multiple generations of the Landsmann tribe with Leora's contemporary plight to establish a meaningful Jewish identity in America. Along the way, Horn engages with a variety of essential Jewish concerns, including Holocaust remembrance, the Ba'al Teshuvah movement, and the resonances of the Hebrew Bible in the contemporary world. The novel culminates in a midrashic tour de force as Horn imagines Bill Landsmann's story through the lens of the biblical Job story.

Horn's second novel, *The World to Come,* is as drenched in Jewish history and texts as her debut. As one reviewer notes, "Horn writes about theology and moral imperatives and the afterlife—as though she didn't realize that *such things just aren't done* in sophisticated literary prose. But that daring is endearing, especially when it flows from deeply sympathetic characters, an encyclopedic grasp of 20th century history and a spiritual sense that sees through the conventional barriers between this life and the one to come—or the one before." The novel opens as the protagonist, Benjamin Ziskind, a former child prodigy and current game show researcher, steals a valuable Chagall painting after a singles' event at New York's Jewish Museum. The reader learns that he has recognized the painting as the one that used to hang in his parents' living room. From there, Horn interweaves an intricate series of narratives through which she imagines, at least in part, Chagall's years teaching art at a Jewish Boys' Colony at Malakhovka in the 1920s (where the artist will meet our protagonist's grandfather-to-be); the travails, and vanished stories, of an obscure Yiddish writer at the colony, Der Nister (the "Hidden One"); Stalin's ultimate purges of Jewish artists and writers in the Soviet Union; and the terrifying Vietnam War experiences of our protagonist's father. Horn's generous recasting of lost Yiddish stories and fabulist tales makes up some of the most imaginative and moving moments of *The World to Come.*

Much of the literature by this youngest cohort of Jewish-American writers might be described as a literature of retrieval and repair. Horn's two works of fiction clearly align her with this growing literary movement. Reflecting on the contrasting fates of Chagall and Der Nister, Horn remarked, "It seems like a vast cultural decision, the casting away of one artist and the canonization of another, but it actually begins as a very personal choice, when we each privately decide what's worth reading, seeing, remembering, and keeping. And it is only those things that we choose to keep that are allowed to extend across the generations and survive us." Horn's novels might be seen as elegant treatises on these matters—fiercely intelligent views regarding which Jewish texts, artists, writers, and lives we ought to best remember.

Bibliography

Charles, Ron. "Divine Inheritance." Review of *The World to Come, Washington Post,* 22 January 2006, BW6.

Cokal, Susann. "Picture Book." Review of *The World to Come, New York Times Book Review,* 19 March 2006, 27.

Gelernter, David. "Redeeming the Lost." Review of *In the Image, Commentary* (December 2002): 72–74.

Halkin, Hillel. "Memorabilia." Review of *The World to Come, Commentary* (March 2006): 76–80.

—**Andrew Furman**

An Hour in Paradise: Stories
Joan Leegant (2003)

JOAN LEEGANT's debut collection of stories, *An Hour in Paradise,* recipient of the 2004 Edward Lewis Wallant Award for Jewish Fiction, captures the deeply conflicted responses to Judaism for a generation coming of age in America at the turn of the 21st century. For many of Leegant's characters, Judaism has become, as one character puts it in the story "The Lament of the Rabbi's Daughters," a "claustrophobic preordained life," a set of laws and restrictions, "the obscure, the arcane." The central tension all the stories in this collection revolve around is the dissatisfaction of a generation caught between two worlds: the world of their fathers and mothers and a world-in-the-making, that is, a place in which the "old rules" of Jewish belief and practice no longer seem to apply to their lives.

In "The Tenth," the collection's opening story, the central character, Rabbi Samuel Steele, recognizes with an acute sense of loss that his synagogue of aged congregants is rapidly becoming obsolete. In the old shul, where with few accoutrements, the Torahs dressed in "plain, worn cloth" appropriate for the old men who reverently open the ark, the rabbi knows himself to reside in the diminishing past. For Rabbi Steele, the old synagogue and its symbolic and real ties with past tradition and ritual stand in defiant contrast to the new synagogues, with their wealth and prosperity, whose solid exteriors barely mask their insubstantial interior. While the changing landscape of American thought and practice militates against the solidity of ancient Hebraic text and identity, Legant finds hope in a new generation of American Jews, who embrace tradition and make it their own. Such a renewal of Jewish identity and faith come about through a dramatic reassessment of what it means to be a Jew at the turn of a new century.

In "The Lament of the Rabbi's Daughters," Judaism is portrayed as stifling and inflexible, not a world in which the rabbi's three daughters believe themselves free to define their own lives in the midst of a rapidly changing and destabilizing world. The rabbi's daughters find themselves uncomfortably scripted to live the lives of their predecessors, mothers and grandmothers, who never deviated from the approved path: "studying at a girls' yeshiva . . . marrying at twenty . . . becoming the dutiful rebbetzin." The rabbi's daughters cannot see a future in this life, only deeply knotted ties to an identity extrinsic to themselves. In an attempt to sever that "intimate Hebraic cord," the daughters, following the biblical injunction to refrain from looking back, walk out of their past lives determined to discover new ones. But what they discover, despite their intentions to reinvent themselves, is that their identities are rooted in Judaism, whose traditions and ethical guidelines protect and sustain them.

In other stories, Israel becomes a place of hoped-for refuge and connection to the past. America, for them, has become a transitory commercial enterprise characterized by a fixation with acquisition at the expense of anything spiritual and enduring. As a result, Jewish identity and history are diluted through, as a character in the story, "Mezivosky," puts it, "a hundred family years of soaking in the great washing machine of America." And for many Jews of this generation, the rise of a Jewish middle class that so defined the 20th century has brought with it an erosion of belief in something greater and more substantial than themselves.

In configurations both despairing and hopeful *An Hour in Paradise* raises the difficult questions: In what form do angels of God appear? Is it possible to atone for one's sins? How does one keep tradition alive in the midst of change? To whom must one be held accountable? Where does one find the courage to perform small acts of compassion?

Bibliography
Bayard, Louis. "Was That Elijah?" *New York Times,* 5 October 2003, A18.
Brawarsky, Sandee. "A Promising Midlife Debut." *Jewish Woman Magazine.* Fall 2003. Available Online. URL: http://www.jwmag.org/site/c.fhLOK0PGLsF/b.2440825/k.4F8D/A_Promising_Midlife_Debut.htm. Accessed November 3, 2007.
—Victoria Aarons

Howl and Other Poems
Allen Ginsberg (1956)

On October 7, 1955, Allen Ginsberg first performed his seminal poem, *Howl,* at the Six Gallery in San Francisco. The event had been organized by Ginsberg and featured Kenneth Rexroth as emcee, and readings by Philip Lamantia, Michael McClure, Philip Whalen, Ginsberg, and Gary Snyder. Although it was reportedly a rowdy, drunken unconventional reading, Ginsberg sobered as he read his work, becoming caught up in the rhythms of *Howl,* an experience he would later describe as "a rabbi reading rhythmically to a congregation" (Ruskin 18). The day after the reading, Lawrence Ferlinghetti, himself a poet and the owner of City Lights Books, sent a telegram to Ginsberg: "I greet you at the beginning of a great career. When do I get the manuscript?" *Howl and Other Poems* appeared as the fourth book in the Pocket Poets Series from City Lights Books in fall 1956. The poem, which had created such a stir the year before, was now completed, accompanied by two additional parts, a footnote, and an introduction by William Carlos Williams.

Ginsberg said, 30 years after *Howl* was published, "I was curious to leave behind after my generation an emotional time bomb that would continue exploding in U.S. consciousness" (Ginsberg, Original, xii). Ginsberg was successful; *Howl*'s continual explosion, however, has been attributed primarily to its content—the "emotional," self-referential madness Ginsberg initiated as acceptable fodder not only for the Beats, but also for subsequent generations of poets. This focus on content is most likely because Ginsberg presented himself as a spontaneous writer, following the cue of his fellow Beat Jack Kerouac, who preached "lingual spontaneity or nothing" (Raskin 168). Ginsberg was actually a meticulous craftsman, and continued to revise *Howl*. Ginsberg's revisions were not simply to the language, but to the form, evidenced by the original drafts and revisions published on the 30th anniversary of *Howl*. In a letter to John Hollander, Ginsberg claimed that *Howl* "was an experiment with form itself" (Raskin 206).

Part I opens with the now famous line "I saw the best minds of my generation destroyed by madness, starving hysterical naked, / dragging themselves through the negro streets at dawn looking for an angry fix." The majority of *Howl* is concerned with chronicling, eulogizing, and glorifying the individuals who, with Ginsberg, were the Beat generation: Jack Kerouac, Neal Cassady, William S. Burroughs, among others. Their glory, however, is not found in pristine language or conventional poetic devices. Ginsberg employs long lines and startling juxtapositions as he pays homage to his colleagues "who bared their brains to Heaven under the El and saw Mohammedan angels staggering on tenement roofs illuminated, / who passed through universities with radiant cool eyes hallucinating Arkansas and Blake-light tragedy among the scholars of war." The aim of Ginsberg's juxtapositions of words and images is not merely for shock value, but to create a physical reaction, some sort of visceral connection between brain and body, a more basic response that fills in the gaps of his poetry for his readers.

Part II continues the use of long lines and juxtaposition, but as a rant against industrial civilization embodied by Moloch. Moloch is the Hebrew name of the pagan god Ba'al and is defined in Ginsberg's annotation (an edition published 30 years after the City Lights edition) as "the Canaanite fire god, whose worship was marked by parents' burning their children as propitiatory sacrifice." Ginsberg communicates the symbolic nature of Moloch as the evils of American consumerism through combining Moloch with other words and images: "Moloch! Solitude! Filth! Ugliness! Ashcans and unobtainable dollars! Children screaming under the stairways! Boys sobbing in armies! Old men weeping in the parks!" The connection between Moloch and the images that follow is intensified by Ginsberg's use of exclamation marks, calling attention to the first word of the line that is subsequently buried by refuse and emotional duress.

Both Part III and the Footnote to *Howl* move away from the grim nature of the Moloch section. Part III directly addresses Carl Solomon, to whom the entirety of *Howl* is dedicated. Ginsberg met Solomon during a brief stay in a psychiatric hospital in 1949. Part III connects Ginsberg to Solomon's madness as he repeats, "I'm with you in Rockland." This connection offers a specific instance of "the best minds of [Ginsberg's] generation destroyed by madness" and subsequently defines the destruction of those minds, as Solomon and Ginsberg are found at the end of Part III with "twenty-five thousand mad comrades all together singing the final stanzas of the Internationale." The Footnote completes the movement of the poem, as in the unified voice of "the best minds" Ginsberg celebrates what he feels should be celebrated: "Holy the supernatural extra brilliant intelligent kindness of soul!"

Howl is the most famous of the collection, but is accompanied by other notable works such as "A Supermarket in California," in which Ginsberg converses in his head with Walt Whitman; "Transcription of Organ Music"; "Sunflower Sutra"; "America"; and "In the Baggage Room at Greyhound." It also features four poems that predate *Howl*: "An Asphodel," "Song," "Wild Orphan," and "In Back of the Real."

By 1997 *Howl and Other Poems* had sold over eight hundred thousand copies. It has been translated into at least 24 languages, including Spanish, Polish, Dutch, Japanese, Chinese, Hungarian, and Italian (Raskin xx), fulfilling Rexroth's prediction at the first reading of *Howl* that it would be a poem to make Ginsberg "famous from bridge to bridge."

Bibliography

Casale, Frank D. "Madness, Speech, and Prophecy in Allen Ginsberg's *Howl*." *Spectacle* 1, no. 2 (Spring 1998): 101–112.

Raskin, Jonah. *American Scream: Allen Ginsberg's Howl and the Making of the Beat Generation.* Berkeley: University of California Press, 2004.

—Sarah E. Jenkins

The Human Stain Philip Roth (2000)

As the third novel of PHILIP ROTH's American Trilogy, *The Human Stain* continues to explore the various themes presented in AMERICAN PASTORAL (1997) and *I Married a Communist* (1998): identity, truth and fiction, perceptions and reality, national obsessions with purity and perfection, public and private spaces. The novel takes place in the late 1990s amid the political turmoil concerning President Clinton's sexual scandal with White House intern Monica Lewinsky. Not only does the novel introduce the dismay of a nation's image stained with the literal stain of Clinton's adulterous indiscretions, but it also brings the very idea of human society's obsession with purity (sexual, racial, intellectual) into acute focus through the life of one man. It is the story of Coleman Silk, an ousted Athena College dean and classics professor who has been labeled a racist and misogynist. As aptly stated by the novel's narrator, Nathan Zuckerman, Coleman's story is presented as stories often are: as truth, as knowledge. The reality, however, is something quite different, something that Roth weaves throughout the work: "You *can't* know anything. The things you *know* you don't know. . . . Even more astonishing is what passes for knowing" (209).

The avenues of knowing and not knowing that appear throughout the novel occur in Zuckerman's retelling of Coleman Silk's life. Through the impotent, disillusioned writer's perspective, the reader is informed of perhaps one of the greatest testimonies to identity and the fine lines between truth and fiction: Coleman Silk's passing. The concept of racial passing is in itself one of the hidden realities of American history, a history stained by inhuman racial discrimination and brutalities. Although Coleman is at first presented as a secular white Jewish professor, Zuckerman later reveals that Coleman (as his name, *Coal* Man, implies) is really a light-skinned black who has passed for white. In an attempt to purge himself of the limitations brought on by his own stain, that of blackness, Coleman opts for the purity of whiteness and the opportunities offered by choosing this particular raced American dream. Coleman rejects his former life and family, closing the door on his black past forever. As a white Jew, Coleman is successful in occupation and in family life. He marries and fathers children under his racial guise, all the while hoping not to stain his children with the mark of his black heritage.

Ironically, it is this same racial divide that comes back to mock Coleman as a white Jew, ultimately stripping him of both occupation and family. After being accused of making a racist remark—referring to two absent students (who turn out to be black) as "spooks"—he resigns as dean and as classics professor. During the social scrutiny that follows Athena College's purgation of Coleman's purported intolerance, Iris, his wife, dies. Coleman blames both the college and the town as the primary stress factors that led to his wife's death, and is determined to write a book, entitled *Spooks,* both to exonerate himself and to expose fully the factors leading to his wife's demise. During this time he meets Zuckerman, already an accomplished novelist, and begs for his assistance in the project. Although Zuckerman refuses the invitation and Coleman eventually decides not to publish the *Spooks* manuscript, the two men become good friends. Through this friendship, and Zuckerman's obvious "publication" of Coleman's story, readers learn of the former professor's budding love affair with an illiterate janitor, Faunia Farley.

In Faunia Farley, another story of staining and passing appears. Some 20-odd years younger than Coleman's age of 71, Faunia is a destitute woman who has suffered a history of emotional, intellectual, and physical abuse and neglect. Many people, like Coleman's feminist Athena College colleague, Delphine Roux, feel that Coleman's actions are despicable and manipulative. To society, Coleman appears to have the upper hand in the love relationship, and he is accused of sexually exploiting someone who is underprivileged. Once again, he feels that his private life has been put on public display and even feels a distancing from his children as a result of the affair. Despite her appearance of poverty and illiteracy, Faunia is in reality a child of privilege, who exercises literacy skills on a regular basis, namely, through writing in a personal journal. She has learned, through her life experiences, however, that passing as a poverty-stricken illiterate is a lifestyle more suited to her American dream. In part her passing occurs as an escape from her past, one stained by the deaths of two children from a marriage to Vietnam veteran Les Farley. It is a stain the resurfaces as Les, who suffers from post-traumatic stress syndrome, begins stalking (and eventually attacks) Faunia and Coleman.

Through Faunia, readers are also introduced to Prince, a black crow who has become so accustomed to human contact that he has forgotten he is a crow, or at least how to act like a crow. According to Faunia (fauna), Prince is an animal, like her and Coleman, trapped in a system of his own choosing and lacking the "right voice" to blend in with other members of the group. Faunia notes that Prince bears a "human stain" like everyone else, "a stain . . . a trail . . . an imprint" (242). Through her voice, Roth makes a condemning statement against the human quest for purity and the idea of truth. The human stain is an innate and inerasable part of life, something that exists but that cannot be defined.

It has been speculated that the character of Coleman Silk is based in part on *New York Times* literary critic Anatole Broyard, an African-American man who passed as white for most of his adult life. This novel was made into a movie in 2003 starring Anthony Hopkins and Nicole Kidman.

Bibliography

Kaplan, Brett Ashley. "Reading Race and the Conundrums of Reconciliation in Philip Roth's *The Human Stain*." In *Turning Up the Flame: Philip Roth's Later Novels*. Newark: University of Delaware Press, 2005.

Parrish, Timothy L. "Ralph Ellison: The Invisible Man in Roth's *Human Stain*." *Contemporary Literature* 45, no. 3 (Fall 2004): 421–459.

—Iris Nicole Johnson

Humboldt's Gift Saul Bellow (1975)

Humboldt's Gift (1975) is a comic portrayal of the spiritual plight of Charlie Citrine, a Chicagoan with a taste for louche types, gangland excitement, and destructive women. He suffers from diminished poetic gifts due to the brutal "Chicago condition," which has recently destroyed his literary mentor and friend Humboldt. The character of Von Humboldt Fleisher is based on Delmore Schwartz, whom Bellow knew at Princeton. Charlie Citrine himself reflects Bellow's reading of the anthroposophist Rudolph Steiner, with whom he was fascinated at the time.

The novel is a panoramic picaresque that deals with the contemporary conflict between the creative mind, the body, American history, and the absurd modern environment. The plot carefully juxtaposes characters possessing an overweening American "hypermasculinity" with characters whose "poetic feminine powers" are all but eclipsed by a capitalistic American striving for dominance, power, and self-aggrandizement. Modernity has all but excluded love, the soul, beauty, and poetic visionary states. As Charlie tries to recover his weakened spiritual powers, he must resist naturalist sex ideologies, technological rationalism, and materialistic sloth. He blames some of Humboldt's failure on his fascination with the ideas of Kinsey, Masters, and Erickson; capitalism; and modernist alienation ethics. Such failed modern ideas seem to have transformed Humboldt from a brilliant young poet to a ruined manic-depressive paranoiac. Charlie attributes Humboldt's final collapse into madness and despair to his reading of Freud's *Psychopathology of Everyday Life*. In Chicago, he concludes, one must erect a buffer zone to protect the sovereignty of the imagination from modern science.

Charlie, 60 years old at this point, must forgo eroticism, media fame, greed, and self-gratification to recover his artistic vision. He must also deal with the mutual betrayals in his relationship with Humboldt, with his persistent longings for his family of childhood, and with his neglected business affairs. The novel abounds in the eccentric and realistic particulars of American life, and provides a rich portrait of Chicago. Typical of all Bellow's novels is the characters' repeated and intimate contact with death as they attempt to transcend brute reality.

Despite its plethora of characters and the fact that its setting somewhat confusingly switches to Madrid at the end of the novel, this masterwork achieved a special popularity with readers and critics, no doubt due to its sheer inventiveness. Consistent with Bellow's concurrent anthroposophical interests, he leaves us with two pictures: Charlie standing on his head in a Madrid hotel room meditating, and Charlie contemplating the miracle of the yellow crocus he sees growing through the cracks of the Chicago city pavement. Finally Charlie realizes that much of what has eluded him is still there to be discovered.

Bibliography

Clayton, John J. "Humboldt's Gift: Transcendence and the Flight from Death." In *Saul Bellow and His Work*. Edited by Edmond Schraepen. Brussels: Centrum voor Taal-en Literatuurwetenschap, Vrije Universiteit Brussel, 1978.

Siegel, Ben. "Artists and Opportunists in Saul Bellow's *Humboldt's Gift*." *Contemporary Literature* 19, no. 2 (Spring 1978): 143–164. Rpt. in *Critical Essays on Saul Bellow*, edited by Stanley Trachtenberg, 158–174. Boston: G.K. Hall, 1979.

—**Gloria L. Cronin**

Hurst, Fannie (1889–1968)

The mid-1920s marked the height of the career of author Fannie Hurst, who was, according to the *New York Times*, "the world's highest paid short-story writer." Hurst, born on October 18, 1889, in Hamilton, Ohio, was the only child of German-Jewish immigrants Rose and Samuel Hurst. She was raised in St. Louis, Missouri, where, unlike many young women of the era, she graduated from high school in 1909. Hurst began writing at age 14, and in December 1904 her first known published story, "An Episode," appeared in her high school newspaper.

Shortly after graduating from high school, Hurst began her studies at Washington University in St. Louis, where she was one of 20 female students entering the class of 1905. She was active in campus life, particularly in the dramatics club and in the campus newspaper *Student Life*, where she served as an editor. In 1909, two weeks before her graduation from college, her story "The Joy of Living," originally written as an assignment for one of her college courses, was published in the *Mirror*, a nationally distributed magazine.

After completing her college degree Hurst convinced her parents that she should move to Manhattan to pursue graduate studies at Columbia University. While she did take some courses at the school, there is no record of her enrolling in a degree-granting program there. Instead, Fannie created her own graduate courses, among the streets and working-class residents of New York City. Here she mined material and developed her literary characters from real people whom she observed and with whom she interacted.

Hurst was interested in the lives of the working class, in particular how minorities, especially women, worked and lived. To understand better the conditions of those outside the dominant culture, she worked in factories, retail shops, and restaurants. She spent countless hours in New York City's night courts observing and developing ideas for her stories. She frequently visited Ellis Island and interacted with arriving immigrants, and explored the ethnic enclaves of Manhattan's Lower East Side. As Joyce Kilmer, writing August 6, 1916, in the *New York Times* remarked, "Miss Hurst's short stories, especially her sympathetic and poignantly realistic studies of the life of the Jewish citizens of New York, have earned for her popular as well as critical approval."

After struggling for years to publish her short stories, she became a sought-after contributor to national magazines, including the *Saturday Evening Post, Cosmopolitan,* and *Colliers*. Many of her novels first appeared serialized in magazines and were later published in book format.

Her works reached a wide audience. Hurst herself commented on what influences popular culture in a March 16, 1924, *New York Times* article: "The American public has not been given an opportunity to demonstrate what it really wants. . . . The canons of taste and culture and intellectuality have been established in every era and in every nation, by the mighty minority. Where is *our* mighty minority?"

She was a social activist, regularly lending her name and talents to a variety of causes, including women's suffrage and workers' rights. She wrote with skill and understanding about the influence of adverse conditions on individuals and their character. As editor Susan Koppleman wrote of Hurst in the introduction to a 2004 compilation of her work, "I believe that the most important social justice advocacy and activities of Fannie Hurst were her short stories" (xi). She was deeply involved in the Harlem Renaissance, and for a time roomed and traveled with her close friend, author Zora Neale Hurston.

In addition to her 18 novels and eight collections of short stories, Hurst's creativity reached into the stage and cinema. Her first stage play, *Back Pay,* was produced on Broadway in 1921 to wide acclaim. Twenty-eight of Hurst's stories and novels were adapted to film, including 1933's IMITATION OF LIFE, produced for the big screen originally in 1934 starring Claudette Colbert and later in 1959 with Lana Turner in the lead role.

In addition to her prolific writing career, she hosted *The Fannie Hurst Showcase* on public television, which featured panel discussions on a variety of issues. In her later years, she would frequently lead public storytelling sessions for children in New York's Central Park.

Hurst had an unconventional marriage to pianist Jacques Danielson, whom she wed in a 1915 civil ceremony. They kept their marriage, which lasted 37 years until Danielson's death, a secret for the first five years, until a reporter accidentally uncovered it. Their arrangement was considered unusual and progressive in that Hurst kept her maiden name and they kept separate homes and separate social lives (Danielson despised public appearances, in contrast to Hurst, who enjoyed socializing). Hurst was often the center of media attention and was as comfortable visiting with her reserved husband as she was in the company of other cultural luminaries, like her good friends Franklin D. and Eleanor Roosevelt.

Hurst died at her home in New York City on February 23, 1968. An excerpt from a eulogy that appeared March 1 of that year in the *New York Times* describes her as "someone who communicated with the common man. . . . She talked to the common people but she also talked to the common good in them."

Hurst was a firm believer in higher education. She bequeathed the rights to her literary estate to Brandeis University and to her alma mater, Washington University, to establish literary scholarships in her name that carry forth her creative legacy into the 21st century.

Bibliography

Koppleman, Susan. *The Stories of Fannie Hurst.* New York: The Feminist Press at the City University of New York, 2004.

Kroeger, Brooke. *Fannie: The Talent for Success of Writer Fannie Hurst.* New York: Times Books, 1999.

—Jacqueline May

Illness as Metaphor Susan Sontag (1978)

Cancer always leads to death. Or so goes the myth SUSAN SONTAG sets out to debunk in *Illness as Metaphor*. Throughout history, societies have chosen to interpret illness and draw conclusions from it rather than accept it. As in her earlier work *AGAINST INTERPRETATION*, Sontag argues that there are things that cannot be interpreted—they simply are. At the core of her argument lies the notion that sentimentalizing and moralizing illness can only result in punishing the victims, condemning them to the world of the dead long before illness kills them. Only by stripping away metaphors and fantasies can we view illness ironically, and therefore in its healthiest way.

Thirty years after the publication of the book, even after numerous medical advancements and treatments for cancer have been discovered, cancer remains one of the leading causes of death in the United States. Sontag claims that because no single definitive cure has been found, cancer remains an illness enshrouded in mystery, and, therefore, enveloped in mythology. It is cancer that primarily holds Sontag's attention in the essay, having herself been terminally diagnosed with the disease in the 1970s and eventually dying from leukemia in 2004. "Her own long fight with cancer gave her pitiless insights into illness and into the psychology of suffering and into the degree of blame all sick people are forced to bear" (Gurganus).

Sontag deconstructs the mythology of cancer through a comparison to an earlier insidious and once always terminal disease: tuberculosis (TB). Unlike TB, cancer is not contagious, but Sontag's essay points to how the fears and fantasies that surround it become as infectious and almost as deadly as the pulmonary bacteria that cause tuberculosis, so much so that the very mention of the word *cancer* can become, in itself, a death sentence. Some cancers have traceable causes, such as asbestos or tobacco. Even so, not everyone who has been exposed to asbestos—nor every smoker—will necessarily get cancer. We attach metaphors to the disease, Sontag tells us, because of this very mystery. The mystery in turn, because it is unsolvable, becomes obscene. In people's minds, cancer becomes a disease that "creeps like a crab," a "demonic pregnancy." Tuberculosis, one almost always assumes, attacks the lungs. But cancer often attacks parts of the body "that are embarrassing to acknowledge," such as the "colon, bladder, rectum, breast, cervix, prostate, [and] testicles."

Cancer then can be mythologized, but is difficult to romanticize. Not so with tuberculosis. Sontag's essay alludes to the many tubercular fantasies found in writing since the time of the romantics. For them and for many writers after them, tuberculosis was the result of too much love and passion (see André Gide's *The Immoralist,* or Henry James' *The Wings of the Dove*). Cancer, on the other hand, was blamed on repression (see Leo Tolstoy's *The Death of Ivan Ilyich*). These literary time lines help to illustrate how the metaphor—and not the truth—becomes entrenched in people's psyches. It may make for good literature but only further confuses patients already grappling with the universal question of the ailing or ill-fated: Why me? Instead, Sontag wanted to empower "readers to take greater responsibility for their illnesses and demand more information and more accountability from doctors" (Giles). Furthermore, Sontag argues, cancer and other diseases are not to be viewed through a moral lens. They are not the result of moral depravity or sin, in the way, for example, that the 10 ancient plagues in the Bible are interpreted as the result of the Egyptian pharaoh shutting his heart to God. The cause of cancer is an uncontrolled division of cells, and all it reveals is "that the body is, all too woefully, just the body."

The last chapter appeals to societies to come to terms with their distorted visions of cancer. This is not easy to do, Sontag admits, as the language of TB and cancer has been lifted and reapplied to the "body politic." Hitler, she tells us, when speaking of Jews, referred to them as "a racial tuberculosis among nations," and later "modernized" his metaphor, comparing the "Jewish problem" to a cancer for which "one must cut out much of the healthy tissue around." Similar political and military metaphors still used by governments today do nothing more than perpetuate the notion that cancer is always lethal. In the end, Sontag hoped that the language of real research and medical advancements would facilitate the necessary revision.

A 1979 review of the book criticized it for lacking a "development of her best insights," primarily, it seems, because it neglects "describing the individual experience," and also because "no subject can be de-mythicised" (Sabini and Lambert). Sontag addressed this criticism directly in her first chapter of *AIDS and Its Metaphors,* published 10 years after *Illness as Metaphor.* She countered that there would be many more first-person stories that would yield "narrative pleasure." Her concern was to show that like cancer, "metaphors and myths" can "kill." It may be impossible to think without

metaphors, but some may be more dangerous than illustrative. Today there is still no sure cure for cancer, but neither is it, in Sontag's words, a curse, punishment, or embarrassment. "And not necessarily a death sentence."

Bibliography

Giles, Patrick. "Susan Sontag, Writer and Witness." *National Catholic Reporter* 41, no. 10 (January 7, 2005): 15.

Gurganus, Allan. "Notes on Sontag." *Advocate,* 1 February 2005, 35.

Sabini, M., and Kenneth Lambert. "Illness as Metaphor (Book)." *Journal of Analytical Psychology* 24, no. 3 (July 1979): 270–272.

Sontag, Susan. *AIDS and Its Metaphors.* New York: Farrar, Straus and Giroux, 1988.

—**Lourdes Fernandez**

Imitation of Life   **Fannie Hurst** (1933)

FANNIE HURST's novel *Imitation of Life* is a story of intricate relationships centered around two young widows who struggle to find security and balance for themselves and their young daughters.

Bea Pullman is a teen left widowed with an infant daughter and paralyzed father to look after. To support the family, Bea takes in boarders and struggles to keep her deceased husband Bill's maple syrup sales route going. Of the many relationships explored in the novel, one of the most complex is formed when Bea encounters Delilah Johnston, another widow with a young daughter of her own. Bea and Delilah form an alternate family of sorts. Breaking social norms of the era, Bea goes out to earn an income while Delilah keeps the household running and looks after Bea's father and the two girls.

Despite the women's respect for each other, there is imbalance and inequality in their relationship stemming from Delilah's African ethnicity and the racial tensions of the period. Delilah is depicted as a stereotypical mammy figure whose role is to look after and nurture others. Yet it is Delilah's accomplished cooking that elevates them all from uncertainty to financial security. The women, with

Bea in charge of business operations and Delilah in charge of the kitchen, open the B. Pullman waffle house, which evolves into a successful national chain of restaurants.

The most distinct relationship of *Imitation of Life* is that of black versus white. In the time in which this novel is set and written, well before civil rights for blacks were established, misconceptions about race greatly impacted American life. Delilah's daughter, Peola, is depicted as a light-skinned African American who, in contrast to her dark-skinned mother, is often mistaken for white. Her ability to "pass" as white is a source of great inner conflict for Peola. The child denies her black heritage so she can enjoy the same privileges she observes other white children experiencing. Delilah is constantly trying to make Peola aware that her place in society as a black woman, as she sees it, is no less significant than that of her white contemporaries. Peola's inner strife causes her to turn against her mother, admonishing her to "just let me pass!" Thus, the character of Peola represents the struggle for balance and equality between black and white. Hurst shows us how, for Peola and others of her generation, there could be no in between; one had to be either black or white.

Bea is also lacking balance in her life. Her devotion to the growing business takes precedence over personal relationships. Her daughter, Jessie, is sent away to boarding school to obtain the best education money can buy, and Bea focuses on building the financial security she believes will make a difference in all their lives. As the story unfolds, Bea comes to realize that without healthy relationships, the most one can really hope to live is an "imitation of life."

In creating this novel, Hurst was not afraid to break with traditional roles of race and gender. By the end of the novel, Peola, as far as the reader knows, adopts an entirely white identity and shuns her mother and heritage. Bea has attained business success not common to women of the era, but her life is devoid of happiness, and she, too, is alienated from her daughter.

Imitation of Life is still a significant novel in that its social commentary regarding the importance of equality and balance is as relevant today as when it was written in 1933.

Bibliography
Caughie, Pamela L. "Let It Pass: Changing the Subject, Once Again." In *Feminism and Composition Studies: In Other Words.* New York: Modern Language Association of America, 1998.
Ravitz, Abe C. *Imitations of Life: Fannie Hurst's Gaslight Sonatas.* Carbondale: Southern Illinois University Press, 1997.

—Jacqueline May

I Never Promised You a Rose Garden
Hannah Green (1964)

Of the nearly 20 novels and story collections brought out by Joanne Greenberg since 1963, *I Never Promised You a Rose Garden* continues to draw the most attention. Published in 1964 under the pseudonym Hannah Green, it was Greenberg's second novel, one that she acknowledges is based heavily on her own experience. Because of its autobiographical foundation, *Rose Garden* became a subject of critical controversy soon after publication when reviewers questioned whether it could more accurately be considered a novel or a fictionalized case study. The uncertainty is best resolved by recognizing the work on its own terms as the author wrote it.

Rose Garden focuses on approximately three years in the life of Deborah Blau, the author's persona, whose frightening psychological aberrations, beyond the understanding of her family, lead to her being institutionalized at the age of 16 against her father's wishes because he prefers to have her near. The novel opens as she rides with her parents to the sanatorium. Diagnosed there as schizophrenic and regarded by most of the hospital staff as probably incurable, Deborah is nevertheless treated by a remarkably patient and open-minded analyst, Dr. Clara Fried, educated as a psychiatrist in Germany, where she had practiced before immigrating to the United States to escape the Nazis. (Dr. Fried is modeled closely on Dr. Frieda Fromm-Reichmann, whose extraordinary care at the Chestnut Lodge psychiatric hospital in Maryland led to Greenberg's gradual return to psychological stability and a virtually new existence.) As Jews, Dr. Fried and Deborah have suffered from the stings of anti-Semitism, which enables the analyst to relate compassionately to the effects of hostility, first on the Blau family and, later, on the sensitive adolescent herself, whose maternal grandfather unwittingly planted the first seeds of her illness. Blau's grandfather had been driven from his native Latvia as a hated Jew and immigrated to the United States, where he made a fortune and dedicated himself to creating a dynasty as a form of vengeance against abusive gentiles. His bitterness and arrogance combined to pressure, first, his daughter to marry into wealth, which she successfully resisted, then to transform Deborah, his lovely blond granddaughter, into a princess through overindulging her from infancy on. Her grandfather's egocentric imposition as an embittered Jew, her father's suppressed sexual attraction to her, which she intuitively perceives, and the anti-Semitic harassment she has faced all merge, creating too much pressure to bear without help. Consequently, she has turned inward and created a new reality in her imagination, the world of Yr, that has gained control over her year by year with its fantastic characters and language. Increasingly, Deborah depends on Yr for guidance and solace to the point that her behavior has become altogether incomprehensible to her family.

The diversified fellow patients and medics whom Deborah meets in the hospital are strikingly individualized by their physical appearance, antic behavior, and developing relationships with the psychotic young woman, but it is Greenberg's dynamic, insightful portrait of the tormented heroine that drives the novel; trapped and goaded to self-mutilation by her psychosis, she simultaneously cooperates yet resists her probing, insistent analyst. Dr. Fried's patient questioning and empathic listening evoke the deeply internalized conflicts and fears that had fabricated a new symbolic life for Deborah and gained enough strength over time to dominate her external existence. Her responses to Dr. Fried surprise her as she becomes aware of the familial roots that underlie much of her illness, especially the double impact on her

mind of her obsessive grandfather and overprotective father. This epiphany subsequently frees her from anger toward them, as well as from the control of Yr, which she readily deletes from her mind at last as she returns, renewed, to the actual world of color and form.

Bibliography

Bail, Paul. "Good Mother, Bad Mother in Joanne Greenberg's *I Never Promised You a Rose Garden.*" In *Women in Literature: Reading through the Lens of Gender.* Westport, Conn.: Greenwood, 2003.

Hornstein, Gail A. *To Redeem One Person Is to Redeem the World: The Life of Frieda Fromm-Reichmann.* New York: Free Press, 2000.

Rubin, Stephen E. "Conversations with the Author of *I Never Promised You a Rose Garden.*" *Psychoanalytic Review* 59 (1972): 201–216.

—Sanford E. Marovitz

In My Father's Court
Isaac Bashevis Singer (1966)

In My Father's Court is one of three memoirs that ISAAC BASHEVIS SINGER wrote about his life in Poland. This memoir recounts Singer's experiences as a boy while living in a Jewish district in Warsaw before and during World War I. Rather than a single narrative, *In My Father's Court* is a collection of vignettes about the moral, social, and religious problems brought before Singer's rabbi father as he acted as a judge and counselor.

Singer was born into a very Orthodox home. Anxious to see their son continue in the family profession, Singer's parents encouraged him to pursue a career as a rabbi. But, after a brief time in rabbinical school, Singer realized that a career as a rabbi did not suit him. He left the school to pursue a literary career.

Singer's father is portrayed in this memoir as extremely pious to the point of irrationality. Singer's mother, however, is extremely practical. In the story "Why the Geese Shrieked," a woman comes to court frightened by apparently cursed geese that continue to shriek after having been slaughtered. Singer's father's solution was to cast the devils out of the geese, but Singer's mother determined that the source of the sound was the geeses' windpipes. As an experiment, Singer's father had windpipes removed and the geese stopped shrieking. Singer interpreted the incident as a victory for reason over piety, and began to question his traditional orthodox upbringing. The contrast between the practicality that his mother demonstrated and the pious belief in miracles that characterized his father was something that the young Singer had to reconcile.

In this memoir, the lessons Singer learns while watching his father sharply contrasted to his early experiences with the libertine gentile world in which his brother Joshua seemed to reside. This contrast influenced Singer's religious doubt and pushed him to question his family's Hasidic tradition. Singer began to read gentile philosophers and explore philosophical questions while also exploring the sensual world and his growing fascination with sex.

The burgeoning questions of human nature, the role of God and religion, and philosophical questions about life that started by Singer's watching his father act as a judge on complex moral and philosophical issues became the motifs that Singer carefully explores in many of his subsequent works. His characters often pushed against the Ten Commandments to test God's laws: Sex was a common subject, and Singer's characters often had multiple lovers or even multiple wives; rabbis struggled with and succumbed to temptations; children associated with demons; and good men became murderers. His more orthodox readers often found his novels and stories outright pornographic. Later in his career Singer wrote novels that explored political ideology and also published several children's books.

Singer was awarded the Nobel Prize in literature in 1978 for his contributions to literature, which included his insights into prewar Jewish life in eastern Europe.

Bibliography

Kresh, Paul. *Isaac Bashevis Singer: The Magician of West 86th Street.* New York: Dial Press, 1979.
Rosen, Jonathan. "The Fabulist: How I. B. Singer Translated Himself into American Culture." New Yorker 80, no. 15 (June 7, 2004).
Singer, Isaac Bashevis. *In My Father's Court.* New York: Farrar, Straus and Giroux, 1966.

—C. Lee Player

Inventing Memory: A Novel of Mothers and Daughters Erica Jong (1997)

ERICA JONG (b. 1942) has long subscribed to Jane Tompkin's assertion that women's literature does culture work; that writing by women engages the actual lives of women, not merely the conventions of literary rhetoric. In *Inventing Memory: A Novel of Mothers and Daughters,* her eighth novel, Jong continues her agenda, begun with the radical FEAR OF FLYING (1973), of teaching women, especially Jewish-American women, to soar above the inhibitions of their bodies and their roles as men's helpmates. With a polyvalent multimedia narrative, Jong creates as well as re-creates four generations of mothers and daughters from one unconventional artistic Jewish family who through the tumultuous 20th century emerge from cocoons of traditional repression to lives of sexual ecstasy and professional fulfillment.

Propelled out of Russia in 1905 by a pogrom that kills her twin brother and her baby son, Sarah Solomon arrives in an America of bowler hats, Irish cops, Italian anarchists, and Jews huddled on New York's Lower East Side. She quickly leaves her sweatshop job, finds work as an artist's assistant, and lives with two men, a *landsman,* Lev Levitsky, and a New Yorker from Edith Wharton's upper class. Pregnant by this elite lover who refuses to marry her, Sarah bears a daughter and marries her Jewish lover. The daughter, Salome, rebels even further, becoming an avant-garde novelist who visits Paris where she has a passionate affair with Henry Miller, discovers her real father, and inherits her father's Berkshire estate. The state is called The Mount, the actual name of Wharton's country home, and in an ironic redressing of the anti-Semitic portraits in Wharton's work, this first generation Jewish-American daughter converts the mansion into a refuge for European Jews fleeing the Holocaust. She marries one of them, and their daughter moves even farther into the counterculture of 1960s America. Sally Sky becomes a famous folksinger, marries an equally famous celebrity, but buckles under the pressures of career and an abusive husband. Becoming an alcoholic, Sally leaves her marriage and daughter.

We meet Sally and all these unconventional women through this abandoned daughter, Sara, who, as she turns 18, discovers her mother, grandmother, and great grandmother living in New York. With their support, she becomes a history graduate student at Columbia University and marries a fellow student who then betrays her. As a single mother working on her dissertation concerning Jewish-American immigrant history, she discovers audio tapes from her great grandmother, manuscripts and diaries of her grandmother, and newspaper interviews of her own mother. The narrative is bracketed by this last daughter's scholarly excursions into the realms of memoir and autobiography, and recovers the various voices alternating chapters of the audio recordings of the founding ancestor, excerpts from the manuscripts of the writer grandmother, and journal entries of the alcoholic folksinger mother. Finally, Sara, the contemporary professor of history, comes to understand the paradoxical subjective nature of memory and gathers strength from these earlier generations. She makes peace with her own neglectful mother as she prepares for the further battles and victories awaiting Jewish-American women seeking to transmit a heritage of liberated and liberating women.

Bibliography

Louit, Robert. "Erica Jong: Writing about Sex is Harder for a Woman." In *Conversations with Erica Jong*. Jackson: University of Mississippi Press, 2002.

Templin, Charlotte. *Feminism and the Politics of Literary Reputation: The Example of Erica Jong.* Lawrence: University Press of Kansas, 1995.

—Annette Zilversmit

Irving, John (1942–)

John Winslow Irving has been a popular and critical success since the publication of his fourth novel, *The WORLD ACCORDING TO GARP* (1978), which remains his most successful and important novel, as well as an intriguing fictional version of his early life and career as an artist. He was born in Exeter, New Hampshire, on March 2, 1942, to a single mother, Helen Frances. According to Josie Campbell, his biological father, John Wallace Blunt, after whom he was originally named, was a pilot shot down over Burma during World War II. The couple divorced before Irving was born, and he had no further contact with his biological father. When he was six, his mother married Colin F. N. Irving, who adopted him, and he changed his name to John Winslow (his mother's maiden name) Irving. Irving was educated at Phillips Exeter Academy, where his adopted father taught Russian history and where, like his protagonist T. S. Garp, he developed an affinity for wrestling and writing. Irving named his first son Colin, presumably after his adopted father, and later endowed the Colin F. N. Irving '41 Lecture Series at Exeter. He graduated cum laude from the University of New Hampshire in 1965, with stops at the University of Pittsburgh and the University of Vienna (Austria), and in 1967 he also completed an M.F.A. degree at the University of Iowa, where he studied with Kurt Vonnegut and wrestled with NCAA wrestling champion Dan Gable. His first novel, *Setting Free the Bears* (1969), came out of his creative thesis as directed by Vonnegut. His time in Vienna, in another parallel to *Garp*, provided the setting and inspiration for this first publication. While in Vienna Irving married Shyla Leary, a painter he had met while taking a German class at Harvard. They had two sons, Colin and Brendan, divorcing in 1982. In 1987 Irving married his agent, Janet Turnbull, with whom he has a son, Everett. In 1992 he was inducted into the National Wrestling Hall of Fame. Irving has received numerous awards, including a Guggenheim, a National Book Award, and an Oscar. He continues to see himself fundamentally as a novelist and has expressed for himself what he wrote about Garp—that compared to writing, everything else can seem something of a letdown.

Irving's literary reputation has not quite lived up to his popular success. Critics seem to be in disagreement regarding the thematic and ideological weight of his work as a whole, but certainly single out *Garp, The Cider House Rules,* and *A Prayer for Owen Meany* as texts particularly worthy of serious scholarly consideration. Irving's style of novel writing has been described most widely as Dickensian; Irving himself has admitted to being a regular and enthusiastic reader of Dickens, noting in an interview with bookreporter.com that he is saving the one Dickens novel he hasn't read, *Our Mutual Friend,* for emergency use. Like Dickens, Irving creates memorable characters, both major and minor, to inhabit his sprawling plots, and then endows them with a unique humanity that goes beyond stereotype and even their status as "typical" Irving characters. As figures out of the mainstream, they can often seem semigrotesque, but Irving always manages to find them a place within an empathetic community. He loves to repeat his standard motifs—bears, wrestling, Vienna, writing, origin-searching, fate, in/fidelity, family, sexualities, danger, death, and so forth—and seems preoccupied with the tension between binaries such as freedom/responsibility, charity/violence, comedy/tragedy, imagination/reality, personal/political, ordinary/fantastic, hope/pessimism, and so forth. Acutely aware of contemporary social issues, Irving takes great care to address them in fundamentally ethical terms. He pays careful attention to detail and wants to get even the minor elements exactly right. He always wraps up his plots neatly with virtually every thread tied up in the end—yet another Dickensian trait—although his endings are not always happy. Irving's other major literary influences include most of the major novelists of the 19th century, American, English, and Russian, as well as 20th-century writers such as Robertson Davies, William Faulkner, Günter Grass, Graham Greene, Gabriel García-Márquez, and Salman Rushdie. All these writers produce lengthy novels that require a certain investment of time and intensity on the part of their readers. Like them, Irving is basically a serious writer of big novels.

His three novels before *Garp,* however, are not all that big, although they embody Irving's typical style, characterization, motifs, and themes. *Setting Free the Bears* is the story of Hannes Graff and Siggy Javotnik off on a motorcycle trip that ends in Siggy's accidental death in a collision with a beehive-loaded truck and leaves Graff to fulfill his friend's dream of setting free all the animals in Vienna's Heitzinger Zoo as a metaphor for Austria's liberation from the 1938 *Anschluss* with Nazi Germany. *The Water-Method Man* (1972) is also a dual-narrated novel, featuring autobiographical chapters dealing with the past narrated by the protagonist, Fred "Bogus" Thumper, which alternate with third-person-narrated chapters dealing with the present. With a complex plot, full of quirky characters and bawdy escapades, the novel aspires to be completely comical farce, with its central symbolic motif being Thumper's attempt to alleviate his pain at urination and ejaculation by using the "water-method"—drinking huge amounts of water—instead of having the surgery that would eliminate the problem altogether. His eventual decision to undergo the surgery portends the amelioration of all his other problems as well. By contrast, *The 158-Pound Marriage* (1974), Irving's least comical novel, features a joyless spouse-swapping plot in which the lives of two couples and their children are almost destroyed by their pursuit of sexual variety. *Garp* combines almost all of the themes and motifs of these three novels, almost as if Irving wrote them in anticipation of this first fully realized novel.

The Hotel New Hampshire (1981) revolves around Winslow and Mary Berry and their five children. As narrated by the middle son, John, the novel has the aura of fantasy as it traces the family's life as hotel managers and inhabitants. It features one of Irving's only Jewish characters, the mysterious Freud, who sells Winslow a motorcycle and a bear in Maine, and whose immigration to America anticipates the rise of the Third Reich and the events of World War II. After the war, Freud persuades the family to move to Vienna to help with his Gasthaus Freud, which proves to be a disaster for everyone involved. *The Cider House Rules* (1985) tackles the issue of abortion with its focus on a Maine orphanage/abortion clinic run by Dr. Wilbur Larch and later, upon his death, by Homer Wells, an orphan who spent his childhood assisting Larch. Although the novel is decidedly pro-choice, Irving balances that position with a pervasive sense of the value of children. It also features a far simpler plot and gentler narrative style. *A Prayer for Owen Meany* (1989), told from the first-person perspective of John Wheelright, takes on the political and social issues of America in the 1950s and 1960s, particularly the Vietnam War. The title character, Owen, as John's best friend, becomes a Christ figure as he anticipates the heroic action that it is his destiny to fulfill.

A Son of the Circus (1994) takes place in India and features a protagonist, Farrokh Daruwalla, who is both an orthopedic surgeon and a writer of detective films. The plot is fairly straightforward, but also revolves around a complicated murder mystery and addresses themes of identity, sexual and otherwise, as well as postcolonial political issues such as the rise of AIDS and the anxiety of cultural hybridity. *A Widow for One Year* (1998) centers on Ruth Cole, a novelist whose career bears certain resemblances to Irving's, and is another one of his writer novels. In fact, it's full of writers: Ted, her father; Marion, her estranged mother; and Eddie, Marion's persistent young admirer. In *The Fourth Hand* (2001) the protagonist, reporter Patrick Wallingford, has his left hand taken off by a lion while he's covering an Indian circus. It's a transplant story of mixed identity, exploring the ethics of substitution and rejection, especially in terms of donor and recipient, but also in terms of other interested parties. *Until I Find You* (2005) chronicles the search of a man, actor Jack Burns, for his father, William. This search is based on two foundational facts he gets from his mother Alice, a tattoo artist: William is a church organist who is addicted to getting tattoos. Again Irving explores the issues of identity and relationships and the difficulty inherent in writing the self.

Irving's novels are all different from one another, but they also have enough in common that they seem to be engaged in a long-term conversation with one another. Populated by a carnivalesque collection of characters, they brim over with narrative energy balanced by serious contemporary themes.

Bibliography

Bloom, Harold, ed. *John Irving*. Philadelphia: Chelsea House, 2001.

Campbell, Josie P. *John Irving: A Critical Companion*. Westport, Conn.: Greenwood, 1998.

Harter, Carol C., and James R. Thompson. *John Irving*. Boston: Twayne, 1986.

—Phillip A. Snyder

Jong, Erica (1942–)

In 1998, looking back over a literary career that had spanned nearly three decades, Erica Jong wrote that she had learned to embrace "a willingness to change, to risk the unknown, to do the very things [she] feared most." Jong's career is marked by a definitive fearlessness interpreted by some as neurotic recklessness, and others as a liberating response to a legacy of cultural restraints. But her daring literary initiative propelled her into the mainstream spotlight and established her a permanent place within literary history. Her openness in writing about sex and women's issues defines her; few other writers inhabit such a provocative space in literature.

Born into New York's Upper West Side, Jong belongs to a legacy of creativity. Her father, Seymour Mann, the child of Polish Jews, was a businessman and musician who performed on Broadway. Eda Mirsky Mann, Jong's mother, was a painter and designer of ceramics and clothing. Jong's maternal grandfather was also a painter, and she spent a great deal of time in his studio, which occupied the top floor of the family's three-floor apartment. Jong's captivation with the arts began as she painted alongside her grandfather, who meticulously educated her in painting. But while her relationship with her grandfather thrived, her relationship with her mother became tentative and Jong admits to her hatred of her mother's "capitulation to her femaleness." Jong often speaks of her mother's anger as something that fueled Jong's own feminism. Eda Mann had been the best draftswoman and painter in her class at the National Academy of Design, and "had every reason to win the top prizes—including the big traveling fellowship—the Prix de Rome." But she was told that as a woman she was expected to marry and bear children, even if that meant wasting her creative gifts. Consequently, Jong began to view womanhood and domesticity as impediments to happiness and freedom. Like many women of her generation, Jong's desires—both to emulate her mother and to escape her example—often conflicted, but this tension fueled her ambitions.

After attending the High School of Music and Art in New York City and graduating from Barnard College in 1963, Jong received a master's degree in 18th-century literature from Columbia University in 1965 and began doctoral studies, but abandoned them to devote full time to writing. During this period she also married and divorced her first husband, fellow Columbia student Michael Werthman. In 1966 she married Allan Jong, a Chinese-American child psychiatrist. When the military sent him to Germany, Jong accompanied him and taught in the University of Maryland Overseas program. Allan Jong provided the inspiration for Bennett Wing in *FEAR OF FLYING* (1973);

likewise, many of the novel's Heidelburg episodes match this period of her life. After they divorced, Jong married Jonathan Fast, the "Josh Ace" in Jong's novels—*How to Save Your Own Life* (1977) and *Parachutes & Kisses* (1984). Jong's marriage to Fast produced her only child, a daughter—Molly Miranda Jong-Fast, who published a novel in 2000. Jong's fourth marriage was to attorney Kenneth Burrows.

The result of Jong's decision to devote herself to writing was an onslaught of published work beginning with the controversial novel *Fear of Flying*, the first of many works that fuse aspects of her own life with their fictional counterparts. With this first novel, Jong was transformed into a celebrity overnight. As with much of her work, the central themes of the novel include openness to sexual and other experiences, and the voyage of liberation and self-discovery. Most remarkable about this work was that it retrieves the erotic life for the middle-class women of America through the celebration of female sexuality. To be sure, her frank, graphically depicted scenes drew much negative criticism as the "zipless fuck" became her most illustrious phrase. But buried not far beneath the surface of *Fear* is an ambivalence regarding the fantasy of frequent, casual (usually extramarital) sex—for accompanying each "zipless fuck" are emotional, psychological, and social repercussions. Although the novel's Isadora Wing longs to be liberated sexually, the thrill of her sexual encounters is linked primarily to the fact that it is adultery—alluring because it is forbidden. Some critics have noted this point as the place where Jong's philosophy disintegrates, for it relies on the institution of marriage—from which her sexual escapades are an escape. Nonetheless, the book proved to be a sensation, and more than 20 million copies have been sold worldwide.

Jong has published consistently, and has written eight novels including FANNY: BEING THE TRUE HISTORY OF THE ADVENTURES OF FANNY HACKABOUT-JONES (1980) and *Sappho's Leap* (2003); six volumes of poetry; a memoir, *Fear of Fifty* (1994); a biography; and other works such as *What Do Women Want? Bread, Roses, Sex, Power* (1998).

Jong's latest book is a collection of essays—*Seducing the Demon: Writing for My Life* (2006). Though best known for her fiction, Jong claims that poetry is the center of her artistic ability. Her first two published works were collections of poetry in 1971 and 1973 (*Fruits and Vegetables* and *Half-Lives*). Most of her poetry, free verse, conversational, and deeply personal, deals with the same themes as her fiction. To Jong's dismay, however, her poetry has been neglected by scholars, which may be why she has focused primarily on fiction and memoir since her last poetry publication (*Becoming Light*, 1991). In addition to various literary awards, in 1998 Jong received the United Nations Award for Excellence in Literature. She has taught writing at the City University of New York, the 92nd Street Y in Manhattan, the Breadloaf Writers Conference in Vermont, The Salzburg Seminar in Austria, and Ben-Gurion University in Israel.

While critics typically have strong opinions about her work, Jong has received far less scholarly attention than her contemporaries. While notables such as Henry Miller and John Updike praised Jong's early work incessantly, her subsequent works garnered little more than book reviews and a handful of critical essays. Critics note that the self-consciousness present in her early work becomes compulsive and tiresome in later work. And rather than a testament to her intellectual stamina, Jong's frequent references to other writers have been called an exhibit of random knowledge. Regardless, Jong utilizes her literary knowledge to address gender, sexuality, and relationships. *Fanny*, especially, is an exception to the undesirable criticism. In *Fanny* Jong rethinks the picaresque 18th-century novel and has her heroine interact with prominent literary figures such as Defoe, Swift, and Fielding. One critic called *Fanny* part of the Jewish fiction tradition based on Jewish motifs including rootlessness, persecution, and humor. INVENTING MEMORY (1997), however, is the only one of Jong's novels that deals explicitly with Jewish issues, telling the story of four generations of Jewish women and reflecting the character Sara Levitsky's quest to retrace her family heritage. But Jong approaches

Jewish history with trepidation, as if she is not quite ready to explore this aspect of her identity. In a recent article, "Mothers, Daughters and the Holocaust," Jong deals directly with the legacy of the Holocaust, however, and reveals the terror she felt in 1955 upon visiting Europe and learning about the previous decade's horrors. She recalls an intense desire to return to New York, where she would not have to think about such atrocities. Perhaps this confession reveals Jong's purposeful avoidance of Jewish themes throughout her literary career. But nearly 40 years later, she is forced to confront the tragedy again with her own teenage daughter—which may mark a turning point in Jong's self-discovery process, one that includes a deeper understanding of her Jewish identity.

Bibliography

Jong, Erica. *Conversations with Erica Jong*. Edited by Charlotte Templin. Jackson: University Press of Mississippi, 2002.

"Erica Jong." Available online. URL: http://www.EricaJong.com. Accessed on March 17, 2006.

—**Monica Osborne**

Kaaterskill Falls Allegra Goodman (1998)

Kaaterskill Falls (1998) is a contemporary Jewish comedy of manners done in an ironic pastoral mode. Elizabeth Shulman, a devout orthodox wife and mother of six daughters, lives in company with a variety of Jewish families and gentile villagers. Significantly, she also inhabited the summer community of the Kirchner Orthodox during three short summers in the 1970s. In actuality, this was the community of ALLEGRA GOODMAN's childhood summer visits, and the community in which her mother grew up.

The book is filled with portraits of tiny children, teenagers, Holocaust survivors, displaced Germans, English, Hungarians, and Syrian Arabs, the ultra-rich Jewish and non-Jewish inhabitants of the local gated communities, and a series of blue-collar non-Jewish types. Central to the immanent ruptures within this American Kaaterskill covenant community is Rav Kirschner, a German Jew who has led several hundred followers out of Germany into Manhattan in 1938 on the eve the Holocaust. In the 1950s he urged them to use reparation payments to buy property in rural Kaaterskill. Goodman bases her portrayal of the community's theology on the teachings of the 19th-century Jewish rabbi, Samson Raphael Hirsch, who encouraged traditionalist Jews to receive a secular education—the better to withstand the challenges of modernity. The brilliant grandson of the famous Rav Jeremiah Solomon Hecht, the founder of German neo-orthodoxy, Goodman's fictional Rav Kirschner also insists that his followers study science, languages, literature, and mathematics. However, he has become increasingly aloof and insular. He visits on his American-born followers a good measure of German contempt, while they in turn adore him as a "real" (i.e., European) pre-Holocaust rabbi. His ancient gender ideologies, rabbinical arrogance, failures as a husband and father, and advanced Parkinson's disease make him difficult for the central protagonist, Elizabeth, to deal with. He is misogynous, remote, tyrannical, and perhaps senile. But, having survived the depredations of anti-Semitism in Europe, he is now faced with the threat of assimilation in America. His German followers are beginning to die off, leaving only the ingenuous American-born flock. Within the "borscht belt" these iconoclasts of the 1950–70 moment face major cultural change and possibly even extinction.

Center stage in the novel is the ambitious and imaginative Elizabeth Shulman, whose religious commitments within patriarchy and the *Kehilla* prevent her from taking refuge in American secular feminism. The book questions the function of women within the patriarchal covenant community as it registers Elizabeth's collision with the small and bounded edges of her Orthodox world. Through a series of disappointments and challenges to her faith, through two disappearing summers, two fading autumns, and two winters of death, a spring of fragile reaffirmation, and a new summer of quiet rejoicing, Elizabeth's soul measures the painful cost of preserving the *Kehilla*. Now, like a chained tiger, Elizabeth perpetually paces in a new condition of deep restiveness.

Full of restraints, miniature portraits, trifles, little cares, everyday happenings, holy and unholy humor, the novel takes for its canvas the modern Jewish Kaaterskill Falls equivalent of an 18th-century Jane Austen village. Like Sara Orne Jewett, Willa Cather, and Flannery O'Connor before her, Goodman brings to life her tiny pastoral retreat, with all its counterpoints of pain, death, tragedy, comedy, local color, and historical fragility. At the heart of the novel lies the elaborate Victorian Frederick Church house on the nearby Olana Estate, the map of Fairyland in the Kaaterskill Public Library, Bierstadt's paintings of the Hudson River Valley, and most important of all, Thomas Cole's famous painting of Kaaterskill Falls. These function as metatexts for this most recent story of the successive communities of American religious romantics who have secluded themselves in the area.

Indeed, *Kaaterskill Falls* recalls a whole series of religious separatists, including the desert patriarchs, the Jews of the Diaspora, the Puritans of the New World, the Hudson River valley romantics, Brook Farm residents, and now, Yiddish-speaking European Holocaust survivors in the form of the Kirschners. Structured talmudically around a complex web of embedded metatexts—literary, artistic, plastic, and painterly—this novel resonates with epigraphs from Psalms, Samuel Johnson, John Keats, Oscar Wilde, Nicholas Breton, and Edna St. Vincent Millay. Their progression marks the seasonal cycles of Elizabeth's passing spiritual states of content, discontent, and fragile reaffirmation.

Bibliography

Avery, Evelyn. "Allegra Goodman's Fiction: From the Suburbs to 'Gan Eden.'" *Studies in American Jewish Literature* 22 (2003): 36–45.

Omer-Sherman, Ranen. "Tradition and Desire in Allegra Goodman's *Kaaterskill Falls*." *MELUS* 29, no. 2 (Summer 2004): 265–289.

—Gloria L. Cronin

Kaddish Allen Ginsberg (1961)

Published in 1961 as part of a collection of poems, *Kaddish* remains one of Allen Ginsberg's best-known works and is often considered his greatest achievement. The complete title of the poem is *Kaddish for Naomi Ginsberg (1894–1956)*. The term "Kaddish" refers to the mourning ritual in Judaism customarily performed at Jewish funerals and memorials. In this instance, it is Ginsberg's attempt to remember and come to terms with the tragic life and death of his mother, Naomi Levy Ginsberg. Naomi's severe mental illness had a tremendous impact on Ginsberg's life and work. More than just a lamentation, *Kaddish* is primarily a celebration of Naomi, her life, and even her death.

The poem is divided into five major parts. Part I, a lyrical rumination on existence, begins with Ginsberg wandering the streets of Manhattan while he imagines his mother walking the same streets as a girl. He wonders what both are walking toward, and as a result asks, "what is this life?" This question becomes a central theme of the poem. Although asked specifically in the context of his mother's life and her journey toward madness, Ginsberg's question extends to the universal; more than just an elegy for his mother, *Kaddish* is an ode to humankind and life itself. Seeking an answer, Ginsberg shares his belief that this world is no more than a dream, a vision. He writes: "That's good! That leaves it open for no regret—no fear radiators, lacklove / torture even toothache in the end—/ Though while it comes it is a lion that eats the soul." Although Ginsberg acknowledges life's inherent suffering, he concludes that if that suffering is just a mirage, then death is liberation. In his mother's case, it freed her from a life plagued by pain and loneliness. Death brought her peace, and Ginsberg's beliefs enabled him to accept her death peacefully as well. Nonetheless, even while admitting the illusory nature of life, Ginsberg still praises it for merely existing: "yet Triumph / to have been here, and changed, like a tree, broken, or flower . . . No flower like that flower, which knew itself in the garden, and fought the / knife—lost." Even a life as marred by torment as his mother's is beautiful solely for being its own, unique self. Ultimately however, Ginsberg reminds us that we are all heading for the same end, the inevitable "Forever" of death.

The bulk of the poem, and by far the longest section, is Part II, in which Ginsberg recounts the life of his mother and its impact on him and the rest of the family. A victim of severe paranoid delusions, Naomi suspected everyone of conspiring against her; the doctors at the various hospitals in which she was committed; her mother-in-law, Buba; her husband, Louis; the government; Hitler himself! Young Ginsberg seemed to be the sole exception. "I was only 12," Ginsberg notes, revealing how difficult her burden of trust must have been. He tells how he took Naomi into the country to rest and escape her delusions. Unfortunately, this resulted in a massive attack of hysteria that concluded with her commitment to yet another mental hospital. Ginsberg could not help but feel responsible: "my fault delivering her to solitude?" After three years of shock therapy and medication Naomi returned home, but soon fled in fear to the house of her sister Elanor. Despite intermittent moments of peace, Naomi's condition worsened, and when she began both verbally and physically assaulting her sister, Ginsberg had her recommitted. On the rare occasions when he visited her, he was horror-struck by her physical deterioration and saddened when his own mother could not recognize him. With his permission she received a debilitating lobotomy in 1948, and ultimately died from a stroke in 1956. Two days after her death, Ginsberg received an enigmatic letter from her: "The key is in the window, the / key is in the sunlight at the window." Ginsberg seems to hope that, at the end of her long, miserable search, Naomi found the key and meaning to life. Part II ends with the brief but accordingly optimistic section entitled "Hymmnn," in which Ginsberg blesses not only death, but all the terror and madness that entailed his mother's existence. He echoes the traditional mourners' Kaddish, which never mentions death, but instead praises God.

The last three parts of the poem are rather brief and serve to sum up its themes. In Part III, Ginsberg looks back on Naomi's life as a whole, trying to make sense out of it, and out of existence, by using her prophetic last words to him. Part IV is a chant, an attempt not to forget the specific details that comprised his mother, and ties her life to the larger social history of the era as well. Finally, Part V concludes with Ginsberg standing over her grave. His final words suggest the intimate, paradoxical bond between life and death: "Lord Lord Lord caw caw caw Lord Lord Lord caw caw caw Lord."

Through the process of writing Kaddish, Ginsberg not only paid homage to his mother, but properly mourned her as well, finally burying his feelings of guilt and grief. He viewed Naomi's illness in spiritual terms rather than mental, and saw her life and death as full of meaning and purpose on its own terms. Likewise, by accepting her insanity, Ginsberg no doubt was also enabled to embrace his own life purpose as a poet, a course that required a similar level of courage and mad devotion. After all, if, as Ginsberg believed, the conventional world is as dream, and a corrupt one at that, and "sanity a trick of agreement," than perhaps the truest, purest moments of one's life can be found in the realms of insanity.

Bibliography

Breslin, James. "Allen Ginsberg: The Origins of 'Howl' and 'Kaddish.'" *Iowa Review* 8, no. 2 (1977): 82–108.
Herring, Scott. "'Her Brother Is Dead in Riverside or Russia': 'Kaddish' and the Holocaust." *Contemporary Literature* 42, no. 3 (Fall 2001): 535–556.

—Eric Izant

Kazin, Alfred (1915–1998)

Irving Howe once wrote that "Immigrant Jewish life left us with a large weight of fear." The gradual decline of the *Partisan Review* (from the 1930s), an anticommunist left journal, and the rise of

Commentary (from 1960, under the editorship of Norman Podhoretz, a neoconservative) reflects the political/cultural milieu in which Alfred Kazin rose to prominence as the preeminent literary critic of American literature. The New York Intellectuals, a group that included Kazin, Irving Howe, Philip Rahv, Sidney Hook, Daniel Bell, Delmore Schwartz, Lionel Trilling, and Meyer Schapiro, were the first Jewish writers from the immigrant milieu who did not crucially define themselves through a relationship to memories of Jewishness. They shared a deep concern for literature as literature, but they often differed in their political sympathies. They also differed in their respect for and knowledge of Judaism, Israel, *Yiddishkeit,* and memories of Jewishness.

Kazin's pathbreaking *On Native Grounds* (1942) and his early studies of Sherwood Anderson and William Faulkner set out to prove that the sons and daughters of immigrants could master American literature. *On Native Grounds* was a passionate celebration of American writers from 1890 to 1940; the last chapter, "America! America!," part of the final section on "the literature of crisis," was a full-throated plea in support of literary nationalism. At 27 this son of Yiddish-speaking immigrants became an instant authority on American literature and culture.

Born in 1915, Kazin grew up in Brooklyn, New York, where his father, Charles, was a house painter, and his mother a dressmaker. After he earned a B.S.S. in 1935 from the City College of New York, he got an M.A. from Columbia University in 1938. He began as an undergraduate writing book reviews for the *New York Times,* the *Herald Tribune,* and the *New Republic.* He began work on a study of American writers in 1938 that culminated in the publication in 1942 of *On Native Grounds.* Showing wide and deep scholarship and balanced criticism, he became a celebrity at a time of cataclysmic change in the world—the rise of Nazism, Stalinist Russia, World War II, and the Holocaust. In a 1962 interview he reflected that his literary and cultural book had catalogued an age that was passing. Writing in the accessible vernacular style so attractive to readers, Kazin's book was the result of five years of 12-hour days reading and writing at the New York Public Library.

In 1951 Kazin penned the first of three personal histories, *A Walker in the City,* his attempt to reclaim a past he was afraid of losing. It speaks of his early years in Brooklyn and also of the cultural and demographic changes that had come about in the neighborhood. A child of poor immigrants, he wrote of the squalid ghetto in New York where he had grown up, and of the family's kitchen, a place that tied him to his family, his ethnicity, and his poverty. Writing of the movement from Brooklyn to Manhattan, the "foreign city," he questioned the marginalization of Jewish and lower-class people.

In the 1950s Kazin taught at Smith and Amherst Colleges. Concerned with the academy's turn to conservatism, he criticized the complacency, self-absorption, and sense of isolation of intellectual America. In *Starting Out in the Thirties* (1965), the second of his personal histories, Kazin reflected on the 1930s, living with his parents in Brownsville (a part of Brooklyn), confident that history was going our way, but growing aware that people like the writer Mary McCarthy were subjecting the idealistic 1930s to the realism of the 1950s and 1960s.

As he moved on to teaching at New York University and the City University of New York, he speculated on the partial successes of contemporary novelists like SAUL BELLOW, NORMAN MAILER, Ralph Ellison, Joyce Carol Oates, and Thomas Pynchon in whom he saw a retreat from the all-encompassing visions of the 19th-century novelists' social and historical solidity. As he argued in *New York Jew* (1978), the third of his personal histories, the world that he, an immigrant outsider, had joined had become a world without heart dominated by the destructiveness of hedonism and power, "Power beyond reason creating a lasting irrationality." He, a Jew, an outsider, had made it, had been accepted—but he deliberately chose to remain an outsider.

In *An American Procession* (1984), his last major work, Kazin dwelled on the American preoccupation with self. Kazin had evolved from a child of immigrants in Brooklyn to a highly respected Jewish critic.

Bibliography

Cook, Richard. "Alfred Kazin." In *Modern American Critics.* Edited by Gregory S. Jay. Detroit: Gale, 1988.

Krupnick, Mark. *Jewish Writing and the Deep Places of the Imagination.* Madison: University of Wisconsin Press, 2005.

Pinsker, Sanford. *Jewish American Fiction 1917–1987.* New York: Twayne, 1992.

Silvers, Robert B. "An Interview with Alfred Kazin." *Horizon* 4 (July 1962).

Solotaroff, Ted, ed. *Alfred Kazin's America.* New York: Harper Collins, 2003.

—Daniel Walden

Klepfisz, Irena (1941–)

Born in the Warsaw Ghetto in April 1941, Klepfisz is the daughter of Michal Klepfisz, a ghetto hero who died a martyr's death on April 20, 1943, the second day of the Ghetto Uprising, and Rose Perczykow, who survived by passing as a Pole. In 1943 Klepfisz was smuggled into a Catholic orphanage on the Aryan side while Rose worked as a maid for Polish families. After Michal's death, Rose and Irena survived by hiding or passing as Poles in the Polish countryside. In 1946, after a brief stay in Lodz, they moved to Sweden, and, in 1949, emigrated to the United States, where English replaced Polish and Swedish, and where Klepfisz also learned Yiddish, adopting the language as an essential element in her identity as a diasporic Jew. She is a quintessential secular Jew, having absorbed Yiddish culture and language from New York's Workmen's Circle school, where she bridged but did not heal "the trauma of her dislocation" (Michelson 787; see also Klepfisz, "Di Mames," 12–16; Schreiber 277–278).

Settled in New York, Klepfisz attended the City College of New York for her undergraduate degree; she earned a doctorate in English literature from the University of Chicago in 1970. In the preface to her collection of essays, she explains that she was never comfortable conforming to traditional linear prose forms; she transgresses, she says, expanding borders both in form and content. "Prose," she contends, "has always been problematic"; "essays have never felt natural" (*Dreams* x). Yet her essays are strong, direct personal statements, unfolding her ideas and her identity as a Jewish lesbian feminist. Klepfisz describes them as public presentations of private discussions (*Dreams* xi), which capture the "zigzag nature of conversations, free association, and fragmentation" (*Dreams* xii). But the clarity of her prose belies the discomfort she claims.

Klepfisz approaches poetry differently, anticipating the "sheer pleasure" of challenging the "empty page," where she continues to break boundaries and test language (*Dreams* xi). Her passion for poetry stems from another child survivor, Elza, who, according to Klepfisz, was a brilliant poet, linguist, and her role model. Elza's suicide, coinciding with Klepfisz's graduation from CCNY, stimulated Klepfisz to write "one depressing poem after another, one atrocity after another, death always the central motif" (*Dreams* 168). This spate of writing released Klepfisz and helped her find her voice, even when writing through Elza's voice, or that of the Yiddish poet Fradel Shtok's. While Klepfisz's strong poems about the Holocaust, "Searching for My Fathers Body," "The Widow and Daughter," "herr captain," "during the war," and "death camp," will inevitably link her to the Holocaust, she has written extensively about other personal subjects: lesbians, love, other women, her years as an office worker ("Work Sonnets").

Her signature poem, "Bashert," blends poetry and prose. Her subject is the randomness of survival and the need to remember. She recites a catalog of possibilities—tactics and accidents of survival during the Shoah—a cadenced dedication that borders on the religious, "almost an incantation" (Schamp 235). She then evokes memories of childhood in Poland, 1944, her graduate student years in Chicago, 1964, her short career as composition teacher at City College, 1971, and a period of time as a thinker/keeper of accounts in Cherry Plain, 1981: "Yes, It's true. All true. I am scrupulously accurate. I keep track of all distinctions . . . Between past and present . . . I have become a keeper of accounts." Later, she sighs, "Like them, my despised ancestors. I have become a keeper of accounts" (*A Few Words* 198–199). Her diction is concrete and specific; her tone of resignation is restrained, realistic, sad, but not hopeless. Life for the working classes in America may be fragile, but life for her ancestors in Europe was a futile struggle. She will not let them or their language be obliterated. Mainly through conversations with survivors and her own research and translations, she resuscitates Yiddish history and biography. As in "Bashert," her later poems often blend Yiddish with English, echoing the rhythm of a nearly lost language in dialogue with a dominant language, neither of which is her native tongue: "The more I translate and interact with Yiddish texts, the more I strengthen my ties—intellectual, imaginative, and emotional—to that past" ("Saranwrap and Tinfoil" 5). Through Yiddish, she assimilates into the present the Jews of Europe whose mother tongue/*mamalushen* had been Yiddish, although they lived in countries where Yiddish was a foreign language.

As a poet activist, Klepfisz is unique. Because she is a child survivor who was too young to have a clear memory of the catastrophe, she writes from the experience of both generations, relying on other survivors' memories about German brutality and about her father and Aunt Gina. Thus, immersed in the Holocaust survivor community, she writes from memory, postmemory, and "inhaled" memory—what others have told her or written. Consistent with the nature of memory, her poetry is not linear; she rearranges space and words to reflect the associative processes of thinking, of breathing, of speaking.

Her commitment to Judaism, socialist/Bundist values, the underdog, secularism, and lesbianism reflects her integrity. Her poetry and prose parallels these interests and her passionate activism. While the early poems, first published in 1971, reveal her preoccupation with the Holocaust, and specifically with the pain of the loss of her father and aunt, her later work broadens to encompass her experiences as a Jewish feminist activist and reflect her commitment to socialist secular Judaism and to the challenge of living Jewishly as a lesbian feminist. Fascinated with the connection of language with

identity and culture, and as a communication tool, she writes in a "constant act of self-creation" (Rich, *A Few Words* 13).

Her work is experimental, personal, narrative, intellectual, and wrestles with issues that concern her: feminism, lesbianism, Jewishness, Middle East politics, and, of course, the Holocaust. Acutely aware of the silence of the world during the Holocaust and of the possibility of offending survivors, she advocates for the Palestinians because she knows that "silence about any form of injustice is wrong" (*Jewish Women's Call for Peace* 44). She writes vigorously about the Palestinians' right to self-determination and Israel's mistreatment of vulnerable Palestinians.

Klepfisz demonstrates her commitment to radical politics not only directly in and through her poetry, but also as a founding editor of *Conditions* (1976–81), and a frequent contributor to *Bridges, Sinister Wisdom,* and other feminist publications. From 1990 to 1992 she was the executive director of the New Jewish Agenda. She currently teaches Jewish women's studies at Barnard College.

Bibliography

Roth, Lawrence. "Pedagogy and the Mother Tongue: Irena Klepfisz's "Di Rayze Aheym/The Journey Home.'" *Symposium* 52, no. 4 (Winter 1999): 269–279.

Schamp, Jutta. "Beyond Association: Difference and Reconfiguration in the Works of Irena Klepfisz, Jyl Lyn Felman, and Rebecca Goldstein." *Zeitschrift für Anglistik und Amerikanistik* 47, no. 3 (1999): 229–243.

Schreiber, Maeera. "The End of Exile: Jewish Identity and Its Diasporic Poetics." *PMLA* 113, no. 2 (March 1998): 273–287.

—Myrna Goldenberg

Kosinski, Jerzy (1933–1991)

Jerzy Kosinski was born in Łódź, Poland, in 1933 to two brilliant young Polish Jews, Micezysław and Elzbieta (Liniecka) Kosinski. Separated from his family from 1939 to 1945, he was assumed dead and spent six years brilliantly evading both

Germans and Polish peasants in the villages of eastern Poland—hence the personal myth of evasion and hiding, brutalization, starvation, beatings, rape, and attempted murder that provides the exotic biographical element of each of his books. During 1942 Kosinski suffered a traumatic accident in which he lost his speech. This was not reversed until 1948, when he suffered another severe shock after a skiing accident. But, when in 1945 he was located by his parents in a Lodz orphanage, he was still speechless.

After 1948 he became a ski and social instructor in Zakopane, Poland. He received a M.A. in political science in 1953, and a M.A. in history in 1955, both degrees conferred by the University of Łód . From 1955 to 1957, while studying in Warsaw, he published on the revolutionary movements of the 19th century and exhibited prize-winning photographs in major international photography salons in Europe. Photography remained a passion throughout his life and finds its way into the subject matter and aesthetics of every work. He escaped to the United States in December 1957 and pursued graduate work at Colombia University from 1958 to 1960. In 1960 he published his first nonfiction work, *The Future Is Ours, Comrade: Conversations with Russians*, under the pseudonym Joseph Novak.

In 1962 he married Mary Hayward Weir in New York. Tragically, she died of a brain tumor in 1968. *The PAINTED BIRD* appeared in 1965, the same year he was granted U.S. citizenship. In this fictional autobiography Kosinski chronicles his childhood experiences during six years in wartime Poland. The historical backdrop is World War II, the Great Depression, the rise of National Socialism, and the rise of European fascism and militarism. It features an unnamed boy's flight from Nazis among mostly Xenophobic depraved Polish villagers who viewed his dark eyes and complexion as foreign and tormented him as a Gypsy or a Jew. Not surprisingly, its revelations on the brutality of Polish peasants caused the book to be banned in Poland. Essentially a bildungsroman, the book describes a series of transformations from innocence to warping experience, in spite of which

the unnamed hero learns incredible survival skills and important lessons about the degradations of human nature. Critical response to this work was very mixed, with some of the most vocal criticism coming from eastern Europe.

In 1966 Kosinski met Katherina (Kiki) Von Frauenhofer, who remained his lifelong companion. In 1968 he published *Steps* and *The Art of the Self: Essays à propos Steps*. *Steps* is a collection of stories featuring a "morphing" character who appears in several stories where he is alternately a wandering boy, a student, a soldier, and an alienated immigrant in a new country, who fatefully runs from collective social control into progressive loss of selfhood. In 1969 he received the National Book Award for *Steps*. He served as president of PEN for two terms, from 1973 to 1975. *The Devil Tree*, published in 1973, presents a series of static images of episodic violence, disorder, mirrors, photographs, and TV watching. In it the protagonist, a victim of Puritanism, becomes a victimizer within the context of the American dream. Whalen, the antihero, becomes entrapped in a baobab tree (devil tree), symbol of the modern condition. It explores issues of self-definition, the philosophy of language, the obliteration of history, muteness, preverbal states, the failure of humane values, sexual violence, and the devil as contemporary society. It sees the apocalypse as Protestant and American in design. *Being There*, published in 1971, focuses on an invisible antihero, Chance, a man without volition and addicted to TV. Central to the novel is Kosinski's fear about how the media is undermining national literacy, thus speeding up cultural homogenization, consumerism, and mechanism. Built on myths of Adam, Eve, and Narcissus and Echo, it traces parallels between Chance and Narcissus. Preoccupied with spiritual defeat of the media-saturated individual, it features images of narcissism, mirrors, autoeroticism, and mindless passivity. *Cockpit*, published in 1975, is a grim, darkly violent, powerful novel in picaresque style. Through its protagonist, Tarden, Kosinski explores the difficulty of maintaining relationships in the face of epistemological difficulties of the 20th century. All

Kosinski's usual themes appear: tricksterism, horror, the maligned writer, the mystery of disconnected human relationships, the individual versus the collective, and the protean nature of 20th-century man. Critics have compared it to the works of John le Carré, the marquis de Sade, and Albert Camus. *Blind Date,* published in 1977, explores the protagonist Levanter's relationships with other survivors, the Socratic quest, the development of the soul, popular culture, time, randomness, and the limits of perception and language. Stylistically it features a series of violent montages, macabre events, cinematographic scenes, and carefully designed tableaux all intended to shock bourgeois readers into an understanding of the spiritual wounds sustained in war. *Passion Play,* published in 1979, revolves around protagonists Fabian and Manuela, through whom Kosinski examines androgyny and transsexuality within patriarchal culture. It is a trenchant exploration of gender identity full of existential meditations and explicit sexual descriptions. *Pinball,* published in 1982, is based on Kosinski's readings of the Jack Henry Abbott incident, and his early reading of theologians Paul Tillich and Abraham Joshua Heschel. It is full of urban anthropology, scenes from the South Bronx, lampoons of contemporary lyrics, and pornographic pastiches. Upon the book's appearance, Geoffrey Stokes and Eliot Fremont-Smith, writing in the *Village Voice,* accused him of plagiarism in an article entitled "Tainted Words." Kosinski was subsequently vigorously and convincingly defended by colleagues and friends John Corry, Barbara Gelb, and Charles Kaiser. *The Hermit of 69th Street: The Working Papers of Norbert Koski,* published in 1988, was inspired by Stokes and Fremont-Smith's accusations of plagiarism and addresses the relationship of the author to his autobiographical and fictional characters.

That same year, Kosinski returned to Poland for the first time since his escape in 1957. The following year, 1989, he returned to Polish national acclaim on the publication in Poland of *The Painted Bird,* the first Polish edition of any of his works. Critics have always balked at the exotic pornographic and violent elements of the novels, and had

difficulty assessing the literary quality of his work. Calvin Trillin complained in his "Uncivil Liberties" (1982) that "the black plague got a more respectful reception than did each new Kosinski novel." In addition, in his later years, Kosinski suffered from accusations that he misrepresented aspects of his life, especially events depicted fictionally in *The Painted Bird,* and also that translators and editors had an unusually large role in fashioning the book. Despite many of his critics and reviewers, Kosinski became a celebrated post–World War II American author, the recipient of numerous grants, fellowships, and writer's awards. His novels, nonfiction, essays, reviews, and lectures all testify to a prolific literary career. Roughly 80 million copies of his novels have been put in circulation in over 20 languages; there are over 600 critical articles and reviews in English alone. Such a stormy and sharply divided reception was in part due to a liberal humanist reviewing community for whom Kosinski's antirealist depictions of human nature as shockingly depraved, sadomasochistic, sexually deviant, and nihilistic seriously unseated their own bourgeois conceptions. Denial of the Jewish Holocaust experience was also a major factor.

Thematically and stylistically, Kosinski shares with such postmodern writers as John Barth, Thomas Pynchon, Günter Grass, Donald Barthleme, Robert Coover, and Ken Kesey the notion of language as a prison house of perception, and the avant-garde as the appropriate site of disruption of the bourgeoise mentality. All of his work reveals a fascination not so much with pseudopornography, but with the notion of escape from the limits of human experience through exotic eroticism, European philosophy, language theory, cultural critique, cinematography, the grotesque, gothic inventiveness, minimalism, tricksterism, media, numbers, fairy tales, märchen, fables, bestiaries, and allied folk forms. His novels typically stage deracinated antiheroes, a series of moments suspended in space, impersonations, electronic devices, technological stratagems, and the landscape of terrorism. Many of the books defend American literary culture, battle "global video-hypnotism," the 20th-century loss of a meaningful web of human relationships, and in Nietzschean fashion warn humankind of its own guilt and horror. His protagonists are solitary beings in conflict with collective powers, often victims themselves of the media. They are all parables of a fictional self divorced from social context and designed to wreak fictional revenge on history as each work probes the relationship between victim and oppressor.

On May 3, 1991, faced with an increasingly serious heart condition and severe depression, Kosinski tied a plastic grocery sack over his head and immersed himself in his bathtub in his West 57th Street New York apartment. His death, he had warned his friends, would be further testimony to the shockingly dehumanizing century of spiritual degradation. Though he considered himself a less than major talent, Kosinski's *The Painted Bird* remains one of the foremost Holocaust novels.

Bibliography

Lavers, Norman. *Jerzy Kosinski*. Boston: Twayne, 1982.

Lilly, Paul. R. *Words in Search of Victims: The Achievement of Jerzy Kosinski*. Kent, Ohio: Kent State University Press, 1988.

—Gloria L. Cronin

Kotlowitz, Robert (1924–)

Robert Kotlowitz is the author four novels that employ his hometown, Baltimore, Maryland, as background: *Somewhere Else* (1972), his first novel, followed by *The Boardwalk* (1977), *Sea Changes* (1986), and *His Master's Voice* (1992). Wryly examining the Jewish immigrant experience, he takes us from the eastern shores of America to Europe and back with America always rising from the horizon like a ripe peach. Kotlowitz's America is the new promised land where a synagogue is just a building and a Jew is just a person. *Somewhere Else* was recognized in 1973 with the National Jewish Book Award.

As a novelist, Kotlowitz explores American Jewish perceptions while gently plumbing concepts of exile and assimilation with ironic charm.

In *Somewhere Else,* four friends carry on a discussion that debates the subjects of oppression and lack of opportunity. With a light touch, Kotlowitz floats existential existence down the hall when one friend blithely equates the meaning of life with "boiled chicken." Kotlowitz's novels quietly assume the Mount Everest of basic questions: Who am I when I am with you? Who am I when I am here and not there? Sigmund Safer, the central character in *His Master's Voice,* tells his wife he "thought he was a goner" when he came to America, but fortuitously he saved himself and her, too, by simply changing his name from Czaferski to Safer. The irony of a person who believes he will be safe within the subterfuge of an Americanized name change while simply ignoring his pronounced Polish accent is just the sort of touching eccentricity with which Kotlowitz imbues his characters.

Over his lifetime, Kotlowitz has forged an admirable and productive career. In addition to being a successful novelist, he worked as a documentary filmmaker and public television producer. *Esquire Magazine* and the *New York Times Magazine,* among others, have published his work. He served as managing editor for *Harper's Magazine* and as senior editor for *Show Magazine.* In 1998 he received the American Prize Fellowship at the American Academy in Berlin, where he analyzed Berlin's role in a postwar, modern Europe.

Some 50 years after World War II, Kotlowitz turned his attention to examining his own war experiences and penned *Before Their Time.* Written in his familiar unsentimental style, Kotlowitz's book is a straightforward telling of his war experience, a poignant memoir both modest and haunting. He beats no drum nor marches to a fife corps, but from the first page his innately masculine writing unfolds his struggle to survive as a G.I. in World War II and underlines his belief in this war. Unveiling the strange dichotomy that is the modern military and war—tedium mixed with terror and beauty, chaos and death—you feel the youth and innocence of these young men thrown together; you know what is coming, yet you want all of them to make it through. Toward the end of the novel, when answering a fellow soldier's question about why "Jooz" always live together, Kotlowitz offers a look at the theory of his own written work, saying "each word must carry its real weight, each answer fit the case."

Robert Kotlowitz is a thoroughly modern American writer. He creates a quintessentially American read, birthing characters that lie gently on the page. Like white marbling in a good steak, the humanity of Kotlowitz's characters cannot be missed: they may seem exotic, but laid bare, we know these people.

Bibliography

Pollack, Eileen. "Judaism, Sacred and Profane." *Washington Post,* 16 April 1992, D4.

Rubin, Merle. "Fiction Roundup: New Novels by Kotlowitz, Gray, and Moore; *Sea Changes,* by Robert Kotlowitz." *Christian Science Monitor,* 28 November 1986, 34.

—Vanessa Lefton

Krim, Seymour (1922–1989)

In the late 1950s Seymour Krim produced the anguished, subjective journalistic pieces in the pages of the *Village Voice* that won him notoriety and led to his editing *The Beats,* a classic 1960 anthology that included critics alongside adherents. Krim published his own essays in *Views of a Nearsighted Cannoneer* (1961), a slim volume printed on cheap paper that won attention with its humorous title and a foreword by Norman Mailer. According to Mailer, Krim's writing "has the guts of New York," and future historians "will say if they have a sense of the past that yes, in the work of Seymour Krim lives one of the truest beats of how horrible, how jarring, how livid and how exciting was this city."

Krim was born in 1922 as the fourth, last, and unplanned child of Abraham and Ida Krim, Yiddish-speaking immigrants who lived in prosperity in Manhattan's Washington Heights neighborhood. His closest sibling in age was nine years his senior. As a boy Seymour attended Kohut, a progressive Jewish school in Harrison, New York. Before long, he began to experience the events that made him a writer. In 1930, when Seymour was seven, his father died. When he was 10, his mother committed suicide by jumping from the roof of her apartment building.

Krim graduated in 1939 from DeWitt Clinton High School in the Bronx, briefly attended the University of North Carolina, returned to New York, and fell under the spell of the critical minds at *Partisan Review.* In the early 1950s he published literary criticism in *Commentary, Commonweal,* and the *Hudson Review,* but the form was a poor fit for his talents and needs. In 1955 he suffered a mental breakdown. This turning point allowed him, as he wrote in "The Insanity Bit," to trust his own "intellect and imagination; for when the climate changes, only the individual vision will stand secure." Krim's vision made him one of the founders of the New Journalism, as he argued for and practiced a style that applied "fictional and avantgarde [*sic*] prose techniques to the actual scene before us."

Krim taught at Pennsylvania State and Columbia Universities, the Iowa Writers' Workshop, and the University of Haifa, Israel. His articles for the *New York Times, New York Magazine, Herald Tribune, Playboy, Washington Post,* and other publications were collected in *Shake It for the World, Smartass* (1970), *You & Me* (1974), and the posthumous *What's This Cat's Story: The Best of Seymour Krim* (1991). *Cannoneer* was reissued in 1968 and billed as an "underground landmark." In 1976 he won a Guggenheim fellowship.

Krim considered himself both too Jewish and not Jewish enough, and he wrote perceptively about the problems faced by acculturated Jews. His manic masterpiece of Jewish introspection is "Epitaph for a Canadian Kike," a frank, outrageous, and comic look at his own Jewish self-hatred. The 1970 essay is Krim's attempt to come to terms with Sam Goodman, a founding member of the rejectionist, scatological, and ugly No!Art movement who represented—to Krim—everything vulgar, unseemly, offensive, and unattractive about being Jewish. Krim was painfully aware that his aversion to Goodman highlighted his own insecurities and fears, and in "Epitaph" all of the rage and insult he directs at Sam only make Krim himself look worse, and he knew it. His ruthless honesty and abandonment of respectability give the essay its lasting power. "I could accept being 'Jewish' very nicely if I didn't look like one, 'act' like one," writes Krim, but he complains that when he sees Goodman and his stereotypical Jewish features—"short, belly sticking out, hooked schnozzola"—he was renewed in his "self-persecution dreads."

Krim's 1980 article about Dr. Joyce Brothers explored similar themes. In "My Sister, Joyce Brothers," Krim views himself and Brothers as representatives of the two poles of Jewish life, the "straights and non-straights," that "can never be totally at ease together." The article seems to signal the end of a certain type of male Jewish writer: attractive, adventurous, foul-mouthed, and self-destructive. Krim admits that bohemianism loses its charm and salutes Brothers as his "straight, smart JAP sister who has survived on a rougher track than I could ever play on."

Bibliography

Stephens, Michael. "A Different King of Two-Fisted, Two-Breasted Terror: Seymour Krim and Creative Nonfiction." *Creative Nonfiction* 2 (1994): 43–62.

—Mark Cohen

Kumin, Maxine (1925–   )

Maxine Kumin was born in Philadelphia in 1925, the fourth child and only daughter of Doll and Peter Winokur. She grew up in a well-to-do household. The family of Reform Jews gave Maxine a Jewish education and celebrated traditional Jewish holidays. However, their proximity to a convent that Maxine attended in the early grades exposed her to Christianity, an experience that confused her and later became the source of a number of poems. Radcliffe College, where she found companions who shared her enthusiasm for literature, opened new horizons for Kumin. Like others who came of age in the World War II era, she married young and had children quickly. Though happily married and devoted to her children, she felt something was missing. That something was writing,

and she began to write light verse and ghostwrite medical articles while doing domestic chores. Enrolling in a poetry workshop in 1957 conducted by John Holmes gave her writing a boost. There she met Anne Sexton, who was, like Kumin, a young mother trying to pursue a writing career at a time when women were expected to be fully satisfied by marriage and motherhood. The two became soul mates, critiquing each other's writing, cowriting children's books, and sharing experiences. Kumin soon was publishing poems in literary journals.

After raising their children in the Boston area, the Kumins moved permanently in the 1970s to a farm in New Hampshire, where raising animals and growing vegetables became the focus of their lives. The Pulitzer Prize for *Up Country,* a collection about living at the farm, established her as a prominent nature poet. Kumin also won many other prizes and received seven honorary doctorate degrees. Primarily a poet, she has also written numerous essays, novels and children's books, and taught at universities throughout the country. Starting out as a formalist, her poetry has become increasingly conversational over the years. Kumin is most renowned for poems written in a private voice, about her experiences with family and at the farm, but she has increasingly written in a public voice about social issues.

Kumin believes that women should write about "their roles and their bodies and their children and their relationships because this is unplowed land." And she has done just that. Writing as a mother ("I have shamelessly drawn on the lives of my children as a sourcebook for my work"), she describes in early poems the pain of separating from young children, and in later poems her sorrow as grown children go off into their adult lives. In recent collections, she portrays her grandchildren in amusing detail, but notes the inevitable, that their generation will eventually take over. Writing as a daughter, she describes her father as the robust man of her childhood, the dying man gasping for breath, and charts her relationship with her mother from adolescent conflict to adult understanding. As a friend, she wrote a series of memorials to Anne Sexton that represent an effort to sustain a connection with the dead poet. Kumin also pioneered writing about women's sexuality and bodies in such poems as "After Love" and "Giving Birth." In all the above, she writes about her life with the openness that, according to Carolyn Heilbrun (*Writing a Woman's Life*), women writers of earlier generations typically could not.

"The life close to nature is compelling," Kumin said in a 1991 interview with Diane George, and she has taken it as the subject of her work, depicting especially her farm in New Hampshire. Often she observes in her poems animal and vegetable life around her with affection and realism—what it is like to split wood, deal with woodchucks, do chores. On a deeper level, she describes bonds between the species, in particular her close connection to her horses, from whom she takes comfort and with whom she has complete, though nonverbal, communication. Aspects of the natural world (in "Summer Meditation," and "Zen of Mowing") suggest the life/death cycle and her own mortality. Finally, her love of nature has compelled her to criticize humankind's exploitation of it. In poems about the endangered manatee and trumpeter swan, Kumin warns us to change our destructive ways. While all the various strains of her nature poetry persist, her approach to this subject has darkened over the years.

The strand of moral/political concern that always existed in Kumin's work has deepened in recent years, engaging such topics as hunger, abuse, and war. In a 1985 collection Kumin moved in a decidedly political direction, with poems portraying conflict in Israel, hunger in the third world, and effects of a possible nuclear war. Later poetry describes the cruelty of war: convoys of Muslim children trying to escape Bosnia and a six-year-old fleeing from death squads in Sudan. In *Jack and Other New Poems* (2005), the poem "Elegy and Rant" dramatizes the abuses of the Patriot Act, and "Eating Babies" predicts our eventual cannibalism, the end product of living in a ruined environment. In six new poems, published in various magazines, Kumin extends her political critique to a series of "torture" poems, which are, in her words, "terser and angrier." In these, she depicts abuses (use of shackles, dogs, beatings) by U.S. soldiers that betray our values as Americans. She explains her new emphasis: "I believe that we poets have to serve as witnesses at least to the injustices around us." Not all critics are pleased with Kumin's public poetry, but young poets feel that her openness gives them the courage to deal with political issues.

Describing herself as "a nonbelieving Jew with a strongly developed Jewish consciousness," Kumin has written a substantial amount of poems on Jewish subjects: her Jewish ancestors, being a Jew in a Christian environment, and Jewish history and morality. In early poems she affectionately describes her immigrant great-grandfather, a tailor, and her mother's growing up Jewish in Radford, Virginia. Noting that her Jewish awareness occurs in Christian settings, Kumin depicts her experience in a convent school humorously in early poems, but more ominously in later poems that recall the powerful effect of the statue of Jesus and being called Christ killer by neighborhood children. Growing up in the era of Hitler (as an adolescent she had nightmares about the Nazis), she was aware of Jewish persecution and provides illustrations of it throughout history: in the biblical world ("Haman's Ears"), in medieval Christian Europe ("11th Century Doors"), during the Holocaust ("Amsterdam Poem"), in the contemporary Middle East ("Poet Visits Egypt and Israel"), and in U.S. history ("Jew Order"). Yet even as she portrays the Jewish plight, she is always aware of the sufferings of others: Persians killed by Jews in revenge for Haman's deeds, African Americans freed from slavery at the same time that the Jew Order was rescinded. Indeed, Kumin affirmed in a recent e-mail message that her Jewish background was influential in her developing the social conscience that she shows in her work and her life.

During 45 years of writing, Kumin has shown herself to be an acute observer of experiences in the life cycle, and of phenomena in the natural and political worlds. Proficient in writing both lyrics of personal experience and poems on moral issues, she fulfills admirably the function she ascribes to the poet, serving as "witness" to the life of our times.

Bibliography

Contemporary Women Poets. Detroit: St. James Press, 1998.

Grosholz, Emily. *Telling the Barn Swallow: Poets on the Poetry of Maxine Kumin.* Boston: University Press of New England, 1997.

Heilbrun, Carolyn G. *Writing a Woman's Life.* New York: W.W. Norton, 1988.

Howard, Ben. "A Secular Believer: The Agnostic Art of Maxine Kumin." *Shenandoah* 52, no. 2 (2002): 141–159.

—Lois Rubin

Kunitz, Stanley (1905–2006)

Though a poet of many honors—including the Pulitzer Prize for poetry, a National Book Award, and service as the U.S. poet laureate at age 95—Stanley Jasspon Kunitz spent nearly 40 years of his eight-decade career in relative anonymity. Born July 29, 1905, in Worcester, Massachusetts, Kunitz experienced familial loss in his early life. He was the third child of Yetta Helen Jasspon and Solomon Z. Kunitz, the latter of whom was a well-known dressmaker whose suicide in a public park six weeks before his only son's birth signaled the bankruptcy of his dressmaking business.

Throughout his childhood, Kunitz knew little of his father. At eight he found a picture of the man he had never known—an event later recounted in "The Portrait." Around the time that he came to know a few details of his father's life, his mother married Mark Dine, with whom Kunitz came to share a close attachment. Six years later, however, Kunitz's stepfather suffered a heart attack and died. Thus, at 14 he had twice lost a father, a double loss that provided a thematic base for much of his poetry.

Kunitz attended Harvard College on a scholarship, graduating summa cum laude in 1926. Encouraged by a professor, he continued his studies at Harvard, where he planned to stay on as a teaching assistant after completing a Ph.D. When the head of the English department informed him that Anglo-Saxon students would resent being taught English literature by a Jew, however,

he finished the requirements for a master's degree and left in 1927. Kunitz's professional life thus began with editing for HW Wilson, a reference company in New York, and reporting for the *Worcester Telegram.*

After serving as a noncombatant in World War II, he accepted a position at Bennington College in Vermont. For the next 40 years, he taught at various universities—including Rutgers, Princeton, Yale, Vassar, and 22 years at Columbia—but he never sought tenure, citing the need for "a revolution every few years" along with his preference for being a poet who taught rather than a professor who wrote poetry.

Kunitz was committed to building community among artists. He had a mutually influential relationship with Theodore Roethke for much of Roethke's life, and Kunitz recommended Sylvia Plath's first collection, *The Colossus,* for publication. His teaching experiences also afforded him ample opportunity to influence the rising generation of poets, including Louise Glück—one of his first students at Columbia. Additionally, Kunitz was a founder of the Fine Arts Work Center in Provincetown, Massachusetts, and Poets House in Manhattan during his later years.

Although his first book of poetry, *Intellectual Things,* was published just three years after he left Harvard, critical acclaim eluded Kunitz for the first four decades of his career. Critics granted that his poetry was technically brilliant, but because he was heavily influenced by Blake, Donne, and Eliot, he was generally dismissed as imitative.

Between his first and second books, a 14-year gap passed—perhaps because of the disappointing critical reception of his first collection. *Passport to War* was published in 1944 while Kunitz served in World War II. Although this second volume contained poems that have now garnered much praise (such as "Father and Son"), it too was largely ignored by critics.

In 1958 when *Selected Poems, 1928–1958*—originally rejected several times—was published by Atlantic Monthly Press, Kunitz's poetry finally received high praise. This third volume was decidedly more narrative than its predecessors, although it also retained traces of the Blakean high rhetoric that characterized the previous two. This collection, however, set Kunitz apart in a way that the others had not: It won the Pulitzer Prize for poetry in 1959. Although this honor gained the admiration of his colleagues, he continued to remain largely unknown as a poet.

The TESTING-TREE (1971) marks what is generally seen as the second chapter in Kunitz's poetry. His first three collections contrast significantly with this later style in which his work takes on a conversational tone and a less disciplined form. The difference in style allowed greater transparency for Kunitz's most significant and serious themes, including the simultaneity of life and death and the suicide of his father, both of which are presented in "The Portrait," "Father and Son," and "Open the Gate." The increased emotional transparency in his poetry combined with his effective treatment of serious issues earned him the praise of many critics.

With increased critical success also came a marked increase in publications: between 1930 and 1971 he published only four volumes of poetry; over the next three and a half decades, however, he published at least 10 more, including *The Lincoln Relics* (1978), *The Wellfleet Whale and Companion Poems* (1983), *Next-to-Last Things* (1985), and *Passing Through* (1995). Although dark topics continued to be a significant theme in Kunitz's poetry, much of his work—especially in his later collections—is optimistic, reflecting his love for his wife, his appreciation for his mother and sisters, and his passion for gardening.

While Kunitz's religious heritage as a Sephardic Jew colored his early experience—forbidding him, for example, from playing on a nearby prep school playground as a young child as recounted in *The Testing-Tree*'s title poem—his family's connection with Judaism was cultural rather than ritual. Almost naturally, therefore, much of his poetry investigates religious—but not necessarily Judaic—themes. Although "An Old Cracked Tune" tells of a 15th-century poet and rabbi, for instance, other poems such as "King of the River" and "The Words of the Preacher" are more universally religious.

Along with the acclaim that began with *The Testing-Tree* and continued with his subsequent collections came belated nominations for various public positions. He served as the New York State poet and the consultant in poetry to the Library of Congress (a precursor to the poet laureate program), and won numerous honors, including the Bollingen Prize and the Levinson Prize, among others. At his death in May 2006, his reputation had long outgrown its earlier boundaries as a poets' poet; today, many see Stanley Kunitz's poetry as some of the most durable of his time.

Bibliography
Goodyear, Dana. "The Gardner." *The New Yorker,* 1 September 2003, 104–111.
Hoffman, Matthew. "Kunitz, Stanley." In *Jewish Writers of the Twentieth Century,* edited by Sorrel Kerbel. New York: Fitzroy Dearborn, 2003.
Ryan, Michael. "Interview with Stanley Kunitz." *American Poetry Observed: Poets on Their Work.* Edited by Joe David Bellamy. Urbana: University of Illinois Press, 1984.

—Melissa Huff

Kushner, Tony (1956–   )

Tony Kushner burst onto the literary scene as an important Jewish-American dramatist with his popular and critically acclaimed *Angels in America: A Gay Fantasia on National Themes.* The two-part Broadway production is set within the political context of the conservative mid-1980's Reagan era and the cultural context of the New York homosexual community during the AIDS epidemic. It is within these themes that Kushner explores America's political turbulence and the harsh realities of personal relationships in a beautifully imaginative treatise that has won him critical acclaim at home and in international theatric circles. For the first part of *Angels,* subtitled *Millennium Approaches,* Kushner earned the prestigious Pulitzer Prize for drama, the Antoinette Perry ("Tony") Award for best Play, and the New York Drama Critics Circle Award for best new play, and the Antoinette Perry Award for *Part Two: Perestroika.*

Born in New York City on July 16, 1956, Kushner spent most of his childhood in Lake Charles, Louisiana. His parents were both classical musicians, but his mother was an amateur actress who exposed Kushner to the wonders of theater through her performances in local plays. Soon Kushner's emerging love of the theater grew to an enchantment with the arts and its power over human emotions. Eagerly encouraged by his mother, Kushner could not resist the fascinating duplicity of the stage. In a 1996 interview with David Savran he recalls "very strong memories of her power and the affect she had on people . . . And then there were other obvious things. I grew up very, very closeted, and I'm sure that the disguise of theatre, the doubleness, and all that slightly tawdry stuff interested me."

Kushner identified himself as homosexual in his late teens. Consequently, acceptance is an important theme in his works as he parallels the histories of "oppression and persecution" experienced in both Jewish and homosexual communities. As a Jewish man, Kushner sees the deep ambivalence in this connection, "because there is a fantastically powerful homophobic tradition within Judaism." His sociopolitical plays, therefore, draw from his own experiences and observations as both a homosexual and a Jew. The bridging of these two cultures in his work is especially noteworthy as it establishes him as a theatrical rarity, and explains the significance of his plays as a gay dramatist.

All of Kushner's plays place the deeper, personal dramas of his characters within the social, cultural, and political context of national/international current events. *Homebody/Kabul* (2002) discusses the influence of Western powers on Afghan history, and *Caroline, or Change* (2002) deals with the relationship between a Jewish family and its African-American maid during the Civil Rights movement. He also adapted several plays written by playwrights and writers such as Bertolt Brecht and Johann Wolfgang von Goethe. Of these, *Angels in America* is considered Kushner's greatest work.

The two parts of *Angels* took Kushner several years to complete. Its wide range of characters, subplots, and split-scene sequences combine to create almost eight hours of dramatic performance. *Millennium Approaches,* the first part of *Angels,* introduces the five main characters: Roy, Joe, Harper, Prior, and Louis, and explores the meaning of the different relationships between the characters: Louis and Prior's gay relationship, Joe and Harper's marriage, and lastly, Louis and Joe's gay relationship. Kushner does all this through well-executed mutual dream scenes and within the context of political commentary on the Reagan administration and social commentary on the prevalence of AIDS within the time period. Part One ends with the appropriate sense of apocalypse as an angel appears to the dying Prior.

Part Two: Perestroika continues the sociopolitical commentary begun in *Millennium Approaches* as we follow the main characters' acceptance of their choices made previously. In having almost all of his characters respond positively to their circumstances, Kushner emphasizes the importance of turning crises into positive experiences. Roy Cohen, however, dies embittered and enshrouded in self-hatred, whereas Prior develops emotionally from his experience with AIDS and shares his personal doctrine on what he has learned from his experience. *Perestroika* ends on a hopeful, even enthusiastic, note, driving home Kushner's central point: Despite tremendous tragedy and difficulty, imagination can foment hope and create beauty from despair.

Angels in America has received an overwhelmingly positive response since its inception in 1991. Critics seem to like Kushner's approach to addressing serious political issues in a realistic social context while simultaneously adding myth and imagination in a manner that eludes the ridiculous. Kushner is also lauded for his ability to intersect the conservative nature of Jewish and Mormon cultures with homosexual characters within the political context of the Reagan era. More recent feminist criticism, however, addresses Kushner's relegation of female characters to marginal roles as opposed to the more prominent male gay persona. Despite this, however, Tony Kushner is largely seen as an important contributor to the American dramatic landscape—openly gay, Jewish, and politically forthright, Kushner unapologetically addresses contentious sociopolitical issues in a manner that fosters hope for the future through imagination.

Bibliography

Raymond, Gerard. "Q & A With Tony Kushner." *Theatre Week* (December 20–26, 1993): 14–20.

Savran, David. "Tony Kushner." In *Speaking on Stage: Interviews with Contemporary American Playwrights,* edited by Philip C. Kolin and Colby H. Kullman. Tuscaloosa: University of Alabama Press, 1996.

—**George Gordon-Smith**

The Last Jew in America
Leslie Fiedler (1966)

LESLIE FIEDLER is principally known for his literary criticism, but his fiction deserves more attention. *The Last Jew in America* is composed of three interrelated novellas: "The Last Jew in America," "The Last WASP in the World," and "The First Spade in the West." Like his earlier works, this book also deals with the twin subjects of inauthenticity and profound alienation in the American heartland, all done in typically Fiedlerian baffled rage. All three are set in the mythical Lewis and Clark City located somewhere between Montana and Wyoming and are worked out with parody and terrible irony.

This American utopia of the Mountain West in Fiedler's accounting is infected with anti-Semitism, racism, homophobia, assimilation, and deracination. Each of the protagonists is a culturally isolated moral coward with no spirituality. "The Last Jew in America" centers on Jacob Moskowitz, a Jew whose family perished in the camps. His leftist affiliations have failed. Though Lewis and Clark City is populated with pseudoacademics and lapsed Jews, he now insists on conducting a Yom Kippur service using a small group of reluctant, long-assimilated first-generation eastern European immigrants. As they unwillingly gather in a Catholic hospital to conduct the ancient service for their dying friend, Moskowitz decides he will become the town's last observant Jew. However, he is a self-deluded fake and an atheist. He has previously tried to buy someone else's share in eternity, and has betrayed an old friendship.

In the "The Last WASP in the World," Vin Hazelbaker, also an assimilated Jew, blasphemously breaks the Yom Kippur fast. He is a love poet devoid of love. A compulsive womanizer, his lifelong sexual encounters are a mockery of selfishness and noncommitment, as is his love poetry. He is an aging sensualist, half eastern European, half American, who ends up in old age screaming down a telephone at no one and, as ever, helplessly erect. No one answers and no one comes. It is the ultimate comment on the failure of human connection.

"The First Spade in the West" features Ned York, a respectable, middle-class black restaurant owner who helps a drunken gay bridegroom home to his nuptials with the elderly woman he has secretly married. As the homosexual groom lies passed out on the floor, Ned sleeps with the old woman, only to find her dead in bed beside him in the morning. Ned Clark is an accepted black businessman in Lewis and Clark City, Kiwanis Man of the Year, a half-breed—part black, part Native American—who is the son of a drifter father and a barmaid mother. Within his character lie exposed all the distressing sociological ironies and impasses of the white middle class he has embraced. Indicative of his self-divisions, he hates gays, Native Americans, and blacks. He constantly feeds an active stomach ulcer, and fakes black American pain as he mangles Leadbelly's famous blues song "When I Was a Cowboy," to which he does not even know the basic chords. Like the gay husband of the dowager, he is also a "Stepin' Fetchit" black man.

Each of these stories focuses on an American sense of restlessness and radical nonbelonging. None of the characters achieves coherence, moral vision, or home. They are all grotesquely materialistic imposters—freaks and misfits—as Fiedler calls such characters. For Jews, gays, Native Americans, and blacks, Lewis and Clark City, the quintessentially Western American city, is absolutely inhospitable. *The Last Jew in American* is Fiedler's most important fictional legacy.

Bibliography

Bluefarb, Sam. "Pictures of the Anti-Stereotype: Leslie Fiedler's Triptych, The Last Jew in America." *College Language Association Journal* 18 (1975): 412–421.

Dewey, Joseph. "Andromeda on the Rocks: The Irony of Belonging in *The Last Jew in America*." In *Leslie Fiedler and American Culture*. Newark: University of Delaware Press, 1999.

—**Gloria L. Cronin**

Lazar Malkin Enters Heaven
Steve Stern (1986)

Steve Stern's third and best-known book of fiction, *Lazar Malkin Enters Heaven,* comprises nine individual stories, all of which take place in or make reference to the Pinch, an old Jewish community that once thrived along North Main Street in Memphis, Tennessee. Most of the characters in *Lazar Malkin* undergo highly unlikely and sometimes downright magical experiences that test belief as well as question identity. Children take flight, the ghosts of dead writers literally haunt their readers, angels marry into the mortal world, and golems are created out of the *mish-mash* of forsaken alleyways. In fabulistic ways, the protagonists of Stern's stories are caught between the real and the imaginary. And it is this unsteady and ambiguous negotiation between these two worlds—the stuff of individuals' dreams and the gritty earth beneath their feet—that best defines Stern's narrative style.

One of *Lazar Malkin*'s most distinctive features is its closely interwoven structure, functioning more as a short story cycle than a traditional collection of loosely linked tales. The short story cycle can be distinguished from the "normal" short story genre in that the various stories that compose the text are all directly linked in some significant fashion (e.g., through setting, protagonist, or theme) in ways that encourage a more holistic reading. It differs from the novel in its weaker narrative unity and the ability of each of its segments to stand alone outside of the book's larger context. The significance of this narrative form in *Lazar Malkin* is that it provides a means through which Stern can narrate subjectivity, yet do so through a "fragmented," yet highly interconnected, structure. Such a form underscores the multifaceted and even postmodern nature of Jewish American identity and the various competing pressures under which present-day identity is forged.

In the first story of the cycle, "Moishe the Just," a boy is convinced that an eccentric bachelor neighbor is one of the *lamed vovnik,* the legendary 36 righteous men whose presence on earth ensures its continued existence. Attempts to prove his theory lead to the boy's untimely death. Morbidity plays a part in the book's other narratives as well, and often in fantastical ways. In "The Gramophone," children of the Pinch concoct an alleyway brew in order to reincarnate the dead. In both "Aaron Makes a Match" and the title story, *Malach ha-Mavet* (the angel of death) comes to earth to collect his dues, in the first case by marrying an elderly spinster and in the second by stuffing the recalcitrant Lazar Malkin, a man who refuses to die, into a sack and carting him off to heaven. And in "The Book of Mordecai," the title character, out of place in his family and adrift from his own time, attempts to re-moor his identity through a reverse memoir, his own personal "Book of Knowledge." As Mordecai recounts backward the defining events of his life, he literally regresses into the figure of his younger days, and by doing so eventually finds his way "home" to the moment of birth, the signifying physical act of individual inscription.

Yet Stern infuses a healthy dose of humor into his narratives, making *Lazar Malkin* a curious work of comic desolation. Young protagonists such as Nathan Siripkin, Shimmele Debrovner, and Aaron Bronsky are hopeless dreamers, 20th-century versions of Tom Sawyer who are caught between fact and fantasy. And in "The Lord and Morton Gruber," a middle-aged "czar" of coin-operated laundries is commanded by God to write a new sacred text, a story whose tone is more akin to a Woody Allen film than it is to the book of Exodus. The final story of the cycle, "The Ghost and Saul Bozoff," revolves around a writer haunted by the ghost of a female Yiddish author who inspires him to make stories out of his Memphis past. He does so, and as a result, creates a text that is surprisingly similar to *Lazar Malkin*, the book readers hold in their hands. Such postmodern metafiction is common in Stern's writing. *Lazar Malkin* is not only about the fractured lives of American Jews, but also (and perhaps more significantly) the ways in which fragmented narratives construct Jewish identity.

Bibliography

Furman, Andrew. "Steve Stern's Magical Fiction of *Tikkun*." In *Contemporary Jewish American Writers and the Multicultural Dilemma: Return of the Exiled.* Syracuse, N.Y.: Syracuse University Press, 2000.

Shechner, Mark. "Steve Stern (1947–)." In *Contemporary Jewish-American Novelists: A Bio-Critical Sourcebook,* edited by Joel Shatzky and Michael Taub. Westport, Conn.: Greenwood, 1997.

—Derek Parker Royal

Lazarus, Emma (1849–1887)

Born to a wealthy New York family in 1849, Emma Lazarus was one of the first Jewish-American writers to achieve literary success. Her poetry and essays, especially between 1882 and 1884, were powerful and unceasing in their intrepid devotion to fighting against hatred and persecution of the Jewish people. Of both German-Jewish and Sephardic descent, Lazarus grew up with three older sisters, two younger sisters, and one younger brother. She was fortunate to be educated by private tutors and to study music, mythology, American and European literature, and German, French, and Italian. Her father, Moses Lazarus, was one of her earliest supporters—even having her *Poems and Translations Written Between the Ages of Fourteen and Sixteen* (1866) printed for circulation among friends and family. Although she lived only to the age of 38, Lazarus spent those years developing herself as a writer and dedicating herself entirely to writing—a feat she was no doubt able to accomplish in part because she was not faced with the burdens of work, marriage, or caring for family members. Around the age of 18, she established a friendship with Ralph Waldo Emerson, who remained one of her mentors until his death in 1882.

Lazarus saw herself first and foremost as an American poet, and like many more widely anthologized 19th-century writers such as Emerson, Walt Whitman, and Emily Dickinson, much of her poetry utilized nature as a prominent theme. Some of her better-known nature poems include "Long Island Sound," "A June Night," and "Niagara." Her understanding of herself as a poet was cultivated by the marked interest taken in her work by Emerson, and through his constant critiques of her writing—ranging from fervent praise to demanding criticism. It was a sharp and painful blow to her when, to Lazarus's surprise, he failed to include her work in his poetry anthology, *Parnassus* (1874). Their friendship apparently recovered from this rift, and although Lazarus subsequently viewed Emerson less idealistically, she continued to praise his work in later essays. The omission of her work from Emerson's collection may have awakened in her a more compelling drive to establish herself as a prolific writer, and consequently the years between the mid-1870s and the mid-1880s were her most productive. She published not only poetry, but also a novel (*Alide: An Episode in Goethe's Life,* 1874), a drama (*The Spagnoletto,* 1876), short stories, translations of Heinrich Heine's work, and essays. She was called a poet of "rare, original power" by the *Illustrated London News,* and the celebrated Russian writer Ivan Turgenev said to Lazarus, "An author who writes as you do . . . is not far from being himself a master." Lazarus was well known by most Americans during the last decade of her life, having published frequently in widely read magazines including *Lippincott's* and *Century.*

Lazarus saw in Americans the potential for a vast array of unique artistic expression to be cultivated, and a great deal of her work, particularly during the last years of her life, was devoted to the immigrant cause. A deep and profound understanding of her two national identities—for while she was a self-identified American, she was also adamant and forthright regarding Jewish concerns—resonates throughout her later work especially. Her poem "The New Colossus" (1883), seen by many as her most important literary contribution and undoubtedly her best-remembered work, asserts her identification with both the Jewish immigrant legacy and her American citizenship. Lazarus's poem was perhaps one of the first to articulate the tensions—between American and Jew, freedom and oppression, silence and speech—that burgeoned beneath the veneer of American culture in the late 19th century. In 1903, 16 years after her death, the words of this sonnet were placed on the pedestal of the Statue of Liberty—a testament to the passion with which they were first penned. "Give me your tired, your poor, your huddled masses yearning to breathe free"—so beckons the "Mother of Exiles" who stands at the "golden door" of Lazarus's land of opportunity and diversity.

Although much of Lazarus's work contributes to the American and immigrant causes, a great deal of her work speaks directly for the Jewish cause. Most of this work was cultivated late in her life, prompting criticism that she realized her Jewish identity only later in life. However, one need not look far to identify Jewish strains even in her earliest work. In addition to poetry that describes her family synagogue ("In the Jewish Synagogue at Newport," 1867), a substantial portion of her early work was dedicated to translating medieval Hebrew poets from German into English, translations that were published in the magazine the

Jewish Messenger in 1879. Moreover, her play *The Dance to Death,* which dealt with the medieval German persecution of Jews, was finalized years earlier than its 1882 publication date. But her advocacy of an international Jewish cause was most apparent in the early to mid-1880s, during which she published essays dealing with provocative Jewish issues. In "Russian Christianity vs. Modern Judaism" (May 1882), she pleaded for a greater awareness of the plight of Russian Jews, while in "Was the Earl of Beaconsfield a Representative Jew?" (April 1882) she depicted Benjamin Disraeli ambiguously. Notably, in "The Jewish Problem" (February 1883), Lazarus identified the perpetual status of Jews as minorities. In connection with her Zionist leanings, her solution was a state in Palestine founded by Jews, for Jews. With this thematic shift in her writing, Lazarus was catapulted into the political sphere, and for the duration of her life she continued to direct her writing to American and European Jews.

One of the first celebrated Jewish writers in American literary history, Emma Lazarus bequeathed a prosperous legacy. Her commitment to Zionism and the Jewish cause—she helped to establish the Hebrew Technical Institute—as well as her devotion to immigrant rights and freedom continue to transform and inspire today.

Bibliography

Jewish Women's Archive. "JWA - Emma Lazarus - Introduction." Available online. URL: http://www.jwa.org/exhibits/wov/lazarus/el1.html. Accessed on March 14, 2006.

Shapiro, Ann R., ed. *Jewish American Women Writers: A Bio-Bibliographical and Critical Sourcebook.* Westport, Conn.: Greenwood, 1994.

                                        —**Monica Osborne**

Letters of Rebecca Gratz
Rebecca Gratz (1929)

The *Letters of Rebecca Gratz* span from 1808 to 1866, and offer a fascinating time capsule of 17th-century life in Philadelphia. The letters also reveal REBECCA GRATZ's anxieties concerning broader issues: the War of 1812, the Mexican War (1846–48), and the Civil War (1861–65), which Gratz foresaw as early as 1832 (Wagenknecht 14–15). Gratz's Civil War letters, written when she was in her 80s, are especially noteworthy, combining the historical importance of an eye witness with the intimacy of personal correspondence. The letters reveal the personal tragedies beneath the historical place names and dates of the Civil War. As a loyal Unionist, Gratz laments the dismissal of General George McClellen (whom she inadvertently calls "Genl McClennel"), and the raggedness of the Union armies. As a woman of action, Gratz chafes at the disturbing business-as-usual apathy in Philadelphia at reports of Confederate ironclads preparing to steam upriver and lay waste to Northern cities. And to her younger brother Benjamin, she offers a moving consolation on the death of his son Cary, killed August 10, 1861, at the Battle of Wilson's Creek, Missouri.

Bibliography

Osterweis, Rollin G. *Rebecca Gratz: A Study in Charm.* New York: Putnam, 1935.

Wagenknecht, Edward. *Daughters of the Covenant: Portraits of Six Jewish Women.* Amherst: University of Massachusetts Press, 1983.

—**Robert S. Means**

Levertov, Denise (1923–1997)

Denise Levertov spent her formative years in pre–World War II England. Her mother, Beatrice Levertoff, was a Welsh Christian. Her father, Paul Levertoff, was a Russian Hasidic Jew who had converted to Christianity and become an Anglican priest. Descended from the famous Hasidic scholar Schneour Zalman, founder of the Habad branch of Hasidism, Paul Levertoff wrote numerous books in many languages, all aimed at the unification of Judaism and Christianity. He was the director of the East London Fund for Jews and made his family home a haven for visiting European and Russian Jews. Many were converting to Christianity, some were simply traveling in England, and others were fleeing Hitler's Germany. The young Denise

and her sister met Jewish booksellers, German theologians, Russian priests, and Viennese opera singers. Denise delighted in the story that she was once dandled on the knee of the son of Theodor Herzl, the famous Zionist.

Since both parents were dedicated to Jewish-Christian dialogue, theological and religious matters dominated the conversation. Beatrice and Paul constantly read aloud to each other and to the children. Denise recalls hearing the English romantic poets read right alongside her father's Hasidic tales and Jewish folk stories. Belief in joyfulness and a mystical apprehension of immanence formed the core of the family religious culture. This twin Hasidic/Christian legacy would characterize everything Levertov wrote. After working as a nurse in London during the war, Levertov lived in several European cities, and published her first book of poems, *The Double Image* (1946). It reflects her immersion in a neoromantic English poetic tradition, as well as in the poetry of Rainer Maria Rilke, George Barker, and Dylan Thomas.

While in Europe she met and married Mitchell Goodman, an American student from Harvard. When the couple moved to New York in 1948, she suffered severe culture shock on two fronts. American culture was challenging enough, but so was the postwar American literary scene. The Beat poets, the San Francisco Renaissance, the New York School, and the South Carolina Black Mountain Poets were all in revolt against the strictures of the New Critics and arguing for open forms. It was Robert Duncan and Robert Creeley, two South Carolinian Black Mountain poets, who initially befriended and sustained Levertov in her transformation into an American poet. Later, William Carlos Williams became an important friend. Levertov's new open, organic, and experimental American style was readily apparent in *Here and Now* (1957), the book that made her an important voice in the American avant-garde. But it was *Overland to the Islands* (1958), and more especially *With Eyes in the Back of Our Heads* (1959), that established her as one of the great American poets. Levertov's 1950s and 1960s poetry reflects the rigorous structural formalism of Ezra Pound, the avant-gardism of Kenneth Rexroth, and the structural exactitude of William Carlos Williams. She had renewed her emphasis on the basic structural elements of the poem such as line, rhythm, diction, and voice. Inside her tightly wrought forms she expressed her own radical disjunctions, intensified her focus on sheer particularity, and diversified her objects of focus.

The events of the 1960s—feminism, the Vietnam War, her own political activism—and the loss of her sister all thrust her into a major spiritual crisis. Her English neoromantic philosophy was no longer an adequate spiritual or philosophical frame for the extreme violence of the historical moment. In *The Jacobs Ladder* (1961), *O Taste and See* (1964), and *The Sorrow Dance* (1967), her shattered faith revealed itself in her shock that most human energy is expended on extinguishing life's mystery. She realized that celebrating this mystery, if she was ever going to be able to do this again, could no longer be done in the idiom of the English neoromantics. The full impact of her spiritual crisis was revealed in *The Sorrow Dance*. While mourning the enormous loss of her sister, she also addresses Vietnam, colonial and capitalist oppression in the third world, ecological devastation, racism, sexism, activism, and the problem of evil. Recovering her spiritual harmony took most of a decade. The religious poetry published throughout the 1970s initially appeared chastened, refined, and cautious. *Relearning the Alphabet* (1970), *To Stay Alive* (1971), *Footprints* (1972), *The Freeing of the Dust* (1975), *Life in the Forest* (1978), and *Collected Earlier Poems* (1979), however, are increasingly poised and joyous. After her conversion to Christianity in 1984, Levertov's poetry resonates even more deeply with a sense of the sacramentality and wholeness of life. *Candles in Babylon* (1982), *Oblique Prayers* (1984), *Breathing the Water* (1987), *Poems 1968–72* (1987), *Door in the Hive* (1989), *Evening Train* (1992), and *The Sands of the Well* (1996) speak joyousness and celebration. She attributed her mystical conviction of the spiritual foundations of life primarily to her Hasidic legacy. As early as 1964 she had written:

"Hasidism has given me since childhood a clear sense of marvels, of wonder. . . . The Hasidim were a little bit like the Franciscans; although in both movements there was also a very great strain of asceticism, yet along with it there was a recognition and joy in the physical world. And a sense of wonder at creation, and I think I have always felt something like that. . . . I think that's what poems are all about" (Sutton 332–338).

From her early work to her last poems she constantly sought to contain the antiphonal strains of Judaism, Christianity, and mysticism. However, it was primarily the Hasidic legacy that energized her vision of the sacramentality of everyday life, and of the sublimity of natural creation. Her preference for spliced images, split vision, juxtapositions, and the inevitable binaries that resulted from her religious legacy are increasingly reconciled. Contained paradoxes became a staple feature of her poetry. Her psychological, moral, and spiritual images usually start in the sensual imagery of concrete particulars and end in spiritual abstractions. Hence poems about cityscapes, landscapes, sublime wilderness, relationships, marriage, and motherhood provide occasions for spiritual meditation about the immanence of God. They are rich in images of seeing, experiencing, bodily responses, food, earth, seeds, animals, seas, rivers, and fountains. But the truly mystical strains of the late poetry are revealed in Levertov's brilliant creation of sounds and echos out of deliberately crafted diction, rhythm, and line progression. She uses these sounds to point to the many kinds of silences that lie within the listening soul. Denise Levertov was a confirmed Jungian, and her religious awareness often revealed itself through the languages of the unconscious: intuition, dream, meditation, fantasy, the suprarational, cycles, rituals, mystical faith, and the natural order. In these increasingly meditative poems monologue takes precedence over dialogue, just as silence finally takes precedence over sound. Stylistically her poetry is characterized by complex and carefully chosen etymologies, images, juxtapositions, binaries, enjambments, and precisely arranged line sequence. Through these she leads the reader into mystical experience often metaphorized in the flower, fruit, and landscape imagery from her English childhood. But, she soon added to her stock nature imagery after repeated exposure to the natural worlds of Mexico, New York, Maine, and the Pacific Northwest.

In the poetry leading up to and after her conversion there is much incarnational imagery. Although she cherished her religious sensibility, her late-life conversion to Christianity seems also to have been prompted by political and social awareness. In her very last interview, granted when she knew she was dying, she told her interviewer: "I think interest in religion is a counter force to the insane rationalist optimism that surrounds the development of all this new technology. . . . our ethical development does not match our technological development. This sense of spiritual hunger is something of a counter force or unconscious reaction to all that technological euphoria. . . . Writing is a form of prayer" (O'Connell). She retained her Hasidic conviction that life was mysterious and to be celebrated, and added to it the belief that Christian community was a viable bridge. Yet in the mosaiclike fragments of memory preserved in *Tesserae: Memories and Suppositions* (1995), her fourth and last prose collection, she attested that the most indelible and enduring of her several religious legacies was her father's Hasidism and her childhood immersion in the prewar world of European Jewry.

Denise Levertov spent the last decade of her life in Seattle, Washington, near one of her most important natural spiritual influences, Mount Rainier. During her final year she published *The Life Around Us: Selected Poems on Nature* and *The Stream and the Sapphire: Selected Poems on Religious Themes*. When she died in December 1997 from complications of lymphoma, she left *This Great Unknowing: Last Poems* (1999), *The Letters of Denise Levertov and William Carlos Williams* (1998), and *The Letters of Robert Duncan and Denise Levertov* (2004) to be published posthumously. In all, she wrote more than 20 volumes of poetry and four books of prose. Her prose works are *The Poet in the World* (1973), *Light up the Cave,* (1981) *New and Selected Essays* (1992), and *Tesserae: Memories and Suppositions*

(1995). During her distinguished life she served as poetry editor of *The Nation Magazine* (1961, 1963–65) and as poetry editor for *Mother Jones* magazine (1975–78). She won the Shelley Memorial Award, Robert Frost Medal, Lenore Marshall Prize, Lannan Award, a Guggenheim Fellowship, and a National Institute of Arts and Letters grant. Though long considered an important American poet, Denise Levertov is increasingly recognized as a profound religious poet whose recurring tropes of spiritual journeying and pilgrimage link each phase of her life and work.

Bibliography

Gelpi, Albert. *Denise Levertov: Selected Criticism.* Ann Abor: University of Michigan Press, 1993.
O'Connell, Nicholas, ed. *At the Field's End: Interviews with 22 Pacific Northwest Writers.* Seattle: University of Washington Press, 1998.
Wagner-Martin, Linda. *Denise Levertov.* New York: Twayne, 1967.
Sutton, Walter. "A Conversation with Denise Levertov." *Minnesota Review,* no. 3–4 (December 1965): 322–338.

—Gloria L. Cronin

Levin, Meyer (1905–1981)

Meyer Levin, Chicago-born, grew up in a Jewish neighborhood on the West Side of that city and obtained his education at the University of Chicago. He worked as a newspaperman to support his own writing, which was a common practice among aspiring writers of the period. As Steve Rubin relates, by the time of his death, Levin had been at work as a writer for nearly 60 years, not only as a novelist, but also as a dramatist, critic, and historian. He is classed with the "second generation of Jewish writers," which also includes HENRY ROTH, MICHAEL GOLD, and DANIEL FUCHS (Rubin 10). This generation faced a popular audience with little interest in the details of Jewish life, despite the precedent set by skilled Jewish writers of the first generation. Levin's work, however, while not successful in itself, was part of a movement that laid the groundwork for successful Jewish writers who followed, including Philip Roth, Bernard Malamud, and Saul Bellow.

Levin once wrote that his most prominent childhood memory is of "fear and shame at being a Jew" (Rubin 2). Portions of his work demonstrate his ambiguous feelings toward his own heritage. His inability to negotiate a comfortable Jewish identity accounts for the absence of Jewish themes or sympathy in his early novels, an absence that exists despite the experience of visiting Palestine five years before the publication of his first novel, an experience that deeply moved him. Levin had written short fiction that treated the subject of American Judaism in those intervening years, but the reception of that short fiction had persuaded him that any success he had as an author would necessarily treat non-Jewish subjects.

Yet, Levin eventually changed his mind; he began again to produce work that centered on Jewish experience. Much of his postwar writing was motivated by a desire to tell the story of the Jews' experiences in the Holocaust. Later in life, he became associated with Zionism, the movement that supported the Jews' return to Palestine as an independent nation. His books *The Settlers* (1972) and *The Harvest* (1978), written near the end of his career, both involve events surrounding the establishment of the Jewish state.

Meyer's reading of *The Diary of Anne Frank* after the war sparked a fierce struggle between him and Anne Frank's father, Otto. The diary had been discovered by the owners of the house where Anne and her family had hidden before being discovered by German officers. Her father had reluctantly shared the diary with relatives, and, at their urging, had even more reluctantly shared it with publishers. It met with great enthusiasm in Europe. When Meyer Levin read the book, he pushed for its American release. He opened a correspondence with Frank's father and promoted the book to publishing houses in the United States. The matter ended on a bitter note when Frank refused to grant Levin the rights for the book's stage adaptation. The rights were instead given to Frances Goodrich and Albert Hackett. Another Jewish writer, Lillian Hellman, had persuaded Frank that the Hacketts would produce a better adaptation, by which she meant a "less Jewish" adaptation. However, most people agree that the book's unexpected success in the United States was due in large part to Levin's glowing review, published in the *New York Times Book Review* on June 15, 1952, the day before the book was released.

Although Levin's work was received tolerably well by the public, it was never the subject of much scholarly discussion. He was an enthusiastic author, however, whose dedication to writing started early and sustained him through a long and prolific career.

Bibliography
Graver, Lawrence. *An Obsession with Anne Frank: Meyer Levin and the Diary.* London: University of California Press, 1995.
Rubin, Steven J. *Meyer Levin.* Boston: Twayne, 1982.
—Andrew Schultz

Lewisohn, Ludwig (1882–1955)

Ludwig Lewisohn was born in Berlin, Germany, to highly assimilated German-Jewish parents, Jacques and Minna. The family moved to South Carolina in 1890. After a distinguished record at Charleston High School, graduating valedictorian, Ludwig graduated with honors from the College of Charleston. His mother encouraged him to become a Methodist (he admitted to being "an American, a Southerner and a Christian" in his youth). Nevertheless, he could not get a much-needed job at the church-affiliated Porter Military Academy because of his Jewish birth. Bitter at his rejection, Ludwig dropped out of school for a year, unable to pay tuition. During this time, he wrote poetry and published his master's thesis, "A Study of Matthew Arnold," in the *Sewanee Review* (1901).

Fortunately, support from family and friends enabled him to go to New York later in 1902 to enter the Ph.D. program at Columbia University. There he became friendly with the poet William Ellery Channing and began his lifelong critical pursuit of Puritan America and his search for his Jewish identity. Though he was a superb student, as usual he was told by two of his senior professors that it would be virtually impossible for a Jewish man to be hired in an English department. Disillusioned, Ludwig again dropped out but published what would have been his Ph.D. dissertation, "Books We Have Made" (1903) in the Charleston paper, a study still of value today.

In 1906, having moved back to Charleston, Ludwig was followed by Mary Arnold Crocker, an Englishwoman, a divorcée with several children, more than 20 years older than he, whom he claimed he had been forced to marry in 1904 because of America's Puritan constraints. Returning to New York with Mary, he published his first novel, *The Broken Snare,* in 1908, with help from Theodore Dreiser. It was superficially a romance novel, but Ralph Melnick calls it "a carefully disguised Jewish polemic against the Puritan Ethos." It marked Lewisohn's departure from being a small-town German-American Christian to a rapidly developing New Yorker, cosmopolitan American, who was entering a life of freedom and creativity.

In 1910 Ludwig took a job at the University of Wisconsin, in the German department. Buttressed by good reviews of his novel and frequent publications in leading journals, he moved to the German department at Ohio State University, where he remained until 1917, when World War I and growing anti-German sentiment forced him out. Despite a fruitful period, during which he published *The Dramatic Works of Gerhard Hauptmann* (1912), *The Modern Drama* (1915), and *The Spirit of Modern German Literature* (1916), Lewisohn had to leave Columbus in 1917 and return to New York City.

Meanwhile, after his mother's death in 1912 and his father's death in 1920, Lewisohn finally embarked on a search for his Jewish identity. He found his niche with the novels *Up Stream* (1922), *The Case of Mr. Crump* (1926), *Roman Summer* (1927), *Mid-Channel* (1929), *The Last Days of Shylock* (1931), and *The Trumpet of Jubilee* (1937).

Most people remember Lewisohn for his aggressive pursuit of a few themes. On the one hand, due to his disastrous marriage, he waged a fierce battle in his novels against the unnatural judicial constraints of a Puritan society. As he wrote in *Up Stream,* "Life among us is ugly and mean and, above all, false in its assumptions and measures. Somehow we must break these shackles and flee and emerge into some kind of sanity, of a closer contact with reality, of nature and of truth." The conflict between marriage and personal freedom, buttressed by a rigid legal system that supported the claims of his wife (who would not give him a divorce for two decades), and his growing interest in a younger woman fueled his critical output. At the same time, beginning in the 1920s he became a Zionist, writing *Israel* (1925), in which he rejected acculturation and assimilation and called for a return to tradition. *The Case of Mr. Crump* is a novelized account of his miserable relationship with Mary. Described by Sigmund Freud as "an incomparable masterpiece" and by Thomas Mann as a "story of the inferno of a marriage," it induced Mary to have it banned in America for its libelous and sexual explicitness. It has, however, sold more than a million copies since its publication.

In a more classical vein, Lewisohn published *Expressionism in America* (1932), a massive, magisterial study of the so-called Puritan values that he criticized as leading to the unjust and unhealthy nature of American life.

In 1939 Mary finally gave Lewisohn a divorce. Meanwhile, his relationship with the younger woman dissolved, though she gave him a son, James, in 1933. In 1939 he met and subsequently married Edna Manley, a marriage that lasted only three years. His fourth wife was Louise Volk, whom he married in the 1940s. By this time, Lewisohn, a passionate critic of Nazi Germany, defender of American Jewry, and spokesman for refugee resettlement in Palestine, had seen his reputation rise, fall, then rise again, in part due to his longtime friendship with Rabbi Stephen Wise, a friend of President Roosevelt. In his last years he became a professor of comparative literature and then university librarian at Brandeis University. Shortly before his death in 1955, he reflected in *In a Summer Season* (1955) on faith and love. "Love . . . How is it to be sought? Where is it to be found?" "Faith . . . is it not almost, Heaven help me, more easily found than love is to be found among the confusions of our lives?" It was a fitting end to a distinguished career, which produced over 85 books, hundreds of poems, thousands of articles, and countless talks and lecture tours.

Bibliography

Lainoff, Seymour. *Ludwig Lewisohn*. Boston: Twayne, 1982.

Melnick, Ralph. *The Life and Work of Ludwig Lewisohn*. Detroit: Wayne State University Press, 1998.

———. "Ludwig Lewisohn: The Early Charleston Years." *Studies in American Jewish Literature* 3 (1983).

—Daniel Walden

The Lights of Earth Gina Berriault (1984)

Set in San Francisco and Chicago in the early 1970s, *The Lights of Earth* is a brief novel about the anguish of erotic loss and the writer's attempt to redeem herself. Cutting close to the bone of Berriault's life and vocation, this novel became a grueling project. Protagonist Ilona Lewis is a writer whose lover of four years, Martin Vandersen, becomes famous when his novel is acclaimed and bought for a movie. Eventually, Martin leaves her for a new lover, and Ilona enters a period of misery. Like her creator, Ilona feels like an outsider yearning for "entry into the light" that radiates from the blessed. Questions of hospitality arise in the novel's frequently recurring doors and thresholds—sites where Ilona faces the ambivalence of entry, welcome, and unwelcome. Her desire to be noticed sets her sharply apart from Berriault, who later borrowed Thomas Merton's famous words to declare her wish to disappear from the world as a means of developing greater compassion.

Ilona endures a crisis as lover, sister, and writer: Forsaken by Martin, she also knows she has forsaken her older brother. A letter from her brother Albert in Chicago renews her shame and guilt over having been, nearly 20 years ago, his caretaker during his early-adulthood mental decline. The narrator describes her environment at that time as menacing, and Albert as a mad person wearing secondhand clothes. Now Ilona, who had sworn to be compassionate to the marginalized individuals she may or may not have been able to understand, suffers from the remembrance of her failure to do so with her brother.

Ilona has taken eros as an "entry into the light." After Martin has begun to live with his new lover, he asks Ilona which people fit into her category of "the blessed." She responds that they are lovers. But, as in this moment, their relation is always triangulated by the imminence or presence of a third party. Torn between eros for Martin and recognition of the third party, Ilona is blessed and cursed with the imagination of the other. It is an ethical imagination, even when the other is a rival disrupting or displacing her solitude with Martin.

Ilona's erotic loss of Martin directs her inward, and toward redeeming her forsaken brother and herself. Shortly after the death of their mother, when he begged her to let him come with her, she had denied him. This action would torment her throughout her life. In these re-creations, Ilona indicts not only herself but also her craft.

Ilona's last night with Martin ends with a phone call at dawn telling her that her brother has died. She flies to Chicago to make funeral arrangements and dispose of his belongings. When Albert's landlady asks what she plans to do with the body, Ilona has to answer with a word that is described but not included in the text. We infer "cremation" from the landlady's response about how her people practice burials. What follows in Ilona's thoughts is one of the very few direct allusions to the Holocaust in Berriault's work. Ilona later denies that there is any godly record that remembers Earth's events, like the Holocaust.

Forsaking and death and loss, even her excruciating loss of Martin, have taken their toll. She wonders if she were not a lover, if there are other ways to enter into life and evade abandonment. Hospitality might be the fundamental figure for both eros and ethics, and for imagination as well. Ilona's writerly hospitality to the "others" she writes about has kept her and her daughter's pitchers full of blessings.

Back in San Francisco Ilona cannot write, so she goes to live for a year in her friend Claud's ex-wife's beach house 20 miles north of the city. Claud, a writer who has stopped writing, stays the first night with her, and during that night she leaves the house and walks down the beach and into the ocean, leaving a light on to direct her back to Claud. She muses as she walks about the "lights of earth," and whether everyone in one's life was such a light, beckoning a person out of the darkness. Her thoughts are interrupted when she is struck by a tremendous wave. Suddenly in danger, she fights to reach the shore again, and hears Claud calling her name in a voice that suggests his need for her presence. So she makes her way back to him as he runs along the sand.

This ending is bare human survival, not some large triumph. Yet Berriault's austere fictional art achieves its own triumph. *The Lights of Earth* is one of the finest recent examples of what Irving Howe has called "a major American tradition, the line of the short novel, exemplified by *Billy Budd, The Great Gatsby, Miss Lonelyhearts,* and *Seize the Day* . . . in which everything—action, form, language—is fiercely compressed, and often enough, dark-grained as well." If it might be called "minimalist," its minimalism is of a kind, of an intensity, that does not shrink our humanity but magnifies and dignifies it. Ilona's choice to live beyond loss presents a singularly fine, austere, and poignant vision of how it is to be on the earth in a darkness lit like the clear night sky.

Bibliography

Lyons, Bonnie. "Didn't I Know You?" In *Passion and Craft: Conversations with Notable Writers.* Urbana: University of Illinois Press, 1998.

Spencer, Elizabeth. "Flotsam of the Heart," *New York Times,* 8 April 1984, 9.

—B. W. Jorgensen

The Little Disturbances of Man
Grace Paley   (1959)

GRACE PALEY was born in 1922, the youngest child of a Jewish family with Ukrainian roots. She dis-covered her passion for writing at a young age while growing up in the Bronx. She was greatly encouraged in her writerly attempts by both her parents, but particularly by her father. At first she focused on poetry, as it seemed to go hand-in-hand with the rhythm of her diverse surroundings. Paley married when she was only 20 and began the life of housewife and mother, much to the dismay of her parents, especially her mother, who would have preferred a less domestic life for her daughter.

Not until she was married did Paley find the prose form in which she could most easily express herself—the short story. She started writing with notable verve, coupling subtle humor and wit with compassion and perception. The strength of her writing, which draws the reader into her characters and into her plots, grows out of her own experience, her life with her family, and her neighborhood in New York City. Paley's observations of common people in everyday situations are an exceptional realistic assessment of the inner life of women, and the circumstances she creates transform the reading into an in-depth analysis of life. The reader gets the impression of sitting in a circle of women, listening to individual stories, misfortunes, and tragedies, as the different narrators find comfort and solace in the company of other women. It is far from gossip; it is confiding in other women, whispering confessions, small truths. Paley's stories are honest and somewhat humorous reflections on decisions and desires that determine the fate of the female protagonists. She succeeds in telling heartbreaking stories in a way that nevertheless cause the reader to laugh heartily once in a while.

Paley's collection of short stories, *The Little Disturbances of Man,* was published to popular success in 1959. The collection includes 10 stories, most of which give us an insight into the lives of women caught in the seemingly inevitable marriage plot. The reader meets women of all ages, all of them trying to coerce, con, lure, and ensnare men into the state of matrimony. This desire for married life is less present in the women's male counterparts. Men and women remain trapped in an eternal attempt to reach what they consider the ultimate purpose of their lives, not acknowledging their conflicting interests, thus remaining in an unhealthy struggle between being caught and catching.

Paley's women long to "arrive," to have their own home, husband, and family. They seem to be born with the wish to settle down. They desire the presence of men or one man in their lives. This is ironic because they consider marriage to be something stable, providing security, although in Paley's stories it does not grant either. "Men are different than women," Joanna states in the story "A Woman, Young and Old." It is the only phrase allowed to her by her older sister Josephine, narrating the story, who (at the tender age of 13) almost succeeds in getting Corporal Brownstar to marry her. Paley shows men's eternal urge for more—there might be something better around the next corner; why stop here? Why settle? The men are not content with stability. Quite the opposite, they consider themselves chained down in marriage, and suffocate in the always ready female embrace. They are on the outlook for constant satisfaction, which the women never seem to get.

In her stories Paley depicts the mothers' feeling accountable for their families and men ignoring both financial and child-rearing responsibilities. Marriages end in divorce, and single mothers, alienated and lonely, struggle to raise their children. Men come and go as they please, popping in and out of the houses and stories either to see the children (rarely so) or (more likely) to have sexual intercourse with the woman they have abandoned. Women are oppressed and used by the men in their lives, harrowed and depressed housewives, prone to disappointing affairs. These issues rising from the conflicting interests of gender are discouraging; however, life goes on for Paley's women.

Bibliography

Cronin, Gloria L. "Melodramas of Beset Womanhood: Resistance, Subversion, and Survival in the Fiction of Grace Paley." In *Studies in American Jewish Literature* 11, no. 2 (Fall 1992): 140–149.

Kamel, Rose. "To Aggravate the Conscience: Grace Paley's Loud Voice." *Journal of Ethnic Studies* 11, no. 3 (Fall 1983): 29–49.

—Sara D. Nyffenegger

The Lost: A Search for Six of the Six Million
Daniel Mendelsohn (2006)

Daniel Mendelsohn's evocative and bittersweet book is a literary and psychological tour de force. A member of the third post-Holocaust generation, the author seeks to clarify the precise details of the life and death of his murdered relatives and to articulate his own relationship to the Shoah. In his global search for answers, Mendelsohn, a secular Jew, blends both quaint techniques such as oral interviews and modern research tools such as the World Wide Web in his exquisitely written quest. A classics professor at Bard College and a regular contributor to such publications as the *New York Review of Books,* the *New York Times Book Review,* and the *New York Times Magazine,* Mendelsohn offers a narrative that juxtaposes diverse literary works including the Hebrew Bible and its classic and contemporary interpreters as well as Greek Literature, Hebrew, Yiddish, German, and Latin. The result illuminates not only the author's familial story but also has much to say about the enduring quality of narrative.

The author recalls that as a boy of six, seven, or eight years of age, when he walked into a room certain of his aunts began weeping. His relatives were from the Ukrainian town of Bolechow, and were far more comfortable speaking Yiddish than English. The reason for their tears is that Daniel was the mirror image of his Uncle Shmiel Jäger, who, along with his wife, Ester, and four daughters—Bronia, Frydka, Lorka, and Ruchele—were murdered by the Germans in World War II. Adding to the pathos of Mendelsohn's tale is that Shmiel came to America before the war, did not like the new country, and returned to Bolechow. Shmiel's brother, Abraham (Aby), Mendelsohn's grandfather, was a refugee who left Europe in the mid-1930s. He kept his brother's letters and some family photos from Europe. Abraham was an Orthodox Jew who told Daniel countless tales of the Bolechow Jewish community. But he never spoke about the murder of Shmiel and his family. Mendelsohn writes that consequently to him, Shmiel's family "seemed not so much dead as lost, vanished not only from the world but—even more terrible to me—from my grandfather's stories."

The Lost is an eloquent memoir dealing with the possibilities and limitations of memory. Interspersing official documents, family photos, and relatives' memories, Mendelsohn achieves some degree of knowledge concerning details of the murder of Shmiel's family. In Bolechow he meets a woman who knew the family. He also discovers that Fydka was hidden by her non-Jewish Polish boyfriend, an act that cost both their lives. The author adds to the richness of his narrative by exploring the mystery of why Shmiel was unable to leave Europe despite his increasingly frantic letters to Abraham against the background of the biblical narrative of Cain and Abel. At one point Shmiel even thought of writing President Roosevelt seeking help to escape the Nazi death machine. What did Abraham tell his brother? Did his letters even get through? All Mendelsohn knows for sure is that his grandfather—a natty dresser—always carried Shmiel's letters, neatly wrapped, in the breast pocket of his jacket.

Mendelsohn's book eloquently reveals three basic facets of the third-generation dilemma. It is axiomatic that this generation makes a pilgrimage to the European birthplace of their grandparents. Further, the third generation depends for aditional knowledge on interviews with family members and others who knew the murdered. Mendelsohn traveled not only to Ukraine, but to Israel and Australia to speak to witnesses and to extended family. Second, his interviews yielded the insight that the Jews from Bolechow were "rich in memories but poor in keepsakes, whereas I was rich in the keepsakes but had no memories to go with them." The implied question is found in Elie Wiesel's novel *The Forgotten:* Can one transfuse memory? Mendelsohn, his brother Matt—whose photos are in *The Lost*—and their sister Jennifer seek just such a transfusion on their European pilgrimage. Third, Mendelsohn becomes aware that certain fundamental things about the Holocaust are simply unknowable, such as the exact manner of the deaths of Shmiel's family. Moreover, he discovers that memory itself can "play tricks," omitting painful details, or be made to fit a certain pattern. Consequently, although he knows a great deal more than when he began his quest, the author feels compelled to imagine various scenarios concerning how Shmiel and his family lost their lives. This memoir underscores the great hovering presence of the Holocaust even in the lives of those born long after the event.

Mendelsohn's first book, *The Elusive Embrace: Desire and the Riddle of Identity,* was a *New York Times* Notable Book of the Year and a *Los Angeles Times* Best Book of the Year. *The Lost* has achieved both commercial and critical success, having received a front-page review in the *New York Times Book Review;* an extensive review in the *New York Review of Books;* as well as being widely reviewed elsewhere, including the *San Francisco Chronicle,* the *New York Observer,* and the *Washington Post Book World. The Lost* was both a *New York Times* and *Boston Globe* best seller. Furthermore, Mendelsohn's book won several distinguished awards: The National Book Critics Circle Award, the National Jewish Book Award, the Salon Book Award, and the American Library Association Medal for Outstanding Contribution to Jewish Literature.

Bibliography

Gold, Sarah F. "Lost . . . and Found," *Publisher's Weekly* 253, no. 32 (August 14, 2006): 173.

Rosenbaum, Ron. "Giving Death a Face," *New York Times,* 24 September 2006, Sec. 7, p. 1.

—Alan L. Berger

Mailer, Norman (1923–2007)

Norman Mailer labored most of his literary career to repudiate "the one personality he found absolutely insupportable—the nice Jewish boy from Brooklyn . . . he had the softness of a man early accustomed to mother-love." Mailer deliberately fashioned himself into the official bad boy of contemporary letters, staking out as his territory the extremes of experience usually excluded from Jewish-American fiction, including murder, rape, orgy, and psychosis. For many years Mailer was more infamous for his misbehavior—drunken brawls, arrests, marrying six times, stabbing one wife—than he was for his work. But as he aged, he mellowed, serving as president of PEN and becoming a respected elder statesman of American letters. He won the National Book Award in 1969, the Pulitzer Prize in 1969 and 1980, and in 2005 was awarded the National Book Medal for distinguished contribution to American letters.

Mailer's heroes tend to be either WASPs or only part Jewish, perhaps because he preferred to think of himself more as an American rather than a Jewish-American writer. His persistent themes are sex, violence, and power in American life, but behind his radicalism is a moral, proselytizing (one might even say rabbinical) streak. Mailer called himself a "left conservative." What gives his work continuity despite its many radical changes in form and style is his quest for a hero fit for our times: a man able to resist the drift of history and help to shape the future.

Mailer had an extremely long and prolific career, beginning in 1948 at the age of 25; he wrote novels, plays, poetry, journalism, essays, and biographies of Marilyn Monroe, Pablo Picasso, and Lee Harvey Oswald. In the 1960s he was one of the innovators of the New Journalism, or "nonfiction novel," and wrote some of the best political reportage in America. A Renaissance man, Mailer also wrote and directed movies, acted in some, helped to found the *Village Voice*, and twice ran for mayor of New York City. From the start, he was a literary celebrity with outsize ambition, determined to make an impact on America. In the opening manifesto of *Advertisements for Myself* (1959) he announced, "The sour truth is that I am imprisoned with a perception which will settle for nothing less than making a revolution in the consciousness of our time."

Mailer came from a middle-class Jewish family and grew up in the Eastern Parkway section of Brooklyn, which he calls "the most secure Jewish environment in America." The precocious Mailer entered Harvard at 16 to study aeronautical engineering but started reading American literature.

He wanted to write the great American war novel, so after graduating Harvard in 1943 he served as a rifleman in the Philippines, which provided the material for his best-selling novel *The NAKED AND THE DEAD* (1948). Today, although it seems rather old-fashioned in form and style, *The Naked and the Dead* remains one of the classic novels of the war. A sweaty, mercilessly realistic view of men at war, it derives from the literary naturalism of the 1930s. Mailer criticizes the overwhelming institutions of modern America that crush the individual and predicts a coming totalitarianism in postwar America.

His second novel, *Barbary Shore* (1951), unsuccessfully mixes political allegory with existential closet drama. Nonetheless, today it seems ahead of its time, an anguished shout of political prophecy from the depths of the Cold War. Mailer's attempt to explore the unconscious motivations of an American society he saw as increasingly perverse and corrupt was leading him away from literary realism and into the feverish distortions of a dream vision.

Mailer next conceived an admittedly "Napoleonic" plan for an eight-novel sequence, a dream epic that consumed his energies for the remainder of the 1950s. The only completed segments are *The Deer Park* and his two best short stories, "The Man Who Studied Yoga" (1952) and "The Time of Our Time" (1959). Sam Slovoda in "The Man Who Studied Yoga" is a failed radical and failed artist subsiding into a middle-class coma, an assimilated Jew whose analyst and wife have effectively hemmed him in. The story anticipates the concerns of his next two novels.

The Deer Park (1955) is a Hollywood novel that explores the corrupt, repressive climate of the 1950s, exposing the interlocking power relationships in America of sex, money, politics, and the dream factory of Hollywood, which keeps the public pacified with illusions.

Advertisements for Myself (1959), a selection of pieces with introductory essays, was a turning point in his career, the most candid confession of the pressures of success and the literary marketplace on the serious American writer since F. Scott Fitzgerald's *The Crack-Up* (1936). Mailer rails against the blandness and conformity of the 1950s and the insignificance of the American writer in that era. The

writing in the autobiographical passages established a new voice, one crackling with energy. Mailer was throwing his hat in the ring in a bid to be the first Jewish president of American letters. From then on, he alternated between novels and nonfiction.

Advertisements includes his notorious essay about the "White Negro" or "philosophical psychopath," a mythical hero concocted out of the psychology of Wilhelm Reich and the influence of the Beat generation, who proves his manhood in the underworld of drugs, crime, and violence, and in the quest for the perfect orgasm. This existential hero, a rebel for the atomic age, is Mailer's instrument in his next few novels for exploring the repressed powers of the instinctual and the irrational.

Mailer now began to write far bolder, more unconventional fiction in a rich, playful, vigorous rhetoric, with characters who were not realistic but deliberate superstereotypes. He centered each work on one strong central hero who embodies the ceaseless war between the White Negro and the nice-Jewish-boy side of Mailer.

"The Time of Her Time" is a breakthrough in Mailer's fiction and anticipates *An American Dream*. The hero is a gentile hipster who seduces a Jewish woman in a sexual struggle for power, which some critics saw as Mailer's attempt to work out his Jewish self-hatred.

Because of its style, narrative energy, and levels of allegorical meaning, *An American Dream* (1965) is one of Mailer's best novels. Mailer now conceives of contemporary America in increasingly fabulous, magical terms. Critics denounced it as self-indulgent and morally repugnant, or praised it as a powerful dream vision of American life. This novel about a man who murders his wife and gets away with it depends on the morality of "The White Negro," that individual acts of violence may be preferable to the collective violence of the bureaucratic superstate.

The 1960s were a turbulent but extremely productive decade for Mailer. As American reality pushed on to new heights of violence and absurdity, so his fiction pushed to comparable extremes of corrosive obscenity in *Why Are We in Vietnam?*

(1967). Like *Huckleberry Finn, Why Are We in Vietnam?* is a savage comedy with a teenage hero, indicting American civilization. A hunting trip to Alaska with a Texas tycoon, complete with excess firepower and helicopters, becomes analogous to the violence of the Vietnam War.

The ARMIES OF THE NIGHT (1968) is one of the most influential works of the New Journalism of the 1960s, a movement in which reporters gave subjective responses or participated in the events they reported. *The Armies of the Night,* Mailer's finest comic work, is written in the third person about a hero, Norman Mailer, recounting the events surrounding his arrest and imprisonment stemming from his participation in an anti–Vietnam War march on the Pentagon in 1967. Mailer as Jewish schlemiel has a foil in his friend and fellow protester, the poet Robert Lowell, whose heroic dignity represents the best of WASP America. Mailer succeeds in capturing and making comprehensible the drift of American history in the 1960s. Later he applied similar novelistic techniques to his reports on the 1968 presidential conventions in *Miami and the Siege of Chicago* (1968) and on man's landing on the moon in *Of a Fire on the Moon* (1970). However, after *The Armies of the Night* the technique and the voice became overly familiar.

The Executioner's Song (1979), a "True Life Novel," recounts the last year in the life of Gary Gilmore, the Utah murderer. From thousands of pages of interviews, Mailer pieced together his own imaginative re-creation, a moving account of the life and death of a charismatic criminal. The work won the Pulitzer Prize, although some critics complained that Mailer was exploiting tragic events and glorifying a vicious criminal.

Mailer's long-promised epic, *Ancient Evenings* (1983), was announced as the first volume of a proposed trilogy intended to range from ancient Egypt into our future. He soon abandoned the trilogy. *Ancient Evenings* is ambitious and innovative in style and point of view, although many critics found Mailer's obsession with sodomy repetitious and the prose purple. Defending the novel against criticism that he was slighting his Jewish heritage, Mailer said he was trying to write about the world before the Judeo-Christian era. The setting of ancient Egypt allowed Mailer to work out on a grand scale his theories about the interconnections of sex, violence, and power. In this historical fantasia, he creates a sweeping panorama of kings, gods, and devils, barbaric violence, and epic fornications, a world as alien as some distant planet.

By comparison, his next novel, *Tough Guys Don't Dance* (1984), is a lightweight thriller about an alcoholic writer who believes he may have committed a murder. Mailer wrote the screenplay for the film version and directed it.

He returned to epic form with *Harlot's Ghost* (1991), a 1,300-page-long chronicle of the CIA from the Berlin airlift to the assassination of John F. Kennedy, focusing on Harry Hubbard, a young agent whose father and whose mentor, Hugh Montague (also known as Harlot), are also in the CIA. Critics took it as evidence that Mailer's work had grown in power and mastery. However, *The Gospel According to the Son* (1997), a novel narrated in the first-person by Jesus Christ, was almost universally panned.

Mailer's work, for all its unevenness, shows a wide scope and flexibility, an epic ambition, and a willingness to experiment and tackle controversial, major themes that place him in the top rank of Jewish-American writers. The irresolvable contradictions in Mailer's personality, between the "nice Jewish boy from Brooklyn" and the all-American wild man, make him remarkably open to a range of experiences and themes alien to most Jewish-American literature.

Bibliography

Bloom, Harold, ed. *Norman Mailer.* Philadelphia: Chelsea House, 2003.

Merrill, Robert. *Norman Mailer Revisited.* New York: Twayne, 1992.

—Andrew Gordon

Malamud, Bernard (1914–1986)

Brooklyn-born Bernard Malamud was the son of Russian immigrant grocers Max and Bertha (Fidelman). Malamud graduated from Erasmus High

School, City College (B.A.), and Columbia University (M.A.). After teaching night school at New York City high schools, he moved his family, wife, Ann, and son, Paul, to Corvallis, Oregon, where he taught for 10 years at Oregon State University. In 1961 he moved his family, now including daughter Janna, to Bennington, Vermont, where he taught at Bennington College for the rest of his career.

Malamud's first novel, *The NATURAL* (1952), introduces his penchant for processing history and myth through his imagination. This allegorical baseball novel about fallen heroes, which was made into a successful film, was followed by *The ASSISTANT* (1957). Set in a grocery store, this book adds personal history to the alchemical mix and produces a story in which an anti-Semitic gentile thief ends up taking the place of his boss, the Jewish grocer, even converting to Judaism, circumcision and all. Here Malamud begins his themes that characterize nearly all of his fiction: To be a good Jew means to be a good human being. The corollary to this theme is how a Jew becomes a good man, which is the subject of *The Magic Barrel* (1958), a short story collection that, like *Idiots First* and *Pictures of Fidelman,* explores a range of social issues, from those confronting new Jewish immigrants to infidelity, poverty, language barriers, black/Jewish relations, suffering, and redemption.

With *A New Life* (1961), Malamud changes pace to expose the vicissitudes of academic life. This satire is set in and inspired by Malamud's experiences teaching at Oregon State. The important short story "The GERMAN REFUGEE" appeared in 1963. But it was *The Fixer* (1966) that cemented Malamud's reputation as an Jewish-American writer, a title he derided, wishing to be considered only a writer. Based on the Mendel Beiliss case, *The Fixer* follows the nonreligious Yakov Bok, an innocent, penniless Jew, through czarist Russia's propaganda machine and prison, where he realizes that a Jew must be political. As with *The Assistant,* the loyalties of Jews and non-Jews are unpredictable. Bok is betrayed by Jews and helped by gentiles, who are killed for doing so. *The Tenants* (1971) also challenges stereotypes, as a black writer and a Jewish writer enact the stormy, mutually destructive

black/Jewish divide of the late 1960s. *Rembrandt's Hat* (1973), a short story collection, and *Dubin's Lives* (1979), about a biographer, were followed by Malamud's last completed novel, the nearly nihilistic GOD'S GRACE (1982). In this work, Calvin Cohn has accidentally survived the earth's nuclear annihilation, and tries to re-create and repopulate civilization on an island of primates. Malamud told an interviewer that "the purpose of the writer is to keep civilization from destroying itself." True to this dictate, in *God's Grace* and elsewhere, Malamud's Jews struggle to be *menschen,* Yiddish for "good human beings," usually while fighting to deny their own Jewish identities. The author's unfinished and posthumously published novel *The People* joins a lonely immigrant Jew with a poor Native American tribe in what appears to be a symbiotic relationship. *The People and Uncollected Stories* was published in 1989; *The Complete Stories* was published in 1997. Using fantasy and history, tragedy and comedy, realism and allegory (complete with talking animals), Malamud develops not only the thematic conflicts of displaced Jews, immigrants, rootlessness, and the absence of faith, but their resolutions in redemptive love, suffering, and sacrifice.

In the context of the Jewish-American literary tradition, Malamud resembles pre–World War II writers ABRAHAM CAHAN, ANZIA YEZIERSKA, and Henry Roth, and post-Holocaust writers ISAAC BASHEVIS SINGER, SAUL BELLOW, and PHILIP ROTH, particularly in his Holocaust works. Malamud's universality, however, is rooted in specificity. His Jewish characters are not only archetypal Jews, but also symbols of suffering humanity. Thus the Jew's rejection of assimilation and acceptance of his own identity is metaphoric of humanity's need to reject conformity and embrace individuality. For Malamud, all of this is in the service of living an ethical life, which he equates with living a Jewish life. In this sense too, then, as he famously said, "All men are Jews, except they don't know it." Interestingly, the recent burgeoning of young American Jewish writers whose fiction embraces living a Jewish life in religious, ritual, and even mystical terms is actually the logical next step following Malamud; he insisted that his Jews accept and acknowledge their born identities. In the current literary landscape, how characters define that Jewish identity is what defines their authors.

Malamud's contribution to American literature has been recognized by the National Book Award and Pulitzer Prize for *The Fixer* (1966), the National Book Award for *The Magic Barrel* (1958), the National Association of Arts and Letters' Gold Medal for Fiction (1983), election to the National Institute of Arts and Letters of the American Academy (1964), and the American Academy of Arts and Sciences (1967). Bernard Malamud was also president of PEN American Center from 1979 to 1981.

Bibliography

Avery, Evelyn. *The Magic Worlds of Bernard Malamud.* Albany: SUNY Press, 2001.

Cappell, Ezra. "Reflecting the World: Bernard Malamud's Post-Holocaust Judaism." In *Modern Jewish Studies,* A Special Issue: The Art of Bernard Malamud. Edited by S. Lillian Kremer. *Yiddish* 13, no. 1 (2002): 31–61.

Smith, Janna Malamud. *My Father Is a Book: A Memoir of Bernard Malamud.* Boston: Houghton Mifflin, 2006.

Watts, Eileen H. "The Art of Racism: Blacks, Jews and Language in *The Tenants.*" *Studies in American Jewish Literature* 15 (1996): 42–48.

—Evelyn Avery

The March E. L. Doctorow (2005)

Published in 2005, *The March* is a historical fiction novel set in 1864 near the conclusion of the American Civil War. The narrative centers around the character of General William Tecumseh Sherman as he marches his 60,000 troops through the heart of the South, carving a 60-mile-wide scar of destruction in their wake. As a result of Sherman's order to live off the land, his soldiers wreak havoc as they pillage homes, steal cattle, burn crops, and accumulate a nearly unmanageable population of freed slaves and refugees who have nowhere else to go. While the direction of the novel's action revolves around the decisions of General Sherman, there is no specific main character. Instead, Doctorow retells Civil War history according to the individual lives of a large and diverse cast of characters—white and black, rich and poor, Union and Confederate—whose lives are caught up in the violence and trauma of the war.

The General Sherman character is an unstable strategic genius who longs for a sense of romance in the war he wages and chafes under the implications of a postwar bureaucracy. Charismatic though often detached, Sherman is idolized by his men and the freed slaves who follow behind in hope of a better future. Pearl is a young, attractive former slave unsure about her future and the attention she is now receiving from the handsome Union soldiers. She must decide whether to follow the advice of other emancipated slaves or choose to seek the possibilities she hopes the conclusion of the war will bring. Colonel Sartorius is a cold yet brilliant field surgeon seemingly numb to the horrors of war due to his close and frequent proximity to his surgical hacksaw. Trained in Germany, Sartorius experiments with new techniques on his patients and becomes consumed with his work, leaving little time for regret, romance, or pain. Arly and Will are two Confederate soldiers who play the part of the Shakespearian fool, alternately offering comic relief and poignant wisdom. Their antics are wild and chaotic and include defecting to the Union, impersonation, and robbing a church to pay for a trip to a brothel. Emily Thompson is a displaced Southern aristocrat who becomes the assistant and lover to the passionless Colonel Sartorius.

The novel ends when the war ends, exposing the cautious optimism of the freed slaves and beleaguered soldiers. The final scene describes the faint smell of gunpowder dissipating through a forest with the lonely image of the boot and shredded uniform of a fallen soldier lying in the dirt. While Doctorow's characters express guarded hope now that the conflict is over, the physical and psychological toll of the war has left its scars on the people and the land. No one is quite sure what to do next.

By focusing on the lives of his characters rather than battles or other historic events, Doctorow stylistically distances himself from other works of historical fiction that seek to glamorize or merely dramatize history. No single person carries a majority of the weight of the narrative. Because of this, what is otherwise well-known Civil War history is retold through multiple viewpoints and voices simultaneously and presented to the reader as a mosaic of complications, confusion, and ambivalence. Structurally, *The March* frequently works in pairs of characters with conflicting backgrounds and needs. Emily and Sartorious, for example, work together in the field hospital and try to cope with the visceral trauma of a never-ending number of grisly operations; Arly and Will struggle for identity and ethics as they defect to the Union Army. Also, several characters in the novel are connected or reused from other Doctorow novels. The impassive Colonel Sartorious hails from *The Waterworks*, and the freed slave Coalhouse Walker is the ostensible father of *Ragtime*'s jazz pianist Coalhouse Walker, Jr. While these references are not crucial to the plot, they hint at a wider mythology for the novel reminiscent of William Faulkner.

The March has been widely praised by critics since its publication and was a New York Times best seller. In 2006 the novel won the PEN/Faulkner fiction award, which Doctorow had previously won in 1990 for his novel *Billy Bathgate*. *The March* also won the 2005 National Book Critics Circle Award and was a finalist for the 2005 National Book Award.

Bibliography

"Just Keep Moving, Regardless of Cost." *Toronto Star*, 26 February 2006, p. D08.
Review of *The March*. *Sunday Telegraph* (London), 29 January 2006, p. 53.

—**Jacob Hodgen**

Margolin, Anna (1887–1952)

Anna Margolin, born Rosa Lebensboym, was an important Yiddish poet writing in the period before World War II. Originally from eastern Europe, Margolin spent time in both Ukraine and Poland before eventually immigrating to the United States and living in New York City. She first started publishing poems in the late 1920s, and her first and only collection of poems, *Lider*, was published in 1929.

At some time in the early 1930s, Margolin sent an unpublished book of her poems to Chaim Nachman Bialik. This fellow Hebrew poet, who was then head of the Hebrew Writer's Union, loved her work. He responded with a short and simple letter that first asked, "Who are you?" and then declared, "Your poems are genuine. You are a true poet. I swallowed up the book as soon as it fell into my hand." This sort of mysterious behavior was characteristic of Margolin, who chose to remain out of the limelight, refusing any kind of celebrity status that would have been quite accessible in her day in the Yiddish community. She was so reclusive, in fact, that many of her contemporaries believed her to be a man hiding under a false name. Toward the end of her life, she lived in common-law status with fellow Yiddish poet Reuven Ayzland. She had at least one child, born during her time in Israel. She is buried in the Workman's Circle Cemetery in Carmel, New York. Her pseudonym, Anna Margolin, is prominent on the gravestone, with her birth name in smaller letters beneath it. Etched on the gravestone itself is the almost complete text to one of her poems, "She with the Cold Marble Breasts."

Writing exclusively in Yiddish, Margolin has been associated with a group of Jewish poets writing within a movement called "Insichism," or Introspectivism. This movement began roughly in 1919 and ended shortly before the beginning of World War II. Introspectivism is characterized by an attempt to express, through poetry, intellectualized emotion. In other words, they sought to look inward to reshape the world to fit their own personal reality. This was usually seen as a rejection of the material world, seeking truth in the imagination. Margolin often toyed with the notion that there is a gap between the mundane material world and the spiritual world, causing the latter to be just beyond our reach. Characters in her poetry would often be depicted as futilely trapped in a dreary material existence, not knowing that if they were but to look inward, they would find their own source of enlightenment. This would often leave her writing poems detailing her relation to the material world, attempting to reshape it according to her inner philosophy.

Margolin also rejected the use of form that was characteristic of many Yiddish poets of the time and, in her own words, was "insulted by the mechanical precision of the conventional rhyme." Along with others in the Introspectivist movement, Margolin rejected what were seen as primarily cultural strictures based on Jewish law, such as practices regarding the use and creation of "graven images." Margolin and other poets often embraced ideas and practices that, in Europe, had been considered taboo or idolatrous, such as pagan imagery. Although she believed in God, she sought to find him through an inner journey rather than necessarily through traditional Jewish practices and customs. In this regard, she was not unlike many other Jews of her generation who were going through an identity crisis, forming communities and family in the New World. It was this search for meaning that drove the Introspectivist movement.

"She with the Cold Marble Breasts," the poem written on Margolin's gravestone, is an interesting example of her writing style. The poem itself details the life of a dead woman who wasted her life "on nothing, on garbage" grounding the figure in the material world. However, other lines in the poem hint that while this woman's life was mired in the material world, there was something otherworldly that allowed her to slip past these worldly chains. A final injunction, "passerby, have pity and be silent—say nothing," encapsulates Margolin's idea that the material world is not worthy of attention, that it is not worth noticing, subtly supporting the Introspectivist notion that real truth can be found only in the imagination.

"Years" is another poem in which Margolin describes the lives of women who, "Half-heartedly play 'Hamlet' in the marketplace." These women again are trapped in the mundane world, laughing in public yet with anger in their eyes. Once more we see the gap between flesh and spirit that Margolin sees as only being bridged by sincere introspection. Margolin criticizes this lifestyle, connecting it to her fellow Jews with the last line, "and seek Thee without ever believing in Thee," speaking, of course, to God. She asserts that simply following rote cultural practices would not bring an individual any closer to God.

A third poem, "Mother Earth," is another embodiment of the Introspectivist ideal, and fits in quite nicely with the rest of Margolin's work. The poem speaks with the voice of Earth itself, a female entity referring to itself as a "dark slave and mistress" to humanity. Earth decries what she calls a "long blind silence" that she is forced to suffer as humans go about their business and neglect to search for a higher purpose or meaning, which is what Earth herself is seeking, yet can achieve only through the actions of individuals, saying, "I seek the sky through you." It is a repetition of the assertion that finding God requires more than going through the motions.

Bibliography

Imber, Samuel J., ed. *Modern Yiddish Poetry: An Anthology.* New York: East and West, 1927.

Liptzin, Sol. *A History of Yiddish Literature.* Middle Village, N.Y.: Jonathan David, 1985.

Mann, Barbara. "Picturing the Poetry of Anna Margolin." *Modern Language Quarterly* (December 2002): 501–536.

Nordell, J. D. "Poetry Microreviews: Drunk from the Bitter Truth: The Poems of Anna Margolin." *Boston Review* September/October 2006.

—M. Ryan Croker

Marjorie Morningstar　**Herman Wouk**　(1955)
One of Herman Wouk's most enduring novels, *Marjorie Morningstar* is the coming-of-age saga of a Jewish-American girl seeking to escape the conventions of her tradition. Set in the 1930s, the tale begins with the introduction of 17-year-old Marjorie Morgenstern, who dreams of one day becoming a famous actress on Broadway. After she rejects a marriage proposal from one of her many suitors, Marjorie's ambitions of stardom are bolstered when, at age 19, she lands a job with a summer-stock company in Camp South Wind. The

company's musical director, Noel Airman, whom Marjorie met the year before, seems unlike any man she has ever known, and the two soon embark on a love affair that proves both thrilling and destructive for Marjorie.

Set largely against the backdrop of New York City, *Marjorie Morningstar* was the first novel dealing with Jewish culture to achieve mass popularity (Beichman 53). To be sure, much of the story's lasting popularity, especially among young women, is its theme of innocence lost. As Laurence W. Mazzeno points out, Marjorie "seems to represent a certain type of American woman, caught between her dreams for self-actualization and her culture's demand that she assume a position befitting her place in that group. Viewed in this light, Marjorie's pursuit of a career as an actress is particularly ironic, for this is a novel about learning one's proper role in life" (60).

Despite its broad appeal, however, *Marjorie Morningstar* features several distinctively Jewish motifs. Embodying these themes are Marjorie's immigrant parents and her beloved uncle, Samson-Aaron, and throughout the book traditions such as the bar mitzvah, the Seder, and dietary laws are established as prominent factors in the Morgenstern family's life. Moreover, Arnold Beichman points out, Wouk's novel proved rare for its era "in that it was dealing directly and specifically with the Jews of New York and how they moved about from one urban neighborhood to another—from the Bronx to Central Park West and then to Park Avenue—as part of Jewish upward mobility" (52–53). Set in sharp contrast to the Morgensterns is Noel, whose real name is Saul Ehrmann, the son of a prominent Jewish judge. Noel's denial of his heritage—indeed, his adoption of a distinctly Christian name—coupled with his shallowness and lazy approach to life establishes his place as the story's villain, despite the superficial charm he clearly possesses (Mazzeno 60–61).

The novel's young heroine is torn between the extremes of tradition and modernism. Deeply in love with Noel, who comes in and out of her life for years, Marjorie's struggle is ultimately one between traditional Jewish views of marriage and

family and Noel's bohemian lifestyle and self-indulgent nature. Further, unable to see Noel for what he truly is, Marjorie dismisses the affection of upstart playwright Wally Wronken, whose work ethic is everything Noel's is not and whose feelings for her are unwavering. Unable to find the success she longs for as actress "Marjorie Morningstar," Marjorie's final attempt to reconcile with Noel is ultimately changed by her chance encounter with Mike Eden, whose efforts to rescue Jews from Nazi Germany shake Marjorie to her core.

Although Wouk's story became the best-selling novel of 1955 (Mazzeno 55), critical response to the work has been mixed. While many critics praised Wouk's depiction of Jewish life, others objected to his didacticism, or charged that his portrayal of Jews is stereotypical (Mazzeno 62–64). Despite such criticism, however, several prominent commentators, including Meyer Levin and Charles Angoff, have noted that *Marjorie Morningstar*'s popular appeal sparked an intense interest in Jewish material: "Instead of being shunted as outsiders," Mazzeno writes, "Jewish writers and Jewish people now had a place in American literature" (65).

Bibliography
Beichman, Arnold. *Herman Wouk: The Novelist as Social Historian.* New Brunswick, N.J.: Transaction Books, 1984.
Mazzeno, Laurence W. *Herman Wouk.* Edited by Frank Day. New York: Twayne, 1994.

—Jay Waitkus

Maus (The Complete Maus, Maus I: My Father Bleeds History and *Maus II: And Here My Troubles Began)*
Art Spiegelman (1986 and 1991)

The two books of the *Maus* series, *Maus I* and *Maus II*, now available together as *The Complete Maus,* are stunning volumes that graphically portray both the Holocaust and its continuing effects. ART SPIEGELMAN, the books' artist and narrator, tells two stories: the experiences of his parents, Vladek and Anja, before, during, and after the Holocaust, and his own troubled existence as an inheritor of their trauma. Representing Jews as mice and Germans as cats, *Maus* is an innovative and bold book that defies conventional discussion about genre while re-raising questions about intergenerational transmission of trauma, the relationship between unique and universal dimensions of the Shoah, and the issue of faith and the death camps. Among the books' numerous recognitions is a 1992 Pulitzer Prize Special Award. *Maus* also appears in a CD version that includes recordings of conversations between Spiegelman and Valdek. Spiegelman is currently preparing *MetaMaus,* a book with a DVD about the making of *Maus.*

Following the book's initial appearance, scholars debated both the appropriateness of a comic format to treat a world historical tragedy and the use of animal figures. Detractors, such as Hillel Halkin, while admitting that Spiegelman intended a serious work, claim that drawing people as animals dehumanizes them. Others, however, such as Geoffrey Hartman, applaud the use of animal imagery. He observes that the books' "metamorphosis of the human figure recognizes that the Shoah has affected how we think about ourselves as a *species* (the human? Race)." *Maus* is now widely regarded as a major contribution to Holocaust studies. It has been translated into many languages, and the use of animal imagery—Americans are dogs, Poles are pigs, Gypsies (Roma) are gypsy moths, French are frogs, Swedes are deer, British are fish, the child of a Jew and a German is drawn as a mouse having cat stripes—has universal resonance; everyone knows what cats do to mice.

Maus contains several levels of narrative. Erin McGlothlin describes these narrative levels as "inner" (Vladek's Holocaust experience), "middle" (scene of Vladek's testimony), and "outer" (memory and representation). The inner level describes Vladek's pre-Holocaust and Holocaust experiences. This level reveals him as a resourceful individual whose knowledge of English, although rudimentary, enables him to meet Anja before the war and helps save both of their lives during the Holocaust. Spiegelman portrays the middle level in carefully drawn scenes that include visual representations of Vladek's tales such as the

hanging of four Jewish people in Sosnowiec, Poland, for violations of Nazi food rationing quotas. Other scenes include a selection (choosing which prisoners are to be gassed the following day) in Auschwitz, Vladek smuggling food to Anja in the women's barracks, and a death march.

The level of memory and representation emphasizes the continuing trauma of Holocaust survivors and their transmission of the trauma to the second generation. In Volume II, Spiegelman draws himself, replete with a mouse mask, seated at his drawing board. Outside his window he has drawn a Nazi guard in Auschwitz pointing his rifle directly at Artie (Spiegelman's childhood self). While the second generation has not experienced the Holocaust, it is the most important event in their lives. Spiegelman feels overwhelmed by the enormity of the Shoah, by his own troubled relationship with Vladek, and by the increasing societal trivialization of Auschwitz. The setting of the book includes eastern Europe, Rego Park, and Florida, emphasizing the omnipresence of the Holocaust and its legacy for the Spiegelman family.

Spiegelman, experiencing writer's block and unable to work on *Maus,* visits Pavel, a survivor psychiatrist from whom he learns several important lessons. Pavel, who also wears a mouse mask and smokes a pipe, contends that Spiegelman is the *real* survivor because of the ridicule he endured from Vladek as a child. Pavel attributes this to Vladek's feelings of survivor guilt. Moreover, the Holocaust teaches no lessons except that nations can get away with it. In addition, Pavel helps Spiegelman realize that the Holocaust is an unmastered and unmasterable trauma. Responding to Spiegelman's question about what Auschwitz felt like, Pavel leans forward and screams BOO! Spiegelman draws himself as a little child. He jumps up and screams YIII! Pavel tells him that Auschwitz felt like that all the time.

Maus recounts the Spiegelman family dynamic in a brutally frank and honest manner. The Holocaust past is a continual presence in their lives, the devastating lens through which the contemporary world is viewed. Spiegelman draws himself as a 10-year-old child who falls while skating with friends who abandon him after he trips. Sobbing, he tells Vladek what happened. His father stops working and exclaims, "**Friends?** Your friends? . . . if you lock them together in a room with no food for a week. . . **THEN** you could see what it is, **FRIENDS!**" Vladek and Anja had a son, Richieu, prior to the Holocaust. He was poisoned by his aunt, who also took her own life and that of her children, to avoid a worse death in Auschwitz. Neither parent ever recovered emotionally from this trauma, and their marriage was deeply troubled. Spiegelman draws the enlarged photo of Richieu that his parents kept in their bedroom. Later he tells Françoise that his childhood was marked by sibling rivalry with a ghost. Anja, who is emotionally ill, takes her own life while Spiegelman is in college.

Anja's suicide is the context for the four-page "Prisoner on Hell Planet: A Case History" segment, which encapsulates the psychological issues in this survivor family. The segment opens with an actual photograph of Anja, and the characters are drawn as human figures. Significantly, Spiegelman draws himself in a striped prisoner uniform. The depth of his own guilt feelings are shown several ways. He is scolded by a survivor for failing to express affection to his mother. The survivor's accusing words are drawn in the same balloon as his words of comfort. Remembering Anja, he writes four epitaphs: "Menopausal Depression," "Hitler Did It," "Mommy," and "Bitch," each accompanied by a relevant image. He then draws himself in a prison cell remembering the last time Anja entered his room asking if he loved her. Spiegelman interpreted the query as her way of tightening the umbilical chord. He mumbles "sure Ma." Spiegelman congratulates his mother for committing the perfect crime; she murdered herself and left her son "to take the rap." The Hell planet refers to both Auschwitz and his own emotional chaos.

Spiegelman's work also raises the issue of religion and the rare instance of Christians who helped Jews. His own estrangement from Judaism is made clear when Vladek recites Kaddish (prayer for the dead, written in Hebrew but from the Aramaic) while Spiegelman reads from the *Tibetan Book of the Dead*. The artist draws the Hebrew letters of the Aramaic prayer. Alan Rosen intelligently argues

that Spiegelman becomes "something of a scribe, transferring into the arena of comics the hand-lettering of a sacred Jewish document." Spiegelman's deceased great grandfather, a deeply religious man, serves as a seer who predicts Vladek's release from a German prisoner of war camp and links the event to the reading of a particular Torah portion. This portion (*parsha Truma*) is also recited when Vladek and Anja marry. Spiegelman was born, and subsequently became a bar mitzvah, at the time of this reading. Although Vladek tells Spiegelman that in Auschwitz "God didn't come," he also relates the tale of a priest who comforted him and a French, non-Jewish prisoner who shared food rations.

In addition to the special Pulitzer prize, *Maus* received the 1988 Angoulême International Comics Festival Awards–Religious Award: Christian Testimony and Prize for Best Comic Book: Foreign Comic Award (1988 and 1993). Volume I was nominated for a National Book Critics Circle Award in 1986, and Volume II was similarly nominated in 1992. The book's continuing impact resides in its having enlarged and enriched Holocaust scholarship in a unique manner that is cross-cultural and international in scope.

Bibliography

McGlothlin, Erin. *Second Generation Holocaust Literature: Legacies of Survival and Perpetration*. Rochester, N.Y.: Camden House, 2006.

Halkin, Hillel. "Inhuman Comedy." *Commentary* (February 1992).

Hartman, Geoffrey H. Introduction to *Holocaust Remembrance: The Shapes of Memory*. Oxford, U.K., and Cambridge, Mass.: Blackwell, 1994.

Rosen, Alan. *Sounds of Defiance: The Holocaust, Multilingualism, and the Problem of English*. Lincoln: University of Nebraska Press, 2005.

—**Alan L. Berger**

Mazel Rebecca Goldstein (1995)

Mazel is REBECCA GOLDSTEIN's fourth novel and the winner of the Edward Lewis Wallant Award and the National Jewish Book Award for Fiction. It takes flight from two related stories published in her 1993 collection, *Strange Attractors*. Both plots center on Phoebe Saunders, a 26-year-old assistant professor of mathematics at Princeton University. She is the daughter of a Barnard classics professor, Chloe Saunders, and the granddaughter of the shtetl-born Yiddish actress and devoted Manhattanite, Sasha Saunders. While *Mazel* features the now tenured 30-year-old Phoebe, who is due any day to give birth to her first child, the novel is actually the story of Sasha's past, which she relates to her granddaughter in her backyard in Lipton, New Jersey.

The first of *Mazel*'s two central themes is the relevance and legacy of history—the understanding and relation of events that make people and families who they are. The second theme concerns the search for home and place, the quest for belonging that, in this case, serves in part as a response to the Jewish inheritance of exile. The two themes often work against each other and produce the tension that fuels the novel, resolving the often turbulent relationship between tradition and free-spiritedness, between the past and the present, and between the varying conditions of reality.

Mazel opens with two stories. The first is a Yiddish folktale, a portion of which is related to the reader at the beginning of each of the novel's five parts, in which two characters, *Mazel* (luck) and *Saychel* (brains), vie with each other for the title of "most important." The second story opens with Sasha's humorous incredulity over Phoebe's return to the more traditional practice of Judaism, embracing the often shtetl-like values that never piqued the interest of her mother, a consummate intellectual, or Sasha, who felt stifled by them and unhesitatingly abandoned them.

The novel is directed by the meaning of place, as indicated by the geographical locations assigned to each of its parts. It opens in Lipton, then shifts to Shluftchev, Galicia, where Sorel (the name Sasha was known by in the old country) was born and raised with her five siblings. Of them all, Sorel was closest to her sister Fraydel, whose intelligence, imagination, and longing for a life to which she had no access ultimately result in her suicide. The family moves to Warsaw after Fraydel's death. Here Sorel comes into her own as a Yiddish actress. With

the memory of Fraydel bringing her luck and an intuitive sense of what to do, she auditions and is welcomed into the Bilbul Art Theater troupe. The actors become stars in Warsaw and take their play abroad, ending in Vilna just before the Germans invaded Poland in 1939. The novel skips over time and place and returns to Lipton, New Jersey to Phoebe's marriage weekend. There, after spending Shabbat in suburban New Jersey, Sasha dramatically announces that "Lipton . . . is Shluftchev . . . with a designer label."

Mazel reviews the lives and fortunes of five generations of one family: Sorel's grandparents, her parents, herself, and her daughter and granddaughter. Finally, the search for home is a search for self-knowledge, but broader than this, it is a search for knowledge of history, roots, and inheritance. To this end, Sorel/Sasha realizes that modernity and tradition both need to be recognized and celebrated. At Phoebe's wedding the three living generations of Saunders women dance together, "their feet barely touching the billowing floor, as they [swirl] in the circles drawn within circles within circles."

Who is valued more in the Saunders family, *Mazel* or *Saychel*? The title of Goldstein's novel reveals the answer, but ultimately Sasha, Chloe, and Phoebe never really have to choose. They are fortunate to be endowed with and protected by *saychel* and *mazel*, and also *sheynkeyt* (beauty), the characteristic of the princess whose hand and heart *Mazel* wins.

Bibliography

Dickstein, Lore. "World of our Mothers," *New York Times*, 29 October 1995.

Meyers, Helene. "The Death and Life of a Judith Shakespeare: Rebecca Goldstein's *Mazel*." *Shofar* 25, no. 3 (2007): 61–71.

—Jessica Lang

Memoirs of an Ex-Prom Queen
Alix Kates Shulman (1972)

When *Memoirs of an Ex-Prom Queen* (1972) was rereleased on its 25th anniversary in 1997, Alix

KATES SHULMAN expressed ambivalent feelings concerning her first novel's continued popularity among a new generation of women. Emerging originally out of Shulman's newfound passion for feminism, the novel was inspired by the author's own involvement in the grassroots protest against the 1968 Miss America Pageant; while marching she fully internalized the seriousness of societal pressures on women to be beautiful. Called "the first important novel to emerge from the women's liberation movement," *Memoirs of an Ex-Prom Queen* may disturbingly hit the mark in its challenges to the oppression of women as much today as it did when it first appeared.

In writing an admittedly semiautobiographical novel, Shulman transposes much of her own life experience onto her protagonist, Sasha Davis. Much like Shulman's own parents, Sasha's lawyer father and homemaker mother are secular Jews, but attention to her heritage amounts to little more than passing references in the text. Jewish identity questions are conscientiously overshadowed by Shulman's more pressing concerns with the women's issues and rights that, in fact, spurred the writing of the novel. Like Shulman, Sasha at a young age abandons her hometown in suburban Ohio for New York City. They both go to graduate school and sacrifice their own careers in marrying young. By drawing on her own experiences and showing Sasha getting divorced, and soon remarrying and having children, Shulman explores a broad spectrum of women's life experiences through which to view the pervasive nature of sexism in society.

The novel begins with Sasha, an all-American beauty and ex-prom queen, traveling across Europe to her graduate-student husband in order to end their marriage. Setting up a pattern that repeats itself throughout the novel, Sasha makes a courageous if brief attempt at self-definition, only to find herself beaten by the social forces and expectations to which she relentlessly tries to conform. On finding herself alone back in New York after a short attempt at independence, she immediately returns to her husband, feeling the weight of her economic and social situation. Before Sasha's return, however, the first-person narrative flashes back to her childhood and youth to chart the alarming yet familiar formation of her white, middle-class femininity in postwar American suburbia. Even as a child, Sasha becomes aware of her body and begins to loathe it, already beginning to worry about whether or not she is beautiful. Despite her parents' cultivation of Sasha's intelligence and passion for reading, Sasha decides in the third grade that only physical beauty is important. The culminating moment of her life occurs when she is crowned prom queen after parading her body before the judges in her high school gym. In an innovative twist on the stereotype of "ugly" feminists, Shulman constructs Sasha as a beautiful combatant against the patriarchal social structure that empowers women solely on the basis of beauty and sexuality. From being harassed by elementary-age boys to becoming the coveted sexual object of the most popular boys in high school, Sasha's world is dominated by an overriding, authoritative male presence.

At least as early as her high school years, Sasha shows her awareness of a male-female power struggle. She devises a game in which she forces herself to stare at men and meet their gaze until either she or the man looks away. Every date for her becomes an expected struggle against a sexual predator. Because the novel is a product of Shulman's own involvement in women's groups that were especially focused on consciousness raising (CR)—the sharing of the women's (particularly sexual) experiences as a means of discussing the personal as political—the author chronicles Sasha's sexual identity formation as a sometimes comical, sometimes tragic political statement. As so many women of the past and present, Sasha faces date rape, rape within marriage (which Sasha fails to recognize as such), sexual harassment at work, and limited career opportunities.

While in college, Sasha goes through a period of rigorous intellectual pursuit that tellingly forces her to ignore her body and completely retreats from society and even her own family life. She discovers a passion for philosophy—a traditionally masculine discipline—and a longing to gather all knowledge together, an experience reminiscent of Shulman's own accounts of her intense college education. Here Shulman introduces Roxanne, a fellow student who becomes Sasha's most enduring and only female friend, through whom Shulman introduces what she views as the only real solution—the bonding of women through shared experiences. As Sasha's second marriage is failing due to her husband's waning interest in her (mostly because of the separation ironically resulting from her passionately throwing herself into the socially designated role of motherhood), the novel ends with Sasha picking up the phone to call Roxanne, who is now a happily divorced and working single mother.

Memoirs of an Ex-Prom Queen puts in concrete detail the issues set forth by earlier, second-wave feminists such as Betty Friedan in *The Feminine Mystique*: the restrictions of traditional marriage and childbearing, birth control and abortion, the educational and vocational sacrifices expected of women, and the sexual objectification of the female body. Even before its original printing, the forthcoming novel had gained underground popularity among women working in the publishing house, so poignantly did it speak to women's very real but until then unarticulated experiences. *Memoirs of an Ex-Prom Queen* continues to be widely studied on college campuses as an essential feminist text.

Bibliography

Altman, Meryl. "Beyond Trashiness: The Sexual Language of 1970s Feminist Fiction." *Journal of International Women's Studies* 4, no. 2 (April 2003): 7–19.

Templin, Charlotte. "Beauty and Gender in Alix Kates Shulman's Memoirs of an Ex-Prom Queen." In *Women in Literature: Reading Through the Lens of Gender*. Westport, Conn.: Greenwood, 2003.

—Sally Giles

Michaels, Anne (1958–)

Within a year of the publication of her first novel, *FUGITIVE PIECES* (1996), Anne Michaels won several of literature's most prestigious awards—including the Guardian Fiction Award (1997) and the Orange Prize for Fiction (1997) in the United Kingdom, the Lannan Literary Award for Fiction in the United States (1997), the City of Toronto Book Award (1997), Chapters/Books in Canada First Novel Award (1997), Heritage Toronto Award of Merit (1997), the Trillium Book Award (1997), and the Martin & Beatrice Fischer Award for Jewish literature (1997) in Canada. Michaels was awarded an estimated $200,000 in prize monies within that year—an amazing sum for a part-time writing instructor at the University of Toronto. She went on to earn other awards and to contract foreign rights with 30 countries for *Fugitive Pieces*. Michaels's books of poetry, *The Weight of Oranges* (1985) and *Miner's Pond* (1991), have also won similar awards and praise. Michaels is also a gifted musician—she plays piano and violin, has composed music for the theater, and is learned in classical music.

Michaels avoids revealing much about her family. She believes that such revelations belong to family members and are, therefore, private. Michaels was born and raised in Toronto, Canada. Her grandfather and her father, Elie David Michaels, emigrated from Poland to Canada in 1931 to avoid the persecution of Jews and for relief from economic deprivation. Family members who remained in Poland were killed by the German invaders during World War II.

The known details of Michaels's own life are few. What she does tell are the simple facts of growing up in Toronto. Although her family was not wealthy, she was raised in a house full of music, books, and discussions of science. Michaels remembers her father playing classical music on the phonograph before and after going to work in his small record shop. More personal events from her family life are recorded in her poetry—especially with regard to her parents and three brothers.

Two poems, "Memoriam" and "Miner's Pond," exemplify Michaels's attention to her family through memories most readers can recognize. In "Memoriam," Michaels remembers a night when she was nine and her mother comforted her: "crying from a dream / you said words that hid my fear. / Above us the family slept on, / mouths open, hands scrolled. / Twenty years later your tears burn the back of my throat." Michaels writes that memories of her parents leave her "starving with mouths full of love" (20). In "Miner's Pond," Michaels recalls a time in 1962 when she and her brothers "pushed" their "father over the edge": "His patience / a unit of time we never learned to measure. / The threat to 'drive into a post' / was a landmark we recognized and raced towards / with delirious intent, challenging the sound barrier of the car roof." Michaels writes that she and her brothers were in the back seat "wild with stories we were living." And with humorous insight into events many families have shared, Michaels notes: "The front seat was another time zone/in which my parents were imprisoned, and from which/ we offered to rescue them, again and again" (*The Weight of Oranges/Miner's Pond* 53).

Michaels insists that her Jewish heritage should not be considered while reading her texts, because her limiting work to her Jewishness is a disservice to her art. "I am not the child of survivors; that's not my autobiography. So why write about those events rather than other events?" Michaels admits that the consequences of the war years "completely altered" the lives of "everyone my family knew." The part of Toronto where Michaels grew up was a haven for European immigrants. And yet Michaels insists that the events surrounding World War II and the Holocaust "are the inheritance of everyone. They're not particular to being Jewish. And the longer we insist that these things be autobiographically imperative, the longer it's going to be before we actually get past that and learn from those events, and begin to understand them as catastrophes of civilisation" (Brown 54).

Mick Brown claims that "To particularise *Fugitive Pieces* as 'a Holocaust novel' would be to limit it." Brown suggests that the novel is about "history, memory and loss, man's capacity for both good and evil—and above all, the pain of having survived when others have died." Brown believes that the novel conveys "the full horror of the Holocaust not by describing its atrocities, but by examining its emotional legacy on those who survived—and those who did not, necessarily, experience it at all"

(Brown 54). Although the central narrators are Jakob Beer (who, as a boy in Poland, watches Nazi Germans murder his parents) and Ben (the son of Holocaust survivors), it is through the tutelage of Athos Roussos—the Greek geologist who smuggles Jacob out of Poland to his home in Zakynthos, Greece—that Jacob learns how to heal. The healing process, however, requires time.

Michaels distinguishes between history and memory: "Knowledge/History is essentially amoral: events occurred. 'Poetic Knowing'/Memory is inextricably linked with morality: history's source is event but memory's source is meaning. Often what we consciously remember is what our conscience remembers" (Michaels, "Cleopatra's Love," 181). For Michaels, memory is also inescapably connected to landscape. She suggests that her poetry and fiction are "like a landscape" or "an archeological/geological slice." Furthermore, Michaels attempts, in her poetry and prose, to "reflect layers of time as well as meaning. Every landscape is a narrative: the static surface is an illusion, and actually reveals all the earth forces that forged and continue to forge the present geological moment." Michaels believes that "the present moment and the past . . . are of equal importance." She therefore explores events "through geology, natural history as well as biography, history" (Michaels, "Unseen Formations," 174). It took Michaels 10 years to write *Fugitive Pieces*. Her research took her to Athens to study in the Jewish Museum of Greece as well as through research on "the war"—both through "original testimony as well as the work of historians." Michaels also studied political theory, geography, geology, cartography, the journals of arctic explorers, Yiddish song books, and translations of *The Psalms* (*Fugitive Pieces* "Acknowledgments" 295). Such study led her to the idea of the "gradual instant"—an idea that is a major theme in *Fugitive Pieces*.

Michaels works are complicated by this archaeology of personal experience, time, history, and landscape. Her metaphors interact within these contexts. For example, she says the problem with evil "is that immorality, or the evil act, seems very particular to a single moment; things seem to occur almost overnight. When, in fact, almost always there's been a gradual movement towards that act." The same metaphor applies to healing. "Grief," writes Michaels, "requires time. If a chip of stone radiates its self, its breath, so long, how stubborn might be the soul. If soundwaves carry on to infinity, where are their screams now? I imagine them somewhere in the galaxy, moving forever towards the psalms" (*Fugitive Pieces*, 55).

Bibliography

Brown, Mick. "A Labour of Love." *Telegraph Magazine.*

Michaels, Anne. "Cleopatra's Love." In *Poetry and Knowing,* edited by Tim Lilburn. Kingston, Canada: Quarry Press, 1995.

———. *Fugitive Pieces.* New York: Vintage International, 1998.

———. "Unseen Formations." In *Sudden Miracles: Eight Women Poets,* edited by Rhea Tregebov. Toronto: Second Story Press, 1991.

———. *The Weight of Oranges/Miner's Pond.* Toronto: McClelland & Stewart, 1997.

—**Suzanne Evertson Lundquist**

The Middle of the Journey
Lionel Trilling (1947)

Although primarily known for his literary criticism, LIONEL TRILLING aspired as a young man to be a novelist and, in his words, became a critic by accident. He published a handful of short stories between 1925 and 1945 before completing his only novel, *The Middle of the Journey,* his last work of fiction. His achievement as a critic, notably established by *The Liberal Imagination* (1950), led him to turn from fiction to the literary-cultural essays for which he is so well known. The passion for ideas and the keen intelligence displayed in his criticism characterize his novel as well. Set in the 1930s, the novel was intended by its author "to draw out some of the moral and intellectual implications of the powerful attraction to communism felt by a considerable part of the American intellectual class during the Thirties and Forties." Trilling himself had felt that attraction and was keenly interested in the period and the lessons it offered concerning strenuously politicized will. He had been drawn tenuously toward communism during 1932–33, but his interest turned to mistrust and hostility. *The Middle of the Journey* is an exploration of the central ideological forces of that seminal era in the development of American intellectuals and serves as a demystification of the Stalinist mentality. The novel vibrates with problems of morality that arise when political commitments become a mask for satisfying the needs of the personal will or when good people give the worst of themselves to ideological politics.

The novel brings together six principal characters who exemplify different social-political tendencies within the liberal community of informed urban people. The main character, John Laskell, an architect specializing in public housing, is a middle-class man of generous sensibilities hoping for a more just and decent world. Although he is "not really a political person," he is sympathetically disposed to communism. Such liberal fellow-traveling was common among urban intellectuals of the period. His fiancée has recently died and he is recovering from a near-fatal bout with scarlet fever. These brushes with death have deeply affected him. He goes from New York City to Connecticut to recover with his friends Arthur and Nancy Croom. Arthur is a professor of economics who anticipates a call to Washington to serve in the New Deal administration of President Franklin Roosevelt. The Crooms, optimistic and utopian, live on the fringe of radical politics and idealize their unreliable handyman, Duck Caldwell, as a member of the sacred proletariat. They misunderstand Duck's wife, Emily, because she does not fit their expectations of the type. Gifford Maxim, whose character Trilling acknowledged was based on Whittaker Chambers, is a mutual friend of Laskell and the Crooms. A former underground agent for the communists, he has made a complete turnabout and become a fervent Christian and now fears assassination. He asks Laskell to get him a job with the *New Era,* a liberal monthly providing a forum for leftist ideas and programs. This will provide him the safety of a visible public identity. Laskell grants the favor. The magazine is published by Kermit Simpson as a way of allaying his liberal compunctions at being wealthy. Laskell delays telling the Crooms of his reflections on death and of Maxim's defection from the Marxist cause, because he knows there is no room for death or political incorrectness in their idealistic, progressive, and fundamentally naive political world. The death of the Caldwells' child and the question of responsibility for that death bring the ideas and relationships of the story to a head. Placing himself in opposition to both the Crooms and Maxim, Laskell goes beyond ideology and arrives at a recognition that human beings are both responsible and conditioned: "An absolute freedom from responsibility—that much of a child none of us can be. An absolute responsibility—that much a divine or metaphysical essence none of us is."

The action of the novel is relatively limited. The dialectic of ideas constitutes its real substance and focus. Is it too much a novel of ideas? This has been the central question in its reception. Some readers find its validity to be an intellectual rather than emotional one. It is finely written, displaying the influence of Henry James and E. M. Forster, but is for some tastes too schematic and argumentative to be a good novel. Even Irving Howe, who admired the book, said that it reads at times "closer to a highly intelligent rumination about a fiction than a fiction itself." There is no definitive way to defend *The Middle of the Journey* against such charges. So much depends on what a reader expects of a novel. Some readers are more engaged by themes and ideas than others and find the interaction of ideas dramatic, aesthetically satisfying, and not without emotional appeal.

Two motifs function significantly in the novel. The first is death. It is Laskell's encounters with and reflections upon death that give perspective to his understanding of political motives and methods. Forster said that "death destroys a man, but the idea of death saves him." Laskell is saved by a new understanding of death. The second is childhood. The motif of childhood functions simultaneously to signify, on the one hand, beginnings and the possibility of growth and learning and, on the other, arrested development, refusal of personal responsibility, and dangerous naïveté. These motifs are enlisted in exploring what one critic delineates as three closely related perennial problems: "the problem of human imperfection and its moral and political implications; the problem of free will and personal responsibility as opposed to determinism and social and metaphysical rather than private guilt; and the problem of how to deal with ugliness, evil, and mortality."

Bibliography

Kimmage, Michael. "Lionel Trilling's *The Middle of the Journey* and the Complicated Origins of the Neo-Conservative Movement." *Shofar* 21, no. 3 (Spring 2003): 48–63.
"Whittaker Chambers and *The Middle of the Journey*." *New York Review of Books*, 17 April 1975, 18–24.

—Stephen Tanner

Miller, Arthur (1915–2005)

Arthur Miller, born in 1915 to a middle-class Jewish family in New York City, grew up in a nominally orthodox household but more likely liberal conservative in fact. His father manufactured ladies coats while his mother, a former school teacher, devoted herself to Arthur, Kermit (his older brother), and Joan (his younger sister). Like a growing number of middle-class American Jewish boys, he was quite at variance with the tradition of his eastern European heritage, an indifferent student, and a promising athlete. In 1928, the year of his bar mitzvah, when his father's business suddenly declined, the family moved to a Brooklyn neighborhood in which many of his relatives already lived. Although the Jews shared the neighborhood with Italians and Irish, there was relative harmony. Unlike Henry Roth, who suffered a lifelong trauma when his family moved from a Jewish neighborhood to a predominantly Christian one, Miller grew up with a comfortable multiethnic ethos.

Miller admitted to worry-free high school years. But reality began to close in as the depression hit. He noticed the effect of mortgage payments on his block. He observed the closed stores and the classmates who dropped out of school to work. He heard quarrels in homes. He saw the lot that was used for football games turned into a junkyard. After graduation he applied for admission to both Cornell University and Michigan University. When he was refused, he went to work for his father.

Working in his father's factory was a revelation. If the economic effects of the Depression had begun to awaken his social conscience, the social conditions in the Seventh Avenue district shocked him. The arrogance, cruelty, hardness, and vulgarity of the buyers affected him in a way he never forgot. He saw his father and the company's salesmen treated badly. In a sketch written at that time, "In Memoriam," he described a salesman named Schoenzeit who commits suicide by jumping in front of a subway train. *Schoenzeit,* which breaks down to *es is shayn zeit* in Yiddish, means "it is already time," or, more literally and ironically, "a nice time." Because Miller spoke Yiddish as a young man, it seems certain that the salesman in the sketch for whom he felt sympathy in the 1930s was the basis for the salesman on whom he based Willie Loman, the protagonist of *Death of a Salesman,* some 17 years later.

At the University of Michigan, to which he was finally admitted conditionally on his second try, he first was exposed to the articulation of the despair and confidence and analysis of the depression and the New Deal. In contrast to the harmony that had prevailed in his early years, he took part in debates and passionately held arguments. At the end of his sophomore year, needing money badly, he wrote a play, *Honors at Dawn,* in four days for which he won the Avery Hopwood Award of $250. The next year his *No Villain* again won the Hopwood Prize. Both plays, reflecting the influence of the decade and of CLIFFORD ODETS, were social protest plays, stressing the necessity of integrity and responsibility in a time of crisis. In *Honors at Dawn,* sibling rivalry and familial strife were part of a 1930s, quasi-Marxist struggle between the evils of capitalism and the goodness of the people. *They Too Arise,* which followed, an expanded and revised version of *No Villain,* was about a middle-class Jewish family reminiscent of both Odets's *Awake and Sing!* and Miller's *Family.* In this way, Miller enunciated his Jewish heritage, his belief in the family and in the millennia-long values of the Jewish people.

In 1938 Miller graduated from Michigan. For a few months he worked for the WPA Federal Theatre's Writing Project. For the next few years he drove a truck and worked as a steamfitter in the Brooklyn Naval Yard. In 1940 he married Mary Slattery, whom he had met at the university.

Miller consistently affirmed his Jewishness as an individual, especially in the first and most important phase of his career, while he, also consistently, sought the comfort of the mainstream with an Irish-American intellectual, a world famous actress and beauty, and a talented photographer from Germany. Meanwhile, writing radio scripts was good practice, although the medium demanded more circumspection than he cared for. He felt that although he was refining his skills, he was writing about what lay outside him. In 1943 he began a new play, *The Man Who Had All the Luck.* Although it closed a week after it opened in November 1944, it served as a preparation for the future. In writing it, according to Miller, "the crux of *All My Sons* . . . was formed; and the roots of *Death of a Salesman* were sprouted."

The idea for *All My Sons,* his next play, came to Miller one evening when a relative told the Millers about a family in her neighborhood in the Midwest whose daughter had turned her father in because he had shipped faulty parts to the army. As Miller remembered the event, "The girl's action astounded me. An absolute response to a moral command." Suddenly the hints in *The Man Who Had All the Luck* came together. As in *They Too Arise,* family loyalty and success were the twin goals.

DEATH OF A SALESMAN is a play about a sane and rational human being, originally a Jewish salesman, who comes to grips finally with the existential question Who am I? in facing the truths of his life. Because Miller was sensitized in relation to the rest of humankind, he had the compulsion to wrestle with the forces surrounding him. Arguing with Eugene O'Neill's interest in the relation of man to God, Miller wrote that his religion had no gods but godlike powers. He spoke of the economic forces that began to weigh heavily on Americans in the early 20th century.

Death of a Salesman, Miller's most celebrated play, derived from "In Memoriam," written in 1932, and an unfinished play written in 1936. Explaining that playwrights often do not know what is beneath the surface of what they have already done, that explanations are often rationalizations after the fact, Miller said:

> The best proof of it is that I started writing *Death of a Salesman* one day in Connecticut. I wrote the whole play. Then, in one of my annual fits of neatness, I decided to clean out closets, suitcases, and so on, and make what I call order. . . . And in the course of that I discovered old notebooks, and in one old notebook which dated back to 1936 when I as at college, there was a play about a salesman of which I'd written an act and a half. I'm saying the obvious, which is that we're bound by a certain unconscious continuity.

With Willy Loman as an outsider in the culture, trying to hold his family together, the play was the epitome of the questions Miller asked: "How may a man make of the outside world a home?" Or, more explicitly: "How may a man make for himself a home in that vastness of strangers and how may he transform that vastness into a home?"

In his early works he was able to dramatize those value conflicts that were close to him. His career, up to and including *Salesman,* pitted his Jewish heritage against his American present. Believing in the values he assimilated from his earliest years through his University of Michigan years, when he was a Jewish boy from New York in Ann Arbor, he focused on the moral dilemma of his time. As a playwright, he saw group identity smashed by external forces and by the demands of individualism and success. On the other hand, at the same time he perceived the ideal world as one in which the individual was one with his society; his conflicts with it were like family conflicts, the opposing sides of which nevertheless shared a mutuality of feeling and responsibility. In this sense, Miller proceeded from his roots. Not certain of who he was but certain of his values, he tried to set forth what happens when a man does not have a grip on the forces of life. The implication was that there must be such a grasp of those forces, or else we are doomed. These are the reasons behind Miller's portrait of Willy. It seems undeniable that in attempting to deal with his moral dilemma, Miller's roots were the barb or spur reflecting his Jewish heritage and sensitivity, and responsible for his continuity of thought and treatment from Brooklyn to Broadway, from adolescence to *Death of a Salesman.*

In the early 1950s the United States witnessed the rise of McCarthyism, as the House Un-American Activities Committee (HUAC) metamorphosed onto a witch hunt investigating Communist influence in the arts. In 1952, after Elia Kazan, who directed *Death of a Salesman,* named names, that is, gave the committee the names of some of his friends who were Communists, Miller traveled to Salem, Massachusetts, to research the town's witch hunts of 1692. *The Crucible,* an allegorical play in which Miller likened the activities of the HUAC to the witch trials in Salem, opened in 1953. Widely criticized in the inflamed atmosphere of the time, it has come to be one of the most frequently produced plays and, with *Death of a Salesman,* acclaimed as a masterpiece. In the meantime, Miller divorced Mary Slattery, married Marilyn Monroe, and continued to turn out socially conscious plays. There was the aborted screenplay, "The Hook," about corrupt labor unions and racketeering on the New Jersey docks, which probably influenced the creation of the film *On the Waterfront.* Next was *A View from the Bridge,* a play that celebrated a young man's freedom to escape the mundane and create his own future; it is also thought to be Miller's reaction to Kazan's betrayal.

After *A View from the Bridge,* and after having been convicted of contempt of Congress for refusing to name names, a conviction overturned a few years later, Miller began work on *The Misfits,* a screenplay he wrote for his wife. Miller said that the filming was one of the lowest points of his life.

The pair divorced just before the film opened in 1961. In a 1992 interview with a French newspaper, Miller called Monroe "highly self-destructive" and said that during their marriage, "All my energy and attention were devoted to trying to help her solve her problems. Unfortunately, I didn't have much success." After Monroe's suicide in 1962, Miller wrote *After the Fall* (1964), a strongly autobiographical work, featuring a Monroe-like character, that dealt with questions of guilt and innocence. In 1962 Miller married Inge Morath, a German photographer, to whom he remained married for 40 years until her death in 2002.

During the 1960s and 1970s, Miller appeared to slow down. *After the Fall* was succeeded by *Incident at Vichy,* the same year he was elected American president of International PEN. *The Price* was produced in 1968; one-acters *Fame* and *The Reason Why* came out in the 1970s, as did *The Creation of the World and Other Business,* and its musical version, *Up from Paradise.* In late 1987 *Timebends,* his autobiography, was published. During the 1990s Miller wrote *The Ride Down Mt. Morgan, The Last Yankee,* and *Broken Glass.* His final play, *Finishing the Picture,* opened in Chicago in 2004; it was based on the filming of *The Misfits.*

On the evening of February 10, 2005, at age 89, Miller died at his home in Roxbury. He is widely held to be one of the greatest dramatists of the 20th century.

Bibliography

Gottfried, Martin. *Arthur Miller: His Life and Work.* Cambridge, Mass.: DaCapo/Perseus, 2003.

Martine, James J., ed. *Critical Essays on Arthur Miller.* Boston: G.K. Hall, 1979.

Miller, Arthur. "A Boy Grew in Brooklyn." *Holiday* 17 (March 1955).

———. "In Memorium." Unpublished Sketch, at the Humanities Research Center, University of Texas, Austin, 1932.

———. "Introduction." *Collected Plays.* New York: Viking, 1957.

———. "Morality and the Modern Drama." Interview with Philip Gelb. *Educational Theatre Journal* 10 (October 1958): 198–199.

Mottram, Eric. "Arthur Miller: Development of a Political Dramatist in America." In *Arthur Miller: A Collection of Critical Essays.* Edited by Robert W. Corrigan. Englewood Cliffs, N.J.: Prentice Hall, 1969.

Nelson, Benjamin. *Arthur Miller: Portrait of a Playwright.* New York: David McKay, 1970.

Ross, George. "Death of a Salesman in the Original." *Commentary* 11 (February 1951): 184–186.

Schlueter, June, and James K. Flanagan. *Arthur Miller.* New York: Ungar, 1987.

—Daniel Walden

The Mind-Body Problem
Rebecca Goldstein   (1983)

The Mind-Body Problem, Rebecca Goldstein's first novel, is the story of Renee Feuer, a lapsed Orthodox Jew, and her marriage to Noam Himmel, mathematical genius and prodigy who, at the age of 12, invented the supernaturals, the "Himmel numbers," and immediately became a much sought-after star in the realm of academe. Although Noam is the center of the mathematical universe, at least in the competitive academic marketplace as depicted by the fawning and sycophantic posturing of the Princeton faculty and graduate students, *The Mind-Body Problem* is Feuer's story, the story of a young woman torn between the religious and the secular worlds, between the rational and the emotional life, between the mind and the body.

Related in first-person narration, Feuer exposes, as she promises to do in the opening line of the novel, "what it's like to be married to a genius." In doing so, however, she tells the story of her life, of her intellectual and emotional insecurities, her evolving sense of coming of age as a woman and a secular Jew who ultimately comes to recognize that "people and their suffering matter," not as an abstraction, but in their particularity (274). A mediocre student in philosophy at Princeton, "majoring in seduction and minoring in parties," it is Renee's seeming good fortune to meet and fall in love with Noam Himmel; their marriage gives her a kind of immediate caché among the

Princeton academics (25). Finally marrying at the precarious age of 22, and not only marrying a Jew, but a "famous genius . . . a real *yiches* [prestige]," Renee falsely believes that she has quelled her mother's anxieties about her future (57). All she seems to have accomplished, however, is to deprive her mother of her raison d'être, the satisfaction that Renee's mother so perversely takes in her continual worry that her daughter's defection from the right and proper conduct of a dutiful Jewish woman will bring the family nothing but *tsuris* (trouble).

Renee, despite her rational instincts, can't quite bring herself to defect entirely from Judaism. Although initially fascinated by Noam's religious indifference and, indeed, cynicism toward those "reasonably intelligent people who haven't outgrown it," Renee finds herself indelibly linked in deeply ambivalent ways to her Jewish legacy (37). Torn between the Orthodox religious life and the equally unsophisticated tendency toward oversimplification by those who reject religion in the name of rationality, Renee admits to "worrying that there may be a God, and worse, that he may be Jewish," in which case she's "in a lot of trouble" (36).

Marrying a secular Jewish mathematical genius, however, who, by his own admission, found early on that he "liked ideas much better than people," does not provide Renee Feuer with the kind of religious-secular compromise that she unconsciously desires. Noam's failure to maintain his mathematical acumen results in the projection of his self-loathing onto his wife (29). But estranged from Noam, Renee fares no better, still torn between the life she desires and the life she believes she should want. Ultimately, she comes to recognize the extent of her own compassion and the reality that "we all do matter. . . . We don't have to justify our existences" (274).

Bibliography
Taylor, Kate. "The Philosopher Novelist." *New York Sun,* 31 May 2006, 16.
Siegel, Laurie. "All That You Can't Leave Behind," *Jerusalem Post,* 11 August 2006, 30.

—Victoria Aarons

The Ministry of Special Cases
Nathan Englander (2007)

"Jews bury themselves the way they live," NATHAN ENGLANDER writes in the opening lines of his second book and first full-length novel, *The Ministry of Special Cases,* "crowded together, encroaching on one another's space." Published eight years after the astonishing success of his earlier volume, *The Ministry of Special Cases* announces its theme in its opening: The book is about burial—burial (at whim) by the government of political dissidents, burial by the Jewish community of its own unwanted past, and burial by individual members of that community of their relations to each other and to themselves. Sitting in the disused Benevolent Self shul, in the final chapter (out of 49), the novel's protagonist, Kaddish Poznan, "stared into the open ark at the sack of bones," a sack that substitutes for that containing his "disappeared" son.

Kaddish Poznan—the name reveals all: Kaddish, the Hebrew prayer for the dead, marking, in this case, an individual who has rejected the dead and who, in fact, spends his working life erasing the names of the dead from gravestones in a cemetery, and Poznan, the Polish town where, in October 1943 Heinrich Himmler revealed to his troops the Nazi exterminationist project aimed against the Jews—in his view, the unsung and never to be sung page of glory in the history of the world. The setting of *Ministry* is Argentina in 1976, during the "dirty war" in which Juan Perón's widow is removed from power by a military junta, and large numbers of children—many of them university students and leftists—are made to "disappear," a term we come to understand to mean "kidnapped," "tortured," and "ransomed" or "killed" (commonly by being dropped from a plane over water).

The book chronicles the fortunes of one family, that of Kaddish Poznan; his wife, Lillian; and their son, Pato. The opening chapters register the growing tensions between father and son, as Poznan pursues his strange job of erasing names from the gravestones of the "cemetery within a cemetery," the perpetual resting place of the Jewish community of Buenos Aires in the 1920s and of pimps and prostitutes now disavowed by their more respectable descendants, while his son pursues his own intellectual interests in radical politics (Herbert Marcuse is mentioned) with his university friends Rafa and Flavia (Pato's mother addresses her anxieties by buying a steel reinforced door for their home). When Pato is snatched one day by government agents, the Poznans pursue a variety of remedies that fill the book's middle chapters: fruitless visits to police stations and to the infamous Ministry of Special Cases, and interviews with neighbors (who see and hear nothing), with terrified friends, with an opportunistic family doctor, with a boastful and gloating military general, and with a young witness working in a bakery across the street whose testimony may have resulted in her own subsequent torture.

All efforts at remedy are abject failures, at best accomplishing nothing, and at worst compounding the difficulty at hand. And in the final third of the book, the situation turns even more bleak. An acquaintance of Poznan's doctor, "the navigator," a man who claims to have dropped the children from his airplane, relates his own story. The religious community fails the family in a particularly spectacular fashion. A Jewish community leader refuses to include the child's name on a list of the missing unless approved by the government. A local rabbi refuses to conduct a burial of the child without a body that the government refuses to supply or even acknowledge. A priest working in the Ministry of Special Cases extorts what little money the Poznan family may have left with the vague hint that their son's safety may be secured if vastly greater sums are made available (a possible ruse, because there is cause to believe the boy already dead).

The congenial tone of Englander's previous book, even when the facts being related are gruesome, has turned nasty here. It is as if a story by ISAAC BASHEVIS SINGER has suddenly turned into one by Franz Kafka (when experienced from the inside) and George Orwell (when experienced from without). The encounter of family members in the famed ministry with a bureaucrat on a snack break (who directs them to the office from which he is currently absent) or with a guard protecting stairwell access to the building who threatens physical violence reflects the former, while the suggestion of the police officer that the son never existed, or of the military general that the missing son is on a beach holiday somewhere, reflects the latter. And although the family is Jewish, the consequences have moved in this book from the specifically Jewish character of the postwar affluent suburban community of FOR THE RELIEF OF UNBEARABLE URGES to the more largely Western humanist setting in which human rights violations are foremost.

But the Jewish connections remain unavoidable. The Ministry of Special Cases reminds us of the special handling of the Nazi's treatment of the Jews, the *Sonderbehandlung,* the Nazi's euphemistically named program of genocide. And in an important sense, the drama of Englander's current book, with its progress from bad to worse, continues the earlier disaster. In the opening chapter of *For the Relief of Unbearable Urges,* "The Twenty-seventh Man," a would-be writer (who has been snatched in 1952 for execution in Stalinist Russia along with other more authentic Yiddish writers that the Russian dictator would make "disappear") composes a story—really more a midrash—with a narrator who thinks the world has ended while he slept and wonders who will say the prayer for the dead. That story is followed in Englander's earlier book by a second, "The Tumblers," set in prewar eastern Europe, in which a group of Jews reminiscent of Singer's "Fools of Chelm" learn about "the trick of the disappearing Jews." It is as if, in other words, in *Ministry,* the "trick" of the "disappearing" or "disappeared" children has recurred 30 years later in Argentina, and the Kaddish has assumed the form of the name of the central character who serves his Jewish community by erasing the memorial markers of their past, as if "saying Kaddish" has become the erasure of the past rather than a symbol of religious mourning.

Perhaps the continuity between Englander's first book and his second continues in other more significant ways. In the first volume, the question of the book, the question constituted materially by the book's existence—did we die during the night? and, if so, who is to say the prayer for the dead?—is given diegetically, which is to say, by a story written within the larger story. There is a passage in the second book with a similar (if not identical) structural status. The writer tells us (the readers) that Pato composed six handwritten notes during his prison stay, notes retrieved by a subsequent young female prisoner, which contained, among other comments, the writer's name, Pato Poznan, but the outside world (and, in particular, Pato's parents) never gets to read these notes. The notes are swallowed by the young girl as "caramels," or little candies, and remain in her stomach (unknown and unexamined) when she is dropped from a plane into the water.

Is not this unread writing, lodged in the belly of the young girl at the bottom of a million tons of water, with the writer's name affixed to each page, like the writing of the 27th prisoner in the earlier book, and, thereby, as was the case with the earlier writing, a version of the book itself? Does not the writing of the son, Pato (or Pablo or Paul), which affirms the writer's name (whatever else its content), contest in an important way the erasing of the names of the past—the "profession" of Pato's father—and which, thus, collaborates in a curious way with the Kafkaesque and Orwellian profession of the military government? And although Englander's current book is not about his family, are we not permitted to wonder whether the writing of this second book, "for my father," as the author affirms on the dedication page, continues the struggle of a son to be heard, to have his name registered in a community that would erase his name from their ranks (if we are to trust the published accounts of the reception of Englander's first book within the Orthodox Jewish community), and thus collaborate in a curious way with the Kafkaesque and Orwellian forces that would seem to act against the human and against the Jews (which, if we are to trust certain writers, are parallel) and to do so ironically in their name? The powerful

and heart-rending exchange between father and son—"I wish you never to have been born" Kaddish says to his son, a sentiment echoed by Pato to his father just before they come to take him away—resonates beyond the fictional contours of Argentina in the 1970s, gathering sparks from the Jewish community in postwar America, and even perhaps from writing as old as Greek tragedy.

"What is left for a man to think when he was raised for ruin and it comes," the unnamed narrator intones in the final chapter. And this sentence—more exclamatory than interrogative—would appear to summarize what has taken place. The book delivers what it promises, both historically (regarding the book as a material registry of a movement from disaster to disaster), and individually (regarding the self-fulfilling prophetic attitude of the three protagonists, one that aligns itself with this perceived history). "Do you know what time it is?" Kaddish's wife, Lillian, asks at one point. And the narrator's commentary in response—"It was the middle of the night"—tells more than the time. With this book, Englander carves out a place for himself as a commentator on the deepest issues of our era, an era riddled by violence, literary writing, and darkness. One looks forward to more from this writer's vital, brilliant, and critical voice, one that, amid other woes than ours, will remain a friend to the human and to the Judaic, and as such one that will refuse the formulaic response of Keats's sheltered burial urn to the violence, literary writing, and darkness it encloses, namely, that "beauty is truth and truth beauty," just as Keats's own brilliant iconoclastic poem itself does.

Bibliography

Englander, Nathan. *For the Relief of Unbearable Urges.* New York: Knopf, 1999.

Levinas, Emmanuel. *Otherwise than Being.* Pittsburgh, Pa.: Duquesne University Press, 1998.

Mason, Wyatt. "Disappearances: Nathan Englander's Novel of Political Terror." *New Yorker* 21 May 2007.

—**Sandor Goodhart**

Miss Lonelyhearts   Nathanael West   (1933)

NATHANAEL WEST's short novel, *Miss Lonelyhearts,* is deceptively simple on the surface. It purports to be a tale of the trials and tribulations of a newspaper columnist pressured into writing the advice column for the editor, but who inadvertently brings on himself a number of serious problems. The so-called Miss Lonelyhearts of the story will not be limited to providing advice to the lovelorn, despite what the title and popular image of such a columnist might lead one to think. By giving in to his editor's request, this columnist takes on a considerable amount of the misery and mental anguish that beset his American readers. Miss Lonelyhearts is found attempting to deal with a variety of social and domestic situations confronting sorely beset individuals lost in the lonely crowd. In addition, the editor who inveigled him into handling this particular column hates him and takes on the persona of a malevolent antagonist bent on bringing about his downfall. Moreover, the story is complicated by West's sometimes distracting symbolism borrowed from Christian and specifically Catholic belief, ritual, and observance, to say nothing of his seeming obsession (in the story) with the persona of Jesus Christ. Not by any means, however, was he so affected as to adopt Jesus as his savior, choosing to regulate his adult life according to what he felt Jesus was calling on him to do.

Miss Lonelyhearts, like West's three other short novels, was written during the Great Depression (1929–1939), and like them, it reflects disillusionment and disappointment of one kind or another. It was not that West was projecting his own hard times or the hard times of his parents, who apparently remained well-to-do during this period, into the story. Rather, the overall tone of *Miss Lonelyhearts,* and its big letdown at the end, suggests some personal idiosyncrasy on West's part, some deeply rooted discontent, perhaps based on his own sense that he was a misfit. The interested reader is referred to James F. Light's excellent biographical and literary sourcebook, *Nathanael West: An Interpretative Study* (Northwestern University Press, 1961).

The idea of an advice columnist counseling troubled readers on personal problems may seem trite, old-fashioned, and commonplace in the 21st century. But when *Miss Lonelyhearts* first appeared in 1933, the idea was still something of a novelty, helping some (if the advice was at all sound), and perhaps amusing others. Yet West may well have drawn the idea of anonymous newspaper counseling from another source, the Yiddish press. James F. Light points out that West's parents were Jewish immigrants. Given the way Jewish immigrants of the period valued a medium in their own language that offered reader-interest features along with news and other forms of information, West's parents may well have been familiar with the Yiddish language newspaper *The Forward,* edited by the writer Abraham Cahan. His popular column, *"Bintel Brief"* (Bundle of Letters), offered the transplanted, confused, often distressed European Jews answers to serious questions about how to get along in this new society and how to deal with family disruption and fragmentation, as well as with other domestic threats. Quite conceivably, West himself might have remembered seeing copies of *The Forward* around the apartment while he was growing up, and might have remembered hearing his parents and their friends discussing the paper's contents or special features, such as the *"Bintel Brief."*

Readers of *Miss Lonelyhearts* will doubtless disagree as to how closely the protagonist's life mirrors or otherwise compares with the New Testament accounts of the life of Jesus Christ. James F. Light makes much of a positive comparison, though he seems to make a bit too much, on occasion. For instance, he relates the name of the protagonist's inimical editor, Shrike (who mocks and satirizes the story and character of the New Testament Jesus), to the thorn bird, shrike. Shrike the editor had nothing to do with the death of Miss Lonelyhearts, who was accidentally shot by a crippled acquaintance he had been trying to help. Yet Light states that the editor's "lack of love and pity justifies the name Shrike, suggestive as it is of the bird that impales its prey upon a cross of torns. Shrike has become the anti-Christ, crucifying those who strive for faith" (82). Yet withal, Light's treatment of *Miss Lonelyhearts* and the Christ dream should be read by anyone seeking clarification of certain features of this short novel.

The narrative is fairly irregular. There are elements that suggest the spasmodic, the absurd, the surreal, the forced articulation of certain episodic fragments. West's temporary residence in Paris and his exposure to Dadaism and surrealism in art there, before he returned to the United States and began writing fiction, has been mentioned as a possible influence on his short novels. With regard to this work, and his three other short novels, it might be just such an exotic, European exposure that makes West's fiction in the first decade of the 21st century more than a literary fossil worn down by time and custom, but rather a voice from the dim past with an odd, contemporary ring.

Bibliography

Jones, Beverly. "Nathanael West's *Miss Lonelyhearts.*" In *Critical Essays on Nathanael West.* New York: G.K. Hall, 1994.

Light, James F. *Nathanael West: An Interpretative Study.* Evanston, Ill.: Northwestern University Press, 1961.

—**Samuel I. Bellman**

More Die of Heartbreak Saul Bellow (1987)

More Die of Heartbreak is modeled on Nikolay Gogol's farce, "The Bridegroom," with its tale of the flight of a bridegroom trapped in a promise of marriage. It is also reminiscent of T.S. Eliot's famous poem "The Love Song of J. Alfred Prufrock." Both focus on failed romance, failed men, and absent mermaids. The stuff of all three is misogynous love lore, comic characters, failed romances, cowardly retreats, and crackpot as well as idealized sexual lore. As Uncle Benn Crader and nephew Kenneth exchange stories of battle wounds received from women, *More Die of Heartbreak* becomes a comic moral allegory of the failure of romance in the 20th century. The poorly fathered Kenneth Trachtenberg has appointed himself the romance guardian of his Uncle Benn

Crader, an eccentric plant morphologist, because he thinks him one of the rare, visionary men of the age. In truth, Kenneth is an arrested child who must secure Uncle Benn as a substitute father and ward off all potential female marauders. When Uncle Benn becomes embroiled in a late-life romance and marriage, the text focuses on a scheming and crass family and all kinds of fraud, legal battles, and betrayals. Ever anxious to say I told you so, Kenneth generates much of the comic action as he engages in farcical, self-serving attempts to rescue his uncle. Through Kenneth's academic credentials as an expert of Western love lore, SAUL BELLOW provides much of the serious intellectual content of the novel that visits gender issues and provides a triple indictment of science, religion, and belles lettres for their failure to illuminate heterosexual love in the late modern moment. Here Bellow explores distortions in human relations, sadomasochism, the interconnection between love and death, modern marriage, the comic misery of human sexuality, and the colossal failure of poetry in human relations.

Bellow also revisits one of his favorite themes, the comic incompatibility of heterosexual love and the male quest for truth. As both Kenneth's and Benn's marriages fail, the full extent of their misogyny is revealed as they blame women for their collective and individual failures to meet male desires perfectly. Kenneth only too eagerly tries to persuade Benn that his superior spiritual nature inevitably attracts educated women who are affected by these emanations but who live in metaphysical darkness. These women, he tells Benn, are parasitic, metaphysically deficient, and in need of "fixing." Meanwhile, the text comically portrays both Benn and Kenneth in need of serious "fixing themselves." Unable to cope, Benn hightails it for the Arctic wastes and his beloved lichens in a hilarious reenactment of the classic bridegroom flight.

In the absence of his true love object, Uncle Benn, Kenneth is now forced to settle for a woman friend whose love for him he has long ignored. His moral awakening begins with his vision of her scoured face wrapped in bandages. Fearing she will never attract him because of his frequently stated preference for perfect classical female beauty, she has had her lumpy, flawed eastern European face sanded by a sadistic dermatologist. Kenneth finally begins to be aware of the cruelty of idealizing female beauty in a world of real women. While men are portrayed in *More Die of Heartbreak* as sexual victims of a droll mortality full of contaminating females, the text does uncover the cultural roots of their misogynous game. And while women are depicted through these two characters as treacherous, metaphysically devoid of value, and stupidly male-identified, the text reveals just how classical love lore and artistic depictions of ideal female beauty have misled misogynous men who fail to deconstruct it in the name of real love. Ultimately the noble, chivalrous, and spiritually enlightened male quest of European mythology is made the butt of Bellow's comedy, since its impossible conditions are always celibacy and bachelorhood. That leaves only three avenues of escape: deception, abandonment, or flight, the perfect stuff of comedy for a writer with Saul Bellow's personal history, intellectual habits, and comic sensibilities. This is a hilarious and endearing tale of two quirky, unreliable narrators both of whom Bellow clearly loves. In it he recaptures much of the old Bellowian comic energy and wit, even though this novel fails to reach the intellectual and artistic stature of *Henderson the Rain King*, *Herzog*, or *Humboldt's Gift*. Its principal legacy is two of 20th-century American literature's most endearing comic characters.

Bibliography

Bach, Gerhard, ed. *The Critical Response to Saul Bellow.* Westport, Conn.: Greenwood Press, 1995.

Bloom, Harold, ed. *Saul Bellow.* New York: Chelsea House, 1986.

—Gloria L. Cronin

Mr. Sammler's Planet Saul Bellow (1970)

Mr. Sammler's Planet reflects New York City at the height of the student radical movements of the 1960s from the perspective of Mr. Arthur Sammler, an old world European aristocrat and elderly Holocaust survivor. At an early age Sammler had become an Anglophile, and later became part of the British H. G. Wells and Bloomsbury intellectual groups. On the eve of World War II while in Europe with his wife and daughter, he is cut off from them by the German invasion of Poland. His wife is murdered, and his Jewish daughter, Shula-Slawa, is hidden by nuns for the duration of the war. Sammler is left for dead in a pit and crawls out from under a pile of dead Jews to a life of continuing terrors. In order to survive he shoots a German soldier in the Zamosht Forest, and subsequently spends the rest of the war hiding by day in a dark tomb. By the time he and his daughter are brought to America by an American relative, Sammler has become neurotic and humanly disengaged. He hates the bizarre world of hippie-era New York, and realizes his curious American-Jewish relatives see him as a sacred object and a leftover from another age. He has become a Swiftian misanthrope and a chronic misogynist.

Saul Bellow structures this book as a focused cultural archaeology of the psychosexual formations of early modern European masculinity, of the intellectual eras Sammler spans, and of his several intellectual mentors. Sammler becomes like an Old Testament prophet prophecying the doom of Western culture, for whom corrupt and stupid femininity is to blame for the wicked sexual mores of the 1960s and for the imminent collapse of modern civilization. However, it is the loving Dr. Elya Gruner, his American rescuer, whose moral example and death finally shock Sammler from coldness to reengagement and love. As he begins to respond to Gruner's love, he refuses Dr. Govinda Lal's Faustian aspirations for colonizing the moon, and declares that he prefers life on this flawed home planet.

In *Mr. Sammler's Planet,* many of Bellow's old moral and philosophical enemies resurface: Faustian romanticism, Rousseau, Nietzsche, Spengler, Darwin, Burkhardt, Schopenhauer, Freud, and Lawrence. Bellow also addresses the racial issues in the Arab-Israeli conflict and in American culture, and makes a general denunciation of the turbulent 1960's counterculture, people whom he saw as destructive, ill-mannered, and corrupt. By this time in his life, Bellow believed civilization to be too fragile to withstand too many more attacks in the 20th century. In the characters of Eisen the Israeli and the gorgeously attired African American pickpocket, Bellow examines contemporary versions of Rousseau's noble savage and Lawrence's truly virile man.

Critics generally disliked this book, complaining that it was sour, that Bellow was clearly tired, that it was a crotchety old man's book, and that it attacked an entire generation. Some few thought it was beautifully adapted to Bellow's middle age, while others complained about its racism, its misogyny, its dismissal of the young, and its problematic depictions of women, blacks, Arabs, Israelis, and the American masses. It remains a complex and troubling work among Bellow's masterworks.

Bibliography

Guttmann, Allen. "Saul Bellow's *Mr. Sammler.*" *Contemporary Literature* 14, no. 2 (Spring 1973): 157–168.

Basu, Biman. "*Mr. Sammler's Planet* Revisited: Bellow's Comment on Intellectual Life." *Saul Bellow Journal* 6, no. 11 (Winter 1987): 18–27.

—Gloria L. Cronin

My Name Is Asher Lev Chaim Potok (1972)

CHAIM POTOK's third novel, *My Name Is Asher Lev,* relates to his childhood when his Yeshiva inexplicably hired an artist to give a course in painting. Normally, an Orthodox school viewed painting as taboo; it was against Jewish tradition and his father thought it a terrible waste of time. But Potok saw Asher Lev as "the metaphor for the problems of the writer." By the time he was 20 he was the inheritor of two utterly antithetical commitments: Modern literature told him no human institution was sacred, while his Jewish tradition maintained the intrinsic sacredness of things.

My Name Is Asher Lev, in a way similar to *The CHOSEN,* tells of a clash between secular and Orthodox Jewish cultures. Born with a supreme gift, Asher is an artist with an enormous talent. Though his father, who travels for the Rebbe, head of the

Ladover Hasidim (modeled on the Brooklyn Lubovitch Hasidim), cannot understand Asher's talent or obsession, he realizes that his son's gift cannot be suppressed and arranges for him to study with a famous secular Jewish artist, Jacob Kahn, who sees art as a religious calling. Kahn qualifies the religiosity of art, however, and he tells Asher that he cannot teach good and evil in art. Asher, forced to choose between art and Jewish tradition, at age 13 (when he would have taken on the responsibility of a bar mitzvah), chooses to try to follow his gift while breaking away from his father's brand of fundamentalism, but not from Judaism.

In Jacob Kahn's eyes, Asher's father, an Orthodox Jew, suffers aesthetic blindness. When Asher's father questions him about "moral blindness," Asher could only reply that he was not hurting anybody. His father responded that such an attitude would lead to hurting someone. Potok explained that there is a good case for art as delectation, for the sheer joy of an aesthetic experience. Like Danny Saunders in *The Chosen,* Asher Lev put personal fulfillment before the needs of the Jewish community. This decision is tenuous and problematic.

Asher Lev's mother, Rivkeh, understands both her husband's view and her son's stance. Rivkeh's angst and suffering impinges on Asher's consciousness and thus leads him to his greatest work.

Influenced by the centrality of religion and also the questioning in the writings of Evelyn Waugh, James Joyce, and Flannery O'Connor, Potok has tried to preserve the languages, traditions, and beliefs of (liberal) Orthodox Judaism while encountering the world of modern art. Asher's notorious painting of the "Brooklyn Crucifixion," which portrays protracted suffering, the suffering of humankind, is explained by a reference to Picasso, hardly a devout Christian, who painted a crucifix in a moment of anguish. To show his mother's suffering, and his own, and to depict the values he got from his parents, he used the Crucifixion.

As Potok put it in 1983, the world he created in *The Chosen* and *My Name Is Asher Lev* is a small esoteric world, not one of good versus evil, of sex and polarization, but one about good people involved in situations that they somehow want to come to terms with in a positive way. In a nutshell, within the context of a core-to-core cultural confrontation, an Orthodox Jew chooses art over community but remains an observant Jew, one who has to find the keys to some truth more important than tradition. Potok's art was full of aesthetic vessels, that is to say, motifs that an artist fills with his own being. This forms the center of *My Name Is Asher Lev.*

Bibliography

Abramson, Edward A. *Chaim Potok.* Boston: Twayne, 1986.

Potok, Chaim. *My Name Is Asher Lev.* New York: Knopf, 1972.

Sternlicht, Sanford. *Chaim Potok.* Westport, Conn.: Greenwood Press, 2000.

—Daniel Walden

The Naked and the Dead
Norman Mailer (1948)

In the 15 months following his discharge from the army in World War II, NORMAN MAILER completed his first published novel, *The Naked and the Dead*. The novel's huge critical and popular success overtook him when he was living with his wife in Paris and studying on the GI Bill at the Sorbonne. The novel topped the best-seller lists for months and was purchased by the movies. Mailer was only 25, and with this book, he began his long career as a literary celebrity.

Today the novel seems rather old-fashioned in form and style when compared with other novels of the 1940s such as Saul Bellow's *Dangling Man* (1944). Nevertheless, *The Naked and the Dead* remains one of the classic novels of World War II, its importance lying in its epic scope and in the profundity and complexity of its themes. It clearly derives from the harsh naturalism of the proletarian fiction of the 1930s—the young Mailer started writing under the influence of John Steinbeck, John Dos Passos, and James T. Farrell—and it stands as a summation and perhaps dead end of that tradition. Mailer did not attempt a novel of precisely this epic form again until 30 years later, in *The Executioner's Song*.

The Naked and the Dead is a sweaty, bleak, mercilessly realistic view of men at war, littered with decaying corpses and filled with the overpowering scent of jungle rot. Death is omnipresent, and the men's violent struggle to preserve their lives and their manhood consumes them. Their unsatisfactory confrontation with the civilian forces that have determined their characters (revealed in compressed "Time Machine" flashbacks) seems only a preparation for the carnage of the battlefield. The novel builds impressive force through raw physical realism in its descriptions of jungle warfare, the massive accumulation of detail, and the various characters' struggle for power and control, which are constantly foiled. Mailer criticizes not the war or the army but the overwhelming institutions of modern America that crush the individual. He is concerned with the drift of history and predicts not freedom coming out of the war, but the possibility of American totalitarianism.

The action takes place on a Pacific island the Americans are trying to recapture from the Japanese. For purposes of contrast, scenes in the officers' camp commanded by the autocratic General Cummings are juxtaposed with scenes in a reconnaissance platoon led by the cruel, hard-driving Texan Sergeant Croft. The link between the two is Lieutenant Hearn, a Harvard graduate and alienated liberal, whose death (he is betrayed by Sergeant Croft, who leads him into a trap) represents the death of American liberalism. Mailer, who divides his attention among all the characters, is interested in the fate of each man.

A division of sympathies also occurs in his treatment of the two Jewish soldiers, Roth and Goldstein. Mailer maintains the same objectivity toward them as he does toward the rest of the mixed platoon, which includes characters from all over America and from different religious faiths and ethnicities. Roth is an upwardly mobile, assimilated Jew. A college graduate, he resembles Hearn: Because he feels superior and distant from the rest of the men, he is universally disliked. The woeful, self-pitying Roth makes a poor soldier. Lacking any defense against the abuse of the platoon, he is goaded to the breaking point. (Mailer always tries to reveal character by pushing his characters to their limits and beyond.) Croft forces the men to climb a mountain, an ultimately pointless mission, and Roth, physically the weakest of the platoon, finally lies down weeping in exhaustion. But when fellow soldier Gallagher hits him, saying, "Get up, you Jew bastard," Roth gets up. "A saving anger, a magnificent anger came to his aid. For the first time in his life he was genuinely furious. . . . It wasn't bad enough that they judged him for his own faults, his own incapacities; now they included him in all the faults of a religion he didn't believe in, a race which didn't exist. . . . A Jew was a punching bag because they could not do without one." Unable to jump a chasm in the mountain, Roth finally knows himself and loses his fear of Croft and the anti-Semitic bully Gallagher. He realizes he could force the patrol to turn back from its senseless mission, but he lacks the courage to refuse and have to face the men afterward. Roth jumps, only to fall to his death.

In contrast to Roth, Goldstein has the courage to endure when pushed beyond his limits. Goldstein was raised in a candy store in Brooklyn. Poorly educated but nourished by his religious faith, he has the survival ability of a peasant. Significantly, his best friend in the platoon is Ridges, a religious fundamentalist and illiterate son of a sharecropper. The two carry their burden, the dying soldier Wilson, for days on a stretcher through the jungle, persisting even after Wilson dies, only to see his body wash away as they try to ford the rapids of a river. In bitter frustration, Goldstein wonders if "all the suffering of the Jews came to nothing." For a time, he feels hopeless: "All the ghettos, all the soul killings, all the massacres and pogroms, the gas chambers, lime kilns—all of it touched no one, all of it was lost." Nevertheless, even if his mission fails, Goldstein perseveres and survives, and he forms a bond of friendship with Ridges through their shared burden. Theirs is the only unselfish male friendship in the novel.

Mailer admires the heroism of ordinary individuals who carry their burdens to the limit, despite the inevitability of failure. His radical criticism of American society seems to espouse a return to traditional values, even if his belief in those values is tempered by an existential pessimism about the vicissitudes of nature and fate.

Bibliography

Thornton, William H. "American Political Culture in Mailer's *The Naked and the Dead*." In *EurAmerica: A Journal of European and American Studies* 22, no. 1 (March 1992): 95–122.

Wilson, Raymond J., III. "Control and Freedom in *The Naked and the Dead*." *Texas Studies in Literature and Language* 28, no. 2 (Summer 1986): 164–181.

—Andrew Gordon

The Natural Bernard Malamud (1952)

BERNARD MALAMUD's *The Natural* opens with 19-year-old Roy Hobbs, a boy from the backwoods, en route to baseball stardom. Traveling by train to major league tryouts with the Chicago Cubs, having been fortuitously discovered by Sam Simpson, former catcher for the St. Louis Browns, Roy believes he is on the verge of a future of promise and unlimited possibility. For Roy Hobbs, baseball fame is the Holy Grail, and with the magical properties of Wonderboy, the bat carved out of wood from a tree split by lightning, he will fight his way to legendary stature. He dreams of future stardom: "when I walk down the street . . . people will say there goes Roy Hobbs, the best there ever was in the game." The journey by train itself would seem to presage the fulfillment of his dream, for during a brief hiatus in the train's journey, Roy disembarks to compete in a contest of skill with Walter Whambold, the Whammer, three-time recipient of the most valuable player award. The contest is only a brief hiatus from Roy's journey, but long enough to strike out the leading hitter of the American League. His victory is an act of will that seals his fate. For in bringing down the baseball idol, Roy wins the rapt attention of Harriet Bird, who previously ascended the train from the deserted platform of the station dressed in black and carrying a black hatbox that she will not relinquish. Bewitched and beguiled by the mysterious woman who boards the train, Roy will joust the crowned warrior, whose weapon fails him in the face of Roy's perfect, "pitiless" pitching. His success in slaying the Whammer, however, shows itself not to be the longed-for portent of victories to come, for the woman in black is a superior opponent and presents a far more dangerous threat, one that Roy, blinded by desire, cannot see. Instead of carrying him to his anticipated destination, the train delivers Roy into the hands of Harriet Bird, the temptress who seeks out famous athletes only to destroy them. Indeed, it is the woman in black who will change Roy's life forever. In an act of pathological self-vindication, Harriet shoots Roy with a gun whose silver bullet, a protection against those who live charmed lives, strikes him down.

When we meet Roy again, it is 15 years later, and, at 34 years old, he is the new left fielder for the floundering New York Knights. When he arrives at the ballpark, the parched field is scorched and cracked, a desolate land of defeat and cessation. The desiccated background is a measure of the psychic landscape, and for Pop Fisher, team manager, it is yet another barren, infertile season for the Knights. Roy's appearance, with Wonderboy in tow, however, brings with it the promise of regeneration and renewal. Where the land cannot, Roy produces life, a rebirth of hope and triumph for the all-but-vanquished Knights. Roy, entering the major leagues at last, becomes the baseball hero that he imagined he would be. His extraordinary batting triumphs make him a baseball legend. The Knights' victories with Roy at bat are magical, mythical, bringing an end to the drought, a "long rain had turned the grass green." Roy changes the team's luck and puts them at long last in the running for the pennant that Pop Fisher "would give his whole life to win."

Roy is, however, a "natural," uncultivated, waiting for fate to play out its hand. Roy is all too easily seduced, initially by Harriet Bird, who disastrously alters the course of his life, and again by Memo Paris, Pop Fisher's niece, a woman solely motivated by the acquisition of material things. Driven by desire for Memo, Roy accepts a bribe to throw the game made to him by the odious owner of the Knights, Judge Banner. To win Memo's affections and blind to her obvious self-interest, Roy, just at the moment in which he might bring the Knights to a final victory, succumbs to his raw fear of losing Memo, and takes the bribe. All of Roy's natural talents at bat and on the field finally cannot stand up to his moral failings and his abdication of responsibility.

Typically, Malamud offers his characters opportunities to show, as one character in the short story "Idiots First," puts it, "what it means to be human." For Malamud, what it means to be human is the recognition of one's responsibility to others, an obligation to a moral world. Such recognition requires the acknowledgment of shared suffering, a condition that Roy Hobbs calamitously rejects. When asked by Iris Lemon, the woman who enigmatically emerges from the midst of the crowded stands unaccountably believing in Roy's goodness, to acknowledge the value of shared suffering in a moral universe, Roy disavows its worth: "All it taught me is to stay away from it. I am sick of all I have suffered." His refusal to acknowledge that anything of value may be learned from suffering prevents him from making the right choice. It is Iris, who hates "to see a hero fail," who offers Roy the chance for redemption and compassion. And although Roy changes his mind at the last moment and tries to win the game, recognizing that "only a homer, with himself scoring the winning run, would truly redeem him," he ultimately, inevitably, strikes out. The novel's conclusion finds Roy Hobbs a fallen hero, one not felled by another, but rather by his own "natural" limitations. Consumed by self-hatred, shattered, and beyond redemption, Roy weeps "bitter tears."

Bibliography
Field, Leslie. "Bernard Malamud." In *Twentieth-Century American-Jewish Fiction Writers.* Detroit: Gale, 1984.

Saperstein, Jeffrey. "Irony and Cliché: Malamud's *The Natural* in the 1980s." *Literature Film Quarterly* 24, no. 1 (1996): 84–87.

—Victoria Aarons

The Nazarene Sholem Asch (1939)

SHOLEM ASCH, in his rich historical romance *The Nazarene,* restructures the Jesus legend. His Rabbi Yeshua is a Jewish Jesus prior to the theological Christian interpretations accumulated over centuries and thrust upon him since his death. In Asch's view, Yeshua was a saintly rabbi. Although a portion of the novel is based on New Testament lore, Asch re-creates the story to exonerate the Jews of Jesus's death, a conception contrary to that in the Gospels.

The Nazarene is composed of a contemporary framing story plus three purportedly eyewitness versions of the Jesus legend: one is related by an ancient Roman Hegemon; a newly discovered fifth gospel by Judah Ish-Kiriot presents a different point of view; and the third narrative is told by an Orthodox Jewish youth. In the framing story, set in Poland in the 1930s, Asch highlights the pervasive anti-Semitism of the day. A young Jewish scholar comes to the residence of elderly Pan Viadomsky, renowned for being a great scholar of antiquity, to help him translate an important document. The Jew, although destitute, is capable, kind, and patient; Viadomsky, on the other hand, is abusive and insolent. The translator is disgusted to discover that Viadomsky is working on a treatise propagating the old blood libel, that Jews use Christian blood in the preparation of matzo. Asch essentially sets up a clear contrast between the blatantly anti-Semitic contemporary Pole and his fictional Nazarene.

The hero of the inner novel, Rabbi Yeshua ben Joseph of Nazareth, is intensely Jewish. He piously celebrates the Sabbath and makes all the proper benedictions. He honors his Jewish mother, a primary law in Judaism. When Yeshua dies, he says the traditional "Hear O Israel" prayer, the verse recited by Jewish martyrs. Most of Yeshua's best qualities derive from basic tenets of the Mosaic law. The famous dictum "Do unto others as you would have them do unto you" comes from the venerable Jewish sage Hillel.

Asch's character Judah Ish-Kiriot is also a man of faith. He makes a hasty, agonizing decision, and he regrets it bitterly. In the novel, Judah is a psychologically complex and believable character; he is impatient and anxious—but not the thief of the Gospels. Other characters, too, who are scarcely given a line each in the four Gospels, are fleshed out by Asch. These include Miriam (Mary), mother of Yeshua; Miriam of Migdal (Mary Magdalene); Herod; and the true villain, Pontius Pilate.

Jochanan, a religious student, narrates the third part of the manuscript. He brokenheartedly concludes, after witnessing his beloved rebbe whipped, tortured, and sentenced to die on the cross (all on Pontius Pilate's orders), that gentle Yeshua is not the longed-for messiah.

The Nazarene, so rich in detail and emotion, became a best seller in English translation in 1939. Abe Cahan, however, mogul editor of the Yiddish *Forverts,* denounced the work as a missionary tract. Although he did his best to destroy Asch's reputation among his Yiddish readers, the novel stands as an imaginative and historical masterpiece.

Bibliography
Fischthal, Hannah Berliner. "*The Nazarene* as a Jewish Novel." *Jewish Quarterly* [London] 41, no. 3 (Autumn 1994): 36–39.

Siegel, Ben. *The Controversial Sholem Asch: An Introduction to His Fiction.* Bowling Green, Ohio: Bowling Green University Popular Press, 1976.

—Hannah Berliner Fischthal

Nemerov, Howard (1920–1991)

A poet, novelist, short story writer, playwright, critic, editor, and teacher, Howard Nemerov is commonly viewed as one of the most distinguished figures of postwar American literature. The elder of two children (his sister was the photographer Diane Arbus), Nemerov was born on March 1, 1920, in New York City to Gertrude Russek and David Nemerov, the latter a philanthropist and connoisseur of the fine arts. His erudite, affluent parents enrolled young Howard first in the exclusive Society for Ethical Culture's Fieldston School, where he excelled at both academics and sports, and Harvard University. While at Harvard, Nemerov began writing poetry and fiction, won the prestigious Bowdoin Prize in 1940 for an essay on Thomas Mann, and received an A.B. degree in 1941. Immediately after college, Nemerov enlisted in the Royal Air Force Coastal Command, then in 1944 joined the Lincolnshire-based Eighth United States Army Air Force as a flying officer. On January 26, 1944, he married Margaret (Peggy) Russell, whom he met in England, and in 1945, deeply marked by the horrors of war (an experience that played a crucial role in Nemerov's development as a poet and humanist), he was discharged from the U.S. Air Force as a first lieutenant.

Upon their return to America, Nemerov and his young wife—their marriage would eventually produce three sons: David, Alexander, and Jeremy Seth—settled in New York City. Much to his father's dismay, Nemerov decided to pursue a career in literature rather than entering the family business. He finished writing his first collection of poetry, *Image and the Law* (1947), during the same year after his release from the military. In 1946 Nemerov accepted a teaching position as an instructor of English at Hamilton College and also became an associate editor of the literary journal *Furioso*, a position he served in until 1951. From 1948 to 1966 he taught at Bennington College (as a member of the faculty of literature). Throughout his career as man of letters, Nemerov earned a living by teaching for a number of other American universities: the University of Minnesota (1958–59), Hollins College (1962–64), Brandeis University (1966–69), and Washington University, St. Louis, first as a visiting Hurst Professor of English (1969–70) and then as Edward Mallinckrodt Distinguished University Professor of English, a position he held from 1976 until his death from cancer of the esophagus on July 5, 1991.

Nemerov was a prolific writer. In addition to 14 books of poetry, including *The Image and the Law, The Salt Garden* (1955), *Mirrors & Windows* (1958), *Trying Conclusions: New and Selected Poems* (1960), *The Next Room of the Dream* (1962), *The Blue Swallows* (1967), and *The Collected Poems of Howard Nemerov* (1977), he wrote three novels—*The Melodramatists* (1949), *Federigo: Or the Power of Love* (1954), and *The Homecoming Game* (1957)—and several collections of short stories, plays, and essays, including *A Commodity of Dreams and Other Stories* (1959), *Poetry and Fiction: Essays* (1963), *Stories, Fables and Other Diversions* (1971), and *Reflexions on Poetry and Poetics* (1972). For his creative output, Nemerov received many awards and honors, most notably fellowships from the Academy of American Poets (1970) and the Guggenheim Foundation (1968–69), a National Endowment for the Arts grant (1966–67), the first Theodore Roethke Memorial Prize for Poetry (1968), the Frank O'Hara Memorial Prize (1971), the National Medal of the Arts (1987), and, for his *Collected Poems*, he won the Pulitzer Prize (1978), the National Book Award (1978), and the Bollingen Prize (1981).

Although Nemerov's voice and writing style developed over the years from academic and formal (mostly influenced by the writings of William Butler Yeats, Wallace Stevens, Allen Tate, and T. S. Eliot) to simple, direct, and elegant, his basic themes and concerns remained constant. Nemerov was essentially an existentialist. All of his poems address, in one way or another, the unbridgeable dichotomy between the mysterious, life-affirming world of nature and the life-denying artifice and alienation of our modern existence. Nemerov was a pessimist, yet along with his poems' underlying skepticism and dark cynicism, his lines were often witty, humorous, and tender, rendering his visions at once intellectually severe, humane, and optimistic. Peter Meinke perhaps says it best when he argues that Nemerov's "modern awareness of contemporary man's alienation and fragmentation, combined with a breadth of wit in the eighteenth century sense of the word, sets Nemerov's writing apart from the other modern writers."

Bibliography

Labrie, Ross. *Howard Nemerov.* Boston: Twayne, 1980.

Meinke, Peter. *Howard Nemerov.* Minneapolis: University of Minnesota Press, 1968.

Mills, William. *The Stillness in Moving Things: The World of Howard Nemerov.* Memphis: Memphis State University Press, 1975.

—Daniele Pantano

The Net of Dreams: A Family's Search for a Rightful Place Julie Salamon (1996)

Written by *Wall Street Journal* and *New York Times* journalist and critic Julie Salamon, this memoir details the life journey of Sanyi and Szimi Salamon from the town of Khust in what is now Ukraine, through the camps of Birkenau and Dachau, to a rural town in Seaman, Ohio.

As part of a growing number of second-generation Holocaust memoirs, *The Net of Dreams* explores the implications of the Holocaust for children of survivors. Salamon writes that her father never spoke of the past and her mother only rarely spoke of it, but it shaped their family's daily life through such things as her father's days of silence or episodes of anger and her mother's optimism. One implication of growing up as a child of a survivor is this silence; she could only hypothesize about their sufferings and never know exactly how they felt about it. Salamon explores the shame of knowing that everything she complained about and suffered through was insignificant in comparison with her parents' sufferings.

Salamon's own journey to know her parents' past more fully begins in 1993 when she decides to visit the movie set of Steven Spielberg's *Schindler's List* in Poland with her mother and stepfather. From there, they visit family members in eastern Europe and the cities of their past. Salamon recounts the history she discovers from her mother's conversations with friends about the 1930s and 1940s. She starts with the story of her mother, Szimi, beginning in Khust during prewar Europe. Her grandfather chose to remain in Khust, despite the warnings to get out, because his business started going well, and he felt proud finally to be able to support his family. Szimi was taken to Birkenau in 1944 and put to work. She was continually grateful for what she had, even in times of poverty. They were eventually freed and she went to Prague, Czechoslovakia. Salamon then inserts the story of her father, Sanyi, growing up in Kis Begany in the Carpathian Mountains. He became a doctor after attending medical school in Prague, married, and had a child. He lost his wife and daughter when they were taken prisoner by the Germans; he was shipped to Dachau and they were gassed. After he escaped, Sanyi met Szimi in Prague. They married and eventually left for New York in search of a more comfortable, peaceful life. In New York Sanyi learned English and completed all the requirements to become a doctor. They made friends, but the city had too many doctors. Sanyi craved a location that required a physician. A friend informed him that rural Seaman, a town in Ohio, desperately needed a doctor, and the family moved there. They were respected and treated kindly; they found the peace they had searched for. Salamon ends the memoir with gratitude for the miracle of her family's ordinariness and the tremendous effort of her parents to overcome their past and give their children a normal life.

Though it was not received as well as her fiction books *WHITE LIES* and *The Christmas Tree*, both best sellers, *The Net of Dreams* received high praise from sources such as *Publishers Weekly* and *Booklist*. Critics have called the memoir unforgettable, poignant, and deeply affecting, declaring it to be well written and filled with compassion and understanding. Several critics criticized the work as being too impersonal, missing the immediacy of the works written by actual survivors.

Bibliography

Berger, Alan L. "Memoir and Memory: The Second Generation Odyssey of Julie Salamon." *Jewish Affairs* 54, no. 2 (Winter 1997).

Fogelman, Eva. "Julie Salamon." In *Holocaust Literature: An Encyclopedia of Writers and Their Work.* New York: Routledge, 2003.

—Marie Horne

"The New Colossus" Emma Lazarus (1883)

EMMA LAZARUS's poem "The New Colossus" is immortalized in a bronze plaque inside the pedestal of the Statue of Liberty. The poem exults in the spirit of welcome idealized in the American founding. It also reflects Lazarus's concern for the condition of European Jewry, many of whom had appeared in the United States as refugees after the Russian pogroms that began in 1881. The poem mythologizes the Statue of Liberty as a symbol of the United States as land of promise for refugees from other nations.

Part of France's motivation in giving the Statue to the United States was to make a political statement to the French people, some of whom anticipated a return to monarchy in France. The official name of the Statue is "Liberty Enlightening the World," a name that reflects the desire of its creators to see democracy spread from American shores to other nations. Representing this ideal in the Statue was intended to remind those who favored a return to monarchy that democracy was the most enlightened form of government. Lazarus's poem, however, rather than envisioning the Statue as a messenger of enlightenment to nondemocratic nations, depicts the statue as a symbol of the U.S. welcome to refugees fleeing those nations. The mythology Lazarus creates in her poem is, therefore, somewhat at odds with the meaning intended by the Statue's sculptor, Frédéric Bartholdi.

Lazarus's title refers to the similarity between the Statue of Liberty and popular descriptions of the *Colossus of Rhodes*. This similarity, frequently noted, depends on written accounts of the *Colossus*, which was destroyed by an earthquake fewer than 60 years after its completion. That statue, included in the popular list of the seven wonders of the ancient world, was built by the people of Rhodes in the third century B.C.E. to celebrate their success in withstanding a siege. Lazarus's poem somewhat incorrectly sees the *Colossus* as a symbol of a conquering nation; the statue was actually built to celebrate their freedom at the end of the siege. Both the Statue of Liberty and the *Colossus of Rhodes* stand at the mouths of their respective harbors. Contrary to the popular belief that Lazarus engages in describing the *Colossus* as having "conquering limbs astride from land to land," most experts believe that it would have been impossible for the statue to have straddled the harbor entrance.

"The New Colossus" was written for an auction being held to raise money for the construction of the pedestal for the Statue of Liberty. Lazarus initially declined to write the poem for the auction but was later persuaded by her friend, the author Constance Carry Harrison. It remains the best-known work of one of America's first successful Jewish literary figures.

Bibliography

James, Alan G. "The Master and the Laureate of the Jews: The Brief Friendship of Henry James and Emma Lazarus." *Henry James Review* 21, no. 1 (Winter 2000): 27–42.

Marom, Daniel. "Who Is the 'Mother of Exiles'? Jewish Aspects of Emma Lazarus' 'The New Colossus.'" *Prooftexts: A Journal of Jewish Literary History* 20, no. 3 (Autumn 2003): 231–261.

—Andrew Schultz

Night Elie Wiesel (1960)

Night (*La Nuit,* 1958) is a classic Holocaust memoir in which the author initiates his lifelong Trial of God [*Din* Torah] and of humanity. Originally published in a 900-page Yiddish volume *Un di Velt Hot Geshvign* (*And the World Remained Silent,* 1955), the work appeared three years later in a 120-page French translation. It was published in English in 1960. The considerably condensed translations of his memoir reveal the author's twofold emphasis: Silence itself deserves to be communicated, and he writes with words against words. Although ELI WIESEL had a difficult time publishing his memoir, and while it initially did not attract much attention, *Night* has become the most read Holocaust memoir, having been translated into many languages. In 2006 the volume appeared in a new translation by Marion Wiesel, the author's wife. Also in that year, the memoir was an Oprah Winfrey Book Club feature.

In the English edition's short space of slightly over 100 pages, Wiesel describes his experiences in the nocturnal inferno that consumed his parents (Shlomo and Sarah), his little sister (Tziporah), and his childhood belief in an omnipotent deity. Part of the memoir's overwhelming power emerges from its contrast to Judaism's master salvation narrative of the Exodus. *Night* attests to an "Anti-Exodus" in which Wiesel juxtaposes the normative teachings of Judaism—ethical action, justice, and a covenanting deity—with the evil of death camps. The memoir reveals in spare language what happened when the "Chosen people became the people chosen, when selection replaced election as the key term to describe the future of a human being" (Langer).

Devoid of chapter headings, *Night* recalls the stages of the Jewish people's extermination as emblemized in the experience of his Romanian village of Sighet: identification (wearing the yellow star), ghettoization, transportation to Auschwitz, and extermination. The young Wiesel was a deeply religious youth. In response to the question "why do you pray," he recalls musing, "Strange question. Why did I live? Why did I breathe?" (4). His memoir attests to the destruction of this pre-Holocaust religious worldview. Writing of his first night in Auschwitz, Wiesel attests: "Never shall I forget that night . . . that turned my life into one long night seven times sealed. . . . Never shall I forget those moments that murdered my God and my soul and turned my dreams to ashes. Never shall I forget those things, even were I condemned to live as long as God Himself. Never" (34).

Night is at the center of all Wiesel's subsequent works. The themes he deals with, such as the unheard witness, the indifference of both God and humanity, his quarrel with the deity, and the few known instances of Christian aid to the Jewish people, accompany the author throughout his voluminous writings. Moshe the Beadle ("servant," or synagogue attendant) taught Wiesel Kabbalah (a form of Jewish mysticism). He was also among the first of Sighet's foreign Jews to be deported. Escaping death, Moshe returned to Sighet to warn the town's remaining Jews. He was, writes Wiesel, "no longer the same. The joy in his eyes was gone. He no longer sang. He no longer mentioned either God or Kabbalah" (7). The witness was ignored; some of Sighet's Jews thought he wanted their pity; others thought he had gone mad. In Wiesel's subsequent works madmen are messengers of the truth.

Wiesel's memoir deals with relationships between fathers and sons, executioners and victims, and Jews and their god. Using language as a physician utilizes a scalpel, Wiesel recalls an incident where a wagon full of starving Jews were fighting over crusts of bread thrown them by townspeople who delighted in seeing the living corpses struggle for precious sustenance. A father was beaten to death by his son for a scrap of bread. But before the son could devour the morsel, he himself was murdered by others in the wagon. Wiesel was at that time 16 years old. This episode, and others where sons abandon fathers on death marches imposed by the Germans, inverts the biblical paradigm of the Akedah (Abraham's binding of Isaac) where a father prepares to sacrifice his son.

Night bears witness that the purpose of death camps was first to dehumanize Jews and then to exterminate them. The power of the camps to turn family members against each other was relentless. Hunger reduced humans to "starved stomachs." Wiesel himself recalls vowing never to abandon his father as several sons in the memoir had. Yet he remembers being separated from Shlomo Wiesel in Buchenwald. Looking for his father, he recalls thinking, "If only I didn't find him! . . . I could use all my strength to fight for my own survival. . . . ." Yet, he writes, "Instantly, I felt ashamed, ashamed of myself forever." (106).

Wiesel's memoir starkly underscores his quarrel with God. The author describes a hanging in the Buna camp that crystallizes the end of his childhood theological certainty. The inmates were forced to march past three people hanging on gallows; two adults and one young boy were executed for sabotage. The adults died almost immediately. The youth, much lighter, took a longer time to expire. Wiesel writes that a prisoner asks, "Where is merciful God, where is He?" The author shares that a voice within him answers: "Where He is? This is where—hanging here from this gallows. . ." (65). Some interpreters wrongly believe that this signals Wiesel's belief in the death of God. It is more accurate to state that Wiesel here announces the impossibility of his unquestioning pre-Holocaust belief in God's justice. As he writes elsewhere in the memoir, "I concurred with Job! I was not denying [God's] existence, but I doubted His absolute justice" (45).

The English version of *Night* concludes with Wiesel looking at himself in the mirror after Buchenwald was freed. "From the depths of the mirror," he writes, "a corpse was contemplating me" (115). The author's searing words signify that a corpse is the most fitting image of humanity after the Holocaust. In the Yiddish version, however, he smashes the mirror with his fist. *Night* marks the conclusion of Wiesel's pre-Holocaust religious worldview. However, it also inaugurates the tension between the faith of the child that he was and the survivor that he is. The memoir is also a type of Kaddish (prayer for the dead) for his father, mother, little sister, and the Jewish world that perished during the Holocaust.

Bibliography

Berger, Alan L. "Faith and God During the Holocaust: Teaching *Night* with the Later Memoirs." In *Approaches to Teaching Wiesel's Night*, edited by Alan Rosen. New York: Modern Language Association of America, 2007.

Culp, Mildred L. "Wiesel's Memoir and God Outside Auschwitz." *Explorations in Ethnic Studies* 4, no. 1 (January 1981): 62–74.

Langer, Lawrence. *Versions of Survival: The Holocaust and the Human Spirit.* Albany: SUNY Press, 1982.

—**Alan L. Berger**

Nissenson, Hugh (1933–)

Hugh Nissenson's novels and short stories graphically portray the eternal conflict between good and evil in a world without divine governance. What makes his work especially intriguing is that it simultaneously acknowledges the human impulse toward religion while denying the possibility of post-Holocaust belief in a transcendent and covenantal deity. Nissenson told an interviewer: "I'm a religious novelist; . . . all my work, one way or another has to do with the major themes of religion: What are we, is there a god, what is our relationship to this god. The religious impulse is something that has interested me all of my life" (Klin). The author's extraordinary tales weave together the archaic worlds of myth and symbol, the crushing events of history, and the personal crises of human existence. Many of his novels integrate original paintings and poetry with his prose.

Brooklyn-born Nissenson reports that his father "loved and feared God" while his mother was an atheist. His search for a credible post-Holocaust moral existence in a world without God was indelibly shaped by three major traumatic events. At age 12 he saw newsreels of the death camps and listened, with his parents, to one of Hitler's raving speeches on the radio. Second, his mother's 31-year-old friend died of breast cancer. Combining human and natural evil, the author writes, "I hate the idea that a just and loving God allows cells to metastasize and men to make gas chambers." The third stage occurred when, as a young journalist in Jerusalem, he covered the 1961 trial of Adolph Eichmann. This experience cost him his faith.

After graduating from Swarthmore College, Nissenson was a Wallace Stegner Literary Fellow at Stanford University. He left a job at the *New York Times* to begin writing full time. He won the Edward Lewis Wallant Memorial Prize for his first collection of short stories, *A Pile of Stones* (1965). Other short stories and journals include *Notes from the Frontier* (1968), *In the Reign of Peace* (1972), and *The Elephant and My Jewish Problem* (1988). In addition, Nissenson has written four novels: *My Own Ground* (1976); *The Tree of Life* (1985), a finalist for the National Book

Award and the PEN-Faulkner Award, *The Song of the Earth* (2001); and *The Days of Awe* (2005). His books have been published in Australia and England. Further, they have been translated into Danish, Finnish, French, and Italian. Nissenson's works have been reviewed in publications such as the *New York Times,* the *New Yorker,* the *Washington Post,* and the *Los Angeles Times.* An Italian Ph.D. dissertation on Nissenson's literary universe appeared in 2006. His short stories reflect Nissenson's grappling with faith and doubt after Auschwitz. His novels, on the other hand, conclude that traditional piety is no longer credible.

Loss of faith in a personal God is the major theological theme in Nissenson's work. He is obsessed by the presence and power of evil, and the absence of God. Moreover, it is *not*—as Martin Buber would have it—that God is in eclipse. Rather, Nissenson claims that God no longer exists except as part of Jewish and Christian myth. Nissenson's novels instead contend that the traditional notion of a transcendent, heavenly deity is no longer realistic after the death camps and gas chambers. In its place there is a competing notion of Mother Earth. Death, moreover, far from being vanquished by life, is a necessary condition of existence. Nissenson's use of language is also noteworthy. Whether employing traditional narrative strategies or breaking the text (into e-mails, phone conversations, or journal entries), the author's use of language embodies the poet Gerard Manley Hopkins's dictum—"spare, original, strange."

My Own Ground portrays Jewish immigrants to America in the early 20th century seduced by the ways of the new land. A Kabbalistic rabbi foresees the Holocaust. His daughter, Hannah, raped by Schlifka, a Jewish pimp—brutal and degrading sex emblemizes the Jewish situation under National Socialism—commits suicide. Reflecting the mythic struggle between Jacob and Esau, Jake Brody, the novel's protagonist, wrestles with the pimp. Moreover, Brody has a dream in which he sees his landlady, Mrs. Tauber, give birth, and begin to devour her own newborn. Symbolically this act conveys the fate of the million and a half Jewish children destroyed by National Socialism.

When asked what is wrong with the human heart, Brody can only wistfully retort, "I wish I knew."

The Tree of Life takes place on the Ohio frontier during the early 19th century. The novel tells the tale of Thomas Keene, a disillusioned Protestant minister robbed of his faith by the death of his wife. Fanny, a widow, initially refuses Keene's marriage proposal because he is an unbeliever. But after witnessing the brutality of a Native American war party, she asks Keene to "help her live without Jesus." The symbol of a Tree of Life, or Cosmic Tree, is a powerful force in the history of religions, ranging from Mesopotamia to ancient India. The Yggdrasil (Cosmic Tree) concept is also present in the religions of central Asia and Siberia. Judaism speaks of the Torah as the "Tree of Life" (*Etz Hayyim*). The Christian cross may also be understood in this manner. These "trees" are viewed variously as an "image of the world," a pole that supports the sky, a means of communication between heaven and earth, and a means of cosmic renewal. Nissenson employs this image in a strikingly different and bold manner. Keene has a vision of a great horned owl's nest in a tree. There he sees the baby owls nesting in the rotting corpse of a duck that their mother had brought them to eat. Nissenson refabulates old myths.

John Firth Baker, the first genetically engineered human being, programmed to be an artist, is the protagonist of *The Song of the Earth,* set in mid-21st century America. The novel warns about the danger of humans usurping divine power, e.g., genetic manipulation, and Baker—a hermaphrodite—dies a violent death amid scenes of sexual excess. But his real tragedy, attests Nissenson, is that his mother did not love him enough at the formative stage of his development, seeking rather to exploit his talents for her own gain. Reflecting the continuing impact of the Holocaust, Baker devotes his attention to the work of Charlotte Solomon, an artist murdered during the Shoah. The novel also espouses the religion of Gaianism, named after Gaia, "our living Motherworld." Like *The Tree of Life,* which concludes with a painting of a Puritan mother embodying death, this novel is replete with terrifying drawings, including an image of Mother Earth, half living and half dead.

The Days of Awe, Nissenson's most Jewish novel, tells the story of Artie and Johanna Rubin. Nissenson told the writer of this article that he is most proud of the fact that *The Days of Awe* is a love story, whereas his earlier works are primarily about violence. The novel's title is taken from the Jewish liturgical year and refers to the 10 days of penance between Rosh Hashannah (the New Year) and Yom Kippur (the Day of Atonement). The Rubins, married 40 years, witness their circle of friends begin to succumb to disease. Johanna herself falls victim to her second, and fatal, heart attack. The novel also addresses the impact of evil as it unfolds in the life of a Holocaust survivor, the violence in Israel, and the victims of September 11, 2001, and their families; Artie and Johanna volunteer to help after the attack. The book has no chapters. E-mails play an important role and readers are given glimpses into intimate details. Cynthia Ozick terms *The Days of Awe* "An amazing novel. It is as if we are eavesdropping on life."

The Days of Awe is also the story of a religious quest. Artie, a secular Jew and an artist, is enamored of Norse mythology, Lévi-Strauss's work on primitive masks, and the richness of mythology; for his bar mitzvah his mother had given him a copy of *Bullfinch's Mythology* as an "antidote" to the Torah. Yet he wants his grandson to be circumcised, even though his daughter has married a non-Jew. Artie "whores after strange gods" while desperately seeking the God of his ancestors. The religion that Artie embraces is one of human relationships; it is the scaffolding on which he hangs his quest for meaning.

Critical response to Nissenson's work has been quite good. His novels and short stories have received striking reviews including by the *New York Times.* Cynthia Ozick believes that Nissenson is an original and exceptional writer. He is currently at work on a new novel dealing with the religious dimension of early America.

Nissenson's novels articulate an aesthetic vision, and aesthetics for him are closely related to holiness. For Nissenson, holiness no longer implies a vertical reference. He writes that "Beauty is a very high form of worship and adoration; a way of keeping the dark at bay." If the task of the writer is to entertain, it is no less to seek a way to acknowledge the religious impulse in a world where death camps and gratuitous violence hold sway. Nissenson, who could not believe in God after such events, ends up positing that love between humans may be the ultimate meaning of divinity.

Bibliography

Berger, Alan L. "Holiness and Holocaust: The Jewish Writing of Hugh Nissenson." *Jewish Book Annual* 48 (1990–1991).

Klin, Richard. Interview with Hugh Nissenson. *January Magazine,* November 2003.

Nissenson, Hugh. "A Sense of the Holy." In *Spiritual Quests: The Art and Craft of Religious Writing.* Edited by William Zinsser. Boston: Houghton Mifflin, 1988.

Smith, Danita. "Depression His Linchpin, A Novelist Keeps Going," *New York Times,* 26 July 2001.

—Alan L. Berger

Noah, Mordecai Manuel (1785–1851)

Noah was born on July 19, 1785, in Philadelphia. His father fought in the Revolutionary War; his mother came from a prominent Sephardic family. After his mother died when he was 10, Noah spent his formative years in Charleston, South Carolina, where he studied law, journalism, and politics. Noah helped found New York University and Mount Sinai Hospital in New York City. During his lifetime he was often compared to James Fenimore Cooper and Washington Irving. He was the country's most famous playwright, with his historical drama about the War of 1812, *She Would Be a Soldier, Or the Plains of Chippewa: An Historical Drama, in Three Acts* (1819), performed for over half a century, typically on July 4 and on President's Day. He is most popularly remembered for his 1825 scheme to build Ararat, a Jewish homeland on the Niagara River near Buffalo, New York. He has been called the "First Jew of America."

As a prominent Jewish presence, Noah promulgated an early form of Zionism. In 1826 he delivered his *Discourse on the Evidences of the American Indians Being the Descendants of the Lost Tribes of Israel,* which was partly an attempt to give historical weight to the newly established United States. In 1844 he delivered an address entitled *Discourse on the Restoration of the Jews,* which speaks forcefully of his belief of the imminent return of Jews to Palestine: "I confidently believe in the restoration of the Jews . . . [and] considered it a duty to call upon the free people of this country to aid us." In 1848 Noah presented his *Address, Delivered at the Hebrew Synagogue, in Crosby-Street, New York, on Thanksgiving Day, to Aid in the Erection of The Temple at Jerusalem* (published in 1849). Noah addressed his major themes regarding the blessings Jews enjoy in the United States due to laws protecting religious freedom and ensuring the separation of church and state (regarding which Noah, Thomas Jefferson, and other leading political figures of the day had exchanged significant correspondence). Such an environment made the United States unique, but it also generated a lack of compassion for the plight of the Jews: "Happy in the enjoyment of every comfort here . . . but when the great events of the restoration which are to fulfill prophecies are talked of, they cling to the home of their birth, and the country of their adoption, and say, 'my destiny is here.'" Emphasizing progressivism and social evolution, Noah spoke of the important roles that citizens play in bringing forth God's plan: "The designs of the Almighty are brought about by human agency; He inclines the hearts of men to execute His great purposes on earth . . . the triumph of liberal opinions, are all His works, through His inscrutable decrees." Noah's comments were part of the groundswell of liberation that is found in the revolutions of 1848 in Europe, to which he also referred in his *Address.*

As a journalist Noah wrote many pieces that were collected in *Essays of Howard, On Domestic Economy* (1820); it was reissued in 1845 as *Gleanings from a Gathered Harvest.* In addition to much editorial writing, Noah served as an editor for several important newspapers and also founded one. He began his editing career with the *New York National Advocate* (1817–26), then moved to the *New York Enquirer* (1826–29), after which he began editing the *New York Evening Star* in 1831. In 1841 Noah founded *Noah's Weekly Messenger,* a popular paper that, even after merging with the *Sunday Times,* paid homage to Noah by keeping his name on the masthead until some 40 years after his death.

Noah enjoyed a prominent political career, serving as U.S. consul to Tunis from 1813 to 1815, during the height of Barbary coast piracy. He wrote *Travels in England, France, and the Barbary States, in the Years 1813–1814* (1819), which offers insights into political and religious tensions of the time. Domestically Noah was active as well, holding, among other posts, the position of sheriff of New York, and delivering prominent addresses that espoused religious tolerance, workers' rights, and an element of progressivism, as seen, for example, in his *Oration Delivered by Appointment Before Tammany Society . . . to Celebrate the 41st Anniversary of American Independence* (1817).

As a creator of dramatic literature, Noah did much to bolster the concept of a unique American literary identity. He wrote a number of plays dealing with the Revolutionary War, such as *Marion, or the Hero of Lake George* (1821), *Oh Yes!, or, the New Constitution* (1822), and *The Siege of Yorktown* (1824), whose first production was notable with Lafayette in the audience. Noah's most popular play, *She Would Be a Soldier. . . ,* was performed over 80 times by 1868. In the play Noah portrays an "Indian Chief" who, after his capture by the Americans, says: "Think you I would be your enemy unless urged by powerful wrongs? No, white man, no! the Great Spirit whom we worship, is also the God whom you adore." For the era, Noah demonstrates a surprising sensitivity toward gender and cultural issues, while staying close to historical events; however, his lasting effects on the Jewish-American literary tradition are difficult to see, given that by the end of the 19th century his style of historical melodrama was no longer in vogue.

It can be argued that Noah's lasting influence has been more cultural and historical than literary. He promulgated an American form of Zionism, and in his *Thanksgiving Day Address* he spoke of the liberalizing effect of social revolution on the fate of Jews, noting that the millions of Christians involved in social change and upheaval "are gradually unloosing the chains of a religious prejudice against us, and feel a deeper interest in our fate and final advent." Of his grand scheme to bring worldwide Jewry to an island in the Niagara River, nothing remains except some relics in a museum.

Bibliography

Bartholomew, Summer Sarah. "Dramatizing American Identity: the Plays of Mordecai Manuel Noah, 1808–1822." A.B. Thesis, Harvard University, 1999.

Weingrad, Michael. "Messiah, American Style: Mordecai Manuel Noah and the American Refugee." *AJS Review* 31, no. 1 (April 2007): 75–108.

—**Brian Adler**

Odets, Clifford (1906–1963)

Clifford Odets's reputation reached its apex in 1930s America. Many of Odets's critics maintain that he failed to fulfill his early promise, but his place in the history of theater and film is nevertheless one of indisputable significance, particularly as regards the Jewish-American experience. As Michael J. Mendelsohn writes in the introduction to *Clifford Odets: Humane Dramatist,* "His body of work constituted the first extended statement in depth about the Jewish experience in America generally" (xiii).

Odets was born in Philadelphia on July 18, 1906, to immigrant parents. His mother was Austrian and his father was Russian; the surname Odets was a shortened form of the Russian surname Gorodetsky, "urban man." As some biographers have pointed out, this alteration seems fitting for a man who would eventually choose to draw attention to the plight of the workers in his plays.

Odets was the first of three children and the only son. After dropping out of high school, he did odd jobs in theater and radio for the next decade, even claiming to be the first disc jockey. He took up with the independent theater company Theatre Guild and attempted to improve his acting skills. Although he was never renowned for his onstage presence, Odets had become involved with the Theatre Guild at a time when theater in America was undergoing an important change.

The focus was shifting from a preoccupation with the stage as a place for artificial amusements to a place for expressing matters of social conscience. Ordinary people and the conflicts at work in their lives became the focus of 1920s and 1930s theater, and the Theatre Guild was one of the best-known and most influential theater companies to embrace this approach. Especially as the Great Depression worsened, playwrights and theater companies responded with realistic drama that showcased the failures of capitalism and embraced the proletariat.

In 1931 Odets cofounded the Group Theater in New York with other Theatre Guild members who shared his leftist political views. It was during the early years of the Group Theater that Odets first began work on *Awake and Sing!* while continuing to take on bit parts as an actor. Although the Group Theater was unwilling to risk performing *Awake and Sing!* initially since Odets was an unknown, another play Odets had written, *WAITING FOR LEFTY,* won a New York playwriting contest and was soon being performed regularly. Odets and *Waiting for Lefty* became the talk of the town, and then of the nation and the world, setting the stage for *Awake and Sing!* and his future works.

Waiting for Lefty is based on the events of a cab strike in New York City in 1934. It is an apt reflection of the times as the working class of America was becoming increasingly disenfranchised and discontented. Odets also briefly joined the American Communist Party in 1934, which would come back to haunt him years later in 1953, when he was investigated by Senator Joseph McCarthy and the House Un-American Activities Committee. Odets had become a screenwriter in Hollywood by this time. He argued that he was not a Communist; his work had merely been based on his sympathy for the working classes. Ultimately, unlike many of his peers in Hollywood, Odets was not blacklisted and continued to work as a screenwriter and director.

During the 1940s Odets became a painter, producing upwards of 600 paintings during the years 1945–57. He fathered two children with Bette Grayson Odets, whom he later divorced. While collaborating on a musical version of *Golden Boy* that would appear on Broadway the following year, Odets died of cancer on August 14, 1963.

In the preface to a collection of his first six plays, Odets wrote "My belief . . . is that the plays will say whatever is to be said; most of them have bones in them and will stand up unsupported" (Odets vii). But the fact that Odets wanted the plays to speak for themselves did not preclude many others from speaking about them. In a 1938 issue of *Time* magazine, the reviewer wrote: "The reason Odets has gained and held a public that, by and large, does not share his Leftish ideas is obviously not the ideas themselves but his rich, compassionate, angry feeling for people, his tremendous dramatic punch, his dialogue, bracing as ozone. In every Odets play, regardless of its theme or its worth, at least once or twice during the evening every spectator feels that a fire hose has been turned on his body, that a fist has connected with his chin."

Odets's work continues to be popular among modern audiences. *Awake and Sing!* was most recently revived on Broadway in 2006, and although it originally opened to mixed reviews in 1935, the play is generally considered his best work. *Awake and Sing!* takes place during the depression. It chronicles the Bergers, a Jewish family living in the Bronx, New York. The piece masterfully encapsulates the hardships experienced by immigrant families during the Depression, in contrast to the perceived American dream. The continuing popularity of *Awake and Sing!* may well have to do with the fact that the play presents an enduring perspective of the immigrant experience in America.

Odets's other works for the stage include *Till the Day I Die, Paradise Lost, Golden Boy, Night Music,* and *Clash by Night.* The playwright also spent many years in Hollywood writing film scripts such as *Sweet Smell of Success, The General Died at Dawn, None but the Lonely Heart* (which he directed), and *The Big Knife.*

Some of Odets's critics, while acknowledging him as the seminal playwright of the 1930s, note in his work an inability to adapt to post-depression changes in America. But others maintain that Odets's importance is inherent in the fact that he made popular, if he did not invent, the social realism that still dominates today's theater. In any case, Odets's work has had an undeniable formative impact on American Jewish playwrights. In *Awake and Sing!* as in Odets's other plays, the Jewish-American characters attempt to reconcile a traditional way of life with the novelty and opportunity of a new homeland. Other themes prevalent in Odets's work include the consequences of poverty, the empowerment of the working class, and concerns of family well-being versus self-realization.

After seeing the 1992 revival of *Awake and Sing!,* John Lahr wrote in the *New Yorker* that Odets's plays "despite their ideological full dress, are a quirky blend of Jewish pessimism and a very American desire to shine . . . The peculiar paradox of 'Awake and Sing' . . . is that it celebrates both the dream and the sure knowledge that a dream is something you wake up from" (Lahr 122). As Odets himself said, "I will reveal America to itself by revealing myself to myself." He continues to do so today as his plays are revived around the world.

Bibliography

Brenman-Gibson, Margaret. *Clifford Odets: American Playwright: the Years from 1906–1940.* New York: Atheneum, 1981.

Lahr, John. "Waiting for Odets." *The New Yorker,* 16 October 1992.

Mendelsohn, Michael. *Clifford Odets: Humane Dramatist.* DeLand, Fla.: Everett/Edwards, 1969.

Schiff, Ellen. "Clifford Odets, Awake and Sing, and the Dawn of the American Jewish Theatre." Available online. URL: http://www2.jewishculture.org/programs/350/icons/schiff/. Accessed on November 12, 2006.

Weales, Gerald. *Odets the Playwright.* London and New York: Methuen, 1985.

—**Brooklyn Bunker Evans**

Olsen, Tillie Lerner (1912–2007)

Uncertainty, one of writer Tillie Olsen's major themes, surrounds her place and date of birth on the American Great Plains. Born in Wahoo, Omaha, or Mead, Nebraska, in 1912 or 1913 (no birth certificate survives) to politically active Jewish immigrant parents who had fled czarist Russia following the 1905 revolution, Tillie Lerner was the second of six children. Her father, Samuel, toiled to support his family in a series of farmhand and packinghouse jobs, while her mother, Ida, struggled to raise the children. Atheists and socialists, the couple came to view the United States both as a place of promise and as a country of decided socioeconomic division. A tenuous upbringing in their shadow would become the inspiration for Olsen's fictional subjects: intergenerational families (in particular mothers and daughters) who confront poverty and deprivation in their search for meaningful accomplishment. Though during the course of a career spanning nearly eight decades she published only a handful of short stories, one novel, a book of essays and speeches, and a few poems, Olsen has earned regard as a feminist writer who in intimately rendered portraits of human anguish chronicles both working-class struggles and limitations on the productivity of women.

The need for resiliency as well as the influence of radical politics during her early years provided rich material for Olsen's literary endeavors. Reared in Omaha, as a child she had jobs caring for her siblings and shelling peanuts after school. A love of learning took hold in Tillie, who became a voracious reader. During her teens she joined both the Young People's Socialist League and the Young Communist League. Leaving Omaha Central High School in the 11th grade to earn a living, over the next several decades she held a string of low-wage jobs, including factory worker, waitress, and secretary. By age 18, she had been arrested and jailed for trying to organize a workers' strike in Kansas City, Missouri. Olsen would come to inscribe in the rhythms and dialogue of her fiction the cadences of a multiethnic workforce, which included blacks and Yiddish speakers.

The nascent author returned to Omaha, next relocating to Faribault, Minnesota, where in 1932 she gave birth to the first of four daughters, Karla, whose paternity Olsen refuses to disclose. The same year, she began writing *Yonnondio: From the Thirties* (1974), which tells the tale of a Midwestern family, the Holbrooks, exploited by the mining, farming, and meatpacking industries. The author's own family obligations forced her to abandon the project, and the novel was not published in its entirety for another 42 years. Olsen's intermittently thwarted ambition would incite her influential view regarding women writers who led what she called "the triple life" of mother-wife-worker, a categorization that over time she developed in a series of essays and talks, eventually collected in *Silences* (1978). Dreams unrealized, along with the silencing of female and other marginalized voices, became standard motifs in her fiction as well.

By 1933 Olsen had landed in California, moving peripatetically until permanently settling in San Francisco, where her activism continued. She was imprisoned in connection with the San Francisco Maritime Strike of 1934, and while jailed that July, "The Iron Throat," a portion of the first chapter of *Yonnondio,* appeared in *Partisan Review.* She published accounts of her arrest and legal proceedings the following month in *New Republic.* Two years later she met and began living with fellow activist Jack Olsen. Marrying in 1943, they had three daughters, Julie, Katherine Jo, and Laurie, born between 1938 and 1948.

Hampered by family responsibilities, activism, and work, Olsen still managed during her forties to enroll in a writing class at San Francisco State

University, in which she drafted her much anthologized "I Stand Here Ironing" (1956), as well as "Hey Sailor, What Ship?" (1953 and 1955). This work in progress earned her a Stegner Fellowship in creative writing at Stanford University, where she completed it and also wrote "O Yes" (1956–57). Additionally, she began the O. Henry–award winning novella "TELL ME A RIDDLE" (1961), first published in *New World Writing* and deemed by critics an "instant classic." Collected in Olsen's most celebrated work to date, *Tell Me a Riddle* (1961), these four stories were originally intended as sections of a novel. Following the extended family of David and Eva of "Tell Me a Riddle" over three generations, they are notable for experiments in form, including fragmented sequences, flashbacks, and extended monologues. Olsen's Jewish socialist background, particularly her firsthand knowledge of injustice, is reflected in the collection as a whole, especially in the character of Eva, who is haunted by the Russian Revolution and the Holocaust. Hospitalized, Eva learns her name appears on the inpatient "Jewish list," but she insists: "Race, human; Religion none."

The burden of "discontinuity," as Olsen herself terms the accumulated weight of habitual disruptions to her writing life, resonates in the nearly 10 years that elapsed before she published another story, "Requa" (1970), in the *Iowa Review,* reprinted in *The Best American Stories of 1971.* Reestablishing the author's themes, "Requa" (the Native-American name of the protagonist's North Pacific town) follows the plight of 14-year-old Stevie, recovering from the death of his mother. During those 10 years since the publication of "Tell Me a Riddle," Olsen's artistic acclaim had grown. Beginning in 1969, over the next decade she held a string of prestigious writing residencies and visiting professorships, including at Amherst College, Stanford, the MacDowell Colony, and Massachusetts Institute of Technology. She also published *Silences* and was awarded a Guggenheim fellowship.

Olsen is likewise the recipient of National Endowment for the Arts fellowships and five honorary degrees from various colleges and universities. In 1988, the year before the death of her husband, Jack, the Modern Language Association convened a special session based on *Silences.* But with "Tell Me a Riddle" assured a place in the canon of American literature, Tillie Olsen's words will continue to champion the lives of the dispossessed for generations to come.

Bibliography
Frye, Joanne S. *Tillie Olsen: A Study of the Short Fiction.* New York: Twayne, 1995.
Pearlman, Mickey, and Abby H. P. Werlock. *Tillie Olsen.* Boston: Twayne, 1991.
—Pauline Uchmanowicz

Once upon a Droshky
Jerome Charyn (1964)
Once upon a Droshky takes place in the nostalgic setting of Charyn's childhood neighborhood in the Bronx. Nostalgia for past Yiddish-American culture is represented by the two main sites of action: Schimmel's cafeteria and the Yiddish theater, both of which are in decline. In these declining sites, there is a conflict between old and new, past and present. The buildings cannot withstand the wear and tear that time creates, just as the Yiddish-American culture cannot survive the rising generation's antihumanist business ethic. Charyn demonstrates this more forcefully with the image of the decaying apartment building that is going to be torn down so that luxury apartments can be built. Such dilapidated buildings are utilized to suggest the inevitability of modernization, which also inevitably dominates minority cultures that attempt to retain their colloquial characteristics.

Language is another element in Charyn's novel that has both nostalgic and thematic value. The first-person narrator and protagonist, Yankel Rabinowitz, speaks distinctly Yiddish-American. This regional use of language, like Twain's *Huckleberry Finn,* personalizes Yankel's character while mediating between the humorous and the darker sides of life. His language also allows for a biting critique of his surrounding social conditions (whether, like Huck Finn, he is completely aware of them or not).

Yankel's first-person narration sets up one of Charyn's oft-used themes: the brilliance behind the fool or antihero. Yankel, an aging minor actor, lives to break moral codes while valuing the Yiddish-American cultural codes of the Lower East Side. His immoral traits (such as dishonesty and womanizing) and biting humor make Yankel the fool an unlikely hero, but his compassion for his fellow tenants elevate Yankel to the status of antihero. He begins a quest to stop his apartment building from being torn down and his friends from getting thrown into the street. His quest is not simply to save an old building—it is to retain a dying past that is being killed by the merciless present.

This conflict between past and present is most dramatically seen in the conflict between father, Yankel, and son, Irving. Irving represents the present and all of its antihumanist qualities. Yankel, who believes his son's profession as a lawyer will save his apartment building, discovers that his son has sold out and is backing the building's destruction. This is the ultimate blow for Yankel, who depends so heavily on cultural and relational ties, believing that the humanist qualities in each will win out over the antihumanist.

Charyn's exploration of the father-son conflict is a familiar theme of many Jewish novels, but the point of view is most often the son's. This reversal of narrators further demonstrates the conflict between past and present by emphasizing the decay of the old and its replacement by the new. Thus even with *Once upon a Droshky*'s humorous moments, the major theme of past versus present creates a sense of despair that at once celebrates Yiddish-American culture and mourns its decline.

Jerome Charyn's first novel, *Once upon a Droshky*, received several scathing reviews in the United States, although as Charyn became a more prolific writer, his popularity in Europe (particularly France) grew. Despite the novel's poor reviews, *Once upon a Droshky* marked Charyn (who was only 26 when the novel was published) as a major emerging writer. His use of minor characters and caricatures and mock heroics and the father-son relationship have led many to compare his writing to Charles Dickens. Of course,

with these similarities to Dickens, differences also abound, such as the setting, language, and theme of the fool and antihero.

Bibliography
Boroff, David. "Stranded on Second Avenue." Review of *Once upon a Droshky. Saturday Review* (February 29, 1964), 34.
Guerard, Albert J. "Charyn's Azazian Prose." *Review of Contemporary Fiction* 12, no. 2 (Summer 1992): 126–142.
Solotaroff, Theodore. "Jewish Camp." Review of *Once upon a Droshky, Commentary* (March 1964), 76–78. Rpt. in *The Red Hot Vacuum and Other Pieces on the Writing of the Sixties*. Edited by Theodore Solotaroff. New York: Atheneum, 1970.
Woolf, Michael. "Charyn in the 1960s: Among the Jews." *Review of Contemporary Fiction* 12, no. 2 (Summer 1992): 143–151.

—Rachel Jeppsen

Osherow, Jacqueline (1956–)

Jacqueline Osherow was raised in an Orthodox Jewish family in Philadelphia, where she developed a love for language. As a youngster she attended the family synagogue, listened to ancient Hebrew, loved singing (particularly Psalms), and became well versed in Hebrew and Jewish religious traditions. She grew up hearing her two sets of immigrant grandparents telling stories in Yiddish, and later absorbed the stories of her Yiddish-speaking father-in-law, a survivor of Auschwitz-Birkenau death camps. This early immersion in language was further developed through formal academic training. As an undergraduate at Radcliffe College, she studied English and American poetry with Robert Lowell and Robert Fitzgerald. Her literary studies continued at Harvard University, where she attended as a Fiske scholar, and at Trinity College, Cambridge, from 1978 to 1979. She completed her studies at Princeton University in 1990 when she received a Ph.D. Osherow's fluency in high culture, language, and poetry, coupled with her knowledge of ancient and contemporary traditions of Judaism, are what shape her poetry. Since she is a now a specialist in Israeli culture, politics, and the Holocaust, this too informs her subject matter. In poems unusually dense in Jewish allusions, she describes how difficult it is to be Jew, a woman, a poet, and a child of the post-Holocaust era. Osherow's recurring subject is the Holocaust, and these poems usually take the form of conversations with survivors. The best of these, "Conversations with Survivors," explains why.

Osherow's poetry is always distinguished by its tightly worked, complex metrics and its brilliant mastery of a wide range of formal verse forms. She writes in sonnets, blank verse narratives, psalms, *ghazals* (an intricately rhyming Persian form), villanelles (19 lines in five tercets and a rhyming couplet), terza rima (the elaborate three-lined rhyming stanzas derived from Dante), and an almost syncopated conversational style. Her meditative works comprise a medley of lengthy reflective passages, spontaneous conversations, ironic interludes, down-to-earth observations, and fascinating digressions. Fortunately, her preference for formalism is relieved in her interposition of lively vernacular aesthetics and conversations. This is difficult poetry, rich in references to learned culture, science, mathematics, astronomy, and popular culture. Whether Osherow writes of foreign landscapes, Israeli deserts, biblical figures, or Renaissance art in Italy, it all eventually becomes the occasion of personal religious ruminations ranging across all emotional extremes.

Jacqueline Osherow has currently published five books of poetry: *Looking for Angels in New York* (1988), *Conversations with Survivors: Poems* (1994), *With a Moon in Transit* (1996), *Dead Men's Praise* (1999), and *The Hoopoe's Crown* (2005). *Dead Men's Praise* (1999) established her as one of the leading poets of her generation. These poems, she explains, are for those who never got to sing at all, the unborn children of the Holocaust. The generations of those who perished are "around somewhere singing hallelujah," but the unborn will never get to hear it or sing it. To suggest the sheer scale of the Holocaust, she often resorts to the scientific language of genetics and references to her Yiddish literary heritage. She confesses that she

is hesitant about her grasp of Yiddish but wants to demonstrate her respect for it. When she refers to Yiddish writers like Perets Markish and Yakov Glatstein, it is to honor their mastery of it and all the lost Yiddish-speaking peoples consumed by the Holocaust. Perets Markish was a Russian-born Yiddish poet who won the Lenin Prize in 1939, only to be murdered in Moscow's Lubyanka prison in 1952 by the Stalinist regime. Yakov Glatstein was a Holocaust survivor and Yiddish poet who first coined the Psalmist's line "Dead Men Don't Praise God." Osherow credits Glatstein's use of the line, and then references Psalm 115 to explain the inspiration for her title poem. In this four-part volume of poems, the most powerful section, "Scattered Psalms," offers a feminist midrash, or commentary, in the manner of many other contemporary Jewish women writers. Later she tries to imagine Yakov Glatstein's sense of emotional betrayal when, after having published his Holocaust experiences as early as 1946, he was totally ignored. She wonders if he thought that all holy praise and psalm singing had ended with the events of the Holocaust, thus questioning whether faith was even possible for those in the death camps. In "Scattered Psalm V" she wonders if her father-in-law ever heard a psalm sung in Auschwitz-Birkenau, and casts doubt on the religious assertion that in the camps one "never saw a righteous man forsaken." In a tribute to the women of the Holocaust, she places references to David with his sling alongside the modern account of the heroic girlfriend of a Vilna partisan who spectacularly disabled a Nazi train full of munitions with a mere ball of yarn and nails. In one of the last of the "Scattered Psalms," she reveals her extensive knowledge of modern astronomy and places her religious and scientific speculations about celestial bodies alongside those of King David. "Space Psalm" combines traditional psalm structure with her own hallelujah's in contemporary idiom. In the poems arising from her art tour of Italy, she expresses deep anger at the cruelty and indifference of Europeans, their anti-Semitic, blood-soaked continent, and their Renaissance paintings revealing anti-Semitic iconography along with persistent traces of Judaic symbols.

The poems on Jewish cemeteries are followed by explanations of life's marvels to a daughter, along with short meditations on nature, birds, and planets. Among these poems are confessional pieces, self-talking, formal lamentations, and much soul-searching. This volume helped established her reputation as a leading poet in the contemporary Jewish literary revival.

The Hoopoe's Crown (2005), her fifth book, is a travelogue of the Holy Land that takes the form of a spiritual journey. It is studded with poems about her personal search for grace, absolution, and faith. She uses mathematical metaphors for expressing a tentative hope in infinite possibility. The poems in this volume are rich in religious language, Judaic allusions, celebration, joy, humorous observation, and spiritual questioning. Her hope of a new world is always tempered by her anguished awareness of the sheer magnitude of human suffering and helplessness. At the core of the poems about Israel she places images of Solomon, wisdom, mothering, and the riddle to suggest the nature of the human acquisition of wisdom. Poems about visiting the Wailing Wall and poems exploring biblical mysteries often serve as the occasion for personal meditations on the difficulty of being a modern Jewish woman under the weight of Jewish tradition. These discursive meditations, essay-style discourses, travel narratives, and lively vernacular conversations are often set in Israeli desert landscape settings that obviously provoke the poet to examine such matters as the nature of spiritual apprehension, major religious mysteries, and the little daily graces. Perhaps the finest poem in this collection is "Slim Fantasia on a Few Words from Hosea."

Jacqueline Osherow is a poet whose imagination has been forged in the deserts and texts of early Judaism. Not surprisingly, it is the deserts of modern Israel, and the deserts surrounding her home in northern Utah, that provide her with a rich source of natural metaphors in which to conduct her spiritual meditations. Her numerous awards include the Guggenheim fellowship, the National Endowment for the Arts fellowship, the Ingram Merrill Foundation fellowship, the Witter Byner Prize from the American Academy and Institute of Arts and Letters, and the Poetry Society of America prize. She currently teaches Hebrew studies, Israeli studies, poetry, and creative writing at the University of Utah, where she is the Distinguished Professor of English.

Bibliography

Maxwell, Glyn. *Times Literary Supplement* Book Review, 31 May 1991, 12.

Schneider, Steven. Review of *Dead Men's Praise*, *Women in Judaism: A Multidisciplinary Journal* 2, no. 2 (Spring 2001).

—Gloria L. Cronin

Ozick, Cynthia (1928–)

Cynthia Ozick was born in New York City on April 17, 1928, to William and Shiphra Regelson Ozick. Her father was the proprietor of the Park View Pharmacy in the Bronx. She graduated Phi Beta Kappa from New York University in 1949 and received a master's degree from Ohio State University in 1950. She describes her college years as "besotted with the religion of Literature," and particularly with Henry James. In 1952 she married a lawyer, Bernard Hallote; they have one daughter.

After college she devoted seven years to a lengthy philosophical novel she eventually abandoned. While writing it, she worked as an advertising copywriter at Filene's department store in Boston. Ozick also composed poetry, primarily formal work on religious topics, which appeared in many literary journals. Her translations of Yiddish poetry can be found in *A Treasury of Yiddish Poetry*, edited by Irving Howe and Eliezer Greenburg (1969). Fluent in Yiddish from childhood, she also studied Hebrew while in college. During her years of apprenticeship, Ozick began her intensive reading of Judaic literature, history, and philosophy. By turning to the oldest Judaic religious sources for her inspiration, Ozick has blazed a trail for other Jewish-American writers to follow.

Ozick's works treat ethnic, religious, and language issues unique to the Jewish artist, and her writing displays an overt reverence for her heritage. Her concern with the creation of a distinctly Jewish literature led to her promotion of "new Yiddish," a language that would be comprehensible to English speakers while preserving the inflections and tone of the waning Yiddish tongue. In general, critics feel that characterization and emotive qualities are Ozick's weak points, while words and ideas are her strengths. Linguistic style and thematic discourse occasionally overpower plot and characterization.

Ozick's critical reputation was established with the publication of *Art & Ardor, Metaphor & Memory,* and other essay collections. She is now well known and highly respected in the critical community. She frequently contributes book reviews, short stories, and poetry to various literary journals. Since the publication of *Trust,* Ozick has received critical acclaim for her attention to language and her thought-provoking arguments about Jewish-American culture. Ozick's stories deal with ideas steeped in Judaic law and history. They are difficult, but only in that they have no fluff. Every word counts, and no image or emotion is wasted. Her works wrestle with theological and philosophical issues—Edmund White wrote in a *New York Times Book Review* appraisal that "Idolatry is Cynthia Ozick's great theme," and other critics have agreed.

She published her first novel, *Trust,* in 1966. Written over six years, each sentence is near perfect; she crafts each paragraph as though it were a poem. But for all its polish, the novel never comes alive; her language is so opaque as to obscures her narrative and dramatic capabilities. The plot begins with the nameless narrator's decision to seek out her father. Her mother, Allegra, is a wealthy, selfish, ambitious woman. Neither her mother's first husband and current lawyer, William, nor her second husband, Enoch, is the narrator's father. Of all the characters, Enoch alone, the only Jew, undergoes a transformation. Endlessly adaptable to circumstance, he embodies the survivor, the mythical Jew. The narrator meets her father, Nicolas Tilbeck, at Duneacres, Allegra's ruined American island estate. While Enoch sides with the Judaic law, Nicholas is a pagan and drifter, Enoch's antithesis. As she watches Tilbeck seduce a guest's fiancée, the narrator notes that she has witnessed the style of her own conception. She has discovered everything she wanted to know, yet remains unchanged by the knowledge. In *Trust,* the intellectual concerns are declaimed in monologues or lengthily debated in dialogue but not fully dramatized or integrated into the novel as a whole. In form, though not in theme, *Trust* is unlike anything else Ozick has published.

Her first set of shorter fiction, *The PAGAN RABBI AND OTHER STORIES* (1971), received high praise when published. The themes developed in *Trust* have been refined. "The Pagan Rabbi" is the story of Rabbi Isaac Kornfield, who forsakes the law and is seduced by nature. In a supernatural episode, Ozick describes his ravishment by the dryad inhabiting the oak from which he ultimately hangs himself. The rabbi's soul, which revels in the law, wars with his earthly desires for natural beauty, and the disciple of Moses succumbs to the charms of nature. While the narrator pities Rabbi Kornfield, Ozick's stance is clearly in favor of living the law. "Envy; or Yiddish in America" is more secular. Edelshtein, a Yiddish poet who cannot find an English translator for his poetry, is consumed by envy of his colleague Ostrover, a famous Yiddish storyteller. Edelshtein's lust for fame is described as another form of idolatry. "Virility" is the story of a mediocre poet who suddenly gains fame when he publishes successive volumes of poetry, each entitled "Virility." His reputation takes a dive when he admits that the poetry is not his own, but was written by an elderly woman, his Tante Rivka. His idolatrous worship of fame brings him no lasting reward. *The Pagan Rabbi and Other Stories* won the B'nai Brith Jewish Heritage Award (1971), the Edward Lewis Wallant Memorial Award (1972), and the Jewish Book Council Award for Fiction (1972).

Her next collection of short fiction, also a winner of the Jewish Book Council Award, *Bloodshed and Three Novellas,* is as concerned with the struggle between the holy and the profane as her earlier works. "Usurpation," a story against story writing, won first prize in the O. Henry short story awards (1975). In the title story, Bleilip, an American Jew visiting a community built by Holocaust survivors finds he cannot escape his Jewish identity and the moral burden of the Holocaust. In contrast, "An Education" has no overtly Jewish theme, but it concerns worship. Una idolizes a young couple and makes herself their slave. Her education begins when she can smash her idols and free herself from bondage. Each story in this collection reiterates one of Ozick's major themes.

Levitation: Five Fictions (1982) was Ozick's next publication. The title story concerns a couple, both second-rate writers, who invite literary giants to a dinner party, but the only guests of honor who arrive are a friend from the seminary and a Holocaust refugee. As the refugee describes his experiences to the group, his voice casts a literal spell on his audience, and the Jews begin to ascend into the air as the others remain below. Lucy, the convert wife, chooses not to complete her conversion by rising with them. Only Jews, the chosen people, will ascend, and conversion cannot cross the gulf of Jewish history. In "Puttermesser: Her Work History, Her Ancestry, Her Afterlife," she relates the saga of Ruth Puttermesser, a serious but dreamy spinster laboring as a civil servant in New York City. In "Puttermesser and Xantippe," Ruth creates a female golem who makes her mayor of New York. As mayor, she magically solves the problems of crime, pollution, and corruption, but when the golem wreaks havoc on the city, Puttermesser must destroy her creation. She loses her position and her golem daughter. Puttermesser usurped the role of God by competing with him in creation; Ozick explores how artists usurp God's role when they create a work of fiction.

In 1989 Ozick published *The Shawl*, which brings together two of her finest short stories, "The Shawl" and "Rosa."

Though best known for these collections of short stories and novellas, Ozick has written three novels in addition to *Trust*. *The Cannibal Galaxy* (1983), wherein she considers the hubris of those who dare rival God by fashioning idols, was well received. It is the tightly constructed story of Joseph Brill and Hester Lilt, and their need to devour others to support their own vanity. In *The Messiah of Stockholm* (1987), she attempts to reconcile her need to create fiction with her desire to remain a follower of Jewish tradition. The story involves Lars Andemening, who has dedicated himself to a search for his supposed father's lost manuscript because he is wholly devoted to literary texts. In her most recent novel, *Heir to the Glimmering World* (2004), Ozick mixes themes of faith, identity, and art in a romantic novel set in New York of the 1930s.

Ozick's 1997 novel, *The Puttermesser Papers*, perhaps her best-known work, is a glorious and brilliant mix of Jewish legend and postmodernism. The story, actually a collection of five vignettes, the first of which appeared in 1982, follows the life of Ruth Puttermesser, a New York City attorney, highly competitive and "something of a feminist." Puttermesser's parents, who live in Florida, urge her to marry, but she has other interests: she studies Hebrew, seeks to rescue Russian Jews, and idolizes George Eliot. By turns a retelling of *Paradise Lost* and a midrash (commentary) on the limits of creativity, Ozick's novel is a stunning example of the relationship between humor and sorrow that brings to mind the work of both Saul Bellow and Isaac Bashevis Singer as it portrays the individual and her attempt to wrest meaning from the chaos of life. Readers are introduced to the 34-year-old lawyer in the novel's first chapter, "Puttermesser: Her Work History, Her Ancestry, Her Afterlife." Here the reader learns the heroine, after resigning from the WASP Wall Street law firm whose all-male staff—which includes three Jews—has no use for her, goes to work for New York City's Department of Receipts and Disbursements. In chapter two "Puttermesser and Xanthippe," Ozick presents her heroine as the first female maker of a golem (a creature made of earth and animated by reciting a special formula). "Putermesser Paired" relates the affair of the now fiftyish heroine with a copy artist who exploits and abandons her. "Puttermesser and the Muscovite Cousin" is a satire on the naïveté of American Jews and the competition between liberal and conservative points of view as represented by the magazines *Tikkun* (called *Shekhina* in the story) and *Commentary*

(*Motherwit*). Puttermesser, now in her sixties, is murdered and raped in the novel's final section "Puttermesser in Paradise."

The most memorable of the sections is titled "Puttermesser and Xanthippe," in which the protagonist makes a golem that she names after Socrates's wife. Although Jewish folklore abounds with tales of the golem, which have been incorporated by contemporary novelists (MICHAEL CHABON's The AMAZING ADVENTURES OF KAVALIER & CLAY, THANE ROSENBAUM's The GOLEMS OF GOTHAM, among others), Puttermesser's golem serves alternately as her daughter and as the being responsible for the protagonist's becoming mayor of New York City, replacing Malachi Mavet (Angel of Death). Puttermesser, following Xanthippe's plan, "resuscitates" the city. However, the golem follows the example of its mythic ancestors and runs amok, compelling Puttermesser to destroy the creature.

The Puttermesser Papers received glowing reviews. Critics from a variety of prestigious publications hailed the author and the work. Reviews appeared in the *New York Times, National Review,* and *Jewish Reader,* among others. While attention was paid to the various themes Ozick raises in the novel, much of the focus was on the golem. Ozick, responding to an interviewer's query about why contemporary Jewish writers are attracted to the figure of the golem, observed: "I suppose imaginative writers will always be drawn to the notion of a manmade creature: after all, every novel is concerned with the theory of the Golem. What else is an invented character?"

In her most recent novel, *Heir to the Glimmering World* (2004), Ozick mixes themes of faith, identity, and art in a romantic novel set in New York of the 1930s. Many scholars have focused their criticism on one of Ozick's major recurring themes: the contradiction between art, or fiction writing, and obeying Jewish law, which forbids the creation of idols. Again and again in the novel and the fiction that follows, characters are torn between the claims of opposing religions. One is pagan, either the worship of nature or the idolatrous pursuit of art, while the other is Judaism, sacred truth. Though in the end Ozick sides with the rabbis in condemning idolatry, part of her worries about possible idolatry is her creation of fiction. This theme, says Eve Ottenburg in her *New York Times Magazine* profile on Ozick, has its deepest impact in a Jewish context. Ozick's characters suffer and struggle in the process of finding out what it means, culturally and religiously, to be Jewish.

Bibliography

Cohen, Sarah Blacher. *Cynthia Ozick's Comic Art: From Levity to Liturgy.* Bloomington: Indiana University Press, 1994.

———. "The Jewish Literary Comediennes." *Comic Relief: Humor in Contemporary American Literature* (1978): 172–186. Rpt. in *Contemporary Literary Criticism,* edited by Jean C. Stine. Detroit: Gale, 1985.

———. "The Fiction Writer-Essayist: Ozick's *Metaphor & Memory.*" *Judaism Quarterly Journal* 39, no. 3 (1990): 276–281. Rpt. in *Contemporary Literary Criticism,* edited by Janet Witalec. Detroit: Gale, 2002.

"Cynthia Ozick." In *Dictionary of Literary Biography,* edited by Daniel Walden. Detroit: Gale, 1984.

Ozick, Cynthia. Interview by Philip Graubart. *The Jewish Reader.* February 2002.

—**Veronica Goosey and Alan L. Berger**

P

The Pagan Rabbi and Other Stories
Cynthia Ozick (1971)

The Pagan Rabbi is a sensitively wrought collection of short stories in which CYNTHIA OZICK illumines her major literary, historical, and religious concerns. She explores the legacy of the Holocaust, the defining difference between Judaism with its concern for history and paganism, which relies on the world of nature, and the role of illusion and deception in human existence. Taken together, the six stories in this collection make up Ozick's midrash (commentary) on the meaning of post-Holocaust life and the danger posed to Jews by American culture. This danger consists in the opposition between Judaism, which is dedicated to memory, and America, which seems afflicted by forgetting. Edelshtein, the protagonist of *Envy; or Yiddish in America,* sarcastically refers to America's Jews as *Amerikaner-geboren;* those born in America do not feel the sting of history on their flesh.

The title story treats the fate of Rabbi Isaac Kornfeld, "a man of piety and brains," who, abandoning his faith and succumbing to the lure of nature, ends by hanging himself with his tallis [prayer shawl] from a tree in a public park. Sheindel, his wife, was born in a concentration camp and survived when, at the last moment, the current to the electric fence was cut. Now a widow with seven daughters, she is visited by Isaac's unnamed friend, a bookseller who intended to marry her.

Poring over the deceased's notebook, written in Greek, Hebrew, and English, the friend discovers the words "Great Pan Lives." Further, the late rabbi's ruminations deal with two categories of soul: humans are "cursed with the indwelling" type, whereas the soul of nature is "free." Isaac Kornfeld couples with Iripomonoeia, a tree-dwelling dryad.

Ozick embodies the distinction between nature and history in opposing the dryad to Rabbi Kornfeld's immortal soul. The dryad rightly observes that the rabbi does not even know his true soul, which, in the form of an old man with matted beard and back "half bent over under the burden of a dusty old" book-laden bag, "conjures" against the dryad—denying multiplicity and spiting Lord Pan. Faced with the stark contrast between two irreconcilable worldviews, Kornfeld is doomed. Although the rabbi's friend calls him an astonishing man, Sheindel responds that her late husband was not what the friend believed him to be. Rather, his reputation was "an illusion." Despite his apparent wisdom and abundant scholarship, the rabbi was pagan at heart. Jewish identity requires unflinching commitment.

Two of the stories in this collection, "Envy; or, Yiddish in America," and "The Suitcase," deal directly with the legacy of the Holocaust. "Envy," which the literary critic Edward Alexander terms "a small masterpiece," is both an elegy for the language of the majority of those martyred in the

Holocaust and a veiled critique of the work of I. B. Singer. Unlike Etruscan or Linear B, whose death "was by mystery not gas," Yiddish was "murdered." The language is inextricably bound to Jewish memory. Edelshtein, the tale's protagonist, attests that "whoever forgets Yiddish courts amnesia of history." Further, he is contemptuous of "writers of Jewish extraction" whose works were praised but who knew nothing.

"Envy" argues that the cultivation of Yiddish is the proper way to memorialize the victims of the Holocaust and to ensure Jewish survival. In Edelshtein's words: "In Talmud if you save a single life it's as if you saved the world. And if you save a language? Worlds maybe. Galaxies. The whole universe." This makes Edelshtein's fruitless and comic search for a translator even more poignant. In contrast to the widely translated, financially successful, and highly popular Yankel Ostrover (the fictional representation of I. B. Singer), Edelshetin labors in obscurity, his Yiddish poems unknown to an American audience. Ozick later modified her insistence on the primacy of Yiddish in a subsequent essay "America: Toward Yavneh," which argued that English is the new Yiddish and its main practitioner is Saul Bellow.

"The Suitcase" deals with a confrontation between a Jew, Genevieve Levin, and a German, Gottfried Hencke, an architect, who had been a pilot in World War I, and whose name conjures the "Hinkle" bomber. Genevieve is the mistress of Hencke's son, also named Gottfried, whose wealthy and unsuspecting wife, Kitty, supports her artist husband. The confrontation occurs against the backdrop of an exhibition of her husband's work that Kitty has arranged at the Nobody Gallery. The preliminary skirmish is touched off when Kitty incorrectly identifies Jung as a famous Jewish psychiatrist. Genevieve replies that he is not a Jew. "That's why he went on staying alive." Genevieve then turns her attention to the elder Gottfried, saying that his son's artwork reminded her of "shredded swastikas."

Hencke senior thinks his son's mistress full of "detestable moral gestures." Adopting the pose that the Holocaust is nobody's fault, Hencke muses, "Who could be blamed for History?" It was, he thinks, a force in itself, like evolution. Further, he favors the philosophical thought of Arthur Schopenhauer, a notorious anti-Semitic thinker. Genevieve then confronts Hencke after first telling him about her thoroughly Jewish family, including four young daughters. The father then seeks to break up his son's affair. In the process he reveals the extent of his anti-Semitism, calling Genevieve a member of an inferior race and noting that rumors abound that the architect Corbusier is a secret Jew. Finally, he observes that when women such as Genevieve are of a blond type, "you can almost take them as our own."

The tale's denouement occurs when Genevieve's pocketbook is stolen. In an effort to prove he did not take her bag—a crime of which he had not been accused—Hencke opens his own suitcase to show her he is not the guilty party. Against the petty theft of a pocketbook stands the enormity of the Holocaust, a crime with which he, like Hitler's architect Albert Speer, denied involvement, thus adding to the list of deceptions with which this story deals.

The collection's final four tales, "The Dock–Witch," "The Doctor's Wife," "The Butterfly and the Traffic Light," and "Virility," all deal with aspects of illusion, deception, and usurpation. "Virility," the strongest of these stories, is illustrative. Edmund Gate, née Elia Gatoff, in eastern Europe, arrives in the United States after a prolonged stay with an elderly aunt in Liverpool, England. Coming to America, he begins his career as a usurper by assuming the first name of his American relative, a crusty newsman appalled by the youth's total lack of poetic talent. Initially, Elia/Edmund's poems receive multiple rejection notes. Suddenly, however, his stories begin to be accepted by magazines that earlier had told him not to bother them.

Upon his return from covering a minor war, the newsman discovers that Gate has become a sought-after poet; his collected poems were published as a book titled "Virility." Moreover, the newsman's sister had become the poet's mistress and publicity agent. A series of "Virility" collections began appearing. The poet went on worldwide reading tours. Critics termed his work "Seminal and hard." "Robust, lusty, male." "Erotic." But it was discovered that Edmund had plagiarized/usurped the poetry of his now deceased Aunt Rivka. When a book containing Rivka's poetry appeared, one critic termed the work "Thin feminine art." Another reviewer wrote, "Distaff talent, secondary by nature. Lacks masculine energy." Ozick clearly indicts the then prevalent practice of gender stereotyping. She ends her tale on an ambiguous note: Gate either has committed suicide or he lives disguised as an old woman.

"The Pagan Rabbi and Other Stories" garnered critical acclaim and was well received by the reading public as well. Moreover, certain of the themes appearing in this collection would reappear in the author's later works, e.g., the motif of flying in her short story "Levitation," or the motif of usurpation in "Usurpation, or Other People's Stories."

Bibliography

Alexander, Edward. *The Resonance of Dust: Essays on Holocaust Literature and Jewish Fate.* Columbus: Ohio State University Press, 1979.

Cohen, Sarah Blacher. *Cynthia Ozick's Comic Art: From Levity to Liturgy.* Bloomington: Indiana University Press, 1994.

—Alan L. Berger

The Painted Bird Jerzy Kosinski (1965)

The Painted Bird appeared the same year JERZY KOSINSKI gained U.S. citizenship. In this fictional autobiography Kosinski mythicizes his childhood experiences during six years in wartime Poland. The large historical backdrop is the Great Depression, World War II, the rise of National Socialism, communism, fascism, and militarism. The central metaphor in the title is from the book of Jeremiah 12:9.

In this novel Kosinski depicts an unnamed Polish Jewish boy's flight from Nazi Germans among mostly depraved Roman Catholic Polish villagers who torment him because his dark eyes and complexion suggest to them he is either a Gypsy or a Jew. Essentially a bildungsroman, the book describes the boy's series of transformations from innocence to bestial and psychotic experience. In the process the unnamed hero learns incredible survival skills and important lessons about the degradations of human nature. However, he becomes deranged through his odyssey of survival and escape, and he experiences a crisis of psychotic proportions involving withdrawal, fantasy, and picaresque nightmare. Through this central narrative of humanity's inescapable complicity in evil, and the transformation of humans into beasts, Kosinski tries to work out the aesthetic problem of how to write a counterlanguage of despair through which to describe the indescribable. Hence his employment of such experimental techniques as displacement, fantasy, collage, and wish fulfillment, combined with sadomasochism, animal torture, and deviant sexuality. On one level the tale is an elaborate history of the archetypal child through various stages of European history. But interwoven within this structure of ancient European fairy tale and myth is the psychological account of fascist/communist terror. Kosinski, a master of the macabre, puts at the base of this tale a jungle fable about hell, filth, savagery, sadism, and violence. Perhaps no other Holocaust writer has managed to combine primitivism, atrocity, the grotesque, and the pain of heightened sexuality as Kosinski has.

Critical response to this work was understandably mixed, with the most vocal criticism coming from eastern Europe. The depictions of the brutality of Polish peasants caused this book to be banned in Poland. But its examination of the brand of Roman Catholicism practiced by these Polish peasants, with their deep-seated superstitions, provides an important historical and sociological account of the times. Outside Poland some critics have considered this book pornographic and distorted, comparable to the works of professional pornographers, or deeply moral, depending on their perspectives. Furthermore, a few critics have complained that Kosinski initially represented as autobiographical many events in the novel that were not. Others have attempted to show that translators and editors had an unusually large role in fashioning the book. Nonetheless, *The Painted Bird* remains one of the most important and problematic works of fiction to come out of the Holocaust.

Bibliography

Hanson, John H. "The Child Archetype and Modern Primitivism: Kosinski's *The Painted Bird.*" *Studies in Literature* 14, no. 3 (1982): 85–95.

Jarniewicz, Jerzy. "The Terror Normality in Jerzy Kosinski's *The Painted Bird.*" *Polish Review* 49, no. 1 (2004): 641–652.

—Gloria L. Cronin

Paley, Grace (1922–2007)

In the tradition of female Jewish writers like TILLIE OLSEN and ANZIA YEZIERSKA, Grace Paley has given voice to people silenced by oppression in American culture. Recognized for her humorous anecdotal style, sensitive portraits of New York ethnic characters, and radical politics, Paley has become one of the most highly acclaimed Jewish writers of post–World War II America.

Born and raised in the Bronx, New York, Paley grew up in a household of oral culture, creative expression, and radical politics. Her parents, Dr. Isaac Goodside and Manya Ridnyik Goodside, were both immigrants from Ukraine. Goodside was a gifted painter and storyteller, and his family spoke English, Yiddish, and Russian. Paley's short stories and poetry would reflect the influences of her family's creativity and oral culture, as well as the colorful life of her immigrant community in the Bronx.

Paley did not launch her career as a fiction writer until she was in her mid-thirties. During her two years of university study (at Hunter College and New York University), she initially showed an interest in writing poetry. At age 17, she studied at the New School for Social Research with W. H. Auden, and much of Paley's poetry reflects his stylistic influence.

In 1942, at age 19, she married Jess Paley, a motion-picture cameraman, with whom she had two children. During their marriage Paley became actively involved in various civic and community organizations, often with a radical political bent. During the mid-1950s, after over 10 years of focusing on her family and working as a typist, she returned to writing—this time fiction.

The LITTLE DISTURBANCES OF MAN, Paley's first collection of short stories, was published in 1959 by Doubleday. The book helped establish Paley in the tradition of post–World War II Jewish fiction that was largely dominated by male authors. The book showcased her talent for ethnic neighborhood sketches, character portraits, monologues in ethnic vernacular, and humorous anecdotes. As the title suggests, the stories focus on seemingly everyday scenarios—an unconventional aunt narrates her love affair with a famous actor to her niece ("Goodbye and Good Luck"); a Jewish daughter often chastized for being loud is chosen to direct her school's Christmas pageant ("The Loudest Voice"). The stories received positive reviews, and many have since become anthologized.

While not overtly political, *The Little Disturbances of Man* reveals Paley's concern for the underdog: She depicts the daily struggles of immigrant culture (mainly Jewish immigrants, although she wrote about other white ethnic groups), as well as the societal restraints on women longing to live passionate and fulfilling lives. Paley's attention to ethnic communities and the repression of women foreshadowed her political involvement. With the publication of her book, she became increasingly involved in political protest, particularly antiwar movements and women's organizations. In 1961, in addition to receiving a Guggenheim fellowship, Paley founded the Greenwich Village Peace Center. Throughout the 1950s and 1960s she engaged in nonviolent protests of American militarization, prison conditions, and nuclear proliferation, and she was arrested on multiple occasions. In addition, Paley participated in the Armed Forces Day Parade, the American Friends Service Committee, the War Resisters League, and Women's Pentagon Action. In 1969 she traveled to Hanoi, North Vietnam at the time, as part of a mission to negotiate the release of prisoners of war. Paley's concern and involvement with central sociopolitical issues helped both to shape her fiction and to illuminate her as a primary contributor to the post–World War II American cultural climate.

Paley's second collection of short stories, *Enormous Changes at the Last Minute* (1974) proved less vibrant and optimistic than her first, focusing more on the hardships of her characters rather than their redemption. Her stories often have a fragmented feel; rather than providing closure (ending in marriage or death, for example), Paley leaves them more open-ended, unfinished—as if the story continues after the narration stops. This effect, as well as her blend of different ethnic vernaculars and other innovative narrative techniques, characterizes her second collection as postmodern.

While Paley again showcases her talent for portraying the everyday lives of immigrants in an ethnic community, often using some of the same characters from *The Little Disturbances of Man*, in this collection she shifts her lens to nonwhite ethnics as well (African Americans, Puerto Ricans, Asian Americans). This shift highlights how post–World War II politics and economics have affected both white and nonwhite ethnic communities and their mobility in and away from New York City. For example, in "The Long Distance Runner," Paley reveals how postindustrial urban renewal has reshaped ethnic communities. Faith, an alter ego for Paley (also featured in *The Little Disturbances of Man*), revisits her old home, now occupied by an African-American family, and moves back in with the new family. On the one hand, the story unifies the experiences of two different immigrant cultures. Yet on the other hand, Paley depicts a white family's mobility from a close-knit but decaying urban ethnic community to suburbia, and contrasts their mobility with that of nonwhite ethnics into urban centers.

Paley's writing career continued to thrive during the 1980s, when she published three collections of poetry: *16 Broadsides* (1980), *Goldenrod* (1982), and *Leaning Forward: Poems* (1985). She also published a third collection of short stories, *Later the Same Day* (1985), which continues both the themes and some of the characters (including Faith) from her earlier collections of short fiction.

In addition to being the first recipient of the Edith Wharton Citation of Merit (1983) and the first official New York State Writer (1989), Grace Paley received a number of other awards and honors, including a National Endowment for the Arts grant (1966), an award for short story writing from the American Institute of Arts and Letters (1970, membership in 1980), a Senior Fellowship by the National Endowment for the Arts (1987), and a Jewish Cultural Achievement Award for Literary Arts (1994). She died at her home in Vermont, where she had been poet laureate for four years (2003–07).

Bibliography

Arcana, Judith. *Grace Paley's Life Stories: A Literary Biography.* Urbana: University of Illinois Press, 1993.
Burns, Alan, and Charles Sugnet. *Grace Paley.* Jackson: University Press of Mississippi, 1997.
Sorkin, Adam J. "'What Are We, Animals?' Grace Paley's World of Talk and Laughter." *Studies in American Jewish Literature* 2 (1982): 144–154.

—Lauren Cardon

Parker, Dorothy (1893–1967)

Dorothy Parker, born Dorothy Rothschild, was a founding member of the Algonquin Roundtable, an important literary salon, and one of the foremost wits of the 20th century. Her acerbic wit and keen observations of life, love, and social issues are memorable not only for their blunt honesty, but also for their sharp turn of phrase. Parker did not limit herself to any one medium; rather, she wrote poetry, short stories, book and theater reviews, and dramatic works (including both plays and movies). It is of interest to note the dark tones that linger in even her lightest work; this may well stem from her earliest memories and experiences.

Dorothy Rothschild was born two months premature, on August 22, 1893. Her father, Jacob Henry Rothschild, was Jewish, and her mother, Annie Eliza Marston, was Scottish. Years later, Parker would often refer to her mixed parentage, though rarely with fondness. When Parker was not quite five years old, her mother died. Jacob remarried and his new wife, Eleanor Frances Lewis, constantly reminded Dorothy that she was a Jew and that, because of said fact, her soul needed saving (Kinney 25). Over time, this shame became thoroughly embedded in Parker's mind; she once stated that if she were ever to write her life story, she would title it *Mongrel*. Such disparaging remarks about her heritage were common for Parker; who was self-conscious about her Jewish background and so compensated for it, utilizing quips and facetiousness whenever it came up.

Parker was sent to elementary school at the Blessed Sacrament Convent. There she was made to feel like an outcast because of her name, her appearance, and her Jewishness. When she was expelled from the Convent for claiming that the "Immaculate Conception was spontaneous combustion," her formal academic education came to a close. She was merely 13. She then attended a finishing school, Miss Dana's (Kinney 26). Much of Parker's knowledge was gained through her own intellectual curiosity. That said, her education and understanding of the world, literature, politics, and more resound throughout her canon.

In 1915 Parker sold her first poem, "Any Porch," to Frank Crowninshield of *Vanity Fair* (Frewin 23). Shortly after that, she was hired to write captions for *Vogue,* then as a drama critic for *Vanity Fair.* In 1920 Parker's position came to an abrupt end. She was fired for going too far with her social satire, choosing to mock the wrong person in a dramatic review: Billie Burke, the wife of one of the magazine's biggest advertisers. In protest, her closest friend and confidante Robert Benchley abdicated his position at the magazine. Together, they opted to work solely for themselves, no longer slaves to the demands of an employer. They rented a cramped office and set to work freelancing.

There was one unfortunate outcome of the Parker-Benchley association: scandal. They were accused of having an affair, though this was untrue. The two were the closest of friends, but their relationship was platonic, so much so that they often joked about how they never could be romantically linked because it would be akin to incest. Parker

did, however, become entangled in several failed romances in the 1920s. The two that affected her most were her marriage to Edwin (Eddie) Pond Parker and her romance with Charles MacArthur. Parker married her husband in June 1917. Shortly after their nuptials, Eddie was sent to do his patriotic duty overseas. The distance proved to be too much; by the time he returned, the union between him and Dorothy had begun to crumble. Though Eddie still loved his wife and asked her to move to Hartford with him, away from the bustle of Manhattan, she declined. She had become accustomed to a life of literature and theater. Instead of just citing this as her reason for leaving her husband, Parker claimed that Eddie's gentile family hated her for being half Jewish (Kinney 38). Therefore, she would never be able to coexist with them. With Eddie gone, the lonely writer soon met Charles MacArthur. Parker, self-conscious and lovestruck, was enamored of the young journalist. His interest, however, quickly waned. He loved all women, not just one (Kinney 39). The relationship ended with an unplanned pregnancy (followed by an abortion) and a failed suicide attempt in which Parker slashed her wrists with one of Eddie's razors. Crushed by rejection, Parker suffered from depression and loneliness, feelings she would call on when writing verse and prose.

Parker's work often contemplated failed romances and explored suicide and death. Despite the emotional weight of the topics on which she wrote, she attacked them with a pointed wit that made them seem quirky, funny, and memorable to her readers. Because of this, they became more personal, more real for the average reader, and they remain that way today. Her pain became other people's pleasure. In the 1920s her writing career flourished. Her first published collection of poems, *Enough Rope* (1926), which included the poem "RÉSUMÉ," was originally compiled with Parker's intent of funding a trip to Europe. Not only did she earn the money necessary to cross the ocean, she also earned acclaim. The book was an instant success and was reprinted 13 times. Readers responded to her masochistic, cynical views on life and liked the bite in her words. Her success led to later publications, which include two more poetry collections: *Sunset Gun* (1928) and *Death and Taxes* (1931), and two short story collections: *Laments for the Living* (1930), and *After Such Pleasures* (1933). Like her poetry, Parker's prose examines people and relationships, focusing specifically on women and their emotional issues. Today, that focus is typically explored from a feminist perspective. Her short stories may deal with themes like war, racism, and marriage, but they do so from the vantage of women—how they discern things, process them, and cope with them. The domestic slant of her work derives from her gender and experience. Possibly one of her best-known short stories is "BIG BLONDE," for which Parker received the 1929 O. Henry award. The story focuses on an aging woman who must come to face bitter reality. It emphasizes the dependence of women on men. Despite trying to emerge as independent figures, women of the early 20th century were still prey to their position in society.

Apart from publishing collections of her poetry and short stories, Parker actively contributed to *The New Yorker*, a new magazine her friend Harold Ross had founded in 1925. Her "Constant Reader" column (of which there would be a total of 46 between 1927 and 1933) mercilessly assessed the writing of many of her contemporaries, including the likes of Katherine Mansfield, Dashiell Hammett, and A. A. Milne. Her reviews helped either to promote or to destroy the writer's reputation (Frewin 120). To this day, Parker's scathing review of Milne's *The House at Pooh Corner* remains unforgettable. She claimed that when she came to the word *hummy* in the book, "Tonstant Weader Fwowed up." Milne's story was too sugary for her and she had no problem voicing her distaste.

In the 1930s Parker moved to Hollywood. The days of the Algonquin wits meeting for lunch and revelry had dried up and a paycheck was much needed. She and her husband, Alan Campbell, whom she married in 1934, worked on films as a team. Though Parker disliked writing for the movies, she was skilled at doing so. Together, the couple worked on 15 movies, including *A Star is Born* (1937), which won an Oscar for Best Original Story.

Literary aspirations and associations aside, Parker was greatly interested in political issues. She was an ardent civil rights activist who never feared making her thoughts known, standing up for what she believed was right, or fighting for those less fortunate. Her leftist politics, however, caused her problems. In the 1920s she was arrested for marching for the release of anarchists Niccola Sacco and Bartolomeo Vanzetti. She was also named as a communist and later faced persecution during the McCarthy era, being scrutinized by the House Un-American Activities Committee. Still, that did not keep her from voicing her opinions and standing for what she believed in. At her passing, Parker bequeathed $20,000 to Dr. Martin Luther King (Keats 307). Even in death, Parker strove to provide some means for equality and justice in the world.

After a life full of highs and lows, lightness and dark, Dorothy Parker died alone of a heart attack in 1967. Without the lasting presence of friends or family, her ashes were left unclaimed for 17 years. Not until the NAACP adopted them did Parker find a final home in a memorial garden in Baltimore.

Bibliography
Frewin, Leslie. *The Late Mrs. Dorothy Parker.* New York: Macmillan, 1986.

Keats, John. *The Life and Times of Dorothy Parker: You Might as Well Live.* New York: Simon & Schuster, 1970.

Kinney, Arthur F. *Dorothy Parker.* Boston: Twayne, 1978.

Pettit, Rhonda S. A *Gendered Collision: Sentimentalism and Modernism in Dorothy Parker's Poetry and Fiction.* Madison, N.J.: Fairleigh Dickinson University Press, 2000.

—Kathena H. DeGrassi

The Pawnbroker
Edward Lewis Wallant (1961)

The most enduring legacy of EDWARD LEWIS WALLANT's most critically acclaimed novel may be the 1964 Sidney Lumet film adaptation of *The Pawnbroker,* starring Rod Steiger, who gives a powerfully subtle performance as Sol Nazerman, the alienated Holocaust survivor who runs a pawn-shop in New York City's Harlem. Although some reviewers argued that the film's excellence exceeds that of the novel, the novel certainly has much to recommend it, beginning with its serious treatment of the Holocaust. While critics have been divided on the accuracy, effectiveness, and sensitivity of Wallant's portrayal of Holocaust survivors, we do know that Wallant interviewed camp survivors before writing *The Pawnbroker,* which remains one of the most significant early literary expressions of the Holocaust's impact on postwar American culture. With its Harlem setting and African-American characters, the novel seems to be reminding mainstream America that we have our own history of racist and genocidal acts, a message that would have echoed nicely throughout the tumultuous civil rights and antiwar decade that followed its 1961 publication.

The pawnshop, operating on the margins of mainstream middle-class American society, becomes a gathering place for the distressed, disadvantaged, and displaced from virtually every ethnic and immigrant group, desperate to get whatever they can in exchange for their most valued possessions. Filled with artifacts of lost lives ranging from wedding rings to men's suits, the pawnshop also becomes a symbolic repository for concentration camp booty, the tangible traces of the Nazis' wholesale destruction of European Jewry. Thus as a contemporary version of the stereotypical Shylockian moneylender and as a figurative double for some concentration camp clerk, Nazerman must isolate himself emotionally from his customers and ignore the problematic parallels that should be obvious to such a well-educated man. As the 15th anniversary of his family's death approaches, which he considers his own death, Nazerman finds himself haunted more and more by the past, less and less able to keep his nightmarish memories in check, either through his Mafia-connected pawn-broker business or his austere isolation within his private bedroom suite at home. He simply cannot distance himself enough.

Nazerman is called out of his routine isolation and customary inaction by five people: Marilyn Birchfield, Mabel Wheatly, Jesus Ortiz, Morton Kantor, and Tessie Rubin. As a gentile, Marilyn, the pleasant community fund-raiser who woos Nazerman with picnics and Sunday outings, represents the possibility of a future without the burdens of the past, both personal and ethnic, even though he finally cannot divest himself of his responsibility for that past. This letting go is difficult for Nazerman, who sees Marilyn as his "life preserver." Mabel, a local prostitute who is also a regular customer and Ortiz's girlfriend, sparks perhaps the most dramatic move Nazerman makes in the novel when she informs him that Murillio, the Mafia boss who launders money through the pawnshop, also owns the bordello for which she works. Because his last view of his wife, Ruth, was of her performing a forced sexual act on an SS guard in the camp bordello, Nazerman cannot allow himself to be connected to Murillio's prostitution business. Amazingly, Murillio permits Nazerman to back out, even after threatening him, understanding finally, gazing at Nazerman's camp tattoo, that death is no threat to the pawnbroker. There is even a touch of respect for Nazerman in Murillio's parting words to him.

Nazerman's assistant, Jesus, in his sacrificial saving of Nazerman's life during a robbery, represents an obvious messianic figure. As an outsider to Nazerman's religious and cultural world, Jesus exemplifies a moving beyond self for the sake of others, an example that Nazerman emulates almost immediately. After Jesus's death, he calls home to arrange for his nephew, Morton, to take Jesus's place as his assistant, and then, after resting, hurries to Tessie's apartment to help his longtime mistress mourn the recent death of her father, Mendel. Both of these acts are incredibly hopeful. Nazerman's reaching out to Morton, an alienated art student, demonstrates the pawnbroker's acknowledgment of his own vulnerability. When he tells Morton that he needs him, Morton responds, making a mutual family commitment all too rare in the novel. Both Jesus and Morton, in their apprenticeship roles, function as surrogates for Nazerman's dead son, David, and their projected partnership suggests a relationship with him that goes beyond economics. Nazerman has provided for Tessie financially and protected her from the aggressive fund-raising efforts of Goberman, a Jewish confidence man and possible Nazi collaborator who plays on collective Jewish guilt for his own profit. Until the end of the novel, however, he cannot even mourn with her because he has had to remain so emotionally distant. Their sexual relationship, for example, is described throughout the novel as devoid of any depth of emotion beyond a pervasive world-weariness that comes out of their shared Holocaust history. For Tessie, it seems to be an economic exchange of sorts; her survival depends on Nazerman's money, for which he's entitled to regular visits that include sex and a meal. Ironically, Nazerman has made of Tessie something of the same thing the Nazis made of his wife, Ruth; his going to her at the end of the novel in empathy represents a necessary amelioration of that relationship, a symbol of his having finally buried his dead and of his moving on toward the future.

Bibliography

Kremer, S. Lillian. "From Buchenwald to Harlem: The Holocaust Universe of *The Pawnbroker*." In *Literature, the Arts, and the Holocaust*. Greenwood, Fla.: Penkeville, 1987.

Parks, John G. "Edward Louis Wallant." In *Holocaust Novelists*. Detroit: Gale, 2004.

—**Phillip A. Snyder**

Pentimento (A Book of Portraits)
Lillian Hellman (1973)

Pentimento is the second of playwright and director Lillian Hellman's trilogy of memoirs. While the first of the trilogy, *An Unfinished Woman* (1969), consists of Hellman writing primarily about herself, and the third, *Scoundrel Time* (1976), focuses on the effects of McCarthyism on Hellman and various associates, *Pentimento* draws on the author's memories of family, friends, and acquaintances. Curiously, these portraits reveal as much about the author as their primary subjects.

In the preface, Hellman explains that the title ("repentance," in Italian) originates from a technical term from the art world denoting the process in which an underlying sketch or image on a canvas is sometimes revealed as upper layers of paint become translucent or transparent with age. Hellman's intent is illustrated by this analogy: She wishes to examine her memory—for images at the surface and others revealed through the passage of time—to observe the differences between layers of remembrance. Several times Hellman admits that memories she had held for years were eventually proven inaccurate or that she had misremembered details or condensed time lines. This apparent candor is offset, however, by Hellman's reputation for writing less-than-honest autobiography—critics of *An Unfinished Woman* protest that it is rife with too-convenient dramatic coincidence—and the book occasionally suffers from questionable facts and conclusions.

Pentimento's seven chapters mostly concentrate on Hellman's relationships and fascination with the title characters but often stray to illuminate others known by the author. The chapters about her uncle Willy and distant cousin Bethe are the most revealing about the author, painting partial portraits of Hellman's family life with her aunts and parents as secondary characters. The section "Theatre" contains many small portrayals of those involved with theater productions but ultimately is a portrait of Hellman's relationship with her work. Dashiell Hammett, Hellman's longtime lover and companion, appears in this chapter and sporadically throughout the book, but readers looking for a thorough character sketch will be disappointed. Even in "Turtle," the chapter that features Hammett, Hellman is careful to limit the information she divulges about him or their relationship.

For the chapter "Julia," Hellman receives the most criticism for writing fiction under the auspices of autobiography. While the author claims that this chapter depicts a friend who worked with the Austrian underground before World War II, critics question whether this chapter is in fact a thirdhand account based on the life of Muriel Gardiner. Also in doubt is Hellman's claim to participation in a 1937 anti-Nazi escapade that involved smuggling cash into Germany at Julia's request.

The strength of Hellman's second memoir lies in the way her portrayal of others manages to reflect a more complete portrait of the author than her first autobiography. Readers who have found the name-dropping and reconstructed conversations of *An Unfinished Woman* tedious may find *Pentimento* more satisfactory because Hellman's recollections focus on others, not herself. The memoir is especially effective when she demonstrates how personal decisions were influenced by her interactions with or observations of others. (Writers looking to learn from the writing, editing, and directing habits Hellman reveals may find it helpful to be familiar with her plays before reading this memoir.) Where the book does center on the author, Hellman describes herself in a nonapologetic tone, sometimes with unflattering frankness about her shortcomings, but just as often with self-congratulatory commentary.

Although she asserts "We [Hellman and people she knew] were disturbed by the anti-Semitism that was an old story in Germany and some of us had sense enough to see it as more than that" (100), for the most part Hellman is reticent in *Pentimento* about her religious background. She limits her few references to her Jewish heritage to brief details such as making German-Jewish food for her father (71) and questioning a distant relative about his family's conversion to Lutheranism (153). And although she often discusses problems she encountered working in the theater and Hollywood, she does not mention any of the prejudice she must have encountered as a Jewish woman writer and director. It is difficult to tell whether Hellman's omissions about her background are due to her lack of religious conviction or her desire to control her public image.

It is unlikely that Hellman expected this memoir to go unchallenged. By using the title *Pentimento*, she defines her book as art and challenges us to determine which is her "truth"—the facts as researched by her critics or the images she has presented as memories.

Bibliography
Hellman, Lillian. *Pentimento.* New York: Signet, 1973.
McCracken, Samuel. "'Julia' and Other Fictions by Lillian Hellman." *Commentary* 77, no. 6 (1984): 35–43.
Weiner, Justus Reid. "Lillian Hellman: The Fiction of Autobiography." *Gender Issues* 21, no. 1 (Winter 2003): 78–83.

—Jeanne Genis

Perelman, S.J. (1904–1970)

Sidney Joseph Perelman was born on February 1, 1904, in Brooklyn, New York, the son of immigrants Joseph and Sophia Perelman. He was raised in Providence, Rhode Island, where, as a young man, he devoured popular novels and frequently attended movies.

S.J., as he would come to be known, served as editor of his high school humor magazine and thus began his lifelong infatuation with words and language. Throughout his career many of his works incorporated wordplay, obscure words and references, irony, non sequiturs, and an overall sense of the ridiculous. Perelman was credited as a wizard with words in many forms according to numerous critics, including his editor at the *New Yorker*, William Shawn.

Perelman's goal was to become a cartoonist, and as a young man he practiced his artwork on old pieces of cardboard he found in his father's dry-goods store. While at Brown University he contributed to the humor magazine as an artist and writer. After leaving college, from which he did not graduate, he secured a cartooning job with the weekly publication *Judge,* where he worked from 1925 to 1929. He then wrote for *College Humor* magazine from 1929 to 1930 (Mitchell 1).

In the 1930s Perelman worked as a screenwriter with the Marx Brothers on some of their early films, including *Monkey Business* and *Horse*

Feathers. He contributed many of the outrageous puns that made the films so popular. He subsequently wrote several books of humor and was a frequent contributor to *The New Yorker.* His series "Cloudland Revisited," which appeared in that magazine, was a sharp-witted response to his adult reviewings of films and rereadings of books he had been enthralled with as a child.

In 1956 Perelman won an Academy Award for his screenwriting adaptation of the Jules Verne classic novel *Around the World in 80 Days.* Perelman's own love of travel and his experiences in and observances of exotic locales throughout the world lent inspiration to several of his own stories, including "Westward Ha?" about his own around-the-world adventures with his friend and fellow artist Al Hirschfeld, who created caricatures in his signature style for the story.

In addition to his travelogues he documented his misadventures as a Pennsylvania farm owner. Perelman described these stories as feuilletons—a French literary term meaning "little leaves." Perelman's "leaves" were witty, wry, and full of self-deprecatory remarks such as "before they made S.J. Perelman, they broke the mold."

Perelman often collaborated with other artists and writers, including his wife, Laura (the sister of author Nathanael West), whom he married in 1929. In 1933 they created the theatrical comedy *All Good Americans.* With Ogden Nash he wrote the book for the musical *One Touch of Venus,* which opened on Broadway in 1943 and had a widely heralded run of over 500 performances.

Throughout his works Perelman is known for observing the world around him and embellishing the absurd he found in everyday life. He would often base unusual juxtapositions in his work on his observances and experiences. He read popular magazines, which he referred to as "sauce for the gander," to find new material for his sketches. He would often take a common word or phrase and change its meaning within the context of what he was writing, often with humorous results. He would sometimes glean a phrase from a newspaper, magazine article, or advertisement, then write a brief satire inspired by the phrase. Such was the case with his 1950s sketch "No Starch in the Dhoti, S'il Vous Plait," inspired by a phrase in a *New York Times Magazine* article. From this Perelman composed a series of imaginary letters that might have been exchanged between a man in India and a Parisian laundry owner.

S.J. Perelman is credited with being one of the few American writers to devote his career solely to humor. When he died in New York City on October 17, 1979, William Shawn's son Wallace commented, "He was utterly serious, but his medium was humor" (*New York Times,* A1).

Bibliography

Cole, William, and George Plimpton. "The Art of Fiction: S.J. Perelman." In *S.J. Perelman: Critical Essays.* Edited by Steven H. Gale. New York: Garland, 1992.

Corliss, Richard. "That Old Feeling: Perelmania." *Time.* Available online. URL: http://www.time.com/time/columnist/corliss/article/0,9565,587750-3,00.html. Accessed on February 5, 2004.

Mitchell, Mitchell. "S.J. Perelman." In *Encyclopedia Brunoiana.* Providence, R.H.: Brown University Library, 1993.

"S.J. Perelman, Humorist, Is Dead." *New York Times,* 18 October 1979, A1, D22.

—Jacqueline May

Piercy, Marge (1936–)

By any standard, Marge Piercy is an exceptionally versatile and prolific writer. To date she has published around 40 books. As an accomplished poet, novelist, and essayist—with a willingness to experiment with new modes of discourse within these traditional genres—she defies easy classification. Piercy always seems to go her own way, leading the charge toward whatever new possibility lies on the horizon. She is also a pragmatic writer with an eye on economics. For example, her official Web site—www.margepiercy.com—reflects this preoccupation with new, practical possibilities and illustrates how Piercy continues to make herself relevant and solvent in the immediate present. It functions primarily as a rather slick marketing device for her books, readings, and workshop services, a necessity for someone who fought hard to be published and who continues to write non-blockbusters for a living. But it also operates as a vehicle for reaching out to her rather broad audience and connecting them especially to her current work. Although she appreciates her privacy, Piercy is not a reclusive writer. What other important contemporary writer would post her resume online? The Web site is clearly the best first stop for both scholars and general readers interested in learning more about Piercy and her work.

Born on March 31, 1936, in Detroit to a working-class family still feeling the economic effects of the Great Depression, Piercy was heavily influenced by her mother, Bert Bernice Bunnin, and her maternal grandmother, Hannah. From her mother, Piercy inherited her capacity for close observation and from her grandmother her sense of storytelling as well as her affection for Jewish religious tradition. Both women have figured in her work, although she had a contentious relationship with her mother for most of her life. Her father was distant, and she consistently refers to her failure to please him. Piercy developed her lifelong love of books and cats from isolating childhood experiences and did well enough in high school to receive a college scholarship to the University of Michigan and then later to Northwestern University. She was at the heart of sixties radicalism, especially in reaction to the escalation of the Vietnam War, and was active in the Students for a Democratic Society (SDS), a left-leaning national college-based protest organization. She was also at the forefront of the feminist movement and still reflects the feminist aphorism "the personal is the political" both in her life and in her writing. In addition, she anticipated the impending sexual revolution in America when she was in college, thus also experienced the nation's catching up to her in terms of its shifting sexual mores. Piercy has been married three times: first, to a French physics major; second, to an American computer scientist with whom she eventually lived in an open marriage; third, to her current husband, Ira

Wood, with whom she has lived rather happily and, she writes, monogamously in Wellfleet, Massachusetts, among their cats and gardens since their 1982 wedding. In recent years Piercy has become more formally connected with Judaism and her local Jewish community with its religious celebrations and rituals. She has also survived successful surgical and other treatments for cataracts and glaucoma.

Sleeping with Cats, Piercy's engaging 2002 memoir, describes these personal experiences in greater detail and provides insights into some of the biographical and ideological contexts of her creative writing. Her charming descriptions of her individual cats and of her intimacies with them are enough to make even the most ardent cat haters rethink that position. These feline characters are developed as fully as any of the people in the memoir and represent for Piercy the most fundamental and constant relationship in her life.

Circles on the Water: Selected Poems is a 1982 collection taken from her first seven volumes of poetry, with an additional seven new poems added, including that feminist declaration of domestic war, "What's That Smell in the Kitchen?" This poem—as well as other widely anthologized poems such as "A Work of Artifice," "Barbie Doll," and "To Be of Use"—illustrates why Piercy's poetry and poetry readings are so popular with a general audience: accessibility and identification. In the poem Piercy takes one of the most common household tasks traditionally assigned to women—cooking—and transforms making dinner into a site for feminist protest and revolution. This accessibility and identification may also explain why she does not have a reputation for being a "serious" contemporary poet in the academic sense: Her poetry can be too transparent with too obvious a didactic message. She has won many literary awards, none of them major.

The Art of Blessing the Day: Poems on a Jewish Theme (1999) revolves around memory and family within the context of Judaism and its framing rituals, particularly on a personal level. Likewise, *My Mother's Body* (1985) includes a poem sequence subtly grounded in Jewish ritual, "The

Chuppah" (Jewish wedding canopy), which celebrates Piercy's marriage to Wood and includes two poems by him. Other poem sequences, such as "The Lunar Cycle" from *The Moon Is Always Female* (1980), underscore Piercy's vision of the interconnectedness of things and the significance of recurring time cycles, especially those connected with nature. "Slides from Our Recent European Trip," a seven-poem sequence from *Available Light* (1988), explores sites in England and France that evoke for Piercy images of life and death, as the past adheres to the present in the concreteness of particular place. She and her husband made this trip to do research for her historical World War II novel, GONE TO SOLDIERS (1987). *Woman on the Edge of Time* (1976) and *He, She, & It* (1991) are dystopian science fiction and fantasy experiments addressing issues of technology, politics, gender, Jewish myth, and magic. *Fly Away Home* (1984) and *The Longings of Women* (1994) articulate the complexities of contemporary female life passages told from various narrative focalizations that feature women of different socioeconomic backgrounds dealing with major life changes. *Three Women* (1999) is a three-generation narrative of a woman who must care for a stroke-ridden mother and a traumatized daughter. Piercy's trifold narrative focus allows readers to see into the consciousness of each of these women. *The Third Child* (2003) is a revisionist Romeo-Juliet story set against the backdrop of Washington politics. *Sex Wars* (2005) is a historical novel set in post–Civil War New York with famous historical characters embedded in a largely fictional plot. Told from multiple viewpoints, an approach Piercy often favors in her novels, the book weaves together a historical fiction of multiple perspectives that also reflects contemporary values and concerns.

Bibliography

Doherty, Patricia. *Marge Piercy: An Annotated Bibliography.* Westport, Conn.: Greenwood, 1997.
Shands, Kerstin W. *The Repair of the World: The Novels of Marge Piercy.* Westport, Conn.: Greenwood, 1994.
Walker, Sue, and Eugenia Hamner, eds. *Ways of Knowing: Essays on Marge Piercy.* Mobile, Ala.: Negative Capability Press, 1991.

—Phillip A. Snyder

The Plot against America
Philip Roth (2004)

Through an alternate rendering of a historical moment in which the American ideal of democracy was threatened by fascism, PHILIP ROTH's *The Plot against America* challenges the notion that "It can't happen here."

The novel rearranges the facts of the 1940 presidential election to have Franklin Delano Roosevelt defeated by the Republican challenger, Charles A. Lindbergh, who had been a prominent national figure since his Atlantic flight in 1927 and further captured the country's sympathy after the mysterious kidnapping and murder of his son. All in all, he was to many a fascinating American hero, despite his political tendencies toward isolationism and anti-Semitism. In Roth's alternate history, Lindbergh, upon his victorious election to the White House, immediately signs an agreement with Adolf Hitler and ultimately keeps the United States out of World War II. Lindbergh's implementation of national programs to disband ethnic solidarity and relocate Jews to various parts of the country is alarming. Roth based his fictional portrayal of Lindbergh on the anti-Semitism Lindbergh publicly professed, as in a 1941 radio address in which he blamed Jews for American involvement in World War II. Cameos of other historical figures such as Henry Ford, Burton K. Wheeler, Fiorello H. La Guardia, and Walter Winchell are also sprinkled throughout Roth's narrative.

Roth explores the underlying thematic element of fear through a fictional re-creation of his own childhood family. The narrator and protagonist, also named Philip Roth, reflects on the turbulence of this period in American history as a mature adult looking through the childhood lens of a much younger self. Autobiographical elements of Roth's life, including the family flat on the southwest edge of Newark, his parents Bess and Herman, and his brother Sandy, seep seamlessly into the narrative. Central to the novel is Roth's exploration of American culture, specifically in regards to familial relationships, as Philip's family reacts to the various political influences in strikingly different ways. Herman, Philip's staunchly patriotic father, is ultimately disappointed by his trust in American democracy. Philip's mother, Bess, tries to protect the children from her own rising fear by maintaining a sense of the normal, giving the narrator occasion to reflect on the absurd juxtaposition of American life and fascist-inspired fear. Sandy, Philip's older brother, is blinded by the guise of Lindbergh's ideology and is co-opted into becoming a sympathizer, causing dissent and bitterness within the family. Seven-year-old Philip, in addition to negotiating his limited understanding of the changes in his family's social dynamic, must also navigate the usual conundrums of boyhood, including the loss of a prized stamp collection, dangerous mischief with friends, and the inexplicable fear of his cousin Alvin's recent war souvenir: the stump where his leg had been.

At the time of publication, *The Plot Against America* was viewed as a political allegory about the Bush administration's war in Iraq. While Roth himself has argued against any sort of political agenda in the narrative, *The Plot against America* serves as an interesting social commentary on American politics and ethnic concerns.

Bibliography

Cooper, Alan. "It Can Happen Here, or All in the Family Values: Surviving *The Plot Against America*." *Philip Roth: New Perspectives on an American Author,* edited by Derek Parker Royal. Westport, Conn.: Praeger, 2005.

Hedin, Benjamin. "A History That Never Happened: Philip Roth's *The Plot Against America*." *Gettysburg Review* 18, no. 1 (2005): 93–106.

Michaels, Walter Benn. "Plots Against America: Neoliberalism and Antiracism." *American Literary History* 18 (2006): 288–302.

—Elise Flanagan

Portnoy's Complaint   Philip Roth (1969)

The final line of PHILIP ROTH's *Portnoy's Complaint* (1969) is a punch line in which the heretofore silent Dr. Spielvogel, a psychoanalyst to whom Alexander Portnoy's complaint is addressed, says, "Now vee may perhaps to begin. Yes?" The beginning at the end signals the cyclical futility and guilt that Roth spills out through his character Portnoy. In fact, *Portnoy's Complaint* is literally one long complaint—an extended comic Jewish monologue that occupies all but the framing devices of the last line and a short preface by Spielvogel, who is plainly a stand-in for Freudian analysis. According to Spielvogel's preface, which is in the form of a diagnostic definition, this malady called "Portnoy's Complaint" surfaces as a result of the battle between libido and morality that erupts "in overriding feelings of shame and the dread of retribution, particularly in the form of castration," creating in effect, as Spielvogel concludes, "the puzzled penis."

The novel is an exploration of this humorous yet disturbingly real and insightful psychological "complaint," specifically as it relates to Portnoy's Newark, New Jersey, upbringing in a middle-class American Jewish family, touching especially on the relationship between Portnoy and his mother, whom he describes as "the most unforgettable character I've met." The "problem" follows Portnoy from kindergarten into adult life. He imagines his mother waiting for him like a witch when he gets home from school; at one point he describes her as she stands over him threatening with a knife; and she pounds on the door of the bathroom yelling at him as he masturbates. Later in life he goes through a series of relationships with women that are all problematized and confused by his guilt-ridden, smothering, yet mutually caring relationship with his mother. In a moment of high comedy Portnoy imagines that his penis falls off from syphilis due to his promiscuity. In the wild fantasy his father shouts, "DON'T TOUCH IT NOBODY MOVE . . ." while his mother crawls on the floor to pick it up and worries aloud that he will never give her grandchildren.

In the background of Roth's exploration of guilt, shame, and eros, the novel delves into what it means to be Jewish in America. Just as he is torn along lines of psychological repression, Portnoy is rent by ethnic and racial tensions. He chases shiksas instead of Jewish girls. He grows up to become a civil rights attorney (a job that Roth admired). The sexual complaint of Portnoy can be seen as a metaphor for the larger problem of Jewish assimilation into American culture, while trying to hang on to the "mother" country. It is the frustration of being able to spread seed "all over" America, yet not being able to touch the Holy Land. That process of absorption—losing traditional values, yet gaining the American dream—creates the same "heavy seas of guilt" and shame as acting out sexually, and suffuses him with similar feelings of powerlessness and impotence. As Portnoy says, "My right mind is simply that inheritance of terror that I bring with me out of my ridiculous past." This ambivalence is illustrated metaphorically in the well known scene in which Portnoy masturbates into an uncooked, un-kosher "maddened piece of liver" that is later cooked, made kosher, and eaten by the family.

Roth, as in most of his novels, also investigates theories of art and literature. In one scene Portnoy recites Yeats's poem "Leda and the Swan" to a girl nick-named "The Monkey," who becomes his central relationship in the novel (except for his mother). The Monkey understands the poem not through an historical or artistic sense, but in a very primitive, emotional-sexual way. Even in the arena of literary criticism Portnoy is psychically caught between two worlds: one represented by tradition and ethics, the other by desire.

With *Portnoy's Complaint*, his fourth book and his third novel, Roth breaks new ground. In the gut-spilling monologue technique, he found a viable comic voice similar to Jewish comedians like Lenny Bruce, thus distancing his writing from previous attempts at a more formal Jamesian style. The almost stream-of-consciousness narrative style of the novel enables Roth to flow smoothly from past to future, from sex to religion, from politics to family, and to develop an unrelenting pace.

Moreover, in the raunchy and ribald language and explicit situations described in the book, Roth rides the crest of the 1960's sexual revolution. The book made Roth a celebrity, and *Portnoy* remained a best seller the entire year of its publication. Ernest Lehman adapted it into the 1972 film starring Richard Benjamin and Karen Black.

Roth also attracted many critics, however, who missed his keen sarcasm and satire. Some felt the sexual language in the book was immoral. Others felt he had betrayed his Jewish heritage and culture and revealed too much about the Jewish family. His biggest critic was Irving Howe, who quipped, "The cruelest thing anyone can do to *Portnoy's Complaint* is to read it twice." He felt Roth's work had been "deeply marred by vulgarity." Bruno Bettelheim, a student of Freud, complained that Roth "refuses to accept the love of his parents and so accept love of anything." And still others felt that his portrayal of women was objectifying.

The fame and infamy created by the publication of the novel did not deter the prolific Roth but instead served as fuel for later writings, especially the Zuckerman novels, in which he investigates issues concerning celebrity, fame, and author identity. For Philip Roth, as for his character Alexander Portnoy, the novel reveals both an unfinished end, and a conclusive beginning.

Bibliography

Strong, Paul. "Firing into the Dark: Sexual Warfare in *Portnoy's Complaint*." *International Fiction Review* 10, no. 1 (Winter 1983): 41–43.

Workman, Mark E. "The Serious Consequences of Ethnic Humor in *Portnoy's Complaint*." *Midwestern Folklore* 13, no. 1 (Spring 1987): 16–26.

—**Kent Chapin Ross**

Potok, Chaim (1929–2002)

Despite mixed reviews from critics, Chaim Potok has won an important place among 20th-century Jewish-American writers because of his wide appeal and his stimulating treatment of what he called "core conflicts"—conflicts within and between characters related to their deepest convictions and commitments. At least one of his novels, *The CHOSEN,* may become an enduring classic.

Potok's fiction is closely linked to his life. Many of his novels reflect his experience growing up in America in an Orthodox Jewish family. The conflict he portrays between traditional and modern is one he himself encountered. As with Asher Lev (in *MY NAME IS ASHER LEV*), his early interest in painting met with a lack of understanding from his parents. Like Reuven (in *The Chosen* and *The Promise*), he received his rabbinical ordination. Like Gershon Loran (in *The Book of Lights*), he was a chaplain in Korea.

He was born Herman Harold Potok on February 17, 1929, in the Bronx, New York, to Jewish emigrants from Poland, who also gave him the Hebrew name Chaim Tzvi. Potok's interest in writing began when he was about 15 with his reading of Evelyn Waugh's *Brideshead Revisited.* Through his high school and college years, Potok read works by Hemingway, Faulkner, Joyce, Mann, Dickens, and Twain, and did writing of his own. Potok received a B.A. in English literature from Yeshiva University in 1950 and a master of Hebrew literature degree from the Jewish Theological Seminary of America in 1954. Upon his graduation from the latter institution, he was ordained a Conservative rabbi. From 1955 to 1957, he served as a U.S. Army chaplain in Korea. While serving there he made several visits to Japan, including Hiroshima, where he confronted the questions of personal identity, cultural conflict, and evil and suffering that influenced much of his subsequent writing. During his service in Korea he began a first novel (never published) about army life. He went on to write another novel that, after considerable rewriting, became *The Chosen* (published in 1967).

Meanwhile, Potok married Adena Sarah Mosevitzsky in 1958; taught during the late 1950s and 1960s at the University of Judaism, Los Angeles, and at the Teachers Institute of the Jewish Theological Seminary; spent a year with his family in Israel in 1963; became managing editor of the magazine *Conservative Judaism* in 1964; and re-

ceived a doctorate in philosophy from the University of Pennsylvania in 1965. He served as editor for the Jewish Publication Society beginning in 1965 and later became chairman of its publications committee. Beginning in 1975 he served as the organization's special projects editor, assisting in the preparation of an English translation of the Hebrew Bible. He and his family spent another four years in Israel (1973–77). During the 1980s and 1990s he taught as a visiting professor at the University of Pennsylvania, Bryn Mawr College, and Johns Hopkins University. In 2000 he was diagnosed with cancer. He died on July 23, 2002, in Merion, Pennsylvania, and is survived by his wife, two daughters, and a son.

After publication of *The Chosen* in 1967, Potok became one of America's most popular writers and published two or more books every decade until the end of his career. His novels include *The Promise* (1969), a sequel to *The Chosen; My Name Is Asher Lev* (1972), the story of an aspiring artist at odds with his family and Hasidic community; *In the Beginning* (1975), which deals with Jewish identity, anti-Semitism, and biblical criticism; *The Book of Lights* (1981), based on Potok's experiences in Korea; *Davita's Harp* (1985), a flawed attempt to write from a woman's point of view, drawing on his wife's experiences; and *The Gift of Asher Lev* (1990), a sequel to his 1972 novel. Unlike his earlier books, Potok's next novel—*I Am the Clay* (1992)—does not focus on Jewish experience; the main characters are Koreans struggling to survive during the Korean conflict. Potok's final works include two children's books (*The Tree of Here,* published in 1993, and *The Sky of Now,* in 1995); *Zebra and Other Stories* (1998); and *Old Men at Midnight* (2001), a collection of three related novellas. Potok also wrote three plays (*Out of the Depths, Sins of the Father,* and *The Play of Lights,* all in the 1990s) and several nonfiction works: *Wanderings: Chaim Potok's History of the Jews* (1978); *Theo Tobiasse: Artist in Exile* (1986); *The Gates of November* (1996), a gripping account of a Jewish family in the Soviet Union; and, cowritten with Isaac Stern, *My First 79 Years: Isaac Stern* (1999). Potok's books brought him the Edward Lewis Wallant Memorial Award, the Athenaeum Award, the National Jewish Book Award, and a nomination for the National Book Award.

Most of Potok's fiction deals with what it means to be a Jew, especially with the conflict between traditional Judaism and the modern world. But because this conflict parallels that experienced by many non-Jews, his work has appealed to a wide audience interested in the tension between the secular and the spiritual, between tradition and modernity, and between individual identity and membership in a community. Though such issues appear in many of his books, nowhere are they presented more powerfully than in his first novel, *The Chosen,* which tells the story of two young Jews, one Hasidic, the other Orthodox but largely Americanized, and their response not only to modern culture but to such events as the Holocaust and the founding of Israel. A well-regarded film based on the novel appeared in 1981.

Some find Potok's plots predictable or inadequately dramatized and his style at times wordy, flat, or plodding. But many critics have responded enthusiastically, finding Potok's work intellectually challenging and emotionally powerful and praising the skill with which he dramatizes intellectual and cultural conflicts. Karl Shapiro called his style "beautifully quiet and gentle." Among other strengths, Potok's defenders point to his potent use of symbolism, his skillful evocations of childhood, and his gift for capturing atmosphere, for incorporating historical background, and for enabling readers to identify with his characters. Potok is perhaps unparalleled in his ability to make the Jewish educational experience, including talmudic study, vivid and interesting. He has also received high praise for the power of his moral concerns, his affirmative view of life and of human nature, and his authentic rendering of Jewish experience. The enduring value of Potok's work derives both from its Jewishness and its universality—that is, from its memorable depiction of a particular culture and its treatment of issues and conflicts with which virtually any reader can identify.

Bibliography
Abramson, Edward. *Chaim Potok.* Boston: Twayne, 1986.
Sternlicht, Sanford. *Chaim Potok: A Critical Companion.* Westport, Conn.: Greenwood Press, 2000.
Walden, Daniel, ed. *Conversations with Chaim Potok.* Jackson: University Press of Mississippi, 2001.
Walden, Daniel, ed. *Studies in American Jewish Literature, Number 4: The World of Chaim Potok.* Albany: State University of New York Press, 1985.
—Bruce W. Young

Properties of Light Rebecca Goldstein (2000)
Properties of Light is a chilling horror story of the Promethean pursuit of scientific truth. Postmodern in theme and style, it is a richly poetic book suffused with learned references from philosophy, literature, quantum mechanics, physics, poetry, and psychology. Goldstein builds her protagonist, David Mallach, (Hebrew for *angel,* or Lucifer) on the historical figure of David Bohm, a Princeton physicist who once worked with Albert Einstein. Bohm later contributed to Robert Oppenheimer's Manhattan Project, out of which came the atom bomb, and subsequently tried to mesh Indian philosophy, cognitive theory, neuropsychology, and quantum mechanics. The fiery death delivered to the Japanese by the atom bomb provided Goldstein her principal metaphor of fiery death. David Mallach's embitterment and subsequent madness is purely fictional.

Once Einstein's likely successor, Mallach now teaches poetry and physics to undergraduates. A mere ghost in his department, he secretly continues his project to solve the original physics problem of the nature of light, the problem that arises from the contradictory claims of quantum mechanics and relativity. We soon learn that he has gone mad, however, and killed his wife because she tried to leave him. Apparently she could no longer serve his project as muse and sex goddess. When a gauche, orphaned young mathematician Justin Childs appears in Olympia, Mallach adopts him as a son, recruits his talents, and offers him his daughter, Dana. Through her mind, both the Mallachs believe, the scientific revelation will come. Ironically, Justin's mathematics are irrelevant. They need him only to stimulate Dana sexually. Since this fractured narration comes mostly from the voice of Justin's ghost, we suspect collaboration has produced his death. When the news breaks that Justin has helped a colleague win the Nobel Prize, Mallach plunges into jealous madness, and the poisonous arrangement traps all three in fiery death or disfigurement. The narrative ends with the ghost of Justin Childs watching the now aging and disfigured Dana Mallach teaching poetry and physics to beginning undergraduates.

This novel is a gothic allegory about the destructive Freudian family drama at the heart of Western intellectual inquiry. In this arrangement women are sexually appropriated, fatherhood betrayed, sons and daughters pitted against each other, and the chosen sons sometimes devoured by the father. The human cost of the Western search for scientific truth, as this book portrays it, seems catastrophic. Since Rebecca Goldstein is a professional philosopher, it is not surprising that she attributes part of the blame to what postmodern philosophers call the epistemological calamity of Western metaphysics: the mind/body/soul split not present in some non-Western philosophy. The physicists' quest for the "properties of light" is an extended metaphor for all truth seeking and allows her to comment on the structuralist pursuit of Ur forms, the scientific search for the "form of forms," the Faustian pursuit of truth, and the erotic quest for enlightenment. Fueling all such quests, Goldstein suggests, is the human terror of finding a chaotic, indifferent, random, or even malicious universe.

Properties of Light has been criticized for its cold atmosphere and the complete absence of felt love. It has been highly praised for its lush metaphorical fusion of poetry, philosophy, psychology, feminist ideology, and science. Critics have been intrigued by the novel's fractal narration, its postmodern thematics, and its feminist agendas. Goldstein has even been identified as a New Humanist because of her novelistic attempt to heal the supposedly catastrophic Enlightenment split between the sciences and the humanities.

Bibliography
Brownrigg, Sylvia. "Love and Other Quantum Leaps." *New York Times,* 17 September 2007, 7:14.
Lowin, Joseph. "Portrait of Rebecca Goldstein." *Haddassah Magazine* 78, no. 19 (June/July 1997).

—**Gloria L. Cronin**

R

Ragtime E. L. Doctorow (1975)

E. L. DOCTOROW's *Ragtime* is a historical novel that features real figures from early 20th-century America, such as Evelyn Nesbit, Emma Goldman, J. P. Morgan, Henry Ford, Harry Houdini, and others, interacting with fictional characters from the nameless nuclear family identified only by their familial relationship roles such as Father, Mother, Mother's Younger Brother, and so on. The book dramatizes the process by which we make history and represents a new historical revisionist view in its preoccupation with the interaction of public and private domains. *Ragtime*'s wealth of historical detail provides a realistic texture that marks the novel as authentic, a texture that then is undercut by surrealistic passages running against its grain. In addition, by effacing its first-person narrator, the "little boy," *Ragtime* pulls its readers into the illusion of omniscient reportage only to reveal its subjective sleight-of-hand in the final chapter with the only use of the first-person narrative "I" of the novel. This first-person revelation functions like a reformatting of the text by opening to question any assumptions readers may have made previously regarding the authority and objectivity of the narrative point of view, intimating that there is as much storytelling magic to the narrative as there is historical fact.

Ragtime begins with a slightly distant ironic tone, describing, for instance, the upper class's naive version of America as exclusively white, re-

fined, ordered, and male-dominated, a perspective clearly benefiting from the authoritative hindsight of the narrator, who knows from the outset that this turn-of-the-century, upper-class isolationism will be shattered, especially within the family on which the narrative focuses. *Ragtime* is the story of the 20th-century reconstitution of the American family: Mother takes in an abandoned black baby and his mother, Sarah; Coalhouse Walker Jr., ragtime pianist and the baby's father, becomes a revolutionary in reaction to the racist destruction of his Model-T Ford and is joined by Mother's Younger Brother; with the deaths of Sarah and Coalhouse, the family makes the baby's adoption permanent; on Father's death, Mother marries Baron Ashkenazy, who is really a Jewish immigrant (Tateh), and adds him and his daughter to the family.

In many ways *Ragtime* is also about the systematic deconstruction of systems—interpretive, economic, productive, philosophical, social, and so forth—especially male systems. Most of the men, for example, are stuck within the systems that give their lives order and meaning but that eventually also destroy them. Only those who can adapt to change and seize new ideological modes of power survive the reconstruction of America in *Ragtime*. Admiral Peary has a system for reaching the North Pole; Father has a system for economic prosperity based on the marketplace for patriotism and a personal penchant for exploration; Coalhouse has a system for stubbornly asserting his notion of manhood in a racist society; Mother's Younger Brother has a system of celebrity worship and revolutionary anarchy; Houdini has a system for escaping physical bondage as popular entertainment; Morgan has a system for determining the cosmic source of his personal prestige and power. However, Peary's system comes from the Eskimo, and its success depends largely on the excellence of Matthew Henson, Peary's African-American employee. Father, despite his efforts, cannot adjust to the social changes occurring around him and dies a bewildered man on the *Lusitania,* an ironic, reversed "immigrant . . . arriving eternally on the shore of his Self" (368). Coalhouse sets his Model-T pride above his love for Sarah and his son, causing her death and his own by his revolutionary actions in pursuit of his personal notion of "justice." Mother's Younger Brother's attachment to Evelyn, Coalhouse, and even Father results in his mad pyrotechnic displays of destruction that culminate in his Mexican Revolution death and also in the ordinance he invents for Father's company, which will wreak far greater destruction during the world wars. Houdini escapes everything but his Oedipal complex and misses his one real opportunity to move into the mystic world by failing to "warn the Duke" (Duke Ellington) and thus escape or delay the start of World War I. Morgan expects his vision quest in the great pyramid to reveal his earlier incarnation as pharaoh but, instead, it shows him to have been a ragged marketplace peddler. Power systems reverse themselves in *Ragtime* as the disempowered, represented by women like Mother and immigrants like Tateh, become empowered by their ability to adapt. Mother goes from a refined subservience to a pragmatic power in her family; Tateh goes from being a Jewish Marxist-socialist to a royal filmmaking entrepreneur in America's capitalistic economy. In literary critic Mikhail Bakhtin's terms, the monologic becomes dialogic, epic discourse replaced by novelistic discourse, and the American family is reconstructed: What begins as Father's Broadview Avenue patrician family unit ends as Mother and Tateh's truly broad-view familial co-op.

Bibliography
Brienza, Susan. "Doctor's *Ragtime*: Narrative as Silhouette and Syncopation." *Dutch Quarterly Review of Anglo-American Letters* 11, no. 2 (1981): 97–103.
Spencer, Luke. "A Poetics of Engagement in E. L. Doctorow's *Ragtime*." *Language and Literature: Journal of the Poetics and Linguistics Association* 5, no. 1 (1996): 19–30.

—Phillip A. Snyder

Ravelstein Saul Bellow (2000)

Ravelstein, Bellow's last book, is ostensibly a tribute to his late friend and colleague Allan Bloom of the University of Chicago. Critics have responded variously to Bellow's "outing" of his homosexual friend in this autobiographical novel, and its clear implication that Bloom died of AIDS. However, none of the critics has questioned Bellow's genuine love for Allan Bloom or the accuracy of his portrait. Playing Boswell to Bloom's Johnson gave Bellow the opportunity to pay tribute to a man who had become his father figure and Jewish soul mate. As Robert Fulford notes: "They weren't the likeliest candidates for friendship. Not many people can make close friends in old age, and Bellow was 64 when they met, Bloom some 15 years younger. Then too, eminence can lead to isolation; a great figure often ceases to spend much time with equals and may live mainly among idolaters. . . . Yet Bellow and Bloom overcame those obstacles, dodged around their mobs of admirers and achieved a rare late-life intimacy." (C14/Front).

Ravelstein also records the jokes, one-liners, gags, Yiddish wit, neuroses, manners, affectations, cultural collisions, intellectual passions, and distinctly Jewish-American voice common to the descendants of Russian Jews. Chick/Bellow comments: "it was our sense of what was funny that brought us together, but that would have been a thin, anemic way to put it" (127). Bloom/Ravelstein is a declared Platonist who believes that the highest purpose of male friendship is the formation of an elite community of potential truth seekers searching for a relationship with their "actuals," or true halves. But he is also a Jew with a moral compass set in Jerusalem. It is to Jerusalem he turns when he is dying. During this final period he urgently tutors Chick about his role in the aftermath of the near-annihilation of Jews in the 20th century. Chick learns that he must never forget the learning of the Jews, half of whom have already been exterminated. As one of the remaining few, it is his obligation to keep on talking into the increasing historical silence. The greatest achievement of this final Bellow book is the fine comic portrait of Bloom/Ravelstein himself, whose appeal is that, for all his efforts to transform himself into an ancient Greek aristocrat, he remains a very Russian-Jewish character with an unmistakable Jewish face, a love of Yiddish wit, and a relentless hatred of the Nazis. "It is impossible to get rid of one's origins," he tells Chick. "It is impossible not to remain a Jew" (190).

Critics have called *Ravelstein* a biographical essay, a eulogy, a memoir, a threnody, a roman à clef, the chronicle of a friendship, a valediction, a Kaddish, and an autoethnography. It is clearly also a mea culpa on Bellow's part for his previous ambivalence about things Jewish and his avoidance of the event of the Holocaust. The biographical content about Bloom/Ravelstein is conflated inside a barely disguised fiction in which Bellow uses Bloom as a site of self-meditation. Through Bloom, he memorializes his own cultural origins, nationality, tribe, and age. It is not surprising, therefore, that the book contains numerous references to Nazi atrocities, and a major scene in which Ravelstein reprimands the careless Chick about tolerating Grielescu (a character based on Mircea Eliade, a known Romanian fascist), a Balkan Nazi sympathizer and Romanian Iron Guardist of their mutual acquaintance. This man is one of the many "sadists who hung living Jews on meat hooks," (16) he angrily reminds Chick. Alongside his tribute to Bloom, Bellow reveals not only the story of his late-life experience of loving Allan Bloom, and watching him enter death, but his own near-death experience due to virulent food poisoning. After a

lifetime of novels centered on their protagonist's death neuroses and male/male relationships that end badly, *Ravelstein* constitutes a final summing up of both these Bellovian themes. Chick/Bellow's fear of death is successfully negotiated, and two male soul mates come together and negotiate a boon companionship. While *Ravelstein* is a meditation on Bloom's and Bellow' shared history, capability for love, intellectual life, historical moment, and indelible Jewish stain, it is also one of the rare literary accounts of a friendship between two famous American intellectuals.

Bibliography
Apple, Sam. "Making Amends." *Jerusalem Report,* 31 July 2000, 46.

Fulford, Robert. "Eulogy to Genius: From a Friend and Fellow Titan." *Citizen's Weekly,* 7 May 2000, C14/Front.

—Gloria L. Cronin

"Résumé" Dorothy Parker (1925)

"Résumé," a disturbing but honest poem, appears in DOROTHY PARKER's poetry collection *Enough Rope* (1926). Originally published in the *New York World* in August 1925, "Résumé" pairs Parker's dark wit with her feelings of futility and weariness. The poem matches despair with grudging acceptance, most certainly the same feelings Parker felt when she composed it.

Dorothy Parker's first suicide attempt took place in January 1923. Shortly after she aborted her lover Charles MacArthur's child, and not long after he left her, Parker realized she was overwhelmed by her feelings of loneliness and rejection. In response, she took one of her estranged husband Edwin (Eddie) Parker's discarded razors and slashed her wrists. The wound was not enough to kill, but it was severe enough to guarantee her a room at the local hospital. There, her closet friend and confidante, Robert Benchley, responded to her action by lecturing, "You might as well live" (Frewin 88). His demand that she get a hold of herself and cope with her dark periods in healthier ways remained with the ailing writer, and she was to utilize it later when writing "Résumé."

A résumé is a catalog of someone's accomplishments detailing one's actions and activities. Plagued by bouts of depression, failed romances, and disillusionment, Parker had a résumé that consisted of a number of failed suicide attempts. Apart from slashing her wrists, she overdosed on veronal (much like her protagonist in "BIG BLONDE"), swallowed shoe polish, and ingested sleeping powder. In "Résumé," the speaker lists some of the different methods available for committing suicide. This morbid catalog consists of cutting one's wrists, drowning, swallowing acid or poison, and shooting, hanging, or gassing oneself. The thought put into the list and the consideration of why various methods of suicide will not work strongly suggests that the speaker has attempted (or at least, carefully considered) executing these various methods. As noted, Parker herself tried several of them, and she clearly formed opinions regarding the others. Her experience helps to shape the poem, forging a dark understanding of why one should choose to endure life, despite reservations.

That said, "résumé" without the accents is the word *resume*. According to the *Oxford English Dictionary*, *resume* means "to continue; to begin again." Understanding Parker's title in this way offers feelings of hope and possibility. But the speaker's point is much different. She longs to explain that, when all approaches to death fail, "You might as well live." She resigns herself to living simply because achieving her desired end is such an insurmountable chore. Parker's signature sarcasm encompasses the piece. It makes the unhappy point that the speaker chooses to continue with the drudgery of the life she has been handed, all because of the difficulties she encounters when contemplating suicide. Nothing—not life, not death—comes easy.

Bibliography
Frewin, Leslie. *The Late Mrs. Dorothy Parker.* New York: Macmillan, 1986.

Pettit, Rhonda S., and Regina Barreca. *The Critical Waltz: Essays on the Work of Dorothy Parker.* Madison, N.J.: Fairleigh Dickinson University Press, 2005.

—Kathena H. DeGrassi

Reznikoff, Charles (1894–1976)

Charles Reznikoff was born in New York City on August 31, 1894. His history as a poet, however, began much earlier. Milton Hindus's biographical essay in *Charles Reznikoff: Man and Poet* relates the event that sparked Reznikoff's determination to have his work published. His maternal grandfather had written poetry, but the family had never read his work. He had died far away from his family on a peddling trip, and only the belongings he had carried with him were returned to his family. His widow saw her husband's poetic work among his possessions and destroyed it. She was afraid of its contents, which she could not read. Reznikoff felt the loss of that precious family heirloom, and this piece of family history gave him the resolve to publish his own work.

Reznikoff's family had come to America after fleeing the pogroms that broke out in czarist Russia following the assassination of Alexander II in 1881. The family's experience in America was a mix of difficulty and optimism. Bigotry in the neighborhood ranged from verbal to physical assault. Reznikoff, however, was a successful student and graduated from high school at the age of 15. He graduated from the New York University Law School, but never pursued a career as a lawyer. He focused instead on his writing, providing for himself with small jobs. He married Marie Syrkin in 1930; she later became a professor at Brandeis University.

Beginning with his first work, *Rhythms*, privately printed in 1918, Reznikoff focuses on the themes of the Jewish-American and Jewish immigrant encounter with the urban environment in New York. He is particularly concerned with the personal, small, intimate objects that surround and inform the tenement dweller. As Paul Auster notes of Reznikoff's writing, "It is a process by which one places oneself between things and the names of things, a way of standing watch in this interval of silence and allowing things to be seen" (151).

The book-length poems *Testimony* and *Holocaust,* both of which are based on legal case histories, most clearly reflect Reznikoff's project. The first volume of *Testimony* (1965) is concerned with the history of America between 1885 and 1890, while the second volume (1968) spans 1891 to 1900. In these poems Reznikoff offers no commentary on the issues arising from the recitation of crimes. Rather, he refines the original legal prose and presents only the facts, the objects, the participants, and the outcomes, trusting the weight of things and events to create the power in his text. A short piece from the first volume of *Testimony* exemplifies this trust in objects.

> *When they told her husband*
> *that she had lovers*
> *all he said was:*
> *one of them*
> *might have a cigar*
> *and set the barn on fire. (104)*

Holocaust (1975), which uses the Nuremberg Trials as source material, demonstrates the same trust in objects, but also suffers a criticism of that trust, as did *Testimony.* Reznikoff was seen by some critics as offering nothing beyond what the trial transcripts already provided. To these critics Reznikoff was simply reciting without guiding the words to any new effect and thereby undermining the power of the events. Other critics, such as Robert Franciosi, see Reznikoff as "attempting to instill the 'bare facts' of the transcribed testimonies with a rhetorical, an emotional power" (243).

Bibliography

Auster, Paul. "The Decisive Moment." In *Charles Reznikoff: Man and Poet,* edited by Milton Hindus. Orono: National Poetry Foundation, University of Maine at Orono, 1984.

Franciosi, Robert. "Detailing the Facts: Charles Reznikoff's Response to the Holocaust." *Contemporary Literature* 29 (1988): 241–264.

Hindus, Milton, ed. *Charles Reznikoff: Man and Poet.* Orono: National Poetry Foundation, University of Maine at Orono, 1984.

　　　　　　　　　　—Matthew Antonio and Andrew Schultz

Rich, Adrienne (1929–)

Adrienne Cecile Rich was born in Baltimore, Maryland, on May 16, 1929. Her father, Arnold Rich, was a physician and a professor of pathology at Johns Hopkins University; her mother, Helen Jones, was a talented pianist and composer. Though Rich's early education was largely her mother's responsibility, it was her father who encouraged her to study poetry and, by allowing her the use of his library, made it possible for Rich to immerse herself in the work of such writers as Tennyson, Keats, Blake, Arnold, Carlyle, Frost, Donne, Stevens, and Yeats. The echoes of many of the writers she discovered as a child in her father's library can be heard clearly in her first two books. W. H. Auden remarks on some of these echoes in his forward to *A Change of World,* Rich's first collection and the winner (selected by Auden) of the prestigious Yale Series of Younger Poets Award:

> They [the poems in *A Change of World*] make no attempt to conceal their family tree: "A Clock in the Square," for instance, is confessedly related to the poetry of Robert Frost, "Design in Living Colors" to the poetry of Yeats. . . .

In 1951, the same year *A Change of World* was published by Yale University Press, Rich graduated with honors from Radcliffe College. A year later she was awarded a grant from the John Simon Guggenheim Memorial Foundation; the $3,000 award allowed her to spend 12 months abroad, during which time she studied literature (English poetry) at Oxford University, worked toward the completion of her second collection of verse, and explored Europe. In summer 1953, while still a Guggenheim fellow, she married Alfred Conrad, a Harvard economics professor. Unlike her mother, however, Rich did not abandon her artistic career for domesticity; instead, she continued to pursue her career as a poet, and in 1955 she published *The Diamond Cutters,* her second book of poems, for which she received the Poetry Society of America's 1955 Ridgely Torrence Memorial Award.

Though Rich was awarded another Guggenheim fellowship in 1959, was honored by the College of William and Mary as the Phi Beta Kappa poet in residence in 1960, and was awarded an Amy Lowell Poetry Traveling Scholarship in 1961, it was not until 1963, eight years after *The Diamond Cutters* was published, that Rich's third volume of poetry appeared. SNAPSHOTS OF A DAUGHTER-IN-LAW, for which Rich received *Poetry Magazine*'s 1963 Hokin Prize for Poetry, marks a turning point in Rich's artistic development. In her essay "'When We Dead Awaken': Writing as Re-Vision," Rich criticizes the title poem of *Snapshots* as being "too literary, too dependent on allusion." Even so, like the other poems in the collection, it is far less "literary" and allusive than any she had written before. *Snapshots* is in many ways Rich's debut collection; in *Snapshots,* she is "able to write, for the first time, directly about experiencing [herself] as a woman."

Three years after the publication of *Snapshots,* Rich moved with her husband and three children from Cambridge, Massachusetts, to New York City, took a job lecturing at Swarthmore College, and published her fourth book, *Necessities of Life,* which was nominated for the National Book Award. In 1967 Rich began teaching at Columbia University as an adjunct professor, leaving Swarthmore in 1968, when she took a position teaching remedial reading in the City College of New York's SEEK (Search for Education, Elevation and Knowledge) program. In 1969 she left Columbia and published *Leaflets,* her fifth collection of poetry. *Necessities of Life* and *Leaflets* are both emotionally charged volumes, each one more conspicuously—more confidently—personal than her previous collections; in both books the pronoun *I,* for example, is voiced by speakers who are completely aware of the power and potential of their own agency.

Rich's sixth collection, *The Will to Change,* was published in 1971, one year before she left her teaching position at CCNY to become the Hurst Visiting Professor of Creative Writing at Brandeis University and one year after her husband's suicide. Winner of the Shelley Memorial Award for Poetry from the Poetry Society of America, *The Will to Change* is a transitional collection; it comments on and complicates many of the concerns that characterize her earlier books while it introduces and investigates those concerns that would become the hallmarks of her later work. The idea of the woman-as-monster, for example, is explored in *The Will to Change* as it is in *Snapshots of a Daughter-in-Law;* the idea that it might be possible to use "the oppressor's language" to effect meaningful, even revolutionary, change—an idea that Rich continues to explore in her poetry and prose—is investigated in *The Will to Change.* More important, *The Will to Change* signals the completion of Rich's transformation from a poet who is also a feminist into a truly feminist poet. In this overtly political book concerned with history at a time when, according to Rich, America had "only the present tense," Rich writes past the difference between the personal and the public—to integrate, successfully and consistently, the poet and the speaker of the poem.

The Will to Change was followed two years later by *Diving into the Wreck,* a volatile collection that has been both praised and reviled by critics. Speaking of the collection's title poem in *Adrienne Rich: The Moment of Change,* Cheri Colby Langdell remarks that "'Diving into the Wreck' is considered by many to be the most important feminist poem of the twentieth century; it may be one of the most important and influential twentieth-century poems written by an American poet." She asserts that the poem "confirmed Rich's place as a founder of women's studies and feminist theory, and . . . helped release a tide of feminist poetry across the world, as others, hearing her voice, were inspired to break their silence." Speaking of one of the collection's most controversial poems, "Rape," in her essay "Ghostlier Demarcations, Keener Sounds," Helen Vendler remarks that "The poem . . . is a deliberate refusal of the modulations of intelligence in favor of an annulling and untenable propaganda, a grisly indictment, a fictitious and mechanical drama denying the simple fact of possible decency." Though artistically uneven, *Diving into the Wreck* was honored as the winner of the 1974 National Book Award. Rich refused to accept the award on her own behalf, accepting it instead (with Audre Lord and Alice Walker) on behalf of all women.

Since winning and declining the National Book Award in 1974, Adrienne Rich has been the recipient of numerous awards and honors, including six honorary doctorates (Smith College, 1979; College of Wooster, 1987; Brandeis University, 1987; City College of New York, 1990; Harvard University, 1990; Swarthmore College, 1991), the National Gay Task Force's Fund for Human Dignity Award (Rich affirmed her lesbianism in *Compulsory Homosexuality and Lesbian Existence* [1980]), the Ruth Lilly Poetry Prize, the 1999 Lannan Foundation Lifetime Achievement Award, the Commonwealth Award in Literature, an Academy of American Poets Fellowship, the 1996 Tanning Award for Mastery in the Art of Poetry, a MacArthur fellowship, the Bollingen Prize for Poetry, the Brandeis Creative Arts Medal in Poetry, the National Poetry Association Award for Distinguished Service to the Art of Poetry, a chancellorship of the Academy of American Poets, the Elmer Holmes Bobst Award in Arts and Letters, the Bay Area Book Reviewers Award in Poetry, the Robert Frost Silver Medal Award from the Poetry Society of America, the William Whitehead Award, the National Medal for the Arts (declined because she disagreed with the Clinton administration's policies regarding art and literature), and the Medal for Distinguished Contribution to American Letters from the National Book Foundation.

Since the publication of *Diving Into the Wreck*, Rich has published 14 books of poetry: *Poems: Selected and New, 1950–1974; Twenty-One Love Poems; The Dream of a Common Language; A Wild Patience Has Taken Me This Far; Sources; Fox; The Fact of a Doorframe; Your Native Land, Your Life; Time's Power; An Atlas of the Difficult World* (winner of the Los Angeles Times Book Award for Poetry, the Lenore Marshall Award, and the Poet's Prize); *COLLECTED EARLY POEMS, 1950–1970; Dark Fields of the Republic* (winner of the Lammy Award for Lesbian Poetry); *Midnight Salvage* and *The School Among the Ruins* (honored as one of *Library Journal*'s Best Poetry Picks of 2004 and winner of the 2004 National Book Critics Circle Award and the 2006 San Francisco Poetry Center Book Award). She has also published five books of prose: *Of Woman Born: Motherhood as Experience and Institution; On Lies, Secrets, and Silence; Blood, Bread and Poetry; What Is Found There: Notebooks on Poetry and Politics;* and *The Arts of the Possible.* She lives in Santa Cruz, California.

Bibliography

Auden, W. H. Foreword to *A Change of World*, by Adrienne Rich. New Haven, Conn.: Yale University Press, 1951.

Baechler, Lea, and A. Walton Litz, eds. *Modern American Women Writers.* New York: Scribners, 1991.

Cucinella, Catherine, ed. *Contemporary American Women Poets: An A-to-Z Guide.* Westport, Conn.: Greenwood Press, 2002.

Langdell, Cheri Colby. *Adrienne Rich: The Moment of Change.* Westport, Conn.: Praeger, 2004.

Rich, Adrienne. *Arts of the Possible: Essays and Conversations.* New York: W.W. Norton, 2001.

Vendler, Helen. *Part of Nature, Part of Us: Modern American Poets.* Cambridge, Mass.: Harvard University Press, 1980.

—Jay Hopler

The Rise of David Levinsky
Abraham Cahan (1917)

ABRAHAM CAHAN's magnum opus, *The Rise of David Levinsky,* began as a series of four installments in *McClure's Magazine* (April–July 1912) entitled "The Autobiography of an American Jew: The Rise of David Levinsky." Though engaging, the series is but a sketch for the full-length novel with its broader portraits of Jewish immigrant life on New York's Lower East Side; the garment manufactory and trade, including the conflicts with organized labor; and the central figure himself, David Levinsky, a pauper with chutzpah as he arrives in New York and a multimillionaire when his narrative is completed. As narrator and central participant, everything is seen through his eyes; telling his story at age 52, Levinsky is the same age Cahan was when he began writing his articles for *McClure's*. Although the novel is often read and discussed primarily as a major contribution to American studies because of its comprehensive picture of urban social and commercial development during a period of mass immigration, the significance of Levinsky himself as a viable character rather than simply an unscrupulous narrator is usually overlooked or minimized in favor of economics and business. This limited reading misses much of the fictive value of Cahan's novel.

Born and reared in Antomir, Russia, Levinsky initially studied to become a Talmud scholar, but his real interests lay elsewhere. Orphaned by the early deaths of his parents, he struggled to learn all he could of the world outside his shtetl, the traditional community of destitute yet mostly pious Jews where the only spoken language is Yiddish, and reading is limited chiefly to the Hebrew Scriptures and other devotional fare. Bright and eager to achieve, he is driven by an insatiable ego that always has him pursuing what he cannot acquire. He confesses in the opening paragraph of his narrative that everything he has seems to be "devoid of significance," and in closing, he acknowledges that he "cannot escape from [his] old self. [His] past and present do not comport well." Although Levinsky honestly admits this, he cannot recognize his hypocrisy; as a Talmud student in Antomir, he was no happier than he is in New York as a secular millionaire and industrial magnate. His inability to perceive his inner self accurately generates much of the ambivalence he betrays throughout his narrative. At 52 he finally realizes that what he can achieve is meaningless once he acquires it.

But if Levinsky is the central unifying figure of the novel, his experience as an immigrant Jew entering America who rises from poverty to extraordinary success as an industrialist is what brought *The Rise of David Levinsky* its acclaim. It is a great American success story in which the shrewd, hardworking narrator advances toward prosperity step by step. From a greenhorn arriving with nothing, he becomes a street peddler; advised to learn how to sew with a Singer sewing machine, he becomes

skilled at piecework and soon acquires his own shop. Gradually he ascends, sliding past questionable ethical practices and exploiting whoever best suits his purposes with glib assurances of forthcoming benefit. Simultaneously, he attempts to seduce one woman after another with varying success, always hoping to find his predestined mate, an idealized, unrealistic figure.

Because Cahan became a devoted reader of W. D. Howells's fiction soon after learning English, it is not surprising that correspondences exist in their work, especially between *The Rise of David Levinsky* and *The Rise of Silas Lapham* (1884), beginning with the titles. Both trace the lives of prominent businessmen and industrialists, highlighting the frustration and embarrassment that accompany climbing the socioeconomic ladder. They also describe in detail the industry in which the protagonists triumph. The parallels prove ironic because ultimately Lapham ascends morally while losing his wealth, whereas Levinsky remains rich and amoral to the end. Perhaps Cahan's allusion to Howells's novel in titling *Levinsky* represents his thanks for the early support he received from the distinguished man of letters. Cahan never lost sight of that debt.

Bibliography

Cahan, Abraham. *The Rise of David Levinsky*. New York: Harper and Brothers, 1917. Reprint, with an Introduction by John Higham. New York: Harper and Brothers, 1960. Reprint with Introduction and notes by Jules Chametzky. New York: Penguin, 1993.

Chametzky, Jules. *From the Ghetto: The Fiction of Abraham Cahan*. Amherst: University of Massachusetts Press, 1977.

Marovitz, Sanford E. *Abraham Cahan*. New York: Twayne, 1996.

—Sanford E. Marovitz

Roiphe, Anne (1935–)

Anne Roiphe, née Anne Roth, was born in New York City on December 25, 1935. In *1185 Park Avenue: A Memoir* (1999), Roiphe records her early years and emerging adulthood in a remarkably candid account of growing up amid the tensions between her parents, Eugene Roth and Blanche Phillips Roth, and amid the anxieties of the era in which she came of age. Her imaginative re-creation of those years traverses the uneasy and volatile terrain of her disturbingly unstable family, as well as the complexities in her developing sense of identity as a Jew and a woman at an erratic and deeply charged period in history. An enormously prolific writer, most of Roiphe's literary work touches on the antinomies and complexities attendant in being a Jew and a woman. As a Jewish feminist writer, Roiphe explores the conditions faced by women and the conflicts that emerge between traditional domestic roles and autonomous self-invention.

Roiphe, whose maternal grandfather made his fortune in the Van Heusen shirt business, attended Smith College in 1953 and received a B.A. in 1957 from Sarah Lawrence College. After a first marriage to the non-Jewish playwright Jack Richardson in 1958, which ended in 1963, she married Herman Roiphe in 1967, a Jewish psychoanalyst who, as she puts it, "understood that family was creation and that skeptical as we remained, closer perhaps to Spinoza than to the Rambam, we nevertheless were Jews, whose memories, personal, collective, and projective, were familiar" (*Testimony: Contemporary Writers Make the Holocaust Personal*, edited by David Rosenberg, 140). In addition to a daughter from her first marriage and her husband's two girls, Anne and Herman Roiphe had two daughters of their own, and her relationship with her daughters has become a large part of Roiphe's literary focus. Roiphe's work centers on feminism, Judaism—contemporary and historical—and family relationships. Much of Roiphe's fiction and essays demonstrate her critical eye for the nuances and ironies of family life. Roiphe is also a well-known journalist, publishing for the *New York Observer* and the *Jerusalem Report*.

To date Roiphe has written 10 novels: *Digging Out* (1967), published under the name Anne Richardson; *Up the Sandbox!* (1970), which was made into a popular movie starring Barbra Streisand; *Long Division* (1972); *Torch Song* (1977); *Lovingkindness* (1987); *The Pursuit of Happiness* (1991); *If You Knew Me* (1993); *Secrets of the City* (2003); and *An Imperfect Lens* (2006), a historical work of fiction based on the cholera epidemic of 1883 in Alexandria, Egypt. Roiphe's publications also include the nonfiction works *Generation Without Memory: A Jewish Journey in Christian America* (1981); *Your Child's Mind: The Complete book of Infant and Child Mental Health Care* (1985), written with Herman Roiphe; *Fruitful: A Real Mother in the Modern World* (1996); *For Rabbit, With Love and Squalor* (2000); and her work of creative nonfiction, *Water from the Well: Sarah, Rebekah, Rachel, and Lea* (2006). Roiphe has also written two memoirs, *1185 Park Avenue* (1999) and *Married: A Fine Predicament* (2002).

Often Roiphe's writing raises issues related to Judaism and to the tensions inherent in the intersections of the secular and religious worlds. Roiphe's work on the Holocaust, including *A Season for Healing: Reflections on the Holocaust* (1988), speaks to her deep commitment to the future of Judaism. In response to the question she poses, "How central to Jewish identity is the Holocaust and how central do we wish it to be?" (*Testimony* 141), Roiphe recognizes that, despite the dangers posed to a religion or a people bound collectively by disaster, "the reality is that the Holocaust has made Jewish existence simultaneously more perilous, as Jews question the covenant and the value of chosenness, and more binding, as Jews feel a sacred connection to those who died, to their mores, their vanished towns, their hopes for their children, to the lost languages and the ancient prayers" (*Testimony,* 142).

Bibliography

Glazer, Miriyam. "*Daughters of Refugees of the Ongoing-Universal-Endless-Upheaval*": Anne Roiphe and the Quest for Narrative Power in Jewish American Women's Fiction. Edited by Jay L. Halio and Ben Siegel. Newark: University of Delaware Press, 1997.

Weaver, Carole McKewin. *Tasting Stars: The Tales of Rabbi Nachman in Anne Roiphe's* Lovingkindness. Edited by Mickey Perlman. Westport, Conn.: Greenwood, 1989.

—Victoria Aarons

Rosen, Jonathan (1963–)

Jonathan Rosen was born February 25, 1963, in New York City. The son of literary parents, Norma, his mother, a fiction writer, and Robert, his late father a professor of comparative literature, Rosen inherited a love of words and writing. He received a degree in English literature from Yale University and was accepted at the University of California at Berkeley, where he completed some graduate work. On returning to New York, Rosen worked at the *Forward* as the culture editor. During this time he also created the Arts and Letters section of the publication. His essays have been published in the *New York Times Magazine, The New Yorker,* and the *American Scholar.* He is the author of three novels: *EVE'S APPLE* (1997), *The Talmud and the Internet: A Journey Between Worlds* (2000), and *Joy Comes in the Morning* (2004). His fourth book, *The Life of the Skies,* was published in 2007. He is the recipient of the Chaim Potok Literary Award, The Reform Judaism Prize, and the Edward Lewis Wallant Award. Currently, he works as a series editor at Nextbook and lives in New York City with his wife and two daughters.

Rosen's first novel, *Eve's Apple,* is a literal and metaphorical exploration of the erotic and grotesque nature of hunger. Set in New York City, a modern-day concrete Eden, the central narrative focuses on the relationship between Joseph Zimmerman and Ruth Simon. As a recovering anorexic, Ruth experiences not only physical hunger, but, more important, a psychological hunger that manifests itself as a desire to create and control her own body. As the narrative voice, Joseph hungers to save Ruth from herself. To do so, he binges on medical texts from the New York City Public Library and steals her private thoughts by reading her diary. When his novice attempts to know Ruth fail, his obsession with her disease leads him to seek further help from Dr. Ernest Flek, a crippled and disenchanted psychiatrist. Through

discussions with Dr. Flek, Joseph soon discovers that, like Ruth, he is bound by the mental and physical appetites and desires of his own body. While Ruth is in France, Joseph begins to understand and accept that his unhealthy obsession with her disease has more to do with himself and less to do with her. Although neither character is healed by the book's end, Joseph's realization does bring with it a sense of hope that the couple will have a future together.

Although Rosen's second book, *The Talmud and the Internet: A Journey Between Worlds,* originally began as an elegy to his grandmother, it cleverly develops into a compelling cyberspace travelogue filled with shadows, snapshots, ashes, artifacts, and fragments. Through its technologically constructed body, Rosen celebrates then reformulates the seeming chaos of cyberspace, as well as that of his own life story or (his)tory. He reconnects the disconnected, retrieves the irretrievable, and reembodies the disembodied bodies not only of different forms of knowledge systems and institutions, but of his own Jewish (his)tory. To connect his genealogical past to his present, Rosen joins the literal beginnings of Jewish history, the Talmud, with that of his present or contemporary connections to the Internet. He achieves this by moving his family's historical, linear beginnings within Judaism into the nonlinear end of time space in the Internet. By invoking the past and examining the present presences in his life, Rosen creates a type of witnessing rooted in the hope, belief, and possibility of a complicated, inconclusive, messy messianic now indicative of our *post* postmodern existence.

Similar to *The Talmud and the Internet,* Rosen's third novel, *Joy Comes in the Morning,* also explores the contradictions and complexities of what it means to be Jewish in the 21st century. Set in New York City, the narrative follows Rabbi Deborah Green as she struggles to negotiate her faith and spirituality along with her dreams and physical desires. Her life is drastically altered when she meets Henry Friedman, an older man who has attempted suicide. Like Rosen's own father, Henry is a German-Jewish survivor of the *Kindertransport,* or childrens' transport, the rescue of some 10,000

Austrian, Czech, and German-Jewish children who were sent to Britain between 1938 and 1939. Deborah's frequent visits with Henry allow her to meet his wife, Helen, and his son Lev, who works as a science reporter. As the narrative develops, the differences between Deborah and Lev seem to dissipate as their interaction as acquaintances develops into a more substantial relationship that eventually results in marriage. It is through relationships like Deborah and Lev's that Rosen explores such contemporary themes as aging and death, belief and skepticism, love and loss, tradition and modernity.

Bibliography

Roach, Korri R. "Jonathan Rosen: A Critical Treatment." Master's thesis, Brigham Young University, Dept. of English, 2005.

Sol, Adam. "'Were It Not for the Yetzer Hara': Eating, Knowledge, and the Physical in Jonathan Rosen's *Eve's Apple*." *Shofar* 22, no. 3 (Spring 2004): 95–103.

—**Korri Roach**

Rosen, Norma (1925–   )

In the essay "Writing as a Woman and a Jew in America," Norma Rosen describes herself as a "third generation Jewish woman in America" who came to Judaism tentatively, a belated entrance into what would come to be a passionate embrace of the weight and impact of Jewish history, culture, and belief (*Accidents of Influence* 133). Norma Rosen was born in New York City on August 11, 1925, the only child of Rose Miller and Louis Gangel. Raised as a secular Jew, the product, as she puts it, of "an immaculate Jewish conception" (*Accidents of Influence* 128), she seems to have been brought up on the periphery of Judaism, like so many other American Jewish children of her generation, with "no religion, no philosophy, no language, no literature, no custom" (*Accidents of Influence* 128). In the essay "On Living in Two Cultures," she describes the ambiguous place of Judaism in the landscape of her early years, her father's occasional forays to Jewish Reform services, coupled with her mother's refusal to participate in the restrictive and claustrophobic rituals of Jewish law.

After completing high school in Brooklyn, Norma Rosen left New York City to attend Mount Holyoke College, where she studied modern dance with José Limon and choreography with Martha Graham. On graduation from college in 1946, she taught English and dance at a private girls' academy. Rosen then went on do graduate work at Columbia University, where she wrote her master's thesis on the writer Graham Greene. Shortly after receiving a master's degree, she studied book design at New York University and, in 1954, was employed by Harper and Row Publishers. Her literary career began in 1959 with the publication of her first two stories, "Apples," published in *Commentary,* and "The Open Window," which appeared in *Mademoiselle.* Rosen's literary coming-of-age would seem to reflect and accompany her growing awareness of what it means to be a Jew and a woman writing in America during an increasingly politicized period of American social history: "Writing, woman, Jew. I name them in the order of discovery," she acknowledges in "Writing as a Woman and a Jew in America" (*Accidents of Influence* 133). In paying homage to these three essential aspects of her identity, she distinguishes the central preoccupations of her long-standing literary career. Such facets of her identity are, for Rosen, intricately and intimately enmeshed. Her nascent awareness of Judaism's influence, despite or perhaps in response to the earlier ambiguities surrounding the place of Judaism in her own life, emerged as a central impulse in her writing. In discussing the beginnings of her literary career, she makes clear Judaism's claims from the start on her work: "When I began to write, I saw to my surprise that for me place, vision, imagination—all the elements that formed my peculiar window—concerned Jews" (*Accidents of Influence* 137).

After a brief first marriage, during which she published under the name Norma Stahl, in 1960 she married Robert Samuel Rosen, a professor of comparative literature. Their marriage brought her closer to the rituals and practices of Judaism and also to the devastating realities of proximate Jewish history. Her husband, whose parents were killed by the Germans, escaped to England on the children's transport in November 1938. Her husband's background may well have been the impetus for Rosen's Holocaust writing, and clearly the Holocaust figures prominently in much of her work. It would seem, moreover, to be the catalyst for her awakening as a Jew. Rosen speaks to this discovery in "Writing as a Woman and a Jew in America":

I had come into my knowledge of the Holocaust and Jewish identity at the same moment. And the knowledge of the former sank into swift and bitter full circle with the latter just in time to darken it, nearly to blot it out, as in an eclipse. My efforts to study and to learn since then, to inform my writing with deeper knowledge of Jews, not only in the accidents of their sociology but in their enduring attachments to the search for belief and meaning—what else are they but an effort to insert my mind into the little space left between the shining of the sun and its darkening? (*Accidents of Influence* 136)

Arguably her most powerful work is that which attempts to negotiate the devastation of the Holocaust and to attempt to articulate the horrors through the eyes of one who can only be a secondhand witness. Rosen's short story "The Cheek of the Trout," for example, is staged against the backdrop of postwar Europe, a landscape to which a grown child of Holocaust victims and his American-born wife return. The man's grief at his enormous loss is seen through the lens of his wife, whose own anger and sorrow in response to the travesties of the past and the near obliteration of history by a new generation of Europeans are terribly complicated by her anguished knowledge that she can only barely attempt to fathom from afar the life that her husband suffered.

Norma and Robert Rosen's first child, Anne Beth, was born in 1961. Their second child, the writer JONATHAN AARON ROSEN, was born in 1963. One can see the influences of domestic and family life in her early work, and also the ways in which

Jewish life and thought came to influence her characters and dramatic situations. Arnold Levine, the Jewish protagonist of Rosen's first novel, *Joy to Levine!* (1962), is an employee of a floundering textbook publishing company, who comically reacts to his father's overbearing nature. Her subsequent work explores a variety of Jewish themes and voices, ranging from scriptural narratives to 20th-century American consciousness to the Holocaust. Her first novel was followed by a collection of short fiction, including her earlier published stories, *Green: A Novella and Eight Stories* (1967); the novel TOUCHING EVIL (1969), which explores the reaction to the Holocaust by those not directly involved with the events of the Nazi genocide but rather those who become "witnesses-through-the-imagination"; *At the Center* (1982), a novel that explores the issue of abortion through the lens of three doctors working in an abortion clinic; *John and Anzia: An American Romance* (1989), a novel that brings to imaginative life the relationship between ANZIA YEZIERSKA and John Dewey; a collection of personal and critical essays, *Accidents of Influence: Writing as a Woman and a Jew in America* (1992); and *Biblical Women Unbound: Counter-Tales* (1996), midrashic readings that give voice to the otherwise silenced stories of women in the Bible. Other works include *A Family Passover* (coauthored with Anne Rosen and Jonathan Rosen 1980) and a number of articles and short fiction.

Bibliography

Goldberg, Marilyn. "The Soul-Searching of Norma Rosen." *Studies in American Jewish Literature* 3 (1983): 202–211.

—Victoria Aarons

Rosenbaum, Thane (1960–)

Thane Rosenbaum is among the forefront of post-Holocaust writers who reflect on their traumatic legacy. The author's parents, both Holocaust survivors, moved from Washington Heights, New York, to Miami Beach when Rosenbaum was a youngster. The Florida locale plays an important role in many of the author's works. Utilizing both the

Jewish mythic imagination and his own personal experience, Rosenbaum writes insightfully and speaks for many daughters and sons of Holocaust survivors who grew up as, in his trenchant phrase, "survivors of survivors." Rosenbaum's protagonists raise three basic questions: How shall I live with the inherited trauma of the Holocaust? What is the relationship of the covenantal deity to death camps? and, How shall I live Jewishly in an indifferent world whose soul has been permanently disfigured by the *Shoah*?

Rosenbaum, the John Whelan Distinguished Lecturer in Law and the Director of the Forum on Law, Culture, and Society at Fordham University in New York City, received a law degree from the University of Miami and worked for several years in a prestigious New York City law firm in which he gravitated toward the firm's pro bono cases. His passion, however, lay elsewhere. To the dismay of his legal colleagues, he left a highly remunerative legal career and devoted himself to writing, teaching, and lecturing on the Holocaust, Jewish literature, human rights, and the legal system. A prolific author, Rosenbaum has published an award winning post-Holocaust trilogy, ELIJAH VISIBLE (1996); *Second Hand Smoke* (1999); and The GOLEMS OF GOTHAM (2002). His nonfiction includes *The Myth of Moral Justice* (2004) and coauthorship of a screenplay for *Second Hand Smoke.*

The author is an insightful critic of culture. Like the prophets of antiquity, he raises his voice in protest over injustice. Rosenbaum is also moved by his prophetic inheritance in seeking to preserve the memory of the Holocaust while voicing disapproval at its trivialization by popular culture. He is a prodigious essayist whose work appears in many anthologies of Jewish writing. Furthermore, he writes opinion pieces and essays for the *New York Times, Wall Street Journal, Los Angeles Times, Washington Post,* and other national newspapers and magazines. These essays deal with matters of Holocaust memory, moral justice, and human rights in the modern world. Rosenbaum's essays are marked by his passionate determination to distinguish between legal and moral justice.

Rosenbaum's post-Holocaust trilogy reveals both the generational transmission of trauma and a psychological "working through" this inheritance. Moreover, theologically, his novels display a movement from indicting God for the death camps to emphasizing the role of humanity in seeking to repair the world. Yet his novels are often comedic, imaginative, and postmodern. Adam Posner, the protagonist in each of the short stories that *Elijah Visible* comprises, represents the stage of post-Holocaust loss and mourning. Duncan Katz, the physically strong and Holocaust-possessed protagonist of *Second Hand Smoke,* who initially seeks literally to overpower the demons of the camps, emblemizes post-Shoah rage. Duncan's half-brother Isaac is an expert in Yoga who seeks to teach Duncan how to cleanse his soul of rage by learning how to breathe.

The Golems of Gotham, Rosenbaum's third novel, stakes out new post-Holocaust literary ground on at least three levels: He brings back the souls of six Holocaust writers who committed suicide; the protagonist, Ariel Levin, is a girl who is the granddaughter of survivors (the third generation)—her grandparents had also taken their own lives; and the author utilizes rites and rituals from the world of Jewish myth and mysticism in suggesting a course between forgetting and becoming psychologically paralyzed by Holocaust inheritance.

Rosenbaum's writings have won critical acclaim. *Elijah Visible* won the Edward Lewis Wallant Book Award. "Cattle Car Complex," the book's first story or chapter, was recorded and performed as part of National Public Radio's *Selected Shorts* series. *Second Hand Smoke,* a finalist for the National Jewish Book Award, has been translated into Dutch. *The Golems of Gotham* has received several awards: selected as one of the top 100 Books of the Year 2002 by the *San Francisco Chronicle;* Noteworthy Books of 2002, *Kansas City Star;* Best Opening Lines of the Year, 2002, *Book Magazine;* Alternate Selection of the Traditions Book Club. Furthermore, the novel received the New York Public Library Award for Best Books for Teenagers 2002–03.

Rosenbaum's Holocaust mystery story, "The Day the Brooklyn Dodgers Finally Died," will be published in *Brooklyn Noir 4 (2010),* and a Hanukkah story, "The Maccabee of Miami Beach," aired on National Public Radio (December 2006). He is also the editor of the nonfiction anthology *Law Literature from Atticus Finch to* The Practice: *A Collection of Great Writing About the Law* (2007 New York: The New Press). Currently, the author is at work on two novels, *The Stranger Within Sarah Stein,* a novel for young adults, and *As If Nothing Happened.*

Bibliography

Berger, Alan L. "Mourning, Rage, and Redemption: Representing the Holocaust: The Work of Thane Rosenbaum." *Studies in Jewish American Literature* 19 (2000): 6–15.

———. "Myth, Mysticism, and Memory: The Holocaust in Thane Rosenbaum's *The Golems of Gotham.*" *Studies in American Jewish Literature* 24 (2005).

Parker, Derek Royal. Interview with Thane Rosenbaum. 2007.

—Alan L. Berger

Rosenfeld, Isaac (1918–1956)

Isaac Rosenfeld was raised in a lower-middle-class home on the North Side of Chicago. His unhappy childhood involved the loss of his mother when he was only 22 months old and his father's second marriage. His growing alienation within his own home and within bourgeois America generally characterized many second-generation Jews in assimilationist America, and Rosenfeld in particular. More than most of his contemporaries, he was emotionally and academically immersed in the rapidly disappearing North Side Chicago immigrant world of *Yiddishkeit.* SAUL BELLOW recalls him as a sickly, yellowish 13-year-old in ridiculous short pants holding forth on Schopenhauer. Isaac spoke Yiddish in his home and studied Yiddish systematically at SHOLEM ALEICHEM schools. Later, he translated Sholem Aleichem's stories from Yiddish, and even wrote some of his own in Yiddish.

Rosenfeld was the first American writer to explore the moment of cultural encounter between Yiddish and English for American letters. His work resonated with the diasporic longing for home and the theme of exile. He suffered poor health, identified with the sickly Jewish intellectual Franz Kafka, disdained physical accomplishments, and pursued American pragmatism and naturalism. His work features his quest for physicality, and has a fascination with such dictators as Hitler, Mussolini, and Stalin, the Moscow show trials of the 1930s, and historical events like the Spanish civil war. With the young Saul Bellow, he was an active Trotskyite and well read in European literature. But while Bellow was more interested in typically masculine physical culture and women, Isaac was sexually alienated and particularly inept with women.

From his earliest years, Rosenfeld was invested in leftist politics and liberal humanism. Beyond this he became convinced that there was some true archetypal pattern to psychic and spiritual life. He soon became deeply interested in the Theory of Signs, gave up his interest in logical positivism, and searched for patterns in the lives of great men like Tolstoy and Gandhi. In 1946 he published his one novel, *Passage from Home,* the story of an estranged adolescent, the failures of the Jewish family, Jewishness as exile, and subsequent elegiac sadness. Its protagonists are alienated from both America and *Yiddishkeit.* A volume of reviews and essays, *An Age of Enormity: Life and Writing in the Forties and Fifties,* was published posthumously in 1962. This uneven collection contains some fine essays and some that are quite mediocre. All resonate with Rosenfeld's humanistic ideas. In 1966 came his uneven volume of short stories, *Alpha and Omega.*

In his decline Rosenfeld lived a disordered life in boarding houses, reacting in self-destructive ways against his father's bourgeois values. His work reflects the recurring subjects of Jews, things Jewish, and the fragile nature of community. The

Holocaust, which affected him dramatically, he announced to be a radical break in history calling into question categories far beyond terror and evil.

During the years 1941–45 he contributed regularly to *Partisan Review, Commentary,* the *New Leader,* and the *Nation.* During the 1940s he won the *Partisan Review's* novelette award for "The Colony," a chapter from a work set in India that he never completed.

As everyday realities became pressing, Rosenfeld increasingly took refuge in the intellectual abstractions explored in *The Age of Enormity.* These essays, written for the general reader, reveal his persistent notion that literature and criticism belong to everyone. Literature, he believed, was for human beings, not scholars, and his essays, though uneven, were clear. Many of his book reviews were treatments of naturalistic and realistic novels. Like Bellow, he hated the "hard-boiled" literature of his contemporaries, and increasingly interested himself in Freudianism, Marxism, and Reichianism. When he could no longer write or function sexually or socially, Reichianism, with its particularly Jewish messianism, promised liberation on both fronts. Though always somewhat ambivalent about Wilhelm Reich's ideas, he nevertheless studied Reichian notions of human sexual categories, regularly interviewing his friends with prurient questions about their sex lives. He even built his own orgone box recommended by Reich for unlocking physical inhibitions. His friends were generally intrigued and amused by it, some even going so far as to try it out themselves.

Rosenfeld's writing career continued to fail despite all these attempts. His second novel, "The Enemy," inspired by his love of Kafka, was rejected. So too was his third novel, "The Empire," focusing on his other hero, Gandhi. Rosenfeld had married Vasiliki Sarantakis after his graduation in 1941, years later the marriage collapsed. He left Chicago for a two-year teaching stint at the University of Minnesota, then returned to the University of Chicago to live in yet another substandard rented room on the North Side. "King Solomon," written soon after his return to Chicago, remains his best piece of fiction and is possibly the source for Mr.

Sammler of Bellow's *MR. SAMMLER'S PLANET.* However, he quickly became withdrawn, depressed, and poverty-stricken. He succumbed to heart failure and died in July 1956. Isaac Rosenfeld was never a prolific writer, nor a long-lived one. But he is remembered as a Greenwich Village bohemian and seer, a potentially important talent, a humorist, and a mentally ill eccentric. He is best remembered now for his memoirs of Saul Bellow and ALFRED KAZIN, and a couple of fine short stories, "The Hand That Fed Me" and "King Solomon." Bellow memorialized him best as a brilliant lost intellectual and artist whose Yiddish heart and soul were defeated by the American experience.

Bibliography

Lyons, Bonnie. "Isaac Rosenfeld's Fiction: A Reappraisal." *Studies in American Jewish Literature* 1, no. 1 (1975): 3–9.

Solotaroff, Theodore. "Isaac Rosenfeld: The Human Use of Literature." *Commentary* 33 (1962): 395–404.

Zipperstein, Steven J. "Isaac Rosenfeld's Dybbuk and Rethinking Literary Biography." *Partisan Review* 69, no. 1 (2002 Winter): 102–117.

—Gloria L. Cronin

Rosten, Leo Calvin (1908–1997)

Best-selling humorist Leo Rosten was one of the most prolific and innovative 20th-century Jewish-American writers, credited with legitimizing the incorporation of Yiddish language and culture into mainstream American society. Long before the appearance of other "crossover" Jewish comedians, such as Mel Brooks or WOODY ALLEN, Rosten's name became synonymous with the integration and success of the European Jewish community in the United States. Over a writing career that spanned more than 60 years, Rosten worked as an essayist, novelist, editor, screenwriter, and social scientist, unleashing his wit on a diverse array of subjects in popular discourse, ranging from behavioral psychology to Hollywood gossip. But, Rosten himself preferred to be defined as a writer of "comic dialect," a field that he claimed consisted of "humor plus anthropology."

At the age of three, Rosten arrived in the United States from his native Poland. Accompanied by his immigrant parents, the family settled in a working-class neighborhood of Chicago, where Rosten attended primary and secondary schools. After completing his undergraduate degree in sociology at the University of Chicago in 1930, he taught English for several years at a night school for adult immigrants. This experience he would later re-create in his first pieces of creative writing, undertaken during a doctoral fellowship in Washington, D.C., where Rosten was researching the political atmosphere of newspaper correspondents in the nation's capital. Afraid of incurring the wrath of his academic advisory committee, Rosten adopted the pen name Leonard Q. Ross and then published, between 1935 and 1937, a series of short stories in the *New Yorker* magazine about the trials of a Jewish immigrant student named Hyman Kaplan, his straight-laced instructor, and his other (mostly) Jewish immigrant classmates. In 1937, the same year he achieved a Ph.D. in political science from the University of Chicago, these short stories were collected and published in book form under the title *The Education of H*Y*M*A*N K*A*P*L*A*N.*

The first H*Y*M*A*N K*A*P*L*A*N stories were subsequently expanded in the sequels *The Return of H*Y*M*A*N K*A*P*L*A*N* (1959) and *O K*A*P*L*A*N! MY K*A*P*L*A*N!* (1976). In essence the plot of these stories is rather simple: There are neither intrigues nor villains; and Hyman Kaplan himself is hardly a hero. The author expressed amazement that the public at large was able to identify so strongly with the story line, sarcastically noting that "Grammar, Spelling, and Punctuation are hardly dramatis personae." Be this as it may, the character of Hyman Kaplan—an immigrant dressmaker whose "Yinglish" ramblings put him at constant odds with his teacher, the reticent Mr. Parkhill—endeared himself to American audiences without their necessarily having grasped the Jewish subtleties in his humor. Kaplan, for example, insists that the plural of "sandwich" is "delicatessen," that the superlative of "failed" is "bankrupt," and that the past participle of "to die" is "funeral." While Kaplan's inappropri-

ate classroom conduct and slapstick demeanor at the American Night Preparatory School for Adults appealed to a large, non-Jewish audience, the combination of his mangled English and tongue-in-cheek Yiddishisms would set the ground for the linguistic ingenuity of Rosten's later work.

Throughout the 1940s Rosten worked for the U.S. Information Service, did postgraduate work at the London School of Economics, and began a successful career as a screenwriter. Among the movies he scripted were *All Through the Night* (1941); the film noir classic *The Dark Corner* (1946), starring Lucille Ball and Clifton Webb; *Lured* (1947); and *The Velvet Touch* (1948). In 1949 he joined the staff of *Look,* where he remained until 1971. As a journalist for the magazine, he worked on a series of articles later compiled into the popular reference volume *A Guide to the Religions of America* (1955). He also authored a collection of critical commentaries on art history, published as *The Story behind the Painting* (1962).

In 1956 Rosten wrote what was arguably his most serious work, *Captain Newman, M.D.* Although laced with comic interludes, this quasi-realistic novel describes the vigilant efforts of an army psychiatrist to rehabilitate, and ultimately to empathize with, the delusional World War II servicemen in his mental ward who are suffering from post-traumatic stress disorder. In what some have called a literary precursor to *M*A*S*H,* the story brings together sociopolitical commentary with uproarious scenes characteristic of Rosten's other comic fiction. *Captain Newman, M.D.* was later turned into a motion picture under the same name in 1963 starring Gregory Peck, Tony Curtis, and Robert Duvall; it was nominated for three Oscars.

Rosten's best-received book is his 1968 classic *The Joys of Yiddish,* a pseudolexicon of Yiddish words and phrases that have made their way into colloquial American English. Arranged in alphabetical order, the "Yiddish-in-English" terms are presented much like the words in a standard dictionary, with explanations given for the possible spellings, pronunciations, and etymologies. The definitions of the words—which are quite often approximate—are followed by example sentences (for clarification), and are subsequently peppered with jokes, anecdotes, or the author's own personal recollections. For instance, in addressing the common confusion between the Yiddish terms *schlemiel* (a simpleton) and *schlimazel* (a chronically unlucky person), Rosten notes how the word *schlemiel* is purported to have come from the name *Shlumiel,* a Hebrew general in the tribe of Simeon known for his bumbling battlefield tactics. On the other hand, explains Rosten, *schlimazel* comes from the German *schlimm* ("bad") and the Hebrew *mazal* ("luck"). So popular was *The Joys of Yiddish* that it was followed by the best-selling *Hooray for Yiddish: A Book about English* (1982), *The Joys of Yinglish* (1989), and the posthumous best seller, *The New Joys of Yiddish* (2001), edited by Lawrence Bush.

In addition to teaching English at Columbia, Yale, Stanford, and New York universities, Rosten wrote more than 30 books of fiction and nonfiction before he died at his home in New York City on February 19, 1997. Although he was often criticized for completely ignoring Sephardic Jewry and for being overly sentimental about his own eastern European Jewish heritage, he will be most remembered for restoring to Ashkenazi Jewry the pride in their *mamaloshen,* or "mother tongue," during an age in which most of the world's speakers of Yiddish had either been exterminated by Nazi Germans or shamed into suppressing their linguistic tradition, mostly out of fear that the latter option all too well recalled the former.

Bibliography

Bronner, Simon J. "Structural and Stylistic Relations of Oral and Literary Humor: An Analysis of Leo Rosten's H*Y*M*A*N K*A*P*L*A*N Stories." *Journal of the Folklore Institute* 19, no. 1 (1982): 31–45.

Foster, Susan E. "Linguistic Literary Treasures: A Study of Yiddish-English Literary Dialect in the Works of Cahan, Yezierska, Gross, Rosten, and Roth." (Master's thesis, Sonoma State University, 2000).

Shiffman, Dan. "The Ingratiating Humor of Leo Rosten's Hyman Kaplan Stories." *Studies in American Jewish Literature* 18 (1999): 93–101.

—**Nathan Devir**

Roth, Henry (1906–1995)

Henry Roth was born in 1906 in Tsymenitz, Galicia (an area formerly in Austria-Hungary, now in Poland) to Herman Roth and Leah Farb. Herman and Leah had been forced into marriage by a strange combination of circumstances, and Herman returned to New York, where he had been living, almost immediately after the ceremony. When Leah and Henry arrived in New York in 1907, he greeted them as burdensome strangers. All of Roth's writing would be about the five years that the unhappily yoked family lived in various dreadful tenement houses in Brownsville, New York; the Lower East Side; the Jewish section of Harlem; and, most painful of all, the non-Jewish section of Harlem on 108 East 119th Street.

While living in the Jewish neighborhoods Henry attended heder (elementary school), but when the unhappy family moved to the non-Jewish neighborhoods, Henry's fragile religious identity was shattered. He picked fights at school, withdrew into himself, and became embarrassed by his mother's agorophobia and Yiddish speech. In order to fit in, he defiantly ate nonkosher foods and resisted Jewish involvement to the point that he had to be forced to become a bar mitzvah.

The family lived in this neighborhood until 1927. In 1924 Henry graduated from DeWitt Clinton High School and entered the College of the City of New York, where he met Professor Eda Lou Walton, a woman 12 years older than he, who ran the literary club. Walton encouraged and supported her protégé, who became her lover for over a decade during which time they lived together in her apartment in Greenwich Village. When Roth met Muriel Parker in 1938 he left Walton. His marriage to Muriel in 1939 lasted until her death in 1990.

In 1930 Roth began writing CALL IT SLEEP, published in 1934 by Robert Ballou. Now a classic of Jewish-American literature, this heavily autobiographical novel focuses on the traumatic emotional life of seven-year-old David Schearl, his loving immigrant mother, Genya, and his enraged paranoid father, Albert. As Alfred's paranoia deepens, he finally turns on them in rage, convinced that David is not his son. Outside the home, anti-

Semitic neighborhood gangs rule the streets, and an older girl lures him into a closet for sexual experimentation. All of these events compound David's sense of dislocation. It is a brilliant Joycean novel which reveals the fractured world of the Jewish immigrant family in America through the eyes of a seven-year-old child. Multiculturalists now mark it as a pioneering work in their field, noting its brilliant linguistic mix of Yiddish, English, Hebrew, and Polish.

Historians consider the book a valuable ethnographic artifact revealing the ghetto conditions of Jewish life on New York's Lower East Side. Heavily influenced by James Joyce's and T. S. Eliot's pioneering use of stream-of-consciousness monologues, Freudian theory, and impressionist techniques, this book is one of American literature's earliest modern experimental novels, and undoubtedly the finest of the 1930s Proletarian Novels. Viewed in hindsight, it is a harbinger of American Jewish literature after World War II.

The novel sold fewer than 2,000 copies when it appeared and soon fell out of print. This devastated Roth and began one of the most legendary writers' blocks of American literary history. It lasted for 30 years and put him in company with Ralph Ellison and J. D. SALINGER. Socialist critics of the day rejected *Call it Sleep*'s self-conscious literary modernism and complained of its self-conscious socialist agenda. Socialist critics for their part dismissed it as too literary and dense with symbolism. When the cultural left collapsed after the Great Depression and before "ethnicity" and "Jewish-American literature" had been officially invented, Roth's reputation was in hiatus. But due to a deliberate literary rehabilitation initiated by Jewish critics Harold Ribalow, LESLIE FIEDLER, Irving Howe, and ALFRED KAZIN, the grounds were laid for the republication of *Call it Sleep* in 1960. Later, faithful agents and editors Roslyn Targ and Peter Mayer carefully orchestrated Roth's literary estate and the appearance of his later work. Not until the aftermath of SAUL BELLOW's winning the Nobel Prize in 1976 and the general rise of Jewish-American letters during the 1970s was Roth seen as a predecessor and a precious missing link.

When the book was largely ignored in 1934, Roth worked on his next book for a few years, then in 1946 he burned the manuscript of what would have been the sequel to *Call it Sleep*. It was a year of madness for him, and the depth of his crisis can be seen in his murdering a puppy. Muriel had given up her career as a serious musician and composer and Henry worked as a newspaper peddler, messenger, English teacher, precision tool grinder, firefighter, ditchdigger, woodcutter, maple syrup salesman, and math and Latin tutor. The 30-year trajectory took him from Greenwich Village radicalism to misanthropic isolation on a waterfowl farm in Maine from 1953 to 1956. In 1956 *Call It Sleep* was mentioned twice in "The Most Neglected Books of the Past Twenty Five Years" in *American Scholar*, an event that paved the way for its being reissued in 1960 in hardcover by Pageant Books. That same year a 30-minute radio adaptation of *Call it Sleep* was also broadcast. Eda Lou Walton lived just long enough to see her protégé begin to take his rightful place in American letters. She died the following year, three years before *Call It Sleep* reappeared as a paperback in 1964, and before Irving Howe's enthusiastic review essay appeared on the front page of the *New York Times Book Review*. This no doubt led to Roth's grant from the National Institute of Arts and Letters in 1965 and the many other honors that followed, such as the Townsend Harris Medal for outstanding achievement by CCNY Alumnus. However, it was with the 1968 D. H. Lawrence fellowship at the University of New Mexico that one of the longest writing blocks in American literary history ended. The Roths spent the year in Lawrence's cottage north of Taos, the pilgrimage site and burial place of his ashes. Here Henry resumed writing and Muriel resumed playing and composing.

The couple made their first trip to Israel in 1972, and returned again in 1977 when Henry was invited to Mishkenot Sha'nanim (Jerusalem's official guesthouse). *Nature's First Green*, a brief autobiographical sketch, appeared in 1979, and later that year Roth began writing the first volume of *Mercy of a Rude Stream*. In 1987 he was awarded the Premio Internazionale Nonino-Percoto in northern Italy.

Later that same year *Shifting Landscape* appeared. The title came from Shakespeare's *Henry VIII*. It fused materials written over many years. Also heavily autobiographical, this novel is set in the 1920s. Protagonist Ira Stigman, another double for high school–aged Henry Roth, has problems with his emerging sexuality and Jewish religious identity. Many other heavily autobiographical fictions followed. Many have called them less fiction than memoir.

When Muriel died in 1990, Henry was devastated. His crowning literary recognition came in 1994 when awarded the prestigious Honorary Doctor of Letters from the University of New Mexico. This was followed by an honorary doctorate from Hebrew Union College, Cincinnati. In 1994 *A Star Shines over Mt. Morris Park,* the sequel to *Call it Sleep,* was published. It was the first of a series of six projected volumes he struggled to write before he died, and despite crippling arthritis, he wrote four volumes, which have appeared under the collective title *Mercy of a Rude Stream. Call it Sleep* begins in 1907 on New York city's Ellis Island and ends with the eight-year-old David Schearl falling asleep on his mother's bed in August 1913. *A Star Shines over Mt. Morris Park* opens in August 1914 and ends in 1920. It also uses materials from Roth's own history and replaces Schearl with Ira Stigman. Ira suffers through anti-Semitism, slum living, a violent father, puberty, religious dislocation, and the torment of his high school years. This time Roth totally confounded the distinction between fiction and autobiography by actually using his own family photographs and a two-page genealogy at the front of the book taken from the Roth/ Farb genealogy, with a few names changed. Ira Stigman's extended family are introduced, and his mother, Leah's, family arrive in New York from Galicia. The book then follows Ira's life into the 1920's. Nearly all of its content is drawn from Roth's own experiences. The *Chicago Sun-Times* reviewer called it "a marvelously poetic chronicle." JONATHAN ROSEN, writing in *Vanity Fair,* called the novel the "comeback of the century." New Mexico–based writer Rudol-

pho Anaya, in a personal letter to Roth, called it an "engrossing masterpiece." Mary Gordon, writing in the *New York Times,* called it "a deliberately unflattering portrait of the garrulity and narcissism of old age. This is something we have not seen before in literature, and if for no other reason, it is valuable as the speech of the tribe until silenced." (Feb. 26, 1995).

Many thought it deficient as a novel. But Paul Gray, writing for *Time* magazine, accurately described it as more of a documentary than a novel. Biographer Steven G. Kellman calls it a an elaborate "psychomachia" in which Roth obsessively worked out his own private issues (303). *A Star Shines over Mt. Morris Park* was followed in 1995 by *A Diving Rock on the Hudson.*

Henry Roth died on October 13, 1995, at Lovelace Hospital, Albuquerque, New Mexico. Crippling arthritis marked his final years. The third of what was to be a six-volume series, *From Bondage,* was posthumously published in 1996, the same year he was posthumously awarded the Ribalow Award from *Hadassah Magazine.* In the following year, February 29 was declared to be Henry Roth Day in New York City. In 1996 *Holding On* and *From Bondage* appeared. Two years later, in 1998, *Requiem for Harlem* was published. Kellman commented that all of Roth's later writing was motivated by a search for some kind of redemption from the long writer's block, and for all the missing continuities in his own life. Located in the archives of the American Jewish Historical Society in New York are some 83 cartons of manuscripts and papers testifying to the literary energy that went into the search for those lost continuities. At the time of his death Roth was an avowed Zionist, an indication that he had at least recovered a strong sense of himself as a Jew.

Bibliography

Kellman, Steven G. *Redemption: The Life of Henry Roth.* New York: W.W. Norton, 2005.
Roth Papers: Archives of the American Jewish Historical Society in New York.

—Gloria L. Cronin

Roth, Philip (1933–   )

Philip Roth was born in Newark, New Jersey, in 1933, the son of American-born parents and the grandson of European Jews who were part of the 19th-century wave of immigration to the United States. He grew up in the city's lower-middle-class section of Weequahic and was educated in Newark public schools. He later attended Bucknell University, where he received a B.A., and the University of Chicago, where he completed an M.A. and taught English. Afterward, at both the University of Iowa and Princeton Universities, he taught creative writing, and for many years he taught comparative literature at the University of Pennsylvania. He retired from teaching in 1992.

His first book was GOODBYE, COLUMBUS AND FIVE SHORT STORIES (1959), a novella and five stories that use wit, irony, and humor to depict Jewish life in postwar America. The book won him critical recognition—SAUL BELLOW said of Roth's precocious literary talents, "Unlike those of us who came howling into the world, blind and bare, Mr. Roth appears with nails, hair, and teeth, speaking coherently." It also brought him condemnation from some within the Jewish community for depicting what they saw as the unflattering side of contemporary Jewish-American experience. Because of stories such as "Defender of the Faith," about a young soldier using his Jewishness to receive special treatment, and "Epstein," where a middle-aged Jewish man turns to adultery as a way out of his uninspired home life, Roth was branded as reckless, self-hating, and even anti-Semitic, a loaded reputation that only increased in subsequent decades.

His first full-length novel was *Letting Go* (1962), a Jamesian realistic work that explores many of the societal and ethical issues of the 1950s. This was followed in 1967 by *When She Was Good*, another novel in the realistic mode that takes as its focus a rare narrative voice in Roth's fiction: a young Midwestern female. But he is perhaps best known—notoriously so, to many—for his third novel, PORTNOY'S COMPLAINT (1969), a wildly comic representation of his middle-class New York Jewish world in the portrait of Alexander Portnoy, whose possessive mother makes him so guilty and insecure that he can find relief only in forbidden sexual practices. *Portnoy's Complaint* was not only a *New York Times* best seller for the entire year 1969, it also made a celebrity of Roth, an uncomfortable position that he would later fictionalize in such novels as *Zuckerman Unbound* (1981) and *Operation Shylock* (1993).

Following the publication of *Portnoy's Complaint,* Roth experimented with different comic modes, at times outrageous, as illustrated in the works "On the Air" (1970), a surrealistic short story that proved even more offensive to some than *Portnoy's Complaint; Our Gang* (1971), a parodic attack on Richard Nixon; *The Breast* (1972), a Kafkaesque rendering of sexual desire; and *The Great American Novel* (1973), a wild satire of both Frank Norris's novelistic quest and the great American pastime, baseball. In *My Life as a Man* (1974), Roth not only introduces his most developed protagonist, Nathan Zuckerman, but for the first time his fiction becomes highly self-reflexive and postmodern. The novel helped to initiate a new direction for Roth that he further honed in one of his most significant literary efforts, the Zuckerman trilogy and epilogue: *The Ghost Writer* (1979), *Zuckerman Unbound, The Anatomy Lesson* (1983), and the novella "The Prague Orgy" (1985). These works trace the development of Roth's alter ego, Nathan Zuckerman, from an aspiring young writer to a socially compromised and psychologically besieged literary celebrity. In THE COUNTERLIFE (1986), a postmodern tour de force and perhaps his most ambitious and meticulously structured novel, Roth brings a temporary end to his Zuckerman writings. It is also the first time the author engages in a sustained examination of the relationship between American and Israeli Jews.

His next four books—*The Facts* (1988), *Deception* (1990), *Patrimony* (1991), and *Operation Shylock*—explore the interplay between "fiction" and "fact," or what Roth has called "the relationship between the unwritten and the written world."

Through his protagonist in these works, a character named Philip Roth, the author questions the genres of autobiography and fiction, and he mischievously encourages the reader to become caught up in this literary game of where one ends and the other begins. Of these four books, only one, *Deception,* is billed as a novel. The other three are subtitled autobiography (*The Facts*), memoir or "true story" (*Patrimony*), or confession (*Operation Shylock*). The most elaborate of these, *Operation Shylock,* is arguably Roth's finest work, leading fellow writer Cynthia Ozick to call it in one of her interviews, "the Great American Jewish Novel" and Roth "the boldest American writer alive."

Roth's next novel, SABBATH'S THEATER (1995), is a return to the outrageous psychosexual (and tragicomic) form that entertained and outraged so many in *Portnoy's Complaint.* Its "hero," the lewd and arthritic puppeteer Mickey Sabbath, is nothing if not a character portrait of transgressive behavior. In his next three novels, however, what is called his American Trilogy, Roth relies once again on Nathan Zuckerman as his agent of focus. AMERICAN PASTORAL (1997), *I Married a Communist* (1998), and *The HUMAN STAIN* (2000) can be read as novels that reflect key moments in late 20th-century American experience—in the 1960s, 1950s, and 1990s, respectively—and each is chronicled by an older Zuckerman, no longer the mischievous and sexually adventurous young writer he once was. In this later trilogy, the aged writer has become somewhat of a recluse devoted exclusively to his writing. Through this writing he reveals the stories of memorable individuals who, in many ways, represent the social, political, and psychological conflicts that defined postwar America.

In *The Dying Animal* (2001) Roth revisits the life of David Kepesh, the protagonist of *The Breast* and *The Professor of Desire* (1977). As in the earlier novels, Kepesh is concerned with the erotic side of existence and, as he puts it, "emancipated manhood." Yet even though its focus is explicitly sexual, this novel, like almost all of Roth's other works, has as its theme the ways in which individuals—specifically men—live with desire in the larger sense of the word. One of the hallmarks of Roth's fiction is the ways in which sexual, communal, familial, ethnic, artistic, and political freedoms play themselves out on the field of contemporary existence. And *The Dying Animal,* along with similarly exuberant works such as *Portnoy's Complaint* and *Sabbath's Theater,* proves tireless in exploring those unrestrained freedoms to their fullest.

The PLOT AGAINST AMERICA (2004) takes Roth into fresh literary territory. It is an alternative history whose premise is the 1940 election of Charles A. Lindbergh to the White House. What, Roth asks, would America have been like had the isolationist and anti-Semitic Lindbergh defeated F.D.R., reached a cordial "understanding" with Adolf Hitler, and kept the United States out of World War II? Reminiscent of the American Trilogy preceding it, *The Plot Against America* continues the author's exploration of American identities, national as well as individual, within the contexts of its history. Many critics feel that Roth's later novels in which he anchors the individual subject within post–World War II American history are his most significant yet.

In *EVERYMAN* (2006) Roth revisits the short novel, or novella, form he explored in such works as *The Breast, Deception,* and *The Dying Animal.* The thematic focus in this novel is not so much on death as on illness and the role it plays in our lives. The protagonist is an anonymous "everyman" figure (reminiscent of the medieval drama) who, from his youngest days, feels the effects of the decaying body and where it ultimately leads.

According to Roth, *Exit Ghost* (2007) is supposed to be the last work in which the perennial Nathan Zuckmerman appears. Unlike his last appearances in the American Trilogy, Nathan is not so much a narrating conduit in *Exit Ghost* as he is the central participant in its various events, all surrounding the topic of cultural celebrity and the suspect genre of literary biography (and this during a time when Roth's own literary biography is currently being written by his friend Ross Miller). This novel is reminiscent of the earlier Zuckerman novels collected in *Zuckerman Bound* (1985), in which Nathan was the point of narrative focus. In it Nathan returns to New York City after decades of self-imposed exile in the Berkshires and inadvertently stumbles onto characters (and problems) he first encountered in *The Ghost Writer*. By bringing his protagonist full circle, Roth underscores many of the themes that have defined his narrative oeuvre and in doing so paints a vivid—and at times, frantic—portrait of the artist as an old man. In 2008 Roth published *Indignation*, a novel about a young Jewish student who attends college in Ohio during the time of the Korean War. Critics disagreed, often sharply, on the novel's worth, with some comparing it to *Portnoy's Complaint* and others to the shorter novels of Roth's later period, such as *Everyman*. Christopher Hitchens, in the *Atlantic*, called *Indignation* a "rather knocked-together novelette," with "thin and flimsy characters." Conversely, David Gates, in the *New York Times*, called it "ruthlessly economical" and cited its "power and intensity."

In addition to his novels and short stories, Roth has also proven to be an accomplished essayist. In collections such as *Reading Myself and Others* (1975) and the more recent *Shop Talk* (2001), he focuses on the act of writing, both his own and that of others. The lengthy interviews that make up *Shop Talk* are a testament to Roth's unwavering and ongoing admiration of some of the most significant writers in the last half of the 20th century. Until 1989 he was the general editor of the Penguin book series "Writers from the Other Europe," which he inaugurated in 1974. That series helped to introduce American audiences to, among others, Milan Kundera, Primo Levi, Aharon Appelfeld, and Ivan Klima.

Unlike many prolific novelists, whose productive qualities may tend to wane over time, Roth has demonstrated a unique ability not only to sustain his literary output, but even surpass the scope and talent displayed in his previous writings. His later fiction is arguably his best work, as demonstrated by the succession of awards he received in the 1990s. His many awards and honors include two National Book Awards (for *Goodbye, Columbus* and *Sabbath's Theater*), two National Book Critics Circle Awards (for *The Counterlife* and *Patrimony*), two PEN/Faulkner Awards (for *Operation Shylock* and *The Human Stain*), a Pulitzer Prize in fiction (for *American Pastoral*), the National Medal of Arts, the National Book Foundation Medal for distinguished contribution to American letters, and, most recently, the PEN/Nabokov Award for lifetime achievement. To call Roth one of the most important American novelists in the past 50 years would be an understatement.

Bibliography
Baumgarten, Murray, and Barbara Gottfried. *Understanding Philip Roth*. Columbia: University of South Carolina Press, 1990.
Cooper, Alan. *Philip Roth and the Jews*. Albany: SUNY Press, 1996.
Halio, Jay L., and Ben Siegel. *Turning Up the Flame: Philip Roth's Later Novels*. Newark: University of Delaware Press, 2005.
Milbauer, Asher Z., and Donald G. Watson, eds. *Reading Philip Roth*. New York: St. Martin's Press, 1988.
Rodgers, Bernard F., Jr. *Philip Roth*. Boston: Twayne, 1978.
Royal, Derek Parker, ed. *Philip Roth: New Perspectives on an American Author*. Westport, Conn.: Greenwood-Praeger, 2005.
———. "Philip Roth's America: The Later Novels." *Studies in American Jewish Literature* 23 (2004): 1–181.
Shechner, Mark. *Up Society's Ass, Copper: Rereading Philip Roth*. Madison: University of Wisconsin Press, 2003.
Shostak, Debra. *Philip Roth—Countertexts, Counterlives*. Columbia: University of South Carolina Press, 2004.

—Derek Parker Royal

Rukeyser, Muriel (1913–1980)

"Muriel, mother of everyone," is how Anne Sexton described the poet, political and social activist, biographer, essayist, novelist, journalist, translator, playwright, traveler, pilot, teacher, and single mother—Muriel Rukeyser. She was, foremost, a poet, but Rukeyser defied categorization because she can be said to have embraced the interconnection between all aspects of life. Rukeyser was born in New York City on December 15, 1913, to wealthy, upwardly mobile, Jewish, American-born parents. Her mother, a bookkeeper, and her father, a partner in a sand-and-gravel company, raised their family on Riverside Drive in New York City. By the time she was in high school, Rukeyser was already a serious poet concerned with issues of social justice.

Rukeyser attended the Ethical Culture Fieldston School in the Bronx, Vassar College, and Columbia University. In 1933, when she was 19 years old, Rukeyser left Vassar and traveled to Alabama to cover the Scottsboro case, in which nine young black men were falsely accused of raping two white women. From there, she traveled to Spain in support of the Spanish Republic at the start of the Spanish civil war; to Gauley Bridge, West Virginia, where hundreds of miners were dying from silicosis due to an industrial disaster; to Hanoi, Vietnam with fellow poet DENISE LEVERTOV, to protest the war with the United States; and to South Korea, to attempt to visit the imprisoned poet Kim Chi Ha on death row. Rukeyser wrote about all these experiences in poems such as "The Gates" and "The Book of the Dead." Rukeyser was arrested for her political convictions, accused of being a communist, attacked by both the Left and the Right, and investigated by the FBI, which had compiled a file on her over 100 pages long. Rukeyser believed strongly that poetry and politics should not be thought of as separate entities. "Oh, for God's sake / they are connected / underneath," she wrote in "Islands," one of many poems about the artificial divisions set up between disciplines and subjects. For Rukeyser, nothing—and no one—stands alone.

At the age of 21, Rukeyser published her first volume of poetry, *Theory of Flight* (1935), which was chosen by Stephen Vincent Benét for the Yale Younger Poets series. The first line in one of the opening poems, "Poem out of Childhood," reveals Rukeyser's insistence on the confluence of poetry and life, of the entanglements between the public and the private: "Breathe-in experience, breathe-out poetry," she writes. Rukeyser drew from a wealth of experiences in her work, and she would go on to publish 15 more volumes of poetry, three biographies, a poetic treatise, one novel, six children's books, translations, as well as many essays, plays, and stories. Her first volume of poetry, inspired by flying lessons she took at the Roosevelt Aviation School, reveals Rukeyser's particular interest in scientific and technological advancement. Indeed, two of the three biographies she wrote were of scientists: *Willard Gibbs* (1942) and *The Traces of Thomas Hariot* (1971). Her other biography, *One Life* (1957), treats the visionary politician and 1940 Republican presidential candidate, Wendell Wilkie. Rukeyser, herself a visionary, saw herself as a dynamic part of everything around her. As such, she was not only a poet "witness" to human suffering, she was an active participant in bringing about change.

Much of her poetry of the 1930s and 1940s attests to her commitment to the impoverished and the oppressed. Unlike most social protest poetry, though, Rukeyser's work is sophisticated, complex, and skillfully written. Along with her contemporaries DELMORE SCHWARTZ, STANLEY KUNITZ, and Karl Shapiro, Rukeyser conjoined realism and modernism, and she was especially influenced by such poets as T. S. Eliot and W. H. Auden.

Though she married, Rukeyser had the marriage annulled after two months, and she later gave birth to a son by another man. In the 1950s she focused on raising her son as a single mother and did not publish. The experience of giving birth and raising a child, though, can be seen in her work published in the 1960s. Moreover, in that period Rukeyser translated poetry by the Mexican poet Octavio Paz and the Swedish poet Gunnar Ekelöf.

During the growth of feminism and the women's movement in the 1970s, Rukeyser became an important teacher and role model for the next generation of women writers. Writers such as Adrienne Rich, Anne Sexton, Sharon Olds, and Alice Walker have all claimed her as a major influence on their work. Two major feminist anthologies of the 1970s even took their titles from poems by Rukeyser: "No More Masks!" and "The World Split Open." During the latter part of her life, Rukeyser taught at Vassar College, the California Labor School, and for many years at Sarah Lawrence College. She died on February 12, 1980, at the age of 66.

Though she remained secular, Rukeyser always maintained a strong sense of her identity as an American Jewish woman. In her poem "To Be a Jew in the Twentieth Century," Rukeyser contemplates the responsibilities that come with being a Jew. Published in 1944, when the events of the Holocaust were just being uncovered, Rukeyser provocatively observe, "To be a Jew in the twentieth century / Is to be offered a gift. If you refuse, / Wishing to be invisible, you choose / Death of the spirit, the stone insanity. / Accepting, take full life." Like many other Jewish-American writers and poets of her time, Rukeyser embraced her Jewish identity as much as her American identity, and she viewed them as being inseparable. "My themes and the use I have made of them," she writes, "have depended on my life as a poet, as a woman, as an American, and as a Jew."

Rukeyser was awarded the Harriet Monroe Poetry Award (1941), a Guggenheim fellowship (1943), the Levinson Prize (1947), election to the National Institute of Arts and Letters (1967), the American Academy of Poets' Copernicus Prize (1977), the Shelley Prize (1977), and grants from the American Academy of Arts and Letters and the National Institute of Arts and Letters.

Because she is so difficult to classify, Rukeyser has often been omitted from anthologies, and many of her works have gone out of print. But there has been a rebirth of interest in Rukeyser, and it is likely that more of her poetry and uncollected writings will soon be available to a new generation of readers.

Bibliography

Herzog, Anne F., and Janet E. Kaufman. *"How Shall We Tell Each Other of the Poet?"* New York: Palgrave, 1999.

Levi, Jan Heller. *A Muriel Rukeyser Reader.* New York: W.W. Norton, 1994.

Rukeyser, Muriel. *The Life of Poetry.* Ashfield, Mass.: Paris Press, 1996.

—**Alexis Wilson**

S

Sabbath's Theater Philip Roth (1995)

In his novel *Sabbath's Theater,* PHILIP ROTH revisits the sexual exploits and violations of social taboos that thoroughly offended readers and the Jewish community in GOODBYE, COLUMBUS (1959) and PORTNOY'S COMPLAINT (1969). Mickey Sabbath, a repulsive, sexually deviant former puppeteer who has few redeeming qualities, is the novel's protagonist. Roth packs the book with so much shock value in his artful attempt to deconstruct our understanding of normality and "deviance" that it makes the exploits of Alexander Portnoy, the protagonist of *Portnoy's Complaint,* seem tame in comparison. With so much graphic overload it is easy to see why critics like Mark Shechner claim that *Sabbath's Theater* is yelling, "Up Society's Ass, Copper!" at the top of its lungs.

Sabbath's Theater received the National Book Award for fiction in 1995. Written and published just a few short years after *Operation Shylock* (1993) and before *American Pastoral* (1997), *Sabbath's Theater* finds itself in a strange position: It is generally accepted to be a great work but is disliked by many readers. Some critics argue that the novel simply rehashes themes established in earlier books. Other critics, such as James Wood and Harold Bloom, have called it one of Roth's greatest.

Within the novel Roth intentionally and masterfully alienates his readers to reveal the false reality that has been sold and consumed by the everyday man through conservative social boundaries. Sabbath is a retired street theater performer and puppeteer living unhappily with his alcoholic wife in the New England town of Madamaska. At every opportunity he has adulterous sex with the equally oversexed Drenka, the innkeeper's wife. The narrative point of view begins to break apart just as Sabbath suffers through a series of unfortunate events that force him to relive his painful past. The eventual disintegration of his childlike, overindulgent reality mirrors Alexander Portnoy's Freudian stream-of-conscience self-analysis in *Portnoy's Complaint.*

Written during the mid-1990s, during the first Clinton administration, *Sabbath's Theater* is the product of a conservative backlash that directly challenges the country's morality police. The character Mickey Sabbath is the portrait of a man abating the anxiety of death with the hopes of rebirth and a second chance through sex. Sabbath, the self-proclaimed "Evangelist of Fornication," has simplified his life philosophy to revolve around sex. His purging of useless activities like the acquisition of wealth, power, and reputation, and his pursuit of painful relationships has allowed him to distance himself from social norms to question their true value in life. While the content of the book may be unusual, the psychological struggle of an aging, 65-year-old retired puppeteer rivals and mirrors the plight of

Hamlet's "to be or not to be" character struggle, especially with the continual reappearance of the ghost of Sabbath's mother, who encourages him to commit suicide. Readers may feel guilty from the pleasure of looking into the soul of a man without social boundaries.

Bibliography

Safer, Elaine B. "The Tragicomic in Philip Roth's *Sabbath's Theater*." In *American Literary Dimensions: Poems and Essays in Honor of Melvin J. Friedman*. Newark: University of Delaware Press, 1999.

Shechner, Mark. *Up Society's Ass, Copper: Rereading Philip Roth*. Madison: University of Wisconsin Press, 2003.

—**Josue Aristides Diaz**

Salamon, Julie (1953–)

Julie Salamon, the American-born daughter of Holocaust survivors, is a novelist and culture writer for the *New York Times*. Raised in Seamon, Ohio, a small town in the northwest of that state, her family members were the town's only Jews. Concerning the impact of the Holocaust on her identity, she observes that it is primal, "especially for somebody whose parents are survivors." One of the primary lessons she learned from her Holocaust inheritance is expressed in her commitment to social justice. She chairs the Bowery Residents Committee, which provides social services and housing to the homeless. Salamon was formerly a film critic and a reporter for the *Wall Street Journal*, and her essays have appeared in *The New Republic, Vanity Fair, Vogue, Bazaar,* and *The New Yorker*. She received a B.A. from Tufts University and a J.D. degree from New York University Law School.

Salamon has written six books, two of which (the novel WHITE LIES and her memoir, *The NET OF DREAMS: A FAMILY'S SEARCH FOR A RIGHTFUL PLACE*) treat her Holocaust inheritance. Two of her books have won awards; *Christmas Tree*—a novella about a relationship between an orphan girl living in a convent and a tiny fir tree—was a New York Times Best Seller, and *Facing the Wind*—a nonfiction account of a family murder—was a New York Times

Notable Book and an NPR Fresh Air Best Book of 2001. *The Devil's Candy: The Bonfire of the Vanities Goes to Hollywood* is an account of the trials and tribulations of director Brian DePalma as he films this box office dud. Salamon's 2003 book, *Rambam's Ladder: A Meditation on Generosity and Why It Is Necessary to Give,* has garnered much attention in the philanthropic world.

The Net of Dreams is a compelling family memoir in which the author shares her relations with her parents and sister with great skill and tenderness. Salamon's mother, Lilly, is energetic and life-affirming. Sanyi, her physician father, although refraining from discussing his own Holocaust past, frequently flies into uncontrollable rages and has dark, brooding moments. Julie discovers only at age 10, and quite by accident—she heard the story from a cousin—that her father's first wife and young daughter had been gassed at Auschwitz. Married and a mother herself, Julie accompanies her mother and stepfather on a pilgrimage to eastern Europe, which has become a ritual among daughters and sons of survivors, where she begins to hear a more detailed account of the Holocaust, the event that has deeply affected her life although it occurred before she was born.

Salamon, always the keen observer, shares with her readers two events that mark the difference between the relationship of the second and third generation to their Holocaust inheritance. The author, a friend of Steven Spielberg, makes arrangements to stop in Poland to watch a portion of the filming of *Schindler's List*. Spielberg's publicist faxes a "cheery message" saying that getting to Auschwitz is easy. Salamon muses, "that may be." However, the real issue is "getting away from it that really is very difficult" (31). In America Roxie, Salamon's four-year-old daughter—the third generation—baulks at eating broccoli. Julie says to the child, "I love it." Her daughter replies: "I'm me and you're you, and we are not the same." This episode reveals much about mother-daughter bonding but also speaks to the issue of how the grandchild of survivors needs to find her own way of relating to the Holocaust.

Bibliography

Berger, Alan L. *Children of Job: American Second Generation Witnesses to the Holocaust.* Albany: State University of New York Press, 1997.

Haberman, Clyde. "Julie Salamon; Growing Up in Ohio in the Shadow of the Holocaust." *New York Times,* 22 May 1996, C1.

Salamon, Julie. "The Long Voyage Home." *Harper's Bazaar,* February 1994, 134–139.

—Alan L. Berger

Salinger, J. D. (Jerome David) (1919–)

Jerome David Salinger was born on January 1, 1919, in New York City to Sol and Miriam Salinger. Sol, the son of a rabbi, worked as an importer of European meats and cheeses. While working in Chicago, Sol met and married Marie Jillich—an Irish Catholic—who later changed her name to Miriam. Though this outward gesture would seem to indicate an embrace of Judaism, the Salingers in fact practiced no religion. The world in which Salinger grew up and eventually chose to write about was the world of the Upper East Side WASP, *not* the world of the eastern European Jewish immigrant.

Sonny, as Salinger was called as a boy, along with his older sister, Doris, led an ordinary childhood. The family lived on Manhattan's Upper West Side until 1932, when Sol moved the family to Park Avenue on the Upper East Side—a sign of his success in the business world. Salinger was enrolled in an expensive private school, but after receiving poor grades his first year, he was asked not to return. Sol sent his 14-year-old son to the Valley Forge Military Academy in Pennsylvania. The two years he spent there were ones of immense growth and change. "Sonny" gave way to "Jerry," and the once introverted boy became involved in several school organizations. With the exception of his English class, in which he excelled, Salinger performed just well enough to pass in his other subjects, and he graduated in 1936 having developed a strong interest in writing.

In fall 1937 Salinger enrolled at New York University's Washington Square College, but after only a year, he dropped out, calling it a "waste of time." Thinking that his son might take over his business, Sol sent him to Europe for several months to study his business firsthand. The trip did not induce Salinger to go into the meat-importing business, though his experiences in Europe would certainly shape his life and his writing.

On his return Salinger decided to try his hand at college again—choosing, for no apparent reason, Ursinus College in Pennsylvania. Again, he dropped out, this time after only nine weeks. By now, though, he knew he wanted to write, but the classes at Ursinus were not helping him. Thus, in spring 1939 Salinger was back in New York City auditing a class at Columbia University taught by Whit Burnett, the highly regarded creative writing professor, as well as founder and editor of the journal *Story*. Salinger's short story "The Young Folks" was published in the 1940 issue of Burnett's journal. Salinger's story, about the emptiness and shallowness of a group of upper-class college kids, brought him $25—his first earnings as a writer. The subject continued to interest him in future stories.

In 1941 Salinger began a 10-year process of developing the character Holden Caulfield, who cemented his fame and status as a writer. From 1941 until 1951, when The CATCHER IN THE RYE was published, Salinger did more than just write. During this period, he joined the army, experienced live combat, met the writer Ernest Hemingway in Paris, had a mild nervous breakdown, married and divorced a French psychologist, developed an interest in Zen Buddhism, published several more short stories in *The New Yorker,* and had one story made into a Hollywood movie. Though he was invited to publish a collection of his short stories, Salinger wanted his novel about a prep school boy in New York to come out first; when it did, *The Catcher in the Rye* remained on the *New York Times* best-seller list for 30 weeks.

The Catcher in the Rye tells the story of Holden Caulfield, who, after having been kicked out of his prep school for poor grades, wanders the streets of New York before succumbing to a nervous breakdown. Holden—the quintessential symbol of disaffected American youth—has one of the most memorable and distinctive literary voices ever written, and *Catcher* remains a staple of high schools across the nation. With its themes of alienation and the superficiality and hypocrisy of the adult world—what Holden incessantly refers to as "phoniness"—*Catcher* has had an enormous impact on subsequent works about jaded youth.

A few years after the success of *The Catcher in the Rye,* Salinger bought a home in Cornish, New Hampshire, and became a recluse. Though he married and continued to publish, he hid from the public spotlight—even going so far as to build a fence around his house. Salinger's second marriage, to 19-year-old Claire Douglas, lasted for 12 years and produced two children—Margaret and Matthew. By 1970 Salinger decided not to publish anymore. In addition to *The Catcher in the Rye,* he had published several short stories that were eventually compiled in three separate books: *Nine Stories* (1953), *Franny and Zooey* (1961), and *Raise High the Roof Beam and Seymour: An Introduction* (1963).

Nine Stories showcases Salinger's superb talent and mastery of the short story form. His subject throughout, though, is young upper-class characters on the verge of a breakdown, and Salinger has received both praise and criticism for this. Norman Mailer famously remarked that Salinger was "no more than the greatest mind ever to stay in prep school." *Franny and Zooey,* as well as *Raise High the Roof Beam, Carpenters and Seymour: An Introduction,* is a joint publication containing two stories about the Glass family. Though Salinger promised "several new Glass stories," only one more was published in the *New Yorker* in 1965—"Hapworth 16, 1924." Salinger still lives in Cornish and has remarried, but everything else about his life is speculation for now.

Bibliography
Alexander, Paul. *Salinger: A Biography.* Los Angeles: Renaissance Books, 1999.
Roemer, Danielle M. "The Personal Narrative and Salinger's *Catcher in the Rye." Western Folklore* 51, no. 1 (January 1992): 5–10.

—Alexis Wilson

Seize the Day Saul Bellow (1956)

Seize the Day is a novella describing a single, pivotal day in the life of Tommy Wilhelm, an ex-traveling salesman who is low on funds, down on his luck, estranged from his wife and children, at odds with his octogenarian father, and under the dubious tutelage of a trickster named Dr. Tamkin—a self-proclaimed psychiatrist who plays the stock market with Wilhelm's last $700. Fast approaching middle age, Wilhelm has led a life of missteps and blunders, particularly his decision to leave college to pursue an ill-fated acting career.

In the first three chapters of *Seize the Day,* Wilhelm has breakfast with his father, Dr. Adler. Wilhelm is hoping for sympathy, guidance, and financial assistance, but his father rejects his bumbling advances. Adler shows his son little sympathy, offers him no money, and gives him only a single piece of "fatherly" advice, as blunt as it is cruel: "I want nobody on my back. Get off! And I give you the same advice, Wilky. Carry nobody on your back" (55). Wilhelm then flees from the dining room in search of Tamkin, who serves as an obvious surrogate for Wilhelm's biological father.

Chapters four through six detail Wilhelm's interactions with Tamkin. The two have breakfast, mirroring Wilhelm's earlier breakfast with Adler. Tamkin tells Wilhelm a number of implausible stories about himself, his patients, and his exploits in the stock market—stories Wilhelm simultaneously believes and disbelieves. Tamkin discusses the connection between moneymaking and murder, waxes eloquent on the differences between real and pretender souls, and presents Wilhelm with a poem that seems to Wilhelm's baffled mind to represent the epitome of stupidity. The two men walk over to the brokerage office to check on their joint investments in lard and rye, then eat lunch in the cafeteria, Tamkin nonchalantly stiffing Wilhelm with the bill. Returning to the brokerage office, Wilhelm discovers that his investments have failed and that Tamkin has fled the scene.

In the novella's final chapter, Wilhelm searches for Tamkin, begs his father for help, and is once again summarily rejected by Adler, who declares, "You want to make yourself into my cross. But

I am not going to pick up a cross. I'll see you dead, Wilky, by Christ, before I let you do that to me" (110). Wilhelm then has an unsatisfactory telephone conversation with his estranged wife, who demands money he does not have. After Margaret abruptly hangs up on him, Wilhelm staggers into the street and stumbles across a large funeral procession. Standing before the corpse of a stranger, Wilhelm begins to cry, his grief and tears bending his head, bowing his shoulders, twisting his face, convulsing his body. And as the sound of the funeral music swells in his ears, he sinks "deeper than sorrow, through torn sobs and cries toward the consummation of his heart's ultimate need" (118).

Seize the Day is thus Wilhelm's futile search for a redemptive father figure. It is also BELLOW's morality tale about the way in which money oppresses the human spirit. Lust for money, obsession about money, and lack of money all contribute to the dissolution of the most important familial relationships in the novella, including Wilhelm's relationships with his children, his wife, and his father. The brokerage house is a symbol of capitalism gone bad. Within its cloistered walls is a veritable carnival of the grotesque, replete with glassy-eyed old men, polygamists, chicken killers, and the racket and clatter of mechanistic determinism. Tamkin embodies the deceptive aspects of stock-market transactions. Tamkin's dubious credentials, his secondhand philosophy, his inflated concern for Wilhelm's well-being, his extravagant stories of marketplace prowess, his strained condemnation of moneymaking aggression, and his canny decision to mischaracterize their joint venture as a gentlemen's experiment in marketplace dynamics all work hand in glove to mesmerize Wilhelm, transforming him into an easy mark who allows himself to be duped by a liar whom he never really believes.

Adler, Wilhelm's biological father, is even worse than Tamkin, his surrogate father. Tamkin confuses and uses Wilhelm, but he risks a portion of his own money in the endeavor, and he seems motivated by greed rather than hate. Wilhelm's father, on the other hand, seems driven by a hidden malice that is one part avarice and two parts contempt. It is not merely that Adler loves his money more than his children; rather, he seems completely incapable of loving anything *but* money—and himself. Neither is Wilhelm free from the general curse. He is occasionally generous with his children, and he struggles to be fair with his wife. But he bitterly resents the claims they make on his income. And although Wilhelm declares that what he most desires is a simple expression of his father's love, the novella makes clear that a check for ten thousand would have done the job just as well.

Nevertheless, Wilhelm remains a surprisingly sympathetic character, in large part because of Bellow's clever manipulation of point of view. In *Seize the Day* the narrator provides full access to Wilhelm's mind and heart. Sometimes the narrator and the protagonist become so completely intertwined that Wilhelm's self-pity gains the flavor—if not the fact—of the narrator's credibility. The narrator grants occasional access to Adler's mind and heart, but only—and this is a key point—when Adler is furious with his son, thereby confirming Wilhelm's bad opinion of his father's character. The narrator offers no access whatsoever to the thought processes and emotional constitutions of Margaret and Tamkin, which has the practical effect of demonizing the former and cloaking the latter in mystery—Wilhelm's perspective exactly. If readers love Tommy Wilhelm (and they frequently do), they do so primarily because the narrator loved him first. Only at the very end of the novella does the narrator begin to pull back—ever so slightly—toward an objective position, which may explain why critics vigorously disagree about the meaning of the book's last image.

Bibliography
Ciancio, Ralph. "The Achievement of Saul Bellow's *Seize the Day." Small Planets: Saul Bellow and the Art of Short Fiction.* East Lansing: Michigan State University Press, 2000.
Cronin, Gloria L. "Bellow's Quarrel with Modernism in *Seize the Day." Encyclia* 57 (1980): 95–102.
                                                    —Daniel Muhlestein

Shaw, Irwin (1913–1984)

A major presence in American literature for over 45 years, Irwin Shaw (born Irwin Gilbert Shamforoff) remains a notable and influential Jewish-American author. Shaw was born in New York City, the son of a Russian immigrant father and a first-generation American mother. His parents were eastern European Jews, but they emphasized assimilation into American society. As a result, Shaw was raised with little formal instruction in Jewish traditions. Despite his parents' pressure to assimilate, Shaw clung to his heritage, insisting on participating in Jewish rites of passage through adolescence. Well into adulthood, however, Shaw called himself "a nonpracticing Jew, but also an atheist" (Shnayerson 23).

Shaw's writing career was launched just two years after graduating from Brooklyn College, when his play *Bury the Dead* (1936) was produced in New York City, establishing him as a writer of note among critics. His second play, *The Gentle People* (1939), likewise received a degree of critical acclaim; but after his fourth play, *The Assassin* (1946), was forced to close early, he "published an angry denunciation of the theatre and came close to abandoning drama" (Giles 4).

Shaw was also a prolific short story and novel writer, genres to which he remained especially faithful after the commercial failure of his fourth play. In his lifetime he published seven collections of short fiction (84 stories in all), among them *Sailor off the Bremen* (1939), *Welcome to the City* (1942), *Act of Faith and Other Stories* (1946), *Mixed Company* (1950), *Tip on a Dead Jockey* (1957), *Love on a Dark Street* (1965), and *God Was Here but He Left Early* (1973). He received the O. Henry Memorial Award first prize in 1944 for his short story "Walking Wounded," and the following year he received the O. Henry Memorial Award second prize for his short story "Gunnar's Passage."

Shaw's first novel, *The Young Lions* (1948), treated major events of World War II, in which he served from 1942 to 1945. *Lions* was heralded as a triumph by critics and later adapted as a film (1958) starring Marlon Brando; both novel and film were fantastic commercial successes. Shaw published his second novel, *The Troubled Air* (1951), after moving to Paris, where he lived for 25 years. During his expatriate years, he published six more novels: *Lucy Crown* (1956), *Two Weeks in Another Town* (1960), *Voices of a Summer Day* (1965), *Rich Man, Poor Man* (1970), *Evening in Byzantium* (1973), and *Nightwork* (1975). After commencing a dual residence on Long Island, New York, and in Klosters, Switzerland, Shaw finished an additional four novels: *Beggerman, Thief* (1977), *The Top of the Hill* (1979), *Bread upon the Waters* (1981), and *Acceptable Losses* (1982). His two novels *Rich Man, Poor Man* and *Beggerman, Thief* were later adapted as ABC dramatizations, contributing to a revival in popular acclaim that characterized Shaw's later years.

Shaw considered himself a "product of [his] times," and his work is accordingly an imaginative response to the major political and social events of the 20th century (Shaw xi). His plays, for example, combine fantasy with social commentary: The primary characters in *Bury the Dead* are deceased soldiers who refuse to be buried, a clear antiwar sentiment indicative of post–World War II attitudes, while the main characters in *The Gentle People* fantasize an escape to a tropical oasis in Cuba, their only hope to free themselves from the hopelessness of the Great Depression.

His short fiction, which Shaw described as "disguised moralizing that . . . set[s] everyday transactions into larger perspective," also offers insight into the social issues of his day (xii). The Great Depression inspired two types of themes in his short fiction: first, stories that depict the despair of the middle and lower classes, and, second, stories that portray wealthy Americans as emotionally and spiritually shallow, a motif most prominently associated with Shaw. Still others of his stories respond to the rise of fascism in Europe and the war, reprove America for ignoring this threat at home and abroad, excoriate anti-Semitism in Europe, and protest the Senator Eugene McCarthy witch hunts of the 1950s. The struggles of American expatriates in Europe are the most prominent theme in stories published after Shaw's move to France; these stories often focus "on the innocent young American confronting a very old and confusing postwar European culture" (Giles 34).

Shaw's *The Young Lions* is his first novelistic treatment of contemporary events. The novel is an all-encompassing vision of the war that follows the lives of three primary characters: Noah Ackerman, a Jewish-American; Michael Whitacre, a dissolute, guilt-ridden Broadway type; and Christian Diestl, a German soldier. Through the lives of these three, Shaw portrays events such as the German occupation of Paris, the Battle of North Africa, the Allied invasion of France, and the liberation of Paris. Shaw explained that the novel was originally conceived as an attempt "to show how we are all linked in this world—soldiers, civilians, the most sophisticated, the most primitive—the link being, in our time, death" (Plimpton 143). Through minor characters who serve as links between the former three, Shaw portrays a complex web of associations, playing out an allegory that highlights "the crucial role of ethical choice in the attainment of human decency" (Giles 104).

Though there is a general consensus among critics that Shaw's short fiction and his *Young Lions* are masterful, his later novels have been attacked by academic critics, largely because of their immense popular success. Some have implied that Shaw panders to popular audiences in his later work, citing the "slickness" of his style and the "sentimentality" of his intellect, which results in a "superficiality" of narrative (Fiedler 71–74). The great majority, however, especially in the last 20 years, have neglected to discuss his work at all. While the critical value of his later work is still open to debate, it is clear that Shaw's contributions to American literature made in his lifetime establish him as an important Jewish-American writer whose legacy will never be entirely forgotten.

Bibliography
Fiedler, Leslie. "Irwin Shaw: Adultery, the Last Politics." *Commentary* 22 (1956): 71–74.
Giles, James R. *Irwin Shaw.* Boston: Twayne, 1983.
Plimpton, George, ed. *Writers at Work: The Paris Review Interviews.* New York: Viking, 1981.
Shaw, Irwin. *Short Stories: Five Decades.* New York: Delacorte, 1978.
Shnayerson, Michael. *Irwin Shaw: A Biography.* New York: Putnam, 1989.

—Scott L. Ross

"The Shawl" Cynthia Ozick (1980)

"The Shawl" is an exquisitely evocative Holocaust short story—CYNTHIA OZICK's most direct encounter with the immediacy of the death camps—which renders the fear, protectiveness, and horror of a Jewish mother and her toddler daughter. Ozick's story of Rosa; her baby, Magda; and her niece, Stella, is a masterpiece of psychological description and economy of language, which leave the reader stunned by the pitilessness of the situation and the brilliance of the author. Rosa Lublin, starving and with breasts long since dried up, wraps Magda in a magical shawl whose fringes the child sucks for nourishment. Stella takes it away. In search of the shawl, 15-month-old Magda wanders out of the barrack. A German guard hurls her against the electrified fence. Rosa watches in horror, stuffing the shawl in her mouth to stifle the scream building within.

In the space of two pages, the tale's omniscient narrator outlines the "choiceless choice" confronting Jewish mothers during the Shoah: Should Rosa give the shawl-encased infant to one of the non-Jewish women watching the Jews marching toward annihilation? What if the woman refused to take Magda? Moreover, if Rosa left the line, even momentarily, she would be shot. The unnamed death camp, described as a "place without pity," is permeated by a "bad wind with pieces of black in it." Human ashes made Stella's and Rosa's eyes tear. Magda made no sound, perhaps, thinks Rosa, because she is deaf and mute. Magda does speak near the end, crying out "maaaa" while looking for the lost shawl. As Magda is hurtling toward her death the "electric voice" emanating from the fence began wildly chattering, "maamaa, maaamaa."

Symbolically, Ozick's shawl plays several roles. On the one hand, it is Magda's mother; nurturing the infant long after the emaciated Rosa is unable to do so. In addition to its maternal function, the shawl also serves as a tallith (prayer shawl) under whose sacred canopy one is protected (Berger). Ironically, this protection also extends to Rosa, whose life is saved even as Magda's is taken, when the shawl stifles the mother's scream, which would have led to her murder. Nazi practice was to send women and their children to the gas chamber. Ozick's use of repetition also brings to mind biblical cadence. Rosa twice describes Stella as being cold, the coldness of hell, which means that she is indifferent to Magda and may in fact contemplate cannibalizing the toddler. Furthermore, the narrator repeats the information that Rosa knew Magda was going to die soon, thus preparing the reader for the narrator's observation that "Rosa saw that today Magda was going to die."

Ozick's bleak tale does, however, contain a seed of hope. Rosa and Stella survive. Furthermore, even in the death camp Rosa is described in flight imagery: "a floating angel," flying—"she was only air"—and "floating." It is as if the author is emphasizing that although the Holocaust hideously wounded Judaism, the tradition survives. History does not triumph over or exterminate Jewish existence. Moreover, Rosa tastes the "cinnamon and almond depth of Magda's saliva" in the shawl. This imagery suggests the contents of the spice box (*besamim*) whose aroma is inhaled by Jews during the havdalah ceremony, which signifies the end of Shabbat (the Sabbath) and the beginning of the ordinary days of the week. The sweetness of the spices sustains the Jewish people during the following six days until the next Shabbat.

"The Shawl," which first appeared in the *New Yorker,* was subsequently linked with Ozick's sequel, "Rosa." This sequel speaks of Rosa and Stella 35 years after the Holocaust and contains disturbing news. It strongly suggests, for example, that Magda had been the child of a German officer who raped Rosa. Stella wants to forget the Holocaust while Rosa is consumed by its memory. Nonwitnessing psychologists and others understand nothing of survivors' continuing Holocaust trauma. Nevertheless, Rosa retains the iconic shawl that ultimately helps her struggle to work through the unmasterable Holocaust past. In addition, Rosa meets a man, also from Warsaw although not a Holocaust survivor, with whom she begins to communicate. Both "The Shawl" and "Rosa" were reprinted in the annual *Best American Short Stories* and received first prize in the annual *O. Henry Prize Stories* volume.

Bibliography
Berger, Alan L. *Crisis and Covenant: The Holocaust in American Jewish Fiction.* Albany: SUNY Press, 1985.
Gordon, Andrew. "Cynthia Ozick's 'The Shawl' and the Transitional Object." *Literature and Psychology* 40, nos. 1–2 (1994): 1–9.
—Alan L. Berger

Shulman, Alix Kates (1932–)

Writer and political activist Alix Kates Shulman was born in the Ohio suburb of Cleveland Heights, which is her model for the fictional Baybury Heights of her first novel, MEMOIRS OF AN EX-PROM QUEEN—the playful yet weighty and influential feminist book for which she is most widely recognized. Her secular Jewish parents—Samuel Simon Kates, a lawyer, and Dorothy Davis Kates, a homemaker involved in local politics—influenced their daughter's tendencies toward political activity and encouraged her intellectual development early in life. Despite their lack of religious fervor, the Kates sent their children (Alix and her adopted brother, Ben) to Hebrew school to cultivate an understanding of and connection to their heritage.

Graduating from Case Western Reserve University with a bachelor's degree at age 20, Shulman anxiously relocated to New York City to escape the suburban strictures of 1950s small-town life. There she entered Columbia University's graduate program in philosophy and at New York University studied mathematics, both subjects considered hard-core male disciplines (a fact that, Shulman admitted contributed to her choosing them). She also completed a master's degree in the humanities. During this time Shulman married her first husband. Shortly after this marriage ended in divorce, she remarried and began to have children; from then on she was passionate about her role as a parent.

While in her 30s, in the midst of her dedication to motherhood, Shulman discovered feminism, which she called "an explanation of all my puzzles." After attending a small women's group meeting that she heard announced on the radio, she soon joined two then fledgling feminist groups, the New York Radical Women and the Redstockings. In consciousness-raising (CR) sessions, women began to share common experiences of oppression caused by marriage, limited career opportunities, and particularly their sexual experiences as manifestations of gender inequality and patriarchal authority. Even feminists of just a few years earlier (such as Betty Friedan in *The Feminine Mystique*) had shied away from articulating in detail the political implications of sexual relationships. Shulman staunchly believed that real change can occur only through women bonding and sharing their experiences, thus raising consciousness about these societal problems. Even her fiction is aimed at raising awareness of widespread cultural and social issues, presenting them through specific characters that represent a much larger group. Consequently, women across generations continue to connect deeply with Shulman's works, seeing their own experiences reflected in the lives of her characters.

When Shulman first began to write, it is ironic that she feared ostracism in feminist circles since professional writers of the time were considered by her peers to be closely tied to the patriarchal establishment. She began writing children's books and was then asked to write a biography of anarchist and first-wave feminist Emma Goldman for a young adult audience. Her intensive study of Goldman's life and writings profoundly influenced not only her later works but her thinking and writing. She gained the courage to write without fear of disapproval. Her first novel, *Memoirs of an Ex-Prom Queen* (1972), became an underground success even before its first printing. In it, the beautiful Sasha Davis—ex-prom queen of a Midwestern suburb—defines herself by the men

around her and how they respond to her physical appearance. While trying to meet patriarchal society's expectations in various phases of her life, she struggles with sexual harassment, date rape, the restrictions of marriage, divorce, abortion, limitations in education and her career, and the strains of motherhood. In reference to her subject, Shulman said, "It was something I passionately needed to write about," and as evidenced by the over 1 million copies sold, it was something women then and now have passionately needed to hear.

In addition to two edited collections of Emma Goldman's essays, an abundance of published articles, and two memoirs, Shulman has written three other novels: *Burning Questions* (1978), *On the Stroll* (1981), and *In Every Woman's Life . . .* (1987). Like *Memoirs of an Ex-Prom Queen, Burning Questions* reflects Shulman's own life experiences. The main character, Zane IndiAnna, leaves her home in suburban Ohio for New York and begins a flirtation with the up-and-coming 1950s beatnik scene. Later, she marries and divorces, and finally discovers a new vitality in the feminist movement and gains a new political consciousness. *On the Stroll* constellates the lives of three marginalized individuals: a pimp named Prince; Robin, the young woman newly arrived in New York, upon whom he is preying; and Owl, a once beautiful but now homeless woman who believes Robin to be her estranged daughter. Delving into a cross-section of humanity usually ignored, Shulman questions the societal forces that lead people into such lives and explores a relatively unexamined realm of feminism.

After 10 years of spending her summers in solitude on an island off the coast of Maine, Alix Kates Shulman wrote her first memoir, *Drinking the Rain* (1995), in which she recounts her Walden-like experiences of living off the land without electricity, a telephone, or running water. The book questions the artificiality of contemporary living standards and pervasive consumerism. In 1999 Shulman published her second memoir, *A Good Enough Daughter,* in which she reflects on her experiences of caring for her aging parents. In being forced to return to the home of her youth,

Shulman discovered the universal inevitability of coming home—returning to one's roots. This return to a consciousness of family life caused her to reflect on her brother's recent death as well as his position as an adopted child. The unique family dynamics surrounding adoption play a prominent role in her work on a forthcoming novel.

Although Shulman acknowledges certain successes of feminism, she argues that women's overall situation has not greatly improved since the movement was launched. She expresses particular concern over the pressures created by heightened standards of female beauty, noting the rise in anorexia and bulimia in girls of even junior high school age. She continues to promote societal change through increased awareness of the oppression of women.

Bibliography

Altman, Meryl. "Beyond Trashiness: The Sexual Language of 1970s Feminist Fiction." *Journal of International Women's Studies* 4, no. 2 (April 2003): 7–19.

Templin, Charlotte. "Beauty and Gender in Alix Kates Shulman's *Memoirs of an Ex-Prom Queen*." In *Women in Literature: Reading through the Lens of Gender*, edited by Jerilyn Fisher and Ellen S. Silber. Westport, Conn.: Greenwood Press, 2003.

—Sally Giles

Side Effects Woody Allen (1980)

Side Effects (1980) is WOODY ALLEN's third book of fiction. It features short stories and plays originally published separately in magazines and newspapers such as the *New Yorker, The New Republic* and the *New York Times*. "Confessions of a Burglar" is original to the collection. All of the stories draw heavily on the ideas of humor, his German-Jewish background on the Lower East Side of Manhattan, literary theory, philosophy, psychoanalysis, Judaism, psychology, and the culture of New York City. Brilliant and quirky, *Side Effects* became a best seller. Its stories employ wit, postmodern effects, parody, realism, and social satire. The collection generally follows the thematic interests of the films

he was making at the time of their conception and perhaps represent a working out of filmic material. Of particular interest here is the comedy of *Love and Death* (1975), the deeper psychological resonances of *Annie Hall* (1978), and the pure drama of *Interiors* (1978).

"Remembering Needleman," a noted Woody Allen humor piece, deals with a deceased genius and takes on the form of a eulogy through which Allen satirizes intellectualism. "The Condemned" takes its stylistic and thematic cues from Kafka, Camus, and French existentialism. It features one Cloquet who decides not to murder his intended victim, Brisseau, but finds himself, nevertheless, under arrest. "By Destiny Denied" experiments with note form and is ostensibly a set of notes for an 800-page novel. No doubt it is Allen's satiric jab at the pretentiousness of monumental modernist novels and his argument for short forms. "My Apology" is a mock Socratic dialogue with its author, Woody Allen, as a condemned philosopher who instead of summoning up the requisite classic stoicism, faces death with characteristically Allenesque comedic panic. Parodies of Kafka, Allen's favorite author, occur in "The Diet," while "Reminiscences: Places and People" is a Joycean parody. "The UFO Menace" is a mock scientific study, rounding out the series of satiric literary "knock-offs." Morality becomes the weighty and serious consideration in "The Shallowest Man."

The Kugelmass Episode, which won the O. Henry Award in 1977 for the best short story, involves Kugelmass, a humanities professor dissatisfied with his life. Seeking diversion, he falls into company with a magician with a magic box. Aided by the magician and his magic box, Kugelmass is transported to the world of Gustave Flaubert's *Madame Bovary*. His subsequent affair with Emma Bovary is initially happy, but ends hilariously and predictably when he transports her back with him to New York City in the late 20th century. She becomes demanding and dissatisfied, and as the story ends Kugelmass is stuck in a literal limbo locked inside the magician's faulty box with a copy of *Remedial Spanish*. It is a typically self-reflexive postmodern story, Allen's most famous, which explores the relationship between reader and text, and reader-response criticism. Central to the exploration, however, is the serious topic of the use and misuse of art to confirm human illusions. Had Allen funneled prodigious talent into literary production only, no doubt he would have been one of the major postmodern American fiction writers of the era.

Bibliography
Charney, Maurice. "Woody Allen's Non Sequitors." *Humor: International Journal of Humor Research* 8, no. 4 (1995): 339–348.
Davis, J. Madison. "The Literary Skills of Woody Allen." *West Virginia University Philological Papers* 29 (1983): 105–111.

—Rachel Mayrer

Sinclair, Jo (1913–1995)

Jo Sinclair is the pen name of Ruth Seid, the author of four published novels, close to 50 published short stories, and nearly 200 unpublished short stories. She was born in Brooklyn, New York, to a poor Jewish family. Ruth experienced early alienation due to a somewhat masculine appearance and behavior, a condition that contributed to a lack of confidence, feelings of fear, and a lifelong struggle with social acceptance. She was even marginalized in her own family, a situation to which she responded accusing her family of being culturally and emotionally illiterate. Her identity as an only partially assimilated Jew during the prewar years that saw an increase of anti-Semitism in America also contributed to Seid's feelings of alienation. As an adult she identified herself as a lesbian. During her frustrated and angry life, she often used writing as a release valve. Lack of acceptance with regards to race or gender-specific traits are common themes in her work.

Despite her painful early emotional life, Sinclair was a successful high school student, participating actively in track and field, drama, and the school newspaper, and graduating as valedictorian. She was financially unable to attend college, however, and after her high school graduation she took a nonliterary job. She continued to write during this time, and published her first story, "Noon Lynching," six years after graduation. Her first novel, *The Wasteland,* was published in 1946. It remained on the best-seller list for several months. It tells the story of a brother and sister undergoing psychotherapy for their social alienation. The brother is subjected to anti-Semitism, and the lesbian sister is subjected to homophobia. The book won the 1946 Harper Prize Novel Award (which included a prize of $10,000) and gave Seid a minor place in the literary canon. Her second novel, however, *Sing at My Wake,* received negative or no critical response when published in 1951.

Seid spent much of her adult life in a lesbian relationship with Helen Buchman, a married woman with two children. She lived with the Buchmans for 23 years until Helen died, then continued to live there for another seven years after her death, despite the predictably strained relationship that existed between her and the surviving members of the family.

Her other most popular work was the novel *The Changelings,* published in 1955. The book deals with the theme of transgenerational transmission of ideas and prejudices. It makes a statement against the idea that children must repeat the negative behavior of their parents. This book somewhat renewed her reputation with the reading public after the failure of *Sing at My Wake.*

Ruth Seid died of cancer in 1995 at the age of 81. She is considered one of the early Jewish-American lesbian writers, and as such, is a precursor of the contemporary generation of such writers.

Bibliography
"Jo Sinclair, Novelist and Memoirist, 81." *New York Times* Available online. URL: http://query.nytimes.com/gst/fullpage.html?res=990CE7D6163AF930A25757C0A96 3958260. Accessed on April 13, 1995.
Wilentz, Gay. "Jo Sinclair (Ruth Seid) (1913–)." *Jewish-American Women Writers: A Bio-Bibliographical and Critical Sourcebook.* Edited by Ann R. Shapiro. Westport, Conn.: Greenwood Press, 1994.

————. "(Re)Constructing Identity: 'Angled' Presentation in Sinclair/Seid's *Wasteland.*" In *Multicultural Literatures through Feminist/Poststructuralist Lenses.* Knoxville: University of Tennessee Press, 1993.

—Elisabeth Sandberg

Singer, Isaac Bashevis (1904–1991)

A Polish-born American journalist, novelist, short story writer, and essayist, Isaac Bashevis Singer was the best-known Yiddish writer of the 20th century. The grandson of two rabbis and son of a third, Singer was born Yitskhok Zynger in 1904, in Leoncin, Poland, a small town 20 miles northeast of Warsaw. He wrote only in Yiddish, but translations of his works made him one of the most beloved authors in English and in other languages. He won the Nobel Prize in literature in 1978. A prolific, indefatigable writer, he brought to life the annihilated Jewish world of eastern Europe. His chief subject was Jewish life in various periods of Poland's history, but primarily the years preceding the Holocaust. He drew on Jewish folk memories, religious customs, and mystical traditions to create a body of work ranging from the realistic to the fantastic. He did so in ways that startled his readers and inspired other writers. He focused especially on the roles of Judaism and Jewishness in the lives of his characters, who were driven by the inner demons of passion and magic, temptation and asceticism, heresy and religious devotion. "A good writer is basically a story-teller," Singer insisted, "not a scholar or a redeemer of mankind."

Singer's knowledge of Jewish psyche and culture was deep, certain, ancestral. From an Orthodox background with numerous rabbis on both sides of the family, Singer read no secular literature until he was 12. His older brother was the novelist Israel Joshua Singer, author of *Yoshe Kalb* and *The Brothers Ashkenazi.* Both rejected rabbinical careers to champion the Haskala or Jewish Enlightenment. Their sister, Esther Kreitman, was also a novelist.

Singer's early years provided a rich source of literary material. When he was four, the family moved to an apartment on Krochmalna Street, in one of Warsaw's poor, overcrowded Jewish quarters. The neighborhood was populated by observant Jews and street vendors, hustlers and beggars, thieves and prostitutes. (Referring to this urban mix as his "literary gold mine," Singer would recall his childhood there in a relatively lighthearted memoir, *In My Father's Court.*) But when, during World War I, the Germans occupied Warsaw, Singer's mother, Basheve, moved the family to her birthplace, the isolated village of Bilgoray. There Singer imbibed the superstitions and folklore, the unyielding religious beliefs and daily practices of a community virtually untouched by modern times. His three years in this small medieval town provided him with subject matter for many of his most vivid shtetl tales. Singer literally re-created in fiction and memoir this cloistered life of eastern Europe's Jews, as it played out in villages, towns, and cities. It was a life of mind-numbing poverty and cruel persecutions, sincere pieties and human hypocrisies, blind faith and demonic superstitions. This Jewish world employed two languages—Hebrew for ritual and prayer and Yiddish for the exigencies of daily life. Singer leaned heavily on this rich heritage. His chosen literary world was the circumscribed but rich one of Polish Jewry from the 17th to the 20th century. Now gone, its vestiges cremated or otherwise obliterated, this world was reshaped in his fiction.

Writing in a language experiencing steady attrition if not extinction, Singer still proved no primitive. Despite exotic materials and idiomatic style, he was a sophisticated craftsman with the easy fluency attained by only the finest writers in any culture. He was a born storyteller, with sure insight and an outrageous compulsion to create. Fable and fantasy, chronicle and saga, children's story and essay issued from his pen—or, more precisely, from his battered "Yiddish" typewriter. Even his least-inspired tales have a tender, gutsy, tragic vitality derived from a sensitive fusion of Yiddish and Western traditions. His little people's pieties and lusts evoke the stark realities not only of Gogol and Dostoyevsky, Isaac Babel, and Isaac Loeb Peretz, but also of Nathaniel Hawthorne and William Faulkner. A veteran journalist, Singer had a healthy respect for the hard fact and objective report. Yet he saw perversity and originality in all existence; "everything alive," he pointed out, was unique, singular, and nonrepeatable. Most of his work appeared first in the *Jewish Daily Forward,* to which he contributed soon after his arrival in America in 1935. He became a *Forward* staff member in 1944 and also wrote sketches for the paper's radio program on New York station WEVD. Singer enjoyed the "very good profession" of newspaper work, but he signed his journalistic fiction Isaac Warshawsky and did not publish it in book form.

One of the few writers to have mastered the entire Judaic tradition, he could enter and articulate any point without a discordant note. Viewing traditional concepts and values with an ambiguous mixture of love, pride, and doubt, he found no easy answers to the eternal questions. What few answers there were, he made clear, the individual must glean for herself or himself. His refusal to champion group, philosophy, or commandment bothered many. For Singer, all humankind constituted the human reality; hence he spared neither Jew nor Christian, neither code nor attitude. Instead, he wove into his fiction the motions, idiom, and humor of ghetto and small-town Jewish life, the shtetl life that was—if little else—integrated and coherent. His precise images laid bare the Jewish grain without pretense or shout. No aspect of life was too trivial or solemn to be reduced to bare motive. Aware of everything, he disdained little. Singer's characters do not perform great deeds; the world has crushed or bypassed them. Yet despite terror, suffering, and disappointment, they accept and even love life, determined to endure. In such novels as *The FAMILY MOSKAT, Satan in Goray, The Magician of Lublin, The Slave,* and *The Manor,* Singer evoked a past rich in the sufferings and joys, shapes and sounds of the Jewish diaspora's last four centuries. However, many critics consider his short stories—especially those collected in *GIMPEL THE FOOL*—to be his greatest works. In later years Singer centered several novels—*Enemies: A Love Story,* and *Shadows on the Hudson,* for example—as well as a number of short stories, on Jewish life in America. His American characters are always foreign born and often Holocaust survivors haunted by their immediate past and disoriented by the American reality. Through them, Singer exposed the internal and external conflicts not only of postwar American Jews but also of an entire society committed to cultural pluralism and assimilation. But it is primarily for his dybbuks and beggars, rabbis and atheists, saints and whores—all bound by common spiritual ties, an expressive common tongue, a common destiny, and frequently a common martyrdom—that Isaac Bashevis Singer will be best remembered. For it is they, together with their American descendants, who constitute the most varied and coherent cavalcade of Jewish life in modern fiction.

Bibliography
Burgin, Richard. "The Sly Modernism of Isaac B. Singer." *American Writing Today.* Edited by Richard Kostelanetz. Troy, N.Y.: Whitston, 1991.
Siegel, Ben. "The Brothers Singer: More Similarities than Differences." *Contemporary Literature* 22, no. 1 (Winter 1981): 42–57.

—Ben Siegel

Sklarew, Myra (1934–   )

Myra Sklarew is a poet who life's work focuses on Jewishness and on the Holocaust. Her scientific training and experience influence her powers of observation. She has frequently included her fields of nonliterary interest in her poetry and prose.

Sklarew was born in 1934 in Baltimore to parents who nurtured both her scientific and her artistic talents. Her father, a biochemist, influenced her choice to study biology because he taught her, by example, to search for answers. In third grade she soothed a favorite teacher who worried about her brothers, soldiers stationed overseas during World War II, by writing stories for her. Her passion for writing has been a major part of her life since then. In 1941 she witnessed her parents' distress at learning the news of Nazi German massacres in Lithuania, the home of her extended family. Thus, science, writing, and the memory of the Holocaust coalesce to form her artistic and analytic work.

Educated at Tufts University, she majored in biology and later did research at the Cold Spring Harbor Biological Laboratory, in Long Island, where she studied bacterial genetics and bacterial viruses. At Yale University Medical School, she was a research assistant to Salvador Luria and Max Delbruck in the Department of Neurophysiology, investigating the frontal lobe function and delayed response memory in Rhesus monkeys. As a pianist, she performed with various ethnic groups and dance bands. She studied sculpture at the Boston Museum of Fine Arts (1952–55), wood and stone carving (1962–66), and oil painting at Skidmore College and American University. However, her major interest has been writing, with an emphasis on poetry. She began teaching poetry at the American University in 1970.

In addition to her appointment as professor, her dedication to literature and writing includes the presidency of the Yaddo artist colony (1987–91), founder and directorship of the MFA Program in Creative Writing (1980–82, and 1984–87), poetry editor of *Lilith Magazine,* and membership in a variety of writing centers and literature panels. She has given countless readings and contributed hundreds of articles and reviews to journals, newspapers, and magazines. The Library of Congress recorded her poetry for the Contemporary Poets' Archive, and besides recognition for teaching and service to the American University, she is the recipient of numerous awards, including the National Book Council (1977), the Di Castagnola Award, Poetry Society of America (1972), the Mayo Gordon Barber Award, Poetry Society of America (1980), four-time winner of the PEN Syndicated Fiction Award, the Anna Davidson Rosenberg Award, Judah Magnes Museum (1998), and a Lucius N. Littauer Foundation grant (2004).

Sklarew is as profound as she is prolific. She is best known for *Lithuania: New and Selected Poems,* 1995, a lengthy narrative of experience based on her 10 visits to Lithuania, where almost all of her mother's family was massacred during World War II. The poem reveals the stories of victims, bystanders, collaborators, rescuers, and witnesses to the atrocities in 1941 and 1942 in Kovno, Stutthof, Ponar, Vilnius, and Keidan, the home of her murdered extended family. *Lithuania* also reflects Sklarew's wide range of subjects, from poems about biblical subjects (such as "Dinah"), to recent history (such as "At the Syrian Border"). The majority of her work revolves around Judaism. She also infuses almost all of her poems with images that evoke the specificity of nature: Birds, gardens, water, and trees set the reader in place and time and create the background of her stories and observations. Her essays and stories, like her poetry, are quiet contemplations of dislocation, of a woman's identity, of remembering, and of isolation. They are direct, emotional, but restrained, sometimes moving beyond the present to the past—an imagined scene set in ancient eras, Jewish history, repeated stories of the Shoah, and responses to contemporary Israel. Her landscape is the landscape of memory without boundaries. Just as she easily bridges the past with the present, in the same way she moves from the United States to Lithuania to Israel, Greece, and other locations embedded in memory. She is rooted in Jewish ritual, history, and culture. "I don't think I ever wrote a poem or story that wasn't a continuation of my ongoing dialogue with Judaism," Sklarew once explained. "Whether I write as an act of memory, so crucial in Judaism, or out of a spiritual longing, that influence is fundamental. Invariably, it's to the Yiddish and Hebrew poets, from the Torah to Ibn Gabirol and Yehuda Halevi in medieval times, to contemporary Israeli writers, that I speak."

Her encounters with witnesses to the Shoah led her to explore the relationship of memory to trauma. The Lithuanians who spoke with her recalled the same events, but differently. She noted that "trauma shaped their memory" and manifests itself in unexpected ways: "Some people would remember something visually with no emotional connection. Others would have an emotional memory with nothing attached to it—no visual accompaniment, no sound, nothing." Her scientific background led her to investigate the complex relationships of experience and the ways in which the mind forms memories of trauma. In *Holocaust* and the *Construction of Memory,* she considers the impact of trauma on the brain.

In "Lie Perfectly Still," the title essay of an unpublished collection of essays on mortality and healing, her scientific training lends a curious detachment to her description of breast cancer surgery and treatment. She recounts her experience of surgery and radiation treatment by juxtaposing the technical information about radiation with her emotional and cognitive responses; she ends in a crescendo of joy and gratitude: "But to be here at all, to be alive in this perishable and exquisite world is a gift beyond all others."

Sklarew's literary uniqueness stems from her exceptional insight into the ways in which she—and by extension other Jews—were shaped by their Judaism. Her work explores Jewish experience and relies heavily on memory, hers and others'. Engaging both the heart and the mind, she writes with a controlled intensity that involves her readers. They are not likely to forget her compelling journeys and reflections.

Bibliography

Gubar, Susan. *Poetry after Auschwitz: Remembering What One Never Knew.* Bloomington: Indiana University Press, 2003.

Goldenberg, Myrna. "Identity, Memory, and Authority: An Introduction to Holocaust Poems by Hilary Tham, Myra Sklarew, and Dori Katz." *Studies in American Jewish Literature* 24 (2005) 137–144.

Getty, Matt. "Poet Probes Science of Tragic Memories." *American University Weekly* 11 (January 2005).

—Myrna Goldberg

Snapshots of a Daughter-in-Law: Poems 1954–1962 Adrienne Rich (1963)

More than 20 books and 50 years later, ADRIENNE RICH's third collection of poetry, *Snapshots of a Daughter-in-Law,* continues to reveal, through carefully chosen diction and form, the tension between one's sense of self and society's mandated conventions. Though heralded as Rich's first overtly "feminist," the 39 poems in this collection raise questions not only of feminine subjugation but of aging, technology, and class dynamics.

In 1951, when she was in her early twenties, Rich entered the male-dominated world of academic poetry with the blessing of W. H. Auden as the winner of the Yale Younger Poets Awards. Auden lauded her commitment to the craft of writing poetry and her "ear and intuitive grasp of much subtler and more difficult matters like proportion, consistency of diction and tone, and the matching of these with the subject at hand." In the forward to Rich's first book, *A Change of World,* Auden introduces Rich's poems like this: "neatly and modestly dressed, speak quietly but do not mumble, respect their elders but are not cowed by them, and do not tell fibs."

The frank and personal poems that characterized Rich's early work found louder and more conflicted companions in *Snapshots of a Daughter-in-Law.* Frustrated by the domestic demands of raising three children before she was 30 and the accompanying guilt that comes with not finding sublime bliss in "wip[ing] the teaspoons," Rich broke from mimicking the traditional style of male poets—Frost, Dylan Thomas, Donne, Auden, and Yeats—from whom she learned the craft. *Snapshots of a Daughter-in-Law* marks the first of many transitions in her work from an academic poet to one anxious to incite political and societal change. This collection spans eight years and introduces the reader to a poet unafraid to divorce from tradition and allow her poems to fill the page in a structure dependent as much on visualization as metrical conventions. Rich does not limit her poems to any particular form or meter. For instance, *Snapshots of a Daughter-in-Law* encompasses 10 stanzas, none alike, and opens with a colorful description of a Shreveport belle to end in abstraction with the single-word lines "delivered/palpable/ours." In an interview, Rich said a writer's job in dealing with abstract subjects like sexism or racism is to "keep the concreteness behind the abstractions visible and alive."

In the title poem Rich's first word is "You." It is directed at a feminine Southern, mother-in-law who directly contrasts with Rich's upbringing as a

Jewish, middle-class daughter. Rich's poetry is not strictly autobiographical, and by traveling from the first to last line, Rich shows that the mother and daughter-in-law are not trapped alone. In contrast to the opening "you," Rich closes the poem with "ours." The malaise, dissatisfaction, and confinement of the poem's female characters belong not only to women but to people in general. The ending "our" need not be limited to the feminist evolution because any societal change requires realization and revision by both sexes. As Rich said in her essay on Ibsen's *When We Dead Awaken,* the exhilarating time of awakening consciousness affects the lives of women and of "men, even those who deny its claims upon them."

In "The Loser," Rich demonstrates that the stereotypes of bride and wife affect male self-conception as well. Expecting the "bourgeois sacrament" to strip the shimmer and beauty from the woman he once loved, Rich surprises us in the second part by having the loser reveal that his lost lover is tougher than he thought and still desirable, despite having three daughters and losing a son. The mundane daily activities of laundry may transform her physical beauty into use, but does not dull the friction of the woman's mind.

Some critics responded negatively to Rich's change in subject matter and form. The book was published in 1956, when women were taught to accept domesticity while men donned suits to join the workforce. Prior to this collection, Rich had strived not to identify herself as a female poet. Friends advised her not to give the collection its title because people would think it was a female diatribe. Rich did not relent, and as predicted, her exposure of the feminine crisis in the kitchen led to critics calling her work too personal and bitter. Even decades after the book was published, Irish poet Derek Mayhom called Rich's work "cold, dishonest, and wicked." However, her controversial work added wood to a growing fire set to incinerate preconceptions of femininity. This is why this collection is as relevant in the new millennium as it was in the 1950s. Rich views her work as encouraging women's liberation instead of falling under the often maligned category "feminism." More so,

throughout her career she tackles cultural and political issues beyond the feminist agenda. She does not write political poetry, but poetry of witness, of dissent, on behalf of those who are generally unheard from. From the Iraq war to middle-class obsession with self-help books, Rich implores people to get energized and involved in change. In "Artificial Intelligence," she questions the creation of computer programs that can play chess and simulate the human mental process. She asks when we will allow technology to subsume all that is innately human, such as writing poetry, and eliminate our reason for being. She refuses to dump her burgeoning political activism into a computer and allow it to solve her "once for all." "Artificial Intelligence" implicates not only society's dependence on technology, but its apathy and inertia to elicit change. Rich's poetry of dissent may have first emerged in *Snapshots of a Daughter-in-Law;* however, her battle to raise awareness continues today.

Bibliography
Gelpi, Barbara Charlesworth, and Albert Gelpi, eds. *Adrienne Rich's Poetry and Prose.* New York: W.W. Norton, 1993.

Martin, Wendy. *An American Triptych: Anne Bradstreet, Emily Dickinson, Adrienne Rich.* Chapel Hill: University of North Carolina Press, 1984.

Rich, Adrienne. *What Is Found There: Notebooks on Poetry and Politics.* New York: W.W. Norton, 1993.

Rothschild, Matthew. "Adrienne Rich: 'I happen to think poetry makes a huge difference.'" *The Progressive* (January 1994).

—Kimberly Jones

Sontag, Susan (1933–2004)

Susan Sontag was born in New York City on January 16, 1933, to Jack and Mildred (Jacobson) Rosenblatt. Her father, the son of Austrian-Jewish immigrants, was a fur trader who died when Sontag was five years old. After his death, Sontag's mother, the daughter of Russian Jewish immigrants, moved Susan and her younger sister, Judith, from New York to Miami and then to Tucson, Arizona, where she met and married Nathan Sontag. The family moved to California in 1946, where Susan graduated from North Hollywood High School at the age of 16. After attending the University of California at Berkeley for a semester, she transferred to the humanities program at the University of Chicago, where she met and married her husband, Philip Rieff, and graduated in 1951. Sontag also earned two master of arts degrees in English literature and philosophy from Harvard University in 1954 and 1955, respectively. While working on her doctoral degree, she won a scholarship to study at Oxford University and, after spending a semester in England, transferred to the University of Paris. After her return to the United States, Sontag divorced Rieff and with her son, David, moved to New York City, where she taught at City College, Sarah Lawrence College, and Columbia University, and also worked as a contributing editor at *Commentary*.

One of the most important public intellectuals and writers of her time, Sontag believed that a good writer should be interested in everything and took this idea to heart. An outstanding creative writer and a profound social critic, she did not limit herself to one area of writing or creative expression. A prolific novelist, short story writer, essayist, dramatist, and filmmaker, Sontag used her writing to address issues of literary interpretation, psychology, religion, popular culture, and politics. In 1963 her first novel, *The Dreams of Hippolyte*, was published as *The Benefactor*. In the first chapter, we learn that Hippolyte has written an article that receives acclaim in the literary world earning him an invitation to the salon of Frau Anders. The remainder of the novel details Hippolyte's distressing dreams and resolves that dreams should not be dismissed, but treated as a higher form of reality. Sontag's second novel, *Death Kit* (1967), reads like a resumption of *The Benefactor*. It tells the story of Dalton Harron, or "Diddy," a businessman and failed novelist who apparently had attempted suicide and is coming to terms with his life. The events of the story take place during Diddy's final coma and are told by the narrator in third person, so that the reader gets the impression that the narrator is not only telling a story about himself but

giving the reader a view of himself as well. Diddy's death, which incorporates events and individuals that actually were a part of his life, reads like a dream in which Diddy attempts to repeat life and get it right the second time.

Literary and artistic interpretation is a topic of central concern for Sontag. Her first collection of essays, *AGAINST INTERPRETATION* (1966), is a compilation of 26 pieces written between 1962 and 1965, some of which previously appeared in the leading magazines of her day, including *Partisan Review, Commentary,* the *Nation, Mademoiselle,* and *Time.* The book, divided into five sections, contains essays that explore literary interpretation, art and the life of an artist, 1960s mainstream theater, current filmmakers, religion, psychoanalysis, and her well-known essay on the importance of "camp" to contemporary culture. Sontag's next collection of essays, *Styles of Radical Will* (1969), contains one of her most important essays, "The Aesthetics of Silence," in which she argues that contemporary art has become a "spiritual project." Art, she suggests, is the main outlet for transcending the painful conflicts of existence. Silence, she argues, is important to contemporary art in that it creates a "cultural clean slate" and calls attention to the limitations of language. *Styles of the Radical Will* also includes the essay "The Pornographic Imagination" and pieces on the place of Romanian exile E. M. Cioran in philosophy and history, the distinctions between theater and film, an antipsychoanalytic reading of Bergman's *Persona,* and the antinarrative structure of the filmmaker Jean-Luc Goddard. This book also marks an important departure for Sontag as she incorporates essays on political topics, including "What's Happening in America," which traces the historical imperialist and racist policies of the U.S. government, and "Trip to Hanoi," in which she reflects on a recent trip to war-stricken Vietnam.

In *On Photography* (1977), a collection of six revised essays Sontag published between 1973 and 1977 in the *New York Review of Books*, Sontag explores the unique qualities of photography as an art form. She argues that unlike literature, which is about the world, photographs are miniatures of the world, without interpretation, that give the viewer instant access to the real and true. *On Photography* won the National Book Critics Circle Award in 1977. In 1978 she published ILLNESS AS METAPHOR, a slim book in which she argues against giving more than a purely medical meaning to illness. Sontag, who wrote this book while undergoing aggressive chemotherapy for breast cancer, argues that illness is often judged in moral or psychological terms and individuals are made to feel a sense of guilt for having caused the onset of their diseases, often inhibiting patients from seeking out a full range of medical interventions.

In 1978, Sontag returned to fiction when she published her most autobiographical book, *I, etcetera,* a collection of short pieces. Among the stories is "Project for a Trip to China," in which she explores the China of her imagination and expresses her desire to recover the memory of her family's time in China. In "Debriefing," Sontag explores the suicide of her friend Susan Taubes. This is the story of Julia, who once sought to make connections between things and individuals on every level but increasingly withdraws from making connections with the world. Sontag also writes about the relationship between parents and children in "Baby" and the complexity of identity in "Dr. Jekyll" and "Unguided Tour."

Under the Sign of Saturn (1980) is a series of narratives and portraits of the intellectual figures who influenced Sontag. These figures include author Paul Goodman, novelist and playwright Antonin Artaud, critical theorist Walter Benjamin, filmmaker Hans Jürgen Syberberg, writer Roland Barthes, and Elias Canetti. In this volume Sontag also criticizes Third Reich filmmaker Leni Riefenstahl for the content of her films as well as her efforts to minimize her involvement with the Nazi Party. Rather than echo others who have given Riefenstahl a hallowed place in the history of cinema as an art form, Sontag relegates her to a prized place in the history of propaganda.

In the 1980s Sontag responded to the death of friends from AIDS by writing two completely different treatments of the disease. The first, a short story, "The Way We Live Now," tells of a person living with AIDS through the eyes of his friends. The story, published in 1986, was reprinted at the beginning of *The Best American Short Stories, 1987.* In 1989 a book-length essay, *AIDS and Its Metaphors,* argued in a manner similar to *Illness as Metaphor* against using AIDS as a metaphor and blaming the patient for the disease.

Over 25 years after the publication of *Death Kit,* Sontag wrote her third novel, *The Volcano Lover* (1992), a departure from her earlier avant-garde fiction. A historical piece set in 1770s London, *The Volcano Lover* tells the story of Sir William Hamilton, an English ambassador who is passionate about collecting works of art and climbing volcanoes. Unlike Sontag's earlier novels, *The Volcano Lover* was a best seller. Staying with this genre, Sontag wrote *Alice in Bed* (1993), a play in eight scenes about Alice James, the sister of William and Henry James, who, after a childhood fraught with illnesses, succumbed to a variety of vague and recurrent illnesses through her adult life that rendered her an invalid. In 2000 Sontag published another historical novel, *In America,* which received that year's National Book Award. The novel tells of a group of Poles, led by Helena Modrzejewska, the renowned Polish actress, who travel to Anaheim, California, in 1876 to establish a utopian community.

In 2001 Sontag published her last collection of essays, *Where the Stress Falls.* In this volume, she considers the writings of Marina Tsvetaeva, Randall Jarrell, Roland Barthes, Machado de Assis, W. G. Sebald, Jorge Borges, and Elizabeth Hardwick, as well as commenting on film, dance, photography, painting, opera, and theater. She also explores her own commitments to activism, writing, and moral issues of the late 20th century. Revisiting the topic of photography, Sontag's final book, *Regarding the Pain of Others,* explores how pictures of warfare are both informed and influenced by the contemporary political and artistic concerns of those who produce and, in turn, view photographs.

In addition to writing essays and fiction, Sontag also directed four feature-length films: *Duet for Cannibals* (1969) and *Brother Carl* (1971), both of which were made in Sweden; *Promised Lands*

(1974), made in Israel during the war of October 1973; and *Unguided Tour* (1983), produced in Italy and based on the short story of the same name. Sontag also served as the president of the American Center of PEN, the international writer's organization, and was a MacArthur Fellow between 1990 and 1995. Sontag died of cancer on December 28, 2004, at the age of 71.

Bibliography

Rollyson, Carl. *Reading Susan Sontag: A Critical Introduction to Her Work.* Chicago: Ivan R. Dee, 2001.

———, Carl and Lisa Paddock. *Susan Sontag: The Making of an Icon.* New York: W.W. Norton, 2000.

Sayers, Sohnya. *Susan Sontag: The Elegiac Modernist.* New York: Routledge, 1990.

—Rebecca Kuhn

Souls on Fire: Portraits and Legends of Hasidic Masters Elie Wiesel (1972)

ELIE WIESEL is the master storyteller of our time. In this stirring collection he brings together a century of the wisdom of various Hasidic masters, beginning with Hasidism's founder, Israel Ba'al Shem Tov (1700–60) and concluding with Menahem Mendl of Kotzk (1789–1859). The author culls the insights of the charismatic zaddikim or rebbes (Hasidic masters) to plumb the depths of their teachings as a guide for our troubled world. He finds parallels between conditions that existed at the beginning of the Hasidic movement and the contemporary world: "Physical and emotional insecurity, fallen idols, the scourge of violence. Where can one go, where can one hide? Despairing of the present, man seeks beauty in legends. Like the Hasid of long ago." The portraits are based on the author's lectures given at the 92nd Street YMHA in New York City.

Hasidism and Hasidic tales have long held a fascination for American audiences. In a world increasingly dominated by technology and the impersonal, tales of wonder-working rebbes and compassionate Hasidic masters have a broad human appeal. Martin Buber, years earlier, popularized the Hasidic world in his two-volume work on Hasidic tales. There is, however, a difference between the work of Buber and Wiesel. Wiesel, in a letter to his then editor, notes that Buber "spoke as an outsider for outsiders, whereas—well, you know what I mean" (Abrahamson). Furthermore, before the appearance of Wiesel's book, Eldridge Cleaver, at that time a member of the Black Panthers, had written a book titled *Soul on Ice.* Cleaver's work deals with the demise of the human spirit and a deadness of the soul. In contrast, Wiesel's book speaks of the sacredness of life and the necessity of combating despair.

What are some of the lessons Wiesel gleans from the vanished world of the Hasidic masters? From the movement's founder comes the insight that "It is in man that God must be loved, because the love of God goes through the love of man." From the great Levi-Yitzhak of Berditchev comes the necessity of reminding God that "He too had to ask forgiveness for the hardships He inflicted on His people. Thence the plural of Yom Kippurim: the request for pardon is reciprocal." Rebbe Nachman of Bratzlav, the Besht's great-grandson, was a spellbinding storyteller. His legacy has crucial implications for the role of stories. Nachman viewed literature through a theological prism, telling his disciples: "Make my tales into prayers." Wiesel hypothesizes that Menachem-Mendel of Kotsk extinguished the Sabbath candles and withdrew from the world because he foresaw that a century later the fires of the Holocaust would consume the Jewish people.

Wiesel retells the tales that he first heard from his maternal grandfather, Dodye Feig, himself a devout Wishnitzer Hasid who perished in the Shoah. The author makes no pretense of scholarly objectivity in presenting, and representing, the tales he heard long ago. Quite the opposite is true. Citing his grandfather, he observes "an objective Hasid is not a Hasid." *Souls on Fire* is neither a scholarly work nor one whose focus is that of history or philosophy. Wiesel himself states that he is a storyteller. Consequently, he views his task as transmitting what was given to him. But this collection is much more. The author lends the tales "his own voice and intonation and sometimes his wonder or simply: his fervor."

Souls on Fire is Wiesel's initial attempt to re-create—if only for an instant and if only in the imagination—the pre-Holocaust Hasidic world. The book received the Prix Bordin, the Eleanor Roosevelt Memorial Award, and the American Liberties Medallion. It was well reviewed in numerous other venues, including the *New York Times.* Wiesel continues to write books that illuminate the Hasidic world: *Four Hasidic Masters: And Their Struggle Against Melancholy* (1978), *Somewhere a Master* (1982), *Sages and Dreamers* (1991), and *Wise Men and Their Tales* (2003). Each of these works presents a different dimension of the teachings of the great Hasidic masters and their tales. Collectively, these books constitute the author's attempt to teach contemporary humanity universal lessons derived from the Hasidic world. Moreover, in works such as *Sages and Dreamers* (1991) and *Wise Men and Their Tales* (2003), he includes biblical and talmudic teachers as well.

Bibliography

Abrahamson, Irving, ed. *Against Silence: The Voice and Vision of Elie Wiesel.* New York: Holocaust Library, 1985.

Gorsky, Jonathan. "Elie Wiesel, Hasidism and the Hiddenness of God." *New Blackfriars* 85, no. 996 (March 2004): 133–143.

—Alan L. Berger

Spiegelman, Art (1948–)

Art Spiegelman, born in Stockholm, Sweden, immigrated to the United States as a child with his Holocaust survivor parents. He was raised in the Rego Park neighborhood of New York City and attended Harpur College in Binghamton, New York, where he studied art and philosophy. He is best known for his Pulitzer Prize–winning MAUS: A SURVIVOR'S TALE, two volumes that relate his parents' Holocaust experience as well as portraying the legacy of this experience in his own life. The book represents Jews as mice and Nazi Germans as cats. Furthermore, the artist draws other nationalities as animals: Americans are dogs; Poles are pigs; Roma (Gypsies) are gypsy moths; and so on.

Spiegelman notes the influence of Franz Kafka in his own work. He refers to Kafka's "Josephine the Singer, or The Mouse Folk," which treats a rodent people (Jews) who live a precarious existence in a world seeking their extermination.

The comic book format of *Maus* bears witness to Spiegelman's advocacy of the serious role comics play in the postmodern world. For the author, comics may best be understood as a "co-mix" of images and words. The resultant text has a stunning effect on readers. *Publishers Weekly* termed *Maus* a "masterpiece of comic literature," while Lawrence Langer describes Spiegelman's work as "a serious form of pictorial literature." Spiegelman had long been a major figure in the world of underground comics. He began experimenting with animal figures to represent Jews (mice wandering in a ghetto) and Germans (cats in SS uniforms) as early as 1972 (Hirt-Manheimer). He and his French-born wife, Françoise Mauly, founded *Raw,* the avant-garde comics magazine, in 1980.

Spiegelman's considerable artistic talent coupled with his experience of growing up in a survivor household has yielded an intense and unrelenting visual text that subversively challenges extant genre distinctions. These images concretize the inner psychic chaos experienced by many Holocaust survivors. This trauma is often absorbed by members of the second generation. *Maus* includes a four-page portion "Prisoner on Hell Planet: A Case History," that portrays humans rather than animals. The artists draws himself as the prisoner. Spiegelman, while an undergraduate, was for a brief time institutionalized in a psychiatric facility. Later, he taught art history and aesthetics of comics at New York's School for Visual arts from 1979 to 1986. He also served as a creative consultant for Topps Bubble Gum Company, where he illustrated, among other things, their "Garbage Pail Kids" trading cards. Spiegelman was a staff artist and writer for the *New Yorker,* and his drawings appear in a variety of publications.

Spiegelman was one of the first artists whose creative work reflects the effects of the September 11, 2001, terrorist attack on the World Trade Center in New York. His provocative work *In The Shadow* of *No Towers,* a two-year cycle of color comics pages, appeared first in Europe, being serialized by *Die Zeit* and *The London Review of Books.* The work later appeared as a book and was one of the *New York Times* Hundred Notable Books of 2004. The Los Angeles Museum of Contemporary Art mounted a major exhibition of Spiegelman's work in its November 2005 "Fifteen Masters of Twentieth-Century Comics" series. Also in that year the French government made Spiegelman a Chevalier de l'ordre des Arts et des Lettres, and he was listed as one of *Time* magazine's 100 most influential people. One year later Spiegelman was made a member of the Art Directors' Club Hall of Fame.

The author's own Jewish identity, like some in the second generation, was initially a source of great inner conflict. His use of comics as a vehicle for serious reflection on the matter of identity makes a signal contribution to the field. While a teenager, he believed that his life would be much easier if he were not Jewish. The Holocaust was terrifying and overwhelmed him. However, in the seventies he began voraciously reading survivor accounts. Listening to his father, Vladek, relate his Holocaust experiences served as the son's "shoehorn with which to squeeze [himself] back into history" (Wechsler). The authenticity of Spiegelman's Holocaust comic panels derives both from his own experience of growing up in a survivor household and from immersion in "drawings and even paintings made by survivors within the camps," which were, he told an interviewer, invaluable preparation for writing volume two of *Maus,* subtitled *And Here My Troubles Began* (Hirt-Manheimer).

In the Shadow of No Towers continued Spiegelman's genre of "autobiographical comic strip." The destruction of the World Trade Center Towers, near where the Spiegelmans live and which he and his wife witnessed, reinforced the admonition of his survivor parents. He recalls that, as a child, his parents constantly told him two things: the world is very dangerous, and he should be ready to flee at a moment's notice. September 11, 2001, confirmed their message. The author confides that 9/11 forced him to "take inventory of everything left in my brain" (*Forward*). After having temporarily abandoned comics because they were "too hard," he made a vow in the immediate aftermath of the terrorist attack that he would again draw comics. The resultant book was the author's attempt to deal with his own trauma as well as the nation's sense of shock and grief. For Spiegelman, comics "offer one of the most effective ways to express emotion, especially emotions related to a complicated and painful disaster" (*Forward*).

Spiegelman's use of comics to represent the lessons and legacies of the Holocaust and other traumatic events has reshaped the artistic landscape. His sensitive drawings compel readers' responses. Furthermore, while reflecting on particular events, e.g., the Holocaust and the destruction of the World Trade Center, his use of animal figures strikes a universal resonance. Spiegelman has also utilized the traditional role of comics in several works: *Open Me . . . I'm a Dog* (1997), a picture book for young children, a coedited series titled *Little Lit,* three comic anthologies for children, and a single volume, *Big Fat Little Lit,* which combines the three *Little Lit* works. However, thanks to Spiegelman's pioneering and visionary work, it is no longer possible to think of comics in a parochial sense as being only for children or only for amusement.

Bibliography

Hirt-Manheim, Aron. "The Art of Art Spiegelman." *Reform Judaism* (Spring 1987).

Langer, Lawrence. "A Fable of the Holocaust." *New York Times Book Review,* 3 November 1991.

Spiegelman, Art. "The Paranoids Were Right." Interview by Alana Newhouse. *Forward,* 6 September 2002.

Wechsler, Lawrence. "Mighty Mouse." *Rolling Stone,* 20 November 1986.

—Alan L. Berger

Stein, Gertrude (1874–1946)

Gertrude Stein was a radically innovative author and an iconic personality. Of German-Jewish descent, she was born in Allegheny, Pennsylvania, on February 3, 1874, the youngest of Daniel and Amelia (Kyser) Stein's five children. Soon after Gertrude's birth, the Stein family moved to Austria and then France before returning to the United States and settling on a farm outside Oakland, California. After Amelia Stein died of cancer, Gertrude and her siblings were raised under Daniel's firm hand until he unexpectedly died three years later.

Soon after, Gertrude followed her beloved brother Leo to the East Coast. There she studied at Harvard Annex (later Radcliffe College) and met one of her lifelong influences, the philosopher William James. Under his tutelage, Stein—his star student—performed some of her first language experiments. She researched a theory called automatic writing, which held that the subconscious mind was capable of writing intelligibly while the conscious mind sustained an unrelated conversation. Stein published two articles on the subject, but ultimately concluded that automatic writing was not possible. She was, however, fascinated by her subjects' unique speech rhythms—a fascination she would later pursue in her writing.

After deciding to stop studying for a medical degree she had been pursuing at Johns Hopkins University, she followed Leo again, this time to Paris. They lived at the now famous address, 27 rue de Fleurus, located in a burgeoning art district, and began filling their apartment with pieces of modern art—many now recognized as the most significant paintings of the 20th century. Though Leo bought many pieces at first, art historians now see Gertrude as the more significant collector, in part thanks to her close friendship with Pablo Picasso, who in turn immortalized Stein in his famous portrait of her. Besides being a mini art gallery, the apartment also became a meeting place for expatriot American authors Ernest Hemingway, Sherwood Anderson, and F. Scott Fitzgerald; French painters Paul Cézanne and Henry Matisse; and a host of others.

Upon moving to Paris, Stein decided to commit herself to writing. While Picasso began experimenting with cubism in painting, she experimented with space and perspective in her writing, trying to make several moments simultaneously present through repetition of sounds and words, syntactical innovation, and fragmentation of her stories' plots. By attempting to strip words of their connotations—and even their denotations—Stein hoped to render language as pliable and abstract as other artistic media, capable of creating "pure" art, unfettered by literary convention or habit. Stein's language experiments, incomprehensible to the general public, were rarely read or praised, and she did not gain fame as an author (though she was a well-known personality) until much later in life.

In 1907 Stein was introduced to Alice B. Toklas, who would become her lifelong partner. Toklas was a small, Polish-Jewish American woman from a well-to-do family in San Francisco. She was immediately drawn to Stein, whom she considered a genius and soon began acting as her secretary, typing Stein's massive The Making of Americans. Meanwhile, Stein and Leo's relationship was deteriorating. Leo was simultaneously resentful of Gertrude's ability to create art and disapproving of what he considered her unintelligible prose. Leo's disapproval caused Gertrude to begin her habit of staying up all night, after visitors had left and Leo was asleep, to do her writing. When Toklas moved into the Steins' apartment in 1909, she served as a welcome reader with whom Gertrude could share her work. Leo moved out of the apartment five years later, growing increasingly critical of his sister. The two would never reconcile. Toklas continued to act as Stein's secretary, shielded her from unwanted visitors, prepared meals, and generally made it possible for the more dominant, self-assured Stein to devote her entire life to writing.

During World War I, Stein and Toklas, though temporarily stranded in England, remained in Paris, dedicating themselves to the war effort. In 1934, upon the successful publication of The Autobiography of Alice B. Toklas and staging of Four Saints in Three Acts, the two traveled to the United States. Stein—who never stopped considering herself American—was warmly welcomed as a celebrity. When World War II broke out, Stein and Toklas, as Jews and lesbians, were forced to seek refuge in a remote French town near Switzerland, where they lived safely until the war's conclusion.

On July 27, 1946, Stein, having developed stomach cancer, died in the American Hospital at Neuilly-sur-Seine in France.

Of Stein's many works—they total nearly 100 in all—her most famous are also ironically her most conventional. *Three Lives: Stories of the Good Anna, Melanctha, and the Gentle Lena* (1909), written early in her career, is frequently read today; Melanchtha is considered one of her finest pieces of fiction. Also still popular is *The Autobiography of Alice B. Toklas* (1933), which Stein wrote in Toklas's voice and which documents the string of famous figures frequenting the couple's apartment. Stein herself was more interested in works such as *Tender Buttons: Objects, Food, Rooms* (1914), in which she created a verbal montage of everyday objects. What she considered her magnum opus—the 900-page *The Making of Americans* (1925)—sat unpublished for many years and was received with little to no critical enthusiasm when it finally did see print. Stein was as diverse as she was prolific, spanning the genres of drama (*Four Saints in Three Acts*), nonfiction (*Lectures in America*), and nearly everything in between. Though the works of which she was most proud are not read frequently today, Stein's legacy lies in her attempts to push the English language to its grammatical limits and in her mentoring of many other great modern artists.

Bibliography

Brinnin, John Malcolm. *The Third Rose: Gertrude Stein and Her World*. Reading, Mass: Addison-Wesley, 1987.

Wagner-Martin, Linda. *"Favored Strangers": Gertrude Stein and Her Family*. New Brunswick, N.J.: Rutgers University Press, 1995.

—Rachel Ligairi

Stern, Steve (1947–   )

Steve Stern was born and raised in Memphis, Tennessee, the son of a grocer father and homemaking mother. Although Stern, like many a young writer, outgrew his hometown in young adulthood, Memphis has remained a privileged space in many of his novels and stories. Overlooking the Mississippi River, itself the locale of the broader American literary mythos, the ethnic neighborhoods of Memphis became the primary setting for many of his works, including *Lazar Malkin Enters Heaven* (1986), *Harry Kaplan's Adventures Underground* (1991), *A Plague of Dreamers* (1994), and *The Wedding Jester* (1999). And just as Mark Twain used the travels of Huck and Jim to explore the 19th-century American crossroads of nation and race, Stern uses his river bluff communities in similar ways to articulate 20th-century narratives of American Jewish identities. With a voice reminiscent of Isaac Bashevis Singer and his folkloric cadence of the fantastic, Stern has taken his mundane and largely assimilated Jewish past and transformed it into a written realm of almost mythic proportions.

Graduating with a B.A. in English from Rhodes College in 1970 and an M.F.A. from the University of Arkansas in 1977, Stern spent the first several years of his postgraduate career adjunct teaching in almost every Memphis institution of higher learning. His career, as well as his relationship with his Jewish heritage, took a fortuitous turn in 1984 when he began working at the Center for Southern Folklore as a transcriber of oral histories. It was here that he inadvertently stumbled upon Memphis's Jewish past through his discovery of the Pinch, an old Jewish ghetto community that had once thrived along the city's North Main Street. This experience, as Stern later recalls, immersed him "into a world that seemed at once as familiar as a homecoming and as strange as discovering the lost city of Atlantis. It was a place where the literal Jewish past . . . kept veering into myth." As a consequence, Stern has taken the long-vanished locale and repopulated it with an unlikely mixture of rabbis and dybbuks, dreamers and golems, and angels that are often unsure which realm they inhabit.

His first two books—*Isaac and the Undertaker's Daughter* (1983), a collection of stories, and *The Moon & Ruben Shein* (1984), a novel—revolve around Jewish characters in search of their identities, and, by the author's own admission, were directly influenced by his ethnographic research with the Center for Southern Folklore. Although not bringing him much critical attention, these works paved the way for a book that helped to establish Stern's literary reputation. *Lazar Malkin Enters Heaven* is a series of nine interconnected tales that function more as a short story cycle than a loose collection of stories. Almost all of the narratives take place in the Pinch, and each is an unsteady mixture of the real and the imaginary. Stories such as "Moishe the Just," "The Gramophone," "Leonard Shapiro Banished from Dreams," and the title piece contain references, if not outright embodiments, of golems, *Malach ha-Mavet* (the angel of death), disembodied souls, and the *lamed vovnikim,* the 36 righteous men whose presence on earth ensures its continued existence. *Lazar Malkin* was published to critical acclaim, yet the attention it drew became, ironically, a stumbling block to Stern's literary fame. A survivor of the old Pinch neighborhood sued him for libel, and although the case was ultimately dropped, Stern's publisher postponed the paperback release of the book and, along with that, the author's hopes of sustained critical attention.

Stern followed *Lazar Malkin* with two more works set in the Pinch, the novel *Harry Kaplan's Adventures Underground* and *A Plague of Dreamers.* The latter is a series of three novellas, interconnected in a cyclical manner similar to *Lazar Malkin* and betraying thematic concerns common to Stern's fiction as a whole: the inextricable link between past and present, the unexpected infusion of magic into an otherwise mundane existence, and the predicament of protagonists caught between two worlds, unable to negotiate either. Stern returned to these issues in his 1999 collection of stories, *The Wedding Jester.* Like *Lazar Malkin,* the text comprises nine tales that interweave the ordinary and the fantastic, but unlike the earlier work, the Pinch does not consume the stories.

Stern continued to expand his narrative reach in *The Angel of Forgetfulness* (2005), a text in which the Pinch is conspicuously absent. His most ambitious work to date, the novel is set on New York's Lower East Side of 1910, a 1960s hippie commune in Arkansas, cold war Prague, and even Paradise itself. Instead of being a series of loosely unified shorter works, *The Angel of Forgetfulness* is a metafictional cycling of three story lines. Each of these tales contains an imaginative artist figure—including Saul Bozoff, who appeared in both *Lazar Malkin Enters Heaven* and *The Wedding Jester*—who is exiled from his community and marginalized as a misfit or idle dreamer. All three narrative strands converge toward the novel's end, collapsed in such a way that the authors seem to become the subjects of their own creations.

Stern is also the author of two children's books—*Mickey and the Golem* (1986) and *Hershel and the Beast* (1987)—and his stories and essays have appeared in a variety of notable publications, including *Epoch, Salmagundi, New England Review, Prairie Schooner, Tikkun,* and The *Jewish Daily Forward.* His work has also garnered numerous awards, including a 1987 Edward Lewis Wallant Award for *Lazar Malkin Enters Heaven* and the National Jewish Book Award in 1999 for *The Wedding Jester.* Stern is also the recipient of an O. Henry Prize (1981), two Pushcart Prizes for short fiction (1997 and 1999), and, most recently, a 2006–07 Guggenheim Foundation fellowship. Such widespread critical attention brought him an invitation from Skidmore College in Saratoga Springs, New York, to serve as their writer-in-residence, a position he currently holds. Much like his perennial artist figure, Saul Bozoff, Steve Stern is a writer drawn to the Jewish past, yet one who refuses to package *Yiddishkeit* into the fictional equivalent of a Hallmark card. Stern's narrative worlds may be magical, yet they are anything but nostalgic, cozy, and safe.

Bibliography

Furman, Andrew. "Steve Stern's Magical Fiction of *Tikkun.*" In *Contemporary Jewish American Writers and the Multicultural Dilemma: Return of the Exiled.* Syracuse, N.Y.: Syracuse University Press, 2000.

—Derek Parker Royal

Sunday Jews Hortense Calisher (2002)

Sunday Jews is a semiautobiographical Jewish family saga written in a neorealist style reminiscent of Jane Austen and Henry James. Elegiac and tragicomic in tone, it comprises a dense historical and anthropological accounting of 20th-century New York Jewish social history. Peter Duffey, a lapsed Catholic, has married Zipporah Zangwill, an assimilated Jewish woman. Now he wonders "In the thicket of opinion, confusion, diffusion, and downright exclusion that is now our America, how will we interface them, our kids?" (292). Through the narrative recounting of family folklore, a murder, affairs, divorces, scandals, and myriad family secrets emerge.

The novel begins with Peter and Zipporah's decision to leave for Italy to conceal Peter's encroaching dementia. As Peter's brilliant mind steadily fades, Zipporah recounts the history of their remarkable marriage and their nurse-companion, Debra, retraces her wanderings with her murdered lover, Lev. Zipporah, HORTENSE CALISHER's center of consciousness, sees as only a clan matriarch and professional anthropologist might. As the convoluted plot unfolds in the manner of a William Faulkner mystery novel with its casually dropped clues, haphazardly accumulated background, and cleverly withheld clues, the individual voices emerge through a clever experimental combination of inner dialogue, direct speech, meditation, brilliant conversations, and metaphorical asides. Calisher's expressionist neorealism is the ideal style for establishing a multivocal communal consciousness, local color, and psychological depth. Interrelated themes of assimilation, Jewish identity, and the existence of a deity unify the text, as do recurring symbols: the Ark of the Covenant, Peter's wristwatch designed by Zach, Italy, Israel, Lev's mysterious package, and Zipporah's primitive religious artifacts.

Zipporah and Peter quickly realize that each is still haunted by religion. Zipporah calls Peter "the Apostle of the in-between" (169), while he retorts "Your theology Zip? . . . you scientists don't believe in personal deity—personally. Yet you yourself run round the world like you got St Vitus's Dance.

Trying to get God to give you the eye" (165). Uncle Lev provides the summary comment when he tells Debra that "the Duffey clan have spent their lives looking for the Law . . . not knowing they already have it" (195).

The Duffeys' secular religion is American democracy itself. Charles, the academic, aspires to a Supreme Court judgeship. The mysterious Gerald makes it big in the stock market. Philip becomes a cultured diplomat. Nellie embraces sexual freedom and pursues social justice as assistant New York City prosecutor. Erika, who has a nose job, becomes the art expert who appoints herself custodian of the family's Jewishness. Zach, the postmodern artist, tries to annihilate classical art. Each has become an "extraordinary thicket of American freedom" (291).

Though their Jewish legacy is principally a moral one, there are still telltale Jewish speech markers, intonations, attitudes, and hand gestures. Jewishness has proved the indelible mark, despite assimilation, free thinking, modernist skepticism, and scientism. None of these are impermeable barriers to belief, Zipporah explains, because "When you deny God you can hear an absence, like the air-suck from a grand concussion elsewhere" (322). Faith in faith itself marks them all (455). When Zipporah is dying, along with her century, grandson Byron, a gay man who has compassionately served at the bedsides of the dying, is her bedside comforter. Grandson Bert, the unbelieving rabbi, speaks the sacred Hebrew words over her as she passes. Bert and Shine, the family's adoptee, run the peace foundation funded by family money.

Debra offers the first clue to the book's title when she tells Zipporah that in her kibbutz "Sunday Jews" were those who did not work hard, or who escaped to become Tel Aviv shopkeepers. "Sunday Jews" also describes those who gather at Zipporah and Peter's famous Sunday afternoons. The reader is left to judge from Zipporah's "book" whether these assimilated American "Sunday Jews" bear the burden of the clan and the larger human family.

Calisher has long been criticized for her ornate style and refusal to write in a fast-paced 1970's minimalist style. Certainly this novel overwhelms with its length and density. Nevertheless, critics call it her best work, and praise its lyrical prose, compassionate meditations, moral depth, and sparkling intelligence.

Bibliography
Allen, Bruce. "The Novellas of Hortense Calisher." *Nation* 265, no. 18 (December 1, 1997): 34–36.
Snodgrass, Kathleen. *The Fiction of Hortense Calisher.* Newark: University of Delaware Press, 1993.
                                   —**Gloria L. Cronin**

Swados, Harvey (1920–1972)

Harvey Swados was a dedicated socialist whose essays pled incessantly for a reform of America's treatment of the working class. He was a skilled essay writer; tradition has it that his persuasive essay for *Esquire*—"Why Resign from the Human Race?"—was the motivation behind the formation of the Peace Corps. Despite the quality and volume of his nonfictional work, Swados was a novelist at heart, and his fiction formed some of his most potent critiques of capitalist society. His experience as a member of the working class, including jobs as a riveter in an aircraft plant, a radio operator in the merchant marine during World War II, and a worker in an automobile plant in New Jersey, formed the values and loyalties that informed the entire body of his work, which returns often to compassionate portraits of the working class.

His first publication was the short story "The Amateurs." It appeared in the University of Michigan's literary periodical, *Contemporary*. More significantly, it reappeared in the collection *The Best Short Stories of 1938*. This collection classed Swados's work with some of the most popular writers of his day, although Swados was still a teenager. This event launched the career of a hardworking writer whose dedication to his craft was constant and enduring. Robin Swados, Harvey's son, describes his father's daily routine: "Highly disciplined, he rarely deviated from his routine of waking each morning at seven and getting to his typewriter by eight, even on weekends or holidays. At the same time, it was equally rare for him to work past five. He often relaxed with a late-afternoon Scotch and an attempt to stumble through a prelude or two on the piano" (xv).

Despite his auspicious beginning and dedicated work ethic, Swados's work never achieved commercial success. Literary critics rarely noticed him or his work. Proponents argue that he was overlooked and undervalued as a writer. His commentary on the tastes of the reading public was harsh at times. In an interview with Herbert Feinstein, Swados argued that "the best writers of the decade have been slighted . . . in favor of those who made more noise . . . [and] become not creative people at all, but public images" (79). Robin Swados relates a comment his father made during the sixties about the lack of attention his work received: "My books have never sold . . . Nevertheless . . . when I consider the miseries of those of my fellow writers who have been treated more like movie stars than creative figures, and whose work has suffered correspondingly, I incline to the belief that my position is more fortunate than theirs" (xii).

Such criticism reveals the position Swados occupied in relation to the popular literary scene of his time. One critic characterized him as a writer who underwent "a heroic struggle to produce art as he believed in it, and as he felt he had to create it, regardless of fashions, expectations, and reception" (xv). His work, though not truly radical in form or content, was sometimes experimental, and one wonders whether his refusal to capitulate to prevailing literary trends or fashions contributed to his lack of commercial success. That his general approach to writing was unconventional can be seen in the way he taught his writing classes at Sarah Lawrence College. GRACE PALEY's *Boston Review* article remembering Harvey Swados recounts the memory of one of his students there: "He sent us on strange, exciting assignments in New York City. We went to the fish market at dawn and watched the boats come in. We sat on hard benches in Night Court, where people who had been arrested lined up before the judge. We wandered all over the city, taking notes on conversations and soaking up smells, textures, and tastes. Afterward, we wrote stories about what we had seen and heard" (Paley).

Although for the most part Swados's place in American literature is still small, his works have gained some critical attention. This article follows the critical summary of Swados's works given by Neil Isaacs in his introduction to *The Unknown Constellations*, the first novel Swados wrote but the last he published (posthumously). *Out Went the Candle* (Isaacs xxiv–xxv), Swados's first novel, is an example of his unconventional writing technique. The book's story is told from five perspectives, a narrative technique that caused enough confusion to give rise to arguments about which character is actually the book's protagonist. The book contained two scenes with sexual content that many readers found offensive, which may have been a factor in its obscurity.

Two of Swados's most popular works are the short story collections *On the Line* and *Nights in the Gardens of Brooklyn*. The former collection (xxv–xxvi) treats the experience of the working-class laborer. Drawn from Swados's own experiences as a laborer, these stories portray the difficulties of the working class in the capitalist system. *On the Line* is an example of Swados's compelling fictional critique of capitalism. Unlike *On the Line*, where the protagonist of each story interacts with the one from the previous story, and where each protagonist is a worker in the same automobile plant, the stories in *Nights in the Gardens of Brooklyn* (xviii–xxx) treat a variety of subjects and themes. The title story, one of the favorite and most often cited of Swados's works by those who knew him and his fiction, is a nostalgic representation of post-World War II New York.

Swados returned to the decentered narrative structure he used in *Out Went the Candle* in *the Will* (xxx–xxxi), this time with a considerably developed talent. The book treats the inability of three men, the sons of two immigrant brothers, to inherit competently their fathers' success. The book was nominated for the 1964 National Book Award, and, despite its eventual elimination, was given high praise by the judges.

Swados wrote several other works that have been praised without being widely read or celebrated. They remain as a reminder of a writer whose dedication to his craft was never rewarded by a public whose tastes he criticized as shallow and skewed by celebrity culture. His works are of great worth to social historians and anthropologists, and have enjoyed critical success with scholars who have characterized him as a writer who was unjustly passed over in favor of lesser contemporaries.

Bibliography

Feinstein, Herbert. "Contemporary American Fiction: Harvey Swados and Leslie Fiedler." *Wisconsin Studies in Contemporary Literature* 2, no. 1 (Winter 1961): 79–98.

Isaacs, Neil D. "Introduction." In *The Unknown Constellations*, by Harvey Swados. Urbana: University of Illinois Press, 1995.

Paley, Grace. "Nights in the Gardens of Brooklyn." *Boston Review* Available online. URL: http://bostonreview.net/BR29.3/paley.html. (Summer 2004). Accessed January 31, 2007.

—**Andrew Schultz**

T

Tell Me a Riddle: A Collection
Tillie Olsen (1961)

TILLIE OLSEN articulates class and gender struggle in *Tell Me a Riddle: A Collection,* a classic in the "socialist feminist" literary canon. Comprising a novella-length title story and three others, all written during the 1950s and intended by the author to be sections of a novel, it discloses the tribulations of a Jewish-immigrant working-class family over three generations. Eva and David of "Tell Me a Riddle" comprise the first generation; their children Clara, Vivi, Hannah, Sammy, Helen, and Davy (killed in World War II) the second; and Jeannine and Carol, offspring of Helen and Lennie, the third. Populated overall by resilient characters, anguished by 20th-century atrocities like the Holocaust and the atomic bomb but still capable of enduring economic deprivation and thwarted opportunity, Olsen's somewhat autobiographical volume features strong women, particularly mothers and daughters, observed in intimate domestic portraits. Read as a short story cycle, its interrelated pieces reveal the paradoxes of what Olsen terms "the triple life" of mother-wife-worker, a "discontinuity" illustrated in *Tell Me a Riddle* through stylistic innovation, including narrative ruptures, flashbacks, interior monologues, imagistic fragments, and random poetry. The experiences of marginalized people, including Yiddish speakers, African Americans, and the multiethnic urban poor likewise arise here in the cadences of Olsen's everyday dialogue.

The first and briefest story, "I Stand Here Ironing," introduces a mother in the midst of performing a routine task while mentally constructing a dialogue with people she considers authority figures, including her daughter's teacher. Emblematic of domestic duty and tumult, the back-and-forth motion of the iron paces the story, mimicking the volley of the first-person protagonist's musings. Looking back over her 19-year-old daughter Emily's life, the narrator recalls herself at that age, when this same child's father abandoned the family. During intervening years, other children have swelled the household, contributing to its discord. The iron at rest calls attention to narrative pauses and interruptions, both literal, as when Emily appears in "real time," and metaphoric, such as occasioned by memory lapses. The mother reflects, "War years. I do not remember them well. I was working, there were four smaller ones now, there was not time for her [Emily]. She had to be a mother, and housekeeper, and shopper."

The motif of everyday suffering recurs in the second story, "Hey Sailor, What Ship?" The title, drawn from a common greeting among seafarers, becomes one of two refrains that persist in the mind of the main character, an aging alcoholic seaman named Michael (Whitey) Jackson (who also refers to himself as M. Norbert Jacklebaum). The second phrase, *"Lennie and Helen and the kids,"* signals Whitey's devotion to longtime friends Helen and Lennie and their children, and his ultimate fall from their grace. Together the two repeating lines symbolize a dichotomy: Whitey must choose between the "itinerate" life of a wanderer and the "settled" life of a married man. Unfolding in the present tense across four sections, the tale chronicles Whitey's hard luck and increasing drunkenness, intolerable to Jeannine, which by degrees excludes him from the family's domestic center. Though the story closes in on Whitey, broke and rootless, the judgmental Jeannine will later resurface, her character redeemed as the granddaughter who nurses an ailing Eva in "Tell Me a Riddle."

Set two years after Whitey's disappearance, "O Yes," in which Lennie and Helen and their children Carol and Jeannine reappear, again deals with the challenges of tenuous friendship, a theme investigated in this third story against the backdrop of race relations. Divided into two sections, narrated in the past and present, respectively, its structure reflects fractures between this white family and that of a black family headed by Mrs. Alva Phillips and including her three children, Parialee (Parry), Lucinda (Lucy), and Buford (Bubbie). The central conflict surrounds 12-year-old Carol and her strong feelings for Parry, a relationship forcibly discontinued because of white prejudice, her middle-class status, and the demands of his working-class existence. In this story Olsen documents social realities that extend beyond the private sphere of domesticity.

Issuing from Jewish-socialist activism of the 1930s and 1940s, the collection's abiding focus on economic injustice culminates in the death of Eva, which transpires in slow stages over the four parts of "Tell Me a Riddle." Framed by an argument between Eva and David, an aging Jewish couple encumbered by their rancorous, 47-year marriage, the novella explores the plight of immigrants who struggle against the historical past. A one-time Russian peasant who revolted against the czarist ruling class during the revolution of 1905, Eva has substituted her former passion for domesticity in an unnamed American city. When Eva is stricken with cancer, David secretly sells their house and takes her traveling to visit their various children, who fade in and out of the narrative. Though resisting religious implications associated with her heritage, Eva's political convictions nevertheless have been shaped by it. Named on a "Jewish" list during a hospital stay, Eva insists: "Race, human; Religion none." The story's title, extracted from a sing-song litany of demands made by a group of her grandchildren, is emptied of playfulness in Eva's beleaguered aside: "(*I know no riddles.*)" Yet she poses her own, "will humankind live or die," pondered in memory fragments that reenact the African slave trade, the horrors of Holocaust crematoriums, and the bombings of Hiroshima and Nagasaki. Here, as in *Tell Me a Riddle* overall, Olsen gives voice to social inequality and suffering, yet manages to celebrate the boundless human spirit.

Bibliography
Frye, Joanne S. *Tillie Olsen: A Study of the Short Fiction.* New York: Twayne, 1995.
Pearlman, Mickey, and Abby H. P. Werlock. *Tillie Olsen.* Boston: Twayne, 1991.
—Pauline Uchmanowicz

The Testing-Tree Stanley Kunitz (1971)

STANLEY KUNITZ was raised in Worcester, Massachusetts, and on returning there before writing *The Testing-Tree,* he was heartbroken at what he saw: an express highway running through his childhood neighborhood and a housing development spanning former fields of play, both a technological nightmare. His town's transformation was the moving force for his writing the poem. His collection of poems published in 1971, which he later renamed *The Testing-Tree,* met with immediate critical acclaim and even was noted on the front page of the *New York Times Book Review.* Kunitz was in his mid-sixties at the time of the book's publication and had never received critical reception equal to that of his peers, despite having won the Pulitzer Prize in 1959.

The poem begins by transporting the reader to Kunitz' distant boyhood, describing his leaving school and passing baseball fields where he will never be skilled enough to compete. Instead, Kunitz selects three stones he will throw in his personal game of baseball. With stones in hand, Kunitz races from school, onto the country road, into a field, through a forest, and reaches his destination: a clearing with a large scarred oak tree. At the tree, Kunitz asks his father to bless his arm so the stones will strike the old oak target. Each stone represents his personal goals of love, poetry, and eternal life. If he hits his target, he will be granted his wish to marry, become a poet, and live forever. The final section of the poem carries the reader to Kunitz's vivid present; he is an older man now, reflecting on his boyhood and seeking solutions to and solace from family shortcomings.

The poem's most imposing image is the old oak tree. For Kunitz, the tree symbolizes his father, who committed suicide before his birth. This suicide devastated his mother, who refused ever to speak to Kunitz about his father and never mentioned his name again. This devastation deeply affected Kunitz. His encounter with the sacred oak tree signifies his longing to know his father and honor him properly as a dutiful son. The father again emerges in the poem's final section as the albino walrus huffing in a well as the well is being filled with dirt. As this well or grave is being filled, the older Kunitz recognizes his father's gentle eyes, but still questions his fault in his father's suicide.

A major theme woven throughout the poem is the Indian influence on Kunitz. As he journeys to the oak tree, the boy Kunitz practices his Indian walk, longing for the tribal past and simplicity to replace the Model A's and tanks of the 20th century. As he follows the steps of Massasoit, he is led to the oak tree. Inscribed on the tree is the name King Philip, who was the son of the Indian Massasoit, and who promoted an Indian alliance against encroaching European settlers in 1675. For the boy Kunitz, this world of Indian legend fuses completely with his world of experience and family suffering. Overall, the poem is an outlet for the author to describe the passing of his magical boyhood and the Indian influence on it. On a personal scale, Kunitz appears in the poem as the solitary self in quest of heroic accomplishment. Though the pain and guilt

of his father's death remain, he assures himself he was ever the dutiful and faithful son.

Bibliography
Henault, Marie. *Stanley Kunitz*. Boston: Twayne, 1980
Kunitz, Stanley. *A Kind of Order, a Kind of Folley: Essays and Conversations*. Boston: Little, Brown, 1975.
———. "The Testing-Tree." *The Poems of Stanley Kunitz 1928–1978*. Boston: Little, Brown 1979.
Orr, Gregory. *Stanley Kunitz: an Introduction to the Poetry*. New York: Columbia University Press, 1985.
—**Daniel W. Newton**

Tevye's Daughters   Sholem Aleichem (1949)

Tevye's Daughters, a collection and translation in English of stories by SHOLEM ALEICHEM (1859–1916), was published in 1949, with an illuminating introduction by Frances Butwin. The book serves, well over half a century later, as a firm basis for understanding and appreciating the story elements and the accompanying songs that constitute the basis of Joseph Stein's phenomenally successful 1960s musical *Fiddler on the Roof*, starring Zero Mostel, with music by Jerry Bock and lyrics by Sheldon Harnick. A wide-screen adaptation of *Fiddler*, directed by Norman Jewison and starring the Israeli actor Chaim Topol, appeared in 1971. Both of these productions are cinematic successors to the 1939 Yiddish-language film *Tevye* (Panavision).

Tevye's Daughters draws on the abundant Jewish literary resources of folklore and biblical lore, historical experience, religious faith and piety, and Jewish methods of coping with their continually endangered lives under pre–World War I Russia's czarist rulers. Moreover, this story collection goes beyond the tragic, pathetic, mixed-blessing experiences of five of Tevye the dairyman's daughters, whose narrative is periodically interrupted by a number of different types of serious or comical (but always diverting) tales. For example, there are accounts of Jewish religious festivals in the towns of Russia and Russian Poland within the restricted Pale of Settlement, stories of Jewish persecution, intimidation, and oppression by Russian officialdom, reports of class conflicts among proletarian, bourgeois, and capitalist segments of Jewish society, and droll railway-carriage anecdotes.

Tevye himself, the purveyor of milk, butter, and cheese to accessible towns beyond his Kasrilevka—Yahupetz and Boiberik especially—is the narrator, bending the ear of his friend Sholom Aleichem, a mostly silent listener and recorder. Tevye is a seriocomic character: garrulous and complaining, prone to asking "why me?" and above all, quoting and misquoting Torah, Talmud, and other reference sources, or else misapplying them. He is forever questioning God's treatment of him and arguing one-sidedly with God, a very familiar and personal presence.

As for the five daughters, Tzeitl, the oldest, is sought after by the rich widower Lazar Wolf, but prefers instead a poor, simple, unlettered tailor, Motel Kamzoil. She winds up with "a household of hungry mouths to feed," but is described by Tevye as "the happiest woman in the world." However, Motel contracts tuberculosis and dies suddenly, leaving her a helpless widow with young children. Hodel marries an older man named Feferel, an agitator devoted to advocating the cause of humanity at large and of workers in particular. She knows he will be sent into exile somewhere for agitating against the authorities. Yet she gladly consents to go with him to the farthest reaches so that she might work at some humble job and visit him once a week, no matter how long his exile.

Chava falls in love with a non-Jew named Fyedka and plans to marry him, which means accepting his Eastern Orthodox religion. The priest tells Tevye that Chava has come under *his* protection, and Tevye considers Chava dead, as far as he is concerned. But when Tevye and his remaining family are suddenly forced to sell all their possessions and leave Kasrilevka, Chava relents, gives up her adopted religious identity and everything that goes with it, and returns to the fold. Schprintze falls in love with a wealthy, young, very spoiled Jewish "swell," who, with his mother, is spending the summer in nearby Boiberik. He falls in love with her and seeks her hand in marriage. But his family of purse-proud elites are alarmed at this threat to their status posed by a poverty-mired toiler like Tevye, and they try to "buy him off," so that he and his daughter will go away. Tevye rejects this shameful offer made by the youth's uncle, and soon the widow and her son leave Boiberik without explanation or farewell. Overcome by grief, Schprintze drowns herself.

Beilke, Tevye's youngest daughter, becomes engaged, through the efforts of a matchmaker, to a wealthy contractor named Padhatzur, who has never been married and now seeks a pretty girl for a mate. He showers her with expensive gifts and, once married, they live like royalty. But he attempts to get Tevye into some kind of work other than that of a dairyman, or, failing that, he tries to send Tevye to America, even to Palestine if need be. In the end Padhatzur turns out to be a boasting, conniving charlatan whose crooked deeds finally catch up with him. He and Beilke lose everything and flee to America, where they become factory workers. Tevye, grieving for his dead wife Golde, and candidly recounting the sad stories of his daughters, nonetheless is able to end his family chronicle on a somewhat cheerful note, and a reaffirmation of his basic faith: "Our ancient God still lives!"

Bibliography

Aleichem, Sholem. *Tevye's Daughters.* Translated and with an introduction by Frances Butwin. New York: Crown, 1949.

Wolitz, Seth L. "The Americanization of Tevye or Boarding the Jewish *Mayflower.*" *American Quarterly* 40, no. 4 (December 1988): 514–536.

—Samuel I. Bellman

Three Lives: Stories of the Good Anna, Melanctha, and the Gentle Leona
Gertrude Stein (1909)

Of all GERTRUDE STEIN's writing, contemporary critics are perhaps most fascinated by "Melanctha," which appears as the second (though it was written last) of three pieces in *Three Lives: Stories of the Good Anna, Melanctha, and the Gentle Lena* (1909). When *Three Lives* was published, at Stein's own expense in part, it was largely ignored. Though Stein's style was not as experimental as it would become a few years later, the prose in this volume is nevertheless far from conventional, thanks to Stein's budding syntactical innovation and focus on repetition. According to Stein, in The AUTOBIOGRAPHY OF ALICE B. TOKLAS, the development of *Three Lives* was influenced by a Cézanne painting hanging in her apartment. The painting, of Cézanne's wife, gives no more detail to its subject than it does to the setting and thus engages in the "democratization of composition," in which each part is as important as the whole (Kimbel 288). This suggests to some that the stories of *Three Lives* are to be read as a short story cycle, though typically they're seen as being only loosely related (Heldrich). Another major influence was Gustave Flaubert's *Trois contes* (1877), which Stein read at her brother Leo's suggestion and on which she clearly modeled *Three Lives*.

"The Good Anna," the first story in *Three Lives,* follows a working-class German immigrant from her job as a devoted (if difficult) servant of Miss Mathilda to her unfulfilled "romance" with Mrs. Lehntman and, finally, her uneventful and unremembered death. Similarly, the last story, "The Gentle Lena," features a German immigrant who is also a servant, this time to her aunt Mrs. Haydon, who marries Lena off to the unwilling German-American tailor Herman Kreder. Lena passively accepts her unhappy marriage, bearing one child after another until she dies in childbirth with the fourth. Neither protagonist is able to alter her circumstances or prevent her death, leading critics to describe both stories in terms of the literary naturalism of the time.

Loosely based on Stein's *Q.E.D.,* which documented (and lightly fictionalized) her troubled love affair with May Bookstaver, "Melanctha" is thematically and stylistically richer. In it, Melanctha, a mulatto, negotiates a series of unsuccessful intimate relationships, at one point falling in love with Doctor Jefferson Campbell. Jeff, who is black, symbolizes both assimilation into white culture and scientific rationality—he is always "thinking," while Melanctha is always "feeling." The disconnect between Melanctha's intuitive energy and Jeff's dependence on logic renders the union unworkable. Lisa Ruddick has argued that this dynamic is evidence of psychologist William James's continued influence on Stein, since Jeff and Melanctha fit into his theories of cognitive processing, with the former paying selective attention to the necessary details in life and the latter taking in all sensations (Ruddick 550). By the end of the story, Melanctha has also been romantically involved with gambler Jem Richards and Rose Johnson, who rejects her in fear that Melanctha's overflowing sexuality will seduce her husband, Sam.

In the original introduction to *Three Lives,* Carl Van Vechten writes glowingly of "Melanctha": "It is perhaps the first American story in which the Negro is regarded as a human being and not as an object for condescending compassion or derision" (x). Since then, some scholars have similarly found in Stein's story a sensitive portrayal of a character who is an outsider by virtue of race. More often, however, contemporary critics see Stein problematically using Melanctha to "pass" as black herself in the tradition of blackface minstrel acts. Others describe Stein's "masking" in terms of modernism's broader fascination with the primitive, exemplified by Picasso's study of African masks. Still others have read "Melanctha" as a model of "modern, hybrid American subjectivity" (Rowe 240) that, while still problematic, warns against the dangers of essentializing identity.

Bibliography
Heldrich, Philip. "Connecting Surfaces: Gertrude Stein's Three Lives, Cubism, and the Metonymy of the Short Story Cycle" *Studies in Short Fiction* 34, no. 4 (Fall 1997): 427–440.
Rowe, John Carlos. "Naming What Is Inside: Gertrude Stein's Use of Names in *Three Lives.*" *Novel: A Forum on Fiction* 36, no. 2 (Spring 2003): 219–243.
—Rachel Ligairi

The Time of the Uprooted **Elie Wiesel** (2005)
The Time of the Uprooted (*Le Temps des déracinés,* 2003) is a gripping novel whose epic sweep encompasses many of the traumatic themes characterizing the 20th century. ELIE WIESEL focuses on the life of Gamaliel Friedman, a hidden child during

the Shoah, to explore the corrosive and continuing effects of the Holocaust's legacy. Consequently, the author deals with several crucial issues: Christianity's teaching of contempt for Judaism; Europe's indifference to the fate of the Jewish people; and the destiny of refugees and victims uprooted from their homes, families, and all that is familiar. Yet the novel moves beyond despair in exploring the key role of friendship; the need for assisting those who have been uprooted; and in emphasizing the author's conviction that storytelling reflects a fundamental need of both humanity and God. Furthermore, this novel is Wiesel's most sustained and detailed depiction of women both during and following the Holocaust.

Gamaliel Friedman, the novel's protagonist, is a Czech-born Jewish youth who flees with his family to Hungary. Wiesel establishes early on in the novel the significant role played by women during the Holocaust. Before her deportation, Gamaliel's mother—to save his life—gives her child to Ilonka, a Christian nightclub singer in Budapest, who at great personal risk hides the youth in her apartment. Ilonka nurtures the youngster and reinforces his love for his birth mother. During his ordeal the boy must assume a Christian identity; his name changes to Péter, he memorizes Christian rituals, and narrowly escapes detection. Following the Holocaust and a traumatic departure from Ilonka, Gamaliel goes first to Vienna, then to Paris, where he and Ilonka had agreed to rendezvous. But she never arrives.

In Paris Gamaliel marries Colette. She wishes to rescue him from his traumatic past. But their relationship ends tragically with his wife's suicide and his estrangement from their two daughters. Collette's despair had arisen because she was unable to help her husband. Because of his Holocaust legacy, he could not be happy. "A refugee," he muses, "is a different kind of being, one from whom all that defines a normal person has been amputated." Her husband could not be happy. Wiesel views the situation as a "double failure"; neither Colette nor Gamaliel was able to undue the Holocaust or to alter his psychic status as a refugee. "But," the author contends, "the story is not an appeal of despair. It is a desperate appeal for hope" (Berger 10).

Gamaliel goes to America, where he and four fellow refugees—Bolek, a Polish survivor; Diego, an anarchist from Lithuania who fought in the Spanish civil war; Yasha, a survivor of Stalinist cruelties; and Gad, a retired agent of the Mossad—comprise an "informal rescue committee" whose task is to help refugees and asylum seekers. To annoy anti-Semites, they call themselves the Elders of Zion, referencing the infamous czarist work that falsely claimed that a small group of rabbis were plotting to take over the world. Although the uprooted are all secularists, Gamaliel continues to seek an understanding of God's relationship to the Shoah. He learns from a mystic, Reb Zusya, who contends that "God is not silent, although He is the God of Silence. He does call out. It is by His silence that He calls to you. Are you answering Him?"

Gamaliel supports himself by being a ghostwriter for well-known novelists. But his passion is devoted to his own *Book of Secrets,* which deals with historic Christian anti-Semitism and its noxious accusation that Jews are Christ killers. One passage in the book reports a conversation between Hananèl ["God have mercy"], a mystic known as the "Blessed Madman," and an Archbishop Baranyi, who imprisons the protagonist and his helper. The prelate offers to save the protagonist and his family if he converts. Hananèl refuses. Moreover, he tells the prelate, "With every Jew you kill, you put your Lord back on the cross." Wiesel's essays (especially *A Jew Today*) and novels (see *A Beggar in Jerusalem*) have always emphasized the difference between the authentic teachings of Jesus and the murderous ways of certain of his followers.

Gamaliel muses on his relationships with two former lovers, Esther and Eve. Esther, whose name means "secret", was a clairvoyant who read palms. Eve was the love of his life. The lives of both Gamaliel and Eve had been uprooted. She lost her husband and young daughter in an automobile accident. Eve believed that she brought bad luck to people. Wiesel describes their relationship as an "encounter . . . in which two lost souls thought they could rescue one another by calling on the love of those who were gone." Eve, like Esther and Colette, disappears from Gamaliel's life. Her reason for leaving? To save the life of Leah, Bolek's daughter whose husband's actions threatened to rob her of her sanity. Eve's intervention and involvement with Leah's husband restored the young woman and devastated Gamaliel.

Bolek tells him of a disfigured and seriously injured hospitalized woman. This nameless person appears to know Hungarian. Is she Ilonka? Gamaliel makes three trips to the hospital but, owing to the ravages of time and the patient's muteness, is unable to determine if she is the person who saved his life. Certain clues indicate that the woman might be Ilonka; she has a pair of Shabbat candlesticks among her possessions. But owing to her condition it is impossible to know her identity for certain. Gamaliel encounters Dr. Lily Rosenkrantz, the patient's physician. He discovers that Lili's life has also been uprooted, her husband inexplicably deserts her, abandoning their two children as well. Although the old woman dies without revealing any information, Rosenkrantz is a healer who may also help Gamaliel. At the novel's end Gamaliel and Lili think about beginning again as dawn breaks and the sun rises, "warming the wounded hearts of the uprooted." Wiesel implies that although Gamaliel's two daughters have denied him, he may have another child with Rosenkrantz (Berger 13).

Wiesel stresses the significance of names in his writings. Gamaliel appears in both the Bible and the Talmud. Living in first-century Palestine, he is a descendant of the great sage Hillel, and the president of the Sanhedrin (rabbinic court). He was known for his wisdom and moderation. Should his namesake perish in the Holocaust, this lineage will be lost. The youngster visits his father, imprisoned by the Nazis, for the final time. The older man admonishes the boy: "You were born a Jew, my son, and a Jew you must remain . . . never forget that you carry the name of my own father: Gamaliel. Try not to dishonor it. You'll take it back as yours when this ordeal is over. Every name has its story. Promise me . . . that one day you will tell that story." The protagonist's survival is simultaneously a continuation of his lineage and a mission to tell the story of Judaism and the Holocaust.

The Time of the Uprooted is a powerful meditation on the human condition. Perhaps the most polished of Wiesel's recent novels, this book emphasizes the significance of persevering in spite of all attempts to destroy the Jews and Judaism. Moreover, his emphasis on the importance of telling the tale makes witnesses of his readers and challenges them to keep the story alive while working to improve the world. This novel was critically acclaimed, reviews appearing in, among other places the *Los Angeles Times*, *Kirkus*, and the *Washington Post*.

Bibliography
Berger, Alan L. "Interview with Elie Wiesel." *Literature and Belief* 26, no. 1 (March 2007): 1–23.
Plank, Karl A. "The Survivor's Return: Reflections on Memory and Place." *Judaism* 38, no. 3 (Summer 1989): 263–277.

—Alan L. Berger

Touching Evil Norma Rosen (1969)

After a first marriage, NORMA ROSEN, née Gangel, married Robert Rosen in 1960, a Judaically educated professor, and gradually became an educated Jewish woman. She and Robert, one of those fortunate few to escape Nazi Germany on a *Kindertransport* to England, had two children, Anne Beth and Jonathan. Her studies in Jewish religion and thought had a lasting impact on her development as a writer and her concerns for the Holocaust.

With *Touching Evil* (1969), a novel about two gentile women's sympathetic response to the Holocaust and to the Eichmann trial in 1961, Norma Rosen created an extraordinarily sensitive response to gentile characters who experience Jewish history vicariously and imaginatively. The novel takes place in New York City in 1961, during Adolf Eichmann's trial in Jerusalem. The first of two epigraphs, a quote from Carl Jung, argues that "Touching evil brings with it the grave peril of succumbing to it. We must, therefore, no longer succumb to anything at all, not even to good." Both Jean Lamb and Hattie Mews are affected by the evil they hear via the Eichmann trial, but choose to live with the knowledge of evil while pursuing that which is greater than good and the knowledge of joy.

Jean first learned of the Shoah (Holocaust) in 1944, as we find out through diary reflections of 1944 and newspaper photos of life and death in the camps; the Eichmann trial confirms Jean's belief that the Holocaust is a central metaphor of her life. Rosen does not picture what happened but creates the impact of the Shoah on Jean and Hattie as they see the survivors and hear their testimony (through translation).

Significantly, the Eichmann trial reaffirms Jean's connection to the Holocaust. Despite the temporal distance, Jean, watching the trial, finds her heart and mind violated again. "I'm up to my ears again in corpses," she says, "those same flesh-less bones that fell on me seventeen years ago. I know now there's nothing to do but heave them off. But they're falling on Hattie for the first time, and I'm with her" (21).

Rosen responds to those who claim that *Touching Evil* universalizes the Holocaust by bringing the Jewish experience into a non-Jewish, universal setting by arguing that her book instead brings something non-Jewish into Jewish experience.

What is so important and significant is the way Rosen pictures the continuing effect on future generations through Hattie's absorption in the trial. Concurring with Jean that the Nazis defiled life itself, that their unspeakable cruelties almost defy belief, the pregnant Hattie has reservations about bringing children into such a world. The destruction of European Jewry also reflects the global indifferences of so many, then and now, to the catastrophe, the insensitivity and apathy paralleling the wish for life to continue as usual. Hattie's husband and her brother-in-law concur that "all this happened to other people." Jean's lover, Loftus, advises Jean to get Hattie to stop watching the trial. He's afraid she might lose her joie de vivre. Jean believes that "there were only two kinds of people . . . those who knew and those who didn't know." For Jean, "Nothing of her life would, after she learns of the existence of the death camps, be as before" (77).

Touching Evil pulls the reader into a larger philosophical view of the Holocaust. The Shoah has transformed our perceptions of humanity. Rosen's feminine deliberation on American reaction reflects those who did not live to testify. It also alerts the reader now and in the future to some of the often overlooked dimensions of the Holocaust.

Bibliography

Rosen, Norma. *Touching Evil.* New York: Harcourt Brace, 1969.
———. "The Holocaust and the American Jewish Novelist." *Midstream* 20 (October 1974).
Rosenberg, Ruth. "Norma Rosen." In *Twentieth Century American Jewish Fiction Writers,* edited by Daniel Walden. Detroit: Gale Research, 1984.

—**Daniel Walden**

The Town Beyond the Wall
Elie Wiesel (1964)

The Town Beyond the Wall (La Ville de la chance, 1962) explores and rejects clinical madness as a response to the Holocaust, although the author implicitly endorses the stance of prophetic or mystical madness, a stance that insists on saying no to a world of violence, torture, and indifference, and on calling God to account. Furthermore, the author treats the troubling phenomenon of the "other" as bystander—the one who watches while evil acts are committed without seeking to intervene. ELIE WIESEL also raises the theological stakes by imagining God as a bystander during the Holocaust. The novel marks a major turning point in Wiesel's literary oeuvre. Whereas his memoir NIGHT and his first two novels, *Dawn* and *The Accident (Le Jour),* end with the protagonist isolated and consumed by the Holocaust dead, Michael, the protagonist in *The Town Beyond the Wall*, begins the painful journey toward human interaction and acceptance of the necessity of dialogue.

The novel is set in a prison in Communist-ruled Hungary. Michael is tortured, compelled to stand facing a wall, and deprived of food and sleep. To save the life of his mysterious friend Pedro, he must refrain from speaking to his interrogators, who falsely accuse him of spying. *Town*, reflecting Wiesel's wish that his prayers be made into tales, is divided not into chapters, but rather four "prayers" (Interview). The First Prayer consists of flashbacks to Michael's Hungarian childhood, the Second Prayer treats his time as a Parisian adolescent, and the Third Prayer recounts his experience as a journalist in Tangier, where he meets Pedro, a smuggler who teaches Michael about the meaning of friendship and the relationship between humanity and God. The Fourth Prayer takes place in a prison cell where Michael, having regained consciousness, encounters three other prisoners: the Religious One, the Impatient One, and the Silent One.

Back in his boyhood town of Szerencsevàros (the city of luck), now without any Jewish presence, Michael stands at the site of the synagogue, now replaced by a new building. As an aside, the author's literary return preceded his actual return. Michael suddenly understands that he has come back to confront the face of indifference as embodied by the man who stared uncaringly from his window as the town's Jews were rounded up for deportation. Between victim and executioner there exists a third category, the spectator. There ensues a dialogue between Michael and the indifferent witness. The protagonist contends that he does not hate the nameless man. Rather, he feels only contempt. Moreover, the indifferent ones are not really living at all, attests Michael. Rather, they "scuttle along the margins of existence." Wiesel, as aphorist, will later observe, "The opposite of love is not hate. It is indifference." Ironically, the indifferent witness finally acts by informing on Michael to the police.

In his prison cell Michael has a discussion with Menachem, the Religious One, and saves the life of two prisoners, one by physically preventing the Impatient One from strangling Menachem, and the second when he obeys Pedro's imagined injunction, "Cure him [The Silent One]. He'll save you." Menachem ("comforter"/"messiah") articulates a religious faith that encompasses the trauma of Auschwitz. "Why," he asks, "does God insist that we come to him by the hardest road?" This possibility of post-Auschwitz faith, even though severely

wounded, marks the first time that a Wieselian protagonist embraces such a possibility. Robert M. Brown importantly notes that in Wiesel's earlier works, each protagonist "saw only his own face, a face of death. It was still night." But at the conclusion of *Town*, "Michael is looking *into the face of another*. He has broken out of isolation into a concern for, and relationship with, another human being." The name of the Silent One is Eliezer ("God has granted my prayer").

The Town Beyond the Wall received great critical acclaim. The French version was awarded the 1963 Prix Rivarol. Wiesel's novel initiates a gradual movement toward embracing the possibility of meaningful post-Auschwitz existence even while acknowledging that faith and belief can never be what they were before the Holocaust. Further, granting the Silent One his own name, Wiesel indicates that he now rejects the option of clinical madness, preferring instead to help humanity and to struggle against and with God.

Bibliography

Berger, Alan L. "Interview with Elie Wiesel." *Literature and Belief*, 26, no. 1 (March 2007): 1–23.

Brown, Robert McAfee. *Elie Wiesel: Messenger to All Humanity*. Notre Dame, Ind.: University of Notre Dame Press, 1983.

Fine, Ellen S. *Legacy of Night: The Literary Universe of Elie Wiesel*. Albany: SUNY Press, 1982.

—Alan L. Berger

Trilling, Lionel (1905–1975)

Lionel Trilling is generally acknowledged as one of the major literary critics of the second half of the 20th century, a period known as "an age of criticism." He is particularly recognized for his role in the postwar redefinition of liberalism. One of the distinctive features of his reputation is the way he is admired by nonliterary intellectuals. He continues to be widely cited outside the area of literary studies. The principal reason for his broad appeal is that he views the study of literature as a study of human life and consequently brings to his consideration of literary texts a concern with large moral, psychological, and cultural questions. His encounter with literature often includes but is not restricted to the critical act narrowly conceived as the description or analysis of a work followed perhaps by a judgment of its aesthetic merits. His deepest interests lay in searching for the animating attitudes and values underlying the literary text and weighing their moral and cultural significance. He assumed that a literary work is saturated with meanings relevant beyond the printed page, that literature has an important and determinate relationship to the real world, to the society and culture that shapes it and is in turn shaped by it. He focuses on literature, as he explains in the preface to *The Liberal Imagination,* "because literature is the human activity that takes the fullest and most precise account of variousness, possibility, complexity, and difficulty."

Lionel Trilling was born in New York City on July 4, 1905, son of David W. and Fannie Cohen Trilling. Both parents were Jewish immigrants from eastern Europe. Although Orthodox Jews, the family's emphasis was on the cultural value of Judaism and its accommodation to the best of the larger world. When the family later moved to 108th Street in Manhattan, Lionel was trained for his bar mitzvah by Max Kadushin, a protégé of Mordecai Kaplan at the Jewish Theological Seminary, where the ceremony was eventually performed. Despite his religious training, he did not, as he later said, "get religion," and by the time he was in college his Jewishness was cultural rather than religious.

After graduation from Dewitt Clinton High School in 1921, Trilling entered Columbia University as a 16-year-old freshman and began an association with that university that lasted until the end of his life. Only a few years of teaching at the University of Wisconsin, Oxford, and Harvard took him away from New York City for any length of time. The big word at Columbia when Trilling was an undergraduate, he tells us, was *intelligence.* John Erskine, one of his teachers, provided a kind of slogan with the title of one of his essays: "The Moral Obligation to Be Intelligent." In this environment, Trilling acquired a keen and lasting respect for intelligence. Moreover, he was converted

to the assumption "that intelligence was connected with literature, that it was advanced by literature."

During his senior year he was introduced to the *Menorah Journal,* the monthly magazine of the Menorah Society. Its broad purpose was to further a secular, humanist, and progressive Jewish consciousness in America. His association with the journal lasted six and a half years, from spring 1925 to fall 1931. In its pages he published book reviews, essays, and four short stories. His commitment to the *Menorah Journal* was social and cultural and had nothing to do with Jewish religion; it appears that the more he studied Jewish identity, the more he recoiled from involving himself in Jewish cultural agony. But although he eventually became disenchanted with the pursuit of ethnic consciousness, his association with the *Menorah Journal* opened the way for his characteristic explorations of manners and morals, self in society, the conditioning influence of class and circumstances, and the interaction of literature and society. Trilling's break with Jewishness was even more complete and permanent than was the rule among second-generation Jewish intellectuals. He acknowledged with pleasure the effect that his Jewish rearing had had on his temperament and mind, but recognized that the impulses of his intellectual life came from other sources and that the chief objects of his thought and feeling were anything but Jewish. While admitting that a Jew of his generation could not "escape" his Jewish origins, he insisted in 1944 that "I cannot discover anything in my professional intellectual life which I can specifically trace back to my Jewish birth and rearing."

He married Diana Rubin in June 1929. She also was later to earn recognition as a literary social critic. A fellowship and the offer of an instructorship at Columbia in 1932 set the direction of his career. He taught for four years while working with only partial success on a doctoral dissertation on Matthew Arnold. At the end of that time he was dismissed, the department spokesman suggesting that "as a Freudian, a Marxist, and a Jew" he would be "more comfortable" elsewhere. In reality Trilling in 1936 was none of those things. He was devastated by the dismissal, but in a few days took the most decisive action of his life. According to Diana, he confronted each of the department members he knew best. "He didn't reason with them, he didn't argue with them. He told them that they were getting rid of a person who would one day bring great distinction to their department; they would not easily find another as good." He was reappointed for another year, which multiplied because he was a changed person. The problems with shaping his book on Arnold disappeared immediately. In 1939 it was published and has remained in print ever since. He was promoted to assistant professor of English, the first Jew of that department to become a member of the faculty. He was appointed university professor in 1970, the highest distinction Columbia University confers on a member of its faculty. By the time his *Matthew Arnold* appeared in 1939, he had published nearly 50 articles in addition to the 20-odd pieces in the *Menorah Journal.* Most of these appeared in the *Nation* and *New Republic,* and a few in *Partisan Review,* on whose advisory board he would serve from 1948 to 1961. The forties were a productive time for him. He continued publishing in these periodicals and began a long association with *Kenyon Review.* In 1943 he published *E. M. Forster* and his famous story "Of This Time, of That Place." Another story, "The Other Margaret," appeared in 1945, and his only novel, *The MIDDLE OF THE JOURNEY,* in 1947. "The Lesson and the Secret" appeared in l949 along with *The Portable Matthew Arnold.* The decade culminated in the l950 publication of *The Liberal Imagination,* a collection of the major essays written during that fertile period.

During most of the 1950s, probably the apex of his reputation, his name was rarely mentioned in print without admiration or at least great respect, but in the late fifties he was sniped at and sometimes roundly attacked. Those who found fault with his work during the last 15 years of his life were mainly those interested in critical theory. Trilling was little interested in literary theory and continued in the humanistic tradition of a moral-cultural approach to literature.

Between 1960 and 1975 his increasing uneasiness with the modern temper found expression in *Beyond Culture: Essays on Literature and Learning* (1965), *Sincerity and Authenticity* (1972, based on the Charles Eliot Norton lectures delivered at Harvard in 1969–70), and *Mind in the Modern World* (1973, a lecture given on receiving the National Endowment for the Humanities first Thomas Jefferson Award). His lasting commitment to teaching was reflected in his editing of *The Experience of Literature* (1967, an anthology with extensive critical commentary) and *Literary Criticism: An Introductory Reader* (1970), and his coediting of *The Oxford Anthology of English Literature* (1973). His profound admiration for Freud resulted in his editing, with Steven Marcus, an abridgment of Ernest Jones's three-volume *The Life and Work of Sigmund Freud* (1970). His achievement was recognized in visiting lectureships at Harvard and Oxford Universities, a Creative Arts Award from Brandeis University, and honorary degrees from Harvard, Northwestern, Case Western Reserve, Brandeis, and Yale universities in the United States and the Universities of Durham and Leicester in England. When he died of cancer in 1975, he was working under a Guggenheim fellowship.

In the eyes of David Daiches, Trilling was the perfect New York intellectual: "Intelligent, curious, humane, well read, interested in ideas, fascinated by other times and places, and immensely knowledgeable about European culture, he is at the same time metropolitan (with the provincialism that goes with true metropolitanism), self-conscious and professional in the practice of literary criticism, very much the *observer* of the great stream of American life that goes on around him, the sophisticated urban observer who is proud of the fact that his observation is undoctrinaire and untainted with snobbism."

Bibliography

Boyers, Robert. *Lionel Trilling: Negative Capability and the Wisdom of Avoidance.* Columbia: University of Missouri Press, 1977.

Shoben, Edward Joseph, Jr. *Lionel Trilling.* New York: Frederick Ungar, 1981.

Tanner, Stephen L. *Lionel Trilling.* Boston: Twayne, 1988.

—Stephen Tanner

U

Uris, Leon (1924–2003)

Author, historian, and screenwriter Leon Uris grew up in Baltimore. Born the son of a shopkeeper couple, Wolf William Uris and Anna (Blumberg) Uris, Leon attended local public schools before entering the U.S. Marine Corps in 1942, where he served a four-year tour of duty in the Pacific, including the battles of Guadalcanal and Tarawa.

On his return from service to San Francisco, Uris married Betty Katherine Beck, with whom he had three children and whom he divorced in 1968. Shortly after his return he began his writing career as a circulation district manager for the *San Francisco Call-Bulletin*. After a series of rejections, he sold his first article to *Esquire* for $300, officially launching his career. With the added confidence, he wrote his first novel, *Battle Cry* (1953), which achieved best-seller status. Next, he adapted the novel for the screen and proved his prowess at screenwriting.

After his second novel, *The Angry Hills* (1955), scored commercially and bombed critically (a pattern that was often repeated throughout his career), Uris began to write his masterpiece: a novel that equally balanced his Hollywood ambition and his desire for historical authenticity. The result was the epic story of the founding of the state of Israel, *Exodus* (1958), named after the famous 1947 immigrant ship that brought Jews from France to Palestine. Writing the 600-page novel was a heavy task that was made more difficult by Uris's lack of formal Jewish education or speaking knowledge of Hebrew. But he spent the next two years of his life researching his topic. He traveled roughly 50,000 miles (12,000 in Israel alone), read over 300 books on the topic, shot over 1,000 photos, and conducted hundreds of interviews.

The effort, was not in vain, as *Exodus* became an instant success. Aside from being a best seller, the novel was also turned into an extremely popular 1960 film, directed by Otto Preminger and starring Paul Newman and Eva Marie Saint. Uris used all of the information he gathered from this project (and more) to write *Mila 18* (1960), but not before releasing *Exodus Revisited* (1959), a photo-essay of his heavily researched topic.

For his next two novels, Uris shifted from his focus on Jewish life and Israel to tackle the Berlin airlift, *Armageddon* (1964), and an iron curtain spy thriller, *Topaz* (1967). Nonetheless, Uris returned to his passion for Jewish themes with *QB VII* (1970), a tale of a Polish camp survivor who sues an American Jewish writer for libel. A number of his novels were made into films—perhaps most famously *Topaz*, directed by Alfred Hitchcock. The novel *QB VII* followed this streak; it was made into a highly rated television miniseries in 1974.

After all of his success with Jewish-themed topics, Uris moved away from such subject matter with

Trinity (1976), an *Exodus*-like attempt at explaining Ireland's history. But he returned to Judaism with *The Haj* (1984) and *Mitla Pass* (1988), only to revisit Ireland with *Redemption* (1995).

Before he died of renal failure in 2003, Uris penned two later novels that fit awkwardly into his canon. With *A God in Ruins* (1999), he focused on the eve of the 2008 presidential election, and with *O'Hara's Choice* (2003), he unfolded a hodgepodge story of a 19th-century Irish-American marine, taking readers from Washington, D.C., to Newport, Rhode Island, and from the Civil War to the end of the 19th century. Fans of Uris agree that these last two novels were so different in style and tone from any of Uris's previous work that they seemed likely to have been heavily edited or possibly written by someone else.

Yet given his impressive career, Uris did not go unrecognized. Among his many novels were numerous best sellers, and many were made into highly successful films. He also won a bounty of awards, including the California Literature Silver and Gold Medal awards, the John F. Kennedy Medal from the Irish/American Society of New York, the Scopus Award from Hebrew University of Jerusalem, and honorary doctorates from the University of Colorado, Santa Clara University, Wittenberg University, and Lincoln College. While much of his work was not a critical success, he was treasured by countless readers over several generations.

Bibliography

Downey, Sharon D., and Richard A. Kallan. "Semi-Aesthetic Detachment: The Fusing of Fictional and External Worlds in the Situational Literature of Leon Uris." *Communication Monographs* 49, no. 3 (1982): 192–204.

Manganaro, Elise Salem. "Voicing the Arab: Multivocality and Ideology in Leon Uris' *The Haj*." *MELUS* 15, no. 4 (1988): 3–13.

Salt, Jeremy. "Fact and Fiction in the Middle Eastern Novels of Leon Uris." *Journal of Palestine Studies* 14, no. 3 (1985): 54–63.

—Holli G. Levitsky

W

Waiting for Lefty Clifford Odets (1935)

Perhaps CLIFFORD ODETS's best received and most acclaimed work is *Waiting for Lefty,* the 1935 agitprop play. The action of the play is drawn from the circumstances surrounding the 1934 strike of taxi drivers in New York City. The play is presented in several vignettes that alternate between a union meeting of taxi drivers and earlier events from the lives of the union members. All of the vignettes portray not only the suffering experienced by the working class and their families, but also depict the hardships suffered as the result of profit-driven business interests, which operate at the expense of workers.

The scenes dedicated to the union meeting explore the voices that both call for and oppose a motion to strike. They demonstrate the difficult decision faced by the workers and the additional complication of ill will on the part of the taxi company, who hires workers to go undercover and arouse antistrike sentiments. Interspersed among these glimpses of the meeting are flashbacks from the lives of several drivers that trace their path of suffering to the current predicament. These scenes represent both young and old workers from within the taxi community as well as scientists and doctors. Their stories tell of suffering from poor wages, a lack of upward mobility, and the need to exchange one's moral values to have a successful career.

The climax comes when the title character, Lefty, whom some in the union desire to consult before making the decision to strike, is reported dead. The play then comes to a close as the taxi drivers join in a repeated call to "STRIKE!"

The formal innovations of *Lefty* reside mainly in the stark stage setting and the interesting use of time. The stage is left as bare as possible, with little done to separate changes of setting between scenes. As the action moves from the union meeting to the other stories, the taxi drivers are still faintly visible to the audience. This encroachment of one scene upon the other along with the nonlinear progression of time creates an interesting method of character and plot development. The overall feel of the play has been described as reminiscent of the German playwright Bertolt Brecht, who is said to have read and admired the work.

Like many of Odets's plays, *Lefty* plays heavily on sentiments of the day that were negative toward big business. These same themes are displayed in other works during the Great Depression, such as John Steinbeck's novel *The Grapes of Wrath.* At first glance *Lefty* would appear to be an inferior work because of the one-dimensional nature of the characters and the predictability of the plot. But the very simplicity of the situation and people helps to convey the depths of human suffering portrayed. The brevity of the scenes, minimal use of props, and definition of characters as mere reactions to their situation are all influences in restricting the audience reaction to a highly focused, emotional response. This simple, strong emotional appeal was often met with an enthusiastic audience response. Some early productions were concluded with the audience joining in the final call to strike.

The harsh criticism of capitalism and the call for organized action by the working class has unmistakable ties to socialist sentiments, which were not unusual during the period. The simplicity of the work, although criticized, helped to create a focus on the human element, while avoiding abstract class politics and overly symbolic gestures. Although the play was written in the space of only three days and was one of Odets's first published works, *Lefty* stands as one of his finest works in content, recognition, and reception.

Bibliography

Cantor, Harold. *Clifford Odets Playwright-Poet.* Metuchen, N.J.: Scarecrow Press, 1978.
Miller, Gabriel, ed. *Critical Essays on Clifford Odets.* Boston: G.K. Hall, 1991.

—**Jason Douglas**

Wallant, Edward Lewis (1926–1962)

Described by David Galloway as a "minor writer with major talent," Edward Lewis Wallant remains an important postwar Jewish-American writer whose promising career was cut short by his premature death at age 36 from a cerebral aneurysm. Born in New Haven, Connecticut, and raised as an only child by his widowed mother and two aunts, Wallant had only limited childhood exposure to the practice of Judaism. His interest and knowledge in his cultural and religious heritage developed largely in adulthood. He and his wife, Joyce, raised their three children in the Reform Jewish tradition. A successful commercial artist working with various New York advertising agencies, Wallant also pursued a writing career in his spare time, publishing his first novel, *The Human Season,* in 1960, which received an award for the finest novel published that year on a Jewish theme. His second

novel, *The PAWNBROKER* (1961), was nominated for the National Book Award, establishing Wallant as a notable emerging writer. His 1962 Guggenheim fellowship allowed him to resign from his art director position and devote himself fully to his writing. At the time of his death in December 1962, Wallant was busy revising his third and fourth novels, *The Tenants of Moonbloom* and *Children at the Gate,* both of which were published posthumously in 1963 and 1964, respectively, after his editor at Harcourt Brace Jovanovich, Dan Wickinden, completed the final revisions.

Because Wallant was so well read, particularly in modernism, his work represents multiple literary traditions and themes, including late 19th- and early 20th-century realism and naturalism, contemporary confessional psychology, immigrant identity and anxiety, materialism, memory's persistence, and transcendental quests within existential contexts. His preoccupation with thematic binaries—individual/society, outsider/insider, despair/hope, ignorance/epiphany, victimization/survival, Jewish/Christian, and so on—tend to make his narratives edge along axes of tension in the direction of a dramatic climax. He seems fond of resolutions that promise some possibility of understanding and unity. The ethic underlying his fiction revolves around the necessity of being individually responsible for others within the community, an ethic that echoes throughout Jewish-American literature.

The Human Season takes place almost solely within the interior of Joe (Yussel) Berman's home during June 1956 as he struggles to come to terms with the death of his wife, Mary, a blonde, middle-class, born-and-bred mainstream American who represents a tangible fulfillment of his immigrant dream of American success. Her loss parallels the loss of this dream, making their home, although still filled with the material accoutrements of success, feel empty to him. The chronological advance of the main narrative is counterpointed by a reverse chronology of flashbacks; as Berman's life moves forward toward whatever fate awaits him, his memory moves backward toward his earliest childhood experiences as a Russian Jew in a figurative reverse diaspora. These memories are tinged with bittersweet nostalgia for the past. The novel concludes with Berman's moving in with his daughter Ruthie and her family, a typically Wallantian return to family and community.

The Pawnbroker, Wallant's most significant novel, was among the first Jewish-American novels to bring the Holocaust to American shores. It addresses themes similar to *The Human Season*: the inevitability of alienation, the persistence of memory, the pervasive atmosphere of loss, the inadequacy of American materialism, the ethical call of responsibility to community, the grounding of identity in Jewish history and culture, and so forth. Like Berman, Sol Nazerman, the pawnbroker of the title, is haunted by memory; his memories, however, are constituted exclusively of horrific images from the brutal treatment he and his family experienced in the Holocaust, with no trace of nostalgia whatsoever. He operates his Harlem pawnbroker shop in supreme indifference to his customers, always driving the hard bargain, sardonically aware of the irony of his embodying the worst Shylockian clichés of Jewish greed. This stereotype, however, is tempered by his generosity to his sister's family, as well as to his mistress, Tessie, and her dying father, both Holocaust survivors. Nazerman is drawn out of his isolation by Marilyn Birchfield, a relentlessly pleasant WASPish fund-raiser for the new neighborhood Youth Center, who offers the romantic possibility of a future separated from the nightmare of his past, and by his assistant, Jesus Ortiz, whose self-sacrifice at the end of the novel calls him to greater empathy and service.

Although *The Children at the Gate* was published after *The Tenants of Moonbloom*, it was drafted long before. The novel features dual protagonists, Angelo DeMarco, a pharmacy delivery-man, and Sammy, an eccentric hospital orderly, whose respective primary and secondary roles in the novel parallel the roles of Nazerman and Ortiz in *The Pawnbroker*. Like Nazerman, DeMarco works on the periphery of American society, among the sick, the dying, and the desperate, alienated from his family. Like Ortiz, Sammy

functions as an atoning Christ figure, particularly in his melodramatic suicide leap onto the wrought-iron fence surrounding the Sacred Heart Hospital, his dead body being displayed with obvious crucifixion associations. In addition, Sammy's strangely moving parables of the grotesque and the marginalized in society function as important ethical touchstones of generosity, such as the story of the pedophile who donates his own corneas to restore a child's sight. Sammy's death seems intended to absolve Lebedov, another hospital orderly, of the attempted rape of a young patient, and to absolve DeMarco also, who may have betrayed Sammy.

The Tenants of Moonbloom differs from Wallant's other three novels in its humorous tone and may suggest the comic direction in which Wallant's latest writing was moving. The author spent summer 1962 on a Guggenheim-financed trip to Europe to gather material for a projected comic novel, *Tannenbaum's Journey*. Wallant's protagonist, Norman Moonbloom, is a failed professional student—accounting, art, dentistry, podiatry, and rabbinical studies—forced to work for his brother collecting rents from an odd assortment of tenement inhabitants while strenuously avoiding any building repairs. Moonbloom goes from reluctant employee to subversive landlord, even using his own money to finance repairs, and thus becomes reborn out of egotism into altruism in the most joyous of Wallant's novel endings.

Bibliography

Galloway, David. *Edward Lewis Wallant.* Boston: Twayne, 1979.

Raney, Stanford. "The Novels of Edward Wallant." *Colorado Quarterly* 17 (1969): 393–405.

—Phillip A. Snyder

Wasserstein, Wendy (1950–2006)

Born and raised in New York City by upper-middle-class Jewish parents Morris (a textile plant owner) and Lola (a former dancer), Wendy Wasserstein and her siblings were raised to be independent overachievers. Wasserstein attended some of the East's most prestigious educational institutions, such as Mount Holyoke College, Yale University, and New York's City University. Her sisters, Sandra and Georgette, and her brother, Bruce, went on to successful business careers, a path Wendy considered but rejected when she was accepted at Yale's School of Drama. Her upbringing is evident in each of the many plays, essays and commentaries she wrote in her more than 40 years as a writer and, like many young people of her era, Wasserstein rebelled against the traditional values of her culture and education to write a body of wry, often bitter, humorous works.

Her early college titles, including "Any Woman Can't," "Happy Birthday, Montpellier Pizz-zazz," and "When Dinah Shore Ruled the Earth," were mostly farcical pieces of biting satire with typical, situational-comic characters. The depth of character and complexity of development for which Wasserstein is so well known, however, can first be seen in *Uncommon Women, and Others* (Phoenix Theatre 1977), which began as Wasserstein's graduate thesis at Yale. The well-received play begins to demonstrate Wasserstein's ability to capture the subtle nuances of realistic female characters, their conversations, and their situations in a manner that is humorous and lighthearted, yet deeply earnest in its presentation of the seriousness and depth of women's issues. Like many of Wasserstein's works, it contains semiautobiographical components, such as the hopeful writer Rita, whose claims to independence are undermined by her need to find a wealthy husband who will support her as she pursues her writing. *Uncommon Women* was followed by Wasserstein's next major play, *Isn't It Romantic* (Phoenix Theatre 1981), which contemplates pressing issues of marriage and children in the lives of women approaching 30. This play was written, tellingly, as the playwright herself was approaching that age. On its heels came the one-act play *Tender Offer* and *The Man in a Case,* one act of the seven-act play *Orchards,* a collection of adaptations of the Russian playwright Anton Chekhov's short stories.

Wasserstein worked regularly with Playwrights Horizons, a critically acclaimed, off-off-Broadway theater company, which produced *Isn't It Romantic; Miami,* a musical about a teen on vacation with his family; and Wasserstein's most celebrated work (and her first produced on Broadway), *The Heidi Chronicles* (Playwrights Horizons 1988), the Pulitzer Prize–winning play about one woman's growing disillusionment with life in post-feminist America.

Wasserstein followed *Heidi* with the plays *The Sisters Rosensweig,* which includes characters based on her sisters, *An American Daughter,* which analyzes liberal politics in Washington, D.C., and the screenplay for *Object of My Affection.*

Wasserstein's many essays were collected in *Bachelor Girls* (1990) and *Shiksa Goddess; or, How I Spent My Forties* (2001), which examines Wasserstein's experiences leading up to the birth of her daughter, Lucy Jane, including her own infertility problems and her sister Sandra's battle with breast cancer. Through these experiences she analyzes, in her typical seriocomic fashion, the many trials and challenges of modern women, touching on themes of romance, aging, single parenthood, divorce, and career in the still-male-dominated world of business. She also wrote a children's book, *Pamela's First Musical* (1996), based on her childhood experiences at Broadway shows with her former dancer mother, which she adapted into a musical with composer Cy Coleman before his death in 2004.

Because her problems with lymphoma had not been widely publicized, Wasserstein's untimely death in January 2006, at age 55, was a shock to many in the entertainment industry. As is customary in honor of theatrical luminaries, Broadway dimmed its streetlights the night after she died.

Bibliography

Barnett, Claudia, ed. *Wendy Wasserstein: A Casebook. Casebooks on Modern Dramatists.* New York: Garland, 1999.

Ciociola, Gail. *Wendy Wasserstein: Dramatizing Women, Their Choices and Their Boundaries.* Jefferson, N.C.: McFarland, 1998.

Wasserstein, Wendy. *The Heidi Chronicles and Other Plays.* New York: Harcourt Brace Jovanovich, 1990.

Wasserstein, Wendy. *Shiksa Goddess; Or, How I Spent My Forties.* New York: Knopf, 2001.

—Jacob Levi Robertson

A Weave of Women   E. M. Broner (1978)

E. M. BRONER–s *Weave of Women*, set in early 1970s Israel, presents a cycle of 15 women's intertwined lives that begins with a birth, follows forms of death in the lives of the women, and comes full circle with the inauguration of a utopian women's community in the Israeli desert. The women, representing different ages, backgrounds, interests, and desires, meet to nourish and support one another in a stone house in East Jerusalem. They include Antoinette, a Shakespearian scholar; Gerda, a German scientist who lost her family in the Holocaust; Vered, a social worker from Poland; Terry, a social activist; Mihal, who is fighting the rabbinate for a divorce from her abusive husband; Hepzibah, the suppressed wife who finally reclaims herself through stepping out of her role as wife and mother and administering a home for girls in Haifa; Tova, an actress; Dahlia, a singer; and Deedee, an Irish exile. In addition to the 12 women, there are three runaway teenage girls: Sula, Simha, and Rina. These women share the stories of their pasts, rely on one another for support, and fight both social and sexual oppression and violence as they also challenge the patriarchal structures of Jewish religion and tradition and the larger Israeli society.

The women's stories are set against a vast tableau of an Israeli society peopled by, among others, politicians, kibbutzniks, social workers, street workers, artists, singers, mystics, Hasidim, Bedouin lovers, rabbis, peaceniks working toward Arab-Israeli reconciliation, and mystical and biblical presences and apparitions. In addition, the drama is enlarged by the specter of the land itself: its multilayered, complex history, its beauty, and its religious and mythic dimensions.

To create a meaningful order for their lives, the women construct Jewish rituals to commemorate the phases of their existence. They reenvision existing rites and rituals (i.e., for birth, death, mourning, and marriage), celebrations for the holidays and prayers (in the marriage vows, for instance, they substitute "life and love" for husband and wife), and compose new ceremonies for aspects of women's lives (i.e., a ceremony to exorcise dybbuks, to forgo false self-images, to celebrate the body). These rituals constitute a powerful retelling of Jewish history and tradition that incorporates the experiences of women's bodies, history, and spirituality.

The novel's stylistic and technical innovations emphasize the interconnectedness of the protagonists' lives. The book moves in an associative rather than a linear fashion, stressing the interwoven nature of the women's experiences and uses stream-of-consciousness and a fragmented style to suggest multiple points of view and perspectives. In addition, the novel's magical realism, its lyrical and allusive prose (i.e., mythic and biblical figures and motifs), its incorporation of parable and incantation, and its sensuous, specific language (particularly noticeable in the treatment of the women's rites) evoke the embodied state of feminine consciousness.

Applauded by critics as "epic" in scope, the novel presents a humanistic and feminist vision of the characters' journeys toward selfhood—their struggles for autonomy, wholeness, and personhood in a more just world. Thus, the book's final utopian vision, the women's creation of a female community in the desert, invokes the expansive sense of tradition that Broner hopes to instill in her readers. As Marilyn French comments in her introduction to the novel, "With her gifted pen and mind, Broner depicts a feminine vision, merges it with a masculine [Judeo-Christian] tradition to create something new, a fully human tradition" (xv).

Bibliography
French, Marilyn. "Introduction." In *Weave of Women* by E. M. Broner. Bloomington: Indiana University Press, l985.
Omer-Sherman, Ranen. "E. M. Broner's Aesthetics of Dispersal in A Weave of Women." *Modern Jewish Studies* 13, no. 4 (2004): 28–39.

—Jan Schmidt

West, Nathanael (1903–1940)

In an attempt to describe the short-lived career of American fiction and screenwriter Nathanael West, one of West's prominent commentators, James F. Light, made much of West's use of dream. Other attempts have focused on themes and influences such as that of French surrealism, symbolism, Dadaism (derived from West's postcollege sojourn in Paris from 1926 to 1927), of Freud and Jung, the grotesque, the fantasy, the hallucinatory tendency, and the quest. Another term may be suggested that cuts across the above designations and encompasses West's lifestyle as well as his creative efforts—the "as if" point of view. Even in such an ethereal story as that of his first novel, *The Dream Life of Balso Snell*, with all of its dreamlike fragments and jarring associations of ideas, it may be read as a series of imaginative possibilities taking the form of "what if so and so instead were such and such?"

West was born in New York City in 1903. His four novels—*The Dream Life of Balso Snell* (1931), *Miss Lonelyhearts* (1933), *A Cool Million: The Dismantling of Lemuel Pitkin* (1934), and *The Day of the Locust* (1939)—were all depression novels. They reflected some of the misery that settled over the United States following the stock market crash of October 24, 1929, and abated in some measure by the time World War II broke out in Europe in fall 1939. Since West's family was not poor, he did not suffer the way that many others did. Instead, he obtained work over the period 1927–31, through a family connection, as hotel night manager of, first, the Kenmore Hall Hotel in New York City, and then the Suffolk Club Hotel. As a serious reader, West became familiar with numerous contemporary American writers, well established or still struggling to make their reputation (or merely a living), and many of them wound up in one or another of these hotels under his part-time management.

Worth noting here is his dramatic writing. His play *Good Hunting: A Satire*, written with Joseph Shrank, was produced in 1938. More important, he wrote screenplays for a number of Hollywood studios. Earl Rovit, in his article on West for *Reference Guide to American Literature,* provides details.

West was a scriptwriter for Columbia Pictures in 1933 and 1938, for Republic from 1936 to 1938, for Universal in 1938, and for RKO from 1938 to 1940. He lived in California during much of this time. West worked on 13 screenplays, most of them with other writers; a few of the screenplays were not credited to him. Among the titles are *Follow Your Heart* (1936), *Ticket to Paradise* (1936), *It Could Happen to You* (1937), *Gangs of New York* (1938), *Born to Be Wild* (1938), *I Stole a Million* (1939), and *Men Against the Sky* (1940).

As for West's "as if" point of view of life, he seemed to be resolutely playing a role meant for someone else's script. Light details West's poor academic record in high school and his finagling his sorry grade record there to get into Brown University. All this, apparently, with no qualms relating to his dishonest conduct or his lack of serious application to his studies, while being genuinely interested in the life of the mind. College life, friendships, and good times triumphed over academic obligations. Being self-consciously Jewish (and coming from an Orthodox family), yet wanting to be accepted by non-Jewish campus elites obliged him, in the early 1920s, to spurn his Jewish connection as much as possible, and act like "the others," though he knew this would not get him into the "right" fraternity. He held athletic champions in high regard and was a devoted follower of the varsity teams at Brown, though he never participated in campus sports. Later, West's fondness for hunting and his interest in guns, despite his utter incompetence with a rifle, would become legendary.

The "as if" pattern shows up in West's novels also. There is a consistent tendency toward caricature, mockery, and absurdity in the first three titles that suggests West was reinventing the social universe by means of radical distortion. The final effect is like a 360-degree funhouse mirror, wired for sound, reflecting a crowd of uninhibited vulgarians.

The Dream Life of Balso Snell begins on a scatological note. Balso finds the original Trojan Horse and determines to enter it, but the only available entry is through the anus, which leads West to the first of many attempted jokes or bits of word play: "O Anus Mirabilis!" evoking John Dryden's 1667 poem "Annus Mirabilis," or "Year of Wonders," commemorating the English sea victory over the Dutch, and the Great London Fire. As Balso enters the lower intestine of the Horse, a Jewish tour guide greets him and offers to conduct him through the channel. There follows a long succession of tasteless anecdotes and anatomical references, as well as a number of sudden odd occurrences. Balso manages to flee this guide and makes his way along the intestinal canal, as he experiences more strange encounters and discoveries.

Among the strange individuals he meets is a naked man, Maloney the Areopagite, a Catholic mystic. Balso finds a packet of themes written by a schoolboy named John Gilson for his teacher, Miss McGeeney. A further sequence of tales emerges, including passages from a crime journal by a Raskolnikov-like character (out of Dostoyevsky's *Crime and Punishment*) confessing to a brutal murder, followed by a treatise on the hypersensitivity of the human nose, described in a book titled *Nosologie* (seemingly out of Laurence Sterne and Edgar Allen Poe). There is a sequence on horribly deformed women, and a faithless lover named Beagle Darwin. Finally, there is a sexual union scene involving Balso and his former sweetheart Mary McGeeney that suggested to one critic the ending of Joyce's *Ulysses*. The chaos and confusion of this novel's mix of bizarre story and dream elements are dispelled by West himself, however, in a clearly stated "as if" decoding of the author's message. "The wooden horse, Balso realized as he walked on, was inhabited solely by writers in search of an audience, and he was determined not to be tricked into listening to another story. If one had to be told, he would tell it."

Miss Lonelyhearts is the story of a newspaper columnist using that pen name for his advice column for the emotionally needy and helpless, who desperately seek his aid and succor. The demanding job, which he had undertaken as a kind of joke, loses its humorous quality for him under the weight of his cynical, shrieking editor, Shrike, and the cumulative pity he experiences as he reads an endless flow of sad complaints and laments from his helpless readers. As time goes by he takes on more and more of their troubles, until he loses his identity and becomes helpless himself, despite his resorting to various palliatives: sex, art, the country, alcohol. Only when he begins to identify with the concept of Christ (one of Shrike's targets of satire) and regard himself "as if" he were the Christ figure does he begin to feel the healing process. One day he finds that a cripple named Doyle with whom he has had some contact (and whose wife he once bedded) is suddenly coming to see him. He views this as a providential event that will allow him to prove his conversion and heal Doyle's handicap. He anticipates the healing to take place through an embrace. When they meet, Miss Lonelyhearts is open-armed to embrace him, but Doyle is carrying a concealed weapon, and a young woman Miss Lonelyhearts was involved with named Betty enters the scene also. In the ensuing confusion, Doyle's gun discharges, killing the succor-seeking and almost justified Miss Lonelyhearts.

A Cool Million contains a good deal of hate material from populist and fascist rhetoric, catchphrases, and symbolism that America was exposed to during President Franklin Delano Roosevelt's first administration (1933–37). Though West's title is quite expressive of the big-money yearning to be noted during this depression period, it also calls up the money hunger of Mark Twain in the late 19th century, and Twain's own story title, *The One Million Pound Bank-Note* (1893). But in format West's is a picaresque novel, a saga of a boy and girl's adventurous journey along the open road of life, experiencing come what may. It is a parody of what is already a parody of serious fiction: the 19th-century Horatio Alger, Jr.'s pulp fictions, exemplified in *Luck and Pluck*, *Ragged Dick*, and the like. Moreover, it combines Voltaire's cheerful *Candide* philosophy with Alger's optimistic work ethos. Here in West's world, adding one set of high hopes to another set of high hopes yields utter disaster. Things do not have to work out for the best, and acting "as if" they do may well lead to sorrow, as in the case of young Lemuel Pitkin and his girlfriend, Betty Prail.

The Day of the Locust, an insider look at late 1930s Hollywood, is perhaps the most coherent and readable of West's novels. The title suggests a biblical plague or a periodic locust plague besieging agricultural workers. Such a plague suggests punishment for an egregious sin. West's novel features the femme fatale, Faye Greener, a movie extra and aspiring actress. Certain men are drawn to her: Homer Simpson, a hotel bookkeeper from Iowa; Tod Hackett, a Hollywood set and costume designer; Earle Shoop, a cowboy from Arizona; Claude Estee, a successful screenwriter; a dwarf named Abe Kusich; and Miguel, a Mexican cock-fight promoter. Through their interactions and observations West displays the depravity, artificiality, and decadence of Hollywood and its movie studios with their simulations of reality. As significant as the title is the artistic project of Tod Hackett: a huge painting called *The Burning of Los Angeles.* This "as if" impressionistic depiction of the supposed city of sin in the day of reckoning is highlighted in the story's final scene. A movie preview draws an enormous crushing crowd, leading to a chaotic situation that somehow becomes merged with the flaming of the city in Tod Hackett's great painting in progress.

Nathanael West was a close friend of the satirical stylist S. J. PERELMAN, who married West's sister. West's wife was Eileen McKenney, whose sister wrote a biography about her entitled *My Sister Eileen,* which was adapted for the stage and then made into a movie.

Bibliography

Light, James F. *Nathanael West: An Interpretive Study.* Evanston, Ill.: Northwestern University Press, 1961.

Nadel, I. B. "The Day of the Locust." In *Reference Guide to American Literature,* edited by Jim Kamp. Detroit: St. James Press, 1994.

Rovit, Earl. "Nathanael West." In *Reference Guide to American Literature,* edited by Jim Kamp. Detroit: St. James Press, 1994.

Siegel, Ben. "Introduction to Nathanael West." In *Critical Essays on Nathanael West,* edited by Ben Siegel. New York: G.K. Hall, 1994.

—**Samuel I. Bellman**

White Lies   Julie Salamon (1987)

White Lies is a moving tale whose author recounts the effects of the Holocaust on the Jewish identity of children of survivors. The inheritance of trauma manifests itself in the life of Jamaica Just, the protagonist of this thinly disguised autobiography. Jamaica, her older sister Geneva, and their survivor parents are the only Jews in a small Ohio town. Dr. Just, their father, harbors a terrible secret from his American-born daughters; his first wife and daughter were murdered in Auschwitz. He himself fought with a local resistance group, serving as their medic. Dr. Just suffers from severe depressive moods and frequent angry outbursts against his wife, Eva. Eva speaks to her daughters dispassionately about her own Holocaust experience, counseling the daughters not to say or do anything to upset their father.

After graduating from college, Jamaica goes to New York City and becomes a newspaper features reporter. In contrast to her editor, an assimilated Jew indifferent to the plight of the less fortunate, Jamaica, true to her surname, strives for justice in an unjust world. Her Holocaust legacy impels the young woman to seek a repair of the world (*tikkun olam*). She therefore views her articles as nothing less than "crusades for betterment." In the course of the novel her editor assigns her three stories that reveal much about Jamaica's second-generation Jewish identity and her quest for social justice amid the general indifference of American culture. She writes about children of survivors; she investigates second-generation welfare mothers; and she interviews a "news junkie," an elderly man who compulsively writes letters to the editor.

Writing about her own experience as a daughter of survivors, Jamaica discusses issues of abiding importance to her peers. She notes the fact of difference both between survivors and their offspring, and between the second generation and children of nonwitnesses. Concerning the former, she notes that, although she had not personally experienced the Holocaust, she nevertheless felt like a "phoenix child, rising out of the ashes of both death and destruction." Jamaica's life is shadowed by the Holocaust. The difference between Jamaica and her husband, Sammy, is also profound. Although he is Jewish, Sammy's American-born parents were stationed at a Texas airbase during the war and told him amusing stories about their experiences. He knows nothing about the Holocaust. Furthermore, reader response to Jamaica's article reveals both enduring anti-Semitism and Holocaust trivialization.

Writing about second-generation welfare mothers, Jamaica indicts government policy and public indifference that result in generational misery. She sees a significant parallel between Lonnie, a young welfare mother, and herself; both had been victimized because of their parents' experience. Jamaica's compassion for those at the margins of society is clearly related to her Holocaust inheritance, as is her outrage at racism and prejudice. Interviewing the "news junkie," Jules Marlin, Jamaica discovers that he is in fact not only a survivor but that he comes from the same Hungarian town as her parents. Jamaica believes that the bond she shares with Marlin is that they both are "capable of feeling outrage." They cannot stand idly by and be indifferent to injustice. Moreover, it is significant that Geneva Just in her role as a physician is also portrayed as one who seeks to alleviate suffering.

White Lies was hailed as a novel that helped readers appreciate the social, psychological, and theological impact of the Holocaust on children of survivors. The novel's autobiographical elements receive fuller exploration in JULIE SALAMON's memoir *The Net of Dreams* (1996), which recounts the author's journey to Poland and Hungary with her mother, Lilly, and her stepfather, Arthur.

Bibliography

Berger, Alan L. *Children of Job: American Second Generation Witnesses to the Holocaust.* Albany: SUNY Press, 1997.

Dickstein, Lore. "Untitled Review." *New York Times,* 7 February 1988, BR21.

—Alan L. Berger

Wiesel, Elie(zer) (1928–)

Elie Wiesel, the 1986 Nobel Peace laureate, is a brand plucked from the fires of the Holocaust.

His memoir *NIGHT* is a classic, known throughout the world. Wiesel is University Professor and Andrew W. Mellon Professor in the Humanities at Boston University, and the author of more than 40 books. His teaching and writing seek to bear witness "for the dead *and* the living." Wiesel was appointed chairman of the United States Holocaust Memorial Council by President Jimmy Carter, and served as the first director of the United States Holocaust Memorial Museum in Washington, D.C. Profoundly anchored in the Jewish tradition, his healing message has universal resonance; his writings and theological insights are cited as much by Christian as by Jewish thinkers. His Nobel citation refers to Wiesel as a "Messenger to all Humanity." He is an indefatigable champion of human rights, and his activities seek to ensure that his own past does not become humanity's future.

Wiesel's vast oeuvre includes both fiction and nonfiction, and addresses a variety of topics: the Bible, the Talmud, Hasidism, the Holocaust, Jewish/Christian relations, Israel and the Middle East, and Zionism. He views these topics through the lens of the Holocaust as he seeks to articulate the possibility of faith and belief in spite of the ethical, moral, and theological chaos wrought by a genocidal universe. His post-Auschwitz literary trial of God (*din Torah*) and of humanity emphasizes that his preoccupations are as much theological as they are literary. Or to put it another way, he utilizes stories to convey questions about God and the covenant. Wiesel's works stress that one can, and should, be angry at God without abandoning the deity.

Wiesel was born in Sighet, Transylvania (in Romania), on September 30, 1928, on the Jewish holiday of Simchat Torah, the only son (there were three daughters: Hilda, Beatrice, and Tzipora) of Shlomo and Sarah. His father owned a small grocery store and was a leader of Sighet's Jewish community. The author's mother was a devotee of the Wishnitz branch of the Hasidic movement. As a youngster Wiesel spent much time with his maternal grandfather, Dodye Feig, from whom he heard countless Hasidic tales whose essence he would subsequently weave into much of his reflections on the post-Holocaust human condition. Deeply religious as a youth, he attests that if it were not for the Holocaust, he would most probably have remained in Sighet and become the principal of a religious school.

The Wiesel family was deported to Auschwitz in April 1944, during the Jewish holiday of Passover. Sarah and Tzipora were gassed immediately upon arrival. Shlomo died in Germany in Buchenwald concentration camp, where he and Elie had subsequently been sent. By the time the war ended, Wiesel had also been imprisoned in Buna and Gleiwitz camps. Refusing repatriation following the war, Eliezer went to France with other Jewish orphans where he spent time at Ambloy, an institution for religious child survivors. While there, he wrote daily in a journal. These "notes" would, after a 10-year period of self-imposed silence, form the basis of *Night*. He subsequently enrolled in the Faculty of Letters at the Sorbonne. Chronically poor, he supported himself in a variety of jobs including choir director, camp counselor, translator, and Hebrew tutor.

Wiesel studied French, the language in which he continues to write, and became a correspondent for several newspapers: *L'Arche* (Paris), *Daily Forward* (New York), and *Yidiot Ahranot* (Tel Aviv). He also traveled to places as disparate as India and South America. During this period Wiesel had a decisive interview with French Catholic novelist François Mauriac, winner of the Nobel Prize in literature, who encouraged him to write a memoir of his Holocaust experience.

Wiesel published an 800-page Yiddish-language memoir, *Un die velt Hot geshvign* (*And the World Remained Silent*), which appeared in Argentina in 1956. Two years later a 120-page French-language edition, *La Nuit* appeared. The English-language version of *Night* was published in 1960. A 50th anniversary edition of his memoir, newly translated by Wiesel's wife, Marion, was published in 2006. The memoir has a foreword by Mauriac.

Night is the foundation of Wiesel's entire body of writing. The memoir speaks of relationships: between the youth and his father; the teenager and God; Wiesel and the world of death camps;

and between the author and the Jewish tradition. He himself contends that *Night* is "both the end and the beginning" of everything. What ended was his traditional and unconditional faith. What began was his continuing search for a viable post-Holocaust faith. Furthermore, *Night* encapsulates key elements of characters and motifs that reappear throughout the author's works. For example, "madmen" or-women frequently proclaim the truth; a child is the protagonist; and biblical paradigms, such as the "binding of Isaac," are inverted.

Wiesel continually worries about the insufficiency of language to tell the story, and he constantly seeks to communicate silence, "silence . . . like language . . . demands to be recognized and transmitted" (*One Generation After*). Also, for Wiesel, stories remain unfinished, and he emphasizes the tragedy of the unheard/disbelieved witness. Wiesel writes of the just man who preached repentance to the uncaring inhabitants of Sodom. A child asks the preacher why he continues when no one listens. The man replies, "I know I cannot [change man]. If I still shout . . . , it is to prevent man from ultimately changing me" (*One Generation After*). *Night* ultimately attests to the changed nature of the post-Holocaust covenantal relationship between God and the Jewish people, and the crucial role of memory.

Wiesel's novels, plays, and cantatas offer a variety of divine images. In *Night* God is hanging on the death camp gallows. Reinforcing the loss of belief in the traditional God of History, Wiesel refers to the deity in *The Accident*, 1962 (*Le Jour*, 1961), as "God, the doorkeeper of the immense brothel that we call the universe." Wiesel's cantata, *Ani Ma'amin: A Song Lost and Found Again*, 1973 (*Ani Maamin:un chant perdue et retrouvé*, 1973) portrays a deity who remains silent, appearing to reject the appeals of Abraham, Isaac, and Jacob to intervene on behalf of the suffering of the Jewish people during the Holocaust. However, the cantata ends with God weeping at the fate of his people. He tells the angels that his children have "defeated" him and silently joins the patriarchs as they return to earth. This God is far from omnipotent; nonetheless, the author continues to believe, perhaps in spite of God. Wiesel observes that "the silence of God is God."

Wiesel's post-Holocaust faith is anchored in a twofold paradox. Even though there is every reason to deny God, he continues to believe perhaps in spite of the deity. Further, the human covenantal partner has the right to accuse God in defense of the Jewish people. This paradox is perhaps nowhere clearer than in his 1979 three-act play, *The Trial of God (Le Procès de Shamgorod tel qu'il se déroula le 25 février 1649*, 1979), which questions God's silence in the face of the suffering of innocence, as well as overturning the traditional response that evil is owing to punishment for sin or a "reproof of love." The play occurs at Purim, a time commemorating the defeat of Haman, an evil prime minister in Persia who sought the eradication of the Jewish people, but who was outwitted by Queen Esther and her uncle Modechai. Wiesel's play is based on a "trial" he witnessed in Auschwitz. Three rabbis, constituting a rabbinical court, presented evidence for and against God in the face of the Holocaust. God is found guilty. Yet the chief rabbi responds, "let us pray."

Berish, an innkeeper whose family had been devastated by a pogrom (government-approved mob violence in czarist Russia), protests God's injustice. The innkeeper sides with the Jewish people. He, like Eliezer in *Night,* is the accuser, God is the accused. God's defender Sam is, in fact, the devil. Consequently, those who justify God at the expense of man understand neither God nor man. In his writings on the Hasidic movement Wiesel emphasizes a shift in his concern from God, "He can take care of Himself," to man. Paraphrasing the Ba'al Shem Tov, founder of 18th-century Hasidism, Wiesel notes that "the way to divine reward leads through human commitment; the way to God leads through your fellow man" (*Somewhere A Master*).

Wiesel's questioning of God results not in answers but in further questions. The author, like the biblical Jacob, wrestles with the deity. He stated in an interview that "ever since Auschwitz he has been trying to find an occupation for God" (Cargas). Gamaliel, the protagonist of *The TIME OF THE UPROOTED*, 2005 (*Le Temps des déracinés*, 2003) discovers the tension between faith and doubt. Rebbe Zusya, Gamaliel's mystical guide, declares that God calls to Gamaliel through his silence. The teacher then asks, "Are you answering Him?" Drawing on the Jewish tradition of arguing with God, Wiesel writes in volume one of his autobiography *All Rivers Run to the Sea*, 1995, (*Tous les fleuves vont á la mer*, 1994) "it is permissible for man to accuse God, provided it be done in the name of faith in God" (84).

Wiesel's novels trace the author's evolution as he focuses on the relationships first articulated in *Night*. His next two books are *Dawn*, 1961 (*L'Aube, 1960*) and *The Accident*, 1962 (*Le Jour*, 1961). The former occurs in pre-Israel Palestine, with Jews fighting the British occupation. If *Night* signifies the end of traditional religious belief, *Dawn* articulates recognition that traditional morality needs to be reexamined in the post-Holocaust world. The protagonists in both the memoir and the novel are portrayed as "Messengers of the dead," who are out of place among the living.

The Accident is the third book of the trilogy. Eliezer, the protagonist, is a Holocaust survivor who fought in Israel's War of Independence. He works in New York City as a journalist for an Israeli newspaper. Struck by a cab while crossing Times Square, he is seriously injured, hovering between life and death, and he spends nearly three months in a hospital. Based on the author's own experience, after which he became an American citizen, the novel explores—and rejects—suicide. Eliezer is convinced that to continue living is a betrayal of the dead. This view is countered by two healers: Doctor Paul Russel saves his life, Gyula (Redemption), a Hasid, alleviates his spiritual despair. *The Accident* is the first of Wiesel's books in which life triumphs, although barely, over death and the possibility of a credible post-Holocaust covenant is introduced.

Wiesel's next book, *The TOWN BEYOND THE WALL*, 1964 (*La ville de la Chance*, 1962) received the French Prix Rivarol. The novel, which is divided into four prayers rather than chapters, explores the themes of friendship, madness, and the role of the bystander. Returning to his birth town after the war, Michael, a Holocaust survivor, is arrested. He remains silent during questioning rather than betray his friendship with the mysterious Pedro. Imprisoned, Michael reaches out to a fellow prisoner, saving his comrade from madness. The protagonist's return is precipitated by his determination to confront the bystander who remained indifferent to the fate of the town's Jews during the Holocaust. Ironically, it is the disinterested witness who informs on Michael, causing his arrest. Wiesel's exploration of indifference leads him to the observation that "the opposite of love is not hate, but indifference."

Wiesel's fifth book, *The Gates of the Forest*, 1966 (*Les Portes de la forêt*, 1964), begins in Europe and ends in America. The author gives special prominence in the epigraph to the saving power of tales, a Hasidic tale dealing with four generations of Hasidic leaders and how tales help them save the Jewish people. Gregor/Gavriel, the protagonist, is a partisan, not a death camp prisoner. His life depends on telling and retelling the story of their commander's death to his fellow partisans. The novel's conclusion occurs in Brooklyn and is based on Wiesel's deceptively simple dialogue with the Lubaviticher Rebbe. The author asked, "Rebbe, how can you believe in *HaShem* (God) after the *Khourban* (Holocaust). He looked at me and said, And how can you not believe after the *Khourban*? Well, that was a turning point in my writing, that simple dialogue" (Abrahamson 63).

Wiesel's next book, *A Beggar in Jerusalem*, 1970 (*Le Mendiant de Jérusalem*, 1968) and winner of that year's Prix Médicis, is the first of his novels in which the Holocaust dead play a saving role. Ostensibly a book about Israel's dramatic victory over its Arab adversaries in the Six Day's War (June 5–11, 1973), Wiesel's novel brings together the wartime fate of Europe's Jews (the Holocaust) and the destiny of Israel's post-Holocaust Jewry (recovering the western wall of the temple built by King Solomon). Peopled with beggars and madmen, the novel, attests Wiesel, encompasses "all my other tales. I wanted it to be the sum total of all my character, of all the visions they had, of all the anxieties I had inherited from them" (Abrahamson 70). One of the novel's preachers explains why the hopelessly outnumbered Israelis won their battle for survival: "Israel won because its army, its people, could deploy six million more names in battle."

Madness is also a prominent theme in Wiesel's work. The madness to which he refers is, however, not clinical. Rather, it is mystical; it enables individuals to see the truth and to reject the falsehoods by which most people live. Both Moshe the Beadle and Madame Schächter in *Night* seek to warn the Jews of their impending doom. Neither is believed. Wiesel uses madness as an epigraph for two of his novels; Dostoyevsky's statement "I have a plan—to go mad" appears in *The Town Beyond the Wall*, whereas Maimonides' observation, "The world couldn't exist without madmen," is from *Twilight*, 1988 (*Le Créspuscule, au loin*, 1987). *Twilight* deals with both madness and friendship. Dr. Raphael Lipkin, a survivor and psychiatrist, finds himself in an institution whose patients identify with biblical characters ranging from Cain and Abel to the Messiah. Wiesel brings back the character of Pedro, for whom Lipkin is still searching following his disappearance shortly after the Holocaust. Madness is also a theme in Wiesel's *Zalmen, or the Madness of God* (1968), treating the Jews of the Soviet Union who, defying Soviet authorities, practiced their tradition, and in his recently published *A Mad Desire to Dance*, 2009 (*Un désir fou de danser*, 2006).

Wiesel's biblical, Talmudic, and Hasidic writings stem from his twofold belief that these sources have contemporary relevance, and that they themselves are in a way "a celebration of memory" (*And the Sea Is Never Full: Memoirs, 1969–*, 1999; . . . *et la mer n'est pas remplie*, 1996). In works such as *Messengers of God*, 1976 (*Célébrations biblique*, 1975), *Five Biblical Portraits* (1981), *Sages and Dreamers: Biblical, Talmudic, and Hasidic Legends* (1991), and *Wise Men and Their Tales* (2003), Wiesel "reads" the past to glean meaning from the tradition's exemplary teachers. Both Hillel and Shammai, Jewish sages in the Talmud whose views are typically presented as opposed, are necessary. Hillel "defends human beings. Shammai defends absolutes." Extrapolating from this, Wiesel writes, "I would like to follow Shammai, as far as *I* am concerned, and to emulate Hillel where others are involved—ideally, to be intransigent with myself and understanding with others."

His Hasidic trilogy SOULS ON FIRE, 1972 (*Célébration hassidique*, 1972), *Four Hasidic Masters and Their Struggle Against Melancholy* (1978), and *Somewhere A Master: Further Hasidic Portraits and Legends* (1982), reveals parallels between the historical situation confronting the Hasidic and the contemporary world. Wiesel stresses two themes in the Hasidic tales: Closeness to God is a key to understanding the acts and aspirations of the Hasidic ambience, but so, too, is friendship. The two notions are related. Wiesel notes that if the Jewish people had had more friends during the Holocaust, the outcome would have been better for both Jews and Christians. Retelling the teachings of Reb Meir of Premishlan, Wiesel writes "when there are people going hungry, they must come first; their well-being must take precedence over all ideals—no, their well-being must become our ideal." The author seeks to infuse the spirit of Hasidism into the post-Holocaust world.

Wiesel began turning his attention to the future of Holocaust memory by writing about the second generation—children of survivors—in the early seventies. He has to date written four novels dealing with this issue: *The Oath* (1973), *The Testament* (1981) (*Testament d'un poète juif assassiné,* 1980), *The Fifth Son* (1985) (*Le Cinquième Fils,* 1983), and *The FORGOTTEN* (1992) (*Oublié,* 1989). These novels explore the traumatic and potentially redemptive dimensions of Holocaust memory by examining the mission of the second generation in transmitting their parents' experience to their own children and to the world at large. Wiesel strongly believes that listening to a witness makes one a witness, however far removed. It is significant that his portrait of the second-generation witness has grown increasingly more vivid with each successive novel. The protagonist in *The Oath* is nameless and suicidal. Listening to a survivor saves his life because he is now obligated to transmit the tale. Grisha, *The Testament*'s protagonist, is mute but transmits his murdered father's book of Holocaust and Stalinist terror. "My father is a book," contends Grisha, "and books do not die." Ariel in *The Fifth Son* is a college professor who teaches the story of the Shoah to his students. Malkiel is the son of a survivor in *The Forgotten*. Elhanan, his father suffering from Alzheimer's disease, must tell his son everything he can remember before it is too late. Wiesel stresses the role of the second generation as a link in the chain of Holocaust memory but differentiates the son from the father. Malkiel will bear witness for Elhanan, but the son knows that memory, unlike blood, cannot be transfused.

Wiesel's books of essays, dialogues, and reflections such as *Legends of Our Time* (1968) (*Le Chant des morts,* 1966), *One Generation After* (1970) (*Entre deux soleils,* 1970), *A Jew Today* (1978) (*Un Juif aujourd'hui,* 1977), *Paroles d'étranger* (1982), and *From the Kingdom of Memory* (1990) are richly suggestive pieces dealing with Jewish identity and its relationship to God: "As a Jew, you will sooner or later be confronted with the enigma of God's action in history" (*One Generation After* 166). Moreover, Wiesel views writing as a mission to "correct injustice" and as a way of "beginning over again" after the Holocaust, just as the Talmud was written in the wake of the destruction of the Jerusalem Temple. Referring to himself in the third person, Wiesel notes that "His mission [as a writer] was never to make the world Jewish but, rather, to make it more human" (*A Jew Today* 16).

Memory is the touchstone of Wiesel's life as writer, witness, and human rights activist. He opposes memory to hatred, which "distorts memory." "The reverse is true," he continues, "memory may serve as a powerful remedy against hatred" (*From the Kingdom of Memory*). Repressive regimes, no less than those who deny the Holocaust, wage war against memory. The suffering of all peoples—Jews, Ethiopians, Palestinians, Miskito Indians, victims of the war in Bosnia and those of Darfur, Sudan—each deserve to be remembered. Moreover, memory can serve as a bond between people: "It is because I remember our common beginnings that I move closer to my fellow human beings" (*From the Kingdom of Memory*). Wiesel notes that for most writers their work is a commentary on their life, whereas for him the reverse is true. The God-intoxicated youth that he was is tempered by the Holocaust survivor that he is, and by the wish that his "prayers be told, to be turned into stories" (interview with Wiesel).

Wiesel has been accorded many honors. In addition to his Nobel Peace Prize, he has received numerous other awards, literary prizes, and honors. A partial list includes the Presidential Medal of Freedom, the U.S. Congressional Gold Medal, the Ellis Island Medal of Honor, and the French Legion of Honor with the rank of Grand Cross, the Humanitarian Award of the International League of Human Rights, and the Brotherhood Award of the Congress of Racial Equality. Wiesel's literary prizes include the French Prix Rivarol, the National Jewish Book Council Literary Award, Prix Médicis, Prix Bordin, French Academy, and the Prix Inter. In addition, he has nearly 150 honorary degrees from colleges and universities in America and abroad. Wiesel's message is one of hope born out of despair.

Bibliography

Abrahamson, Irving, ed. *Against Silence: The Voice and Vision of Elie Wiesel.* New York: Holocaust Library, 1985.

Berger, Alan L. "Interview with Elie Wiesel." *Literature and Belief* 26, no. 1 (March 2007): 1–23.

Cargas, Harry James. "Positive Ambiguity: The Religious Thought of Elie Wiesel." *Spiritual Life* (Summer 1970).

—Alan L. Berger

Wolf, Emma (1865–1932)

As an American-born Jew from a prominent San Francisco family and a native Californian residing in the middle-class comfort of the Pacific Heights section of San Francisco, Emma Wolf contributed to multiple literary traditions by working at the intersections of American literature, Jewish-American literature, regional literature, and women's literature.

Emma Wolf was one of eight daughters of Alsatian immigrants, Annette (née Levy) and Simon Wolf and the fourth of their 11 children. Wolf's sister Alice was also a published author whose interfaith marriage may have provided kindling for the plot of Wolf's first novel. Emma's brother, Julius, was president of the Grain Exchange in San Francisco. Wolf's classmate, Rebekah Bettleheim Kohut, who became the president of the New York branch of the National Council of Jewish Women and a committed social activist on New York's Lower East Side, offers in her autobiography, *My Portion* (1925), a recollection of Emma Wolf as a "brilliant authoress" and recalls their "meaningful exchanges of innermost thoughts" as they "meditated the thorny path which the Jew traveled." Wolf's family belonged to the Sutter Street Reform synagogue, Emanu-El, where Wolf composed a tribute to her father who died when she was 13, an event that marked the inception of her future career. Under a portrait of Emma Wolf in the *American Jewess,* the journal's founder and editor, Rosa Sonneschein, confirms that Wolf's "literary genius developed at a tender age."

Wolf's nascent literary activity contrasts with the restrictions that impinged on her personal life. Polio incapacitated an arm, she never married, and she was confined to a wheelchair in the Dante Sanitarium in San Francisco during the last 16 years of her life. Despite these circumstances, Wolf did not live an entirely sheltered life; she was a member of the Philomath Club, a Jewish women's club that was invested in literary and social issues. Nineteenth-century clubs were exclusionary, barring Jews and "colored" from membership, a practice to which Wolf alludes in her fourth novel when "the colored and Jewish women" are singled out for their service to the soldiers during the Spanish-American War. Wolf's Jewish heroine, Jean Willard, bristles at such "fine distinctions."

Notwithstanding her physical and social limitations, Wolf enjoyed the accolades of a long, productive literary career, publishing five novels, one novella, and 10 short stories. Two surviving poems appeared in the San Francisco–based, English-language monthly, the *American Jewess* (1895–99), to which Wolf also contributed a review of Israel Zangwill's "Dreamers of the Ghetto." Although

Wolf's correspondence with Zangwill does not survive, Zangwill's letters to his American protégé were brought to scholarly attention by Barbara Cantalupo. Wolf's fiction is freighted with the questions and contingencies that counterbalanced her life as an American-born Jew of French rather than eastern European or Iberian extraction, as a 19th-century Jewish writer on America's Western frontier, and as a woman writing during an era of male hegemony.

Among Wolf's novels, her first, *Other Things Being Equal* (1892), and her fourth, *Heirs of Yesterday* (1900), are immersed in the problems, paradoxes, and pleasures of Jewish life at the close of the 19th century. In these two works Wolf addresses the complications that accompany disenfranchised women and career-driven men who negotiate hybridized identities as Americans and Jews. Wolf's Jewish novels chart not only the social shifts that characterized American culture of the period, but the rituals and laws that prescribed specific roles for Jewish women who lived in both secular and religious communities.

Other Things Being Equal scrutinizes the struggle of a young Jewish woman, tellingly named Ruth, who wants to marry a non-Jew, Dr. Herbert Kemp, without abnegating her commitment to her Judaism or the wishes of her beloved father. Ruth is torn between her affection for the physician who has assiduously attended her parents and the obligation she feels to the Fifth Commandment in honoring her father's objection to such an interfaith union. Wolf was comfortable with the Americanized adaptations of Reform Judaism, which did not embrace interfaith marriage; however, *Other Things Being Equal* tenders the possibility that Jews can sustain their Judaism even as they enter non-Jewish alliances. The social and religious implications of intermarriage provide Wolf with the opportunity to expand on the dilemmas surrounding Jewish affirmation and American assimilation.

Other Things Being Equal enjoyed immediate success, was widely reviewed, and secured Wolf's regional and national reputation. *Other Things Being Equal* attracted favorable reviews in leading national newspapers including the *Chicago Tribune,* Boston's *Literary World,* and Philadelphia's *Public Ledger.* In 1895 Gustav Danziger's "The Jew in San Francisco: The Last Half Century" confirms Wolf's growing acclaim, noting that "Miss Wolf, the author of *Other Things Being Equal,* has met with some success as a writer" (403). Again in 1904, the *Overland Monthly and Out West Magazine* (1868–1935) included Wolf in an article devoted to "San Francisco Women Who have Achieved Success." In 2002 Wayne State University Press reissued the revised 1916 edition of *Other Things Being Equal* with an informative introduction and thereby secured Emma Wolf's place on the roster of early Jewish-American women writers who experience literary longevity despite their marginalized and minority status in American letters.

Even amid the relative tolerance that prevailed in San Francisco, the mid- to late-19th century was marred by several widely publicized instances of anti-Semitism. Wolf's novel *Heirs of Yesterday* (1900) examines this period of Jewish discrimination and secondary citizenship. Wolf presciently echoes the sentiments of her coreligionist Emma Lazarus (1849–87) in urging Jews not to forsake their ethnic, religious and cultural inheritance for the nebulous pluralism of American identity. *Heirs of Yesterday,* is set once again in the familiar milieu of Pacific Heights and the adjoining military installation, the Presidio, where the novel's central figure watches on May 25, 1898, the first deployment of U.S. troops to the Philippine Islands at the outset of the Spanish-American War. Wolf contrasts Jean Willard, a Jewish-American woman who affirms that as a Jew she carries in her very being the history of all Jews, with Harvard-trained Dr. Philip May, the son of German-Jewish immigrants who rejects his Jewish identity, discarding every vestige of his Jewish birthright from his persona as he reinvents himself as an American. Dr. May disavows his Jewish inheritance and distances himself from family connections for educational, professional, and social advancement, asserting, "You see I should be making a move in the wrong direction were I to identify myself unnecessarily with any Jewish club, Jewish anything, or Jewish anybody" (*Heirs* 36). Wolf insists in *Heirs of Yesterday* that the assimilated Jew—Philip May—is still a Jew because American society retains its nativist predilections and, more important, Wolf suggests that Jews who remain either forgetful of their tribal identity or willfully neglectful of Judaism are as misguided as the society that rejects them.

Wolf's secular novels navigate the paradoxes facing women at the close of the 19th century as they acquired new paradigms on which to pattern their lives. The Progressive Age, despite its welcome reforms, was a destabilizing period for women in America as the ideals of traditional womanhood were refashioned to the contours of the era's New Woman. Far from embracing a protofeminist imperative, Wolf in *A Prodigal in Love* (1894) and *The Joy of Life* (1896) interrogates the seemingly untenable options of choosing between abortion or unwed motherhood, womanly self-sacrifice or illicit romance, premarital relations or lifetime isolation, careerism or marriage. In *The Joy of Life*, Barbara Gerish, a college graduate, vacillates between her identification with contrasting models for women, wavering between conventional and progressive inclinations. Grappling with the issues of suffrage, careerism, and maternity, Gerish tries to decipher what it means to be a woman in the closing decade of the 19th century.

A Prodigal in Love provides Wolf with an agency through which to explore the tropes of female propriety, premarital sexuality, abortion, divorce, and encoded patterns of feminine morality that place honor and self-sacrifice above a woman's personal happiness. In *Writing Their Nations: The Tradition of Nineteenth-Century American Jewish Women Writers*, Diane Lichtenstein suggests that when Eleanor Herriott marries Hall Kenyon, she assumes a traditional role, but as she assists her husband in editing and rewriting his book, Eleanor uncovers the transformative power of language, finding an avenue of empowerment.

Wolf's short story "One-Eye, Two-Eye, Three-Eye" appeared in 1896 in the *American Jewess,* and between 1902 and 1911 nine additional stories and a novella, *The Knot,* were published in the tony magazine *The Smart Set,* which was edited by George

Jean Nathan and H. L. Menken. Barbara Cantalupo observes that Wolf's short fiction reflects the problems that specifically beset modern love after the turn of the century: adultery, divorce, abortion, careerism, intermarriage, and children born outside of marriage. Although Wolf's progressive feminism is on display in her short fiction, her gendered advocacy is offset by a decidedly traditional perspective on the role of women in contemporary society. In the short fiction as in her novels, Wolf modulates her feminism with traditional values, alternately embracing reform while acknowledging her allegiance to the past, accepting the ambiguity of her stance as both an "heir to yesterday" and a New Woman in a progressive age.

The Knot (1909), a novella published in the *The Smart Set,* reiterates Wolf's passionate belief in the emotional intensity of love, whereas Wolf's last novel, *Fulfillment: A California Novel* (1916), undermines the sentimentality of love without undervaluing its omnipresence. In Wolf's final work, Gwendolyn Heath discovers she is involved with a married man and additional complications involving marriage, divorce, and abortion further complicate her life; nevertheless, Wolf's last novel implies that women can find fulfillment in work as well as marriage.

Emma Wolf died on October 31, 1932, in the same City by the Bay where she had lived her entire life. She was eulogized in the same synagogue where many years before she had, in turn, eulogized the temple's cantor. It is impossible to characterize Wolf's fiction as representing a sustained worldview because Wolf's thoughtful independence from conventional norms as progressive expectations demarcates her collective works. Wolf directed her creative energy into exposing the dilemmas of Jewish identity, exploring the assimilative inclination of Reform Jews, and investigating the status of women. In her Jewish novels Wolf does not promulgate assimilative remedies for conflicting national, regional, and cultural identities, nor does her secular fiction promote predictable resolutions for the conflicts that beset the New Woman. Instead, Wolf's characters learn to live in a world of differences rather than yield to normative paradigms of the day that tended toward the Americanization of ethnic, religious, and cultural distinctions and transformative feminist advocacy. As Jews, Wolf's protagonists are different, and as much as some of the characters might consider themselves no different from their fellow Americans, in the late 19th century Jews lived in a world apart—sometimes by choice and sometimes ghettoized by discrimination. Confronting the anxiety of displacement, Wolf penned her novels as a means of mediating rather that easing or erasing difference, a social and literary legacy that has been reactivated in subsequent generations of Jewish-American women writers, who, like Wolf, confront the history of their distinctive identity.

Bibliography

Irwin, E. P. "San Francisco Women Who Have Achieved Success." *Overland Monthly and Out West Magazine* 44, no. 5 (November 1904): 512ff.

Lichtenstein, Diane. *Writing Their Nations: The Tradition of Nineteenth-Century American Jewish Women Writers.* Bloomington: Indiana University Press, 1992.

—Dena Mandel

Women in Their Beds: New and Selected Stories Gina Berriault (1996)

Women in Their Beds: New and Selected Stories is the final collection of short stories published by GINA BERRIAULT (1926–99) before her death. The book contains nine new stories and 26 selected from the author's previous publications. Winner of the National Book Critics Circle Award, the Rea Foundation Prize, and the PEN/Faulkner Award, *Women* is a compilation of narratives dense with detail and awash, sometimes painfully, with the internal conflicts experienced by Berriault's characters.

Asked if her life experience was an important factor in creating a variety of characters and settings, Berriault replied, "I never thought I had a wide scope. The way to escape from the person who you figure you may be is to become many others in your imagination. And that way you can't be categorized as a regional writer or a Jewish writer or a feminist writer, and even though you may be confined by the circumstances of your life, you're roaming out in the world, your imagination as your guide" (Lyons and Oliver 719). Throughout *Women*, Berriault's imagination is our guide to ordinary people, their internal dialogues as real as our own, their conflicts distinctive and at the same time so familiar they invoke compassion. The stories center on the theme of isolation, but this separation is more than just personal burden—it is the common thread that binds us each to the other.

In the title story, Berriault addresses this connection directly when Angela, the main character, reveals how she tries to imagine the lives of hospital patients: "'I try to imagine them when they were girls, but I can't,' she told the head nurse, Nancy, and the nurse, already verging into that same anonymity of aging, turned her head for Angela to see her deliberately uncomprehending face. 'Why would you ever think to do that anyway?'" (7). Angela, isolated from the patients by her position as a staff member, and isolated from the rest of the staff through her idealism, attempts to reach outside of her seclusion. She looks for parallels between herself and others in an effort to both understand isolation and find comfort in this slim connection to her sister women.

Much of this book concentrates on female characters (and sometimes reflects on their beds as symbols of isolation), but regardless of the gender of Berriault's characters, they are almost always marginalized by age, social or economic status, and physical or mental illness. While she did not want to be singled out as a Jewish writer, Berriault's background may have influenced her recurring use of isolation and marginalization as subject matter for her fiction. About growing up, Berriault said, "No one, all through my school years (except for a teacher who must have felt a kinship with Hitler) suspected that I was Jewish, and I must have been one-of-a-kind in that small California town" (Lyons and Oliver 715).

Berriault's stories featuring children as main characters (for example, "The Woman in the Rose-colored Dress" and "The Stone Boy") are exceptional portrayals of the intricacy of adolescent estrangement, but it is selections such as "Who Is It Can Tell Me Who I Am?" that highlight with stunning intimacy the recognition of the similarities between the self and the other. The strength of Berriault's writing is best described in a review of two of her earlier books, *The LIGHTS OF EARTH* and *The Infinite Passion of Expectation: Twenty-five Stories,* in which it is pointed out that the constant in her work "is the precise and unflinching psychological and moral exploration of people at important moments of realization, of how they come to terms with their lot, are undone by it, or transcend it" (Davenport 125).

The intense nature of *Women* is both an asset and a possible limitation. While it is difficult to criticize Berriault's writing style or thematic choices, it is conceivable that the average reader may find the combination of pervasive sadness and the density of detail and language overwhelming at times. Potential readers should keep in mind that *Women* is a collection of beautiful but tension-filled stories—slices of realism with sharp and penetrating edges.

Bibliography

Berriault, Gina. *Women in Their Beds: New and Selected Stories.* Washington D.C.: Counterpoint, 1996.

Davenport, Gary. "The Blessed and the Forsaken." Review of *The Infinite Passion of Expectation: Twenty-five Stories* by Gina Berriault, *The Lights of Earth* by Gina Berriault, and *Love Medicine* by Louise Erdrich. *Kenyon Review* 7, no. 4 (Fall 1985): 122–125.

Lyons, Bonnie, and Bill Oliver. "'Don't I Know You?': An Interview with Gina Berriault." *Literary Review* 37, no. 4 (Summer 1994): 714–723.

—**Jeanne Genis**

The World According to Garp
John Irving (1978)

Garp is the novel that made JOHN IRVING's career and set him firmly on the road to critical and popular success. The paperback version won the American Book Award for 1979, selling over 3 million copies in its first two years. It became an award-winning 1982 film directed by George Roy Hill and starring Robin Williams. Furthermore, this novel's success sparked the reissue of his previous three novels and set up public anticipation for his subsequent work. Modern Library published a special 20-year commemorative edition of *Garp* in 1998, with a new introduction by Irving. *Garp* embodies everything that critics and reviewers have found characteristic of Irving's writing: motifs such as wrestling, bears, Vienna, New England, writers, sexualities, fate, death, marriage, and so forth, as well as key binaries such as affection/violence, comedy/tragedy, imagination/reality, personal/political. It also represents Irving's energetic prose style: his Dickensian creativity with character and plot development, his penchant for ironic reversal, his flirtations with the grotesque, and his underlying humanity.

One of the foremost contemporary examples of the *Künstlerroman* (artist novel), *Garp* tells the story of infamous writer T. S. Garp, from his immaculate conception to his perfidious assassination, including embedded excerpts from his work and letters, as well as his pithy observations. The text has a biographical, retrospective tone and structure to its narrative. Garp's mother, Jenny Fields, a nurse by both temperament and vocation, conceives her son by clambering atop one of her patients, a burned and brain-damaged ball-turret gunner whose constant erections provide her an opportunity to conceive the child she wants without long-term emotional complications. She names her son T. S. for his father's rank, technical sergeant, and Garp for the only sound his father is capable of making. Jenny takes a nurse position at Steering School, a private New England boy's school, where she works only until Garp graduates, after which they both go to Vienna, Austria, intent on becoming writers. While at Steering, Garp meets Helen Holm, the studious daughter of Coach Holm, the wrestling coach. She helps develop his vocational ambition—to become a novelist. Garp and Helen marry. At Steering Garp also begins his lifelong struggle with lust, in the form of Cushie Percy, daughter of the secretary of

Steering School. As Garp's first and foremost critic and confessor, Helen tends, from the beginning, to be more seriously critical of his writing than of his sexual escapades.

In Vienna Jenny writes her famous feminist autobiography, *A Sexual Suspect,* and Garp writes "The Pension Grillparzer." After their return to America, Jenny's novel becomes a great public sensation as a touchstone for the women's movement, while Garp's novella is rejected. Although Garp becomes a successful writer, in the eyes of the general public he will never emerge from his mother's shadow. After Helen receives a Ph.D. in English, Helen and Garp settle down to domestic life, she as a college professor and he as a novel-writing househusband. Although a doting and concerned father, always on the lookout for the "Under Toad," which threatens to pull his family under, Garp continues to be challenged by his lust. Both he and Helen become involved in extramarital affairs. They have two boys, Duncan and Walt, the latter of whom is killed by a freak automobile accident that also emasculates Helen's graduate student lover, Michael Milton. Out of their mourning over the loss of Walt, they have a third child, and name her Jenny. Garp's mother, by this time, has set up a center for troubled women at the Fields estate at Dog's Head Harbor, New Hampshire, where the family moves to recuperate immediately after the accident. They end up back at Steering School, Helen teaching and Garp coaching wrestling. Jenny Fields is assassinated by a misogynist hunter with a deer rifle while she is speaking at a small New Hampshire rally in support of a woman running for governor. Garp is assassinated at age 33 by Pooh Percy, a radical Ellen Jamesian, who holds him responsible for all crimes perpetrated by men, especially against her sister Cushie. Ironically, the real Ellen James, an orphaned rape victim whose tongue was cut out by her rapists to prevent identification, hates the women who cut out their tongues as a gesture of sisterhood with her. But she loves Garp, her adoptive father, and his writing, which is almost always misread by feminists.

Such a skeletal and bittersweet plot summary, however, cannot do justice to the novel. For example, its narrative play, with the embedded narratives by Garp, explores the fine line between auto/biography and fiction. Its Christ imagery, with Garp at the center, underscores the seriousness of its enterprise while also discouraging too strict an archetypal reading. Its sense of carnival, with all the semigrotesque characters and multi-voiced perspectives, celebrates difference and tolerance. Its sense of mutual caring and forgiveness, tinged with comedic color and sometimes black humor, balances its pervasive sense of impending doom and makes *Garp* a thoroughly humane text.

Bibliography

McKay, Kim. "Double Discourse in John Irving's *The World According to Garp.*" *Twentieth Century Literature* 38, no. 4 (Winter 1992): 457–475.

Morris, Ann R. "The Importance of Names in Garp's and Irving's World." *Notes on Contemporary Literature* 14, no. 5 (Nov. 1984): 3–4.

—Phillip A. Snyder

Wouk, Herman (1915–)

Hailed for writing compelling, richly detailed novels, Herman Wouk is best known for his fictional accounts of World War II and his forays into Jewish life. His works, including MARJORIE MORNINGSTAR, *The Caine Mutiny, The Winds of War,* and *War and Remembrance,* are meticulously researched and have won admiration for their historical accuracy. His skillfully crafted novels and satires deal primarily with moral dilemmas during times of war and peace, as well as with the Jewish-American experience.

Wouk (pronounced *woke*) was born in New York City in 1915, the son of Abraham Isaac Wouk and the former Esther Levine, both Russian-Jewish immigrants. Wouk graduated from Townsend Harris High School at age 16 and attended New York's Columbia University as a comparative literature and philosophy major. He was a staff writer for the school's publication *The Spectator* and served as editor for the school's humor magazine, *The Jester.* He graduated with a B.A. in 1934 and worked as a scriptwriter for radio comedy programs.

In 1941 he began working for the U.S. Treasury Department producing radio broadcasts to promote the sale of government bonds. Following the Japanese attack on Pearl Harbor in December 1941, he joined the navy and was commissioned as an officer. He served aboard two destroyer-minesweepers in the Pacific theater, the USS *Zane* and the USS *Southhard,* until 1946. He credited his experiences in the U.S. Navy as a major influence on his later writing and part of his education: "I learned about machinery, I learned how men behaved under pressure, and I learned about Americans." He began his first fictional novel, *Aurora Dawn,* a satire of the New York radio industry, during his off-duty hours at sea. The story was published in 1947 to critical acclaim.

Perhaps Wouk's best-known work is *The Caine Mutiny* (1951), which was loosely based on his experiences during the war, although he was quick to point out that the events central to its drama were purely fiction. The book tells the tale of the USS *Caine* under the command of Captain Philip Francis Queeg, who loses control of his ship during a typhoon. The story used language rich in metaphor and focused on characters of a kind that had not been seen before in a modern war novel raising questions of loyalty, patriotism, and adherence to military code. *The Caine Mutiny* earned the 1952 Pulitzer Prize in fiction and soon topped best-seller lists, becoming one of the most popular English-language novels of the 20th century. The story was so successful in print that it quickly spawned a stage adaptation, a television production, and an immensely popular movie. The film version starring Humphrey Bogart as Captain Queeg was produced in 1954, the same year that *The Caine Mutiny Court-Martial,* Wouk's two-act play based on the novel, was published and produced on Broadway.

The Winds of War (1971) is an epic story of relationships between actions of individuals and the events leading up to the Japanese attack on Pearl Harbor. In contrast to the film versions of *The Caine Mutiny* and MARJORIE MORNINGSTAR, which Wouk felt were "mere thin skims of the story lines"

when it came time to bring this story to the screen and that of *War and Remembrance* (1978), he chose the small screen instead, explaining "I opted for television, with its much broader time limits, for the *Winds of War* . . . [aired for a total of] Sixteen hours!" (NYT).

Marjorie Morningstar (1955) marked Wouk's first publication about the Jewish faith. It is the story of a modern young Jewish-American woman and her struggles to find a balance among her religion, the confining middle-class values of her family, and her aspirations to become an actress. Wouk then produced two studies of Judaism and American-Jewish life, *This Is My God* (1959), a personal examination of Orthodox Judaism, and *The Will to Live On* (2000).

In the 1970s Wouk endowed a Jewish communal residence for Columbia University students and served on its advisory board for a number of years. For this he was honored in 2002 with an award for outstanding contribution to Jewish life at Columbia. Many of his personal papers, including the 2,119-page manuscript for *The Caine Mutiny,* are preserved in Columbia's Manuscript Library.

On his philosophy of creating, Wouk is quoted as saying, "If [the artist] understands his responsibility and acts on it—taking the art seriously always, himself never quite—he can make a contribution equal to, if different from, that of the scientist, the politician, and the jurist."

A distinct influence on American popular culture, his early works first widely published and well received in the mid-20th century continue to sell in the 21st century, and the resulting screen adaptations are still widely viewed. Herman Wouk's stories have become a vital part of American literature and popular culture.

Bibliography

Mazzeno, Laurence W. *Herman Wouk.* Edited by Frank Day. New York: Twayne, 1994.

Wouk, Herman. "Herman Wouk: 'A Faithful Adaptation." *New York Times,* 14 June 1981.

—Jacqueline May

Yezierska, Anzia (ca 1885–1970)

The woman some referred to as the "Cinderella of the Sweatshops," Anzia Yezierska, burst onto the American literary scene with a prose style vibrant with Yiddish expressions and scented with pungent old world cadences, which gave an air of authenticity and vigor to her portraits of Jewish immigrants and to the stories of their struggle in a bewildering and unfamiliar world.

Anzia Yezierska was born in a Polish shtetl near the border with Russia around 1885. The youngest of nine children, Anzia lived with her family in a squalid mud hut. At the age of 15 (she kept changing the date of her birth until her death), Anzia and the rest of her family came to New York City, where they joined Meyer, the oldest son, who had immigrated to America several years before. Immediately after, they decided to change their names to Mayer, and it was only in her late twenties that Anzia resumed using her original name.

The "Mayer" family lived in a tenement apartment on Manhattan's Lower East Side. Her father, like the stubborn patriarch in BREAD GIVERS, concentrated daily on the study of the sacred texts, while her mother worked long hours to support the family. Like her, Yezierska worked as a domestic, and later went to work in the sweatshops and factories, in which many immigrants like her toiled away. All she could claim as education were a few years of elementary school. While working in the sweatshops, Anzia managed to learn English at night school.

Although her older sisters married early, Anzia, like the protagonist of her semiautobiographical novel, *Bread Givers,* chose not to marry and moved into the Clara de Hirsch Home for Working Girls, a residential trade school for young immigrant Jewish women founded by German Jews. While at the Hirsch Home, Yezierska devised a plan to continue her education. Somehow she managed to produce a high-school diploma and win a four-year scholarship to Columbia University. The official plan was to study domestic science. At least this is what her patrons at the East Side settlement house were told she intended to do. While at Columbia's Teachers College between 1901 and 1905, Yezierska focused on a teaching career, but in her spare time she read poetry and continued to polish and refine her English. She was determined to become a good teacher.

For five years, from 1908 to 1913, she taught elementary school in New York. She taught her classes with dedication and competence. But her "hungry" heart longed for poetry.

In 1910 Yezierska was briefly married to an attorney and then to a schoolteacher who spent most of his free time writing textbooks. In 1912 she gave birth to a daughter. But marriage and motherhood proved stifling to Anzia. After several trial separations, she left her husband in 1916 and moved to San Francisco with their daughter. Finally, Anzia entrusted her daughter to her husband, who, to her mind, was a better parent. After two divorces and a romantic, platonic relationship with the philosopher and Columbia professor John Dewey, who eventually became her mentor and encouraged her to publish her work, Yezierska decided to dedicate herself entirely to writing fiction.

The passionate encounter between Yezierska and Dewey is enlaced in the texture of *All I Could Never Be* (1932) and *Red Ribbon on a White Horse* (1950). In these literary representations, their love story becomes a modern parable about the impossibility of transcending cultural barriers and the inevitable failure of such utopian enterprises. This theme reappears frequently in her work and is entwined with the story of the immigrant woman's struggle to become a true American.

The Free Vacation House, her first short story, was written in 1913 during a difficult period in her life, and published in 1915. A beginner's work, this is a harsh commentary on charity and the negative effects on its recipients.

In 1919 Yezierska's short story "The Fat of the Land" was accepted for publication. Her first collection of short stories, entitled *Hungry Hearts,* was published by Houghton Mifflin in 1920. Two years later, the movie with the same title was launched in Hollywood by Samuel Goldwyn, who offered her a contract and a substantial sum of money. Yezierska left Hollywood as fast as she left her husbands; both were too oppressing.

In 1923 Yezierska published another collection of short stories, *Children of Loneliness,* as well as her first novel, *Salome of the Tenements.* A silent film based on this novel was directed by Sidney Alcott in 1925. The same year she published *Bread Givers,* which is considered by many to be her most powerful novel and is taught today in literature and women's studies departments across the country. Published four years earlier than Virginia Woolf's *A Room of One's Own,* this novel shows women the way to financial and political independence. In 1927 she published Arrogant Beggar and in 1932, *All I Could Never Be.*

The depression years were especially tough on Yezierska. She spent most of the days cataloging the trees in Central Park. Nonetheless, she continued to publish articles, essays, and book reviews. In 1950 a fictionalized autobiography brought her back into the limelight. Her *Red Ribbon on a White Horse* is a powerful work, written by a mature writer.

In the tumult of the sixties, Yezierska was all but forgotten, yet she continued to write stories about the difficulties of aging, a topic now explored by many fine writers including Philip Roth, who has published his own reflections, entitled Everyman. She died in 1970 in California. Since the publication of *The Open Cage: An Anzia Yezierska Collection* in 1979, American readers have shown a renewed interest in Yezierska's writings, in part because of the work of feminist scholars and women's activism and in part because of a new appreciation of her passionate portrayals of Jewish immigrants.

Bibliography

Duncan, Erika. "The Hungry Jewish Mother." In *The Lost Tradition: Mothers and Daughters in Literature.* Edited by Cathy N. Davidson and E. M. Broner. New York: Ungar, 1980.

Schoen, Carol B. *Anzia Yezierska.* Boston: Twayne, 1982.

—Gila Safran Naveh

The Yiddish Policemen's Union
Michael Chabon (2007)

The Yiddish Policemen's Union, Michael Chabon's eighth novel, is a dazzlingly written work of the imagination. The author combines alternate history; the detective noir genre; Yiddish expressions, both real and faux; biblical symbolism; miracle cures; and messianic yearnings in telling his tale of exile and the possibility of redemption. Following the 1948 fall of the state of Israel, Chabon transports the remaining Jews to Sitka, in Alaska's panhandle, where in their latest diaspora they become the "frozen chosen." Trouble looms for the Jews as the 60-year period of their Alaskan exile draws to a close. Under the terms of the American government mandate, the territory is to revert to U.S. control, thereby once again scattering the Jews. Except that this time, there is an attempt to hasten the Messiah's coming that involves distinctively secular means.

The novel's conceit lies in utilizing a history that might have been. Chabon appears to have taken a cue from PHILIP ROTH'S *The PLOT AGAINST AMERICA,* which imagines that the anti-Semitic and isolationist aviator Charles Lindbergh, "Lucky Lindy," had been elected president. *The Yiddish Policemen's Union* draws on a shadowy plan to relocate Jews in Alaska offered by Harold Ickes, President Franklin D. Roosevelt's secretary of the interior. The plan was squelched by an Alaskan politician, Anthony Dimond, whom Chabon kills off in the novel. Furthermore, it is doubtful whether FDR ever seriously considered this proposal. Moreover, the author skillfully employs the linguistic argot of classic private detectives such as Raymond Chandler's Philip Marlowe and the iconic Sam Spade. But in this case, the detective protagonist and all of Sitka's Jews speak primarily Yiddish, occasionally lapsing into "American." Hovering in the background is the dark shadow of the Holocaust, which Chabon calls the Destruction, and the millennial messianic yearning of the Jewish people in their Diaspora setting.

Meyer Landsman is a down-on-his luck divorced detective who discovers the body of Mendel Shpilman, son of Rabbi Heskel Shpilman, corrupt leader of the Verbover Hasidim, who has disowned him. Mendel, an apparent derelict, may also have been the Messiah. He was believed to be the Zaddik ha-Dor (the righteous man of the generation). A child prodigy who learned many languages at an early age, Mendel was known for his ability to heal the sick and pronounce beneficial blessings, which, among other things, enabled barren women to conceive. Yet, on the eve of his arranged marriage, Shpilman, who may also have been gay, disappears into the murky world of drug addiction. Moreover, the murdered man was a chess master. The novel's dramatic tension is heightened by Chabon's metaphoric use of chess

vocabulary, *Zwischenzug* is "an unexpected move in the orderly unfolding of a chess game," whereas *Zugszwang* means that even when you have no good moves, "you still have to move," as a template for both the Jewish situation and discovering the identity of a murderer.

Landsman (his name implies relatedness, as in countryman) and Berko Shemets, his half–Tlingit Indian and half-Jewish partner, investigate the murder. They discover a complex web of events involving a shadowy alliance between Rabbi Shpilman, Washington D.C.'s Globocops, a Christian evangelist named Cashdollar, the Federal District of Sitka, and the native Tlingit population. Furthermore, Landsman's sister Naomi, a pilot who had flown Mendel to the Beth Tikkun (House of Retreat) Center, dies in a mysterious plane crash. At stake is the fate of the Holy Land—the plot involves blowing up the Dome of the Rock, thereby sowing dissension among the Arabs and enabling Jews to return to Israel, and the implementation of an evangelical theological worldview that may well eventuate in World War III. A subplot involves the tension between religious fanaticism (Rabbi Heskel Shpilman and Cashdollar) and secularism (Landsman and Bina ["wisdom"] his ex-wife who is now his commanding officer).

The Yiddish Policemen's Union is both a parody and a parable of Jewish history. Chabon believes that messianic yearning is an inescapable paradox. As the Verbover Hasidim prepare to bury Mendel Shpilman, the author writes "Every generation loses the messiah it has failed to deserve." Moreover, the paradox is heightened, notes Chabon, because "a messiah who actually arrives is no good to anybody." One interpretation of this comment suggests that a messiah who failed to arrive during the Holocaust need not bother to appear now. Chabon also reverses crucial mythic concepts in Jewish history. The *Akedah,* Abraham's binding of Issac, a biblical sacrifice averted, becomes Landsman's "sacrifice" of Django, his unborn son aborted by Bina at her husband's insistence because he might have had a fatal genetic disease. The longing for a return to the Holy Land—"Jews have been tossed out of the joint three times now—in 586 B.C.E., in

70 C.E. and with savage finality in 1948"—seems more remote than ever.

Chabon' s novel juxtaposes biblical injunctions and contemporary efforts to hasten the Messiah's arrival. The sacred text requires the sacrifice of a red heifer, without blemish, on the altar of the rebuilt (third) Temple in Jerusalem. When this occurs, the Messiah will come. Landsman and Berko come across a red heifer grazing in a pasture owned by the Beit Tikkun Retreat Center. Not content to wait for the arrival of the Messiah, the Verbover Hasidm, with help from Cashdollar and the Globocops, utilize the Retreat Center to cover their clandestine operations, which include gathering weapons and support to take Jerusalem by force, thereby hastening the messianic coming.

The dream of returning to Zion has, following the Holocaust, become a permanent nightmare. Jewish attempts to repair or improve the world (*tikkun 'olam*) have failed. Landsman lives in the Zamenhof, a seedy hotel. But Ludwik Lazar Zamenhof, a Polish-Jewish thinker, invented Esperanto—the universal language—designed to bring people together. Moreover, the hotel is located on Max Nordau Street. Nordau, a physician by training, was a fervent Zionist. Korczak Platz and Ringelblum Avenue are named in honor of two Jewish martyrs of the Holocaust. Janos Korzak chose to go to the gas chamber with the residents of his orphanage. Emanuel Ringelblum was the historian of the Warsaw ghetto. Yet the dream continues, but on a personal rather than national level. At novel's end Landsman and Bina reconcile.

Chabon introduces his readers to a variety of colorful characters: Inspector Willie Dick is a Tlingit midget; Doctor Rudolph Buchbinder, "the mad dentist of Ibn Ezra Street," is a fervent Zionist willing to do anything—including resort to violence to hasten the messiah's return; Itzak Zimbalist, "the boundary maven," an expert at determining the exact placement of an 'eruv (an area exempted from prohibitions which apply outside the designated area), and Alter Litvak, a demolition expert. Further, Chabon's Holocaust survivors are inheritors of trauma, which leaves deep psychic scars. Jews who had fought in the European underground come to Alaska and build an extensive series of tunnels called the *untershtat* (under the city) in case the Alaskan authorities decide to exterminate Jews. As if to underscore the precariousness of the Jewish situation on the eve of reversion, the refrain "strange times to be a Jew" is repeated at significant points in the novel.

Chabon's novel has received much favorable critical attention. The author's uncanny ability to conjure imaginative scenarios continues to attract and enrich his readers. As in his earlier work *The AMAZING ADVENTURES OF KAVALIER & CLAY,* Chabon weaves mythic and mystical elements of the Jewish tradition into a richly suggestive tale. *Yiddish Policemen's Union* was reviewed in such prestigious newspapers and journals as the *New York Times, Washington Post, Times Literary Supplement, Commonweal,* and *Commentary.* Moreover, The American Library Association named it a Notable Book, one of only five titles so designated. Yet certain critics, notably Ruth Wisse, questioned the depth of Chabon's novel. Wisse is especially critical of the author's misuse of Yiddish—she terms it "mock Yiddish"—and his ahistorical appropriation of such figures as Emanuel Ringelblum and Jacob Glatstein. Nevertheless, Columbia Pictures has purchased the film rights to Chabon's novel, and it is reasonable to assume that a film version will be forthcoming.

Bibliography

Chabon, Michael. "The Language of Lost History." *Harper's Magazine,* October 1997, 32–33.
Wisse, Ruth R. "Slap Shtick." *Commentary* 124, no. 1 (July/August 2007).

—Alan L. Berger

Z

Zangwill, Israel (1864–1926)

Although he was not the first or the only early writer of ghetto life, Israel Zangwill is considered the father of modern Jewish literature, especially British-Jewish literature. In his short story collections *Ghetto Tragedies* (1893) and *Ghetto Comedies* (1907), and his novellas *The King of the Schnorrers* (1894) and *The Celibates' Club* (1898), Zangwill showed his talent as an early realist writer and moralist, portraying late 18th-century life in London's East End Jewish ghetto. His skill at going beyond merely describing conditions and subjects, and infusing his stories with humor and optimism, won him an international readership. But as a dramatist (where he most wished for success), Zangwill first succeeded with a romance, *Merely Mary Ann* (1903), and then failed with didactic social dramas.

Born in London's Whitechapel ghetto and educated at the Jews Free School in Whitechapel, then later at Bristol and at London University, Zangwill returned to Jews Free School and taught until 1888. There he collaborated with fellow pupil-teacher Louis Cowen on his first work, a privately published pamphlet about market day in the ghetto entitled *Motza Kleis* (1882), which was later expanded and enlarged to become *Children of the Ghetto* (1892). Zangwill continued his collaboration (under the name J. Freeman Bell) with Cowen on his first book-length work, *The Premier and the Painter* (1888), a fantasy modeled after Mark Twain's *The Prince and the Pauper*.

Zangwill began writing stories as a boy, and perfected his skill writing for newspapers, including *The Jewish Standard,* and the humorous paper he founded in 1890, *Ariel: The London Puck*. Zangwill's first successes were humorous story collections, including *The Bachelors' Club* (1891), later married with *The Old Maid's Club* (1892), to become *The Celibates' Club: Being the United Stories of the Bachelors' Club and Old Maids' Club* (1898). But Zangwill achieved international recognition with the publication of *Children of the Ghetto: A Study of a Peculiar People* (1892). Commissioned by the Jewish Publication Society of America, the portrayal of Jewish life in *Children of the Ghetto* is credited with building public awareness and support that ultimately prevented passage of anti-Jewish legislation in Parliament.

Some contemporary reviews of Zangwill's work criticized him for exaggeration and melodrama that sometimes approached burlesque (as in the 1898 unsigned review in *Nation* of *Dreamers of the Ghetto*). On the other hand, in his 1914 essay, Holbrook Jackson praised Zangwill for going beyond the stereotypes of Shakespeare's Shylock and Dickens's Fagin, while keeping Jews unique and not seeking simply to homogenize them into a human melting pot. Later critics, however, have questioned Zangwill's realism. Writing in 1964,

Harold Fisch saw Zangwill combining historical fact with his own message to make a definite point. No wonder, for Zangwill had become a committed Zionist after his pivotal meeting in 1895 with Theodor Herzl (1860–1904), the founder of modern Zionism. From this point on, Zangwill's artistic and political life began to merge into one.

Zangwill's portrayals of Jewish life and culture were meant for both gentile and Jewish audiences, intended to be both instructive and corrective. His stories revealed the tragedy and nobility of life in the ghetto, and also the generational schisms that exist between Jewish factions. Often his stories were about the problems of confronting and choosing between orthodoxy versus assimilation, intra- versus intermarriage, resistance versus apathy, until, ultimately, Harold Fisch finds Zangwill himself confronted with the ambivalence of the ghetto. The ghetto is a place of gathering, Orthodoxy, identity, safety, but its very insularity and isolation is the seed of its downfall. The ghetto is finite, a school that one must move beyond to continue learning.

Ghetto Tragedies (1893) originally comprised four short stories. These four were later included with seven additional stories and published as *They Walk in Darkness* (1899), and in 1907, the 11 stories were republished under the original title, *Ghetto Tragedies*. The stories explore the folly of trusting humanity over God, the effect of debilitating factions and disunity within Judaism, and the need for a person of action to confront and correct the in-fighting and indecision

In *The King of the Schnorrers: Grotesques and Fantasies* (1894), comprised of the title novella and 14 short stories, the hero is the legendary Jewish beggar, the Schnorrer, an insolent, ironic, itinerant philosopher and critic. Zangwill created his most memorable character in the caustic and comedic Manasseh Bueno Barzillai Azevedo da Costa, the "King of the Schnorrers," who manipulates the foibles and weaknesses of the wealthy members of the local Sephardic community, as Joseph Udelston says, wreaking havoc on the little community and its institutions as he deigns to accept its charity, triumphing in every test of wit he encounters.

The Grey Wig: Stories and Novellas (1903) consists of eight short stories, including a murder mystery. And finally, Udelson sees *Ghetto Comedies* (1907), a collection of 14 stories, as coming at a turning point in Zangwill's life, as he voiced an opposition to Zionism. *Ghetto Comedies* was the last Jewish fiction Zangwill would produce, as he turned more to lecturing, essays, drama, and social reform, and the collection well demonstrates Zangwill's exhausted creativity.

Although his later plays were not successful, Zangwill's first play, *Merely Mary Ann* (adapted from his 1893 short story of the same title, and first produced in 1903), reportedly earned Zangwill more money than all his ghetto books combined. *Merely Mary Ann* is the story of a struggling musician, Lancelot, in love with a servant girl, Mary Ann. When Mary Ann inherits a fortune and changes her name to Marian, Lancelot decides she is now too good for him, and instead devotes himself to his musical compositions. After achieving his own success, Lancelot and Mary Ann/Marian are finally reunited.

Zangwill's later plays, including *The War God* (1911), *The Next Religion* (1912), *Too Much Money* (1918)—all with plots revealed in their titles—went beyond romance to didacticism, and were not commercial successes. Also, later in his career, Zangwill tried his hand at essays, travel writing, drama, and fiction with non-Jewish themes, but this later work was never as successful as his stories about life in the London ghetto.

Bibliography
Fisch, Harold. "Israel Zangwill: Prophet of the Ghetto." *Judaism* 13 (1964): 407–421.
Udelson, Joseph H. *Dreamer of the Ghetto: The Life and Works of Israel Zangwill.* Tuscaloosa: University of Alabama Press, 1990.

—**Robert S. Means**

PRIMARY SOURCE BIBLIOGRAPHY

Aleichem, Sholem
Adventures of Mottel the Cantor's Son (1953)
*Collected Stories of Sholom Aleichem: Vol. 1: The Old
    Country* (1946)
*Collected Stories of Sholom Aleichem: Vol. 2: Tevye's
    Daughters* (1949)
The Great Fair (1955)
Inside Kasrilevke (1948)
Old Country Tales (1966)
Selected Stories (1954)
Stories and Satires (1959)
Wandering Star (1952)
Sholom Aleichem Panorama (1948)

Allen, Woody (includes films)
Annie Hall (1977)
Crimes and Misdemeanors (1989)
The Curse of the Jade Scorpion (2001)
Don't Drink the Water (1966)
Everything You Always Wanted to Know About Sex*
    (*But Were Afraid to Ask) (1972)
From A to Z (1960)
Getting Even (1971)
Hannah and Her Sisters (1986)
Husbands and Wives (1992)
Interiors (1978)
Love and Death (1975)
Manhattan (1979)
Manhattan Murder Mystery (1993)
Match Point (2005)
Mighty Aphrodite (1995)
Play It Again, Sam (1972)
The Purple Rose of Cairo (1985)

Side Effects (1980)
Sleeper (1973)
Stardust Memories (1980)
Take the Money and Run (1969)
The Third Woody Allen Album (1968)
What's New, Pussycat? (1965)
Without Feathers (1975)
Woody Allen (1964)
Woody Allen, Volume 2 (1965)

Antin, Mary
From Plotzk to Boston (1899)
The Promised Land (1912)
They Who Knock at Our Gates (1914)

Asch, Sholem
Amerikaner dertseylungen (*American Stories*, 1918)
The Apostle (1943)
Chaim Leyderer's tsurik-kumen (1927) (*Chaim Leyderer's
    Return*, 1938)
Der brenendiker dorn (*Burning Bush*, 1946)
Der man fun natseres (*The Nazarene*, 1939)
Der tilim yid (*Salvation*, 1934)
Di kishufmakherin fun kastilien (*The Witch of Castile*,
    1921)
Di muter, 1919 (*Mother*, 1930)
Dos gezang fun tol, 1938 (*Song of the Valley*, 1939)
Dos shtetl (1905)
Farn mabl (1929–31; *Three Cities*, 1933)
Got fun nekome, 1907 (*God of Vengeance*, 1918)
Grosman un zun (*Grosman and Son*, 1954)
Ist River (*East River*, 1946)
Kiddush haShem (1924)

Mary (1949)
Motke ganiv (1916)
Moyshe (*Moses*, 1951)
Onkl mozes, 1918 (*Uncle Moses*, 1938, 1920—various
    dates listed)
Reb Shloyme nogid (*Wealthy Shloyme*, 1913)
Toyt-urteyl (*Death Sentence*, 1924)

Asimov, Isaac

Asimov's Guide to the Bible (1968–1969)
Asimov's Guide to Shakespeare (1970)
Azazel (1988)
Banquets of the Black Widowers (1984)
Biochemistry and the Human Metabolism (1957)
Casebook of the Black Widowers (1980)
Foundation (1951)
Foundation's Edge (1982)
Foundation and Earth (1985)
Foundation and Empire (1952)
I, Asimov (1994)
I, Robot (1950)
In Memory Yet Green (1979)
The Intelligent Man's Guide to Science (1960)
More Tales of the Black Widowers (1976)
Prelude to Foundation (1988)
Puzzles of the Black Widowers (1990)
The Realm of Numbers (1959)
The Return of the Black Widowers (2003)
The Roving Mind (1983)
Second Foundation (1953)
The Sensuous, Dirty Old Man (1971)
Tales of the Black Widowers (1974)
Yours, Isaac Asimov (1995)

Bellow, Saul

The Actual (1997)
The Adventures of Augie March (1953)
The Bellarosa Connection (1989)
Dangling Man (1944)
The Dean's December (1982)
Henderson the Rain King (1959)
Herzog (1964)
Him With His Foot in His Mouth (1984)
Humboldt's Gift (1975)
It All Adds Up (1994)
The Last Analysis (1964)
Mr. Sammler's Planet (1970)
More Die of Heartbreak (1987)
Ravelstein (2000)
Seize the Day (1956)

A Theft (1989)
To Jerusalem and Back: A Personal Account (1976)
The Victim (1947)

Berriault, Gina

Conference of Victims (1962)
The Descent (1960)
The Great Petrowski (1999)
The Infinite Passion of Expectation: Twenty-Five Stories
    (1982)
The Lights of Earth (1984)
The Mistress and Other Stories (1965)
The Son (1966)
The Tea Ceremony: The Uncollected Writings (2003)
Women in Their Beds (1996)

Bitton–Jackson, Livia

A Decade of Zionism in Hungary, the Formative Years:
    The Post–World War I Period: 1918–1928 (1971)
Biblical Names of Literary Jewesses (1973)
Elli: Coming of Age in the Holocaust (1980)
I Have Lived a Thousand Years: Growing Up in the
    Holocaust (1997)
The Jewess As a Fictional Sex Symbol (1973)
Madonna or Courtesan: The Jewish Woman in Christian
    Literature (1983)
My Bridges of Hope: Searching for Life and Love after
    Auschwitz (1999)

Broner, E. M.

The Body Parts of Margaret Fuller (1976)
Bringing Home the Light: A Jewish Woman's Handbook
    of Ritual (1999)
Ghost Stories (1995)
Her Mothers (1985)
"Higginson: An American Life" (2005)
Mornings and Mourning: A Kaddish Journal (1994)
Summer is a Foreign Land (1962)
A Weave of Women (1978)
Women's Haggadah (1994)

Bukiet, Melvin

After (1996)
"Machers and Mourners" (1997)
Stories of an Imaginary Childhood (1992)

Cahan, Abraham

The Imported Bridegroom, and Other Stories of the New
    York Ghetto (1898)

The Rise of David Levinsky (1917)
The White Terror and the Red (1905)
Yekl (1896)

Calisher, Hortense
Sunday Jews (2002)

Chabon, Michael
The Amazing Adventures of Kavalier & Clay (2000)
The Final Solution: A Story of Detection (2004)
The Yiddish Policeman's Union (2007)

Charyn, Jerome
Back to Bataan (1993)
Black Swan (2000)
Blue Eyes (1975)
Bronx Boy (2002)
Captain Kidd (1999)
Dark Lady from Belorusse (1997)
The Education of Patrick Silver (1976)
Eisenhower, My Eisenhower (1971)
Gangsters and Gold Diggers: Old New York, the Jazz Age, and the Birth of Broadway (2003)
The Green Lantern: A Romance of Stalinist Russia (2004)
The Man Who Grew Younger (1967)
Marilyn the Wild (1976)
Metropolis: New York as Myth, Marketplace, and Magical Land (1986)
Movieland: Hollywood and the Great American Dream Culture (1989)
On a Darkening Green (1965)
Once upon a Droshky (1964)
Raised by Wolves: The Turbulent Art and Times of Quentin Tarantino (2006)
Savage Shorthand: The Life and Death of Isaac Babel (2005)
Secret Isaac (1978)

Cohen, Arthur Allen
Acts of Theft (1980)
An Admirable Woman (1983)
Artists and Enemies: Three Novellas (1987)
The Carpenter Years (1967)
In the Days of Simon Stern (1973)
Herbert Bayer: The Complete Works (1984)
A Hero in His Time (1976)
The Myth of the Judeo-Christian Tradition (1970)
The Natural and the Supernatural Jew (1963)

A People Apart: Hasidism in America (1970)
The Tremendum: A Theological Interpretation of the Holocaust (1981)
"Why I Choose To Be a Jew" (1959)

Cohen, Sarah Blacher
American Klezmer (2006)
Comic Relief: Humor in Contemporary American Literature (1978)
Cynthia Ozick's Comic Art (1994)
Danny Kaye: Supreme Court Jester (2001)
Henrietta Szold: Woman of Valor (2000)
Jewish Wry: Essays on Jewish Humor (1986)
The Ladies Locker Room (1987)
Making a Scene: The Contemporary Drama of Jewish-American Women (1997)
Molly Picon's Return Engagement (1994)
Saul Bellow's Enigmatic Laughter (1974)
Sofie, Totie and Belle (1990)
Soul Sisters (2007)

Doctorow, E. L.
Big as Life (1966)
Billy Bathgate (1989)
The Book of Daniel (1971)
Drinks Before Dinner: a Play (1978)
Lives of the Poets (1984)
Loon Lake (1980)
The March (2005)
Ragtime (1975)
Reporting the Universe (2003)
Sweet Land Stories (2004)
The Waterworks (1994)
Welcome to Hard Times (1960)
World's Fair (1985)

Elman, Richard
Cathedral-Tree-Train (1992)
A Coat for the Czar (1959)
Lilo's Diary (1968)
Namedropping: Mostly Literary Memoirs (1998)
The Poorhouse State: The American Way of Life on Public Assistance (1966)
The Reckoning (1969)
Tar Beach (1991)
The Twenty-Eighth Day of Ehul (1967)

Englander, Nathan
For the Relief of Unbearable Urges (1999)

"How We Avenged the Blums" (2005)
The Ministry of Special Cases (2007)

Epstein, Helen
*Children of the Holocaust: Conversations with Sons and
    Daughters of Survivors* (1979)
The Companies She Keeps (1985)
Joe Papp: An American Life (1994)
Music Talks (1987)
Under a Cruel Star
*Where She Came From: A Daughter's Search for her
    Mother's History* (1997)

Fast, Howard
Alice (1963)
Being Red (1990)
The Case of the Angry Actress (1984)
Citizen Tom Paine (1943)
Freedom Road (1944)
The Immigrants (1977)
The Last Frontier (1941)
Lord Baden-Powell of the Boy Scouts (1941)
Lydia (1964)
Moses, Prince of Egypt (1958)
The Naked God (1957)
Phyllis (1962)
Shirley (1963)
Spartacus (1951)
Sylvia (1960)
Two Valleys (1933)
The Unvanquished (1942)

Ferber, Edna
American Beauty (1931)
Cimarron (1930)
Dawn O'Hara, the Girl Who Laughed (1911)
Giant (1952)
"The Homely Heroine" (1910)
Ice Palace (1958)
A Kind of Magic (1963)
Our Mrs. McChesney (1915)
A Peculiar Treasure (1939)
Saratoga Trunk (1941)
Showboat (1926)
So Big (1924)

Fiedler, Leslie
Being Busted (1969)
"Come Back to the Raft Ag'in Huck Honey" (1948)

An End to Innocence (1955)
Freaks: Myths and Images of the Secret Self (1978)
In Dreams Awake (1976)
The Inadvertant Epic (1980)
Last Jew in America (1966)
Love, Death and the American Novel (1960)
Messengers Will Come No More (1974)
No! in Thunder: Essays on Myth and Literature (1973)
Olaf Stapelton: A Man Divided (1982)

Foer, Jonathan Safran
Everything Is Illuminated (2002)
Extremely Loud and Incredibly Close (2005)

Fuchs, Daniel
The Apathetic Bookie Joint (1979)
The Golden West: Hollywood Stories by Daniel Fuchs (2005)
Homage to Blenholt (1936)
Love Me or Leave Me (1955)
Low Company (1937)
Panic in the Streets (1950)
Summer in Williamsburg (1934)
West of the Rockies (1971)

Ginsberg, Allen
Howl and Other Poems (1956)
The Fall of America (1973)
Kaddish and Other Poems (1961)
Glass, Montague Marsden
Abe and Mawruss (1911)
Elkan Lubliner: American (1912)
Potash and Perlmutter (1910)
Worrying Won't Win (1918)
You Can't Learn 'Em Nothin' (1930)

Gold, Herbert
Age of Happy Problems (1962)
Birth of a Hero (1951)
Fathers: A Novel in the Form of a Memoir (1967)
Family: A Novel in the Form of a Memoir (1981)
The Great American Jackpot (1969)
He/She (1980)
Love and Like (1960)
The Man Who Was Not with It (1956)
The Prospect Before Us (1954)
Salt (1963)
Slave Trade (1979)
Swiftie the Magician (1974)
Waiting for Cordelia (1977)

Goldstein, Rebecca (Newberger)

Betraying Spinoza (2006)
The Dark Sister (1991)
Incompleteness (2005)
The Late-Summer Passion of a Woman of Mind (1989)
Mazel (1995)
The Mind-Body Problem (1983)
Properties of Light (2000)
Strange Attractors (1993)

Goodman, Allegra

The Family Markowitz (1996)
Kaaterskill Falls (1998)
Paradise Park (2001)
Total Immersion (1989)

Gratz, Rebbecca

Letters of Rebecca Gratz (1929)

Green, Hannah

I Never Promised You a Rose Garden (1964)

Hecht, Ben

Casino Royale (1967)
The Cat That Jumped Out of the Story (1947)
A Child of the Century (1954)
Count Bruga (1926)
The Egoist (1923)
Erik Dorn (1921)
Fantazies Mallare (1922)
A Farewell to Arms (1932)
The Florentine Dagger (1923)
The Front Page (1928)
Gargoyles (1922)
Gone With the Wind (1939)
Gunga Din (1939)
His Girl Friday (1940)
Humpty Dumpty (1924)
A Jew in Love (1931)
Letters from Bohemia (1964)
Miracle of the Bells (1947)
Monkey Business (1931)
Nothing Sacred (1937)
Notorious (1946)
1001 Afternoons in New York (1941)
Perfidy (1961)
Scarface (1932)
The Sensualists (1959)
Some Like It Hot (1959)

Spellbound (1945)
Tales of Chicago Streets (1924)
Twentieth Century (1934)
Viva Villa (1934)
Wuthering Heights (1939)

Heller, Joseph

Catch as Catch Can (2003)
Catch-22 (1961)
Catch-22: A Dramatization (1971)
Clevinger's Trial (1973)
Closing Time (1994)
God Knows (1984)
Good as Gold (1979)
No Laughing Matter (1986)
Picture This (1988)
Portrait of an Artist, as an Old Man (2000)
Something Happened (1975)
We Bombed in New Haven (1969)

Hellman, Lillian

Another Part of the Forest (1947)
The Autumn Garden (1951)
The Children's Hour (1937)
Days to Come (1936)
The Little Foxes (1939)
Pentimento (1974)
Scoundrel Time (1977)
The Searching Wind (1944)
Toys in the Attic (1960)
An Unfinished Woman (1969)
Watch on the Rhine (1941)

Hoffman, Eva

After Such Knowledge (2004)
Exit into History (1993)
Lost in Translation (1989)
The Secret (2001)
Shtetl: The Life and Death of a Small Town and the World of Polish Jews (1997)

Horn, Dara

In the Image (2002)
The World to Come (2006)

Hurst, Fannie

"Back Pay" (1921)
Imitation of Life (1933)
"The Joy of Living" (1909)

Irving, John
The Cider House Rules (1985)
The Fourth Hand (2001)
The Hotel New Hampshire (1981)
The 158-Pound Marriage (1974)
A Prayer for Owen Meany (1989)
Setting Free the Bears (1968)
A Son of the Circus (1994)
Until I Find You (2005)
The Water-Method Man (1972)
A Widow for One Year (1998)
The World According to Garp (1978)

Jong, Erica
Becoming Light (1991)
Fanny: Being the True History of the Adventures of Fanny Hackabout-Jones (1980)
Fear of Flying (1973)
Fear of Fifty (1994)
Fruits and Vegetables (1971)
Half-Lives (1973)
How to Save Your Own Life (1977)
Inventing Memory: A Novel of Mothers and Daughters (1997)
Parachutes and Kisses (1984)
Sappho's Leap (2003)
Seducing the Demon: Writing for My Life (2006)
What Do Women Want? Bread, Roses, Sex, Power (1998)

Kazin, Alfred
An American Procession (1984)
On Native Grounds (1942)
Starting Out in the Thirties (1965)
A Walker in the City (1931)

Klein, A. M.
The Second Scroll (1931)

Kosinski, Jerzy
The Art of the Self: Essay a Propos "Steps" (1968)
Being There (1971)
Blind Date (1977)
Cockpit (1975)
The Devil Tree (1973)
The Future Is Ours, Comrade: Conversations with Russians (1960)
The Hermit of 69th Street: The Working Papers of Norbert Koski (1988)
The Painted Bird (1965)

Passion Play (1979)
Pinball (1982)
Steps (1968)

Kotlowitz, Robert
Before Their Time (1999)
The Boardwalk (1977)
His Master's Voice (1992)
Sea Changes (1986)
Somewhere Else (1972)

Krim, Seymour
Shake It for the World, Smartass (1970)
Views of a Nearsighted Cannoneer (1961)
What's This Cat's Story: The Best of Seymour Krim (1991)
You and Me (1974)

Kumin, Maxine
Jack and Other New Poems (2005)
Up Country (1972)

Kunitz, Stanley
Intellectual Things (1930)
The Lincoln Relics (1978)
Next-to-Last Things (1985)
Passing Through (1995)
Passport to War (1944)
Selected Poems, 1928–1958 (1958)
The Testing-Tree (1971)
The Wellfleet Whale and Companion Poems (1983)

Kushner, Tony
Angels in America: A Gay Fantasia on National Themes (1991)
Caroline, or Change (2003)
Homebody/Kabul (2001)

Lazarus, Emma
Alide: An Episode in Goethe's Life (1874)
The Dance to Death (1882)
"The Jewish Problem" (1883)
"The New Colossus" (1883)
Poems and Translations Written Between the Ages of Fourteen and Sixteen (1866)
"Russian Christianity vs. Modern Judaism" (1882)
The Spagnoletto (1876)
"Was the Earl of Beaconsfield a Representative Jew?" (1882)

Leegant, Joan
An Hour in Paradise: Stories (2003)

Levertov, Denise
Breathing the Water (1987)
Candles in Babylon (1982)
Collected Earlier Poems (1979)
Door in the Hive (1989)
The Double Image (1946)
Evening Train (1993)
Footprints (1972)
The Freeing of the Dust (1975)
Here and Now (1957)
The Jacobs Ladder (1961)
The Letters of Denise Levertov and William Carlos Williams (1998)
The Letters of Robert Duncan and Denise Levertov (2004)
The Life All Around Us: Selected Poems on Nature (1997)
Life in the Forest (1978)
Light up the Cave (1981)
New and Selected Essays (1992)
O Taste and See (1964)
Oblique Prayers (1984)
Overland to the Islands (1958)
Poems 1968–72 (1987)
The Poet in the World (1973)
Relearning the Alphabet (1970)
The Sands of the Well (1996)
The Sorrow Dance (1966)
Tessserae: Memories and Suppositions (1993)
This Great Unknowing: Last Poems (1999)
To Stay Alive (1971)
The Stream and the Sapphire: Selected Poems on Religious Themes (1997)
With Eyes in the Back of Our Heads (1959)

Levin, Meyer
The Harvest (1978)
The Settlers (1972)
Lewisohn, Ludwig
The Case of Mr. Crump (1930)
The Dramatic Works of Gerhard Hauptmann (1917)
Expressionism in America (1937)
In a Summer Season (1955)
Israel (1925)
The Last Days of Shylock (1931)
Mid-Channel (1929)
The Modern Drama (1915)
Roman Summer (1927)

The Spirit of Modern German Literature (1916)
The Trumpet of Jubilee (1937)
Up Stream (1922)
Malamud, Bernard
The Assistant (1957)
The Complete Stories (1997)
Dubin's Lives (1979)
The Fixer (1966)
The German Refugee (1966)
God's Grace (1982)
Idiots First (1963)
The Magic Barrel (1958)
The Natural (1952)
A New Life (1961)
The People and Uncollected Stories (1989)
Pictures of Fidelman (1969)
Rembrandt's Hat (1973)
The Tenants (1971)

Mailer, Norman
Advertisements for Myself (1959)
An American Dream (1965)
Ancient Evenings (1983)
Armies of the Night (1968)
Barbary Shore (1951)
The Deer Park (1955)
The Executioner's Song (1979)
The Gospel According to the Son (1997)
Harlot's Ghost (1991)
"The Man Who Studied Yoga" (1959)
Miami and the Siege of Chicago (1968)
The Naked and the Dead (1948)
Of a Fire on the Moon (1971)
"The Time of Our Time" (1998)
Tough Guys Don't Dance (1984)
Why Are We in Vietnam? (1967)

Margolin, Anna
Lider (1929)

Mendelsohn, Daniel
The Lost: A Search for Six of the Six Million (2006)
The Elusive Embrace: Desire and the Riddle of Identity (1999)

Michaels, Anne
Fugitive Pieces (1996)
Miner's Pond (1991)
The Weight of Oranges (1985)

Miller, Arthur
All My Sons (1947)
The Crucible (1953)
Death of a Salesman (1949)
Honors at Dawn (1936)
The Man Who Had All the Luck (1944)
No Villain (1936)
They Too Arise (1937)

Nemerov, Howard
The Blue Swallows (1967)
The Collected Poems of Howard Nemerov (1959)
A Commodity of Dreams and Other Stories (1959)
Federigo: Or the Power of Love (1954)
The Homecoming Game (1957)
The Image and the Law (1947)
The Melodramatists (1949)
Mirrors & Windows (1958)
The Next Room of the Dream (1962)
Poetry and Fiction: Essays (1963)
Trying Conclusions: New and Selected Poems (1992)
Reflexions on Poetry and Poetics (1972)
The Salt Garden (1955)
Stories, Fables and Other Diversions (1971)

Nissenson, Hugh
The Days of Awe (2005)
The Elephant and My Jewish Problem (1988)
In the Reign of Peace (1972)
My Own Ground (1976)
Notes from the Frontier (1968)
A Pile of Stones (1965)
The Song of the Earth (2001)
The Tree of Life (1985)

Noah, Mordecai Manuel
Address, Delivered at the Hebrew Synagogue, in Crosby-Street, New York, on Thanksgiving Day, to Aid in the Erection of The Temple at Jerusalem (1849)
Discourse on the Evidences of the American Indians Being the Descendants of the Lost Tribes of Israel (1837)
Discourse on the Restoration of the Jews (1845)
Essays of Howard, On Domestic Economy (1820)
Marion, or the Hero of Lake George (1822)
Oh Yes!, or, the New Constitution (1814)
Oration Delivered by Appointment Before Tammany Society . . . to Celebrate the 41st Anniversary of American Independence (1817)

She Would Be a Soldier, Or the Plains of Chippewa: An Historical Drama, in Three Acts
The Siege of Yorktown (1824)
Thanksgiving Day Address (1848)
Travels in England, France, and the Barbary States, in the Years 1813–1814 (1819)

Odets, Clifford
Awake and Sing! (1935)
The Big Knife (1949)
Clash by Night (1942)
The General Died at Dawn (1936)
Golden Boy (1937)
Night Music (1940)
None but the Lonely Heart (1944)
Paradise Lost (1936)
Sweet Smell of Success (1957)
Till the Day I Die (1935)
Waiting for Lefty (1935)

Olsen, Tillie
"Requa" (1970)
Silences (1978)
Tell Me a Riddle (1961)
Yonnondio: From the Thirties (1974)

Osherow, Jacqueline
Conversations with Survivors: Poems (1994)
Dead Men's Praise (1999)
The Hoopoe's Crown (2005)
Looking for Angels in New York (1988)
With a Moon In Transit (1996)

Ozick, Cynthia
Art and Ardor (1983)
Bloodshed and Three Novellas (1976)
The Cannibal Galaxy (1983)
Heir to the Glimmering World (2004)
Levitation: Five Fictions (1982)
The Messiah of Stockholm (1987)
Metaphor and Memory (1991)
The Pagan Rabbi and Other Stories (1971)
"Rosa" (1983)
"The Shawl" (1989)
Trust (1966)

Paley, Grace
Enormous Changes at the Last Minute (1974)
Goldenrod (1982)

Later the Same Day (1985)
Leaning Forward: Poems (1985)
The Little Disturbances of Man (1959)
16 Broadsides (1980)

Parker, Dorothy
After Such Pleasures (1932)
"Big Blonde" (1929)
Death and Taxes (1931)
Enough Rope (1926)
Laments for the Living (1930)
A Star Is Born (1937)
Sunset Gun (1928)

Piercy, Marge
The Art of Blessing the Day: Poems on a Jewish Theme (1999)
Circles on the Water: Selected Poems (1982)
Fly Away Home (1984)
Gone to Soldiers (1987)
He, She, and It (1991)
The Longings of Women (1994)
The Moon Is Always Female (1980)
My Mother's Body (1985)
Sex Wars (2005)
Sleeping with Cats (2002)
The Third Child (2003)
Three Women (1999)
Woman on the Edge of Time (1976)

Potok, Chaim
The Book of Lights (1981)
The Chosen (1967)
Davita's Harp (1985)
The Gates of November (1996)
The Gift of Asher Lev (1990)
I Am the Clay (1992)
My First 79 Years: Isaac Stern (1999)
My Name Is Asher Lev (1972)
Old Men at Midnight (2001)
Out of the Depths (1990)
The Play of Lights (1992)
The Promise (1969)
Sins of the Father (1990)
The Sky of Now (1995)
Theo Tobiasse: Artist in Exile (1986)
The Tree of Here (1993)
Wanderings: Chaim Potok's History of the Jews (1978)
Zebra and Other Stories (1998)

Reznikoff, Charles
Holocaust (1975)
Rhythms (1918)
Testimony (1965)

Rich, Adrienne
Arts of the Possible (2001)
An Atlas of the Difficult World (1991)
Blood, Bread and Poetry (1986)
A Change of World (1951)
Collected Early Poems 1950–1970 (1993)
"Compulsory Heterosexuality and Lesbian Existence" (1980)
Dark Fields of the Republic (1995)
The Diamond Cutters (1955)
Diving into the Wreck (1973)
The Dream of a Common Language (1978)
The Fact of a Doorframe (1984)
Fox (2001)
Leaflets (1969)
Of Woman Born: Motherhood as Experience and Institution (1976)
On Lies, Secrets, and Silence (1979)
Midnight Salvage (1999)
Necessities of Life (1966)
Poems: Selected and New, 1950–1974 (1974)
The School Among the Ruins (2004)
Snapshots of a Daughter-in-Law (1963)
Sources (1983)
Time's Power (1988)
Twenty-One Love Poems (1977)
What Is Found There: Notebooks on Poetry and Politics (1993)
A Wild Patience Has Taken Me This Far (1981)
The Will to Change (1971)
Your Native Land, Your Life (1986)

Roiphe, Anne
Digging Out (1967)
1185 Park Avenue: A Memoir (1999)
For Rabbit, with Love and Squalor (2000)
Fruitful: A Real Mother in the Modern World (1996)
Generation without Memory: A Jewish Journey in Christian America (1981)
If You Knew Me (1993)
An Imperfect Lens (2006)
Long Division (1972)
Lovingkindness (1987)
Married: A Fine Predicament (2002)

The Pursuit of Happiness (1991)
A Season for Healing: Reflections on the Holocaust (1988)
Secrets of the City (2003)
Torch Song (1977)
Up the Sandbox! (1970)
Water from the Well: Sarah, Rebekah, Rachel, and Lea (2006)
Your Child's Mind: The Complete Book of Infant and Child Mental Health Care (1985)

Rosen, Jonathan

Eve's Apple (1997)
Joy Comes in the Morning (2004)
The Life of the Skies (2008)
The Talmud and the Internet: A Journey Between Worlds (2000)

Rosen, Norma

Accidents of Influence: Writing as a Woman and a Jew in America (1992)
At the Center (1982)
Biblical Women Unbound: Counter-Tales (1996)
A Family Passover (1980)
Green: A Novella and Eight Stories (1967)
John and Anzia: An American Romance (1989)
Joy to Levine! (1962)
Touching Evil (1969)

Rosenbaum, Thane

Elijah Visible (1966)
Golem's of Gotham: A Novel (2002)
The Myth of Moral Justice (2004)
Second Hand Smoke (1999)

Rosenfeld, Isaac

Alpha and Omega (1966)
An Age of Enormity: Life and Writing in the Forties and Fifties (1962)
"The Colony" (1945)
Passage from Home (1946)

Rosten, Leo

All Through the Night (1942)
Captain Newman, M.D. (1961)
The Dark Corner (1945)
*The Education of H*Y*M*A*N K*A*P*L*A*N* (1937)
Hooray for Yiddish: A Book about English (1982)

The Joys of Yiddish (1968)
Joys of Yinglish (1989)
Lured (1947)
The New Joys of Yiddish (2001)
*O K*A*P*L*A*N! MY K*A*P*L*A*N!* (1976)
*The Return of H*Y*M*A*N K*A*P*L*A*N* (1959)
The Story behind the Painting (1961)
The Velvet Touch (1948)

Roth, Henry

Call It Sleep (1934)
A Diving Rock on the Hudson (1995)
From Bondage (1996)
Holding On
Mercy of a Rude Stream: A Star Shines over Mt. Morris Park (1994)
Nature's First Green (1979)
Requiem for Harlem (1998)
Shifting Landscape (1987)

Roth, Philip

American Pastoral (1997)
The Anatomy Lesson (1983)
The Breast (1972)
The Counterlife (1986)
Deception (1990)
The Dying Animal (2001)
Everyman (2006)
Exit Ghost (2007)
The Facts (1988)
Goodbye, Columbus and Five Short Stories (1995)
The Ghost Writer (1979)
The Great American Novel (1973)
The Human Stain (2000)
I Married a Communist (1998)
Indignation (2008)
Letting Go (1962)
My Life as a Man (1979)
Operation Shylock (1993)
Our Gang (1971)
Patrimony (1991)
The Plot Against America (2004)
Portnoy's Complaint (1969)
The Prague Orgy (1985)
Reading Myself and Others (1975)
Sabbath's Theater (1995)
Shop Talk (2001)
When She Was Good (1967)
Zuckerman Unbound (1981)

Rukeyser, Muriel

One Life (1957)
Theory of Flight (1935)
The Traces of Thomas Hariot (1971)
Willard Gibbs (1942)

Salamon, Julie

The Christmas Tree (1996)
*The Devil's Candy: The Bonfire of the Vanities Goes to
    Hollywood* 1991)
Facing the Wind (2001)
*The Net of Dreams: A Family's Search for a Rightful
    Place* (1996)
*Rambam's Ladder: A Meditation on Generosity and Why
    It Is Necessary to Give* (2003)
White Lies (1987)

Salinger, J. D.

The Catcher in the Rye (1951)
Franny and Zooey (1961)
Nine Stories (1953)
Raise High the Roof Beam and Seymour: An Introduction
    (1963)
Schaeffer, Susan Fromberg
Anya (1976)

Schwartz, Delmore

Delmore Schwartz and James Laughlin: Selected Letters
    (1993)
The Ego Is Always at the Wheel: Bagatelles (1986)
Genesis (1943)
In Dreams Begin Responsibilities (1938)
Last and Lost Poems (1979)
Portrait of Delmore (1986)
Selected Essays of Delmore Schwartz (1970)
Selected Poems: Summer Knowledge (1967)
Shenandoah (1941)
Vaudeville for a Princess (1950)

Shaw, Irwin

Acceptable Losses (1982)
Act of Faith and Other Stories (1946)
The Assassin (1945)
Beggerman, Thief (1977)
Bread upon the Waters (1981)
Bury the Dead (1936)
Evening in Byzantium (1973)
The Gentle People (1939)
God Was Here but He Left Early (1973)

Love on a Dark Street (1965)
Lucy Crown (1956)
Mixed Company (1950)
Nightwork (1975)
Rich Man, Poor Man (1970)
Sailor off the Bremen (1939)
Tip on a Dead Jockey (1957)
The Top of the Hill (1979)
The Troubled Air (1950)
Two Weeks in Another Town (1960)
Voices of a Summer Day (1965)
Welcome to the City (1942)
The Young Lions (1948)

Shulman, Alix Kates

Burning Questions (1978)
Drinking the Rain (1995)
A Good Enough Daughter (1999)
In Every Woman's Life . . . (1987)
Memoirs of an Ex-Prom Queen (1972)
On the Stroll (1981)

Sinclair, Jo

The Changelings (1955)
Sing at My Wake (1951)
The Wasteland (1946)

Singer, Isaac Bashevis

Enemies: A Love Story (1972)
The Family Moskat (1966)
Gimpel the Fool and Other Stories (1957)
In My Father's Court (1967)
The Magician of Lublin (1960)
The Manor (1967)
Satan in Goray (1955)
Shadows on the Hudson (1998)
The Slave (1962)

Skibell, Joseph

A Blessing on the Moon (1997)
The English Disease (2003)

Sklarew, Myra

Holocaust and the Construction of Memory (2008)
Lithuania: New and Selected Poems (1995)

Sontag, Susan

Against Interpretation (1966)
AIDS and Its Metaphors (1989)

Alice in Bed (1993)
The Benefactor (1963)
Brother Carl (1972)
Death Kit (1967)
Duet for Cannibals (1969)
I, etcetera (1978)
Illness as Metaphor (1978)
In America (2000)
On Photography (1977)
Promised Lands (1974)
Regarding the Pain of Others (2003)
Styles of Radical Will (1969)
Under the Sign of Saturn (1980)
Unguided Tour (1983)
The Volcano Lover (1992)
Where the Stress Falls (2001)

Spiegelman, Art

In The Shadow of No Towers (2004)
Maus I: My Father Bleeds History (1986)
Maus II: And Here My Troubles Began (1991)
Open Me . . . I'm a Dog (1997)

Stein, Gertrude

The Autobiography of Alice B. Toklas (1933)
Libretto from *Four Saints in Three Acts* (1934)
Lectures in America (1935)
The Making of Americans (1925)
Tender Buttons: Objects, Food, Rooms (1914)
Three Lives: Stories of the Good Anna, Melanctha, and the Gentle Lena (1909)
Q.E.D. (1903)

Stern, Steve

The Angel of Forgetfulness (2005)
Harry Kaplan's Adventures Underground (1991)
Hershel and the Beast (1987)
Isaac and the Undertaker's Daughter (1983)
Lazar Malkin Enters Heaven (1986)
Mickey and the Golem (1986)
The Moon and Ruben Shein (1984)
A Plague of Dreamers (1994)
The Wedding Jester (1999)

Swados, Harvey

"The Amateurs" (1938)
Nights in the Gardens of Brooklyn (1960)
On the Line (1957)
Out Went the Candle (1955)

The Unknown Constellations (1995)
The Will (1963)

Trilling, Lionel

Beyond Culture: Essays on Literature and Learning (1965)
The Liberal Imagination (1950)
Matthew Arnold (1939)
The Middle of the Journey (1947)
Mind in the Modern World (1973)
Sincerity and Authenticity (1972)

Uris, Leon

The Angry Hills (1955)
Armageddon (1964)
Battle Cry (1953)
Exodus (1957)
Exodus Revisited (1959)
A God in Ruins (1999)
The Haj (1984)
Mitla Pass (1988)
Mila 18 (1960)
O'Hara's Choice (2003)
QB VII (1970)
Redemption (1995)
Topaz (1967)
Trinity (1976)

Wallant, Edward Lewis

Children at the Gate (1964)
The Human Season (1960)
The Pawnbroker (1961)
The Tenants of Moonbloom (1963)

Wasserstein, Wendy

"An American Daughter" (1997)
"Any Woman Can't" (1973)
Bachelor Girls (1990)
"Happy Birthday, Montpellier Pizz-zazz" (1974)
The Heidi Chronicles and Other Plays (1988)
"Isn't It Romantic" (1981)
"Miami" (1986)
"The Man in a Case" (1986)
"Object of My Affection" (1998)
"Orchards" (1986)
"Pamela's First Musical" (1996)
Shiksa Goddess; or, How I Spent My Forties (2001)
"The Sisters Rosensweig" (1993)
"Tender Offer" (1983)

"Uncommon Women, and Others" (1975)
"When Dinah Shore Ruled the Earth" (1975)

West, Nathanael
Born to Be Wild (1938)
A Cool Million: The Dismantling of Lemuel Pitkin (1934)
The Day of the Locust (1981)
The Dream Life of Balso Snell (1931)
Follow Your Heart (1936)
Gangs of New York (1938)
Good Hunting: A Satire (1938)
I Stole a Million (1939)
It Could Happen to You (1937)
Men Against the Sky (1940)
Miss Lonelyhearts (1933)
Ticket to Paradise (1936)

Wiesel, Elie
The Accident (1962)
All Rivers Run to the Sea (1995)
Ani Ma'amin: A Song Lost and Found Again (1973)
A Beggar in Jerusalem (1970)
Dawn (1961)
The Fifth Son (1985)
Five Biblical Portraits (1981)
The Forgotten (1989)
Four Hasidic Masters: and Their Struggle Against Melancholy (1978)
From the Kingdom of Memory (1990)
The Gates of the Forest (1964)
A Jew Today (1978)
Legends of Our Time (1968)
A Mad Desire to Dance (2009)
Messengers of God (1976)
Night (1958)
The Oath (1973)
One Generation After (1970)
Paroles d'étranger (1982)
Sages and Dreamers: Biblical, Talmudic, and Hasidic Legends (1991)
And the Sea Is Never Full: Memoirs, 1969– (1999)
Somewhere A Master: Further Hasidic Portraits and Legends (1982)
Souls on Fire: Portraits and Legends of Hasidic Masters (1972)
The Testament (1980)
The Time of the Uprooted (2005)
The Town Beyond the Wall (1962)
The Trial of God (1979)
Twilight (1987)

Un di Velt Hot Geshvign (And the World Remained Silent) (1955)
Wise Men and Their Tales (2003)
Zalmen, or the Madness of God (1968)

Wolf, Emma
Fulfillment: A California Novel (1916)
Heirs of Yesterday (1900)
The Joy of Life (1896)
The Knot (1909)
"One-Eye, Two-Eye, Three-Eye" (1896)
Other Things Being Equal (1892)
A Prodigal in Love (1894)

Wouk, Herman
The Caine Mutiny (1951)
The Caine Mutiny Court-Martial (1953)
Marjorie Morningstar (1955)
This Is My God (1959)
The Will to Live On (2000)
The Winds of War (1971)
War and Remembrance (1978)

Yezierska, Anzia
All I Could Never Be (1932)
Arrogant Beggar (1927)
Bread Givers (1925)
Children of Loneliness (1923)
Hungry Hearts (1920)
Red Ribbon on a White Horse (1950)
Salome of the Tenements (1923)

Zangwill, Israel
The Bachelors' Club (1891)
The Celibate's Club: Being the United Stories of the Bachelors' Club and Old Maids' Club (1898)
Children of the Ghetto: Being Pictures of a Peculiar People (1892)
Ghetto Comedies (1907)
Ghetto Tragedies (1893)
The Grey Wig: Stories and Novellas (1903)
The King of the Schnorrers: Grotesques and Fantasies (1894)
Merely Mary Ann (1903)
Motza Kleis (1882)
The Next Religion (1912)
The Old Maid's Club (1892)
The Premier and the Painter (1888)
Too Much Money (1918)
The War God (1911)

BIBLIOGRAPHY OF SECONDARY SOURCES

Aarons, Victoria. "The Legacy of the Disinherited: Thane Rosenbaum's Holocaust Fiction." In *What Happened to Abraham? Reinventing the Covenant in American Jewish Fiction.* Newark: University of Delaware Press, 2005.

Abrahamson, Irving, ed. *Against Silence: The Voice and Vision of Elie Wiesel.* New York: Holocaust Library, 1985.

Abramson, Edward. *Chaim Potok.* Boston: Twayne, 1986.

Adlam, Carol. "Anton Chekhov and Lillian Hellman: Ethics, Form and the Problem of Melodrama." In *Chekhov 2004: Chekhov Special Issues in Two Volumes, Vol. 2, Chekhov and Others.* Keele, U.K.: Keele University Students Union, 2006.

Aleichem, Sholem. *Tevye's Daughters.* Translated and with an introduction by Frances Butwin. New York: Crown, 1949.

Alexander, Edward. *Isaac Bashevis Singer.* Boston: Twayne, 1980.

———. *The Resonance of Dust: Essays on Holocaust Literature and Jewish Fate.* Columbus: Ohio State University Press, 1979.

Alexander, Paul. *Salinger: A Biography.* Los Angeles: Renaissance Books, 1999.

Allen, Bruce. "The Novellas of Hortense Calisher." *Nation* 265, no. 18 (1 December 1997): 34–36.

Alphen, Ernst van. "Second-Generation Testimony, Transmission of Trauma, and Postmemory." *Poetics Today* 27, no. 2 (Summer 2006): 473–488.

Alter, Robert. "Heirs of the Tradition." *Rogue's Progress: Studies in the Picaresque Novel.* Cambridge, Mass.: Harvard University Press, 1964.

Altman, Meryl. "Beyond Trashiness: The Sexual Language of 1970s Feminist Fiction." *Journal of International Women's Studies* 4, no. 2 (April 2003): 7–19.

Amis, Martin. "A Chicago of a Novel." *Atlantic* (October 1995): 114–120, 122–127.

Apple, Sam. "Making Amends." *Jerusalem Report,* 31 July 2000, 46.

Arcana, Judith. *Grace Paley's Life Stories: A Literary Biography.* Urbana: University of Illinois Press, 1993.

Ashton, Dianne. *Rebecca Gratz: Women and Judaism in Antebellum America.* Detroit: Wayne State University Press, 1997.

"Asimov, Isaac." *Contemporary Authors: A Bio-Bibliographic Guide to Current Writers in Fiction, Non-Fiction, Poetry, Journalism, Drama, Motion Pictures, Television, and Other Fields.* Edited by Tracy Watson. Farmington Hills, Mich.: Gale Group, Thompson Learning, 2004.

Atlas, James. *Bellow.* New York: Random House, 2000; London: Faber, 2001; New York: Modern Library, 2002.

Atlas, James. *Delmore Schwartz: The Life of an American Poet.* New York: Farrar, Straus & Giroux, 1977.

Auden, W. H. "Foreword." *A Change of World,* by Adrienne Rich. New Haven, Conn.: Yale University Press, 1951.

Auster, Paul. "The Decisive Moment." In *Charles Reznikoff: Man and Poet.* Edited by Milton Hindus. Orono, Me.: National Poetry Foundation, University of Maine at Orono, 1984.

Avery, Evelyn. "Allegra Goodman's Fiction: From the Suburbs to 'Gan Eden.'" *Studies in American Jewish Literature* 22 (2003): 36–45.

Avery, Evelyn G., ed. *The Magic Worlds of Bernard Malamud.* Albany: SUNY Press, 2001.

Baba, Minako. "The Young Gangster as Mythic American Hero: E. L. Doctorow's *Billy Bathgate.*" *MELUS* 18, no. 2 (Summer 1993): 33–46.

Bach, Gerhard, ed. *The Critical Response to Saul Bellow.* Westport, Conn.: Greenwood Press, 1995.

Baechler, Lea, and A. Walton Litz, eds. *Modern American Women Writers.* New York: Scribner, 1991.

Bail, Paul. "Good Mother, Bad Mother in Joanne Greenberg's *I Never Promised You a Rose Garden.*" In *Women in Literature: Reading through the Lens of Gender.* Westport, Conn.: Greenwood, 2003.

Banville, John. "Grave Thoughts from a Master: A Blank Style Masks the Magical Craft of the Novelist." *Guardian* (London). 29 April 2006, 7.

Barnett, Claudia, ed. *Wendy Wasserstein: A Casebook. Casebooks on Modern Dramatists.* New York: Garland, 1999.

Basu, Biman. "*Mr. Sammler's Planet* Revisited: Bellow's Comment on Intellectual Life." *Saul Bellow Journal* 6, no. 11 (Winter 1987): 18–27.

Baumgarten, Murray, and Barbara Gottfried. *Understanding Philip Roth.* Columbia: University of South Carolina Press, 1990.

Bayard, Louis. "Was That Elijah?" *New York Times,* 5 October 2003, A18.

Baym, Nina, ed. *Norton Anthology of American Literature,* 5th ed. New York: W.W. Norton, 1998.

Behlman, Lee. "The Escapist: Fantasy, Folklore, and the Pleasures of the Comic Book in Recent Jewish American Holocaust Fiction." *Shofar* 22, no. 3 (Spring 2004): 56–71.

Beichman, Arnold. *Herman Wouk: The Novelist as Social Historian.* New Brunswick, N.J.: Transaction Books, 1984.

Berger, Alan L. "Bearing Witness: Second Generation Literature of the 'Shoah.'" *Modern Judaism* 10, no. 1 (1990): 43–63.

———. *Children of Job: American Second Generation Witnesses to the Holocaust.* Albany: SUNY Press, 1997.

———. *Crisis and Covenant: The Holocaust in American Jewish Fiction.* Albany: SUNY Press, 1985.

———. "Faith and God During the Holocaust: Teaching *Night* with the Later Memoirs." In *Approaches to Teaching Wiesel's* Night. Edited by Alan Rosen. New York: Modern Language Association of America, 2007.

———. "Holiness and Holocaust: The Jewish Writing of Hugh Nissenson." *Jewish Book Annual* 48 (1990–91).

———. "Interview with Elie Wiesel." *Literature and Belief* 26, no. 1 (March 2007): 1–23.

———. "Memoir and Memory: The Second Generation Odyssey of Julie Salamon." *Jewish Affairs* 54, no. 2 (Winter 1997).

———. "Mourning, Rage, and Redemption: Representing the Holocaust: The Work of Thane Rosenbaum." *Studies in Jewish American Literature* 19 (2000): 6–15.

———. "Myth, Mysticism, and Memory: The Holocaust in Thane Rosenbaum's *The Golems of Gotham.*" *Studies in American Jewish Literature* 24 (2005).

———. "Transfusing Memory: Second-Generation Postmemory in Elie Wiesel's *The Forgotten.*" *Obliged by Memory: Literature, Religion, Ethics: A Collection of Essays Honoring Elie Wiesel's Seventieth Birthday.* Edited by Steven T. Katz and Alan Rosen. Syracuse, N.Y.: Syracuse University Press, 2006.

Berriault, Gina. *Women in Their Beds: New and Selected Stories.* Washington, D.C.: Counterpoint, 1996.

Bertonneau, Thomas F. "The Mind Bound Round: Language and Reality in Heller's *Catch-22. Studies in American Jewish Literature* 15 (1996): 29–41.

Bigsby, Christopher. *The Cambridge Companion to Arthur Miller.* Cambridge, New York: Cambridge University Press, 1997.

Bloom, Harold, ed. *E.L. Doctorow.* Philadelphia: Chelsea House, 2002.

———. ed. *John Irving.* Philadelphia: Chelsea House, 2001.

———, ed. *Norman Mailer*. Philadelphia: Chelsea House, 2003.

Bloom, Harold, ed. *Saul Bellow*. New York: Chelsea House, 1986.

Bluefarb, Sam. "Pictures of the Anti-Stereotype: Leslie Fiedler's Triptych, The Last Jew in America." *College Language Association Journal* 18 (1975): 412–421.

Boken, Julia B. "Gina Berriault." In *American Short Story Writers Since World War II*. Detroit: Thomson Gale, 1993.

Bordewyk, Gordon. "Nathanael West and *Seize the Day*." In *Critical Essays on Nathanael West*. New York: G.K. Hall, 1994.

Boroff, David. "Stranded on Second Avenue." Review of *Once upon a Droshky. Saturday Review*, February 29, 1964, 34.

Boyers, Robert. *Lionel Trilling: Negative Capability and the Wisdom of Avoidance*. Columbia: University of Missouri Press, 1977.

Brater, Enoch, ed. *Arthur Miller's America: Theatre and Culture in a Time of Change*. Ann Arbor: University of Michigan Press, 2005.

Brauner, David. "Breaking the Silences: Jewish-American Women Writing the Holocaust." *Yearbook of English Studies* 31 (2001): 24–38.

Brawarsky, Sandee. "A Promising Midlife Debut." *Jewish Woman Magazine*. Fall 2003. Available Online. URL: http://www.jwmag.org/site/c.fhLOK0PGLsF/b.2440825/k.4F8D/A_Promising_Midlife_Debut.htm. Accessed November 3, 2007.

Brenman-Gibson, Margaret. *Clifford Odets: American Playwright: The Years from 1906–1940*. New York: Atheneum, 1981.

Brenner, Rachel Feldhay. *"The Almost Meeting": The Quest for the Holocaust in Canadian Jewish Fiction*. In "Studies in Judaism: Methodology in the Academic Teaching of the Holocaust." Edited by Zev Garber, Alan L. Berger, and Richard Liebowitz. Lanham: University Press of America, 1988.

Breslin, James. "Allen Ginsberg: The Origins of 'Howl' and 'Kaddish.'" *Iowa Review* 8, no. 2 (1977): 82–108.

———. "Gertrude Stein and the Problems of Autobiography." *Georgia Review* 33, no. 4 (Winter 1979): 901–913.

Brienza, Susan. "Doctor's *Ragtime*: Narrative as Silhouette and Syncopation." *Dutch Quarterly Review of Anglo-American Letters* 11, no. 2 (1981): 97–103.

Brinnin, John Malcolm. *The Third Rose: Gertrude Stein and Her World*. Reading, Mass.: Addison-Wesley, 1987.

Bronner, Simon J. "Structural and Stylistic Relations of Oral and Literary Humor: An Analysis of Leo Rosten's H*Y*M*A*N K*A*P*L*A*N Stories." *Journal of the Folklore Institute* 19, no. 1 (1982): 31–45.

Brown, Mick. "A Labour of Love." *Telegraph Magazine*.

Brown, Robert McAfee. *Elie Wiesel: Messenger to All Humanity*. Notre Dame, Ind.: University of Notre Dame Press, 1983.

Brownrigg, Sylvia. "Love and Other Quantum Leaps." *New York Times*, 17 September 2007, 7:14.

Budick, Emily Miller. "Rebecca Goldstein: Jewish Visionary in Skirts." *Hollins Critic* 34, no. 2 (April 1997): 1–13.

Burgard, Peter J. "Two Parts Ibsen, One Part American Dream: On Derivation and Originality in Arthur Miller's *Death of a Salesman*." *Orbis Litterarum: International Review of Literary Studies* 43, no. 4 (1988): 336–353.

Burgin, Richard. "The Sly Modernism of Isaac B. Singer." *American Writing Today*. Edited by Richard Kostelanetz. Troy, N.Y.: Whitston, 1991.

Burns, Alan, and Charles Sugnet. *Grace Paley*. Jackson: University Press of Mississippi, 1997.

Burstein, Janet. "Traumatic Memory and American Jewish Writers: One Generation after the Holocaust." *Yiddish* 11, nos. 3–4 (1999): 188–197.

Butler, Robert J. "The Woman Writer as American Picaro: Open Journeying in Erica Jong's *Fear of Flying*." *Centennial Review* 31, no. 3 (Summer 1987): 306–328.

Butwin, Julius and Frances. Foreword to *The Old Country* by Sholem Aleichem. New York: Crown, 1946.

Cahan, Abraham. *The Education of Abraham Cahan*. Vols. 1 and 2 of *Bleter fun mayn lebn*. Edited by Leon Stein, Abraham B. Conan, and Lynn Davidson, introduction by Leon Stein. Philadelphia: Jewish Publication Society of America, 1969.

———. *The Rise of David Levinsky*. New York: Harper and Brothers, 1917. Reprint, with introduction by John Higham, New York: Harper and Brothers, 1960. Reprint, with introduction and notes by Jules Chametzky. New York: Penguin, 1993.

Campbell, Josie P. *John Irving: A Critical Companion.* Westport, Conn.: Greenwood, 1998.

Cantor, Harold. *Clifford Odets Playwright-Poet.* Metuchen, N.J.: Scarecrow Press, 1978.

Cappell, Ezra. Interview with Sarah Blacher Cohen, 26 July 2006, Albany, N.Y.

———. "Reflecting the World: Bernard Malamud's Post-Holocaust Judaism." In *Modern Jewish Studies,* A Special Issue: The Art of Bernard Malamud. Edited by S. Lillian Kremer. Yiddish 13, no. 1 (2002): 31–61.

———. "Sarah Blacher Cohen." *Encyclopedia of Ethnic American Literature.* Edited by Emmanuel S. Nelson. Greenwood Press, 2005.

Cardon, Lauren. "*Herzog* as 'Survival Literature.'" *Saul Bellow Journal* 20, no. 2 (Fall 2004): 85–108.

Cargas, Harry James. "Positive Ambiguity: The Religious Thought of Elie Wiesel." *Spiritual Life* (Summer 1970).

Casale, Frank D. "Madness, Speech, and Prophecy in Allen Ginsberg's Howl." *Spectacle* 1, no. 2 (Spring 1998): 101–112.

Caughie, Pamela L. "Let It Pass: Changing the Subject, Once Again." In *Feminism and Composition Studies: In Other Words.* New York: Modern Language Association of America, 1998.

Chametzky, Jules. *From the Ghetto: The Fiction of Abraham Cahan.* Amherst: University of Massachusetts Press, 1977.

Charles, Ron. "Divine Inheritance." Review of *The World To Come, Washington Post,* 22 January 2006, BW6.

Charney, Maurice. "Woody Allen's Non Sequitors." *Humor: International Journal of Humor Research* 8, no. 4 (1995): 339–348.

Ciancio, Ralph. "The Achievement of Saul Bellow's *Seize the Day." Small Planets: Saul Bellow and the Art of Short Fiction.* East Lansing: Michigan State University Press, 2000.

Ciociola, Gail. *Wendy Wasserstein: Dramatizing Women, Their Choices and Their Boundaries.* Jefferson, N.C.: McFarland, 1998.

Clark, Thomas. "Allen Ginsberg." In *Writers at Work:The Paris Review Interviews* 3, no. 1 (1968): 279–320.

Clayton, John J. "Humboldt's Gift: Transcendence and the Flight from Death." In *Saul Bellow and His Work.* Edited by Edmond Schraepen. Brussels: Centrum voor Taal-en Literatuurwetenschap, Vrije Universiteit Brussel, 1978.

Cohen, Arthur Allen. "Why I Choose to Be a Jew." *Harper's Magazine,* April 1959, 61–66.

Cohen, Sarah Blacher. *Cynthia Ozick's Comic Art: From Levity to Liturgy.* Bloomington: Indiana University Press, 1994.

———. "The Fiction Writer-Essayist: Ozick's *Metaphor & Memory." Judaism Quarterly Journal.* 39, no. 3 (1990): 276–281. Reprinted in *Contemporary Literary Criticism.* Edited by Janet Witalec. Detroit: Gale, 2002.

———. "From Critic to Playwright: Fleshing Out Jewish Women in Contemporary Drama." In *Talking Back: Images of Jewish Women in American Popular Culture.* Edited by Joyce Antler. Hanover, N.H.: Brandeis University Press, 1998.

———. "The Jewish Literary Comediennes." *Comic Relief: Humor in Contemporary American Literature* (1978): 172–186. Reprinted in *Contemporary Literary Criticism.* Edited by Jean C. Stine. Detroit: Gale, 1985.

Cokal, Susann. "Picture Book." Review of *The World to Come. New York Times Book Review,* 19 March 2006, 27.

Cole, William, and George Plimpton. "The Art of Fiction: S.J. Perelman." In *S.J. Perelman: Critical Essays.* Edited by Steven H. Gale. New York: Garland, 1992.

Coles, Diane. "Profesion: Renaissance Man: Arthur A. Cohen." *Present Tense* 9 (Fall 1981): 32–35.

Contemporary Women Poets. Detroit: St. James Press, 1998.

Cook, Richard. "Alfred Kazin." In *Modern American Critics.* Edited by Gregory S. Jay. Detroit: Gale, 1988.

Cooper, Alan. "It Can Happen Here, or All in the Family Values: Surviving *The Plot Against America." Philip Roth: New Perspectives on an American Author.* Edited by Derek Parker Royal. Westport, Conn.: Praeger, 2005.

———. *Philip Roth and the Jews.* Albany: SUNY Press, 1991.

Corliss, Richard. "That Old Feeling: Perelmania." *Time.* Available online. URL: http://www.time.com/

time/columnist/corliss/article/0,9565,587750-3,00.html. Accessed on February 5, 2004.

Cronin, Gloria L. *A Room of His Own: In Search of the Feminine in the Novels of Saul Bellow.* Syracuse, N.Y.: Syracuse University Press, 2000.

———. "The Complex Irony of Grace: A Study of Bernard Malamud's *God's Grace.*" *Studies in American Jewish Literature* 5 (1986): 119–128.

———. "Melodramas of Beset Womanhood: Resistance, Subversion, and Survival in the Fiction of Grace Paley." In *Studies in American Jewish Literature* 11, no. 2 (Fall 1992): 140–149.

———. "Seasons of Our (Dis)Content, or Orthodox Women in Walden: Allegra Goodman's *Kaaterskill Falls.*" In *Connections and Collisons: Identities in Contemporary Jewish-American Women's Writing.* Edited by Lois Rubin. Newark: University of Delaware Press, 2005.

Cucinella, Catherine, ed. *Contemporary American Women Poets: An A-to-Z Guide.* Westport, Conn.: Greenwood Press, 2002.

Culp, Mildred Louise. "E. L. Doctorow." In *Twentieth-Century American-Jewish Fiction Writers.* Detroit: Gale, 1984.

———. "Wiesel's Memoir and God Outside Auschwitz." *Explorations in Ethnic Studies* 4, no. 1 (January 1981): 62–74.

Davenport, Gary. "The Blessed and the Forsaken." Review of *The Infinite Passion of Expectation: Twenty-five Stories* by Gina Berriault, *The Lights of Earth* by Gina Berriault, and *Love Medicine* by Louise Erdrich. *Kenyon Review* 7, no. 4 (Fall 1985): 122–125.

Davis, J. Madison. "The Literary Skills of Woody Allen." *West Virginia University Philological Papers* 29 (1983): 105–111.

Dewey, Joseph. "Andromeda on the Rocks: The Irony of Belonging in *The Last Jew in America.*" In *Leslie Fiedler and American Culture.* Newark: University of Delaware Press, 1999.

Dickstein, Lore. "Untitled Review." *New York Times,* 7 February 1988, BR21.

Doherty, Patricia. *Marge Piercy: An Annotated Bibliography.* Westport, Conn.: Greenwood Press, 1997.

Donnelly, Pat. "Not Yet 30, but Feeling Older." *Gazette,* 28 October 2006, J6.

Downey, Sharon D., and Richard A. Kallan. "Semi-Aesthetic Detachment: The Fusing of Fictional and External Worlds in the Situational Literature of Leon Uris." *Communication Monographs* 49, no. 3 (1982): 192–204.

Drucker, Sally Ann. "Yiddish, Yidgin, and Yezierska." *Yiddish* 6, no. 4 (1987): 99–113.

Duncan, Erika. "The Hungry Jewish Mother." In *The Lost Tradition: Mothers and Daughters in Literature.* Edited by Cathy N. Davidson and E. M. Broner. New York: Ungar, 1980.

"Edna Ferber Is Eulogized Here as Champion of Great Causes." *New York Times,* 19 April 1968, 47.

"Edna Ferber, Novelist, 82 Dies." *New York Times,* 17 April 1968, 1.

Elman, Richard. *Namedropping: Mostly Literary Memoirs.* Albany: SUNY Press, 1998.

———. *The Poorhouse State: The American Way of Life on Public Assistance.* New York: Pantheon Books, 1966.

"Erica Jong." Available online. URL: http://www.EricaJong.com. Accessed on March 17, 2006.

Fetherling, Doug. *The Five Lives of Ben Hecht.* Toronto, Canada: Lester and Orpen Limited, 1977.

Feuer, Menachem. "Almost Friends: Post-Holocaust Comedy, Tragedy, and Friendship in Jonathan Safran Foer's *Everything is Illuminated.*" *Shofar* 25, no. 2 (Winter 2007): 24–48.

Fiedler, Leslie. "Irwin Shaw: Adultery, the Last Politics." *Commentary* 22 (1956): 71–74.

Feinstein, Herbert. "Contemporary American Fiction: Harvey Swados and Leslie Fiedler." *Wisconsin Studies in Contemporary Literature* 2, no. 1 (Winter 1961): 79–98.

———. "Bernard Malamud." In *Twentieth-Century American-Jewish Fiction Writers.* Detroit: Gale, 1984.

Fine, Ellen S. *Legacy of Night: The Literary Universe of Elie Wiesel.* Albany: SUNY Press, 1982.

Fisch, Harold. "Israel Zangwill: Prophet of the Ghetto." *Judaism* 13 (1964): 407–421.

Fischer, G. K. *In Search of Jerusalem: Religion and Ethics in the Writings of A.M. Klein.* Montreal: McGill-Queen's University Press, 1975.

Fischthal, Hannah Berliner. "*The Nazarene* as a Jewish Novel." *Jewish Quarterly* [London] 41, no. 3 (Autumn 1994): 36–39.

———. "Sholem Asch and the Shift in His Reputation: 'The Nazarene' as Culprit or Victim?" Ph.D. diss., City University of New York, 1994.

————. "Uncle Moses." *When Joseph Met Molly: A Reader on Yiddish Film*. Edited by Sylvia Paskin. Nottingham, U.K.: Five Leaves, 1999.

Fogelman, Eva. "Julie Salamon." In *Holocaust Literature: An Encyclopedia of Writers and Their Work*. New York: Routledge, 2003.

Foster, Susan E. "Linguistic Literary Treasures: A Study of Yiddish-English Literary Dialect in the Works of Cahan, Yezierska, Gross, Rosten, and Roth." Master's Thesis, Sonoma State University, 2000.

Fox, Margalit. "Susan Sontag, Social Critic With Verve, Dies at 71." *New York Times,* 29 December 2004, A1,18.

Franciosi, Robert. "Detailing the Facts: Charles Reznikoff's Response to the Holocaust." *Contemporary Literature* 29 (1988): 241–264.

Fredericksen, Brooke. "Home Is Where the Text Is: Exile, Homeland, and Jewish American Writing." *Studies in American Jewish Literature* 11, no. 1 (Spring 1992): 36–44.

Freedman, Carl, ed. *Conversations with Isaac Asimov*. Jackson: University of Mississippi Press, 2005.

French, Marilyn. "Introduction." In *Weave of Women* by E. M. Broner. Bloomington: Indiana University Press, l985.

Frewin, Leslie. *The Late Mrs. Dorothy Parker*. New York: Macmillan, 1986.

Friedell, Deborah. "Bird of the Baskervilles." *New York Times*. Available online. URL: http://www.nytimes.com/2004/11/14/books/review/14FRIEDEL.html?ex=116909640 0&en=890f7b4977a9299c&ei=5070. Accessed on November 14, 2004.

Friedman, Lawrence S. *Understanding Isaac Bashevis Singer*. Columbia: University of South Carolina Press, 1988.

Frye, Joanne S. *Tillie Olsen: A Study of the Short Fiction*. New York: Twayne, 1995.

Fuchs, Daniel. *The Apathetic Bookie Joint*. New York: Methuen, 1979.

Fulford, Robert. "Eulogy to Genius: From a Friend and Fellow Titan." *Citizen's Weekly,* C14/Front.

Furman, Andrew. "Steve Stern's Magical Fiction of *Tikkun*." In *Contemporary Jewish American Writers and the Multicultural Dilemma: Return of the Exiled*. Syracuse, N.Y.: Syracuse University Press, 2000.

Galloway, David. *Edward Lewis Wallant*. Boston: Twayne, 1979.

Gelernter, David. "Redeeming the Lost." Review of *In the Image, Commentary* (December 2002): 72–74.

Gelpi, Albert. *Denise Levertov: Selected Criticism*. Ann Abor: University of Michigan Press, 1993.

Gelpi, Barbara Charlesworth, and Albert Gelpi, eds. *Adrienne Rich's Poetry and Prose*. New York: W.W. Norton, 1975.

Gentry, Marshall Bruce. "Newark Maid Feminism in Philip Roth's *American Pastoral*." *Shofar* 19, no. 1 (Fall 2000): 74–83.

Gessen, Keith. "Horror Tour." *New York Review of Books* 52, no. 14 (September 22, 2005): 68–72.

Giles, James R. *Irwin Shaw*. Boston: Twayne, 1983.

Giles, Patrick. "Susan Sontag, Writer and Witness." *National Catholic Reporter* 41, no. 10 (7 January 2005): 15.

Glazer, Miriyam. '*Daughters of Refugees of the Ongoing-Universal-Endless-Upheaval': Anne Roiphe and the Quest for Narrative Power in Jewish American Women's Fiction*. Edited by Jay L. Halio and Ben Siegel. Newark: University of Delaware Press, 1997.

"Gold, Herbert." In *Contemporary Literature Criticism: Criticism of the Works of Today's Novelists, Poets, Playwrights, Short Story Writers, Scriptwriters, and Other Creative Writers*. Detroit: Gale, 1973.

Gold, Sarah F. "Lost . . . and Found." *Publisher's Weekly* 253, no. 32 (14 August 2006): 173.

Goldberg, Marilyn. "The Soul-Searching of Norma Rosen." *Studies in American Jewish Literature* 3 (1983): 202–211.

Goldenberg, Myrna. "Identity, Memory, and Authority: An Introduction to Holocaust Poems by Hilary Tham, Myra Sklarew, and Dori Katz." *Studies in American Jewish Literature* 24 (2005): 137–144.

Goldman, Mark I. "Delmore Schwartz." In *Twentieth-Century American-Jewish Fiction Writers*. Detroit: Gale, 1984.

Goldstein, Rebecca. "Dark Afterthoughts on Fiction and the Self." *Dark Clock* 1 (March 2004): 92–97.

Gonshak, Henry. "'Rambowitz' versus the 'Schlemiel' in Leon Uris' *Exodus*." *Journal of American Culture* 22, no. 1 (Spring 1999): 9–16.

Goodyear, Dana. "The Gardner." *The New Yorker,* 1 September 2003, 104–111.

Gordon, Andrew. "Cynthia Ozick's 'The Shawl' and the Transitional Object." *Literature and Psychology* 40, nos. 1–2 (1994): 1–9.

Gorsky, Jonathan. "Elie Wiesel, Hasidism and the Hiddenness of God." *New Blackfriars* 85, no. 996 (March 2004): 133–143.

Gottfried, Martin. *Arthur Miller, His Life and Work.* Cambridge: DaCapo Press, 2003.

Goudie, Jeffrey Ann. Review of *Ghost Stories, Women's Review of Books* 12, nos. 10–11 (July 1995): 34.

Graeber, Laurel. "New and Noteworthy Paperbacks." *New York Times,* 22 February 1998, Sec. 7, p. 7.

Gratz, Rebecca. *Letters of Rebecca Gratz.* Edited, and with an introduction and notes by Rabbi David Philipson. Philadelphia: Jewish Publication Society of America, 1929.

Graver, Lawrence. *An Obsession with Anne Frank: Meyer Levin and the Diary.* London: University of California Press, 1995.

Greenberg, Jonathan. "Nathanael West and the Mystery of Feeling." *Modern Fiction Studies* 52, no. 3 (Fall 2006): 588–612.

Grödal, Hanne Tang. "Words, Words, Words." *Dolphin: Publications of the English Department, University of Aarhus* 18 (Spring 1990): 21–26.

Grosholz, Emily. *Telling the Barn Swallow: Poets on the Poetry of Maxine Kumin.* Boston: University Press of New England, 1997.

Gubar, Susan. "Empathic Identification in Anne Michaels's *Fugitive Pieces*: Masculinity and Poetry after Auschwitz." *Signs* 28, no. 1 (Fall 2002): 249–276.

———. *Poetry After Auschwitz: Remembering What One Never Knew.* Bloomington: Indiana University Press, 2003.

Guerard, Albert J. "Charyn's Azazian Prose." *Review of Contemporary Fiction* 12, no. 2 (Summer 1992): 126–142.

Gurganus, Allan. "Notes on Sontag." *Advocate,* 1 February 2005, 35.

Guttmann, Allen. "The Rise of a Lucky Few: Mary Antin and Abraham Cahan." In *The Jewish Writer in America: Assimilation and the Crisis of Identity.* New York: Oxford University Press, 1971.

Guttmann, Allen. "Saul Bellow's *Mr. Sammler.*" *Contemporary Literature* 14, no. 2 (Spring 1973): 157–168.

Haberman, Clyde. "Julie Salamon; Growing Up in Ohio in the Shadow of the Holocaust." *New York Times,* 22 May, 1996, C1.

Hadda, Janet. *Isaac Bashevis Singer: A Life.* New York, Oxford: Oxford University Press, 1997.

Halio, Jay L., and Ben Siegel, eds. "Immersions in the Postmodern: The Fiction of Allegra Goodman." In *Daughters of Valor: Contemporary Jewish-American Women Writers.* Newark: University of Delaware Press, 1998.

———, and Ben Siegel. *Turning Up the Flame: Philip Roth's Later Novels.* Newark: University of Delaware Press, 2005.

Halkin, Hillel. "Inhuman Comedy." *Commentary* (February 1992).

———. "Memorabilia." Review of *The World To Come, Commentary* (March 2006): 76–80.

Hamer, Katharine. "The Price of Fame: Cheap." *Vancouver Sun,* 18 November 2006, pg. C11.

Hamilton, Carole L. "Reading between the Lines of Gina Berriault's 'The Stone Boy.'" *Short Stories in the Classroom.* Edited by Carole L. Hamilton and Peter Kratzke. Urbana, Ill.: NCTE, 1999.

Hammond, Karla. "A Conversation with Marge Piercy." *Pulp* 1, no. 1 (1978): 10–12.

Hanson, John H. "The Child Archetype and Modern Primitivism: Kosinski's *The Painted Bird.*" *Studies in Literature* 14, no. 3 (1982): 85–95.

Harter, Carol, and James R. Thompson. *E. L. Doctorow.* Boston: Twayne, 1990.

———, and James R. Thompson. *John Irving.* Boston: Twayne, 1986.

Hartman, Geoffrey H. "Introduction: Darkness Visible." In *Holocaust Remembrance: The Shapes of Memory.* Edited by Geoffrey Hartman. Oxford and Cambridge, Mass.: Blackwell, 1994.

Heber, Janice Stewart. "The X-Factor in E. L. Doctorow's *Billy Bathgate*: Powerless Women and History as Myth." *Modern Language Studies* 22, no. 4 (Autumn 1992): 33–41.

Hedin, Benjamin. "A History That Never Happened: Philip Roth's *The Plot Against America.*" *Gettysburg Review* 18, no. 1 (2005): 93–106.

Heilbrun, Carolyn G. *Writing a Woman's Life.* New York: W.W. Norton, 1988.

Heldrich, Philip. "Connecting Surfaces: Gertrude Stein's Three Lives, Cubism, and the Metonymy of the Short Story Cycle." *Studies in Short Fiction* 34, no. 4 (Fall 1997): 427–440.

Heller, Joseph. *God Knows.* New York: Knopf, 1984.

Hellman, Lillian. *Pentimento.* New York: Signet, 1973.

Henault, Marie. *Stanley Kunitz.* Boston: Twayne, 1980.

Henriksen, Louise Levitas. "Afterword." In *The Open Cage: An Anzia Yezierska Collection.* New York: Persea Books, 1979.

Henry, Matthew A. "Problematized Narratives: History as Fiction in E. L. Doctorow's *Billy Bathgate.*" *Critique* 39, no. 1 (Fall 1997): 32–41.

Herzog, Anne F., and Janet E. Kaufman. *"How Shall We Tell Each Other of the Poet?"* New York: Palgrave, 1999.

Hindus, Milton, ed. *Charles Reznikoff: Man and Poet.* Orono, Me.: National Poetry Foundation, University of Maine at Orono, 1984.

Hirsch, Marianne. *Family Frames: Photography, Narrative, and Postmemory.* Cambridge, Mass.: Harvard University Press, 1997.

Hirt-Manheim, Aron. "The Art of Art Spiegelman." *Reform Judaism* (Spring 1987).

Hitchens, Christopher. "Susan Sontag: Remembering an Intellectual Heroine." *Slate.* Available online. URL: http://www.slate.com/id/2111506/. Accessed on December 29, 2004.

Hoffman, Eva. "After Such Knowledge: Memory, History, and the Aftermath of the Holocaust." *Kirkus Reviews,* 15 November, 2003.

Hoffman, Matthew. "Kunitz, Stanley." In *Jewish Writers of the Twentieth Century.* Edited by Sorrel Kerbel. New York: Fitzroy Dearborn, 2003.

Hornstein, Gail A. *To Redeem One Person Is to Redeem the World: The Life of Frieda Fromm-Reichmann.* New York: Free Press, 2000.

Howard, Ben. "A Secular Believer: The Agnostic Art of Maxine Kumin." *Shenandoah* 52, no. 2 (2002): 141–159.

Humm, Peter. "Reading the Lines: Television and New Fiction." In *Re-Reading English.* New York: Methuen, 1982.

Hunter, Jeffrey W., ed. "Tony Kusher." In *Contemporary Literary Criticism, Vol. 203: Criticism of the Works of Today's Novelists, Poets, Playwrights, Short Story Writers, Scriptwriters, and Other Creative Writers.* Detroit: Thomson Gale, 2005.

Illig, Joyce. "An Interview with Saul Bellow." *Publishers Weekly,* 22 October 1973, 74–77.

Imber, Samuel J., ed. *Modern Yiddish Poetry: An Anthology.* New York: East and West Publishing Co., 1927.

Irwin, E. P. "San Francisco Women Who Have Achieved Success." *Overland Monthly and Out West Magazine* 44, no. 5 (November 1904): 512ff.

Isaacs, Neil D. Introduction to *The Unknown Constellations,* by Harvey Swados. Urbana: University of Illinois Press, 1995.

Jackson, Livia Bitton. *Elli: Coming of Age in the Holocaust.* New York: Times Books, 1980.

———. *I Have Lived a Thousand Years: Growing Up in the Holocaust.* New York: Simon & Schuster Books for Young Readers, 1997.

James, Alan G. "The Master and the Laureate of the Jews: The Brief Friendship of Henry James and Emma Lazarus." *Henry James Review* 21, no. 1 (Winter 2000): 27–42.

Jarniewicz, Jerzy. "The Terror Normality in Jerzy Kosinski's *The Painted Bird.*" *Polish Review* 49, no. 1 (2004): 641–652.

Jewish Women's Archive. "JWA - Emma Lazarus - Introduction." Available online. URL: http://www.jwa.org/exhibits/wov/lazarus/el1.html. Accessed on March 14, 2006.

"Jo Sinclair, Novelist and Memoirist, 81." *New York Times* Available online. URL: http://query.nytimes.com/gst/fullpage.html?res=990CE7D6163AF930A25757C0A96 3958260. Accessed on April 13, 1995.

Johnson, Gary. "The Presence of Allegory: The Case of Philip Roth's *American Pastoral.*" *Narrative* 12, no. 3 (2004): 233–248.

Johnston, Georgia. "Narratologies of Pleasure: Gertrude Stein's *The Autobiography of Alice B. Toklas.*" *Modern Fiction Studies* 42, no. 3 (1996): 590–606.

Jones, Beverly. "Nathanael West's *Miss Lonelyhearts.*" In *Critical Essays on Nathanael West.* New York: G.K. Hall, 1994.

"Just Keep Moving, Regardless of Cost." *Toronto Star,* 26 February 2006, p. D08.

Kamel, Rose. "To Aggravate the Conscience: Grace Paley's Loud Voice." *Journal of Ethnic Studies* 11, no. 3 (Fall 1983): 29–49.

Kandiyoti, Dalia. "'Our Foothold in Buried Worlds': Place in Holocaust Consciousness and Anne Michaels's *Fugitive Pieces*." *Contemporary Literature* 45, no. 2 (Summer 2004): 300–330.

Kaplan, Brett Ashley. "Reading Race and the Conundrums of Reconciliation in Philip Roth's *The Human Stain*." In *Turning Up the Flame: Philip Roth's Later Novels*. Newark: University of Delaware Press, 2005.

Kartiganer, Donald. "Fictions of Metamorphosis: From *Goodbye, Columbus* to *Portnoy's Complaint*." In *Reading Philip Roth*. New York: St. Martin's Press, 1988.

Kaul, Arthur J., ed. *American Literary Journalists, 1945–1955*. Detroit: Gale Research, 1997.

Keats, John. *The Life and Times of Dorothy Parker: You Might as Well Live*. New York: Simon & Schuster, 1970.

Kersell, Nancy D. "Phantoms Past and Present in Holocaust Fiction." *Kentucky Philological Review* 14 (March 1999): 16–20.

Kellman, Steven G. *Redemption: The Life of Henry Roth*. New York: W.W. Norton, 2005.

Kellerman, S. G., and Irving Malin, eds. *Leslie Fiedler and American Culture*. Newark: University of Delaware Press, 1991.

Kessler-Harris, Alice. "Introduction." In *The Open Cage: An Anzia Yezierska Collection*. New York: Persea Books, 1979.

Kibler, James E., Jr., ed. *American Novelists since World War II*. Detroit: Gale Research, 1980.

Kiernan, Robert F. *Saul Bellow*. New York: Continuum Press, 1989.

Kimmage, Michael. "Lionel Trilling's *The Middle of the Journey* and the *Complicated Origins of the Neo-Conservative Movement*." *Shofar* 21, no. 3 (Spring 2003): 48–63.

Kinney, Arthur F. *Dorothy Parker*. Boston: Twayne, 1978.

———. "The Other Dorothy Parkers." In *The Critical Waltz: Essays on the Work of Dorothy Parker*. Madison, N.J.: Fairleigh Dickinson University Press, 2005.

Klin, Richard. Interview of Hugh Nissenson. *January Magazine*, November 2003.

Koppleman, Susan. *The Stories of Fannie Hurst*. New York: Feminist Press at the City University of New York, 2004.

Kotzen, Kip, and Thomas Beller, ed. *With Love and Squalor: 14 Writers Respond to the Work of J. D. Salinger*. New York: Broadway Books, 2001.

Krafchick, Marcelline. *World Without Heroes: The Brooklyn Novels of Daniel Fuchs*. Rutherford, N.J.: Fairleigh Dickinson University Press, 1988.

Kravitz, Bennett. "The Culture of Disease or the Disease of culture in *Motherless Brooklyn* and *Eve's Apple*." *Journal of American Culture* 26, no. 2 (June 2003): 171–179.

Kremer, S. Lillian. "From Buchenwald to Harlem: The Holocaust Universe of *The Pawnbroker*." In *Literature, the Arts, and the Holocaust*. Greenwood, Fla.: Penkeville, 1987.

———. *Witness through the Imagination: Ozick, Elman Cohen, Potok, Singer, Epstein, Bellow, Steiner, Wallant, Malamud: Jewish-American Holocaust Literature*. Detroit: Wayne State University Press, 1989.

Kresh, Paul. *Isaac Bashevis Singer: The Magician of West 86th Street*. New York: Dial Press, 1979.

Kroeger, Brooke. *Fannie: The Talent for Success of Writer Fannie Hurst*. New York: Times Books, 1999.

Krondorfer, Bjorn. "Review of *After Such Knowledge: Memory, History, and the Legacy of the Holocaust* by Eva Hoffman." *Holocaust and Genocide Studies* (October–November 2004): 291–293.

Krupnick, Mark. "Assimilation in Recent American Jewish Autobiographies." *Contemporary Literature* 34, no. 3 (1993): 457–462.

———. *Jewish Writing and the Deep Places of the Imagination*. Madison: University of Wisconsin Press, 2005.

Kunitz, Stanley. *A Kind of Order, a Kind of Folley: Essays and Conversations*. Boston: Little, Brown, 1975.

———. "The Testing-Tree." *The Poems of Stanley Kunitz 1928–1978*. Boston: Little, Brown, 1979.

Labrie, Ross. *Howard Nemerov*. Boston: Twayne, 1980.

Lahr, John. "Waiting for Odets." *The New Yorker*, 16 October 1992.

Lainoff, Seymour. *Ludwig Lewisohn.* Boston: Twayne, 1982.

Langdell, Cheri Colby. *Adrienne Rich: The Moment of Change.* Westport, Conn.: Praeger, 2004.

Langer, Lawrence. "A Fable of the Holocaust." *New York Times Book Review,* 3 November 1991.

———. *Versions of Survival: The Holocaust and the Human Spirit.* Albany: SUNY Press, 1982.

Lambert, Carol. "Friendship in *The Gates of the Forest*: Friends as 'Ladders.'" In *Is God Man's Friend? Theodicy and Friendship in the Novels of Elie Wiesel.* New York: Peter Lang, 2006.

Lavers, Norman. *Jerzy Kosinski.* Boston: Twayne, 1982.

Lax, Eric. *Woody Allen: A Biography.* Cambridge, Mass.: Da Capo Press, 2000.

Leer, Norman. "The Double Theme in Malamud's *The Assistant*: Dostoevsky with Irony." *Mosaic* 4, no. 3 (Spring 1971): 89–102.

Lenart-Cheng, Helga. "Autobiography as Advertisement: Why Do Gertrude Stein's Sentences Get Under Our Skin?" *New Literary History* 34, no. 1 (Winter 2003): 117–133.

Levi, Jan Heller. *A Muriel Rukeyser Reader.* New York: W.W. Norton, 1994.

Lichtenstein, Diane. *Writing Their Nations: The Tradition of Nineteenth-Century American Jewish Women Writers.* Bloomington: Indiana University Press, 1992.

Light, James F. *Nathanael West: An Interpretative Study.* Evanston, Ill.: Northwestern University Press, 1961.

Lilly, Paul R. *Words in Search of Victims: The Achievement of Jerzy Kosinski.* Kent: Kent State University Press, 1988.

Liptzin, Sol. *A History of Yiddish Literature.* Middle Village, N.Y.: Jonathan David, 1985.

Louit, Robert. "Erica Jong: Writing about Sex Is Harder for a Woman." In *Conversations with Erica Jong.* Jackson: University Press of Mississippi, 2002.

Lowin, Joseph. "Portrait of Rebecca Goldstein." *Hadassah Magazine* 78, no. 19 (June–July 1997).

Lyons, Bonnie. "Isaac Rosenfeld's Fiction: A Reappraisal." *Studies in American Jewish Literature* 1, no. 1 (1975): 3–9.

———. "Didn't I Know You?" In *Passion and Craft: Conversations with Notable Writers.* Urbana: University of Illinois Press, 1998.

———, and Bill Oliver. "'Don't I Know You?': An Interview with Gina Berriault." *Literary Review* 37, no. 4 (Summer 1994): 714–723.

MacAdams, William. *Ben Hecht: The Man Behind the Legend.* New York: Scribner, 1990.

MacArthur, Kathleen L. "Shattering the American Pastoral: Philip Roth's Vision of Trauma and the American Dream." *Studies in American Jewish Literature* 23 (2004): 15–26.

Macilwee, Michael. "Saul Bellow and Norman Mailer." *Saul Bellow Journal* 19, no. 1 (Winter 2003): 3–22.

Malamud, Bernard. *Idiots First.* New York: Dell, 1965.

Maliszewski, Paul. "Lie, Memory: Michael Chabon's Own Private Holocaust." *BookForum: The Review for Art, Fiction, & Culture* 12, no. 1 (April–May 2005): 4–8.

Manganaro, Elise Salem. "Voicing the Arab: Multivocality and Ideology in Leon Uris' *The Haj.*" *MELUS* 15, no. 4 (1988): 3–13.

Mann, Barbara. "Picturing the Poetry of Anna Margolin." *Modern Language Quarterly* (December 2002): 501–536.

Marom, Daniel. "Who Is the 'Mother of Exiles'? Jewish Aspects of Emma Lazarus' 'The New Colossus.'" *Prooftexts: A Journal of Jewish Literary History* 20, no. 3 (Autumn 2003): 231–261.

Marovitz, Sanford E. *Abraham Cahan.* New York: Twayne, 1996.

Martin, Wendy. *An American Triptych: Anne Bradstreet, Emily Dickinson, Adrienne Rich.* Chapel Hill: University of North Carolina Press, 1984.

Martin, J. B. *Ben Hecht.* Ann Arbor, Mich.: UMI Research Press, 1985.

Maxwell, Glyn. Book Review. *Times Literary Supplement,* 31 May 1991, 12.

Mazzeno, Laurence W. *Herman Wouk.* Edited by Frank Day. New York: Twayne, 1994.

McCracken, Samuel. "'Julia' and Other Fictions by Lillian Hellman." *Commentary* 77, no. 6 (1984): 35–43.

McDonald, Brian. "'The Real American Crazy Shit': On Adamism and Democratic Individuality in

American Pastoral." *Studies in American Jewish Literature* 23 (2004): 27–40.

McGlothlin, Erin. *Second Generation Holocaust Literature: Legacies of Survival and Perpetration*. Rochester, N.Y.: Camden House, 2006.

McGrath, Charles. "Roth, Haunted by Illness, Feels Fine." *New York Times,* 25 April 2006, E1.

McKay, Kim. "Double Discourse in John Irving's *The World According to Garp*." *Twentieth Century Literature* 38, no. 4 (Winter 1992): 457–475.

McNett, Gavin. "Festival of Wrath." *New York Times,* 9 January 2002, F21.

Meanor, Patrick. "Michael Chabon." In *American Novelists Since World War II: Fifth Series*. Detroit: Thomson Gale, 1996.

Meinke, Peter. *Howard Nemerov*. Minneapolis: University of Minnesota Press, 1968.

Melnick, Ralph. *The Life and Work of Ludwig Lewisohn*. Detroit: Wayne State University Press, 1998.

Mendelsohn, Michael. *Clifford Odets: Humane Dramatist*. DeLand, Fla.: Everett / Edwards, 1969.

Merrill, Robert. *Norman Mailer Revisited*. New York: Twayne, 1992.

Merrill, Sam. "*Playboy* Interview: Joseph Heller." In *Conversations with Joseph Heller*. Edited by Adam J. Sorkin. Jackson: University Press of Mississippi, 1993.

Meyer, Adam. "Putting the 'Jewish' Back in 'Jewish American Fiction': A Look at Jewish American Fiction from 1977 to 2002 and an Allegorical Reading of Nathan Englander's 'The Gilgul of Park Avenue.'" *Shofar* 22, no. 3 (Spring 2004): 104–120.

Meyer, Gerald. "Howard Fast: An American Leftist Reinterprets His Life." *Science & Society* 57, no. 1 (Spring 1993): 86–91.

Meyers, Helene. "The Death and Life of a Judith Shakespeare: Rebecca Goldstein's *Mazel*." *Shofar* 25, no. 3 (2007): 61–71.

Michaels, Anne. "Cleopatra's Love." In *Poetry and Knowing*. Edited by Tim Lilburn. Kingston, Canada: Quarry Press, 1995.

———. *Fugitive Pieces*. New York: Vintage International, 1998.

———. "Unseen Formations." In *Sudden Miracles: Eight Women Poets*. Edited by Rhea Tregebov. Toronto: Second Story Press, 1991.

———. *The Weight of Oranges/Miner's Pond*. Toronto: McClelland & Stewart, 1997.

Michaels, Walter Benn. "Plots Against America: Neoliberalism and Antiracism." *American Literary History* 18 (2006): 288–302.

Milbauer, Asher Z., and Donald G. Watson, eds. *Reading Philip Roth*. New York: St. Martin's Press, 1988.

Miller, Arthur. "A Boy Grew in Brooklyn." *Holiday* 17 (Mar. 1955).

———. *Collected Plays*. New York: Viking Press, 1957, 1981.

———. *Death of a Salesman: Revised Edition* (Viking Critical Library). New York: Penguin, 1996.

———. "In Memoriam." Unpublished Sketch, at the Humanities Research Center, University of Texas, Austin, 1932.

———. "Introduction." *Collected Plays*. New York: Viking, 1957.

———. "Morality and the Modern Drama." Interview with Philip Gelb. *Educational Theatre Journal* 10 (October 1958): 198–199.

Miller, Gabriel, ed. *Critical Essays on Clifford Odets*. Boston: G.K. Hall, 1991.

———. *Daniel Fuchs*. Boston: Twayne, 1979.

Mills, William. *The Stillness in Moving Things: The World of Howard Nemerov*. Memphis: Memphis State University Press, 1975.

Miles, Barry. *Ginsberg: A Biography*. London: Virgin Publishing Ltd., 2001.

Miron, Dan. "Sholom Aleichem." CD-Rom Edition. Jerusalem: Keter, 1971.

Mitchell, Mitchell. "S.J. Perelman." In *Encyclopedia Brunoiana*. Providence, R.I.: Brown University Library, 1993.

"Montague Marsden Glass." *Columbia Encyclopedia*. 6th ed. 2007.

Morris, Ann R. "The Importance of Names in Garp's and Irving's World." *Notes on Contemporary Literature* 14, no. 5 (November 1984): 3–4.

Morris, Christopher, ed. *Conversations with E. L. Doctorow*. Jackson: University Press of Mississippi, 1999.

Mottram, Eric. "Arthur Miller: Development of a Political Dramatist in America." In *Arthur Miller: A Collection of Critical Essays*. Edited by Robert W.

Corrigan. Englewood Cliffs, N.J.: Prentice Hall, 1969.

Nadel, I. B. "The Day of the Locust." In *Reference Guide to American Literature.* Edited by Jim Kamp. Detroit: St. James Press, 1994.

Navasky, Victor. *Naming Names.* New York: Viking Press, 1980.

Nelson, Benjamin. *Arthur Miller.* New York: David McKay, 1970.

Nissenson, Hugh. Review of *The Chosen, New York Times Book Review,* 7 May 1967.

———. "A Sense of the Holy." In *Spiritual Quests: The Art and Craft of Religious Writing.* Edited by William Zinsser. Boston: Houghton Mifflin, 1988.

Nitzsche, Jane Chance. "'Isadora Icarus:' The Mythic Unity of Erica Jong's *Fear of Flying.*" *Rice University Studies* 64, no. 1 (1978): 89–100.

Nordell, J. D. "Poetry Microreviews: Drunk from the Bitter Truth: The Poems of Anna Margolin." *Boston Review* (September/October 2006).

O'Connell, Nicholas, ed. *At the Field's End: Interviews with 22 Pacific Northwest Writers.* Seattle: University of Washington Press, 1998.

Omer-Sherman, Ranen. "E. M. Broner's Aesthetics of Dispersal in A Weave of Women." *Modern Jewish Studies* 13, no. 4 (2004): 28–39.

———. "Tradition and Desire in Allegra Goodman's *Kaaterskill Falls.*" *MELUS* 29, no. 2 (Summer 2004): 265–289.

Orr, Gregory. *Stanley Kunitz: An Introduction to the Poetry.* New York: Columbia University Press, 1985.

Osterweis, Rollin G. *Rebecca Gratz: A Study in Charm.* New York: Putnam, 1935.

Paley, Grace. "Nights in the Gardens of Brooklyn." *Boston Review.* Available online. URL: http://bostonreview.net/BR29.3/paley.html. Summer 2004. Accessed on January 31, 2007.

Parker, Dorothy. "Big Blonde." In *The Portable Dorothy Parker.* New York: Viking Press, 1973.

Parker, Derek Royal. Interview of Thane Rosenbaum, 2007.

———. "Fictional Realms of Possibility: Reimagining the Ethnic Subject in Philip Roth's *American Pastoral.*" *Studies in American Jewish Literature* 20 (2001): 1–16.

———, ed. *Philip Roth: New Perspectives on an American Author.* Westport, Conn.: Greenwood-Praeger, 2005.

———. "Philip Roth's America: The Later Novels." *Studies in American Jewish Literature* 23 (2004): 1–181.

———. "Postmodern Jewish Identity in Philip Roth's *The Counterlife.*" *Modern Fiction Studies* 48, no. 2 (Summer 2002): 422–443.

Parks, John G. "Edward Louis Wallant." In *Holocaust Novelists.* Detroit: Gale, 2004.

Parrish, Timothy L. "The End of Identity: Philip Roth's *American Pastoral.*" *Shofar* 19, no. 1 (Fall 2000): 84–99.

———. "Ralph Ellison: The Invisible Man in Roth's *Human Stain.*" *Contemporary Literature* 45, no. 3 (Fall 2004): 421–459.

"'Partners Again'—Hilarious." *New York Times,* 2 May 1922, p. 27.

Pearlman, Mickey, and Abby H. P. Werlock. *Tillie Olsen.* Boston: Twayne, 1991.

Pettit, Rhonda S. *A Gendered Collision: Sentimentalism and Modernism in Dorothy Parker's Poetry and Fiction.* Madison, N.J.: Farleigh Dickinson University Press, 2000.

———, and Regina Barreca. *The Critical Waltz: Essays on the Work of Dorothy Parker.* Madison, N.J.: Fairleigh Dickinson University Press, 2005.

Phillips, John, and Anne Hollander. "Lillian Hellman." In *Writers at Work: The Paris Review Interviews.* New York: Viking, 1967.

Pinsker, Sanford. *Jewish American Fiction 1917–1987.* New York: Twayne, 1992.

Plank, Karl A. "The Survivor's Return: Reflections on Memory and Place." *Judaism* 38, no. 3 (Summer 1989): 263–277.

Plimpton, George, ed. *Writers at Work: The Paris Review Interviews.* New York: Viking, 1981.

Pollack, Eileen. "Judaism, Sacred and Profane." *Washington Post,* 16 Apr. 1992, D4.

Pollock, Zailig, ed. *A.M. Klein Complete Poems: Part 1—Original Poems, 1926–1934.* Toronto: University of Toronto Press, 1990.

Potok, Chaim. *My Name Is Asher Lev.* New York: Knopf, 1972.

Pratt, Norma Fain. "Culture and Radical Politics: Yiddish Women Writers, 1890–1940." *Ameri-*

can *Jewish History* 70, no. 1 (September 1980): 68–90.

Raney, Stanford. "The Novels of Edward Wallant." *Colorado Quarterly* 17 (1969): 393–405.

Rapf, Joanna E. "Sidney Lumet and the Politics of the Left: The Centrality of Daniel." *Literature Film Quarterly* 31, no. 2 (2003): 148–155.

Raskin, Jonah. *American Scream: Allen Ginsberg's* Howl *and the Making of the Beat Generation.* Berkeley: University of California Press, 2004.

Ravitz, Abe C. *Imitations of Life: Fannie Hurst's Gaslight Sonatas.* Carbondale: Southern Illinois University Press, 1997.

Raymond, Gerard. "Q & A with Tony Kushner." *Theatre Week,* 20–26 December 1993, 14–20.

Reed, Whittemore. "Safari among the Wariri." *New Republic* 140, 16 March 1959, 17–18.

"Review of *The March.*" *Sunday Telegraph* (London), 29 January 2006, 53.

Rich, Adrienne. *Arts of the Possible: Essays and Conversations.* New York: W.W. Norton, 2001.

———. *What Is Found There: Notebooks on Poetry and Politics.* New York: W.W. Norton, 1993.

Richler, Mordecai. "He Who Laughs Last." *New York Times,* 23 September 1984, sec. 7, p. 1.

Rideout, Walter B. "The Long Retreat." In *The Radical Novel in the United States: Some Interrelations of Literature and Society.* Cambridge, Mass.: Harvard University Press, 1956.

Roach, Korri R. "Jonathan Rosen: A Critical Treatment." Master's thesis, Brigham Young University. Department of English, 2005.

Rodgers, Bernard F., Jr. *Philip Roth.* Boston: Twayne, 1978.

Roemer, Danielle M. "The Personal Narrative and Salinger's *Catcher in the Rye.*" *Western Folklore* 51, no. 1 (January 1992): 5–10.

Rollyson, Carl. *Reading Susan Sontag: A Critical Introduction to Her Work.* Chicago: Ivan R. Dee, 2001.

———. *Susan Sontag: The Making of an Icon.* New York: Norton, 2000.

Rollyson, Carl, and Lisa Paddock. *Susan Sontag: The Making of an Icon.* New York: W.W. Norton, 2000.

Rosen, Alan. *Sounds of Defiance: The Holocaust, Multilingualism, and the Problem of English.* Lincoln: University of Nebraska Press, 2005.

Rosen, Gerald. *Zen in the Art of J. D. Salinger.* Berkley, Calif.: Creative Arts Book Company, 1977.

Rosen, Jonathan. "The Fabulist: How I. B. Singer Translated Himself into American Culture." *The New Yorker* 80, no. 15 (7 June 2004): 93.

———. "Writer, Interrupted: The Resurrection of Henry Roth." *The New Yorker* 88, no. 22 (August 1, 2005): 74–79.

Rosen, Norma. *Touching Evil.* New York: Harcourt Brace, 1969.

———. "The Holocaust and the American Jewish Novelist." *Midstream* 20 (October 1974).

Rosenberg, Ruth. "Norma Rosen." In *Twentieth-Century American-Jewish Fiction Writers.* Edited by Daniel Walden. Detroit: Gale, 1984.

Rosenbaum, Ron. "Giving Death a Face." *New York Times,* 24 September 2006, sec. 7, p. 1.

Ross, George. "Death of a Salesman in the Original." *Commentary* 11 (February 1951): 184–186.

Roth, Lawrence. "Pedagogy and the Mother Tongue: Irena Klepfisz's "Di Rayze Aheym/The Journey Home."" *Symposium* 52, no. 4 (Winter 1999): 269–279.

Roth Papers: Archives of the American Jewish Historical Society in New York.

Roth, Philip. *The Plot Against America.* New York: Houghton Mifflin, 2004.

Rothschild, Matthew. "Interview with Adrienne Rich." *The Progressive.* Available online. URL: http://www.progressive.org/rothrich9401.htm. Accessed on January 6, 2007.

Rovit, Earl. "Nathanael West." In *Reference Guide to American Literature.* Edited by Jim Kamp. Detroit: St. James Press, 1994.

Rowe, John Carlos. "Naming What Is Inside: Gertrude Stein's Use of Names in *Three Lives.*" *Novel: A Forum on Fiction* 36, no. 2 (Spring 2003): 219–243.

Rubin, Merle. "Fiction Roundup: New Novels by Kotlowitz, Gray, and Moore; *Sea Changes,* by Robert Kotlowitz." *Christian Science Monitor,* 28 November 1986, 34.

Rubin, Stephen E. "Conversations with the Author of *I Never Promised You a Rose Garden.*" *Psychoanalytic Review* 59 (1972): 201–216.

Rubin, Steven J. *Meyer Levin.* Boston: Twayne, 1982.

Rubin, Steven J. "Style and Meaning in Mary Antin's *The Promised Land*: A Reevaluation." *Studies in American Jewish Literature* 5 (1986): 29–34.

Ruderman, Judith. *Joseph Heller*. New York: Continuum, 1991.

Rukeyser, Muriel. *The Life of Poetry*. Ashfield, Mass.: Paris Press, 1996.

Ryan, Michael. "Interview with Stanley Kunitz." *American Poetry Observed: Poets on Their Work*. Edited by Joe David Bellamy. Urbana: University of Illinois Press, 1984.

"S. J. Perelman, Humorist, Is Dead." *New York Times*, 18 October 1979, A1, D22.

Sabini, M., and Kenneth Lambert. "Illness as Metaphor (Book). *Journal of Analytical Psychology* 24, no. 3 (July 1979): 270–272.

Safer, Elaine B. *Mocking the Age: The Later Novels of Philip Roth*. Albany: SUNY Press, 1996.

———. "The Tragicomic in Philip Roth's *Sabbath's Theater*." In *American Literary Dimensions: Poems and Essays in Honor of Melvin J. Friedman*. Newark: University of Delaware Press, 1999.

Salamon, Julie. "The Long Voyage Home." *Harper's Bazaar*, February 1994, 134–139.

Salt, Jeremy. "Fact and Fiction in the Middle Eastern Novels of Leon Uris." *Journal of Palestine Studies* 14, no. 3 (1985): 54–63.

Sanders, Ronald. *The Downtown Jews: Portraits of an Immigrant Generation*. New York: Harper & Row, 1969.

Saperstein, Jeffrey. "Irony and Cliché: Malamud's *The Natural* in the 1980s." *Literature Film Quarterly* 24, no. 1 (1996): 84–87.

Savran, David. "Tony Kushner." In *Speaking on Stage: Interviews with Contemporary American Playwrights*. Edited by Philip C. Kolin and Colby H. Kullman. Tuscaloosa: University of Alabama Press, 1996.

Sayers, Sohnya. *Susan Sontag: The Elegiac Modernist*. New York: Routledge, 1990.

Schaeffer, Susan Fromberg. "The Writer on Her Work." In *Anya*. New York: W.W. Norton, 2004.

Schamp, Jutta. "Beyond Association: Difference and Reconfiguration in the Works of Irena Klepfisz, Jyl Lyn Felman, and Rebecca Goldstein." *Zeitschrift fur Anglistik und Amerikanistik* 47, no. 3 (1999): 229–243.

Schiff, Ellen. "Clifford Odets, Awake and Sing, and the Dawn of the American Jewish Theatre." Available online. URL: http://www2.jewishculture.org/programs/350/icons/schiff/.2. Accessed on November 12, 2006.

Schneider, Steven. Book Review of *Dead Men's Praise, Women in Judaism: A Multidisciplinary Journal* 2, no. 2 (Spring 2001).

Schoen, Carol B. *Anzia Yezierska*. Boston: Twayne, 1982.

Schreiber, Maeera. "The End of Exile: Jewish Identity and Its Diasporic Poetics." *PMLA* 113, no. 2 (March 1998): 273–287.

Schulz, Max F. "The Family Chronicle as a Paradigm of History." *The Achievement of Isaac Bashevis Singer*. Edited by Marcia Allentuck. Carbondale and Edwardsville: Southern Illinois University Press, 1969.

Schumacher, Michael. *Dharma Lion: A Biography of Allen Ginsberg*. New York: St. Martin's Press, 1994.

Schwartz, Richard A. *Woody, From Antz to Zelig: A Reference Guide to Woody Allen's Creative Work, 1964–1998*. Westport, Conn.: Greenwood Press, 2000.

Scott, Robert F. "'Sweets' and 'Bitters': *Fanny* and the Feminization of the Eighteenth-Century Novel." *Midwest Quarterly* 42, no. 1 (Autumn 2000): 81–93.

Shands, Kerstin W. *The Repair of the World: The Novels of Marge Piercy*. Westport, Conn.: Greenwood Press, 1994.

Shapiro, Ann R., ed. *Jewish American Women Writers: A Bio-Bibliographical and Critical Sourcebook*. Westport, Conn.: Greenwood Press, 1994.

Shaw, Irwin. *Short Stories: Five Decades*. New York: Delacorte, 1978.

Shechner, Mark. "Steve Stern (1947–   )." In *Contemporary Jewish-American Novelists: A Bio-Critical Sourcebook*. Edited by Joel Shatzky and Michael Taub. Westport, Conn.: Greenwood Press, 1997.

———. *Up Society's Ass, Copper: Rereading Philip Roth*. Madison: University of Wisconsin Press, 2003.

Shiffman, Dan. "The Ingratiating Humor of Leo Rosten's Hyman Kaplan Stories." *Studies in American Jewish Literature* 18 (1999): 93–101.

Shnayerson, Michael. *Irwin Shaw: A Biography*. New York: Putnam, 1989.

Shoben, Edward Joseph, Jr. *Lionel Trilling.* New York: Frederick Ungar, 1981.

Shostak, Debra. *Philip Roth—Countertexts, Counterlives.* Columbia: University of South Carolina Press, 2004.

Sicher, Efraim, ed. *Holocaust Novelists.* Detroit: Gale, 2004.

Siegel, Ben. "Artists and Opportunists in Saul Bellow's Humboldt's Gift." *Contemporary Literature* 19, no. 2 (1978): 143–164. Reprinted in Critical Essays on Saul Bellow. Edited by Stanley Trachtenberg. *Critical Essays on American Literature.* Boston: G.K. Hall, 1979.

———. "The Brothers Singer: More Similarities than Differences." *Contemporary Literature* 22, no. 1 (Winter 1981): 42–57.

———. *The Controversial Sholem Asch: An Introduction to his Fiction.* Bowling Green, Ohio: Bowling Green University Popular Press, 1976.

———, ed. *Critical Essays on E. L. Doctorow.* New York: G.K. Hall, 2000.

———. "Introduction to Nathanael West." In *Critical Essays on Nathanael West.* Edited by Ben Siegel. New York: G.K. Hall, 1994.

Siegel, Laurie. "All That You Can't Leave Behind." *Jerusalem Post,* 11 August 2006, 30.

Siegel, Lee. "Review of *Namedropping.*" *New York Times Book Review,* 23 August 1998, 11–13.

Silvers, Robert B. "An Interview with Alfred Kazin." *Horizon* 4 (July 1962).

Singer, Elliot, and David Wittenberg. "Cornell Sun Interviews Best-Selling Novelist." *Cornell Sun,* 21 November 2006.

Singer, Isaac Bashevis. *In My Father's Court.* New York: Farrar, Straus and Giroux, 1966.

Skibell, Joseph. "In the Invisible Courtyards of Chaim Skibelski." *New York Times Sophisticated Traveler Magazine,* 8 November 1998.

Smith, Danita. "Depression His Linchpin, A Novelist Keeps Going." *New York Times,* 26 July 2001.

Smith, Janna Malamud. *My Father Is a Book: A Memoir of Bernard Malamud.* Boston: Houghton Mifflin, 2006.

Smith, Larry. "Herbert Gold: Belief and Craft." *Ohioana Quarterly* 21 (1978): 148–156.

Snodgrass, Kathleen. *The Fiction of Hortense Calisher.* Newark: University of Delaware Press, 1993.

Sol, Adam. "'Were It not for the Yetzer Hara:' Eating, Knowledge, and the Physical in Jonathan Rosen's *Eve's Apple.*" *Shofar* 22, no. 3 (Spring 2004): 95–103.

Solomon, Deborah. "The Fabulist." *New York Times Magazine,* 8 April 2007, 18.

Solotaroff, Theodore, ed. *Alfred Kazin's America.* New York: Harper Collins, 2003.

———. "Isaac Rosenfeld: The Human Use of Literature." *Commentary* 33 (1962): 395–404.

———. "Jewish Camp." Review of *Once upon a Droshky. Commentary* Mar. 1964, 76–78. Reprinted in *The Red Hot Vacuum and Other Pieces on the Writing of the Sixties.* Edited by Theodore Solotaroff. New York: Atheneum, 1970.

Sontag, Susan. *AIDS and Its Metaphors.* New York: Farrar, Straus and Giroux, 1988.

Sorkin, Adam J. "'What Are We, Animals?' Grace Paley's World of Talk and Laughter." *Studies in American Jewish Literature* 2 (1982): 144–154.

Spencer, Elizabeth. "Flotsam of the Heart." *New York Times,* 8 April 1984, 9.

Spencer, Luke. "A Poetics of Engagement in E. L. Doctorow's *Ragtime.*" *Language and Literature: Journal of the Poetics and Linguistics Association* 5, no. 1 (1996): 19–30.

Spiegelman, Art. "The Paranoids Were Right." Interview by Alana Newhouse. *Forward,* 6 September 2002.

Spignesi, Stephen J. *The Woody Allen Companion.* Kansas City, Mo.: Andrews and McMeel, 1992.

Stahl, Nanette, ed. *Sholem Asch Reconsidered.* New Haven, Conn.: Beinecke, 2004.

Stanley, Sandra Kumamoto. "Mourning the 'Greatest Generation': Myth and History in Philip Roth's *American Pastoral. Twentieth-Century Literature* 51, no. 1 (2005): 1–24.

Stark, John. "Alienation and Analysis in Doctorow's *The Book of Daniel.*" *Critique* 16, no. 3 (1975): 101–110.

Steed, J. P. "Malamud's *God's Grace* and the Theme of Reversal: Or, Old Joke, Better Version." *Studies in American Jewish Literature* 20 (2001): 17–28.

Stephens, Michael. "A Different King of Two-Fisted, Two-Breasted Terror: Seymour Krim and Creative Nonfiction." *Creative Nonfiction* 2 (1994): 43–62.

Stern, David. "Malamud: Seen and Unseen." In *The Magic Worlds of Bernard Malamud.* Albany: State University of New York Press, 2001.

Stern, Richard G. "Lillian Hellman on her Plays." *Contact* 3 (1959): 113–119.

Sternlicht, Sanford. *Chaim Potok: A Critical Companion.* Westport, Conn.: Greenwood Press, 2000.

Strong, Paul. "Firing into the Dark: Sexual Warfare in *Portnoy's Complaint.*" *International Fiction Review* 10, no. 1 (Winter 1983): 41–43.

Sutton, Walter. "A Conversation with Denise Levertov." *Minnesota Review,* nos. 3–4 (December 1965): 322–338.

Tanner, Stephen L. *Lionel Trilling.* Boston: Twayne, 1988.

Taylor, Kate. "The Philosopher Novelist." *New York Sun,* 31 May 2006, 16.

Templin, Charlotte. "Beauty and Gender in Alix Kates Shulman's Memoirs of an Ex-Prom Queen." In *Women in Literature: Reading Through the Lens of Gender.* Westport, Conn.: Greenwood Press, 2003.

———, ed. *Conversations with Erica Jong.* Jackson: University Press of Mississippi, 2002.

———. *Feminism and the Politics of Literary Reputation: The Example of Erica Jong.* Lawrence: University Press of Kansas, 1995.

Thornton, William H. "American Political Culture in Mailer's *The Naked and the Dead.*" In *EurAmerica: A Journal of European and American Studies* 22, no. 1 (March 1992): 95–122.

Tuerk, Richard. "Assimilation in Jewish-American Autobiography: Mary Antin and Ludwig Lewisohn." *A/B: Auto/Biography Studies* 3, no. 2 (Summer 1987): 26–33.

Udelson, Joseph H. *Dreamer of the Ghetto: The Life and Works of Israel Zangwill.* Tuscaloosa: University of Alabama Press, 1990.

Vendler, Helen. *Part of Nature, Part of Us: Modern American Poets.* Cambridge, Mass.: Harvard University Press, 1980.

Vogel, Dan. "From Milkman to Salesman: Glimpses of the Galut." *Studies in American Jewish Literature* 10, no. 2 (Fall 1991): 172–178.

Wagenknecht, Edward. *Daughters of the Covenant: Portraits of Six Jewish Women.* Amherst: University of Massachusetts Press, 1983.

Wagner-Martin, Linda. *"Favored Strangers": Gertrude Stein and Her Family.* New Brunswick, N.J.: Rutgers University Press, 1995.

———. *Denise Levertov.* New York: Twayne, 1967.

Walden, Daniel, ed. *Conversations with Chaim Potok.* Jackson: University Press of Mississippi, 2001.

———, ed. *Studies in American Jewish Literature, Number 4: The World of Chaim Potok.* Albany: SUNY Press, 1985.

Walker, Sue, and Eugenia Hamner, eds. *Ways of Knowing: Essays on Marge Piercy.* Mobile, Ala.: Negative Capability Press, 1991.

Wasserstein, Wendy. *The Heidi Chronicles and Other Plays.* New York: Harcourt Brace Jovanovich, 1990.

———. *Shiksa Goddess; Or, How I Spent My Forties.* New York: Knopf, 2001.

Watts, Eileen H. "The Art of Racism: Blacks, Jews and Language in *The Tenants.*" *Studies in American Jewish Literature* 15 (1996): 42–48.

Weales, Gerald. *Odets the Playwright.* London and New York: Methuen, 1985.

Weaver, Carole McKewin. *Tasting Stars: The Tales of Rabbi Nachman in Anne Roiphe's* Lovingkindness. Edited by Mickey Perlman. Westport, Conn.: Greenwood Press, 1989.

Wechsler, Lawrence. "Mighty Mouse." *Rolling Stone,* 20 November 1986.

Weiner, Justus Reid. "Lillian Hellman: The Fiction of Autobiography." *Gender Issues* 21, no. 1 (Winter 2003): 78–83.

Weissbrod, Rachel. "*Exodus* as a Zionist Melodrama." *Israel Studies* 4, no. 1 (Spring 1999): 129–152.

"Whittaker Chambers and The Middle of the Journey." *New York Review of Books,* 17 April 1975, 18–24.

Wilentz, Gay. "Jo Sinclair (Ruth Seid) (1913–   )." *Jewish-American Women Writers: A Bio-Bibliographical and Critical Sourcebook.* Edited by Ann R. Shapiro. Westport, Conn.: Greenwood Press, 1994.

———. "(Re)Constructing Identity: 'Angled' Presentation in Sinclair/Seid's *Wasteland.*" In *Multicultural Literatures through Feminist/Poststructuralist Lenses.* Knoxville: University of Tennessee Press, 1993.

Wilson, Jonathan. "*Herzog*'s Fictions of the Self." In *Saul Bellow: A Mosaic.* New York: Peter Lang, 1992.

Wilson, Raymond J., III. "Control and Freedom in *The Naked and the Dead.*" *Texas Studies in Lit-*

erature and Language 28, no. 2 (Summer 1986): 164–181.

Winchell, Mark Roydon. *Leslie Fiedler.* Boston: Twayne, 1985.

———. *"Too Good To Be True:" The Life and Work of Leslie Fiedler.* Columbia: University of Missouri Press, 2002.

Wohlgelernter, Maurice. "Herbert Gold: A Boy of Early Autumn." *Studies in American Jewish Literature* 10, no. 2 (Fall 1991): 136–171.

Wolitz, Seth L. "The Americanization of Tevye or Boarding the Jewish *Mayflower.*" *American Quarterly* 40, no. 4 (December 1988): 514–536.

Woodson, Jon. *A Study of Joseph Heller's* Catch-22: *Going Around Twice.* New York: Peter Lang, 2001.

Woolf, Mike. "Charyn in the 1960s: Among the Jews." *Review of Contemporary Fiction* 12, no. 2 (Summer 1992): 143–151.

———. "Exploding the Genre: The Crime Fiction of Jerome Charyn." In *American Crime Fiction: Studies in the Genre.* New York: St. Martin's Press, 1988.

Workman, Mark E. "The Serious Consequences of Ethnic Humor in *Portnoy's Complaint.*" *Midwestern Folklore* 13, no. 1 (Spring 1987): 16–26.

Wouk, Herman. "Herman Wouk: 'A Faithful Adaptation.'" *New York Times,* 14 June 1981.

Zipperstein, Steven J. "Isaac Rosenfeld's Dybbuk and Rethinking Literary Biography." *Partisan Review* 69, no. 1 (Winter 2002): 102–117.

LIST OF CONTRIBUTORS

Victoria Aarons, Trinity University

Brian Adler, Valdosta State University

Matthew Antonio, University of South Florida

Samuel I. Bellman, California State Polytechnic University, Pomona

Rosalind Benjet, Dallas Jewish Historical Society/ Independent Scholar

Josef Benson, University of South Florida

Alan L. Berger, Florida Atlantic University

Sarah Bylund, Emerson College

Ezra Cappell, University of Texas at El Paso

Lauren Cardon, Tulane University

Ben Child, Independent Scholar

Mark Cohen, Independent Scholar

M. Ryan Croker, Brigham Young University

Gloria L. Cronin, Brigham Young University

Kathena H. DeGrassi, The State University of New York at New Paltz

Nathan Devir, Penn State University

Josue Aristides Diaz, Texas A & M University

Jason Douglas, Brigham Young University

Emily Dyer, Brigham Young University

Brooklyn Bunker Evans, Brigham Young University

Mary Kathleen Eyring, Independent Scholar

Lourdes Fernandez, Florida Atlantic University

Ellen S. Fine, Kingsborough Community College of the City University of New York

Hannah Berliner Fischthal, St. Johns University

Elise Flanagan, Florida Atlantic University

Andrew Furman, Florida Atlantic University

Jeanne Genis, Florida Atlantic University

Sally Giles, University of California, San Diego

Myrna Goldenberg, Johns Hopkins University and the University of Maryland

Sandor Goodhart, Purdue University

Veronica Goosey, Brigham Young University

Andrew Gordon, University of Florida

George Gordon-Smith, Independent Scholar

Holly Rose Hansen, Independent Scholar

Trenton Hickman, Brigham Young University

Jacob Hodgen, Brigham Young University

Jay Hopler, University of South Florida

Marie Horne, Brigham Young University

Melissa Huff, Independent Scholar

Eric Izant, Independent Scholar

Sarah E. Jenkins, Brigham Young University

Iris Nicole Johnson, Texas A & M University, Commerce

Kimberly Jones, Independent Scholar

B. W. Jorgensen, Brigham Young University

Aaron Keeley, Independent Scholar

Rebecca Kuhn, Florida Atlantic University

Jessica Lang, the City University of New York

Vanessa Lefton, Florida Atlantic University

Holli G. Levitsky, Loyola Marymount University

Anna Lewis, Brigham Young University

Rachel Ligairi, Independent Scholar

Suzanne Evertsen Lundquist, Brigham Young University

Dena Mandel, University of Alaska

Sanford E. Marovitz, Kent State University
Jacqueline May, Florida Atlantic University
Rachel Mayrer, University of Delaware
Robert S. Means, Brigham Young University
Asher Z. Milbauer, Florida International University
Daniel K. Muhlestein, Brigham Young University
Gila Safran Naveh, University of Cincinnati
Caren S. Neile, Florida Atlantic University
Daniel W. Newton, Brigham Young University
Sara D. Nyffenegger, University of Zürich
Monica Osborne, Purdue University
Daniele Pantano, Florida Southern College
C. Lee Player, Independent Scholar
Korri Roach, University of Colorado at Boulder
Jacob Levi Robertson, Independent Scholar
Kent Chapin Ross, Texas A & M University, Commerce
Scott L. Ross, Brigham Young University
Derek Parker Royal, Texas A & M University
Lois Rubin, Penn State University

Elisabeth Sandberg, Woodbury University
Jan Schmidt, The State University of New York
Andrew Schultz, Independent Scholar
Ben Siegel, California State Polytechnic University, Pomona
Phillip A. Snyder, Brigham Young University
Stephen Tanner, Brigham Young University
Pauline Uchmanowicz, The State University of New York at New Paltz
Joe Vogel, Independent Scholar
Jay Waitkus, Florida Atlantic University
Daniel Walden, Penn State University
Brian Wall, Independent Scholar
Eileen H. Watts, Torah Academy of Greater Philadelphia
Eliot Wilcox, Orem Public Library
Ginna Wilkerson, University of South Florida
Jacob Wilkes, Independent Scholar
Alexis Wilson, Indiana University
Bruce W. Young, Brigham Young University

INDEX

Note: **Boldface** page numbers indicate main entries.

A

Aaron, Eliezer. *See* Fiedler, Leslie
"Aaron Makes a Match" (Stern) 162
Abbott, Jack Henry 152
"About the Typefaces Not Used in This Edition" (Foer) 90
Abraham, Pearl xxiv
Accident, The (Wiesel) 300, 315, 316
Accidents of Influence (Rosen) 253
acculturation. *See also* assimilation
  Lewisohn (Ludwig) on 169
  Yezierska (Anzia) on 37
"Act of Defiance, An" (Rosenbaum) 67
Actual, The (Bellow) 28–29
Admirable Woman, An (Cohen) 53
Adrienne Rich: The Moment of Change (Langdell) 247
Adventures of Augie March, The (Bellow) xxi, **3–4,** 27
Advertisements for Myself (Mailer) 174, 175
aesthetics 4, 282
"Aesthetics of Silence, The" (Sontag) 282

After (Bukiet) 40
"After Love" (Kumin) 156
After Such Knowledge (Hoffman) 126
After the Fall (Miller) 192
Against Interpretation (Sontag) **4–5,** 134, 282
Age of Enormity, An: Life and Writing in the Forties and Fifties (Rosenfeld) 255, 256
Age of Happy Problems (Gold) 106
aging
  Berriault (Gina) on 322
  Englander (Nathan) on 92
  Miller (Arthur) on 62, 63
  Parker (Dorothy) on 31
  Rosen (Jonathan) on 252
  Roth (Philip) on 73, 266–267
  Salinger (J. D.) on 46
  Wasserstein (Wendy) on 309
  Yezierska (Anzia) on 327
agitprop play 306
AIDS and Its Metaphors (Sontag) 135, 283
AIDS epidemic 158, 159, 283
alcohol abuse
  Chabon (Michael) on 48
  Jong (Erica) on 139
  Parker (Dorothy) on 31
  Richler (Mordecai) on 25, 26

Aleichem, Sholem **5–7**
  Rosenfeld (Isaac) and 255
  Tevye's Daughters **295–296**
Alexander, Edward 224
Alger, Horatio, Jr. 312
Algonquin Roundtable 228
Algren, Nelson 72
Alice in Bed (Sontag) 283
Allen, Woody **7–8,** 256
  Side Effects 8, **275–276**
All Good Americans (Perelman and Perelman) 234
All I Could Never Be (Yezierska) 327
All My Sons (Miller) 190
All Rivers Run to the Sea (Wiesel) 316
"Amateurs, The" (Swados) 291
Amazing Adventures of Kavalier and Clay, The (Chabon) xxiv, **8–9,** 88, 329
"America" (Ginsberg) 35, 36
American Daughter, An (Wasserstein) 309
American dream
  Asch (Sholem) on 19
  Cahan (Abraham) on 249
  Doctorow (E. L.) on 65
  Kosinski (Jerzy) on 151
  Mailer (Norman) on 175
  Miller (Arthur) on 62

Odets (Clifford) on 215
Roth (Philip) on 111–112, 130, 131, 238
Wallant (Edward Lewis) on 307
Yezierska (Anzia) on 17, 37
American Dream, An (Mailer) 175
American Jewess (magazine) 319, 321
American Jewish Committee xx
American Klezmer (Cohen) 55
American Pastoral (Roth) **9–10,** 112, 130, 262, 266
American pragmatism 255
American Procession, An (Kazin) 148
American Trilogy (Roth) 9, 57, 130, 262
"America: Toward Yavneh" (Ozick) 225
Anatomy Lesson, The (Roth) 9, 57, 261
Anaya, Rudolpho 260
Ancient Evenings (Mailer) 176
Anderson, Margaret 116
Anderson, Maxwell 63
Anderson, Sherwood xviii, 22, 116, 121, 148, 287
Angel of Forgetfulness, The (Stern) 289
Angels in America: A Gay Fantasia on National Themes (Kushner) 158, 159
Angoff, Charles 181
Angry Hills, The (Uris) 304
Ani Ma'amin: A Song Lost and Found Again (Wiesel) 315
animal imagery
Kumin (Maxine) using 155, 156
Malamud (Bernard) using 104–105
Roth (Philip) using 131
Spiegelman (Art) using 182–183, 285, 286
animal rights activism 91
Annie Hall (film) 7–8, 275

anorexia 74, 75, 251
Another Part of the Forest (Hellman) 121
anthroposophy 28, 131, 132
anticommunist hysteria 59. *See also* McCarthyism
antihero 15, 63, 151, 152, 218
Antin, Mary xviii, **10–12**
The Promised Land xvii, 10, 11, 37
antirealism 50, 152
anti-Semitism xvi, xvii, xx
Aleichem (Sholem) on 295
Asch (Sholem) on 204
Bellow (Saul) on 27
Chabon (Michael) on 8
in colonial times xiv, xv
in czarist Russia xiii, xvi, 5, 42, 245, 316
Fiedler (Leslie) on 87, 161
Glass (Montague Marsden) on 103
Green (Hannah) on 137
Hellman (Lillian) on 233
Jong (Erica) on 86
Mailer (Norman) on 202
Malamud (Bernard) on 21–22, 99, 177
Osherow (Jacqueline) on 219
Ozick (Cynthia) on 225
Piercy (Marge) on 111
Roth (Henry) on 259, 260
Roth (Philip) on 58, 236, 262, 328
Shaw (Irwin) on 271
Sinclair (Jo) on 276
Singer (Isaac Bashevis) on 79
Wiesel (Elie) on 298
Wolf (Emma) on 320, 322
anti-utopian character 72
anti–Vietnam War movement
Elman (Richard) on 68
Ginsberg (Allen) on 101
Mailer (Norman) on 15, 16, 176
Piercy (Marge) on 235

Anya (Schaeffer) xxii, **12–13**
"Any Porch" (Parker) 229
"Any Woman Can't" (Wasserstein) 309
Apathetic Bookie Joint, The (Fuchs) 94
"Apples" (Rosen) 252
Apprenticeship of Duddy Kravitz, The (film) 14–15
Apprenticeship of Duddy Kravitz, The (Richler) **13–15**
Arendt, Hannah 4, 53
Argentina 193–195
Armageddon (Uris) 304
Armies of the Night, The (Mailer) **15–16,** 176
Arnold, Matthew 4, 302–303
Around the World in 80 Days (Verne) 234
Arrogant Beggar (Yezierska) **17–18,** 327
Art & Ardor (Ozick) 54–55, 221
Artaud, Antonin 283
"Artificial Intelligence" (Rich) 281
Art of Blessing the Day: Poems on a Jewish Theme, The (Piercy) 235
Art of the Self: Essays à propos Steps, The (Kosinski) 151
Asch, Sholem **18–19**
The Nazarene 19, **204**
Ashkenazim xiii, xv–xvi, 258
As I Lay Dying (Faulkner) 110
Asimov, Isaac **19–21**
Asimov, Stanley 21
Assassin, The (Shaw) 271
assimilation
Calisher (Hortense) on 290
Fiedler (Leslie) on 161
Goodman (Allegra) on 145
Kotlowitz (Robert) on 153
Lewisohn (Ludwig) on 169
Malamud (Bernard) on 177
Rosenfeld (Isaac) on 255
Roth (Philip) on 58, 112, 238
Singer (Isaac Bashevis) on 79
Stein (Gertrude) on 297

Wolf (Emma) on 320, 321
Zangwill (Israel) on 331
Assistant, The (Malamud) **21–22,**
    177
atheism
    Asimov (Isaac) on 20
    Fiedler (Leslie) on 161
    Foer (Jonathan Safran) on 90
    Schaeffer (Susan Fromberg) on
        13
atomic bomb 240, 293, 294
At the Center (Rosen) 253
Auden, W. H. 56, 246, 264, 280
"Aunt Jennifer's Tigers" (Rich) 56
Aurora Dawn (Wouk) 325
Austen, Jane 44, 146, 290
Auster, Paul 245–246
"Authors in the Classroom"
    (Calisher) 43
autobiographical elements
    Bellow (Saul) using 243
    Berriault (Gina) using 30, 170
    Broner (E. M.) using 39
    Cahan (Abraham) using 42
    Calisher (Hortense) using 44,
        290
    Chabon (Michael) using 48
    Charyn (Jerome) using 50
    Cohen (Sarah Blacher) using 55
    Doctorow (E. L.) using 65
    Gold (Herbert) using 106
    Green (Hannah) using 136
    Hecht (Ben) using 72
    Irving (John) using 140
    Jong (Erica) using 142–143
    Kunitz (Stanley) using 294–295
    Mailer (Norman) using 15–16,
        175
    Miller (Arthur) using 192
    Olsen (Tillie) using 293
    Parker (Dorothy) using 31
    Potok (Chaim) using 239
    Rich (Adrienne) using 281
    Roth (Henry) using 45, 258, 260
    Roth (Philip) using 58, 73,
        236–237, 262

Salinger (J. D.) using 46
Shulman (Alix Kates) using
    185
Sontag (Susan) using 283
Spiegelman (Art) using
    181–183, 285, 286
Wasserstein (Wendy) using 118,
    309
Yezierska (Anzia) using 37, 326
autobiographical form
    Cohen (Arthur Allen) using 53
    Doctorow (E. L.) using 32
    Gold (Herbert) using 83–84
    Hecht (Ben) using 118
    Jong (Erica) using 139
    Kosinski (Jerzy) using 151, 226
    Michaels (Anne) using 95
    Richler (Mordecai) using
        24–26
autobiography
    by Antin (Mary) 10, 11
    by Asimov (Isaac) 21
    by Bitton-Jackson (Livia) 33
    by Calisher (Hortense) 44
    by Cohen (Sarah Blacher) 54
    by Elman (Richard) 69
    by Fast (Howard Melvin) 83
    by Ferber (Edna) 86
    by Hellman (Lillian) 122,
        232–233
    by Jong (Erica) 143
    by Kotlowitz (Robert) 153
    by Mendelsohn (Daniel) 173
    by Piercy (Marge) 235
    by Roth (Henry) 259
    by Salamon (Julie) 206, 267,
        313, 314
    by Shulman (Alix Kates)
        274–275
    by Singer (Isaac Bashevis)
        137–138, 277
    by Stein (Gertrude) 22–23
    by Wiesel (Elie) xxii, 207–209,
        300, 314, 315
*Autobiography of Alice B. Toklas,
    The* (Stein) **22–23,** 287, 288, 297

*Autobiography of an American Jew,
    The* (Cahan). *See Rise of David
    Levinsky, The* (Cahan)
automatic writing 287
Autumn Garden, The (Hellman)
    121
Available Light (Piercy) 236
Awake and Sing! (Odets) 190, 214,
    215
Ayzland, Reuven 179

B

Ba'al Shem Tov 284, 316
Babel, Isaac 277
"Baby" (Sontag) 283
Bachelor Girls (Wasserstein) 309
Bachelors' Club, The (Zangwill)
    330
Back Pay (Hurst) 133
Bad Companions (Roughhead)
    121
Baile, David 14
Bakhtin, Mikhail 243
Ballard, J. G. 105
Ballou, Robert 258
Barbary Shore (Mailer) 175
"Barbie Doll" (Piercy) 235
Barfield, Owen 28
Barker, George 165
Barney's Version (Richler) **24–26**
Barthes, Roland 283
Barth, John 58, 152
Barthleme, Donald 152
Bartholdi, Frédéric 207
baseball 51, 65, 177, 202–204, 261,
    294–295
"Bashert" (Klepfisz) 149–150
Battle Cry (Uris) 304
Beat movement xx, xxi, 100–102,
    128–129, 175
Beats, The (Krim) 154
Before Their Time (Kotlowitz)
    153–154
Beggar in Jerusalem, A (Wiesel)
    317

Beggerman, Thief (Shaw) 271
Beichman, Arnold 181
Beiliss, Mendel 177
Being Busted (Fiedler) 88
Being Red (Fast) 83
Being There (Kosinski) 151
Bellarosa Connection, The (Bellow) 28
Bell, Daniel 148
Bellow, Saul xx, xxi, xxiv, **26–29**
   The Adventures of Augie March xxi, **3–4,** 27
   Cohen (Sarah Blacher) on 54
   Fuchs (Daniel) and 93
   on Gold (Herbert) 107
   on Hecht (Ben) 72
   Henderson the Rain King 27, **122–124,** 198
   Herzog 27, **124–125,** 198
   Humboldt's Gift 28, **131–132,** 198
   Kazin (Alfred) on 148
   Levin (Meyer) and 168
   Mailer (Norman) and 201
   Malamud (Bernard) and 177
   More Die of Heartbreak 28, **197–198**
   Mr. Sammler's Planet xxii, xxiii, 28, **198–199,** 256
   Ozick (Cynthia) and 222, 225
   Ravelstein 29, **243–244**
   Rosenfeld (Isaac) and 255, 256
   on Roth (Philip) 111, 261
   Roth (Henry) and 259
   Seize the Day 27, 125, **269–270**
Benchley, Robert 229, 244
Benefactor, The (Sontag) 282
Benét, Stephen Vincent 264
Benjamin, Walter 283
Berriault, Gina **29–31**
   The Lights of Earth 30, **170–171,** 323
   Women in Their Beds: New and Selected Stories 30, **322–323**
Betraying Spinoza (Goldstein) 107
Bettelheim, Bruno 238

Beyond Culture: Essays on Literature and Learning (Trilling) 303
Bialik, Chaim Nachman 179
biblical elements. *See also* Christ imagery
   Aleichem (Sholem) using 295
   Asch (Sholem) using 204
   Broner (E. M.) using 310
   Chabon (Michael) using 49, 327, 328–329
   Doctorow (E. L.) using 35
   Heller (Joseph) using 104
   Roth (Philip) using 57–58
   Wiesel (Elie) using 208, 285, 315, 316, 317
Biblical Women Unbound: Counter-Tales (Rosen) 253
Bibliography of Jewish Life in the Fiction of America and England (Schneider) xvii
"Bicentennial Man" (Asimov) 20
Big as Life (Doctorow) 64
"Big Blonde" (Parker) **31–32,** 230, 245
Big Fat Little Lit (Spiegelman) 286
bildungsroman 48, 81, 106, 151, 226
Billy Bathgate (Doctorow) **32–33,** 65, 179
"Bingo by the Bungalow" (Rosenbaum) 67
"Bintel Brief" (advice column) xvii, 196
bird imagery 22
Birth of a Hero (Gold) 106
Bitton-Jackson, Livia **33–34**
Black Swan (Charyn) 50
Blake, William 100, 102, 157, 158
Blessing on the Moon, A (Skibell) **34–35**
Blind Date (Kosinski) 152
Blood, Bread and Poetry (Rich) 56
Bloodshed and Three Novellas (Ozick) xxii, 221–222
Bloom, Allan 29, 243–244
Bloom, Harold 123, 266

Bodenheim, Maxwell 116, 117
Body Parts of Margaret Fuller, The (Broner) 38
Bohm, David 108, 240
Book of Daniel, The (Doctorow) 32, **35–36,** 64
Book of Lights, The (Potok) 239
"Book of Mordecai, The" (Stern) 162–163
"Book of the Dead, The" (Rukeyser) 264
"Books We Have Made" (Lewisohn) 169
Bread Givers (Yezierska) **36–38,** 326, 327
Breast, The (Roth) 261, 262
Brecht, Bertolt 159, 306
Breton, Nicholas 146
"Bridegroom, The" (Gogol) 197
Brideshead Revisited (Waugh) 239
Bringing Home the Light: A Jewish Woman's Handbook of Ritual (Broner) 39
Broken Snare, The (Lewisohn) 169
Broner, E. M. xxi, **38–39**
   A Weave of Women xxii, 38–39, **310**
Bronx Boy (Charyn) 50
Brooks, Juanita xv
Brooks, Mel 256
Brothers Ashkenazi, The (Singer) 79
Brothers, Joyce 155
Brown, Mick 187
Brown, Robert M. 300
Broyard, Anatole 131
Brustein, Robert 120
Buber, Martin 70, 210, 284
Buchman, Helen 276
Bukiet, Melvin Jules xxii, xxiv, **39–40**
Burke, Billie 229
Burnett, Whit 268
Burning Questions (Shulman) 274
Burns, Robert 46
Burroughs, William S. 100, 101, 129
Burton, Richard 123

Bury the Dead (Shaw) 271
"Butterfly and the Traffic Light,
  The" (Ozick) 225
Butwin, Frances 295
"By Destiny Denied" (Allen) 275

C

Cahan, Abraham **41–42**
  Asch (Sholem) and 19, 204
  Forward (newspaper) of xvii,
    41–42, 196
  Malamud (Bernard) and 177
  The Rise of David Levinsky xvii,
    42, **248–249**
  West (Nathanael) and 196
  Yekl 37, 41
Caine Mutiny, The (Wouk) 324, 325
Calisher, Hortense xix, xxi, **43–44**
  Sunday Jews 44, **290–291**
Call It Sleep (Roth) xix, **44–45,**
  258–259
"Camera Eye" (Dos Passos) 93
Campbell, Alan 230
Campbell, Josie 139
Camus, Albert 30
cancer 134–135
Canetti, Elias 283
Cannibal Galaxy, The (Ozick) 222
Cantalupo, Barbara 320, 321
Can't Learn 'Em Nothin' (Glass) 103
Capone, Al 32
Captain Kidd (Charyn) 50
Captain Newman, M.D. (Rosten)
  257
Caregivers, The (Cohen) 55
Caroline, or Change (Kushner) 159
Carpenter Years, The (Cohen) 53
cartoons 233. *See also* comic books
Case of Mr. Crump, The (Lewisohn)
  169
Case of the Angry Actress, The
  (Fast) 82
Cassady, Neal 100, 129
Catch-22 (Heller) **46–47,** 103, 104,
  120

Catcher in the Rye, The (Salinger)
  xx, **45–46,** 268–269
Cathedral-Tree-Train (Elman)
  68–69
Cather, Willa xviii
"Cattle Car Complex" (Rosen-
  baum) 67, 254
Caylor, Rose 117, 118
Celibates' Club, The (Zangwill)
  330
Center for Southern Folklore 288,
  289
Cézanne, Paul 22, 287, 297
Chabon, Michael xxii, xxiii, **47–49**
  *The Amazing Adventures of Ka-
    valier and Clay* xxiv, **8–9,** 48,
    88, 329
  *The Final Solution: A Story of
    Detection* 49, **88–89**
  The Yiddish Policemen's Union
    49, **327–329**
Chagall, Marc 127
Chandler, Raymond 49, 328
Changelings, The (Sinclair) 276
Change of World, A (Rich) 56, 246,
  280
Channing, William Ellery 168
charity. *See* philanthropy
Charles Reznikoff: Man and Poet
  (Hindus) 245
Charyn, Jerome **49–51**
  Once Upon a Droshky 50,
    217–218
Cheated, The (West). *See* Day of the
  Locust, The (West)
"Cheek of the Trout, The" (Rosen)
  253
Cheever, John 48
Chekhov, Anton 309
Chicago
  Bellow (Saul) on 3, 27, 131, 132
  Hecht (Ben) on 72, 116, 117
Chicago School 116, 117
Child of the Century (Hecht) 118
Children at the Gate (Wallant)
  307, 308

Children of Loneliness (Yezierska)
  327
*Children of the Ghetto: A Study of
  a Peculiar People, The* (Zangwill)
  330
Children of the Holocaust (Epstein)
  xxiii, 71
Children's Hour, The (Hellman) 121
Chosen, The (Potok) **51–52,** 199,
  239, 240
Christ imagery. *See also* biblical
  elements
  Asch (Sholem) using 204
  Cohen (Arthur Allen) using 53
  Irving (John) using 324
  Mailer (Norman) using 176
  Malamud (Bernard) using 22
  Wallant (Edward Lewis) using
    308
  West (Nathanael) using
    196–197, 312
Christmas Tree, The (Salamon)
  206, 267
"Chuppah, The" (Piercy) 235–236
Cider House Rules, The (Irving)
  140, 141
Circles on the Water: Selected Poems
  (Piercy) 235
Citizen Tom Paine (Fast) 82
City Lights Books 101, 128
City of God (Doctorow) 65–66
civil rights 106, 230
Civil War
  Doctorow (E. L.) on 66,
    178–179
  Gratz (Rebecca) on 165
  Whitman (Walt) on 35–36
Cleaver, Eldridge 284
Cleland, John 80
Clinton, Bill 130
cloning 126
Closing Time (Heller) 120
"Cloudland Revisited" (Perelman)
  234
Coat for the Czar, A (Elman) 68
Cockpit (Kosinski) 151

cognitive processing 297

Cohen, Arthur Allen xxii, **52–53**

Cohen, Robert xxii

Cohen, Sarah Blacher **53–56**

Collected Early Poems (Rich) **56–57,** 248

colonialism xiv–xv, 27, 123, 166

"Colony, The" (Rosenfeld) 256

Colossus, The (Plath) 157

Columbus, Christopher xiii, xiv

"Come Back to the Raft Ag'in, Huck Honey" (Fiedler) 87

comedy of manners 145

comic books 8–9, 48, 182, 233, 285–286

comic relief 6, 178. *See also* humor

coming-of-age story
  by Broner (E. M.) 38
  by Chabon (Michael) 48
  by Doctorow (E. L.) 65
  by Elman (Richard) 68
  by Goldstein (Rebecca) 192
  by Horn (Dara) 126
  by Roiphe (Anne) 250
  by Roth (Philip) 111
  by Salinger (J. D.) 46, 268–269
  by Wasserstein (Wendy) 119
  by Wouk (Herman) 180

"Comin' Thro' the Rye" (Burns) 46

Commentary (journal) xx, 112, 148, 154, 282

communism. *See also* socialism
  Fast (Howard Melvin) on 82–83
  Fiedler (Leslie) on 87
  of Odets (Clifford) 215
  of Olsen (Tillie) 216
  of Parker (Dorothy) 230
  of Rosenfeld (Isaac) 255
  of Rukeyser (Muriel) 264
  Singer (Isaac Bashevis) on 80
  Trilling (Lionel) on 188

"Condemned, The" (Allen) 275

Conference of Victims (Berriault) 30

"Confessions of a Burglar" (Allen) 275

Conrad, Joseph 123

consciousness raising (CR) 185, 274

"Constant Reader" (Parker) 230

Contemporary Jewish Record xx

Convergence of Birds: Original Fiction and Poetry Inspired by the Work of Joseph Cornell, A (Foer) 90

"Conversations with Survivors" (Osherow) 219

Cool Million: The Dismantling of Lemuel Pitkin, A (West) 311, 312

Cooper, James Fenimore 211

Coover, Robert 58, 152

"Corpse Plant, The" (Rich) 57

Corry, John 152

"Cosmic Corkscrew" (Asimov) 20

Counterlife, The (Roth) 9, **57–59,** 261

Cowan, Phillip 11

Cowen, Louis 330

Crack-Up, The (Fitzgerald) 175

Creeley, Robert 165

Crime and Punishment (Dostoyevsky) 21, 22

crime fiction. *See* detective fiction

Crocker, Mary Arnold 169

Crucible, The (Miller) xx, **59–60,** 191

Cunningham, E. V. 82

Curry, Margery 116

cyberspace travelogue 251

D

Dadaism 197, 311

Daiches, David 303

Dance to Death, The (Lazarus) 164

Dangling Man (Bellow) xx, xxi, 27, 201

Danielson, Jacques 133

Danny Kaye: Supreme Court Jester (Cohen) 55

Danziger, Gustav 320

Dark Lady from Belorusse (Charyn) 50

Dark Sister, The (Goldstein) 108

Darwin, Charles 105

Davies, Robertson 140

Davita's Harp (Potok) 239

Dawn (Wiesel) 300, 316

Dawn O'Hara, The Girl Who Laughed (Ferber) 86

Day of the Locust, The (West) **61–62,** 311, 313

Days of Awe, The (Nissenson) 211

"Day the Brooklyn Dodgers Finally Died, The" (Rosenbaum) 255

Dead Men's Praise (Osherow) 219

Dean's December, The (Bellow) 28

death. *See also* suicide
  Bellow (Saul) on 123, 124, 244
  Berriault (Gina) on 170
  Broner (E. M.) on 310
  Foer (Jonathan Safran) on 77, 90
  Ginsberg (Allen) on 146–147
  Goldstein (Rebecca) on 240, 241
  Klepfisz (Irena) on 149
  Kumin (Maxine) on 156
  Mailer (Norman) on 201
  Michaels (Anne) on 95
  Nissenson (Hugh) on 210–211
  Parker (Dorothy) on 31, 229, 245
  Rich (Adrienne) on 57
  Rosen (Jonathan) on 252
  Roth (Philip) on 73, 262, 266
  Salinger (J. D.) on 46
  Sontag (Susan) on 134–135, 282
  Stein (Gertrude) on 297
  Stern (Steve) on 162
  Trilling (Lionel) on 189
  Wallant (Edward Lewis) on 231–232
  Wiesel (Elie) on 208, 316

Death Kit (Sontag) 282, 283

Death of a Salesman (Miller) xx, 59, **62–64,** 190–191

"Debriefing" (Sontag) 283

Deception (Roth) 58, 261, 262

*Decline and Fall of the Roman
   Empire* (Gibbon) 20
Deer Park, The (Mailer) 175
"Defender of the Faith" (Roth)
   111, 261
Defoe, Daniel 80
Dell, Floyd 116
DePalma, Brian 267
depression era
   Bellow (Saul) on 3, 27
   Doctorow (E. L.) on 65
   Fuchs (Daniel) on 93–94
   Gold (Herbert) on 84
   Miller (Arthur) on 189–190
   Odets (Clifford) on 214, 215,
      306
   Shaw (Irwin) on 271
   West (Nathanael) on 61, 196,
      311, 312
Descent, The (Berriault) 30
detective fiction
   by Calisher (Hortense) 290
   by Chabon (Michael) 88–89,
      327, 328
   by Charyn (Jerome) 50
   by Fast (Howard Melvin) 82
*Devil's Candy: The Bonfire of the
   Vanities Goes to Hollywood, The*
   (Salamon) 267
Devil Tree, The (Kosinski) 151
Dewey, John 253, 327
Diamond Cutters, The (Rich) 56,
   247
Diary of a Young Girl (Frank) 168
Dickens, Charles 6, 44, 79, 140,
   218, 239
Dickinson, Emily 163
"Diet, The" (Allen) 275
Digging Out (Roiphe) 250
Dillingham, Mary S. 11
Dimond, Anthony 328
Dine, Mark 157
disability 54, 55
*Discourse on the Restoration of the
   Jews* (Noah) 212

Diving into the Wreck (Rich) 56,
   247–248
Diving Rock on the Hudson, A
   (Roth) 260
"Divorce as Moral Act" (Gold) 106
"Dock-Witch, The" (Ozick) 225
Doctorow, E. L. xxii, **64–66**
   Billy Bathgate **32–33,** 65, 179
   The Book of Daniel 32, **35–36,** 64
   The March 66, **178–179**
   Ragtime 64–65, 66, 179,
      242–243
"Doctor's Wife, The" (Ozick) 225
Donne, John 157
Dos Passos, John 36, 65, 93, 201
Dostoyevsky, Fyodor 21, 22, 277
Double Image, The (Levertov) 165
Doyle, Arthur Conan 88, 89
"Dreamers of the Ghetto" (Zang-
   will) 319–320
Dream Life of Balso Snell, The
   (West) 311–312
Dreams of Hippolyte, The (Sontag)
   282
Dreiser, Theodore 3, 121, 169
Dreyfuss, Richard 14–15
Drinking the Rain (Shulman)
   274–275
Drinks Before Dinner: A Play (Doc-
   torow) 65
"Dr. Jekyll" (Sontag) 283
drug abuse 100–102. *See also* alco-
   hol abuse
Dubin's Lives (Malamud) 177
Duffy, Sherman 116
Duncan, Robert 165
Dutch West India Company xiv
Dying Animal, The (Roth) 73, 262
Dylan, Bob 102
dystopian themes 81

E

East River (Asch) 19
"Eating Babies" (Kumin) 156

eating disorder. *See* anorexia
Ebert, Robert 15
"Education, An" (Ozick) 222
*Education of H*Y*M*A*N
   K*A*P*L*A*N, The* (Rosten) 257
Egotist, The (Hecht) 117
Eichmann, Adolf 209, 299, 300
Einstein, Albert 107, 240
Eisenhower, My Eisenhower
   (Charyn) 50
"Elegy and Rant" (Kumin) 156
Elijah Visible: Stories (Rosenbaum)
   xxiii, **67–68,** 254
Eliot, T. S. xviii, 4, 157, 197, 259, 264
"Eli the Fanatic" (Roth) 112
Elkan Lubliner: American (Glass)
   103
Elli: Coming of Age in the Holocaust
   (Bitton-Jackson) 33
Ellis Island National Immigration
   Center xvi
Ellison, Ralph 3, 148, 259
Ellmann, Richard 68
Elman, Richard **68–69**
*Elusive Embrace: Desire and the
   Riddle of Identity, The* (Men-
   delsohn) 173
Emerson, Ralph Waldo xviii, 163
Emma McChesney series (Ferber)
   86
"Empire, The" (Rosenfeld) 256
End to Innocence, An (Fiedler) 87
"Enemy, The" (Rosenfeld) 256
Englander, Nathan xxii, **69–70**
   The Ministry of Special Cases
      69, **193–195**
   *For the Relief of Unbearable
      Urges* xxiv, 69, **92–93,** 194
English Disease, The (Skibell) 35
*Enormous Changes at the Last Min-
   ute* (Paley) 228
Enough Rope (Parker) 229–230, 244
"Envy; or Yiddish in America"
   (Ozick) 221, 224–225
"Episode, An" (Hurst) 132

epistolary novel 27
"Epitaph for a Canadian Kike"
    (Krim) 154–155
"Epstein" (Roth) 261
Epstein, Helen xxii, xxiii, **70–71**
Erik Dorn (Hecht) **72–73,** 117
Eros and the Jews (Baile) 14
erotic reader responses 4
Erskine, John 302
*Essays of Howard, On Domestic
    Economy* (Noah) 212
eugenics movement xviii
Eugenides, Jeffrey 90
Evans, Mary 48
Everyman (Roth) **73,** 262, 327
Everything Is Illuminated (Foer)
    74, 77, 78, 89, 90
Eve's Apple (Rosen) **74–75,** 251
evolution 105
Ewing, Samuel 114
Executioner's Song, The (Mailer)
    176, 201
existentialist themes
    by Allen (Woody) 275
    by Bellow (Saul) xxi, 27, 123
    by Fuchs (Daniel) 94
    by Kosinski (Jerzy) 152
    by Mailer (Norman) 175
    by Nemerov (Howard) 205
Exit Ghost (Roth) 57, 262–263
Exit Into History (Hoffman) 125
Exodus (Uris) **76–77,** 304
Exodus Revisited (Uris) 304
Expressionism in America
    (Lewisohn) 169
*Extremely Loud and Incredibly
    Close* (Foer) **77–78,** 89, 90

F

Facing the Wind (Salamon) 267
Fackenheim, Emil 70
Fact of a Doorframe, The (Rich) 56
Facts, The (Roth) 261, 262
Fall of America, The (Ginsberg) 102

family. *See also* father-daughter rela-
    tionship; father-son relationship;
    mother-daughter relationship;
    mother-son relationship
    Bellow (Saul) on 124
    Calisher (Hortense) on 44
    Doctorow (E. L.) on 242, 243
    Foer (Jonathan Safran) on 90
    Green (Hannah) on 137
    Hellman (Lillian) on 121, 232,
        233
    Jong (Erica) on 138
    Kumin (Maxine) on 155
    Michaels (Anne) on 186–187
    Miller (Arthur) on 190, 191
    Olsen (Tillie) on 216, 217
    Roiphe (Anne) on 250
    Roth (Henry) on 45
    Roth (Philip) on 236–237
    Salamon (Julie) on 267
    Schaeffer (Susan Fromberg) on
        13
    Shulman (Alix Kates) on
        274–275
    Singer (Isaac Bashevis) on 79
    Wallant (Edward Lewis) on
        231
*Family: A Novel in the Form of a
    Memoir* (Gold) 106, 107
Family Markowitz, The (Goodman)
    112
Family Moskat, The (Singer)
    79–80, 278
Fannie Hurst Showcase (television
    program) 133
*Fanny: Being the True History of the
    Adventures of Fanny Hackabout-
    Jones* (Jong) **80–81,** 143
Fanny Hill (Cleland) 80
fantasy
    by Asimov (Isaac) 20
    by Berriault (Gina) 30
    by Chabon (Michael) 48–49
    by Kosinski (Jerzy) 226
    by Malamud (Bernard) 177

    by Piercy (Marge) 236
    by Rosenbaum (Thane) 109
    by Shaw (Irwin) 271
    by Stern (Steve) 162–163, 288,
        289
Fantazies Mallare (Hecht) 117
Farrell, James T. 45, 201
Farrow, Mia 8
Fast, Howard Melvin xx, **81–83**
Fast, Jonathan 143
"Father and Son" (Kunitz) 158
father-daughter relationship
    Green (Hannah) on 137
    Kumin (Maxine) on 155
    Yezierska (Anzia) on 37
*Fathers: A Novel in the Form of a
    Memoir* (Gold) **83–84,** 106, 107
father-son relationship
    Bellow (Saul) on 269–270
    Charyn (Jerome) on 218
    Englander (Nathan) on
        193–194, 195
    Kunitz (Stanley) on 295
    Malamud (Bernard) on 22
    Miller (Arthur) on 62
    Roth (Henry) on 45
    Wiesel (Elie) on 91, 208
"Fat of the Land, The" (Yezierska)
    327
Faulkner, William xviii, 66, 110,
    140, 148, 179, 239, 277
Fear of Flying (Jong) **84–86,** 138,
    142–143
Feinstein, Herbert 291
Feminine Mystique, The (Friedan)
    186
feminism xxi–xxii
    Irving (John) on 324
    of Jong (Erica) xxii, 80, 81, 142
    of Klepfisz (Irena) 149, 150
    of Piercy (Marge) 235, 236
    of Roiphe (Anne) 250
    Roth (Philip) on 130
    of Rukeyser (Muriel) 264
feminist criticism 159

feminist works
   by Broner (E. M.) 38, 310
   by Jong (Erica) 80, 81
   by Olsen (Tillie) 216, 293, 294
   by Osherow (Jacqueline) 219
   by Parker (Dorothy) 230
   by Rich (Adrienne) 56, 57,
      247–248, 280–281
   by Shulman (Alix Kates)
      185–186, 273, 274, 275
   by Wasserstein (Wendy) 119
   by Wolf (Emma) 321, 322
Ferber, Edna xvii, **86–87**
Ferlinghetti, Lawrence 101, 128
feuilleton 6
Fiddler on the Roof (musical) 6,
   119, 295
Fiedler, Leslie xx, **87–88**
   The Last Jew in America 87,
      161–162
   Roth (Henry) and 45, 259
Fielding, Henry 80
Fifth Son, The (Wiesel) 91, 318
"Final Problem, The" (Doyle) 89
*Final Solution: A Story of Detection,
   The* (Chabon) 49, **88–89**
"First Spade in the West, The"
   (Fiedler) 161–162
Fisch, Harold 331
Fitzgerald, F. Scott xviii, 22, 175,
   287
Fitzgerald, Robert 218
Fixer, The (Malamud) 177, 178
Flaubert, Gustave 297
Florentine Dagger, The (Hecht) 117
Fly Away Home (Piercy) 236
Foer, Jonathan Safran xxii, **89–91**
   Everything Is Illuminated **74,**
      77, 78, 89, 90
   *Extremely Loud and Incredibly
      Close* **77–78,** 89, 90
folklore 288–289, 295
folktales 13
food 17–18, 74–75, 251
Forbes, Frederick E. 123

forgiveness 21, 35
Forgotten, The (Wiesel) **91–92,**
   173, 318
formalism 155, 219
Forster, E. M. 189, 303
For the Relief of Unbearable Urges
   (Englander) xxiv, 69, **92–93,** 194
Forward (newspaper) xvii–xviii,
   41–42, 79, 196, 251, 278
Foundation series (Asimov) 20
"Fountain City" (Chabon) 48
*Four Hasidic Masters: And Their
   Struggle Against Melancholy* (Wi-
   esel) 285, 318
Fourth Hand, The (Irving) 141
Franciosi, Robert 246
Francis of Assisi, Saint 21, 22
Frank, Anne 168
Franklin, Benjamin xv
Frank, Waldo xviii, xix
Franny and Zooey (Salinger) 269
Freedman, Janis 29
Freedom Road (Fast) 82
Free Vacation House, The (Yezierska)
   327
Fremont-Smith, Eliot 152
French, Marilyn 39, 310
Freudian analysis
   Bellow (Saul) on 122, 123, 131
   Goldstein (Rebecca) on 241
   Rosenfeld (Isaac) on 256
   Roth (Henry) on 259
   Roth (Philip) on 237, 266
   West (Nathanael) on 311
Freud, Sigmund
   Jong (Erica) on 85
   on Lewisohn (Ludwig) 169
   Potok (Chaim) on 51
   Trilling (Lionel) on 303
Friedan, Betty 186
Friedell, Deborah 89
Friedman, Elli Livia. *See* Bitton-
   Jackson, Livia
Friedman, Lawrence S. 79, 80
From Bondage (Roth) 260

From Here to Eternity (Jones) 110
Fromm-Reichmann, Frieda
   136–137
From Plotzk to Boston (Antin) 11
"From the Diary of One Not Born"
   (Singer) 100
Front Page, The (Hecht and
   MacArthur) 117
Fuchs, Daniel xix, **93–94,** 167
Fugitive Pieces (Michaels) **95–96,**
   186, 187
Fulfillment: A California Novel
   (Wolf) 321
Fulford, Robert 243
Fuller, Edmund 105
Furioso (journal) 205
Future Is Ours, Comrade, The
   (Kosinski) 151

G

Gable, Dan 139
Galloway, David 307
Gandhi, Mohandas (Mahatma)
   255, 256
Gangel, Norma. *See* Rosen, Norma
gangsters 32–33
García-Márquez, Gabriel 140
Gardiner, Muriel 233
Gargoyles (Hecht) 117
garment industry xvii, 103
Garp (Irving). *See World According
   the Garp, The* (Irving)
"Gates, The" (Rukeyser) 264
Gates of November, The (Potok)
   239
Gates of the Forest, The (Wiesel)
   97–98, 317
Gay, Peter 51
Gelb, Barbara 152
"Gentle Lena, The" (Stein) 297
"Gentleman from Cracow, The"
   (Singer) 100
Gentlemen of the Road (Chabon)
   49

Gentle People, The (Shaw) 271

George, Diane 156

"German Refugee, The" (Malamud) **98–99,** 177

ghazals 219

Ghetto Comedies (Zangwill) 330, 331

Ghetto Tragedies (Zangwill) 330, 331

"Ghost and Saul Bozoff, The" (Stern) 163

Ghost Stories (Broner) 39

Ghost Writer, The (Roth) 9, 57, 261

Giant (Ferber) 86

Gibbon, Edward 20

Gift of Asher Lev, The (Potok) 239

"Gilgul of Park Avenue, The" (Englander) 92

Gilmore, Gary 176

Gimpel the Fool and Other Stories (Singer) **99–100,** 278

Ginsberg, Allen xx, **100–102**
    "America" 35, 36
    Howl and Other Poems xxi, 101, **128–130**
    Kaddish xxi, 100, 101, **146–147**

Ginsberg, Naomi Levy 100, 101, 146–147

"Giving Birth" (Kumin) 156

Glass, Montague Marsden **102–103**

Glatstein, Yakov 219

Gleanings from a Gathered Harvest (Noah) 212

Glück, Louise 157

Gödel, Kurt 107

God in Ruins, A (Uris) 305

God Knows (Heller) **103–104,** 120

God of Vengeance (Asch) 18

God's Grace (Malamud) **104–105,** 177

Goethe, Johann Wolfgang von 159

Gogol, Nikolay 197, 277

Gold, Herbert **106–107**
    Fathers: A Novel in the Form of a Memoir **83–84,** 106, 107

Gold, Michael xix, 37, 167

Goldberg, Myra xxiv

Golden Boy (Odets) 215

Goldman, Emma 274

Goldstein, Rebecca Newberger xxii, xxiii, **107–108**
    Mazel 108, **183–184**
    The Mind-Body Problem 107–108, **192–193**
    Properties of Light 108, **240–241**

golem
    Chabon (Michael) on xxiv, 8–9, 48
    Ozick (Cynthia) on 222, 223
    Rosenbaum (Thane) on xxiv, 109
    Stern (Steve) on 289

Golems of Gotham: A Novel, The (Rosenbaum) xxiii, xxiv, **109,** 254

Gone to Soldiers (Piercy) **109–111,** 236

Goodall, Jane 105

"Good Anna, The" (Stein) 297

Good as Gold (Heller) 103–104

"Goodbye and Good Luck" (Paley) 227

Goodbye, Columbus and Five Short Stories (Roth) **111–112,** 261, 266

Good Enough Daughter, A (Shulman) **274–275**

Good Hunting: A Satire (West) 311

Goodman, Allegra xxii–xxiv, **112–113**
    Kaaterskill Falls 113, **145–146**

Goodman, Kenneth Sawyer 116, 117

Goodman, Paul xx, 283

Goodman, Sam 154–155

Goodrich, Frances 168

Gordon, Mary 260

Gospel According to the Son (Mailer) 176

Gottlieb, Robert 120

Goudie, Jeffrey Ann 39

Gould, Stephen Jay 105

Grabau, Amadeus William 11, 12

"Gramophone, The" (Stern) 162, 289

Grapes of Wrath, The (Steinbeck) 306

Grass, Günther 140, 152

Gratz, Rebecca xiv, xvii, **114–115**
    Letters of Rebecca Gratz **164–165**

Gray, Paul 260

Great American Jackpot, The (Gold) 106

Great American Novel, The (Roth) 261

Great Depression. *See* depression era

Great Petrowski, The (Berriault) 30

Green, Hannah, *I Never Promised You a Rose Garden* **136–137**

Green: A Novella and Eight Stories (Rosen) 253

Greenberg, Joanne. *See* Green, Hannah

Greene, Graham 140, 252

Green Lantern: A Romance of Stalinist Russia, The (Charyn) 50

Greenwich Village Peace Center 227

Grey Wig: Stories and Novellas, The (Zangwill) 331

"Grimaces" (Hecht) 72

"Grocery Store, The" (Malamud) 21

Group Theater 214

Guide to the Religions of America, A (Rosten) 257

"Gunnar's Passage" (Shaw) 271

H

Hackett, Albert 168

Hackett, Francis 116

Haj, The (Uris) 305

Hale, Edward Everett 11

"Halfway" (Rich) 57

Halkin, Hillel 182

Hammett, Dashiell 49, 121, 122, 230, 232
Hansen, Harry 117
"Happy Birthday, Montpellier Pizz-zazz" (Wasserstein) 309
"Hapworth 16, 1924" (Salinger) 269
Hardwick, Elizabeth 4
Harlot's Ghost (Mailer) 176
Harrison, Constance Carry 207
Harry Kaplan's Adventures Underground (Stern) 289
Hartman, Geoffrey 182
Harvest, The (Levin) xix, 168
Hasidic Judaism xiii, xxiv
    Levertov (Denise) on 165, 166
    Potok (Chaim) on 51, 240
    Singer (Isaac Bashevis) on 138
    Wiesel (Elie) on 97, 284, 316, 317, 318
Hawthorne, Nathaniel xviii, 277
He, She, & It (Piercy) 236
Heart of Darkness (Conrad) 123
Hecht, Ben **116–118**
    Erik Dorn **72–73,** 117
    Fuchs (Daniel) and 93
Hecht, Hattie 11
Hechtian man 72
Heidi Chronicles (Wasserstein) 118, 119
Heidi Chronicles and Other Plays (Wasserstein) **118–119,** 309
Heilbrun, Carolyn 156
Heiney, Donald 48
Heirs of Yesterday (Wolf) 320–321
Heir to the Glimmering World (Ozick) 222, 223
Heller, Joseph **119–120**
    Catch-22 **46–47,** 103, 104, 120
    God Knows **103–104,** 120
Hellman, Lillian **120–122,** 168
    Pentimento (A Book of Portraits) 122, **232–233**
Hemingway, Ernest xviii, xxiii
    Bellow (Saul) and 27, 123
    Hellman (Lillian) and 121

Potok (Chaim) and 239
Salinger (J. D.) and 268
Stein (Gertrude) and 22, 287
Henderson the Rain King (Bellow) 27, **122–124,** 198
Henrietta Szold: Woman of Valor (Cohen) 55
Here and Now (Levertov) 165
Hermit of 69th Street: The Working Papers of Norbert Koski, The (Kosinski) 152
Her Mothers (Broner) 38
Hero in His Time, A (Cohen) 53
Herriman, George 51
Herskovits, Melville J. 123
Herzl, Theodor 331
Herzog (Bellow) 27, **124–125,** 198
Heschel, Abraham Joshua 152
He/She (Gold) 106
heterosexuality
    Bellow (Saul) on 197
    Rich (Adrienne) on 56
    Sontag (Susan) on 5
"Hey Sailor, What Ship?" (Olsen) 217, 293–294
Hicks, Granville xix
Higginson: An American Life (Broner) 38
high culture. *See also* popular culture
    Chabon (Michael) on 48
    Sontag (Susan) on 4–5
Himmler, Heinrich 193
Him with His Foot in His Mouth (Bellow) 28
Hindus, Martin 80
Hindus, Milton 245
Hirsch, Marianne 91
Hirsch, Samson Raphael 145
His Master's Voice (Kotlowitz) 153
historical revisionist view 242
historical works
    by Asch (Sholem) 18–19, 204
    by Calisher (Hortense) 44, 290
    by Doctorow (E. L.) 64–65, 66, 178–179, 242

by Fast (Howard Melvin) 81–82
by Horn (Dara) 126, 127
by Jong (Erica) 80–81
by Kosinski (Jerzy) 226
by Malamud (Bernard) 177
by Michaels (Anne) 187
by Piercy (Marge) 236
by Reznikoff (Charles) 246
by Roiphe (Anne) 250
by Rosen (Jonathan) 251
by Sontag (Susan) 283
by Uris (Leon) 76
"History as a Novel: The Steps of the Pentagon" (Mailer) 15
Hitchcock, Alfred 304
Hitler, Adolf 135, 236, 262
Hoffman, Eva **125–126**
Holding On (Roth) 260
holistic narrative 12
Hollander, John 129
Hollywood. *See also* screenplays
    Mailer (Norman) on 175
    West (Nathanael) on 61–62, 313
Holmes, John Clellon 100, 155
Holocaust
    Bellow (Saul) on 124, 244
    Berriault (Gina) on 170
    Bitton-Jackson (Livia) on 33
    Chabon (Michael) on 8–9, 48, 49, 89, 328
    Cohen (Arthur Allen) on 53
    Englander (Nathan) on 69–70, 193, 194
    Foer (Jonathan Safran) on 74, 78, 89, 90
    Goodman (Allegra) on 145
    Jong (Erica) on 139, 144
    Klepfisz (Irena) on 149, 150
    Kosinski (Jerzy) on 151, 152, 226–227
    Kumin (Maxine) on 156
    Levin (Meyer) on 168
    Malamud (Bernard) on 21–22, 98–99, 105
    Mendelsohn (Daniel) on 172–173

Michaels (Anne) on 95, 187

Olsen (Tillie) on 217, 293, 294

Osherow (Jacqueline) on 219

Ozick (Cynthia) on 224, 225, 272–273

Potok (Chaim) on 240

Reznikoff (Charles) on 246

Roiphe (Anne) on 250

Rosenbaum (Thane) on 254, 255

Rosenfeld (Isaac) on 256

Rosen (Norma) on 253, 299, 300

Singer (Isaac Bashevis) on 79

Skibell (Joseph) on 34–35

Spiegelman (Art) on 181–183, 285, 286

Uris (Leon) on 76

Wallant (Edward Lewis) on xxii, 231, 308

Wiesel (Elie) on xxii, 207–209, 298–299, 300, 314, 315

Holocaust (Reznikoff) 246

Holocaust survivors xxii, xxiii. *See also* post–Holocaust

Bellow (Saul) on xxii, 198

Bukiet (Melvin Jules) on 39, 40

Chabon (Michael) on 329

Epstein (Helen) on 71

Hoffman (Eva) on 126

Osherow (Jacqueline) on 219

Ozick (Cynthia) on 221–222, 224

Rosenbaum (Thane) on 67–68, 109, 254

Salamon (Julie) on 206, 267, 313–314

Schaeffer (Susan Fromberg) on 12–13

Singer (Isaac Bashevis) on 278

Sklarew (Myra) on 278, 279–280

Wiesel (Elie) on 91–92, 97–98, 318

Homage to Blenholt (Fuchs) 93–94

Homebody/Kabul (Kushner) 159

"Homely Heroine, The" (Ferber) 86

homosexuality. *See also* lesbianism

Asch (Sholem) on 18

Bellow (Saul) on 243

Chabon (Michael) on 9, 48

Fiedler (Leslie) on 161

Ginsberg (Allen) on 101

Kushner (Tony) on 158, 159

Rich (Adrienne) on 56, 57

Sinclair (Jo) on 276

Stein (Gertrude) on 22, 287

Honors at Dawn (Miller) 190

"Hook, The" (Miller) 191

Hook, Sidney 148

Hoopoe's Crown, The (Osherow) 220

Hopkins, Gerald Manley 210

Horn, Clayton W. 101

Horn, Dara xxiii, **126–127**

horror story 240

Hotel New Hampshire, The (Irving) 140–141

Hour in Paradise, An: Stories (Leegant) **127–128**

House at Pooh Corner, The (Milne) 230

Houses of the City, The (Berriault) 29

House Un-American Activities Committee (HUAC) 59, 83, 122, 191, 215, 230

Howe, Irving xxiii, 45, 148, 171, 189, 238, 259

Howells, W. D. 41, 42, 249

"Howl" (Ginsberg) xx, xxi, 100, 101, 128–129

Howl and Other Poems (Ginsberg) xxi, 101, **128–130**

How to Save Your Own Life (Jong) 143

Huebsch, Ben 27

human cloning 126

Human Season, The (Wallant) 307–308

Human Stain, The (Roth) 9, 112, **130–131,** 262

Humboldt's Gift (Bellow) 28, **131–132,** 198

humor

Aleichem (Sholem) using 5, 6

Allen (Woody) using 7, 275

Asimov (Isaac) using 20

Bellow (Saul) using 27, 28, 122, 123, 197, 198

Bukiet (Melvin Jules) using 40

Charyn (Jerome) using 217, 218

Cohen (Sarah Blacher) using 54, 55

Doctorow (E. L.) using 178

Elman (Richard) using 69

Foer (Jonathan Safran) using 74, 90

Fuchs (Daniel) using 94

Goldstein (Rebecca) using 184

Goodman (Allegra) using 113, 146

Heller (Joseph) using 46, 103, 104

Hellman (Lillian) using 121

Irving (John) using 140

Jong (Erica) using 80, 81

Kotlowitz (Robert) using 153

Krim (Seymour) using 154

Kumin (Maxine) using 156

Mailer (Norman) using 15, 16, 176

Michaels (Anne) using 187

Nemerov (Howard) using 205

Osherow (Jacqueline) using 220

Ozick (Cynthia) using 222

Paley (Grace) using 171, 227

Parker (Dorothy) using 228, 229, 244, 245

Perelman (S. J.) using 233, 234

Richler (Mordecai) using 14

Rosenbaum (Thane) using 109, 254

Rosten (Leo Calvin) using 256–258

Roth (Philip) using 58, 237, 238, 261
Salinger (J. D.) using 46
Shulman (Alix Kates) using 185
Singer (Isaac Bashevis) using 278
Stern (Steve) using 163
Wallant (Edward Lewis) using 308
Wasserstein (Wendy) using 309
West (Nathanael) using 61, 311–312
Yezierska (Anzia) using 37
Zangwill (Israel) using 330
Humpty Dumpty (Hecht) 117
Hungry Hearts (Yezierska) 327
Hurst, Fannie xvii, **132–133**
    Imitation of Life 133, **135–136**
Hurston, Zora Neale 133

I

I, Asimov (Asimov) 21
I, Robot (Asimov) 20
I Am the Clay (Potok) 239
Ibsen, Henrik 63, 281
Ice Palace (Ferber) 86
Ickes, Harold 328
"Idiots First" (Malamud) 203
"I Don't Love You Anymore" (Heller) 119
"If the Aging Magician Should Begin to Believe" (Foer) 90
I Have Lived a Thousand Years: Growing Up in the Holocaust (Bitton-Jackson) 33
Illig, Joyce 3
Illness as Metaphor (Sontag) **134–135,** 283
Image and the Law (Nemerov) 205
I Married a Communist (Roth) 9, 112, 130, 262
Imitation of Life (Hurst) 133, **135–136**

immigrant experience
    Antin (Mary) on 11
    Asch (Sholem) on 19
    Bellow (Saul) on 3
    Cahan (Abraham) on xvii, 41, 248–249
    Glass (Montague Marsden) on 103
    Gold (Herbert) on 83–84
    Hoffman (Eva) on 125
    Hurst (Fannie) on 132
    Kazin (Alfred) on 148
    Kosinski (Jerzy) on 151
    Kotlowitz (Robert) on 153
    Lazarus (Emma) on 164, 207
    Malamud (Bernard) on 21, 177
    Nissenson (Hugh) on 210
    Odets (Clifford) on 215
    Olsen (Tillie) on 294
    Paley (Grace) on 227, 228
    Reznikoff (Charles) on 245
    Rosten (Leo Calvin) on 257
    Roth (Henry) on 45, 258–259
    Stein (Gertrude) on 297
    Wallant (Edward Lewis) on 231
    Yezierska (Anzia) on 17, 37, 326
Immigrants, The (Fast) 83
Imperfect Lens, An (Roiphe) 250
Imported Bridegroom, and Other Stories of the New York Ghetto, The (Cahan) 41
In America (Sontag) 283
In a Summer Season (Lewisohn) 169–170
Incident at Vichy (Miller) 192
Incompleteness (Goldstein) 107
Indignation (Roth) 263
I Never Promised You a Rose Garden (Green) **136–137**
In Every Woman's Life . . . (Shulman) 274
Infinite Passion of Expectation: Twenty-Five Stories, The (Berriault) 30, 323
"In Memorium" (Miller) 190, 191

In Memory Yet Green (Asimov) 21
In My Father's Court (Singer) **137–138,** 277
"Insanity Bit, The" (Krim) 154
Insichism 179–180
Intellectual Things (Kunitz) 157
Interiors (film) 275
In the Beginning (Potok) 239
In the Days of Simon Stern (Cohen) xxii, 53
In the Image (Horn) 126
In the Shadow of Man (Goodall) 105
In the Shadow of No Towers (Spiegelman) 285–286
"In the Woods" (Rich) 57
"In This Way We Are Wise" (Englander) 92
Introspectivism 179–180
Inventing Memory: A Novel of Mothers and Daughters (Jong) **138–139,** 143
involuntary trauma therapy 124
Irving, Colin F. N. 139
Irving, John **139–141**
    The World According the Garp 139, 140, **323–324**
Irving, Washington 114, 211
Isaac and the Undertaker's Daughter (Stern) 288–289
Isaac Sidel Quartet (Charyn) 50
Isaacs, Neil 292
Isn't It Romantic (Wasserstein) 118–119, 309
Israel xxiii
    Bellow (Saul) on 27, 28
    Broner (E. M.) on 38, 310
    Englander (Nathan) on 70, 92
    Klepfisz (Irena) on 150
    Leegant (Joan) on 128
    Levin (Meyer) on 168
    Lewisohn (Ludwig) on 169
    Osherow (Jacqueline) on 219, 220
    Potok (Chaim) on 240

Roth (Philip) on 57, 58
Singer (Isaac Bashevis) on 80
Skibell (Joseph) on 34
Sklarew (Myra) on 279
Uris (Leon) on 76, 304
Wiesel (Elie) on 317
"I Stand Here Ironing" (Olsen) 217, 293
It All Adds Up (Bellow) 28
Ivanhoe (Scott) 114, 115

J

Jack and Other New Poems (Kumin) 156
Jackson, Holbrook 330
Jacobs Ladder, The (Levertov) 166
James, Henry 44, 189, 220, 283, 290
James, William 283, 287, 297
"Jerusalem" (Rich) 57
Jesus. *See* Christ imagery
"Jewbird, The" (Malamud) 35
"Jew in American Fiction, The" (Lebowich) xvi–xvii
"Jew in San Francisco: The Last Half Century, The" (Danziger) 320
"Jewish Problem, The" (Lazarus) 164
Jewish Publication Society 239
Jewish women
    Bitton-Jackson (Livia) on 34
    Broner (E. M.) on 38–39
    Cohen (Sarah Blacher) on 54, 55
    Goodman (Allegra) on 145–146
    Jong (Erica) on 85–86, 138–139, 143
    Osherow (Jacqueline) on 219
    Rosen (Norma) on 252
    Rukeyser (Muriel) on 264–265
    Wolf (Emma) on 320
    Yezierska (Anzia) on 37, 326
Jews without Money (Gold) xix, 37
Joffe, Charles 7

John and Anzia: An American Romance (Rosen) 253
John Reed Clubs xix
Johnson Act of 1924 xvi
Johnson, Samuel 146
Joint Anti-Fascist Refugee Committee 83
Jones, Ernest 303
Jones, James 110
Jong, Allan 142
Jong, Erica xxi, xxii, **142–144**
    Fanny: Being the True History of the Adventures of Fanny Hackabout-Jones 80–81, 143
    Fear of Flying **84–86,** 138, 142–143
    Inventing Memory: A Novel of Mothers and Daughters **138–139,** 143
"Josephine the Singer, or The Mouse Folk" (Kafka) 285
"Joy" (Singer) 100
Joyce, James 3, 44, 45, 125, 199, 239, 259, 312
Joy Comes in the Morning (Rosen) 251–252
Joy of Life, The (Wolf) 321
"Joy of Living, The" (Hurst) 132
Joys of Yiddish, The (Rosten) 257–258
Joy to Levine! (Rosen) 253
Jung, Carl 299
Jungian analysis 24, 166, 311
Junk-Dealer's Daughter (Cohen) 54

K

Kaaterskill Falls (Goodman) 113, **145–146**
Kaddish 67, 98, 105, 146, 183, 193, 209, 244
Kaddish (Ginsberg) xxi, 100, 101, **146–147**
Kafka, Franz 40, 194, 195, 255, 256, 275, 285

Kaiser, Charles 152
Kaplan, Harry 289
Kavalier and Clay (Chabon). *See Amazing Adventures of Kavalier and Clay, The* (Chabon)
Kazan, Elia 191
Kazin, Alfred xx, **147–149**
    Rosenfeld (Isaac) on 256
    Roth (Henry) and 45, 259
Keaton, Diane 7, 8
Keats, John 69, 146, 195
Kellman, Steven G. 260
Kemeny, John 14
Kerouac, Jack 100, 129
Kesey, Ken 152
Kiddush haShem (Asch) 18
Kiernan, Robert F. 123
King of the Schnorrers (Zangwill) 330, 331
"King Solomon" (Rosenfeld) 256
Klepfisz, Irena **149–150**
Knickerbocker Literary Club xvi
Knot, The (Wolf) 321
Kober, Arthur 121, 122
Kocheff, Ted 14
Kohut, Rebekah Bettleheim 319
Konigsberg, Allan Stewart. *See* Allen, Woody
Koppleman, Susan 133
Kosinski, Jerzy xxii, **150–153**
    The Painted Bird 151, 152, **226–227**
Kotlowitz, Robert **153–154**
Krauss, Nicole 89–90
Krazy Kat cartoons 51
Kreitman, Esther 277
Krim, Seymour **154–155**
Kristallnacht 98
"Kugelmass Episode, The" (Allen) 275–276
Kumin, Maxine **155–157**
Kundera, Milan 74
Kunitz, Stanley **157–158**
    Rukeyser (Muriel) and 264
    The Testing-Tree 158, **294–295**

Künstlerroman 48, 323
Kurtz, Seymour xv
Kushner, Tony **158–160**
kvetching 6

L

Ladies Locker Room, The (Cohen)
   55
Lahr, John 215
Lamantia, Philip 128
"Lament of the Rabbi's Daughters,
   The" (Leegant) 127, 128
Langdell, Cheri Colby 247
Langer, Lawrence 285
language experiments 287
Lasser, Louise 7
Last Analysis, The (Bellow) 27
Last Frontier, The (Fast) 82
Last Jew in America, The (Fiedler)
   87, **161–162**
"Last One Way, The" (Englander)
   92
"Last WASP in the World, The"
   (Fiedler) 161
Later the Same Day (Paley) 228
*Late-Summer Passion of a Woman
   of Mind, The* (Goldstein) 108
Law of Return 57
Lawrence, D. H. 3
Lazar Malkin Enters Heaven
   (Stern) **162–163**, 288, 289
Lazarus, Emma **163–164**
   "The New Colossus" xvi, 11,
      164, **207**
   Wolf (Emma) and 320
Lazarus, Emmanuel xv
Lazarus, Josephine 11, 12
Lazarus, Moses xvi, 163
Leaflets (Rich) 247
Leary, Shyla 139
Leary, Timothy 102
Lebensboym, Rosa. *See* Margolin,
   Anna
Lebowich, Joseph xvi–xvii
Lecky, William xv

"Leda and the Swan" (Yeats) 238
Leegant, Joan xxiii
   An Hour in Paradise: Stories
      127–128
Lehman, Ernest 238
Lennon, John 119
"Leonard Shapiro Banished from
   Dreams" (Stern) 289
Lerner, Tillie. *See* Olsen, Tillie
   Lerner
lesbianism
   Asch (Sholem) on 18
   Klepfisz (Irena) on 149, 150
   Rich (Adrienne) on 56, 57
   Sinclair (Jo) on 276
   Stein (Gertrude) on 22, 287
"Lesson and the Secret, The"
   (Trilling) 303
Letters from Bohemia (Hecht) 118
Letters of Rebecca Gratz (Gratz)
   114, **164–165**
Letting Go (Roth) 261
Levertoff, Beatrice 165
Levertoff, Paul 165
Levertov, Denise **165–167**, 264
Levinas, Emmanuel 29, 70
Levine, Richard 16
Levin, Meyer xix, **167–168**
   Fuchs (Daniel) and 93
   on Wouk (Herman) 181
Lévi-Strauss, Claude 211
"Levitation" (Ozick) 226
Levitation: Five Fictions (Ozick)
   xxii, 222
Lewinsky, Monica 130
Lewisohn, Ludwig 93, **168–170**
Liberal Imagination, The (Trilling)
   188, 302, 303
Lichtenstein, Diane 321
Lider (Margolin) 179
"Lie Perfectly Still" (Sklarew) 280
*Life and Works of Sigmund Freud,
   The* (Jones) 303
Light, James F. 196–197, 311
"Light at Birth, The" (Berriault)
   30

Lights of Earth, The (Berriault) 30,
   170–171, 323
Lindbergh, Charles A. 236, 237,
   262, 328
literary criticism
   by Asimov (Isaac) 21
   by Cohen (Sarah Blacher) 53–54
   by Fiedler (Leslie) xx, 87, 88,
      161
   by Kazin (Alfred) xx, 148
   by Ozick (Cynthia) 221
   by Parker (Dorothy) 230
   by Sontag (Susan) 282
   by Trilling (Lionel) xx, 188,
      301–303
   by Wolf (Emma) 319–320
literary nationalism 148
Lithuania: New and Selected Poems
   (Sklarew) 279
"Little Blue Snowman of Washing-
   ton Heights, The" (Rosenbaum)
   67
Little Disturbances of Man, The
   (Paley) xxii, **171–172,** 227, 228
Little Foxes, The (Hellman) 121
Little Lit (Spiegelman) 286
Little Review (journal) 116, 117
Lives of the Poets (Doctorow) 65
"Living in Sin" (Rich) 56
logical positivism 255
"Long Distance Runner, The"
   (Paley) 228
Longings of Women, The (Piercy)
   236
Look (magazine) 257
Loon Lake (Doctorow) 32, 65
"Lord and Morton Gruber, The"
   (Stern) 163
*Lord Baden-Powell of the Boy
   Scouts* (Fast) 82
"Loser, The" (Rich) 281
"Lost, in a Sense" (Rosenbaum) 67
*Lost: A Search for Six of the Six Mil-
   lion, The* (Mendelsohn) **172–173**
Lost in Translation (Hoffman) 125
"Loudest Voice, The" (Paley) 227

Love and Death (film) 275

Love and Death in the American Novel (Fiedler) 87

Love and Like (Gold) 106

"Love Song of J. Alfred Prufrock, The" (Eliot) 197

Lovingkindness (Roiphe) xxii

Low Company (Fuchs) 93, 94

Lowell, Robert 16, 176, 218

Lumet, Sidney 230

"Lunar Cycle, The" (Piercy) 236

M

MacAdams, William 72

MacArthur, Charles 117, 229, 244

"Maccabee of Miami Beach, The" (Rosenbaum) 255

Mad Desire to Dance, A (Wiesel) 317

Madonna or Courtesan: The Jewish Woman in Christian Literature (Bitton-Jackson) 33–34

Magic Barrel, The (Malamud) 177, 178

magic realism
  of Broner (E. M.) 310
  of Bukiet (Melvin Jules) 40
  of Chabon (Michael) 48
  of Foer (Jonathan Safran) 90
  of Skibell (Joseph) 34, 35

Mailer, Norman xx, **174–176**
  The Armies of the Night **15–16,** 176
  Kazin (Alfred) on 148
  Krim (Seymour) and 154
  The Naked and the Dead 110, 175, **201–202**
  on Salinger (J. D.) 269

Making of Americans, The (Stein) 287, 288

Malamud, Bernard xx, xxi, xxii, **176–178**
  Asch (Sholem) and 19
  The Assistant **21–22,** 177
  Fuchs (Daniel) and 93

"The German Refugee" **98–99,** 177

God's Grace **104–105,** 177
  Gold (Herbert) and 107
  Levin (Meyer) and 168
  The Natural 177, **202–204**
  Skibell (Joseph) and 35

Mandelstam, Osip 53

Manhattan Project 240

Manhattan Rhapsody (Bukiet) 40

Man in a Case, The (Wasserstein) 309

Mankiewicz, Helen 117

Mann, Eda Mirsky 142

Mann, Seymour 142

Mann, Thomas 79, 169, 205, 239

Mansfield, Katherine 230

Man Who Grew Younger, The (Charyn) 50

Man Who Had All the Luck, The (Miller) 190

"Man Who Studied Yoga, The" (Mailer) 15, 175

Man Who Was Not with It, The (Gold) 106

March, The (Doctorow) 66, **178–179**

Marcus, Steven 303

Margolin, Anna **179–180**

Marjorie Morningstar (Wouk) xx, **180–181,** 324, 325

Markish, Perets 219

"Marriage in the Sixties, A" (Rich) 56

martyrdom 18–19, 36, 91

Marx Brothers 233–234

Masao Masuto series (Fast) 82

materialism
  Bellow (Saul) on 131
  Ginsberg (Allen) on 100, 101, 129
  Kosinski (Jerzy) on 151
  Malamud (Bernard) on 203
  Margolin (Anna) on 179, 180
  Miller (Arthur) on 59
  Roth (Philip) on 111–112

Salinger (J. D.) on 46
Shulman (Alix Kates) on 274
Wallant (Edward Lewis) on 307, 308
West (Nathanael) on 61

Matisse, Henry 22, 287

Mauriac, François 315

Maus (Spiegelman) **181–183,** 285, 286

Mayer, Peter 259

Mayhom, Derek 281

Mazel (Goldstein) 108, **183–184**

Mazzeno, Laurence W. 181

McCarthyism xx, 59, 122, 191, 215, 230, 232, 271

McCarthy, Mary 4, 148

McChesney series (Ferber) 86

McClellen, George 165

McClure, Michael 101, 102, 128

McGlothlin, Erin 182

McKenney, Eileen 313

McMurtry, Larry 106–107

Meinke, Peter 206

"Melanctha" (Stein) 296, 297

Melnick, Ralph 169

melting pot 3, 19

Melting Pot, The (Zangwill) 11

Melville, Herman xviii

Memoirs of an Ex-Prom Queen (Shulman) **184–186,** 273, 274

"Memoriam" (Michaels) 186–187

Menahem Mendl 284

Mencken, H. L. 116, 117

Mendelsohn, Daniel
  The Lost: A Search for Six of the Six Million **172–173**
  Skibell (Joseph) and 34

Mendelsohn, Michael J. 214

Menorah Journal 302, 303

Mercy of a Rude Stream (Roth) 259, 260

Merely Mary Ann (Zangwill) 330, 331

Merton, Thomas 170

Messiah of Stockholm, The (Ozick) 222

messianism 18–19, 34
  Chabon (Michael) on 327,
    328–329
  Cohen (Arthur Allen) on 53
  Rosenfeld (Isaac) on 256
  Wallant (Edward Lewis) on
    231
metafiction 58, 163, 289
MetaMaus (Spiegelman) 182
Metaphor & Memory (Ozick) 221
Meyer, Gerald 83
"Mezivosky" (Leegant) 128
Miami (Wasserstein) 309
Michaels, Anne xxiii, **186–188**
  Fugitive Pieces **95–96**, 186, 187
Middle of the Journey, The (Trill-
  ing) **188–189**, 303
Mila 18 (Uris) 304
Millay, Edna St. Vincent 146
Miller, Arthur xix, **189–192**
  The Crucible xx, **59–60**, 191
  Death of a Salesman xx, 59,
    62–64, 190–191
Miller, Henry 143
Milne, A. A. 230
Mind-Body Problem, The (Gold-
  stein) 107–108, **192–193**
Mind in the Modern World (Trilling)
  303
"Miner's Pond" (Michaels) 186,
  187
minimalism 152, 171
Ministry of Special Cases, The
  (Englander) 69, **193–195**
Miron, Dan 6, 7
Misfits, The (Miller) 191
*Mission to Gelele the King of
  Dahomey, A* (Burton) 123
Miss Lonelyhearts (West) **196–197**,
  311, 312
Mistress and Other Stories, The
  (Berriault) 29–30
Mitle Pass (Uris) 305
Model World and Other Stories, A
  (Chabon) 48

modernism. *See also* postmodern-
  ism
  of Bellow (Saul) 131
  Fiedler (Leslie) on 87, 88
  Potok (Chaim) on 240
  of Roth (Henry) 259
"Moise" (Hecht) 72
"Moishe the Just" (Stern) 162, 289
Moll, Elick 103
Molly Picon's Return Engagement
  (Cohen) 55
Monaghan, Pat 69
Monroe, Harriet 116
Monroe, Marilyn 191, 192
Moon Is Always Female, The
  (Piercy) 236
Moon & Ruben Shein, The (Stern)
  288–289
morality play 73
More Die of Heartbreak (Bellow)
  28, **197–198**
Mormons xv
*Mornings and Mourning: A Kaddish
  Journal* (Broner) 39
mother-daughter relationship
  Broner (E. M.) on xxii, 39
  Jong (Erica) on 138–139
  Kumin (Maxine) on 155
  Olsen (Tillie) on 293
  Ozick (Cynthia) on 272–273
  Salamon (Julie) on 267
"Mother Earth" (Margolin) 180
"Mothers, Daughters and the
  Holocaust" (Jong) 144
mother-son relationship
  Roth (Henry) on 45
  Roth (Philip) on 237, 261
Motza Kleis (Zangwill and Cowen)
  330
"Mourners and Machers" (Bukiet)
  40
Mr. Sammler's Planet (Bellow)
  xxii, xxiii, 28, **198–199**, 256
multivoiced narrative 36, 110, 324
Mumford, Lewis xviii

"My Apology" (Allen) 275
*My Bridges of Hope: Searching for
  Life and Love after Auschwitz*
  (Bitton-Jackson) 33
My First 79 Years: Isaac Stern
  (Potok and Stern) 239
My Life as a Man (Roth) 9, 261
My Mother's Body (Piercy)
  235–236
My Name Is Asher Lev (Potok)
  199–200, 239
My Own Ground (Nissenson) 210
My Portion (Kohut) 319
"My Sister, Joyce Brothers" (Krim)
  155
Mysteries of Pittsburgh, The
  (Chabon) 48
mystical elements xxii
  Asimov (Isaac) using 20
  Broner (E. M.) using 310
  Chabon (Michael) using 329
  Charyn (Jerome) using 50
  Cohen (Arthur Allen) using 53
  Levertov (Denise) using
    166–167
  Rich (Adrienne) using 56
  Rosenbaum (Thane) using 109,
    254
  Singer (Isaac Bashevis) using
    277
  Wiesel (Elie) using 298, 300,
    316, 317
Myth Criticism 87
Myth of Moral Justice, The
  (Rosenbaum) 254

N

Nabokov, Vladimir 48
Naked and the Dead, The (Mailer)
  110, 175, **201–202**
Naked God, The (Fast) 83
*Namedropping: Mostly Literary
  Memoirs* (Elman) 69
Nash, Ogden 234

Nathanael West: An Interpretative Study (Light) 196–197
nationalism, literary 148
Natural, The (Malamud) 177, **202–204**
naturalism
    of Mailer (Norman) 175, 201
    of Rosenfeld (Isaac) 255, 256
    of Stein (Gertrude) 297
    of Wallant (Edward Lewis) 307
nature
    Kumin (Maxine) on 155, 156
    Lazarus (Emma) on 163
    Ozick (Cynthia) on 224
    Sklarew (Myra) on 279
Nature's First Green (Roth) 259
Nazarene, The (Asch) 19, **204**
Necessities of Life (Rich) 57, 247
negative capability 69
Nemerov, Howard **205–206**
neo-orthodoxy 145
neorealism 44, 290
Net of Dreams: A Family's Search for a Rightful Place, The (Salamon) **206–207**, 267, 314
"New Colossus, The" (Lazarus) xvi, 11, 164, **207**
New Criticism 87
New Humanism 241
New Journalism 15, 154, 174, 176
New Life, A (Malamud) 177
New Masses, The (journal) xix
"new Yiddish" (language) 221
New York City
    Allen (Woody) on 7, 275
    Bellow (Saul) on 198
    Cahan (Abraham) on 248–249
    Calisher (Hortense) on 43, 44, 290
    Chabon (Michael) on 8, 9
    Charyn (Jerome) on 50
    colonial Jewish settlements in xiv
    Doctorow (E. L.) on 65
    Foer (Jonathan Safran) on 77

Gold (Herbert) on 106
Hurst (Fannie) on 132
Kushner (Tony) on 158
Odets (Clifford) on 306–307
Paley (Grace) on 171
Reznikoff (Charles) on 245
Rosenbaum (Thane) on 109
Roth (Henry) on 44–45, 259
Roth (Philip) on 261
Wouk (Herman) on 181
New Yorker, The (magazine) 230, 233, 234, 257
New York Intellectuals 148
New York Jew (Kazin) 148
New York Radical Women 274
Night (Wiesel) xxii, 91, **207–209**, 300, 314, 315, 317
Nights in the Gardens of Brooklyn (Swados) 292
nihilism xxi, 10
Nimrod, Naomi 39
Nine Stories (Salinger) 269
Nissenson, Hugh xxii, **209–211**
Noah, Mordecai Manuel **211–213**
Noah's Weekly Messenger (newspaper) 212
No!Art movement 154
No! in Thunder: Essays on Myth and Literature (Fiedler) 87
nonfiction novel (New Journalism) 15, 154, 174, 176
nonfiction works
    by Asimov (Isaac) 20–21
    by Charyn (Jerome) 50
    by Elman (Richard) 68
    by Epstein (Helen) 70, 71
    by Fiedler (Leslie) 87
    by Foer (Jonathan Safran) 90
    by Goldstein (Rebecca) 107
    by Hoffman (Eva) 125–126
    by Roiphe (Anne) 250
    by Rosenbaum (Thane) 254
    by Rosten (Leo Calvin) 257, 258
    by Salamon (Julie) 267
    by Stein (Gertrude) 288

by Swados (Harvey) 291
by Wiesel (Elie) 314
"Noon Lynching" (Sinclair) 276
Norris, Frank 261
"No Starch in the Dhoti, S'il Vous Plait" (Perelman) 234
Novak, Joseph. *See* Kosinski, Jerzy
"Novel as History: The Battle of the Pentagon, The" (Mailer) 15
No Villain (Miller) 190

O

Oates, Joyce Carol 74, 90, 106–107, 148
Oath, The (Wiesel) 91, 318
Object of My Affection (Wasserstein) 309
O'Connor, Flannery 199
Odets, Clifford xix, **214–216**
    Miller (Arthur) and 63, 190
    Waiting for Lefty 214–215
Of a Fire on the Moon (Mailer) 16, 176
"Of This Time, of That Place" (Trilling) 303
O'Hara's Choice (Uris) 305
*O K*A*P*L*A*N! MY K*A*P*L*A*N!* (Rosten) 257
Olaf Stapelton: A Man Divided (Fiedler) 88
"Old Cracked Tune, An" (Kunitz) 158
Old Maid's Club, The (Zangwill) 330
Olds, Sharon 264
Olsen, Jack 216
Olsen, Tillie Lerner xxi–xxii, **216–217**
    Paley (Grace) and 227
    Tell Me a Riddle: A Collection 37, 217, **293–294**
On a Darkening Green (Charyn) 50
Once Upon a Droshky (Charyn) 50, **217–218**

"One-Eye, Two-Eye, Three-Eye" (Wolf) 321
158-Pound Marriage, The (Irving) 140
O'Neill, Eugene xviii, 63, 190
One Touch of Venus (Perelman and Ogden) 234
"On Living in Two Cultures" (Rosen) 252
On Million Pound Bank-Note, The (Twain) 312
On Native Grounds (Kazin) 148
On Photography (Sontag) 282–283
"On the Air" (Roth) 261
On the Line (Swados) 292
On the Road (Kerouac) 100
On the Stroll (Shulman) 274
Open Cage: An Anzia Yezierska Collection, The (Yezierska) 327
Open Me . . . I'm a Dog (Spiegelman) 286
"Open the Gate" (Kunitz) 158
"Open Window, The" (Rosen) 252
Operation Shylock (Roth) 261, 262, 266
Oppenheimer, Robert 240
Optimist, The (Gold) 106
Orchards (Wasserstein) 309
Orthodox Judaism xvi, xxiv
    Cohen (Sarah Blacher) on 55
    Englander (Nathan) on 69, 70, 92
    Goldstein (Rebecca) on 107, 108, 192, 193
    Goodman (Allegra) on 113, 145–146
    Potok (Chaim) on 51, 52, 199, 200, 239
    Singer (Isaac Bashevis) on 79, 80, 137, 138, 277
    Wouk (Herman) on 325
    Zangwill (Israel) on 331
Orwell, George 194, 195
Osherow, Jacqueline xxiii, 218–220
O Taste and See (Levertov) 166

"Other Margaret, The" (Trilling) 303
Other Things Being Equal (Wolf) 320
Ottenburg, Eve 223
Our Gang (Roth) 261
Our Mrs. McChesney (Ferber) 86
Our Mutual Friend (Dickens) 140
Out Went the Candle (Swados) 292
Overland to the Islands (Levertov) 165
"O Yes" (Olsen) 217, 294
Ozick, Cynthia xxii, xxiv, 220–223
    Cohen (Sarah Blacher) and 54
    Horn (Dara) and 126
    on Nissenson (Hugh) 211
    The Pagan Rabbi and Other Stories xxii, 221, 224–226
    Rosenbaum (Thane) and 109
    on Roth (Philip) 262
    "The Shawl" 222, 272–273

P

paganism 224
Pagan Rabbi and Other Stories, The (Ozick) xxii, 221, 224–226
Painted Bird, The (Kosinski) 151, 152, 226–227
Pale of Settlement (Russia) 5–6, 295
Paley, Grace xx, xxi, 227–228
    The Little Disturbances of Man xxii, 171–172, 227, 228
    on Swados (Harvey) 291–292
Pamela's First Musical (Wasserstein) 309
"Pants in the Family, The" (Rosenbaum) 67
Parachutes & Kisses (Jong) 143
Paradise Park (Goodman) 113
Park Avenue: A Memoir (Roiphe) 249–250
Parker, Dorothy 228–230
    "Big Blonde" 31–32, 230, 245
    "Résumé" 31, 229, 244–245

Parker, Edwin (Eddie) Pond 229, 244
Parker, Muriel 258, 259, 260
Parnassus (Emerson) 163
Partisan Review (journal) xix, xx, 5, 147, 154, 216, 256, 303
Passage from Home (Rosenfeld) 255
Passport to War (Kunitz) 157
Pater, Walter 4
Patrimony (Roth) 73, 261, 262
Pawnbroker, The (film) 230–231
Pawnbroker, The (Wallant) xxii, 230–232, 307, 308
Peace Corps 291
Penn, William xiv
Pentagon, march on (1967) 15, 16, 176
Pentimento (A Book of Portraits) (Hellman) 122, 232–233
People, The (Malamud) 177
Perelman, Laura 234
Perelman, S. J. 233–234
    on Heller (Joseph) 120
    West (Nathanael) and 313
Peretz, Isaac Loeb 277
Peretz, Yitskhok Leybush 18
philanthropy
    of Gratz (Rebecca) xiv, 114, 115
    Richler (Mordecai) on 25
    Salamon (Julie) on 267
    Yezierska (Anzia) on 17
Philipson, David 114
photography
    by Kosinski (Jerzy) 151
    Sontag (Susan) on 5, 282–283
picaresque novels
    by Bellow (Saul) 3, 131
    by Chabon (Michael) 48
    by Jong (Erica) 80, 143
    by Kosinski (Jerzy) 151, 226
    by West (Nathanael) 312
Picasso, Pablo 22, 287
Piercy, Marge 234–236
    Gone to Soldiers 109–111, 236

Pile of Stones, A (Nissenson) 209
Pinball (Kosinski) 152
Plague of Dreamers, A (Stern) 289
Plath, Sylvia 157
Playwrights Horizons 309
Plot Against America, The (Roth)
    49, **236–237,** 262, 328
Poe, Edgar Allan 88
"Poem out of Childhood"
    (Rukeyser) 264
*Poems and Translations Written
    Between the Ages of Fourteen and
    Sixteen* (Lazarus) 163
poetry
    by Antin (Mary) 11
    by Elman (Richard) 68–69
    by Ginsberg (Allen) 100–102,
        128–130, 146–147
    by Jong (Erica) 143
    by Klepfisz (Irena) 149–150
    by Kumin (Maxine) 155, 156
    by Kunitz (Stanley) 157–158,
        294–295
    by Lazarus (Emma) xvi, 11,
        163–164, 207
    by Levertov (Denise) 165–167
    by Margolin (Anna) 179–180
    by Michaels (Anne) 186–187
    by Nemerov (Howard) 205
    by Osherow (Jacqueline)
        218–220
    by Ozick (Cynthia) 220, 221
    by Paley (Grace) 171, 227, 228
    by Parker (Dorothy) 228–230,
        244–245.31
    by Piercy (Marge) 110, 235–236
    by Rich (Adrienne) 56–57,
        246–248, 280–281
    by Rukeyser (Muriel) 264–265
    by Sklarew (Myra) 278, 279
pogroms xiii, 5, 11, 37, 42, 138,
    245, 316
*Poorhouse State: The American Way
    of Life on Public Assistance, The*
    (Elman) 68

popular culture
    Chabon (Michael) on 8, 9, 48
    Fiedler (Leslie) on 88
    Hurst (Fannie) on 132–133
    Rosenbaum (Thane) on 254
    Sontag (Susan) on 4–5
    Wasserstein (Wendy) on 119
"Pornographic Imagination, The"
    (Sontag) 282
Portnoy's Complaint (Roth) xxiii,
    24, **237–238,** 261, 266
"Portrait, The" (Kunitz) 157
positivism, logical 255
postfeminism 44, 309
post–Holocaust era xx–xxiv. *See
    also* Holocaust survivors
    Bellow (Saul) on 27
    Englander (Nathan) on 92
    Nissenson (Hugh) on xxii, 209
    Osherow (Jacqueline) on 219
    Ozick (Cynthia) on 224, 225
    Richler (Mordecai) on 13–14
    Rosenbaum (Thane) on 109
    Singer (Isaac Bashevis) on 278
    Wallant (Edward Lewis) on 231
    Wiesel (Elie) on 97–98,
        298–299, 301, 314, 315–319
postmodernism xxiii
    of Allen (Woody) 276
    of Chabon (Michael) 89
    Fiedler (Leslie) on 87, 88
    of Foer (Jonathan Safran) 90
    of Goldstein (Rebecca) 240,
        241
    of Goodman (Allegra) 113
    of Kosinski (Jerzy) 152
    of Ozick (Cynthia) 222
    of Paley (Grace) 228
    of Rosen (Jonathan) 74–75
    of Rosenbaum (Thane) 254
    of Roth (Philip) 58, 261
    of Skibell (Joseph) 35
    of Spiegelman (Art) 285
    of Stein (Gertrude) 23
    of Stern (Steve) 162, 163

post-traumatic stress disorder
    131, 257
Potok, Chaim xxi, **238–240**
    The Chosen **51–52,** 199, 239,
        240
    My Name Is Asher Lev **199–200,**
        239
Pound, Ezra 165
pragmatism 255
Prairie Schooner (quarterly)
    xxii–xxiii
Prayer for Owen Meany, A (Irving)
    140, 141
Premier and the Painter, The
    (Zangwill and Cowen) 330
Previn, Soon-Yi 8
"Primer for the Punctuation of
    Heart Disease, A" (Foer) 90
"Prisoner on Hell Planet: A Case
    Story" (Spiegelman) 183, 285
Prodigal in Love, A (Wolf) 321
Progressive era 64–65, 321
"Project for a Trip to China"
    (Sontag) 283
proletarian fiction xvii–xix, 201,
    259. *See also* working class
*Proletarian Literature in the United
    States* (Hicks) xix
Promised Land, The (Antin) xvii,
    10, 11, 37
Promise, The (Potok) 239
Properties of Light (Goldstein) 108,
    240–241
Prose, Francine 90
Prospect Before Us, The (Gold) 106
Proust, Marcel 44
"Providential Match, A" (Cahan)
    41
Psalm Jew (Asch) 19
pseudopornography 152
psychiatry
    Green (Hannah) on 136–137
    Jong (Erica) on 85
    Rosen (Jonathan) on 251
    Rosten (Leo Calvin) on 257

psychoanalysis. *See also* Freudian
  analysis; Jungian analysis; Reichian
  analysis
    Hecht (Ben) on 72
    Potok (Chaim) on 51
    Richler (Mordecai) on 24, 25
    Roth (Philip) on 237
    Sinclair (Jo) on 276
psychology 51
Puritan America xv, 168–169
pusherke 14
"Puttermesser and the Muscovite
  Cousin" (Ozick) 222–223
"Puttermesser and Xantippe"
  (Ozick) 222, 223
"Puttermesser: Her Work His-
  tory, Her Ancestry, Her Afterlife"
  (Ozick) 222
"Puttermesser in Paradise" (Ozick)
  223
"Puttermesser Paired" (Ozick) 222
Puttermesser Papers, The (Ozick)
  222–223
Pynchon, Thomas 148, 152

Q

QB VII (Uris) 304
quest story
    by Bellow (Saul) 123, 124
    by Chabon (Michael) 48
    by Charyn (Jerome) 218
    by Doctorow (E. L.) 36
    by Foer (Jonathan Safran) 74
    by Goldstein (Rebecca) 184, 241
    by Jong (Erica) 81, 143
    by Nissenson (Hugh) 211
    by West (Nathanael) 311

R

"Rabbi Double Faults, The"
  (Rosenbaum) 67
Rabinowitch, Solomon. *See*
  Aleichem, Sholem

racism xviii. *See also* anti-Semitism
    Bellow (Saul) on 123
    Doctorow (E. L.) on 242, 243
    Fiedler (Leslie) on 87, 161–162
    Olsen (Tillie) on 294
    Roth (Philip) on 130
    Salamon (Julie) on 314
    Stein (Gertrude) on 297
    Wallant (Edward Lewis) on 231
Ragtime (Doctorow) 64–65, 66,
  179, **242–243**
Rahv, Philip xix, 148
*Raise High the Roof Beam, Carpen-
  ters and Seymour: An Introduction*
  (Salinger) 269
*Rambam's Ladder: A Meditation on
  Generosity and Why It Is Necessary
  to Give* (Salamon) 267
Ransom, John Crowe 64
"Rape" (Rich) 247–248
Rappoport, Nessa xxii, xxiv
Ravelstein (Bellow) 29, **243–244**
reader-response criticism 276
Reading Myself and Others (Roth)
  263
realism
    of Allen (Woody) 275
    of Cahan (Abraham) 41, 42
    of Calisher (Hortense) 44
    of Doctorow (E. L.) 64, 242
    of Mailer (Norman) 175, 201
    of Odets (Clifford) 215
    of Paley (Grace) 171
    of Rosenfeld (Isaac) 256
    of Roth (Philip) 261
    of Wasserstein (Wendy) 118
    of West (Nathanael) 61
    of Zangwill (Israel) 330
"Reb Kringle" (Englander) 92
redemption
    Chabon (Michael) on 327
    Cohen (Arthur Allen) on 53
    Malamud (Bernard) on 21, 22
    Skibell (Joseph) on 34, 35
Redemption (Uris) 305

Red Ribbon on a White Horse
  (Yezierska) 327
Redstockings 274
Reform Judaism xvi, 320, 321
Regarding the Pain of Others
  (Sontag) 283
Reichian analysis 24, 175, 256
Reich, Tova xxi
religion. *See also* biblical elements;
  Christ imagery
    Aleichem (Sholem) on 295, 296
    Asch (Sholem) on 18–19, 204
    Broner (E. M.) on 310
    Calisher (Hortense) on 290
    Cohen (Arthur Allen) on 52–53
    Doctorow (E. L.) on 65
    Fiedler (Leslie) on 161
    Goldstein (Rebecca) on 192,
      193
    Goodman (Allegra) on 113
    Heller (Joseph) on 104
    Hellman (Lillian) on 233
    Kunitz (Stanley) on 158
    Leegant (Joan) on 127–128
    Levertov (Denise) on 166, 167
    Lewisohn (Ludwig) on 169–170
    Miller (Arthur) on 190–191
    Nissenson (Hugh) on 209, 210,
      211
    Osherow (Jacqueline) on 219,
      220
    Ozick (Cynthia) on 220, 221,
      222, 223, 224
    Potok (Chaim) on 199, 240
    Roiphe (Anne) on 250
    Rosen (Jonathan) on 251
    Rosen (Norma) on 252–253
    Roth (Henry) on 260
    Schaeffer (Susan Fromberg) on
      13
    Skibell (Joseph) on 34–35
    Spiegelman (Art) on 183
    Wiesel (Elie) on 97–98,
      208–209, 284–285, 300–301,
      314, 315–319

Wouk (Herman) on 325
Zangwill (Israel) on 331
Rembrandt's Hat (Malamud) 177
"Remembering Needleman"
    (Allen) 275
"Reminiscences: Places and People"
    (Allen) 275
"Requa" (Olsen) 217
Requiem for Harlem (Roth) 260
"Résumé" (Parker) 31, 229,
    244–245
Return of H*Y*M*A*N
    K*A*P*L*A*N, The (Rosten) 257
"Return of the Griffins" (Berriault)
    29
"Reunion" (Englander) 92
Revolutionary War xiv–xv, 211, 212
Rexroth, Kenneth 128, 129, 166
Reznikoff, Charles **245–246**
Rhythms (Reznikoff) 245
Ribalow, Harold 259
Rich, Adrienne **246–248**
    Collected Early Poems **56–57,**
        248
    Rukeyser (Muriel) and 264
    Snapshots of a Daughter-in-Law:
        Poems 1954–1962 56, 247,
        280–281
Richardson, Anne. *See* Roiphe, Anne
Richardson, Samuel 80
Richler, Mordecai
    The Apprenticeship of Duddy
        Kravitz **13–15**
    Barney's Version **24–26**
    on Heller (Joseph) 104
Rich Man, Poor Man (Shaw) 271
Rideout, Walter B. 82
Riefenstahl, Leni 283
Rilke, Rainer Maria 165
Rise of David Levinsky, The
    (Cahan) xvii, 42, **248–249**
Rise of Silas Lapham, The (Howells)
    42, 249
Robot series (Asimov) 20
Roethke, Theodore 157

Roiphe, Anne xxi, **249–251**
Roiphe, Herman 250
Rollins, Jack 7
"Romancing the Yohrzeit Light"
    (Rosenbaum) 67
"Room after Room" (Foer) 90
Room of One's Own, A (Woolf) 327
Roosevelt, Eleanor 133
Roosevelt, Franklin D. 133, 173,
    188, 236, 262, 312, 328
Roosevelt, Theodore 11
"Rosa" (Ozick) 222, 273
Roscoe, John 123
Rosen, Alan 183
Rosenbaum, Thane xxii, **253–255**
    Elijah Visible: Stories xxiii,
        67–68, 254
    The Golems of Gotham: A Novel
        xxiii, xxiv, **109,** 254
Rosenberg trial 36, 64
Rosenfeld, Isaac xix, xx, **255–256**
    Bellow (Saul) and 27, 28
Rosenfeld, Paul xviii
Rosen, Harlene 7
Rosen, Jonathan xxii, xxiv,
    251–252, 253
    Eve's Apple **74–75,** 251
    on Roth (Henry) 260
Rosen, Norma xxi, **252–253**
    Touching Evil 253, **299–300**
Rosenzweig, Franz 52
Ross, Harold 230
Ross, Leonard Q. *See* Rosten, Leo
Calvin
Rosten, Leo Calvin **256–258**
Roth, Anne. *See* Roiphe, Anne
Roth, Henry xix, **258–260**
    Call It Sleep xix, **44–45,** 258–259
    Fuchs (Daniel) and 93
    Levin (Meyer) and 167
    Malamud (Bernard) and 177
    Miller (Arthur) and 189
Roth, Philip xx–xxiv, **261–263**
    American Pastoral **9–10,** 112,
        130, 262, 266

The Counterlife 9, **57–59,** 261
Everyman **73,** 262, 327
Fuchs (Daniel) and 93
Gold (Herbert) and 107
Goodbye, Columbus and Five
    Short Stories **111–112,** 261, 266
The Human Stain 9, 112,
    130–131, 262
Levin (Meyer) and 168
Malamud (Bernard) and 177
The Plot against America 49,
    236–237, 262, 328
Portnoy's Complaint xxiii, 24,
    237–238, 261, 266
Sabbath's Theater 73, 262,
    266–267
Rothschild, Dorothy. *See* Parker,
Dorothy
Roughhead, William 121
Rovit, Earl 311
Rubin, Steve 167
Ruddick, Lisa 297
Rukeyser, Muriel xix, xx, **263–265**
Rushdie, Salman 74, 140
Russia, czarist
    Aleichem (Sholem) on 295
    anti-Semitism in xiii, xvi, 5, 42,
        245, 316
    Malamud (Bernard) on 177
    Pale of Settlement in 5–6, 295S

S

Sabbath's Theater (Roth) 73, 262,
    266–267
Sacco, Niccola xix, 230
Sages and Dreamers (Wiesel) 285
Salamon, Julie xxii, **267–268**
    Epstein (Helen) and 71
    The Net of Dreams: A Family's
        Search for a Rightful Place
        206–207, 267, 314
    White Lies xxiii, 206, 267,
        313–314
Salem Witchcraft Trials 59, 191

Salinger, J. D. **268–269**
    The Catcher in the Rye xx,
    45–46, 268–269
    Gold (Herbert) and 107
    Roth (Henry) and 259
Salome of the Tenements (Yezierska)
    327
Salt (Gold) 106
Samantha (Fast) 82
Sandburg, Carl 116
San Francisco Renaissance 101
Sappho's Leap (Jong) 143
sarcasm 40
Satan in Goray (Singer) 79
satire
    by Allen (Woody) 275
    by Bellow (Saul) 123
    by Berriault (Gina) 30
    by Glass (Montague Marsden)
        103
    by Gold (Herbert) 106
    by Goodman (Allegra) 113
    by Jong (Erica) 80, 85
    by Malamud (Bernard) 177
    by Ozick (Cynthia) 222
    by Parker (Dorothy) 229
    by Roth (Philip) 58, 111, 112,
        238, 261
    by Wasserstein (Wendy) 309
    by West (Nathanael) 311, 312,
        313
    by Wouk (Herman) 324, 325
Saul Bellow's Enigmatic Laughter
    (Cohen) 54
Savran, David 159
"Scattered Psalms" (Osherow)
    219
Schaeffer, Susan Fromberg, *Anya*
    xxii, **12–13**
Schapiro, Meyer 148
Schechner, Mark xxiii
Schindler's List (film) 206, 267
Schindler, Solomon 11
schizophrenia 136–137
schlemiel 14, 15, 16, 176, 258
schlimazel 258

Schneiderman, Harry xviii
Schneider, Rebecca xvii
Schopenhauer, Arthur 225
Schultz, Dutch 32–33
Schwartz, Delmore xix, xx, 27, 28,
    131, 148, 264
science fiction, by Asimov (Isaac)
    19–20
scientific truth 240, 241
Scottsboro case 264
Scott, Sir Walter 114, 115
Scoundrel Time (Hellman) 122, 232
screenplays
    by Allen (Woody) 7–8
    by Berriault (Gina) 30
    by Fast (Howard Melvin) 83
    by Fuchs (Daniel) 93, 94
    by Hecht (Ben) 118
    by Mailer (Norman) 176
    by Miller (Arthur) 191
    by Odets (Clifford) 215
    by Perelman (S. J.) 233–234
    by Richler (Mordecai) 14
    by Rosenbaum (Thane) 254
    by Rosten (Leo Calvin) 256, 257
    by Uris (Leon) 76, 304
    by Wasserstein (Wendy) 309
    by West (Nathanael) 61, 311
SDS. *See* Students for a Demo-
    cratic Society
Searching Wind, The (Hellman) 121
*Season for Healing: Reflections on
    the Holocaust* (Roiphe) 250
Second Hand Smoke (Rosenbaum)
    xxiii, 254
Secret, The (Hoffman) 126
secularism xxi
    Cahan (Abraham) on xvii, 249
    Calisher (Hortense) on 290
    Englander (Nathan) on 70
    Goldstein (Rebecca) on 192, 193
    Goodman (Allegra) on 145
    Klepfisz (Irena) on 149, 150
    Nissenson (Hugh) on 211
    Potok (Chaim) on 51, 52, 199,
        240

Singer (Isaac Bashevis) on
    79–80
    Wolf (Emma) on 321
Seeger, Pete 109
Seid, Ruth. *See* Sinclair, Jo
Seize the Day (Bellow) 27, 125,
    269–270
Selected Poems, 1928–1958
    (Kunitz) 157–158
Sephardim xiii, 158, 258, 331
September 11, 2001, terrorist attack
    77, 90, 211, 285–286
Setting Free the Bears (Irving) 139,
    140
Settlers, The (Levin) xix, 168
sex/sexuality
    Chabon (Michael) on 48
    Fiedler (Leslie) on 161
    Gold (Herbert) on 106
    Goldstein (Rebecca) on 241
    Irving (John) on 140, 323–324
    Jong (Erica) on 81, 84–86, 138,
        142, 143
    Kosinski (Jerzy) on 152, 226
    Kumin (Maxine) on 156
    Mailer (Norman) on 174, 175,
        176
    Nissenson (Hugh) on 210
    Piercy (Marge) on 110
    Richler (Mordecai) on 14
    Roth (Henry) on 45, 260
    Roth (Philip) on 130, 238, 261,
        262, 266
    Shulman (Alix Kates) on 185,
        274
    Singer (Isaac Bashevis) on 138
    Wallant (Edward Lewis) on
        232
    West (Nathanael) on 312
Sexton, Anne 155–156, 263, 264
sexual orientation. *See* heterosexu-
    ality; homosexuality
Sex Wars (Piercy) 236
Shalienberger, Moses xv
"Shallowest Man, The" (Allen) 275
Shamforoff, Gilbert. *See* Shaw, Irwin

Shandeling, Arline. *See* Berriault, Gina

Shapiro, Karl 240, 264

Shaw, Irwin **271–272**

"Shawl, The" (Ozick) 222, **272–273**

Shawn, William 233

Shechner, Mark 24, 266

Sherwood, Robert 63

"She with the Cold Marble Breasts" (Margolin) 179, 180

She Would Be a Soldier, Or the Plains of Chippewa (Noah) 211, 212

Shifting Landscape (Roth) 260

Shiksa Goddess; or, How I Spent My Forties (Wasserstein) 309

Shoah. *See* Holocaust

Shop Talk (Roth) 263

Showboat (Ferber) 86

shtetl xiii, 14, 18, 37, 184, 249, 277, 278

Shtetl (Hoffman) 125–126

Shtok, Fradel 149

Shulman, Alix Kates xxiii, **273–275**
    Memoirs of an Ex-Prom Queen **184–186,** 273, 274

Shuster, Joe 8, 48

Side Effects (Allen) 8, **275–276**

Sidel series (Charyn) 50

Siegel, Harry 74

Siegel, Jerry 8, 48

Siege of Chicago (Mailer) 176

Siege of Yorktown, The (Noah) 212

"Silver Dish, A" (Bellow) 28

Simon, Andrea 34

Sincerity and Authenticity (Trilling) 303

Sinclair, Jo xx, **276–277**

Sing at My Wake (Sinclair) 276

Singer, Isaac Bashevis xx, xxiv, **277–278**
    Asch (Sholem) and 19
    Englander (Nathan) and 194, 195
    The Family Moskat **79–80,** 278
    Gimpel the Fool and Other Stories **99–100,** 278

Malamud (Bernard) and 177

In My Father's Court **137–138,** 277

Ozick (Cynthia) and 222, 225

Rosenbaum (Thane) and 109

Skibell (Joseph) and 35

Stern (Steve) and 288

Singer, Israel Joshua 79, 277

Sisters Rosensweig, The (Wasserstein) 309

Six Gallery Reading 101, 128

Skibell, Joseph, *A Blessing on the Moon* **34–35**

Sklarew, Myra **278–280**

slang 106

Slave Trade (Gold) 106

Sleeping with Cats (Piercy) 235

"Slides from Our Recent European Trip" (Piercy) 236

"Slim Fantasia on a Few Words from Hosea" (Osherow) 220

Smart Set, The (magazine) 321

Snapshots of a Daughter-in-Law: Poems 1954–1962 (Rich) 56, 247, **280–281**

Snyder, Gary 101, 102, 128

So Big (Ferber) xvii, 86

Social Darwinism xviii

socialism xvii–xix, 41, 42. *See also* communism

social issues xix
    Cahan (Abraham) on 41, 42
    Charyn (Jerome) on 217
    Glass (Montague Marsden) on 103
    Hurst (Fannie) on 133
    Kushner (Tony) on 158, 159
    Malamud (Bernard) on 177
    Miller (Arthur) on 62, 63, 190
    Odets (Clifford) on 214–215, 215
    Parker (Dorothy) on 229
    Richler (Mordecai) on 13
    Roth (Henry) on 259
    Roth (Philip) on 237
    Shaw (Irwin) on 271

socialist feminism 293

social justice 263–264, 267, 313

social protest movement 5

social protest plays 190

Solomon, Carl 101, 129

Something Happened (Heller) 103–104, 120

Somewhere a Master (Wiesel) 285, 318

Somewhere Else (Kotlowitz) 153

"Song of Myself" (Whitman) 35–36

Song of the Earth, The (Nissenson) 210–211

Sonneschein, Rosa 319

Son of the Circus, A (Irving) 141

Sontag, Susan xxi, xxii, **281–284**
    Illness as Metaphor **134–135,** 283
    Against Interpretation **4–5,** 134, 282

Son, The (Berriault) 30

Sophie, Totie and Belle (Cohen) 55

Sorrow Dance, The (Levertov) 166

Soul on Ice (Cleaver) 284

Soul Sisters (Cohen and Koch) 55

Souls on Fire: Portraits and Legends of Hasidic Masters (Wiesel) **284–285,** 318

South Carolina Black Mountain Poets 165

"Space Psalm" (Osherow) 219

Spanish-American War 319, 320

Spanish civil war 83, 255, 264, 298

Spanish Inquisition xiv

Spartacus (Fast) 82

Spiegelman, Art xxii, **285–286**
    Epstein (Helen) and 71
    Maus **181–183,** 285, 286

Spielberg, Steven 206, 267

Stahl, Norma. *See* Rosen, Norma

stand-up comedy 7

Stardust Memories (film) 7

Star Shines over Mt. Morris Park, A (Roth) 260

Starting Out in the Thirties (Kazin) 148

Statue of Liberty xvi, 11, 164, 207

Steinbeck, John 201, 306

Steinberg, Milton 52

Steiner, Rudolph 28, 131

Stein, Gertrude xviii, **286–288**

    The Autobiography of Alice B. Toklas **22–23,** 287, 288, 297

    Three Lives: Stories of the Good Anna, Melanctha, and the Gentle Leona 288, **296–297**

Stein, Joseph 295

Stein, Leo 287

Steps (Kosinski) 151

Sterne, Lawrence 80

Stern, Isaac 239

Stern, Steve xxii, xxiii, xxiv, **288–289**

    Lazar Malkin Enters Heaven **162–163,** 288, 289

Stevenson, Robert Louis 48

Stokes, Geoffrey 152

"Stolen Pleasures" (Berriault) 30

"Stone Boy, The" (Berriault) 30

Stories of an Imaginary Childhood (Bukiet) 40

"Storm Warnings" (Rich) 56

Strange Attractors (Goldstein) 108

stream-of-consciousness narrative 46, 238, 259, 266, 310

Strindberg, August 63

Stubbs, Katherine 17

Students for a Democratic Society (SDS) 235

Stuyvesant, Peter xiv

Styles of Radical Will (Sontag) 282

suicide

    Goldstein (Rebecca) on 184

    Kunitz (Stanley) on 295

    Malamud (Bernard) on 99

    Miller (Arthur) on 62, 190

    Ozick (Cynthia) on 221, 224

    Parker (Dorothy) on 31, 229, 245

    Rosenbaum (Thane) on 109, 254

    Sontag (Susan) on 282, 283

    Spiegelman (Art) on 183

    Wallant (Edward Lewis) on 308

    Wiesel (Elie) on 316

"Suitcase, The" (Ozick) 224, 225

Sully, Thomas 114

Summer in Williamsburg (Fuchs) 93

Summerland (Chabon) 48–49

Sunday Jews (Calisher) 44, **290–291**

Sunflower, The (Wiesenthal) 35

"Supermarket in California, A" (Ginsberg) 129

surrealism 51, 197, 242, 261, 311

Swados, Harvey **291–292**

Swados, Robin 291

Swiftie the Magician (Gold) 106

Syberberg, Hans Jürgen 283

Sylvia (Fast) 82

T

Take the Money and Run (film) 7

Talmud and the Internet: A Journey Between Worlds, The (Rosen) 251

Talmudic study 51, 251, 317

Tar Beach (Elman) 68

Targ, Roslyn 259

Taubes, Susan 283

Tea Ceremony: The Uncollected Writings, The (Berriault) 30

teen angst 46

Telling, The (Broner) 39

Tell Me a Riddle: A Collection (Olsen) 37, 217, **293–294**

Tenants, The (Malamud) 177

Tenants of Moonbloom, The (Wallant) 307, 308

Tender Buttons: Objects, Food, Rooms (Stein) 288

Tender Offer (Wasserstein) 309

"Tenth, The" (Leegant) 127–128

terza rima 219

Tesserae: Memories and Suppositions (Levertov) 167

Testament, The (Wiesel) 91, 318

Testimony (Reznikoff) 246

Testing-Tree, The (Kunitz) 158, **294–295**

Tevye's Daughters (Aleichem) **295–296**

Thackeray, William 65

Thanksgiving Day Address (Noah) 212, 213

Theatre Guild 214

Theft, A (Bellow) 28

theological writings 52, 53. *See also* religion

"Theory of Flight" (Rukeyser) 264

Theory of Signs 255

"There Are Such Springlike Nights" (Rich) 57

They Too Arise (Miller) 190

They Walk in Darkness (Zangwill) 331

They Who Knock at Our Gates (Antin) 11

Third Child, The (Piercy) 236

This Is My God (Wouk) 325

Thomas, Dylan 165

Thomas, Richard 83

Thoreau, Henry David xviii, 54

Thousand and One Afternoons in Chicago, A (Hecht) 117

"Three Laws of Robotics" (Asimov) 20

Three Lives: Stories of the Good Anna, Melanctha, and the Gentle Leona (Stein) 288, **296–297**

Three Women (Piercy) 236

Tillich, Paul 152

"Time of Her Time, The" (Mailer) 16, 175

"Time of Our Time, The" (Mailer) 175

Time of the Uprooted, The (Wiesel) **297–299,** 316

"To Be a Jew in the Twentieth Century" (Rukeyser) 264–265

"To Be of Use" (Piercy) 235

To Jerusalem and Back: A Personal Account (Bellow) 28

"To Judith, Taking Leave" (Rich) 56–57

Toklas, Alice B. 22–23, 287

Tolstoy, Leo 255

Tompkin, Jane 138

Topaz (Uris) 304

Torres, Luis de xiv

torture poems 156

Total Immersion (Goodman) xxiv, 112

Touching Evil (Rosen) 253, **299–300**

Tough Guys Don't Dance (Mailer) 176

Town Beyond the Wall, The (Wiesel) 97, **300–301,** 316–317

Toys in the Attic (Hellman) 121–122

transcendentalism 11, 28

transparency 4

Treasure Island (Stevenson) 48

Tree of Life, The (Nissenson) 210

Trial of God, The (Wiesel) 316

Trillin, Calvin 152

Trilling, Diana xx, xxiv, 302, 303

Trilling, Lionel xx, xxiv, 148, **301–303**

  The Middle of the Journey **188–189,** 303

Trinity (Uris) 305

"Trip to Hanoi" (Sontag) 282

Trois Contes (Flaubert) 297

Troubled Air, The (Shaw) 271

Trust (Ozick) 221

tuberculosis 134, 135

"Tumblers, The" (Englander) 92, 194

Turgenev, Ivan 164

Turnbull, Janet 139

Twain, Mark 6, 217, 239, 288, 312

"Twenty-seventh Man, The" (Englander) 92, 194

Two Valleys (Fast) 82

U

Udelston, Joseph 331

"UFO Menace, The" (Allen) 275

Ulysses (Joyce) 125, 312

"Unacknowledged Legislator, The" (Bukiet) 40

Unbearable Lightness of Being, The (Kundera) 74

"Uncivil Liberties" (Trillin) 152

Uncle Moses (Asch) 19

Uncommon Women and Others (Wasserstein) 118, 309

unconscious repetition compulsion 124

Under the Sign of Saturn (Sontag) 283

Unfinished Woman, An (Hellman) 122, 232, 233

"Unguided Tour" (Sontag) 283

universalism xviii

Unknown Constellations, The (Swados) 292

"Unsaid Word, An" (Rich) 56

Until I Find You (Irving) 141

Unvanquished, The (Fast) 82

Up Country (Kumin) 155

Updike, John 48, 74, 107, 143

Up Stream (Lewisohn) 169

Up the Sandbox! (Roiphe) 250

Uris, Leon xx, **304–305**

  Exodus **76–77,** 304

U.S.A. Trilogy (Dos Passos) 36

"Usurpation" (Ozick) 221–222, 226

utopian themes 81, 82

V

Vanity Fair (magazine) 229

Van Vechten, Carl 297

Vanzetti, Bartolomeo xix, 230

"Variant Text" (Goodman) 112

Vendler, Helen 247–248

Verne, Jules 234

"Very Rigid Search, The" (Foer) 90

Victim, The (Bellow) xx, xxi, 27

Vietnam War. *See also* anti–Vietnam War movement

  Heller (Joseph) on 120

  Irving (John) using 141

  Levertov (Denise) on 166

  Mailer (Norman) on 175–176

  Roth (Philip) on 9–10

View from the Bridge, A (Miller) 191

Views of a Nearsighted Cannoneer (Krim) 154

Village Voice (newspaper) 152, 154, 174

"Virility" (Ozick) 221, 225–226

visual materials 77, 90

Volcano Lover, The (Sontag) 283

Voltaire 312

Vonnegut, Kurt 139

W

Waiting for Cordelia (Gold) 106

Waiting for Lefty (Odets) 214–215, **306–307**

Walden (Thoreau) 54

Waldman, Anne 102

Waldman, Ayelet 49

Walker, Alice 264

Walker in the City, A (Kazin) 148

"Walking Wounded" (Shaw) 271

Wallant, Edward Lewis xx, **307–308**

  The Pawnbroker xxii, **230–232,** 307, 308

Walton, Eda Lou 258, 259

War and Remembrance (Wouk) 324, 325

War of 1812 xv, 165, 211

Washington Times 14

Wasserstein, Wendy xxiii, **308–310**
   *Heidi Chronicles and Other
      Plays* **118–119,** 309

Wasteland, The (Sinclair) xx, 276

"Was the Earl of Beaconsfield a
   Representative Jew?" (Lazarus)
   164

Watch on the Rhine (Hellman)
   121

Water-Method Man, The (Irving)
   140

Waterworks, The (Doctorow) 65,
   66, 179

Waugh, Evelyn 199, 239

"Way We Live Now" (Sontag) 283

Weave of Women, A (Broner) xxii,
   38–39, **310**

We Bombed in New Haven (Heller)
   120

Wedding Jester, The (Stern) 289

Weidman, Jerome 103

Weight of Oranges, The (Michaels)
   186

Weimar Republic 98

Weinstein, Eli 13

Weinstein, Nathaniel Wallenstein.
   See West, Nathanael

Welcome to Hard Times (Doctorow)
   32, 64

Wells, H. G. 3

Werewolves in Their Youth (Chabon)
   48

West, Nathanael xix, **311–313**
   The Day of the Locust **61–62,**
      311, 313
   Miss Lonelyhearts **196–197,**
      311, 312

West of the Rockies (Fuchs) 94

"Westward Ha?" (Perelman) 234

Whalen, Philip 128

Wharton, Edith 44, 138

"What's Happening in America"
   (Sontag) 282

What's New, Pussycat? (Allen) 7

"What's That Smell in the
   Kitchen?" (Piercy) 235

"When Dinah Shore Ruled the
   Earth" (Wasserstein) 309

When She Was Good (Roth) 261

When We Dead Awaken (Ibsen)
   281

"'When We Dead Awaken': Writing
   as Re-Vision" (Rich) 247, 281

Where She Came From (Epstein)
   xxiii, 71

Where the Stress Falls (Sontag) 283

White, Edmund 221

White Lies (Salamon) xxiii, 206,
   267, **313–314**

White Terror and the Red, The
   (Cahan) 42

Whitman, Walt xviii, 35–36, 98,
   99, 100, 129, 163

Whittemore, Reed 123

"Who Is It Can Tell Me Who I Am"
   (Berriault) 323

Why Are We in Vietnam? (Mailer)
   175–176

"Why I Choose To Be a Jew"
   (Cohen) 52

"Why Resign from the Human
   Race?" (Swados) 291

"Why the Geese Shrieked" (Singer)
   137–138

Wickinden, Dan 307

Widow for One Year, A (Irving)
   141

Wiesel, Elie xxiv, **314–319**
   The Forgotten **91–92,** 173, 318
   The Gates of the Forest **97–98,**
      317
   Night xxii, 91, **207–209,** 300,
      314, 315, 317
   Rosenbaum (Thane) and 109
   *Souls on Fire: Portraits and
      Legends of Hasidic Masters*
      284–285, 318
   The Time of the Uprooted
      297–299, 316

The Town Beyond the Wall 97,
   300–301, 316–317

Wiesel, Marion 208

Wiesenthal, Simon 35

"Wig, The" (Englander) 92

Wilde, Oscar 146

Wilkie, Wendell 264

Williams, Roger xiv

Williams, William Carlos 101, 128,
   165, 166

Williamsburg Trilogy (Fuchs) xix,
   93–94

Will to Change, The (Rich) 247

Will to Live On (Wouk) 325

Winds of War, The (Wouk) 324, 325

Wise Men and Their Tales (Wiesel)
   285

Wise, Stephen 169

Wisse, Ruth 329

Witch of Castille, The (Asch) 18

With Eyes in the Back of Our Heads
   (Levertov) 165

Wolf, Emma xvii, **319–322**

Wolfe, Thomas xviii

Woman on the Edge of Time
   (Piercy) 236

"Woman, Young and Old, A"
   (Paley) 172

women. *See also* feminism; Jewish
   women
   Bellow (Saul) on 197–198
   Berriault (Gina) on 322
   Broner (E. M.) on xxii, 310
   Doctorow (E. L.) on 243
   Ferber (Edna) on 86
   Goldstein (Rebecca) on 241
   Hellman (Lillian) on 121
   Hurst (Fannie) on 133
   Jong (Erica) on 80–81, 84–86,
      138–139, 142, 143
   Kumin (Maxine) on 155, 156
   Olsen (Tillie) on 216, 293
   Osherow (Jacqueline) on 219
   Paley (Grace) on xxii, 171–172,
      227

Parker (Dorothy) on 230
Piercy (Marge) on 235, 236
Rich (Adrienne) on 247–248, 280–281
Roiphe (Anne) on 250
Shulman (Alix Kates) on 185–186, 274, 275
Wasserstein (Wendy) on 118–119, 309
Wiesel (Elie) on 298
Wolf (Emma) on 320, 321
Wouk (Herman) on 181
Yezierska (Anzia) on 327
Women in Their Beds: New and Selected Stories (Berriault) 30, **322–323**
Women's Haggadah (Broner and Nimrod) 39
Wonder Boys (Chabon) 48
Wood, Ira 235
Wood, James 266
Woolf, Virginia 38, 327
working class xvii–xviii
   Aleichem (Sholem) on 296
   Hurst (Fannie) on 133
   Odets (Clifford) on 214–215, 306, 307
   Olsen (Tillie) on 216, 294
   Swados (Harvey) on 291, 292
"Work of Artifice, A" (Piercy) 235
World According the Garp, The (Irving) 139, 140, **323–324**
World's Fair (Doctorow) 32, 65
World to Come, The (Horn) 126–127
World War II. *See also* Holocaust
   Heller (Joseph) on 46–47, 104, 120
   Kosinski (Jerzy) on 151
   Kotlowitz (Robert) using 153
   Mailer (Norman) on 175, 201–202
   Piercy (Marge) on 110–111, 236

Rosten (Leo Calvin) on 257
Shaw (Irwin) on 271, 272
Wouk (Herman) on 324, 325
Worrying Won't Win (Glass) 103
Wouk, Herman xxi, **324–325**
   Marjorie Morningstar xx, **180–181**, 324, 325
wrestling 139, 323, 324
"Writing as a Woman and a Jew in America" (Rosen) 252, 253
Writing Their Nations: The Tradition of Nineteenth-Century American Jewish Women Writers (Lichtenstein) 321

Y

"Years" (Margolin) 180
Yeats, William Butler 238
Yekl (Cahan) 37, 41
Yezierska, Anzia xvii, xviii, **326–327**
   Arrogant Beggar **17–18**, 327
   Bread Givers **36–38**, 326, 327
   Malamud (Bernard) and 177
   Paley (Grace) and 227
   Rosen (Norma) on 253
Yiddish language
   Antin (Mary) using 11
   Asch (Sholem) using 18, 204
   Cahan (Abraham) using 41
   Chabon (Michael) using 327, 328, 329
   Charyn (Jerome) using 50, 217
   decrease in use of xxi
   development of xiii
   in *Forward* (newspaper) xvii–xviii, 41–42, 196
   Glass (Montague Marsden) using 103
   Klepfisz (Irena) using 149, 150
   Margolin (Anna) using 179
   Miller (Arthur) using 190

Ozick (Cynthia) using 220, 221, 224–225
Rosenfeld (Isaac) using 255
Rosten (Leo Calvin) using 256, 257–258
Singer (Isaac Bashevis) using 79, **277**
Wiesel (Elie) using 315
Yezierska (Anzia) using 37, 326
Yiddish Policemen's Union, The (Chabon) 49, **327–329**
"Yinglish" (language) 257
Yonnondio: From the Thirties (Olsen) 216
Young, Brigham xv
"Young Folks, The" (Salinger) 268
Young Lions, The (Shaw) 271, 272
Yours, Isaac Asimov (Asimov) 21

Z

Zalmen, or the Madness of God (Wiesel) 317
Zangwill, Israel **330–331**
   Antin (Mary) and 11
   Wolf (Emma) and 319–320
Zen Buddhism 102
Zionism xviii, xxi
   Chabon (Michael) on 329
   Englander (Nathan) on 70
   of Lazarus (Emma) 164
   of Levin (Meyer) 168
   of Lewisohn (Ludwig) 169
   of Noah (Mordecai Manuel) 212
   of Roth (Henry) 260
   Singer (Isaac Bashevis) on 80
   of Zangwill (Israel) 331
Zuckerman Bound (Roth) 262–263
Zuckerman Unbound (Roth) 57, 261
zwischenmensch 51
Zynger, Yitskhok. *See* Singer, Isaac Bashevis